Limited-dependent and qualitative variables in econometrics

G. S. MADDALA
Department of Economics
University of Florida

CAMBRIDGE UNIVERSITY PRESS

Cambridge
London   New York   New Rochelle
Melbourne   Sydney

Published by the Press Syndicate of the University of Cambridge
The Pitt Building, Trumpington Street, Cambridge CB2 1RP
32 East 57th Street, New York, NY 10022, USA
296 Beaconsfield Parade, Middle Park, Melbourne 3206, Australia

First published 1983

Printed in the United States of America

Library of Congress Cataloging in Publication Data
Maddala, G. S.
Limited-dependent and qualitative
variables in econometrics.

(Econometric Society monographs in
quantitative economics; 3)
Bibliography: p.
Includes index.
1. Econometrics. I. Title. II. Title:
Qualitative variables in econometrics.
III. Series.
HB139.M355   1983   330′.028   82-9554
ISBN 0 521 24143 X

Contents

Preface

This book deals with the usual regression and simultaneous-equations models when the dependent variables are qualitative, truncated, or censored. This has been an area of great interest in econometrics in recent years. The book covers in more or less elementary fashion many of the models commonly used in this field. It does not cover the area of analysis of panel data; including this topic would have made the book very unwieldy.

I would like to thank Forrest D. Nelson for our early collaborative work that stimulated my interest in this area. I would like to thank Angus Deaton, Lung-fei Lee, Daniel McFadden, and Robert P. Trost for going through the book in detail, correcting errors, and suggesting methods of improvement. R. P. H. Fishe, David Goldenberg, David Grether, and Forrest Nelson also provided useful comments. They are not, however, responsible for any errors that may remain, nor for any omissions. I would like to thank Betty Sarra for carefully typing the different versions, the National Science Foundation for providing me research funds to work in this area, and the Center for Econometrics and Decision Sciences at the University of Florida for support. I would also like to thank Colin Day and his associates at Cambridge University Press for their careful production of this book.

G. S. MADDALA

to
KAMESWARI, TARA, *and*
VIVEK

CHAPTER 1

Introduction

The purpose of this book is to present methods for the analysis of some econometric models in which the dependent variables are either qualitative or limited in their range. These models are commonly encountered in empirical work that analyzes survey data, although we shall also give examples of some time-series models. In a certain sense every variable we consider in practice, at least in econometric work, is limited in its range. However, it is not necessary to apply the complicated analysis described in this book to all these problems. For instance, if we believe that prices are necessarily positive, we might postulate that they have a log-normal distribution rather than the normal. On the other hand, in the limited-dependent-variable models discussed in this book, the variables are limited to their range because of some underlying stochastic choice mechanism. It is models of this kind that we shall be concerned with in this book. Similarly, there are many qualitative variables that are often used in econometric work. These are all usually known as dummy variables. What we shall be concerned with in this book are models in which the dummy variables are endogenous rather than exogenous. The following simple examples will illustrate the types of models that we shall be talking about. These examples can be conveniently classified into three categories: (a) truncated regression models, (b) censored regression models, and (c) dummy endogenous models.

1.1 Truncated regression models

Example 1: Negative-income-tax experiment

The negative-income-tax experiment provides detailed information on a sample of households with incomes below some threshold. Suppose we

1

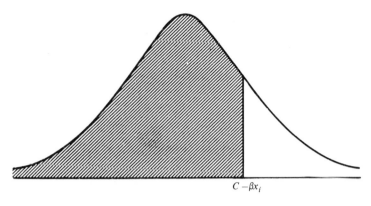

$$C - \beta x_i$$

Figure 1.1. Truncated normal distribution

wish to use these data to estimate an earnings equation:

$$y = f(\text{education, age, experience, etc.})$$

Then we need to take into consideration the fact that the dependent variable is truncated at a certain point. Observations with values of y above a threshold value are not included in the sample. This problem has been analyzed by Hausman and Wise (1976, 1977) and will be discussed in detail in Chapter 6.

To see why the ordinary least-squares (OLS) method gives biased estimates in this case, suppose we want to estimate the effect on earnings (y) of years of schooling (x). The regression equation is

$$y_i = \beta x_i + u_i \tag{1.1}$$

where $u_i \sim IN(0, \sigma^2)$. We observe y_i only if $y_i \leqslant c$, where c is a given constant. This condition implies that

$$\beta x_i + u_i \leqslant c \quad \text{or} \quad u_i \leqslant c - \beta x_i \tag{1.2}$$

Clearly, $E(u_i \,|\, u_i \leqslant c - \beta x_i)$ is not equal to zero. In fact, it will be a function of x_i. Thus the residual is correlated with the explanatory variable x_i, and we get inconsistent estimates of the parameter β if we use the OLS method. In this case, because β is expected to be positive, and because $E(u_i \,|\, u_i \leqslant c - \beta x_i)$ decreases with increasing values of x_i, we get the result that the OLS estimator of β will be downward-biased;[1] that is,

[1] This follows from the well-known result about the least-squares bias from omitted variables, which says $E(\text{OLS estimate}) = (\text{true coefficient of the included variable}) + (\text{true coefficient of the omitted variable}) \times (\text{the regression coefficient from a regression of the excluded variable on the included variable}).$

estimating the effect of years of schooling on income from the data generated by the negative-income-tax experiment gives us an underestimate of the true effect.

Example 2: Schooling and earnings of low achievers

On this topic, see Hansen et al. (1970). Suppose we have a sample of military rejects – those who scored below the thirtieth percentile on the Armed Forces Qualification Test (AFQT). We wish to estimate an "intelligence" equation:

$$AFQT = f(\text{education, age, socioeconomic characteristics, etc.})$$

Again, we need to take into account the fact that the dependent variable is truncated. The OLS method will give biased estimates.

The least-squares bias arising from the truncation of the dependent variable also arises when we classify observations on the basis of the values of the dependent variable or when we aggregate observations on the basis of the dependent variable. The aggregation bias problem has been discussed by Feige and Watts (1972).

1.2   Censored regression models

Example 3: Demand for durable goods

If we have survey data on consumer expenditures, we find that most households report zero expenditures on automobiles or major household goods during any year. However, among those households that make any such expenditures, there will be wide variation in the amounts. Thus there will be a lot of observations concentrated around zero. Tobin (1958) analyzed this problem by formulating the regression model

$$
\begin{aligned}
y &= x\beta + u \quad \text{if } y > 0 \\
y &= 0 \quad \text{otherwise}
\end{aligned}
\tag{1.3}
$$

where y is expenditures and x is a set of explanatory variables. An alternative and perhaps a better way of formulating the model is the following:

Let y be the expenditure the individual can afford and y^* be "threshold" expenditure (the price of the cheapest automobile acceptable to the individual):

$$
\begin{aligned}
y &= x\beta + u \\
y^* &= z\gamma + v
\end{aligned}
\tag{1.4}
$$

The observed expenditures are y if $y > y^*$ and zero otherwise. In this alternative formulation the threshold y^* is not necessarily zero and can vary from individual to individual. We shall describe the methods for analyzing both models (1.3) and (1.4) in Chapter 6.

Example 4: Changes in holdings of liquid assets

Consider a change in a household's holding of liquid assets during a year. This variable can be positive or negative, but it cannot be smaller than the negative of the household's assets at the beginning of the year, because one cannot liquidate more assets than one owns. Here again the threshold is nonzero and is different for different individuals.

Example 5: Married women in the labor force

Let y^* be the reservation wage of the housewife based on her valuation of time in the household. Let y be the market wage based on an employer's valuation of her effort. The woman participates in the labor force if $y > y^*$. Otherwise she does not. In any given sample we have observations on y for those women who participate in the labor force, and we have no observations on y for those who do not. For these women we know only that $y^* \geq y$. Given these data, we have to estimate the coefficients in the equations explaining y^* and y, as in model (1.4). The analysis is similar to that in the case of automobile demand. This problem has been analyzed by Nelson (1975, 1977). There are more complicated versions of the labor-supply model that have been analyzed by Heckman (1974), Hanoch (1980a, b), and others. One interesting example of the problem of women in the labor force is that involving nurses. There are some nurses (particularly married nurses) who choose not to work because the value of their time at home is greater than their market wage. There is an interesting policy problem here concerning whether to spend money in training more nurses or to raise the wages of nurses so that some of those already trained who have chosen to stay at home can be brought into the labor force.

Examples 1 and 2 are illustrations of truncated regression models, and examples 3, 4, and 5 are illustrations of censored regression models. The distinction between the two is as follows:[2]

[2] See Aitchison and Brown (1957, Chapter 9). See also Kendall and Stuart (1967, p. 522) for a discussion of the difference between truncating and censoring.

Suppose that y is $N(\mu, \sigma^2)$ and that all our observations are for $y \geqslant T$. We do not have any observations for $y < T$. Then T is called the point of truncation, and the density of y, which is called a truncated normal distribution, is

$$
\begin{aligned}
g(y) &= \frac{1}{\sigma(2\pi)^{1/2}} \exp\left[-\frac{1}{2\sigma^2}(y-\mu)^2\right] \bigg/ \int_T^\infty \frac{1}{\sigma(2\pi)^{1/2}} \exp\left[-\frac{1}{2\sigma^2}(y-\mu)^2\right] dy \\
&= \frac{1}{\sigma}\phi\,\frac{y-\mu}{\sigma} \bigg/ \left[1-\Phi\left(\frac{T-\mu}{\sigma}\right)\right]
\end{aligned}
\tag{1.5}
$$

where ϕ refers to the standard normal density function and Φ refers to the cumulative normal.

On the other hand, suppose we have a sample of size n, of which n_1 observations are less than T and $n_2 = n - n_1$ observations are equal to or greater than T, and only for these n_2 observations are the exact values known. This is the case of a censored distribution.

The joint density of the observation is

$$
\binom{n}{n_1}\left[\Phi\left(\frac{T-\mu}{\sigma}\right)\right]^{n_1} \prod_{i=1}^{n_2} \frac{1}{\sigma(2\pi)^{1/2}} \exp\left[-\frac{1}{2\sigma^2}(y_i-\mu)^2\right]
\tag{1.6}
$$

In this case we do not have the exact values for n_1 observations, but we do have the information that they are all less than T. The maximum-likelihood estimates of the parameters μ and σ^2 in this case are obtained by maximizing (1.6) with respect to these parameters.

In the econometric literature it is customary to use the term *truncated normal distribution* to describe both of these cases; the term *censored distribution* is rarely used.[3] This is perhaps justified, because in analyses of both these models we shall be making use of the properties of the truncated normal distribution. In any case, it is important to note the definitions commonly used in the statistical literature and to bear in mind the distinction between the two problems. In the regression context, we do not have any observations on either the explained variable y or the explanatory variables x in the case of the truncated regression model if the value of y is above (or below) a threshold. This is the case with the data generated by the negative-income-tax experiment. In the case of the censored regression model, we have data on the explanatory

---

[3] Amemiya (1973) discussed a regression model in which the dependent variable is truncated normal. However, the model he considered is what is known in the statistical literature as the censored model. Nelson (1977) discussed a censored regression model (although the model is not a simple regression model).

variables x for all the observations. As for the explained variable y, we have actual observations for some, but for others we know only whether or not they are above (or below) a certain threshold. This is the model considered by Tobin.

1.3   Dummy endogenous variables

Example 6: Effects of unions on wages

Suppose we are given data on wages and personal characteristics of workers and we are told whether or not they are unionized. A naive way of estimating the effects of unionization on wages is to estimate a regression of wages on the personal characteristics of the workers (age, race, sex, education, experience, etc.) and a dummy variable that is defined as

$$D = 1 \quad \text{for unionized workers}$$
$$D = 0 \quad \text{otherwise}$$

The coefficient of D then measures the effect of unions on wages. Here the dummy variable D is exogenous. However, this is not a satisfactory method for analyzing the problem, because the dummy variable D is not exogenous but endogenous. The decision to join or not to join the union is determined by the expected gain. This is the formulation used by Lee (1978). Alternative formulations of endogenizing the dummy variable D in this example are somewhat mechanical approaches to this problem. All these studies will be discussed in Chapter 11.

Both examples 5 and 6 can also be called self-selectivity models. The data are generated by self-selection of individuals – the choices of individuals whether or not to participate in the labor force, whether or not to join the union,[4] and so forth. The earliest discussion of this problem in the context of labor supply was that of Lewis (1974). Some further examples of this follow.[5]

Example 7: Returns to college education

If we are given data on incomes of a sample of individuals, some with college educations and others without, our analysis must take into

[4] Of course, in the unions example, there are other problems, such as restriction of entry and union selectivity, in addition to the self-selectivity of the workers. There may also be some employer selectivity that makes employers more selective in their choices of employees if the employees are unionized.

[5] Models with self-selection are discussed in Chapter 9.

account the fact that those who have college educations are those who chose to go to college, and those who do not have college educations are those who chose (for their own reasons) not to go to college. A naive and commonly used way of analyzing these differences is to define a dummy variable

$D = 1$ if the person went to college

$D = 0$ otherwise

and estimate an earnings function with D as an extra explanatory variable. However, this is not a satisfactory solution to the problem, because the dummy variable D is itself determined by the choices of individuals on the basis of expected income and other factors. There have been many efforts made to include ability as an extra variable in the equations for earnings. However, in addition to the ability bias there is also a selectivity bias. The two are not mutually exclusive. Perhaps one should model the two factors taking into account the fact that persons with more ability are also capable of making the correct choices, so that the difference between expected incomes from the different choices is almost the same as the actual difference.

There has been a lot of discussion on returns to college education and whether or not college matters. However, in all these studies the usual regressions have been dummy-variable regressions (with perhaps some explanatory variables and IQ scores added). This is not a correct measure, because of the self-selectivity involved in the data. Also, a question is often asked: What would have been the average income for those who did not go to college if they had gone to college? Again, the answers to such questions are not obtained from simple dummy-variable regressions. See the work of Griliches et al. (1978), Kenny et al. (1979), and Willis and Rosen (1979).

Example 8: Demand for housing

In studies of demand for housing it is customary to analyze the demand for owner-occupied housing and the demand for rental housing separately, or else to regress housing expenditures (imputed rent for owner-occupied housing) on other explanatory variables and a dummy variable defined as

$D = 1$ for owner-occupied housing

$D = 0$ otherwise

Again, there is a self-selectivity problem here: Some individuals choose to own houses, and others choose to rent. In the estimated demand functions this choice must be taken into account. This problem has been analyzed by Trost (1977), Lee and Trost (1978), and Rosen (1979).

Example 9: Effects of fair-employment laws

Landes (1968) studied the effects of fair-employment legislation on the status of blacks. Landes used the regression model $y_i = \alpha X_i + \beta D_i + u_i$, where y_i is the wage of blacks relative to that for whites in state i, X_i is the vector of exogenous variables for state i, $D_i = 1$ if the state i has a fair-employment law ($D_i = 0$ otherwise), and u_i is a residual. The regression coefficient β is hypothesized to be positive. Landes found a marginally significant positive coefficient for β.

In this formulation, D_i is exongenous. However, the presence of a law is not an exogenous event. States in which blacks would fare well without a fair-employment law may be more likely to pass such a law if legislation depends on the concensus. On the other hand, one can argue for the reverse case that in states with much market discrimination, the demand for antidiscrimination legislation on the part of blacks is high, and this leads to a greater probability of fair-employment legislation in such states. Heckman (1976a) reanalyzed the Landes data allowing for the endogeneity of the dummy variable D_i.

Example 10: Compulsory school attendance laws

This example is similar to example 9 involving fair-employment laws. The passage of the legislation is itself an endogenous variable. This example has been discussed by Edwards (1978).

The foregoing examples illustrate the wide class of models in which limited-dependent-variable methods are applicable. We still have not discussed the multivariate log-linear models considered by Nerlove and Press (1973, 1976) or the several applications of the conditional logit model pioneered by McFadden (1974). These will be discussed in Chapters 5 and 3, respectively. We also have not discussed disequilibrium models, which will be considered in Chapter 10. Elaborating the illustrative examples for all these models would make this list far too lengthy.

Much of what will be discussed in subsequent chapters depends on the assumption that the underlying random variables have a (univariate or multivariate) normal distribution. Not much is known about the robustness of the results to departures from normality. We shall discuss the available results at the appropriate places.

In the case in which there is only one underlying random variable u, some alternative functional forms have been suggested. These are the following:

1. *Logistic distribution.* Actually, this is the cumulative distribution of the hyperbolic-secant-square (sech^2) distribution whose density function is given by

$$f(u) = \frac{e^u}{(1 + e^u)^2} \, du \quad -\infty < u < \infty \tag{1.7}$$

The cumulative distribution is

$$F(Z) = \frac{e^Z}{1 + e^Z} \tag{1.8}$$

which is the logistic function. The advantage of this distribution is that the distribution function has, unlike the normal, a closed-form expression given by (1.8). However, given the fast computer programs to evaluate the cumulative normal, this is not a major advantage today. The logistic and cumulative normal differ very little, and only at the tails. Hence, unless the sample size is very large, the empirical results obtained from the two will be very close.

The logistic function has been used frequently only in cases in which the dependent variable is binary (taking only two values, say 0 and 1), and then we refer to it as logit analysis (as opposed to probit analysis, in which the underlying variable u has a normal distribution). In actual practice, one need not confine the use of this function to only binary variables. One can as well use it to estimate any of the models given by equations (1.3)–(1.6).

2. *Cauchy distribution.* The main thing that characterizes the sech^2 distribution in equation (1.7) is that it has thicker tails than the normal. This is all the more true of the Cauchy distribution, whose density function is (in the standard form):

$$f(u) = \frac{1}{\pi} \cdot \frac{1}{1 + u^2} \tag{1.9}$$

The cumulative distribution function of this is

$$F(z) = \frac{1}{2} + \frac{1}{\pi} \tan^{-1} z$$

The general form of (1.9) is

$$f(u) = \frac{1}{\pi} \frac{1}{[1 + (x - \theta)/\lambda]^2} \tag{1.10}$$

Table 1.1. *Comparisons of Cauchy and normal distributions*

	Pr$(X \leqslant x)$	
x	Cauchy	Normal
0	0.5000	0.5000
0.4	0.6211	0.6063
0.6	0.6720	0.6571
1.0	0.7500	0.7500
2.0	0.8524	0.9113
3.0	0.8976	0.9785
4.0	0.9220	0.9965

A comparison of the Cauchy and the normal distributions is given in Table 1.1.[6] This shows how much thicker the tails of the Cauchy distribution are as compared with those of the normal. The cumulative normal and the logistic, on the other hand, agree much more closely (see Cox, 1970, Table 2.1., p. 28).

3. *Burr distribution.* This has been discussed by Burr (1942). The density function is given by

$$f(u) = \frac{cku^{c-1}}{(1 + u^c)^{k+1}} \quad (c, k > 0, \ u > 0) \tag{1.11}$$

and the cumulative distribution function is given by

$$F(z) = 1 - \frac{1}{(1 + z^c)^k} \quad (c, k > 0) \tag{1.12}$$

All these distributions have the property that the cumulative distributions have closed-form expressions. However, as mentioned earlier, this is not important, because of present-day computer technology. The Burr distribution has the advantage that it can handle random variables that take on only positive values. With the normal and the logistic distributions, one can handle such variables by considering the appropriate log-transforms, that is, by assuming that $\log u$ instead of u follows a normal (or sech^2) distribution. Other feasible alternatives are the gamma distribution and the beta distribution.

As mentioned earlier, unless samples are very large and the observations at the tails exert a large influence, one obtains similar results using

[6] This is based on Table 1 from Johnson and Kotz (1970, p. 155).

probit analysis and logit analysis. However, when comparing the results of probit versus logit analysis, one must take account of the fact that the variance of a standard normal is 1, whereas the variance of the standard sech^2 distribution given by (1.7) is $\pi^2/3$. Thus, one must multiply the logit coefficients by $(3/\pi)^{1/2}$ to get coefficients comparable to the probit coefficients. Amemiya (1981) suggested that multiplying the logit coefficients by 1/1.6 or 0.625 is slightly better. This transformation actually brings the logistic distribution closer to the distribution function of the standard normal. More discussion of logit versus probit analysis is contained in the next chapter. In the univariate case, there is perhaps not much difference between the cumulative normal and the logistic distributions. However, as we shall see later, when we discuss models involving bivariate and multivariate distributions, the multivariate logistic has very restrictive properties as compared with the multivariate normal. These problems will be discussed in Chapter 5.

In subsequent chapters we shall first discuss discrete regression models, the simple limited-dependent-variable models, and then move on to more complicated models. Throughout this book, $\log x$ means $\log_e x$.

One problem we have omitted from our discussion (mentioned briefly in section 2.17 of Chapter 2) is that of analysis of panel data with qualitative and limited-dependent-variable models. A great amount of work has been done in this area in recent years, and going through it would make this book unusually lengthy.

$y = 3$ if the individual has completed college but not a higher degree

$y = 4$ if the individual has a professional degree

In studies of marketing research, one often considers attitudes of preference that are measured on a scale 1, 2, 3, 4, 5. For instance,

$y = 1$ if intensely dislike

$y = 2$ if moderately dislike

$y = 3$ if neutral

$y = 4$ if moderately like

$y = 5$ if intensely like

This is an example of an ordered categorical variable.

The methods of analysis are different for models with categorical and noncategorical variables. In the following sections we shall first discuss binary dependent variables, then the different kinds of categorical variables, and finally the noncategorical variables.

2.2   The linear probability model

The term *linear probability model* is used to denote a regression model in which the dependent variable y is a binary variable taking the value of 1 if the event occurs and 0 otherwise. Examples of this include purchases of durable goods in a given year, participation in the labor force, the decision to marry, and the decision to have children. We write the model in the usual regression framework as

$$y_i = \beta'x_i + u_i \tag{2.1}$$

with $E(u_i) = 0$. The conditional expectation $E(y_i \mid x_i)$ is equal to $\beta'x_i$. This has to be interpreted in this case as the probability that the event will occur given the x_i. The calculated value of y from the regression equation, $\hat{y}_i = \hat{\beta}'x_i$, will then give the estimated probability that the event will occur given the particular value of x. In practice, these estimated probabilities can lie outside the admissible range $(0, 1)$.

Because y_i takes the value of 1 or 0, the residuals in equation (2.1) can take only two values: $1 - \beta'x_i$ and $-\beta'x_i$. Also, given our interpretation of equation (2.1) and the requirement that $E(u_i) = 0$, the respective probabilities of these events are $\beta'x_i$ and $1 - \beta'x_i$. Thus we have

u_i	$f(u_i)$
$1 - \beta'x_i$	$\beta'x_i$
$-\beta'x_i$	$(1 - \beta'x_i)$

Hence,

$$\mathrm{Var}(u_i) = \beta'x_i(1 - \beta'x_i)^2 + (1 - \beta'x_i)(\beta'x_i)^2$$
$$= \beta'x_i(1 - \beta'x_i)$$
$$= E(y_i)[1 - E(y_i)]$$

Because of this heteroscedasticity problem, the ordinary least squares (OLS) estimates of β from equation (2.1) will not be efficient. Goldberger (1964, p. 250) suggested the following procedure: First, estimate (2.1) by OLS. Next, compute $\hat{y}_i(1-\hat{y}_i)$ and use weighted least squares; that is, defining

$$w_i = [\hat{y}_i(1 - \hat{y}_i)]^{1/2}$$

we regress y_i/w_i on x_i/w_i. The problems with this procedure are the following:

1. In practice, $\hat{y}_i(1-\hat{y}_i)$ may be negative, although in large samples there is a very small probability that this will be so. However, McGillivray (1970) showed that $\hat{y}_i(1-\hat{y}_i)$ is a consistent estimator for $E(y_i)[1-E(y_i)]$.

2. Because the residuals u_i are obviously not normally distributed, the least-squares method is not, in general, fully efficient; that is, there are nonlinear procedures that are more efficient than the least-squares procedure. As will be seen in the next section, this criticism does not affect the significance tests, provided one makes the additional assumption that the explanatory variables have a multivariate normal distribution.

3. The most important criticism concerns the formulation itself – that the conditional expectations $E(y_i \mid x_i)$ be interpreted as the probability that the event will occur. In many cases $E(y_i \mid x_i)$ can lie outside the limits $(0, 1)$.

2.3   The linear discriminant function

In spite of the fact that the residuals in the linear probability model are not normally distributed, one can justify its use because of the correspondence that exists between the linear discriminant function and the linear probability model (Ladd, 1966). We shall first discuss the linear discriminant function and then its relationship to the linear probability model.

In linear discriminant analysis we try to find a linear function, say $\lambda'x$, of k explanatory variables, that provides the best discrimination between the two groups corresponding to $y=1$ and $y=0$. It makes intuitive sense that λ should be chosen so that the variance of $\lambda'x$ between groups is maximum relative to its variance within groups (λ and x are k-dimensional vectors).

Suppose that there are n_1 observations for which $y=1$ and n_2 observations for which $y=0$. Denote the values of x in these groups by x_1 and x_2, respectively. Define

$$\bar{x}_1 = \frac{1}{n_1} \sum_i x_{1i}$$

$$\bar{x}_2 = \frac{1}{n_2} \sum_i x_{2i}$$

$$\bar{x} = \frac{1}{n_1 + n_2} (n_1 \bar{x}_1 + n_2 \bar{x}_2) \tag{2.2}$$

and

$$S = \frac{1}{n_1 + n_2 - 2} \left[\sum_i (x_{1i} - \bar{x}_1)(x_{1i} - \bar{x}_1)' + \sum_i (x_{2i} - \bar{x}_2)(x_{2i} - \bar{x}_2)' \right] \tag{2.3}$$

Then the between-group variance of $\lambda'x$ is $\lambda'(\bar{x}_1 - \bar{x}_2)^2$. The within-group variance of $\lambda'x$ is $\lambda'S\lambda$. Thus, we choose λ to maximize

$$\phi = \frac{\lambda'(\bar{x}_1 - \bar{x}_2)^2}{\lambda'S\lambda}$$

This gives

$$\hat{\lambda} = S^{-1}(\bar{x}_1 - \bar{x}_2) \tag{2.4}$$

The means of the discriminant functions in the two samples are, respectively,

$$\bar{y}_1 = \hat{\lambda}'\bar{x}_1 = (\bar{x}_1 - \bar{x}_2)'S^{-1}\bar{x}_1$$
$$\bar{y}_2 = \hat{\lambda}'\bar{x}_2 = (\bar{x}_1 - \bar{x}_2)'S^{-1}\bar{x}_2$$

Given a new observation with characteristics, say, x_0, we calculate

$$y_0 = \hat{\lambda}'x_0 = (\bar{x}_1 - \bar{x}_2)'S^{-1}x_0$$

and assign it to the first group if y_0 is closer to $\bar{y}_1$ than to $\bar{y}_2$. If $\bar{y}_1$ is greater than $\bar{y}_2$, y_0 will be closer to $\bar{y}_1$ than to $\bar{y}_2$ if

$$|y_0 - \bar{y}_1| > |y_0 - \bar{y}_2|$$

that is, if

$$y_0 > \tfrac{1}{2}(\bar{y}_1 + \bar{y}_2)$$

Thus the cutoff point is the average of the two means. The square of the difference between the means is often called the Mahalanobis generalized distance and is denoted by D^2. Thus, $D^2 = (\bar{y}_1 - \bar{y}_2)^2$.

$$D^2 = (\bar{x}_1 - \bar{x}_2)' S^{-1} (\bar{x}_1 - \bar{x}_2) \tag{2.5}$$

If $S = I$, this is nothing but the Euclidean distance between the points $\bar{x}_1$ and $\bar{x}_2$.

To apply any test of significance, we need to make the assumption of normality. The usual assumption made is that the explanatory variables in the two groups come from normal populations with means μ_1 and μ_2, respectively, and the same covariance matrix Σ. Under this assumption, to test whether or not there are significant differences between the two groups, we use the ratio

$$F = \frac{n_1 n_2 (n_1 + n_2 - k - 1)}{(n_1 + n_2)(n_1 + n_2 - 2)k} D^2 \tag{2.6}$$

as an F ratio with degrees of freedom k and $(n_1 + n_2 - k - 1)$, where k is the number of explanatory variables. This is the test (known as Hotelling's T^2 test) for the hypothesis $\mu_1 = \mu_2$, assuming normality for the distribution of x and a common covariance matrix Σ.

The method outlined here in deriving λ is distribution-free, but the F test is not. Also, the cutoff point $\frac{1}{2}(y_1 + y_2)$ can be improved on if we have some prior probabilities that x belongs to either population, and if we are given the costs of misclassification.

2.4   Analogy with multiple regression and the linear probability model

Fisher (1936) also suggested an analogy between multiple regression and discriminant analysis. Suppose we define a dummy variable as follows:

$$y = \frac{n_2}{n_1 + n_2} \quad \text{if the individual belongs to } \pi_1 \text{ (first group)}$$

$$y = -\frac{n_1}{n_1 + n_2} \quad \text{if the individual belongs to } \pi_2 \text{ (second group)}$$

where n_1 and n_2 are the numbers of sample observations in π_1 and π_2. This gives $\bar{y} = 0$, where $\bar{y}$ is the sample mean of y over all $n_1 + n_2$ observations. We also define

$$\bar{x} = \frac{1}{n_1 + n_2} (n_1 \bar{x}_1 + n_2 \bar{x}_2) \tag{2.7}$$

where $\bar{x}_1$ and $\bar{x}_2$ are, respectively, the means of x in the two subsamples corresponding to the two groups. Let us use $\Sigma_{1,2}$ to denote summation over all $n_1 + n_2$ observations, Σ_1 to denote summation over the n_1 observations in the first group, and Σ_2 to denote summation over the n_2 observations in the second group.

Consider the multiple regression of y on x, that is, the estimation of α and β in

$$E(y_i) = \alpha + \beta'x_i$$

The normal equations are

$$\sum_{1,2}(x_i - \bar{x})(x_i - \bar{x})'\hat{\beta} = \sum_{1,2} y_i(x_i - x) \tag{2.8}$$

and $\hat{\alpha} = -\hat{\beta}'\bar{x}$ (because $\bar{y} = 0$). Now $\Sigma_{1,2}\, y_i\bar{x} = 0$, because $\Sigma y_i = 0$, and

$$\sum_{1,2} y_i x_i = \frac{n_2}{n_1 + n_2} \sum_1 x_i - \frac{n_1}{n_1 + n_2} \sum_2 x_i = \frac{n_1 n_2}{n_1 + n_2}(\bar{x}_1 - \bar{x}_2)$$

Also,

$$\sum_{1,2}(x_i - \bar{x})(x_i - \bar{x})' = \sum_1 (x_i - \bar{x})(x_i - \bar{x})' + \sum_2 (x_i - \bar{x})(x_i - \bar{x})' \tag{2.9}$$

The first term in (2.9) can be written as

$$\sum_1 (x_i - \bar{x}_1 + \bar{x}_1 - \bar{x})(x_i - \bar{x}_1 + \bar{x}_1 - \bar{x})'$$

$$= \sum_1 (x_i - \bar{x}_1)(x_i - \bar{x}_1)' + n_1(\bar{x}_1 - \bar{x})(\bar{x}_1 - \bar{x})'$$

(since the cross-product terms vanish). Similarly, the second term in (2.9) can be written as

$$\sum_2 (x_i - \bar{x}_2)(x_i - \bar{x}_2)' + n_2(\bar{x}_2 - \bar{x})(\bar{x}_2 - \bar{x})'$$

Also, using (2.2), $n_1(\bar{x}_1 - \bar{x})(\bar{x}_1 - \bar{x})' + n_2(\bar{x}_2 - \bar{x})(\bar{x}_2 - \bar{x})'$ can be simplified to $[n_1 n_2/(n_1 + n_2)](\bar{x}_1 - \bar{x}_2)(\bar{x}_1 - \bar{x}_2)'$. Noting the definition of S in (2.3), we finally have

$$\sum_{1,2}(x_i - \bar{x})(x_i - \bar{x})' = (n_1 + n_2 - 2)S + \frac{n_1 n_2}{n_1 + n_2}(\bar{x}_1 - \bar{x}_2)(\bar{x}_1 - \bar{x}_2)'$$

If we define

$$\theta = (\bar{x}_1 - \bar{x}_2)'\hat{\beta} \tag{2.10}$$

the normal equations (2.8) can be written as

$$(n_1 + n_2 - 2)S\hat{\beta} = \frac{n_1 n_2 (1 - \theta)}{n_1 + n_2}(\bar{x}_1 - \bar{x}_2) \tag{2.11}$$

or

$$\hat{\beta} = \frac{n_1 n_2 (1 - \theta)}{(n_1 + n_2)(n_1 + n_2 - 2)} S^{-1}(\bar{x}_1 - \bar{x}_2)$$

$$= \frac{n_1 n_2 (1 - \theta)}{(n_1 + n_2)(n_1 + n_2 - 2)} \hat{\lambda} \tag{2.12}$$

Thus the regression coefficients $\hat{\beta}$ are proportional to the discriminant coefficients $\hat{\lambda}$ derived in (2.4). We can easily show that the constant of proportionality is nothing but $RSS/(n_1 + n_2 - 2)$, where RSS is the residual sum of squares from the regression of the dummy variable y on x. To see this, note that

$$\sum y_i^2 = n_1 \left(\frac{n_2}{n_1 + n_2} \right)^2 + n_2 \left(-\frac{n_1}{n_1 + n_2} \right)^2 = \frac{n_1 n_2}{n_1 + n_2}$$

The regression sum of squares is

$$\hat{\beta}' \frac{n_1 n_2}{n_1 + n_2}(\bar{x}_1 - \bar{x}_2) = \frac{n_1 n_2}{n_1 + n_2}\theta$$

Hence, the residual sum of squares is $[n_1 n_2/(n_1 + n_2)](1 - \theta)$, and $R^2 = \theta$. Thus, equation (2.12) can be written as

$$\hat{\beta} = \hat{\lambda}\frac{RSS}{n_1 + n_2 - 2} \tag{2.13}$$

Thus, once we have the regression coefficients and the residual sum of squares from the dummy-dependent-variable regression, we can very easily obtain the discriminant-function coefficients.

The linear probability model is only slightly different from the formulation of Fisher. In the linear probability model we define

$$y = 1 \quad \text{if the individual comes from } \pi_1$$
$$y = 0 \quad \text{if the individual comes from } \pi_2$$

This merely amounts to adding $n_1/(n_1 + n_2)$ to each observation of y as defined by Fisher. Thus, only the estimate of α of the constant term changes, and $\hat{\beta}$ and other statistics are the same as before.

The F statistic to test for the significance $\beta = 0$, as though y_i had a normal distribution, is

$$F = \frac{R^2/k}{(1 - R^2)/(n_1 + n_2 - k - 1)}$$

$$= \frac{\theta/k}{(1-\theta)/(n_1 + n_2 - k - 1)}$$

with k and $n_1 + n_2 - K - 1$ degrees of freedom. But from (2.10) and (2.12) we have

$$\theta = (\bar{x}_1 - \bar{x}_2)'\hat{\beta} = \frac{n_1 n_2 (1 - \theta)}{(n_1 + n_2)(n_1 + n_2 - 2)} (\bar{x}_1 - \bar{x}_2)' S^{-1}(\bar{x}_1 - \bar{x}_2)$$

Thus

$$\frac{\theta}{1 - \theta} = \frac{n_1 n_2}{(n_1 + n_2)(n_1 + n_2 - 2)} D^2$$

where D^2 is as defined in (2.5). Hence,

$$F = \frac{n_1 n_2 (n_1 + n_2 - k - 1)}{(n_1 + n_2)(n_1 + n_2 - 2)k} D^2$$

This is exactly the same formula as (2.6).

By a similar derivation one can show that the t statistics for testing $\lambda_i = 0$ (or $\beta_i = 0$ in the linear probability model) really do have t distributions with $n_1 + n_2 - k - 1$ degrees of freedom, despite the binary form of the dependent variable. These are all exact (not asymptotic) F tests and t tests conditional on the joint normality of the x's. Also, the tests for any subsets of λ (or β) can be carried out in the usual manner, as in a linear hypothesis.[1]

Suppose we divide the vector x into (x_1, x_2), where x_1 has k_1 $(<k)$ variables. A test for the hypothesis that the k_1 variables in x_1 are sufficient for discrimination is given by

$$F = \frac{n_1 + n_2 - k - 1}{k - k_1} \cdot \frac{C(D^2 - D_1^2)}{1 + CD_1^2}$$

where D^2 and D_1^2 are the Mahalanobis distances with the full set x and the subset x_1, respectively, and

$$C = \frac{n_1 n_2}{(n_1 + n_2)(n_1 + n_2 - 2)}$$

This has an F distribution with degrees of freedom $k - k_1$ and $n_1 + n_2 - k - 1$ (Rao, 1970). It can be shown that this statistic is the same as the F statistic for testing the linear hypothesis $\beta_2 = 0$ if the vector β is correspondingly partitioned into (β_1, β_2).

---

[1] Note that for all these tests we have to assume that the x's are jointly normally distributed in each group. This excludes binary and truncated x's.

2.5   The probit and logit models

An alternative approach, called by Goldberger (1964) the *probit analysis model,* is to assume that there is an underlying response variable y_i^* defined by the regression relationship

$$y_i^* = \beta'x_i + u_i \tag{2.14}$$

In practice, y_i^* is unobservable. What we observe is a dummy variable y defined by

$$\begin{align} y &= 1 \quad \text{if } y_i^* > 0 \\ y &= 0 \quad \text{otherwise} \end{align} \tag{2.15}$$

In this formulation, $\beta'x_i$ is not $E(y_i | x_i)$ as in the linear probability model; it is $E(y_i^* | x_i)$.

From the relations (2.14) and (2.15) we get

$$\begin{align} \text{Prob}(y_i = 1) &= \text{Prob}(u_i > -\beta'x_i) \\ &= 1 - F(-\beta'x_i) \end{align} \tag{2.16}$$

where F is the cumulative distribution function for u.

In this case the observed values of y are just realizations of a binomial process with probabilities given by (2.16) and varying from trial to trial (depending on x_i). Hence, the likelihood function is

$$L = \prod_{y_i=0} F(-\beta'x_i) \prod_{y_i=1} [1 - F(-\beta'x_i)] \tag{2.17}$$

The functional form for F in (2.17) will depend on the assumptions made about u_i in (2.14). If the cumulative distribution of u_i is the logistic, we have the *logit model.* In this case,

$$F(-\beta'x_i) = \frac{\exp(-\beta'x_i)}{1 + \exp(-\beta'x_i)} = \frac{1}{1 + \exp(\beta'x_i)}$$

Hence,

$$1 - F(-\beta'x_i) = \frac{\exp(\beta'x_i)}{1 + \exp(\beta'x_i)} \tag{2.18}$$

In this case we say that there is a closed-form expression for F, because it does not involve integrals explicitly. Not all distributions permit such a closed-form expression. For instance, in the *probit model* (or, more accurately, the *normit* model) we assume that u_i are $IN(0, \sigma^2)$. In this case,

$$F(-\beta'x_i) = \int_{-\infty}^{-\beta'x_i/\sigma} \frac{1}{(2\pi)^{1/2}} \exp\left(-\frac{t^2}{2}\right) dt \tag{2.19}$$

It can be easily seen from (2.19) and the likelihood function (2.17) that we can estimate only β/σ, and not β and σ separately. Hence, we might as well assume $\sigma=1$ to start with.

Because the cumulative normal distribution and the logistic distribution are very close to each other, except at the tails, we are not likely to get very different results using (2.18) or (2.19), that is, the logit or the probit method, unless the samples are large (so that we have enough observations at the tails). However, the estimates of β from the two methods are not directly comparable. Because the logistic distribution has a variation $\pi^2/3$, the estimates of β obtained from the logit model have to be multiplied by $3^{1/2}/\pi$ to be comparable to the estimates obtained from the probit model (where we normalize σ to be equal to 1).

Amemiya (1981) suggested that the logit estimates be multiplied by $1/1.6 = 0.625$, instead of $(3^{1/2}/\pi)$ saying that this transformation produces a closer approximation between the logistic distribution and the distribution function of the standard normal. He also suggested that the coefficients of the linear probability model $\hat{\beta}_{LP}$ and the coefficients of the logit model $\hat{\beta}_L$ are related by the relationships

$$\hat{\beta}_{LP} \simeq 0.25\hat{\beta}_L \quad \text{except for the constant term}$$
$$\hat{\beta}_{LP} \simeq 0.25\hat{\beta}_L + 0.5 \quad \text{for the constant term}$$

Thus, if we need to make $\hat{\beta}_{LP}$ comparable to the probit coefficients, we need to multiply them by 2.5 and subtract 1.25 from the constant term.

An alternative way of comparing the models would be to (a) calculate the sum of squared deviations from predicted probabilities, (b) compare the percentages correctly predicted, and (c) look at the derivatives of the probabilities with respect to a particular independent variable. Let x_{ik} be the kth element of the vector of explanatory variables x_i, and let β_k be the kth element of β. Then the derivatives for the probabilities given by the linear probability model, probit model, and logit model are, respectively,

$$\frac{\partial}{\partial x_{ik}}(x_i'\beta) = \beta_k$$

$$\frac{\partial}{\partial x_{ik}}\Phi(x_i'\beta) = \phi(x_i'\beta)\beta_k$$

$$\frac{\partial}{\partial x_{ik}}L(x_i'\beta) = \frac{\exp(x_i'\beta)}{[1 + \exp(x_i'\beta)]^2}\beta_k$$

These derivatives will be needed for predicting the effects of changes in one of the independent variables on the probability of belonging to a

Table 2.1. *Comparison of the probit, logit, and linear probability models: loan data from South Carolina*

Variable[a]	Linear probability model	Logit model	Probit model
AI	1.489 (4.69)[b]	2.254 (4.60)	2.030 (4.73)
XMD	−1.509 (5.74)	−1.170 (5.57)	−1.773 (5.67)
DF	0.140 (0.78)	0.563 (0.87)	0.206 (0.95)
DR	−0.266 (1.84)	−0.240 (1.60)	−0.279 (1.66)
DS	−0.238 (1.75)	−0.222 (1.51)	−0.274 (1.70)
DA	−1.426 (3.52)	−1.463 (3.34)	−1.570 (3.29)
NNWP	−1.762 (0.74)	−2.028 (0.80)	−2.360 (0.85)
NMFI	0.150 (0.23)	0.149 (0.20)	0.194 (0.25)
NA	−0.393 (1.34)	−0.386 (1.25)	−0.425 (1.26)
Const.	0.501	0.363	0.488

Note: Total number of observations = 750; number of applications rejected = 250; number of applications accepted = 500. To make the coefficients comparable to one another, we have multiplied the logit coefficients by 0.625 and the coefficients of the linear probability model by 2.5 and then subtracted 1.25 from the constant term, as explained in the text.
[a] AI, applicant's + coapplicant's incomes (in 10^5 dollars); XMD, debt minus mortgate payment (in 10^3 dollars); DF, 1 if female; DR, 1 if nonwhite; DS, 1 if single; DA, age of house (in 10^2 years); NNWP, (neighborhood % nonwhite) $\times 10^3$; NMFI, neighborhood mean family income (in 10^5 dollars); NA, neighborhood average age of homes (in 10^2 years).
[b] t ratios in parentheses.

group. In the case of the linear probability model, these derivatives are constant. In the case of the probit and logit models, we need to calculate them at different levels of the explanatory variables to get an idea of the range of variation of the resulting changes in the probabilities.

As an illustration, we consider data on a sample of 750 mortgage loan applications in the Columbia, South Carolina, metropolitan area. There were 500 loan applications accepted and 250 loan applications rejected. Define

$y = 1$ if the loan application was accepted

$y = 0$ if the loan application was rejected

Table 2.1 shows the results for the linear probability model, and logit model, and the probit model. The linear probability model was estimated by ordinary least squares (not weighted least squares). Thus the correction for heteroscedasticity has not been made. The coefficients of the discriminant function can thus be obtained from these estimates by using the formula (2.13).

The likelihood function (2.17) can be written as

$$L = \prod_{i=1}^{n} \left(\frac{1}{1 + \exp(\beta'x_i)} \right)^{1-y_i} \left(\frac{\exp(\beta'x_i)}{1 + \exp(\beta'x_i)} \right)^{y_i} \quad (2.20)$$

$$= \frac{\exp(\beta') \sum_{i=1}^{n} x_i y_i}{\prod_{i=1}^{n} [1 + \exp(\beta'x_i)]} \quad (2.21)$$

Define $t^* = \sum_{i=1}^{n} x_i y_i$. To find the maximum-likelihood (ML) estimate of β, we have

$$\log L = \beta't^* - \sum_{i=1}^{n} \log[1 + \exp(\beta'x_i)]$$

Hence, $\partial \log L / \partial \beta = 0$ gives

$$S(\beta) = -\sum_{i=1}^{n} \frac{\exp(\beta'x_i)}{1 + \exp(\beta'x_i)} x_i + t^* = 0 \quad (2.22)$$

These equations are nonlinear in β. Hence, we have to use the Newton–Raphson method or the scoring method to solve the equations. The information matrix is

$$I(\beta) = E\left(-\frac{\partial^2 \log L}{\partial \beta \partial \beta'} \right)$$

$$= \sum_{i=1}^{n} \frac{\exp(\beta'x_i)}{[1 + \exp(\beta'x_i)]^2} x_i x_i' \quad (2.23)$$

Starting with some initial value of β, say β_0, we compute the values $S(\beta_0)$ and $I(\beta_0)$. Then the new estimate of β is, by the method of scoring,

$$\beta_1 = \beta_0 + [I(\beta_0)]^{-1} S(\beta_0)$$

In practice, we divide both $I(\beta_0)$ and $S(\beta_0)$ by n, the sample size. This iterative procedure is repeated until convergence. In the present case it is clear that $I(\beta)$ is positive definite at each stage of iteration. Hence, the iterative procedure will converge to a maximum of the likelihood function, no matter what the starting value is. If the final converged estimates are denoted by $\hat{\beta}$, then the asymptotic covariance matrix is estimated by $[I(\hat{\beta})]^{-1}$. These estimated variances and covariances will enable us to test hypotheses about the different elements of $\hat{\beta}$.

After estimating β, we can get estimated values of the probability that the ith observation is equal to 1. Denoting these estimated values by $\hat{p}_i$, we have

$$\hat{p}_i = \frac{\exp(\hat{\beta}'x_i)}{1 + \exp(\hat{\beta}'x_i)}$$

Equation (2.22) shows that

$$\sum \hat{p}_i x_i = \sum y_i x_i \tag{2.24}$$

Thus, if x_i includes a constant term, then the sum of the estimated probabilities is equal to $\sum y_i$ or the number of observations in the sample for which $y_i = 1$. In other words, the predicted frequency is equal to the actual frequency. Similarly, if x_i includes a dummy variable, say 1 for female, 0 for male, then the predicted frequency will be equal to the actual frequency for each sex group. Similar conclusions follow for the linear probability model by virtue of the fact that equations (2.24) are the least-squares normal equations in that case.

In any case, after estimating $\hat{\beta}$ and then $\hat{p}_i$ by the logit model, it is always good practice to check whether or not equations (2.24) are satisfied.

For the probit model, we substitute expression (2.19) in equation (2.17).

Let us denote by $\phi(\cdot)$ and $\Phi(\cdot)$ the density function and the distribution function, respectively, of the standard normal. Then for the probit model the likelihood function corresponding to (2.20) is

$$L = \prod_{i=1}^{n} [\Phi(\beta'x_i)]^{y_i} [1 - \Phi(\beta'x_i)]^{1-y_i}$$

and the log-likelihood is

$$\log L = \sum_{i=1}^{n} y_i \log \Phi(\beta'x_i) + \sum_{i=1}^{n} (1 - y_i) \log[1 - \Phi(\beta'x_i)]$$

Differentiating $\log L$ with respect to β yields

$$S(\beta) = \frac{\partial \log L}{\partial \beta} = \sum_{i=1}^{n} \frac{[y_i - \Phi(\beta'x_i)]}{\Phi(\beta'x_i)[1 - \Phi(\beta'x_i)]} \phi(\beta'x_i) x_i$$

The ML estimator $\hat{\beta}_{ML}$ can be obtained as a solution of the equations $S(\beta) = 0$.

These equations are nonlinear in β, and thus we have to solve them by an iterative procedure. The information matrix is

$$I(\beta) = E\left(-\frac{\partial^2 \log L}{\partial \beta \partial \beta'}\right)$$

$$= \sum_{i=1}^{n} \frac{[\phi(\beta'x_i)]^2}{\Phi(\beta'x_i)[1 - \Phi(\beta'x_i)]} x_i x_i'$$

As with the logit model, we start with an initial value of β, say β_0, and compute the values $S(\beta_0)$ and $I(\beta_0)$. Then the new estimate of β is, by the method of scoring,

$$\beta_1 = \beta_0 + [I(\beta_0)]^{-1}S(\beta_0)$$

Note that $I(\beta)$ is positive definite at each stage of the iteration. Hence, the iterative procedure will converge to a maximum of the likelihood function no matter what the starting value is. If the final converged estimates are denoted by $\hat{\beta}$, then the asymptotic covariance matrix is estimated by $[I(\hat{\beta})]^{-1}$. These can be used to conduct any tests of significance.

2.6 Comparison of the logit model and normal discriminant analysis

There have been many studies on the relative performances of the logit model and discriminant analysis in analyzing models with dichotomous dependent variables. The reason for this interest is that ordinary least-squares procedures can be used to estimate the coefficients of the linear discriminant function, whereas maximum-likelihood methods are required for estimation of the logit model. Given the high-speed computers now available, computational simplicity is no longer an adequate criterion.

If the independent variables are normally distributed, the discriminant-analysis estimator is the true maximum-likelihood estimator and therefore is asymptotically more efficient than the logit maximum-likelihood estimator (MLE). However, if the independent variables are not normal, the discriminant-analysis estimator is not even consistent, whereas the logit MLE is consistent and therefore more robust (see section 4.4 for some examples of this). Press and Wilson (1978) calculated the probability of correct classification for the two estimators in two empirical examples in which the independent variables were dummy variables, and thus the assumption of normality was violated. In both examples, the logit MLE did slightly better than the discriminant-analysis estimator. The criterion of the goodness of prediction in their study was the probability of correct classification defined by

$$P(\beta'x_i \geqslant 0 \mid y_i = 1)Q + P(\beta'x_i < 0 \mid y_i = 0)(1 - Q)$$

where $Q = \text{Prob}(y_i = 1)$.

The close relationship between the logit model and the discriminant function discussed here does not hold good except under very special circumstances in the case of McFadden's (1974) conditional logit model. This model is discussed in section 2.12 and Chapter 3. The relationship between this logit model and discriminant analysis has been discussed by McFadden (1976a).

2.7   The twin linear probability model

Goldberger (1964) used the name twin linear probability model to describe the following situation. Suppose we have data on y for those individuals for whom $y > 0$ (e.g., for those who bought cars). In this method we fit a linear probability model for the $(0, 1)$ dichotomous variable and a classical regression model for the subsample for which $y > 0$. The explanatory variables can be the same in both the functions. This was the method used by Fisher (1962) to analyze consumer durable-goods expenditures in 1957. The linear probability function was estimated for all 762 observations. The dependent variable was defined as $y = 1$ if any expenditure was made, $y = 0$ otherwise. The usual regression equation was fitted for 359 observations based on the data for the people who made purchases. Here the dependent variable was the actual expenditure. In this model,

$$E(y) = P(y > 0) \quad [E(y \mid y > 0)] \tag{2.25}$$

The first expression in (2.25) is obtained from the linear probability model, and the second expression is obtained from the usual regression function. A similar approach was followed by Cragg (1971); he applied the probit model rather than the linear probabilty model to the $(0, 1)$ decision.

The twin linear probability model is subject to the same criticisms as the linear probability model discussed earlier. In addition, one can also criticize the two-stage decision framework. The model implies that individuals first decide whether or not to buy and then decide on how much to spend if they decide to buy. In actual practice these decisions are simultaneous rather than sequential. This same argument can be made against the model discussed by Cragg (1971). Later we shall discuss models in which these decisions are considered simultaneously.

2.8   The case of multiple observations: minimum chi-square methods

With multiple observations (as with grouped data), however, the linear probability model is not subject to as many criticisms as with ungrouped data. Suppose we have n_i observations corresponding to x_i, and suppose that for m_i the event occurred, and for $n_i - m_i$ the event did not occur. Then the empirical probabilities are

$$\hat{p}_i = \frac{m_i}{n_i}$$

Suppose we write the theoretical probabilities as

$$p_i = \beta' x_i \tag{2.26}$$

This is a *linear probability function*, so called because the probability p_i is expressed as a linear combination of the regressors x_i. We can write equation (2.26) as

$$\hat{p}_i = \beta' x_i + u_i \tag{2.27}$$

where $u_i = \hat{p}_i - p_i$.

In large samples (i.e., n_i large for all i) we have $\hat{p}_i \simeq p_i$ and $E(u_i) \simeq 0$. Also, $\text{Var}(\hat{p}_i) = p_i(1-p_i)/n_i$, which can be estimated by $\hat{p}_i(1-\hat{p}_i)/n_i$ if n_i is large. Thus, one can use a weighted least-squares method to estimate β in (2.27) using as weights

$$w_i = \left(\frac{n_i}{\hat{p}_i(1-\hat{p}_i)} \right)^{1/2}$$

The method just described is called the *minimum chi-square method*.

In a log-linear model, we assume, instead of (2.26),

$$\log p_i = \beta' x_i \tag{2.28}$$

In this case we write

$$\log \hat{p}_i = \beta' x_i + u_i \tag{2.29}$$

where $u_i = \log \hat{p}_i - \log p_i$. Expanding $\log \hat{p}_i$ around p_i in a Taylor series, we get

$$\log \hat{p}_i = \log p_i + (\hat{p}_i - p_i) \frac{1}{p_i} + \text{higher-order terms}$$

Hence, $u_i \simeq (1/p_i)(\hat{p}_i - p_i)$. In large samples, $E(u_i) \simeq 0$, and

$$\text{Var}(u_i) = \frac{1}{p_i^2} \cdot \frac{p_i(1-p_i)}{n_i} = \frac{(1-p_i)}{n_i p_i}$$

Again, we can estimate this by $(1-\hat{p}_i)/n_i \hat{p}_i$. Now, in weighted least-squares estimation of (2.29) we use $[n_i \hat{p}_i/(1-\hat{p}_i)]^{1/2}$ as weights. This is the minimum chi-square method for the log-linear model.

In the logit model, we assume, instead of (2.26) and (2.28),

$$\log \frac{p_i}{1-p_i} = \beta' x_i \tag{2.30}$$

Again, we write

$$\log \frac{\hat{p}_i}{1-\hat{p}_i} = \beta' x_i + u_i \tag{2.31}$$

where $u_i = \log[\hat{p}_i/(1-\hat{p}_i)] - \log[p_i/(1-p_i)]$. Using a Taylor-series expansion of $\log[\hat{p}_i/(1-\hat{p}_i)]$ around p_i, we get, omitting higher-order terms, as before,

$$u_i \simeq (\hat{p}_i - p_i)\left(\frac{1}{p_i} + \frac{1}{1-p_i}\right) = \frac{1}{p_i(1-p_i)}(\hat{p}_i - p_i)$$

Hence, in large samples, $E(u_i) \simeq 0$, and

$$\text{Var}(u_i) = \frac{1}{[p_i(1-p_i)]^2} \cdot \frac{p_i(1-p_i)}{n_i} = \frac{1}{n_i p_i(1-p_i)}$$

Again, we can estimate $\text{Var}(u_i)$ by $1/[n\hat{p}_i(1-\hat{p}_i)]$ and use the weighted least-squares method for (2.31). This is known as the *minimum logit chi-square method*. The method is due to Berkson (1953).

In any case, with multiple observations, so long as the sample sizes in each cell are sufficiently large, and provided $\hat{p}_i$ is not equal to 1 or 0, the linear probability model is not subject to the criticisms made earlier. It is no different in spirit from the log-linear model or the logit model. There is also another reason to belive that the linear probability model is not entirely meaningless. This is because of its intimate connection with the linear discriminant function discussed earlier in section 2.4.

Cox (1970, p. 33) suggested the use of

$$\log \frac{\hat{p}_i + (2n_i)^{-1}}{1 - \hat{p}_i + (2n_i)^{-1}}$$

in place of $\log[\hat{p}_i/(1-\hat{p}_i)]$ in (2.31). The advantage of this is that the logits are defined even when $\hat{p}_i$ is 0 or 1, which is not the case with (2.31). Cox gave other justifications for this transformation.

It can be shown that the minimum logit χ^2 estimator is consistent and asymptotically normal, with the same asymptotic covariance matrix as the ML estimator given by the inverse of the expression in (2.23). With grouped data, the expression $I(\beta)$ in (2.23) becomes

$$\sum_{i=1}^{k} \frac{n_i \exp(\beta'x_i)}{[1 + \exp(\beta'x_i)]^2} x_i x_i'$$

where k is the number of groups and n_i is the number of observations in the ith group.

In the normit model, we assume that $p_i = \Phi(\beta'x_i)$, where $\Phi(\cdot)$ is the distribution function of the standard normal. We write $\Phi^{-1}(p_i) = G(p_i) = \beta'x_i$. $G(p_i)$ is called the *normit* of p_i. Again, we write

$$G(\hat{p}_i) = \beta'x_i + u_i$$

Expanding $G(\hat{p}_i)$ around p_i and omitting higher-order terms, we get

$$G(\hat{p}_i) = G(p_i) + (\hat{p}_i - p_i) \frac{dG(p_i)}{dp_i}$$

But $d\Phi^{-1}(p_i)/dp_i = [\phi(p_i)]^{-1}$, where $\phi(\cdot)$ is the density function of the standard normal. Hence, we have

$$u_i = \frac{\hat{p}_i - p_i}{\phi(p_i)} \quad \text{and} \quad \text{Var}(u_i) = \frac{p_i(1 - p_i)}{n_i \phi(p_i)^2} = w_i^2$$

In the minimum normit chi-square method, we minimize

$$\sum_i \frac{[G(\hat{p}_i) - \beta' x_i]^2}{w_i^2}$$

with respect to β. We use an iterated weighted least-squares method, as before, substituting $\hat{w}_i$ for w_i.

In the next section we shall present some evidence on the comparison between the results for raw microdata and grouped data. With microdata we maximize the likelihood function (2.17). With grouped data we use the weighted least-squares methods.

The foregoing analyses can be extended to other functional forms. For instance, Zellner and Lee (1965) discussed *"Gompit analysis"* based on the Gompertz curve

$$F(\beta' X) = e^{-e^{\beta' X}}$$

In this case, the likelihood function (2.17) is somewhat more complicated, and thus analysis based on individual data is more complicated than the probit or logit analysis. However, with grouped data, because we have $\log\log(1/p) = \beta' X$, we use the same procedure as before and write

$$\log\log\left(\frac{1}{\hat{p}_i}\right) = \beta' X_i + u_i \tag{2.32}$$

where $u_i = \log\log(1/\hat{p}_i) - \log\log(1/p_i)$. Using a Taylor-series expansion of $\log\log(1/\hat{p}_i)$ around p_i, we get, omitting higher-order terms, as before,

$$u_i \simeq (\hat{p}_i - p_i)\left(-\frac{1}{p_i \log p_i}\right)$$

Hence, in large samples, $E(u_i) \simeq 0$, and

$$\text{Var}(u_i) = \frac{1}{(p_i \log p_i)^2} \cdot \frac{p_i(1 - p_i)}{n_i} = \frac{1 - p_i}{n_i p_i} \cdot \frac{1}{(\log p_i)^2}$$

Again, we estimate $\text{Var}(u_i)$ by substituting $\hat{p}_i$ for p_i in this expression and use the weighted least-squares method for the estimation of β in equation (2.32). This is the *minimum Gompit chi-square method.*

Another functional form one can use is the distribution considered by Burr (1942). The analysis based on this distribution can be called *"Burrit analysis."* The distribution function is now given by

$$F(\beta'x) = 1 - \frac{1}{[1 + (\beta'x)^c]^k} \quad (c, k > 0, \ \beta'x > 0)$$

The expressions for both the microdata and the grouped data are now messier than in the logit model.

2.9   Illustrative examples with grouped data

Warner (1978) considered the problem of prediction of attrition for first-term enlisted personnel in the U.S. Navy. Define

$y = 1$ if the person leaves the navy before completion of the first enlistment

$y = 0$ otherwise

Warner estimated four models: (a) linear probability model with individual observations, (b) linear probability model with grouped observations, (c) logit model with individual observations, and (d) logit model with grouped observations. The dependent variable was whether or not the person was lost before the end of the enlistment. The independent variables were years of education, mental ability (as measured by the Armed Forces Qualification Test, AFQT), marital status, age, and race. Education was split into three categories (less than 12 years, 12 years, and more than 12 years). The AFQT scores were split into five categories. Age was split into three categories (less than 18 years, 18 or 19 years, and more than 19 years). The various combinations of education level, mental ability, age, race, and marital status gave rise to $3 \times 5 \times 3 \times 2 \times 2 = 180$ cells into which individuals could fall. These were the grouped data. The sample consisted of 30,000 individuals drawn from a total of 67,000 male recruits in 1973. In the estimation of the linear probability model, the method of correction for heteroscedasticity suggested by Goldberger was applied. However, in cases in which the estimate of p from the ordinary least-squares regression was less than zero, Warner used $\hat{p}$ as 0.02, using a suggestion by Nerlove and Press (1973, pp. 54–5). Although this procedure can be applied to get around the problem of negative weights in the generalized least-squares (GLS) estimation of β, the problem of interpreting the resulting equation as a probability model still remains.

Table 2.2 shows the results. The important thing to note is that the

Table 2.2. A comparison of estimates of parameter values: individual and grouped data

Variable	Individual linear	Grouped linear	Individual logit	Grouped logit
Ed <12	−0.105 (17.04)	−0.109 (14.14)	−0.672 (21.23)[a]	−0.656 (14.42)
Ed >12	0.028 (3.88)	0.032 (3.79)	0.349 (4.51)	0.284 (2.87)
Mental group I	0.084 (9.95)	0.084 (9.65)	1.179 (9.32)	1.040 (6.00)
Mental group II	0.021 (3.96)	0.020 (3.09)	0.201 (4.50)	0.208 (3.60)
Mental group III	−0.053 (7.70)	−0.052 (6.20)	−0.345 (7.71)	−0.342 (6.00)
Mental group IV	−0.098 (12.46)	−0.097 (10.04)	−0.581 (12.98)	−0.571 (9.75)
Dependents	−0.046 (4.82)	−0.039 (3.61)	−0.349 (5.52)	−0.403 (5.21)
Age <18	−0.031 (4.16)	−0.024 (2.56)	−0.145 (3.24)	−0.166 (3.14)
Age >19	−0.027 (4.30)	−0.022 (3.51)	−0.185 (4.13)	−0.169 (3.24)
Race (non-Caucasian)	0.027 (3.61)	0.037 (4.15)	0.136 (3.04)	0.081 (1.28)
Constant	0.881 (25.70)	0.882 (20.79)	1.959 (61.96)	1.950 (40.87)
N	30,000	137	30,000	137

[a] t values in parentheses.

estimates from the individual observations and the grouped data are very close. The coefficients of the linear discriminant function in the last column are proportional to those of the linear probability model estimated by ordinary least squares. The reason that they are not exactly proportional to those in the first column of Table 2.2 and that the standard errors are also different is that the results in the first column are those for the weighted least-squares estimation of the linear probability model.

One can compare the predictive powers of the different equations in several ways. We shall discuss this issue in greater detail in section 2.11. Because the navy usually uses a score on the AFQT test as a cutoff score, Warner computed selection ratio, hit rate, and false-positive and false-negative rates for the individual linear and logit models for AFQT scores from 60 to 100. He found that for scores below 74 or above 82, the two models gave the same numbers of hits, false positives, and false negatives. In the range between 74 and 82, the logit model gave higher rates of hits and false negatives, but a lower rate of false positives, than the linear model.

Presumably, the proper way of comparing the two models and of finding the optimal cutoff score on the AFQT test is to specify a loss function that gives the losses entailed in the false-positive and false-negative classification. Warner, however, did not attempt this exercise. Regarding the comparison of grouped logit and grouped linear models, Warner computed $\sum (P_i - \hat{P}_i)^2$ and $\sum N_i (P_i - \hat{P}_i)^2$. On both these measures the grouped logit model was better than the grouped linear model. However, we shall see later, in section 2.11, that these are not the appropriate summary predictive measures of performance.

2.10   Polychotomous variables: unordered variables

Until now we have considered binary or dichotomous variables. Categorical variables that can be classified into many categories are called polychotomous variables. As mentioned earlier, we have to discuss the unordered, sequential, and ordered categories separately.

Case 1: Unordered variables: the multinomial logit model

Suppose there are m categories. Let $P_1 P_2 \ldots P_m$ be the probabilities associated with these m categories. Then the idea is to express these probabilities in binary form. Let

$$\frac{P_1}{P_1 + P_m} = F(\beta_1' x)$$

$$\frac{P_2}{P_2 + P_m} = F(\beta_2'x)$$

$$\frac{P_{m-1}}{P_{m-1} + P_m} = F(\beta_{m-1}'x) \tag{2.33}$$

These imply

$$\frac{P_j}{P_m} = \frac{F(\beta_j'x)}{1 - F(\beta_j'x)} = G(\beta_j'x) \quad (j = 1, 2, \ldots, m-1) \tag{2.34}$$

Because

$$\sum_{j=1}^{m-1} \frac{P_j}{P_m} = \frac{1 - P_m}{P_m} = \frac{1}{P_m} - 1$$

we have

$$P_m = \left[1 + \sum_{j=1}^{m-1} G(\beta_j'x) \right]^{-1} \tag{2.35}$$

and hence, from (2.34),

$$P_j = \frac{G(\beta_j'x)}{1 + \sum_{j=1}^{m-1} G(\beta_j'x)} \tag{2.36}$$

One can consider the observations as arising from a multinomial distribution with probabilities given by (2.35) and (2.36). Although, in principle, any of the previously mentioned underlying distributions of u can be used, from the computational point of view the logistic is the easiest to handle. In this case $G(\beta_j'x)$ in (2.35) is nothing but $\exp(\beta_j'x)$, and equations (2.35) and (2.36) can be written as

$$P_j = e^{\beta_j'x}/D \quad (j = 1, 2, \ldots, m-1)$$

and

$$P_m = 1/D \tag{2.37}$$

where

$$D = 1 + \sum_{k=1}^{m-1} e^{\beta_j'x}$$

This model is commonly referred to as the *multinomial logit model*.

We shall now consider estimation of model (2.37) based on samples of size n. Each of the n individuals will fall into one of the k categories, with probabilities given by (2.37). Let x_i denote the vector of observations on the variables x for individual i. Then the probabilities P_{ij} $(j=1, 2, \ldots, m-1)$ and P_{im} for the ith individual are obtained by substituting x_i for x in equations (2.37). We also define a set of dummy variables:

$y_{ij} = 1$ if the ith individual falls in the jth category

$y_{ij} = 0$ otherwise

Then the likelihood function for the multinomial logit model can be written as

$$L = \prod_{i=1}^{n} P_{i1}^{y_{i1}} P_{i2}^{y_{i2}} \ldots P_{im}^{y_{im}} \tag{2.38}$$

or

$$\log L = \sum_{i=1}^{n} \sum_{j=1}^{m} y_{ij} \log P_{ij} \tag{2.39}$$

because

$$P_{ij} = \frac{\exp(x_i' \beta_j)}{1 + \sum_{k=1}^{m-1} \exp(x_i' \beta_k)} \quad (j = 1, 2, \ldots, m-1)$$

and

$$P_{im} = \frac{1}{1 + \sum_{k=1}^{m-1} \exp(x_i' \beta_k)}$$

We get, on simplifying the relevant expressions,

$$\frac{\partial P_{ij}}{\partial \beta_j} = P_{ij}(1 - P_{ij})x_i$$

$$(j, k = 1, 2, \ldots, m-1)$$

$$\frac{\partial P_{ij}}{\partial \beta_k} = -P_{ij} P_{ik} x_i$$

and

$$\frac{\partial P_{im}}{\partial \beta_j} = -P_{ij} P_{im} x_i$$

Hence, we have

$$\frac{\partial \log L}{\partial \beta_k} = \sum_{i=1}^{n} \left[\frac{y_{ik}}{P_{ik}} P_{ik}(1 - P_{ik}) + \sum_{\substack{j=1 \\ j \neq k}}^{m} \frac{y_{ij}}{P_{ij}} (-P_{ij} P_{ik}) \right] x_i$$

$$= \sum_{i=1}^{n} \left[y_{ik} - P_{ik} \left(\sum_{j=1}^{m} y_{ij} \right) \right] x_i$$

$$= \sum_{i=1}^{n} (y_{ik} - P_{ik}) x_i \tag{2.40}$$

because

$$\sum_{j=1}^{m} y_{ij} = 1$$

Thus, the equations to solve for obtaining the ML estimates are

$$\sum_{i=1}^{n} (y_{ik} - P_{ik})x_i = 0 \quad (k = 1, 2, \ldots, m - 1) \tag{2.41}$$

Equations (2.41) are similar to equation (2.24) in the case of the simple logit model and can be interpreted similarly. For instance, if x_i consists of a constant term, then the predicted and actual frequencies will be identical for each of the m categories. Similarly, if x_i contains a dummy variable denoting, say, sex, then the predicted frequencies and actual frequencies will be identical for each of the two sex groups in each of the m categories.

The equations (2.41) are nonlinear in β_k, because P_{ik} is a nonlinear function of all the β's. However, one can use some iterative procedure like the Newton–Raphson method. Differentiating equations (2.40) again, we get

$$\frac{\partial^2 \log L}{\partial \beta_k \partial \beta_k'} = - \sum_{i=1}^{n} P_{ik}(1 - P_{ik})x_i x_i' \tag{2.42}$$

and

$$\frac{\partial^2 \log L}{\partial \beta_k \partial \beta_l'} = \sum_{i=1}^{n} P_{ik} P_{il} x_i x_i' \tag{2.43}$$

Thus the matrix of second derivatives is easily seen to be negative definite. Hence, there is a unique maximum, and the iterative procedure converges to the maximum.

For the starting values, one can obtain them from the simple logit models in equations (2.33) or from the discriminant-function coefficients described in Chapter 4. Many commonly used computer programs use the discriminant-function coefficients as starting values. Some use the Davidon–Fletcher–Powell algorithm rather than the Newton–Raphson method. The asymptotic covariances of the ML estimates are given by the elements of the inverse of the information matrix, whose diagonal blocks are given by equation (2.42) and nondiagonal blocks by equation (2.43), both expressions with signs changed. The relationship between the multinomial logit model and discriminant analysis is discussed in Chapter 4.

2.11 Measures of goodness of fit

A goodness-of-fit measure is a summary statistic indicating the accuracy with which a model approximates the observed data (like the R^2 measure in the familiar linear regression model). In the case in which the dependent variables are qualitative, accuracy can be judged either in terms of the fit between the calculated probabilities and observed response frequencies or in terms of the model to forecast observed responses.

We can discuss the goodness-of-fit measures for individual data and grouped data. For individual data we can compute the direct R^2 or the indirect pseudo-R^2 derived from the likelihood-ratio test. The direct R^2 method can be used only in the case of binary dependent variables. Note that the predicted value is a probability, whereas the actual value is either 0 or 1. The correlation between a binary dependent variable and a probabilistic predictor thereof was studied by Morrison (1972). Morrison argued that the low R^2 values one usually obtains when calculating correlations between a binary dependent variable and the predicted probabilities need not imply that the model is not good. Morrison derived an upper bound on R^2 on the assumption that the predictor has a beta distribution. Goldberger (1973) subsequently generalized this result. The upper bound on R^2 derived there is as follows.

Let Y be a random variable that takes on the values 1 and 0 with probabilities p and $1-p$, respectively. Here p, a known function of explanatory variables, is distributed over the unit interval with density function $f(p)$, expectation $E(p)$, and variance $V(p)$. The squared correlation between Y and p is given by

$$R^2 = \frac{[\text{Cov}(Y,p)]^2}{\text{Var}(Y) \cdot \text{Var}(p)}$$

Now $E(Y) = E(p)$ and $E(Y^2) = E(p)$. Hence, $\text{Var}(Y) = E(p) - E^2(p)$. Also, $E(Y,p) = E(p^2)$. Hence,

$$\begin{aligned}
\text{Cov}(Y,p) &= E(Y,p) - E(Y) \cdot E(p) \\
&= E(p^2) - E^2(p) = V(p)
\end{aligned}$$

Thus,

$$R^2 = \frac{[V(p)]^2}{V(p)V(Y)} = \frac{V(p)}{V(Y)} = \frac{V(p)}{E(p) - E^2(p)}$$

If $f(p)$ is the beta distribution with parameters α and β, then $E(p) = \alpha/(\alpha + \beta)$, and $V(p) = \alpha\beta/[(\alpha + \beta + 1)(\alpha + \beta)^2]$. Thus, $R^2 = 1/(\alpha + \beta + 1)$, which is the result Morrison obtained. Goldberger argued that this is merely the population squared correlation coefficient between Y and p and that there is no reason why the sample R^2 must be less than this. He argued that "for a binary variable as with a continuous variable, the proper upper bound on R^2 is unity."[2]

---

[2] The point in Goldberg's argument is that R^2 is a measure of the proportion of variance explained in the binary model, just as in the standard model, and the better the fit, the smaller α and β will be in Morrison's

The foregoing discussion is valid only for binary-dependent-variable models. For multinomial logit models, we cannot calculate an R^2, and it is better to define a goodness-of-fit measure based on the likelihood-ratio test statistic. To see this, let us consider defining R^2 in relation to the likelihood-ratio test statistic for a linear regression model.

Consider the standard linear regression model:

$$y = \alpha + \sum_{j=1}^{m} \beta_j x_j + u \quad [u \sim IN(0, \sigma^2)]$$

Let L_Ω be the maximum of the likelihood function when maximized with respect to all the parameters, $\alpha, \beta_1, \beta_2, \ldots, \beta_m$, and let L_ω be the maximum when maximized with respect to α only (setting all the β's equal to zero). Then we have the goodness-of-fit measure

$$R^2 = 1 - \left(\frac{L_\omega}{L_\Omega}\right)^{2/n} \tag{2.44}$$

where n is the sample size.

For the multinomial logit model considered in equations (2.37), again let L_Ω denote the maximum of the likelihood function when maximized with respect to all the parameters β_j (each vector β_j is assumed to contain a constant term α_j), and let L_ω be the maximum when maximized with respect to the constant term α_j only. If n_j is the number of observations in the jth category, then, clearly, $\exp(\hat{\alpha}_j) = n_j/n_m$ for $j = 1, 2, \ldots, m-1$. Hence, we get

$$L_\omega = \prod_{j=1}^{m} \left(\frac{n_j}{n}\right)^{n_j} \tag{2.45}$$

One can think of using a measure like (2.44) in the logit model as well, but the problem is that even though $R^2 \to 0$ as $L_\Omega \to L_\omega$, the upper bound of R^2 is much less than 1, unlike the case of the linear model. The reason is that the likelihood function (2.38) achieves an absolute maximum of 1.

Thus, we can write the maximum value of L as

$$L_{\max} = 1 \tag{2.46}$$

Hence, we have

$$\prod \left(\frac{n_j}{n}\right)^{n_j} = L_\omega \leqslant L_\Omega \leqslant L_{\max} = 1 \tag{2.47}$$

result. It is possible to define R^2 for the multinomial logit models. See the attempts of Cragg and Uhler (1970) and McFadden (1974) in the discussion that follows.

or

$$\frac{L_\omega}{L_{\max}} \leqslant \frac{L_\omega}{L_\Omega} \leqslant 1 \tag{2.48}$$

so that R^2 defined by (2.44) must lie in the range

$$0 \leqslant R^2 \leqslant 1 - (L_\omega)^{2/n} \tag{2.49}$$

This obviously does not provide a good measure of the goodness of fit, because even if the model fits perfectly, the resulting R^2 will be much less than 1.

A better measure is the pseudo-R^2, defined as

$$\text{pseudo-}R^2 = \frac{1 - (L_\omega/L_\Omega)^{2/n}}{1 - (L_\omega/L_{\max})^{2/n}} = \frac{L_\Omega^{2/n} - L_\omega^{2/n}}{1 - L_\omega^{2/n}} \tag{2.50}$$

where L_ω is given by (2.45), $L_{\max} = 1$, and L_Ω is obtained from the computer program that maximizes the likelihood function. Cragg and Uhler (1970) suggested the use of the pseudo-R^2 in equation (2.50).[3]

To get an idea of the magnitude of the difference between the R^2 given in (2.44) and the pseudo-R^2 given in (2.50), consider the results of Cragg and Uhler (1970, Table 1, p. 400). The reported pseudo-R^2 is 0.3444. Because the reported likelihood-ratio test statistic is 333.2, we have

$$-2\log_e\left(\frac{L_\omega}{L_\Omega}\right) = 333.2$$

Because the sample size is 986, we get $(L_\omega/L_\Omega)^{2/n} = 0.7132$, or the R^2 given by (2.44) is 0.2868. Because $(L_\omega/L_{\max})^{2/n}$ in this example is 0.1667, the upper bound for R^2 given by (2.49) is 0.8333. On the other hand, the ratio 0.2868/0.3444 is equal to 0.8327, which is close enough.

In a binary-choice model with, say, $n_1 = 10$ and $n_2 = 30$, we have, from (2.45),

$$L_\omega = \left(\frac{1}{4}\right)^{10}\left(\frac{3}{4}\right)^{30}$$

and $L_\omega^{2/n}$ is approximately 1/3, and thus the upper bound on the empirical R^2 is 0.67.

Coming next to the case of grouped data, one can consider the usual Pearson chi-square, $\sum_j (O_j - E_j)^2/E_j$, where O_j is the observed frequency and E_j is the expected frequency in the jth group. However, Tsiatis (1980) argued that a better measure is

$$(O - E)'V^{-1}(O - E) \tag{2.51}$$

---

[3] Another pseudo-R^2 measure (McFadden, 1974) is $R^2 = 1 - (\log L_\Omega)/(\log L_\omega)$.

where $O - E$ is the vector of observed frequencies minus expected frequencies in the different cells, and V is the (asymptotic) covariance matrix of $O - E$.

We can also define a pseudo-R^2 measure in the case of grouped data, as we did earlier with individual data, by analogy with the linear regression model with heteroscedastic errors. With grouped data, the minimum χ^2 estimator is, as discussed in section 2.8, a weighted least-squares estimator applied to a heteroscedastic regression model. To derive a pseudo-R^2 measure, we consider the analogous normal regression model with heteroscedastic errors. Consider the model

$$y = X\beta + u$$

where $u \sim N(0, D)$, where D is a known nonsingular matrix. Then

$$\hat{\beta} = (X'D^{-1}X)^{-1}X'D^{-1}y$$

The weighted residual sum of squares is

$$\text{WSSR}_u = (y - X\hat{\beta})'D^{-1}(y - X\hat{\beta})$$

The subscript u denotes unrestricted.

With the restriction that all the explanatory variables have zero coefficients, the constrained estimate of β is

$$\hat{\beta}_c = (e'D^{-1}e)^{-1}e'D^{-1}y$$

where e is a vector of 1's. The constrained weighted residual sum of squares is

$$\begin{aligned} \text{WSSR}_c &= (y - e\hat{\beta}_c)'D^{-1}(y - e\hat{\beta}_c) \\ &= y'D^{-1}y - \frac{(y'D^{-1}e)^2}{e'D^{-1}e} \end{aligned}$$

The R^2 that Buse (1973) defined is

$$R^2 = \frac{\text{WSSR}_c - \text{WSSR}_u}{\text{WSSR}_u}$$

In the minimum logit χ^2 estimation, $y_i = \log(\hat{p}_i / (1 - \hat{p}_i))$, and D is a diagonal matrix with the ith diagonal element $1/[n\hat{p}_i(1 - \hat{p}_i)]$.

Other measures of the goodness of fit in qualitative-response models can be found in the work of Amemiya (1981).

2.12   Multinomial logit and McFadden's conditional logit

The multinomial logit model has been used by Theil (1969) to study choices of transportation modes, by Cragg and Uhler (1970) to study the number of automobiles demanded, by Uhler and Cragg (1971) to study the structure of asset portfolios of households, and by Schmidt and Strauss (1975b) to study the determinants of occupational choice. There are many more illustrations in the literature, but the examples cited are sufficient for our purpose.

McFadden (1974) also suggested a logit model (he called it the "conditional logit model") and derived it from random utility models. This model will be discussed in the next chapter, but the main difference between the McFadden logit model and the multinomial logit (MNL) model considered here is that the McFadden model considers the effects of choice characteristics on the determinants of choice probabilities as well, whereas the MNL model considered here makes the choice probabilities dependent on individual characteristics only.[4]

As an illustration, consider the two studies on occupational choices by Boskin (1974) and Schmidt and Strauss (1975b). In the study by Boskin, there are several occupations, and each is characterized by three variables: present value of potential earnings, training cost/net worth, and present value of time unemployed. Let x_{ij} denote the vector of the values of these characteristics for occupation j as perceived by individual i. The probability that individual i chooses occupation j is

$$P_{ij} = \frac{\exp(\beta' x_{ij})}{\sum_{k=1}^{m} \exp(\beta' x_{ik})} \qquad (2.52)$$

where m equals the number of possible occupations in the choice set. Note the difference between this model and the multinomial model given by (2.37), where the P_j have different coefficient vectors β_j. In the model (2.52), the vector β gives the vector of implicit prices for the characteristics.[5] Thus, the problem analyzed here is similar to that analyzed in the hedonic-price-index problem. Boskin obtained a different set of "implicit prices" for the characteristics for white males, black males, white females, and black females. These coefficients tell us the relative valuations of the three characteristics mentioned earlier by these different groups. Also, if we are given a new occupation not considered in the estimation procedure and the characteristics of the new occupation,

---

[4] Algebraically, though, the MNL and conditional logit models are totally equivalent. Start from the MNL model $P_i/P_1 = \exp[(\beta_i - \beta_1)x]$ and assume $x = (z_1, z_2, \ldots, z_n)$ and $\beta_i = (0, \ldots, \alpha, \ldots, 0)$ to get the conditional logit form $P_i/P_1 = \exp[\alpha(z_i - z_1)]$. Alternatively, start from the conditional logit form $P_i/P_1 = \exp[\alpha(z_i - z_1)]$ and assume $\alpha = (\beta_1, \beta_2, \ldots, \beta_m)$ and $Z_i = (0, \ldots, x, \ldots, 0)$ to get the MNL form $P_i/P_1 = \exp[\beta_i - \beta_1)x]$.

[5] It is clear from the expression in (2.52) that one needs some normalization (say setting the first element of β to be equal to 1).

as perceived by an individual, then we can use the estimated coefficients to predict the probability that this individual will join this occupation. Thus, the main use of the model (2.52) is to predict the probability of choice for a category not considered in the estimation procedure but for which we are given the vector of characteristics x_{ij}.

By contrast, the model on occupational choice considered by Schmidt and Strauss (1975b) is the usual multinomial model given by equations (2.37). Suppose there are m occupations and y_i is the vector of individual characteristics for individual i (age, sex, years of schooling, experience, etc.). Then the probability that the individual with characteristics y_i will choose the ith occupation is

$$P_{ij} = \exp(\alpha'_j y_i) \left/ \sum_k \exp(\alpha'_k y_i) \right. \tag{2.53}$$

with some normalization like $\alpha_m = 0$. In (2.52) the number of parameters to be estimated is equal to the number of characteristics of the occupations. In (2.53) the number of parameters to be estimated is equal to the number of individual characteristics multiplied by $m - 1$, where m is the number of occupations. The questions answered by the models are different. In (2.53) we estimate the parameters; then, given a new individual with specified characteristics, we can predict the probability that the individual will choose one of the m occupations considered.

Boskin gave estimates of the weights that different groups attach to the different characteristics. These are presented in Table 2.3. The numbers show the relative weights attached to the different characteristics by the different groups. Given the fact that in equation (2.52) one needs a normalization rule, we cannot compare the absolute values of the coefficients in the different groups in Table 2.3. It is the relative values that we can compare (e.g., $-18.74/0.875$ for white females versus $-20.78/0.378$ for black females, etc.).

Schmidt and Strauss (1975b) considered the multinomial model with individual characteristics: education, experience, race, and sex. After estimating the parameters, one can predict the probability that an individual with a specified set of characteristics will choose any particular occupation. Table 2.4 presents their calculated probabilities for 1970. (They calculated for 1960 and 1967 also, and for different regions in 1967, etc. However, because the results are similar, we are presenting results for one year only.) They concluded, on the basis of these results, that there is strong evidence in favor of race and sex discrimination.

Of course, one can combine the two models given by (2.37) and (2.52) and write

Table 2.3. *Relative weights of occupational characteristics in the conditional logit decision model*

	Population group			
Variable	White males	Black males	White females	Black females
Present value of potential earnings	1.084 $(0.075)^a$	0.072 (0.013)	0.875 (0.076)	0.378 (0.132)
Training cost/net worth	−0.001 (0.001)	−0.010 (0.001)	−0.005 (0.002)	−0.012 (0.002)
Present value of time unemployed	−0.051 (0.090)	−4.35 (0.57)	−18.74 (1.61)	−20.78 (1.82)

^{a} Figures in parentheses are asymptotic standard errors.
Source: Boskin (1974, Table 3, p. 395).

Table 2.4. *Probability of being in each occupation given average education and experience in 1970*

	Occupation				
Race-sex combination	Menial	Blue collar	Craft	White collar	Professional
Black female	0.396	0.188	0.011	0.219	0.187
Black male	0.222	0.368	0.136	0.073	0.202
White female	0.153	0.146	0.018	0.492	0.192
White male	0.089	0.296	0.232	0.169	0.214

$$P_{ij} = \frac{\exp(\beta'x_{ij} + \alpha_j'y_i)}{\sum_{k=1}^{m}\exp(\beta'x_{ik} + \alpha_k'y_i)} \tag{2.54}$$

The multinomial logit model in equation (2.37) is now seen to be a special case of this general model.

McFadden (1974) considered an example of shopping-mode choices in which he took into account both the mode characteristics x_j (transit walk time, transit wait plus transfer time, auto vehicle time, etc.) and individual characteristics y_i (ratio of number of autos to number of workers in the household, race, occupation – blue collar or white collar).

In his discussion of choices of models of transport, Theil (1969) specified the following model: Let D_1 be bus, D_2 train, D_3 car; x_1, x_2, and x_3

are the respective travel times, and y is income. Then he specified the model as

$$\log \frac{P(D_r \mid x_1, x_2, x_3, y)}{P(D_s \mid x_1, x_2, x_3, y)} = \alpha_r - \alpha_s + (\beta_r - \beta_s)\log y + \gamma \log\left(\frac{x_r}{x_s}\right) \tag{2.55}$$

The implied probabilities P_j are

$$P_j = \frac{\exp(\alpha_j + \beta_j \log y + \gamma \log x_j)}{\sum_{k=1}^{3} \exp(\alpha_k + \beta_k \log y + \gamma \log x_k)}$$

which are of the same form as (2.37), except that the explanatory variables are in log form.

Cragg and Uhler (1970) used the multinomial model to study these decisions: (a) no change; sell a car, replace a car, purchase additional car, and (b) number of cars owned (1, 2, 3, or more). Strictly speaking, neither of these can be treated as a standard multinomial model. They are both cases of ordered-response models, as discussed in the following section. Cragg and Uhler also considered in the first case a series of binary choices that can be described diagramatically:

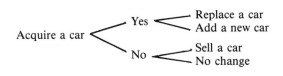

They reported that this gave a lower likelihood value than a multinomial model that considered all choices simultaneously.[6] However, for the second case they considered that a sequence of binary choices would perhaps be quite appropriate. This can be shown diagramatically:

Buy second car $<$ Yes, buy more cars $<$ Yes / No / No

However, in the second case, concerning the number of cars held, Cragg and Uhler had the following numbers of observations:

[6] The total numbers of observations in the four categories in the first case were 677, 46, 205, and 58, respectively, in 1961 and 723, 51, 160, and 52, respectively, in 1962. The data consist of 986 spending units from the re-interview portion of the 1960, 1961, and 1962 surveys of consumer finances. Because the same units were present in both samples, one could make use of information on the previous year's decision in estimating the equation for 1962.

Year	One car	Two cars	Three or more cars
1960	624	139	4
1961	597	155	7
1962	581	165	8

Thus, given the small numbers of observations in the third category, it is doubtful that it would be worthwhile to consider a trichotomous-choice model. A simple binary-choice model (single car versus multiple cars) will be adequate.

2.13 Polychotomous variables: ordered-response models

Case 2: Ordered-response models

Suppose we have three ordered categories. Some examples are the following: less than high school, high school, college education; dead, severely affected, unaffected; buy maximum coverage, partial coverage, no coverage in insurance. In such cases we define the model as follows: The individual falls in category 3 if $u < \beta'x$, in category 2 if $\beta'x < u < \beta'x + c$, and in category 1 if $u > \beta'x + c$, where $c > 0$. Thus, we have

$$
\begin{aligned}
P_3 &= F(\beta'x) \\
P_2 &= F(\beta'x + c) - F(\beta'x) \\
P_1 &= 1 - F(\beta'x + c)
\end{aligned}
\tag{2.56}
$$

For the distribution function F, we can use the logistic or cumulative normal.[7]

The ordered-response model was first considered by Aitchison and Silvey (1957) and Ashford (1959), who used the cumulative normal for F in (2.56) and gave a maximum-likelihood analysis. Gurland et al. (1960) discussed more general functional forms for F in (2.56), including the logistic, and also gave the analysis by weighted least squares. Cox (1970, Chapter 7) discussed the case in which F has the logistic distribution. The extension of the foregoing model to the case of m ordered categories is straightforward. We can write equations (2.56) as

$$
P_m = F(\beta'x)
$$

[7] An obvious generalization of the model in (2.56) is to make both thresholds different functions of x, so that $P_3 = F(\beta'_1 x)$ and $P_2 = F(\beta'_2 x) - F(\beta'_1 x)$.

$$P_{m-1} = F(\beta'x + \alpha_1) - F(\beta'x)$$
$$P_{m-2} = F(\beta'x + \alpha_1 + \alpha_2) - F(\beta'x + \alpha_1)$$

and so forth.

These equations imply

$$P_m = F(\beta'x)$$
$$P_m + P_{m-1} = F(\beta'x + \alpha_1)$$
$$P_m + P_{m-1} + P_{m-2} = F(\beta'x + \alpha_1 + \alpha_2)$$
$$\cdots$$

$$P_m + P_{m-1} + \cdots + P_2 = F(\beta'x + \alpha_1 + \alpha_2 + \cdots + \alpha_{m-2}) \qquad (2.57)$$

and

$$P_1 = 1 - F(\beta'x + \alpha_1 + \alpha_2 + \cdots + \alpha_{m-2})$$

where $\alpha_1, \alpha_2, \ldots, \alpha_{m-2} > 0$. In actual practice we do not impose the condition that c in equations (2.56) or $\alpha_1, \alpha_2, \ldots, \alpha_{m-2}$ in equations (2.57) must be positive. The maximum-likelihood estimates usually will yield positive estimates for these parameters. If not, then one can assume that there is some specification error in the model. In the examples of Aitchison and Silvey and Gurland et al. cited earlier, the estimates were indeed positive. Ashford did not estimate the parameter c in (2.56).

McKelvey and Zavoina (1975) used the ordinal-level probit model to analyze the determinants of congressional voting on the 1965 Medicare bill. They also wrote a computer program based on the Newton–Raphson iteration method that gives the output that one usually gets from a standard regression model. We shall now discuss in detail the ordinal probit model with m categories. Instead of defining the α's as in (2.57), we shall define a set of constants α_i such that $\alpha_1 = -\infty$, $\alpha_m = +\infty$, and $\alpha_1 < \alpha_2 < \cdots < \alpha_m$. This will facilitate the notation in the writing of the likelihood equations.

Let the underlying response model be described as

$$Y_i = \beta'x_i + u_i \quad (i = 1, 2, \ldots, n)$$

where Y is the underlying response variable, x is a set of explanatory variables, and u is the residual. Y is not observed, but we know which of the m categories it belongs to. It belongs to the jth category if

$$\alpha_{j-1} < Y < \alpha_j \quad (j = 1, 2, \ldots, m)$$

Because Y is observed only ordinally, we shall use the normalization rule (as in a simple probit model) that $\text{Var}(u) = 1$. Thus, $u_i \sim IN(0, 1)$.

We shall now define a set of ordinal variables

$Z_{ij} = 1$ if Y_i falls in the jth category
$Z_{ij} = 0$ otherwise $(i=1,2,\ldots,n, \ \ j=1,2,\ldots,m)$

$$\text{Prob}(Z_{ij} = 1) = \Phi(\alpha_j - \beta'x_i) - \Phi(\alpha_{j-1} - \beta'x_i)$$

where Φ is the cumulative standard normal. The likelihood function for the model is

$$L = \prod_{i=1}^{n} \prod_{j=1}^{m} [\Phi(\alpha_j - \beta'x_i) - \Phi(\alpha_{j-1} - \beta'x_i)]^{Z_{ij}}$$

and the log-likelihood function is

$$L^* = \log L = \sum_{i=1}^{n} \sum_{j=1}^{k} Z_{ij} \log[\Phi(\alpha_j - \beta'x_i) - \Phi(\alpha_{j-1} - \beta'x_i)]$$

For compactness of notation let us write

$$Y_{i,j} = \alpha_j - \beta'x_i$$
$$\phi_{i,j} = \phi(\alpha_j - \beta'x_i)$$

Noting that $\partial\Phi(x)/\partial x = \phi(x)$ and $\partial\phi(x)/\partial x = -x\phi(x)$, and defining the Kronecker delta

$$\delta_{j,k} = 1 \quad \text{if } j = k$$
$$\delta_{j,k} = 0 \quad \text{otherwise}$$

we get

$$\frac{\partial L^*}{\partial \beta} = \sum_{i=1}^{n} \sum_{j=1}^{m} Z_{ij} \frac{\phi_{i,j-1} - \phi_{i,j}}{\Phi_{i,j} - \Phi_{i,j-1}} x_i = 0$$

and   (2.58)

$$\frac{\partial L^*}{\partial \alpha_k} = \sum_{i=1}^{n} \sum_{j=1}^{m} Z_{ij} \frac{\delta_{j,k}\phi_{i,j} - \delta_{j-1,k}\phi_{i,j-1}}{\Phi_{i,j} - \Phi_{i,j-1}} = 0$$

Equations (2.58) must be solved iteratively. One method is the Newton–Raphson method. McKelvey and Zavoina (1975) reported good results for the convergence of this method. The second partial derivatives are as follows:

$$\frac{\partial^2 L^*}{\partial\beta\partial\beta'} = \sum_{i=1}^{n} \sum_{j=1}^{m} \frac{Z_{ij}}{(\Phi_{i,j} - \Phi_{i,j-1})^2}$$
$$\times [(\Phi_{i,j} - \Phi_{i,j-1})(Y_{i,j-1}\phi_{i,j-1} - Y_{i,j}\phi_{i,j})$$
$$- (\phi_{i,j-1} - \phi_{i,j})^2]x_i x_i'$$

$$\frac{\partial^2 L^*}{\partial\beta\partial\alpha_k} = \sum_{i=1}^{n} \sum_{j=1}^{m} \frac{Z_{ij}}{(\Phi_{i,j} - \Phi_{i,j-1})^2}$$

$$\times \left[(\Phi_{i,j}-\Phi_{i,j-1})(Y_{i,j}\phi_{i,j}\delta_{j,k}-Y_{i,j-1}\phi_{i,j-1}\delta_{j-1,k})\right.$$
$$\left.-(\phi_{i,j-1}-\phi_{i,j})(\phi_{i,j}\delta_{j,k}-\phi_{i,j-1}\delta_{j-1,k})\right]x_i$$

and

$$\frac{\partial^2 L^*}{\partial\alpha_k\partial\alpha_l}=\sum_{i=1}^{n}\sum_{j=1}^{m}\frac{Z_{ij}}{(\Phi_{i,j}-\Phi_{i,j-1})^2}$$
$$\times \left[(\Phi_{i,j}-\Phi_{i,j-1})(Y_{i,j-1}\phi_{i,j-1}\delta_{j-1,k}\delta_{j-1,l}-Y_{i,j}\phi_{i,j}\delta_{j,k}\delta_{j,l})\right.$$
$$\left.-(\phi_{i,j}\delta_{j,k}-\phi_{i,j-1}\delta_{j-1,k})(\phi_{i,j}\delta_{j,l}-\phi_{i,j-1}\delta_{j-1,l})\right]$$

Pratt (1981) showed, as in the case of the simple probit model, that the matrix of second partial derivatives of L^* is everywhere negative definite. Hence, we are sure that the Newton–Raphson iterative procedure will converge to the global maximum of the likelihood function. McKelvey and Zavoina (1975) reported that the procedure always converged very rapidly, with the convergence taking between four and ten iterations, depending on the number of parameters to be estimated. We had similar experience and also found that the iterative procedure converged to the same value with different initial values.

Denoting by $\hat{\theta}$ the final parameter estimates, we evaluate the matrix of second partial derivatives of L^* at $\hat{\theta}$. This matrix, with the sign reversed, is the information matrix, and the inverse of the information matrix gives the estimates of the (asymptotic) variances and covariances of the different parameters. One can use these to perform any desired tests of significance. If one desires to test the significance of a subset of the parameters, one can apply the familiar likelihood-ratio tests.

2.14   Polychotomous variables: sequential-response models

Case 3: Sequential-response models

The case of sequential-response models is easy to analyze, because the likelihood functions for these models can be maximized by maximizing the likelihood functions of dichotomous models repeatedly.

Consider the example

$Y=1$ if the individual has not finished high school

$Y=2$ if the individual has finished high school but not college

$Y=3$ if the individual has completed college but not a professional degree

$Y=4$ if the individual has a professional degree

Then the probabilities can be written as (Amemiya, 1975)

$$P_1 = F(\beta_1' x)$$
$$P_2 = [1 - F(\beta_1' x)]F(\beta_2' x)$$
$$P_3 = [1 - F(\beta_1' x)][1 - F(\beta_2' x)]F(\beta_3' x) \qquad (2.59)$$
$$P_4 = [1 - F(\beta_1' x)][1 - F(\beta_2' x)][1 - F(\beta_3' x)]$$

The parameters β_1 can be estimated from the entire sample by dividing it into two groups: not finished high school, finished high school. The parameters β_2 can be estimated from the subsample of high school graduates by dividing it into two groups: not finished college, finished college. The parameters β_3 can be estimated from the subsample of college graduates by dividing it into two groups: no professional degree, professional degree. In each case the binary models can be estimated by the probit or logit method.

The model on automobile demand discussed by Cragg and Uhler (1970) is another kind of a sequential-decision model. It consists of a series of binary decisions.

P_1 = probability of replacing a car
P_2 = probability of adding a new car
P_3 = probability of selling a car
P_4 = probability of no change

Then, if the sequential decision is as shown in section 2.12, we can write the probabilities as

$$P_1 = F(\beta_1' x)F(\beta_2' x)$$
$$P_2 = F(\beta_1' x)[1 - F(\beta_2' x)]$$
$$P_3 = [1 - F(\beta_1' x)]F(\beta_3' x)$$
$$P_4 = [1 - F(\beta_1' x)][1 - F(\beta_3' x)]$$

The parameters β_1 can be estimated by considering the whole sample and partitioning it into those who acquire new cars and those who do not, using a binary model. The parameters β_2 can be estimated by considering the subsample of individuals who acquire new cars and partitioning it into those who replace cars and those who buy new cars. The parameters β_3 can be estimated by considering the subsample of individuals who do not acquire new cars and partitioning it into those who sell cars and those with no change.

In any case, the sequential models are very easy to handle provided we make the probability of choice at each stage independent of the choice at the previous stage. More complicated sequential models will be discussed in later chapters. One point that needs to be emphasized is that these models are valid only if the random factors influencing responses at various stages are independent.

2.15   Noncategorical variables: Poisson regression

There are several cases in which the dependent variable assumes discrete values $0, 1, 2, 3, \ldots$, but it is not a categorical variable. Examples of this are the number of accidents in a county, the number of accidents on a natural-gas pipeline, the number of patents issued, and so forth. We have data on other explanatory variables for each observation, and our interest centers on the effect of each of these explanatory variables on the explained variable. In the case of accidents on a natural-gas pipeline, one of the explanatory variables could be a regulatory variable, and our interest would be in studying the effect of the regulations on the number of accidents. In such cases a Poisson regression model would be very appropriate.[8]

We assume that the explained variables $Y_1, Y_2, \ldots, Y_n$ have independent Poisson distributions with parameters $\lambda_1, \lambda_2, \ldots, \lambda_n$, respectively. Hence,

$$\text{Prob}(Y_i = r) = \exp(-\lambda_i) \, \frac{(\lambda_i)^r}{\gamma!} \tag{2.60}$$

We shall assume that λ_i are log-linearly dependent on the explanatory variables. Thus,

$$\ln \lambda_i = \beta_0 + \sum_{j=1}^{p} \beta_j x_{ij} \tag{2.61}$$

The likelihood function is given by

$$L = \prod_{i=1}^{n} \left(\exp(-\lambda_i) \, \frac{\lambda_i^{Y_i}}{Y_i!} \right)$$

$$= \exp\left(-\sum_i \lambda_i + \beta_0 \sum_i Y_i + \sum_{j=1}^{p} \beta_j \sum_i x_{ij} Y_i \right) \left(\prod_i Y_i! \right)^{-1}$$

Hence,

$$\ln L = -\sum_i \lambda_i + \beta_0 \sum_i Y_i + \sum_{j=1}^{p} \beta_j \sum_i x_{ij} Y_i - \sum_i \ln(Y_i!) \tag{2.62}$$

[8] However, it should be pointed out that the usefulness of the Poisson model is limited by the fact that the variance is equal to the mean, which is rarely obviously true in the sort of data we might use.

We can easily see that this model is an exponential family with sufficient statistics given by

$$T_0 = \sum_i Y_i \quad \text{and} \quad T_j = \sum_i x_{ij} Y_i \quad (i = 1, 2, \ldots, p) \qquad (2.63)$$

Differentiating (2.62) with respect to β_0 and β_j, because $\partial \lambda_i / \partial \beta_0 = \lambda_i$ and $\partial \lambda_i / \partial \beta_j = x_{ij} \lambda_i$, we get

$$T_0 = \sum_i \hat{\lambda}_i$$

$$T_j = \sum_i x_{ij} \hat{\lambda}_i \quad (j = 1, 2, \ldots, p) \qquad (2.64)$$

where

$$\hat{\lambda}_i = \exp\left(\hat{\beta}_0 + \sum_{j=1}^{p} \hat{\beta}_j x_{ij} \right)$$

Equations (2.64) can be solved iteratively using, for example, the Newton–Raphson method. The matrix of second derivatives is given by

$$\frac{\partial^2 \log L}{\partial \beta_j \partial \beta_k} = -\sum_i x_{ij} x_{ik} \lambda_i \quad (j, k = 0, 1, 2, \ldots, p)$$

with $x_{i0} = 1$. The inverse of this matrix with the negative sign will give the asymptotic covariance matrix of the ML estimates.

As an illustration, Holland (1973) used data on the number of new chemical entities created by each of fifty chemical firms for a certain five-year period. The explanatory variables used were

$$X_1 = \ln(\text{sales})$$
$$X_2 = \ln(\text{expenditures on research and development})$$
$$X_3 = \ln(\text{an index of diversity of the company's product line})$$

The estimated values (with asymptotic standard errors in parentheses) were

$$\hat{\beta}_0 = -7.179 \ (1.809)$$
$$\hat{\beta}_1 = 0.680 \ (0.237)$$
$$\hat{\beta}_2 = -0.094 \ (0.195)$$
$$\hat{\beta}_3 = 0.314 \ (0.324)$$

The variable X_2 is clearly not at all significant. Dropping this variable and reestimating gave the following results:

$$\hat{\beta}_0 = -6.638 \ (1.402)$$
$$\hat{\beta}_1 = 0.587 \ (0.138)$$
$$\hat{\beta}_3 = 0.316 \ (0.323)$$

Possibly X_3 can also be dropped. The only significant variable appears to be sales. Holland claimed that the fact that $\hat{\beta}_1$ is less than 1 indicates that several smaller companies provide a more productive base for new inventions than do a few larger companies.

Hausman et al. (1981) used the Poisson regression model to study the effects of R&D expenditures on patents issued. They used panel data and extended the simple Poisson regression model discussed here by allowing for individual-firm-specific effects as well as a disturbance term in equation (2.61). We shall not go into the details here, because they involve problems beyond the scope of the present chapter.

An analysis of the Poisson regression model can also be found in the work of El Sayyad (1973) and Lancaster (1974). In addition to the ML estimation, Lancaster suggested some weighted least-squares methods. Actually, in the Poisson regression model considered earlier, it is assumed that the size of the relevant population is constant (e.g., the number of miles driven in the case of car accidents, the length of natural-gas pipelines in the case of pipeline accidents, etc.). If N_i is the size of the population corresponding to Y_i (so that the rate of occurrence is Y_i/N_i), then we ought to define (2.61) as

$$\log \lambda_i = \log N_i + \beta_0 + \sum_j \beta_j x_{ij}$$

In the example that Holland considered, N_i was assumed to be the same for all observations, and thus $\log N_i$ got absorbed in the constant term.

The weighted least-squares estimator suggested by Lancaster is based on asymptotic expansions as $N_i \to \infty$. The estimator is

$$\hat{\beta} = (X'YX)^{-1}X'Yq \tag{2.65}$$

where q is an $n \times 1$ vector with jth element $q_j = \log Y_j$ (if $Y_j = 0$, put $Y_j = 0.5$, say). $X = (x_{ij})$ is an $n \times p$ matrix of observations on the explanatory variables (measured as deviations from the mean). Y is an $n \times n$ diagonal matrix with the jth diagonal term $= Y_j$.

El Sayyad arrived at the same formula (2.65) using a Bayesian argument. A particular term in the Poisson likelihood function is

$$e^{-\lambda} \frac{\lambda^Y}{Y!}$$

which can be written as

$$\lambda \cdot e^{-\lambda} \frac{\lambda^{Y-1}}{Y!}$$

which is proportional to λ times a gamma density with parameter Y.

Noting that for large Y the log of a gamma variate is normally distributed with mean $\log Y$ and variance $1/Y$, we have

$$e^{-\lambda}\lambda^{Y-1}\,d\lambda \propto \exp\left(\frac{-Y(\log\lambda - \log Y)^2}{2}\right)d\log\lambda$$

or

$$e^{-\lambda}\lambda^{Y} \propto \exp\left(\frac{-Y(\log\lambda - \log Y)^2}{2}\right)$$

Hence, the Poisson likelihood function can be written approximately as a product of normal density functions. Combining this with a diffuse prior leads to a multivariate normal distribution for β, with mean $(X'YX)^{-1}X'Yq$ and variance $(X'YX)^{-1}$, because

$$\exp\left(\frac{-\Sigma_j Y_j(\log\lambda_j - \log Y_j)}{2}\right)$$

$$= \exp\left[-\frac{1}{2}(X\beta - q)'Y(X\beta - q)\right] \propto \exp\left[-\frac{1}{2}(\beta - \hat{\beta})(X'YX)(\beta - \hat{\beta})\right]$$

with $\hat{\beta}$ defined in (2.65).

2.16   Estimation of logit models with randomized data

Very often one has to conduct surveys in which the questions are very sensitive: "Have you had an abortion?" "Do you use drugs?" It has been found that in such cases respondents often suppress information and give false answers. However, if some anonymity is achieved, respondents are more likely to give honest answers. To this end, Warner (1965) suggested the *randomized response technique*, in which the respondent is asked to answer either the sensitive question or the result of a random experiment. For instance, in the case of the question "Do you use drugs?" we give the respondent a box consisting of predetermined proportions of red, blue, and white balls. The person is asked to draw a ball at random and report the result as

1   if it is a red ball
0   if it is a blue ball
1   if it is a white ball and the person uses drugs
0   if it is a white ball and the person does not use drugs

Extensions of this method to quantitative schemes of randomization that are suitable for surveys conducted by mail have been discussed in the literature. We need not go through these here, but it is important to note that all these studies have been directed only at obtaining estimates of the proportions of people who have certain characteristics (e.g., percentages of people using heroin, LSD, etc.; percentages of women having had zero, one, or two abortions, etc.). None of these authors has discussed the methodology for analyzing the determinants of these factors. That is what we shall now discuss.

To take the simplest case, consider the question "Do you use drugs?" We are given the results of the answers from a randomized-response experiment and all the explanatory variables X (age, sex, education, parents' income, etc.). We want to estimate the effect of each of these variables on drug use. In the absence of a randomized experiment, we use a logit model. Let the observations be

$$y = 1 \quad \text{if the person uses drugs}$$
$$y = 0 \quad \text{otherwise}$$

Then we estimate the parameter β by maximizing the likelihood function

$$L = \prod_{y_i=1} \frac{e^{\beta'X_i}}{1 + e^{\beta'X_i}} \prod_{y_i=0} \frac{1}{1 + e^{\beta'X_i}}$$

Here

$$\text{Prob}(y_i = 1) = \frac{e^{\beta'X_i}}{1 + e^{\beta'X_i}}$$

With randomized response, we do the following: Suppose there is a box with red, blue, and white balls. If the ball drawn is red, the respondent gives the answer 1; if the ball drawn is blue, the respondent gives the answer 0; if the ball drawn is white, the respondent answers the question whether or not he uses drugs. He answers 1 if he uses, 0 otherwise. Assuming the proportions of red, blue, and white balls are P_1, P_2, and $1 - P_1 - P_2$, and letting the true probability of using drugs be denoted by Π_i, then

$$\text{Prob}(y_i = 1) = P_1 + (1 - P_1 - P_2)\Pi_i$$
$$\text{Prob}(y_i = 0) = P_2 + (1 - P_1 - P_2)(1 - \Pi_i)$$

Assuming that the true probability[9] Π_i can be written as $e^{\beta'X_i}/(1+e^{\beta'X_i})$, we get the likelihood functions to be maximized as

$$L = \prod_{y_i=1}\left(P_1 + (1-P_1-P_2)\frac{e^{\beta'X_i}}{1+e^{\beta'X_i}}\right) \prod_{y_i=0}\left(P_2 + (1-P_1-P_2)\frac{1}{1+e^{\beta'X_i}}\right)$$

$$(2.66)$$

[9] The probability of using drugs has an i subscript because the model assumes the probability of using depends on the characteristics X. So different individuals will have different probabilities of using drugs.

Let us define

$$C_1 = \frac{P_1}{1 - P_1 - P_2}$$

$$C_2 = \frac{P_2}{1 - P_1 - P_2}$$

$$R_i = C_1 + (1 + C_1)e^{\beta'X_i}$$

$$S_i = 1 + C_2 + C_2 e^{\beta'X_i}$$

Then, from equation (2.66), we get

$$\log L = \text{constant} + \sum_i \left[y_i \log R_i + (1 - y_i) \log S_i - \log(1 + e^{\beta'X_i}) \right]$$

$$\frac{\partial \log L}{\partial \beta} = 0 \Rightarrow \sum_i \left[\frac{y_i(1 + C_1 + C_2)e^{\beta'X_i}}{R_i S_i} - \frac{e^{\beta'X_i}}{S_i(1 + e^{\beta'X_i})} \right] X_i = 0 \tag{2.67}$$

and

$$\frac{\partial^2 \log L}{\partial\beta\partial\beta'} = \sum_i \left[\frac{y_i(1 + C_1 + C_2)e^{\beta'X_i}}{R_i S_i} \cdot \left(\frac{1 + C_2}{S_i} + \frac{C_1}{R_i} - 1 \right) \right.$$
$$\left. - \frac{e^{\beta'X_i}}{1 + e^{\beta'X_i}} \cdot \frac{1}{S_i}\left(\frac{1 + C_2}{S_i} - \frac{e^{\beta'X_i}}{1 + e^{\beta'X_i}} \right) \right] X_i X_i' \tag{2.68}$$

Using equations (2.67) and (2.68), we can get the ML estimates of β by the Newton–Raphson iterative procedure and also get an estimate of the asymptotic covariance matrix of the estimates.

  None of the randomized-response surveys that we know of have any data on the exogenous variables X, because the main emphasis in these surveys has been on merely estimating some population proportion (e.g., abortion rate, rate of drug use, etc.) rather than studying the determinants of the sensitive factors under consideration.[10] What we have discussed in this section is a method that enables us to measure the effect of the exogenous variables X on the true probability Π_i for the occurrence of the sensitive variable (in this example, the use of drugs).

2.17   Estimation of logit and probit models from panel data

All analysis in the preceding sections was for data from a single cross section. There are many instances in which we have data on a time series

---

[10] For some results with artificially randomized data, see the work of Maddala and Trost (1978).

of cross sections. It is beyond the scope of this chapter to go through this area in great detail. We shall briefly mention some of the models considered.

Heckman and Willis (1976) considered the model

$$y_{it}^* = \beta x_{it} + \epsilon_{it} \quad (i = 1, 2, \ldots, N, \ t = 1, 2, \ldots, T)$$
$$y_{it} = 1 \quad \text{if } y_{it}^* > 0$$
$$y_{it} = 0 \quad \text{otherwise}$$
$$\epsilon_{it} = u_i + v_{it}$$
$$E(\epsilon_{it}, \epsilon_{i't'}) = \sigma_u^2 + \sigma_v^2 \quad \text{if } i = i', \ t = t'$$
$$= \sigma_u^2 \quad \text{if } i = i', \ t \neq t'$$
$$= 0 \quad \text{if } i \neq i'$$

The model is like the variance-components model in the literature on analysis of panel data. Butler and Moffitt (1982) provided an efficient computational algorithm for this model. Avery et al. (1981) suggested some instrumental-variable estimators for this model. Chamberlain (1980) considered cases in which u_i are random as well as fixed effects. For the fixed-effects model, he suggested conditional maximum-likelihood methods, that is, considering the likelihood function conditional on sufficient statistics for the incidental parameters.

Heckman (1982a, b) considered distributed-lag models of the form

$$y_{it}^* = \alpha y_{i, t-1} + \beta x_{it} + u_{it}$$

This model can be termed a lagged-dummy model. Grether and Maddala (1982) analyzed a model of the form

$$y_{it}^* = \alpha y_{i, t-1}^* + \beta x_{it} + u_{it}$$

This model can be termed a lagged-index model. With y_{it}^* observed as a dummy variable when we consider distributed-lag models, we can consider lagged values of both the latent and observed variables.

As mentioned earlier, it is beyond the scope of this book to go into these models in detail. The reader should consult the previously mentioned studies.

CHAPTER 3

Probabilistic-choice models

This chapter continues with the multinomial logit model discussed in section 2.12. It derives the multinomial logit model from a theory of probabilistic choice. We then discuss its limitations and examine some extensions of this model (the multinomial probit model, the nested logit model, the generalized extreme-value model, etc.).

3.1   McFadden's conditional logit model

In the previous chapter we discussed the multinomial logit model as an extension of the simple logit model for dichotomous variables. There it was pointed out that there is a difference in the way the multinomial logit model was derived and discussed in some of the statistical literature and the way it was discussed by McFadden. The latter discussion is related to the hedonic-price problem in econometrics and the theory of probabilistic choice discussed by several psychologists. In this chapter we shall discuss the multinomial logit model and its extensions as developed by McFadden (1973, 1974, 1976a, 1978, 1979, 1982, in press).

We start with the assumption that consumers are rational in the sense that they make choices that maximize their perceived utility subject to constraints on expenditures. However, there are many errors in this maximization because of imperfect perception and optimization, as well as the inability of the analyst to measure exactly all the relevant variables. Hence, following Thurstone (1927), McFadden assumed that utility is a random function.

Suppose that an individual faces m choices. We can define an underlying latent variable Y_i^* to denote the level of indirect utility associated with the ith choice. The observed variables Y_i are defined as

$$Y_i = 1 \quad \text{if} \quad Y_i^* = \text{Max}(Y_1^*, Y_2^*, \ldots, Y_m^*)$$
$$Y_i = 0 \quad \text{otherwise}$$

We shall assume that there are no ties. Write $Y_i^* = V_i(X_i) + \epsilon_i$, where X_i is the vector of attributes for the ith choice and ϵ_i is a residual that captures unobserved variations in tastes and in the attributes of alternatives and errors in the perception and optimization by the consumer.

If the residuals ϵ_i are independently and identically distributed with the type I extreme-value distribution whose cumulative distribution function (CDF) is

$$F(\epsilon_i < \epsilon) = \exp(-e^{-\epsilon}) \tag{3.1}$$

and whose probability density function (PDF) is

$$f(\epsilon_i) = \exp(-\epsilon_i - e^{-\epsilon_i}) \tag{3.2}$$

then we can show that

$$\text{Prob}(Y_i = 1 \mid X) = \frac{e^{V_i}}{\sum_{j=1}^m e^{V_j}} \tag{3.3}$$

which is the same as equation (2.39) in Chapter 2, with $V_i = \beta' X_i$. This result can be shown as follows: The condition $Y_i^* = \text{Max}(Y_1^*, Y_2^*, \ldots, Y_m^*)$ implies

$$\epsilon_i + V_i > \epsilon_j + V_j \quad \text{for all } j \neq i$$

or

$$\epsilon_j < \epsilon_i + V_i - V_j \quad \text{for all } j \neq i$$

Hence, if $\epsilon_1, \epsilon_2, \ldots, \epsilon_m$ are identically and independently distributed (IID), with CDF given by (3.1), then

$$\text{Prob}(Y_i = 1) = \text{Prob}(\epsilon_j < \epsilon_i + V_i - V_j) \quad \text{for all } j \neq i \tag{3.4}$$

$$= \int_{-\infty}^{\infty} \prod_{j \neq i} F(\epsilon_i + V_i - V_j) \cdot f(\epsilon_i) \, d\epsilon_i \tag{3.5}$$

where $F(\cdot)$ and $f(\cdot)$ are given by (3.1) and (3.2), respectively. Now

$$\prod_{j \neq i} F(\epsilon_i + V_i - V_j) f(\epsilon_i) = \prod_{j \neq i} \exp(-e^{-\epsilon_i - V_i + V_j}) \exp(-\epsilon_i - e^{-\epsilon_i})$$

$$= \exp\left[\epsilon_i - e^{-\epsilon_i}\left(1 + \sum_{j \neq i} \frac{e^{V_j}}{e^{V_i}}\right)\right]$$

If we write

$$\lambda_i = \log\left(1 + \sum_{j \neq i} \frac{e^{V_j}}{e^{V_i}}\right) = \log\left(\sum_{j=1}^{m} \frac{e^{V_j}}{e^{V_i}}\right) \tag{3.6}$$

we can write (3.5) as

$$\int_{-\infty}^{\infty} \exp(-\epsilon_i - e^{-(\epsilon_i - \lambda_i)}) \, d\epsilon_i$$

$$= \exp(-\lambda_i) \int_{-\infty}^{\infty} \exp(-\epsilon_i^* - e^{-\epsilon_i^*}) \, d\epsilon_i^* \quad \text{where } \epsilon_i^* = \epsilon_i - \lambda_i$$

$$= \exp(-\lambda_i)$$

$$= \frac{e^{V_i}}{\sum_{j=1}^{m} e^{V_j}}$$

If we have a set of N individuals facing m choices, we can define

$Y_{tj}^* =$ the level of indirect utility for the tth individual making the jth choice

$Y_{tj} = 1$ if the tth individual makes the jth choice

$Y_{tj} = 0$ otherwise

We shall assume that

$$Y_{tj}^* = \beta'X_{tj} + \alpha_j'Z_t + \epsilon_{ij}$$

where Z_t are individual-specific variables and X_{tj} is the vector of values of the attributes of the jth choice as perceived by the tth individual. Then

$$P_{tj} = \text{Prob}(Y_{tj} = 1) = \frac{e^{\beta'X_{tj} + \alpha_j'Z_t}}{\sum_{k=1}^{m} e^{\beta'X_{tk} + \alpha_k'Z_t}} \tag{3.7}$$

which is equation (2.54).

3.2   The Luce model

The model in equation (3.3) has the property referred to as "independence of irrelevant alternatives" (IIA). This is because the odds ratio for the ith and jth choices is $\exp(V_i)/\exp(V_j)$, which is the same irrespective of the total number m of choices considered. If the individual is offered an expanded choice set, that does not change this odds ratio.

Luce (1959) derived the model given by equation (3.3) starting from the IIA axiom on the choice probabilities. For this reason this model is also referred to as the Luce model. The multinomial logit model is a special case of the Luce model in which V_i is a linear function of the attributes X_i.

The model specified by equation (3.4) is called the strict-utility model. McFadden (1973) showed that a necessary and sufficient condition for the Luce model given by equation (3.3) to be equivalent to the strict-utility model (3.4) is that the ϵ_i be independently and identically distributed with the extreme-value distribution given by (3.1).

The Luce model has been used in transportation planning by McFadden (1974) and McFadden and Reid (1975). Given data on the characteristics of different models of transportation, the characteristics of the individuals, and the choices made, we can estimate the parameters β and α in (3.7). Then, given a new travel mode with given characteristics, we can estimate the probabilities with which different individuals will choose this mode of travel.

The primary drawback of the Luce model is that the IIA assumption is inappropriate in many applications. As pointed out by Debreu (1960), this model predicts too high a joint probability of selection for two alternatives that are in fact perceived as similar rather than independent by the individual. For instance, suppose X_1, X_2, and X_3 are the attributes of a trip by red bus, blue bus, and auto, respectively. Suppose consumers treat the two buses as equivalent and are indifferent between auto and bus. Then one expects

$$P(1 \mid X_1, X_2) = P(1 \mid X_1, X_3) = P(2 \mid X_2, X_3) = 1/2$$

and

$$P(1 \mid X_1, X_2, X_3) = P(2 \mid X_1, X_2, X_3) = 1/4$$

The relative odds of alternatives 1 and 3 depend on the presence of alternative 2. They are $1:1$ if choice 2 is not present. They are $1:2$ if choice 2 is present. This is inconsistent with the Luce model.

3.3   The multinomial probit model

The restrictions imposed by the IIA property of the Luce model are very unappealing in many applications. One appealing alternative is the multinomial probit (MNP) model, in which the residuals ϵ_i in the random-utility model have a multivariate normal distribution. This model was first proposed by Thurstone (1927) and has been applied to psychological-choice data by Bock and Jones (1968). Hausman and Wise (1978) applied the multinomial probit model to the transit-choice problem and compared the results with those of the multinomial logit and independent probit models (the independent probit model is the one in which the ϵ_i have independent normal distributions). The multinomial probit can be applied only for a small number of alternatives (at most three or four), because the computations involve evaluating multiple integrals, as can be seen with the following case.

Consider the case of three alternatives:

$$Y_1^* = V_1 + \epsilon_1$$
$$Y_2^* = V_2 + \epsilon_2$$
$$Y_3^* = V_3 + \epsilon_3$$

Assume that the residuals $(\epsilon_1, \epsilon_2, \epsilon_3)$ have a trivariate normal distribution with mean vector zero and covariance matrix Σ given by

$$\Sigma = \begin{bmatrix} \sigma_1^2 & \sigma_{12} & \sigma_{13} \\ \sigma_{12} & \sigma_2^2 & \sigma_{23} \\ \sigma_{13} & \sigma_{23} & \sigma_3^2 \end{bmatrix}$$

Consider the probability that the first alternative will be chosen. This is

$$\text{Prob}(Y_1^* > Y_2^*, \ Y_1^* > Y_3^*) = \text{Prob}(\epsilon_2 - \epsilon_1 < V_1 - V_2, \ \epsilon_3 - \epsilon_1 < V_1 - V_3)$$

Write

$$\eta_{21} = \epsilon_2 - \epsilon_1, \quad \eta_{31} = \epsilon_3 - \epsilon_1, \quad V_{12} = V_1 - V_2, \quad \text{and} \quad V_{13} = V_1 - V_3$$

η_{21} and η_{31} have a bivariate normal distribution with covariance matrix

$$\Omega_1 = \begin{bmatrix} \sigma_1^2 + \sigma_2^2 - 2\sigma_{12} & \sigma_1^2 - \sigma_{13} - \sigma_{12} + \sigma_{23} \\ \sigma_1^2 - \sigma_{13} - \sigma_{12} + \sigma_{23} & \sigma_1^2 + \sigma_3^2 - 2\sigma_{13} \end{bmatrix}$$

Thus the probability that alternative 1 will be chosen is given by

$$P_1 = \int_{-\infty}^{V_{12}} \int_{-\infty}^{V_{13}} f(\eta_{21}, \eta_{31}) \, d\eta_{21} \, d\eta_{31}$$

where $f(\eta_{21}, \eta_{31})$ has a bivariate normal distribution with covariance matrix Ω_1 and mean vector zero. The probabilities P_2 and P_3 can be similarly calculated.

With four alternatives it is easy to see that we end up with trivariate integrals, and this can be very costly. For more than four alternatives the computations are almost impractical. Two alternative methods have been suggested recently for approximating MNP choice probabilities at moderate cost. The first, which is a Monte Carlo method used by Lerman and Manski (1982), starts with given values of V_i and draws vectors $(\epsilon_1, \epsilon_2, \ldots, \epsilon_m)$ from a multivariate normal distribution, and the frequency with which utility is maximized at alternative i is recorded. What this procedure amounts to is a search procedure on both the V_i and the covariance matrix of the errors Σ. Clearly, even this can get computationally cumbersome.

The second approach is based on the Clark (1961) approximation described in the Appendix at the end of this book. It approximates the distribution of the maximum of normal variates with that of a normal variate. This approximation is good for nonnegatively correlated variates of equal variances, but it is poor for negative correlations or unequal variances. The Clark method consideres trivariate normal random variables (X_1, X_2, X_3) and approximates the bivariate distribution of $[(X_1, \mathrm{Max}(X_2, X_3)]$ by a bivariate normal distribution with the same first and second moments. The approximation rests on the fact that these moments for $[X_1, \mathrm{Max}(X_2, X_3)]$ can be calculated exactly in a straightforward manner. For the multinomial probit model with m choices, we have to apply the Clark approximation repeatedly, $m-2$ times. Details of this can be found in the work of Daganzo (1980). Because this approximation is poor for negative correlations or unequal variances, it is doubtful that the multinomial probit model is worth all the computational trouble when the number of choices is greater than four.

3.4   The elimination-by-aspects model

The multinomial probit model is one way of taking account of the similarities of alternatives. An alternative method is the elimination-by-aspects (EBA) model proposed by Tversky (1972*a, b*). The EBA model views choice as a covert sequential process. It is assumed that each alternative is described by a set of aspects (or characteristics) and that at each stage of the process an aspect is selected (from the ones included in the available alternatives) with a probability that is proportional to its weight. The selection of the aspect eliminates all the alternatives that do not contain the selected aspect, and the selection continues until a single alternative remains. Aspects that are common to all the alternatives under consideration do not affect the choice probabilities.

A somewhat similar model is the lexicographic model. With the lexicographic model, one specifies the ordering of relevant attributes a priori. One chooses the alternative that is best with regard to the first attribute, then moves on to the second attribute and selects the alternative that is best with regard to that attribute, and so on. For instance, in purchasing a car, one might have an ordering of automatic transmission, price, gas mileage, and body appearance, in that order. At the first step, cars without automatic transmissions are eliminated. At the next step, cars above a certain price are eliminated, and so on. However, the EBA model differs from this in that there is no fixed prior ordering of aspects (or attributes); the choice process is inherently probabilistic.[1]

Suppose there are four aspects with (utility) values V_1, V_2, V_3, and V_4. Suppose there are three alternatives Z_1, Z_2, and Z_3. These alternatives, along with their associated aspects (or attributes), are as follows:

$$Z_1 = (V_1, V_4)$$
$$Z_2 = (V_2, V_4)$$
$$Z_3 = (V_3)$$

Note that those aspects common to all choices do not enter the decision process and hence are eliminated. Also, the probability that each aspect will be chosen is proportional to its value. For example, if V_1, V_2, or V_3 is chosen, this immediately determines the corresponding choice. If V_4 is chosen, then Z_3 is eliminated, and then there is a further choice between Z_1 and Z_2. Thus,

Prob$(1 \mid Z_1, Z_2, Z_3)$ = (probability that V_1 will be chosen as the first aspect) + (probability that V_4 will be chosen as the first aspect) × (probability that V_1 will be chosen as the second aspect)

$$= \frac{V_1}{V_1 + V_2 + V_3 + V_4} + \frac{V_4}{V_1 + V_2 + V_3 + V_4} \frac{V_1}{V_1 + V_2}$$

Note that at each stage, aspects common to the alternatives at that stage do not enter the choice process. Similarly, if

$$Z_1 = (V_1, V_4, V_5)$$
$$Z_2 = (V_2, V_4, V_6)$$
$$Z_3 = (V_3, V_5, V_6)$$

and $S = \sum_{j=1}^{6} V_j$, we have

$$P(1 \mid Z_1, Z_2, Z_3) = \frac{V_1}{S} + \frac{V_4}{S} \frac{V_1 + V_5}{V_1 + V_5 + V_2 + V_6}$$

$$+ \frac{V_5}{S} \frac{V_1 + V_4}{V_1 + V_4 + V_3 + V_6}$$

$$= \text{Prob}(V_1 \text{ chosen first}) + \text{Prob}(V_4 \text{ chosen first}) \times \text{Prob}(V_1 \text{ or } V_5 \text{ chosen second}) + \text{Prob}(V_5 \text{ chosen first}) \times \text{Prob}(V_1 \text{ or } V_4 \text{ chosen second})$$

[1] A sufficient, but not necessary, condition for EBA is choice by maximizing a randomly chosen lexicographic preference.

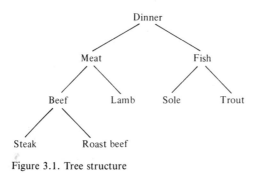

Figure 3.1. Tree structure

Tversky showed that the EBA model is consistent with random preference maximization. As with the multinomial logit and multinomial probit models, in econometric applications we shall have to make the V_i parametric functions of measured attributes. The EBA model becomes computationally infeasible for large choice sets. This problem has been discussed further by McFadden (1982). The EBA model does not have the latent-variable characterization that we have given to the multinomial logit and multinomial probit models. The EBA model has not been used in any econometric applications.

3.5   The hierarchical elimination-by-aspects model

In the EBA model, if there are n aspects, the total number of subsets one must consider is $2^n - 2$, and this can get very large. Recognizing this problem, Tversky and Sattath (1979) specialized the EBA model to the situation in which the alternatives are represented by a tree graph. The example they considered involves the choice of a dinner entrée from five alternatives: steak, roast beef, lamb, trout, and sole. The tree structure is shown in Figure 3.1. When aspects have a tree structure, the EBA model reduces to the elimination-by-tree (EBT) model or the hierarchical elimination-by-aspects (HEBA) model. In this case the subject selects a link from the tree (with probability proportional to its length) and eliminates all the alternatives that do not include that link. The same process is applied to each selected branch until only one alternative remains.

Suppose that the (utility) values associated with the different aspects specific to each of the choices are as follows:[2]

---

[2] It should be pointed out that this example on choice of meal is purely for illustrative purposes. It is nice in theory but not very practicable because of the difficulty in defining and measuring objective attributes of meat, fish, etc.

Steak	V_1
Roast beef	V_2
Lamb	V_3
Trout	V_4
Sole	V_5
Beef	V_6 (steak, roast beef)
Meat	V_7 (steak, roast beef, lamb)
Fish	V_8 (trout, sole)

Assume that the V's are normalized so as to sum to 1 (i.e., $\sum V_i = 1$). Then, in the HEBA model,

Prob(steak will be chosen) = (probability meat will be chosen)
$$\times \text{ (probability beef will be chosen)}$$
$$\times \text{ (probability steak will be chosen)}$$
$$= (V_1 + V_2 + V_3 + V_6 + V_7)$$
$$\times \frac{V_1 + V_2 + V_6}{V_1 + V_2 + V_6 + V_3} \frac{V_1}{V_1 + V_2}$$

Note that the members of the string of transition probabilities defining the HEBA model are conditional probabilities.

On the other hand, the corresponding probability in the EBA model is

$$\text{Prob(steak)} = V_1 + V_6 \frac{V_1}{V_1 + V_2}$$
$$+ V_7 \left(\frac{V_1}{V_1 + V_2 + V_3 + V_6} + \frac{V_6}{V_1 + V_2 + V_3 + V_6} \cdot \frac{V_1}{V_1 + V_2} \right)$$

This corresponds to all the sequences V_1, (V_6, V_1), (V_7, V_1), (V_7, V_6, V_1) by which steak can be chosen.

Although it involves fewer parameters than the EBA model, the HEBA model also has not found many econometric applications.

3.6   The nested multinomial logit model

An alternative to the HEBA model considered in the previous section is the nested multinomial logit (NMNL) model due to McFadden. McFadden (1981) argued that numerical experiments indicate that the HEBA (or EBT) and NMNL models give virtually identical fits to data. The NMNL model is computationally tractable for large problems. Computationally, it involves the sequential use of the multinomial logit program. In many econometric applications with several explanatory variables, it is better to use the NMNL model rather than the HEBA model.

As an illustration, consider the problem of choice of housing location (McFadden, 1978). Suppose a consumer faces a residential location problem, with a choice of communities indexed $i = 1, 2, \ldots, C$ and dwellings $j = 1, 2, \ldots, N_i$ in community i. The consumer will have a utility U_{ij} for alternative (i, j) that is a function of the attributes of this alternative, such as accessibility, quality of public services, and neighborhood and dwelling characteristics, as well as the consumer's characteristics, such as age, family size, and income. The consumer will choose the alternative that maximizes his utility.

As in the previous sections, we write $U_{ij} = V_{ij} + \epsilon_{ij}$, where V_{ij} is a function of all the measured characteristics and ϵ_{ij} is a residual that captures the effects of unmeasured variables, personal idiosyncracies, imperfections in perception and maximization, and so forth. If we assume that ϵ_{ij} are indepedently and identically distributed with the extreme-value distribution (3.1), then the probability P_{ij} that the (i, j)th alternative will be chosen is given by

$$P_{ij} = e^{V_{ij}} \left/ \sum_{m=1}^{C} \sum_{n=1}^{N_m} e^{V_{mn}} \right. \tag{3.8}$$

Suppose that

$$V_{ij} = \beta' X_{ij} + \alpha' Y_i \tag{3.9}$$

where X_{ij} is the vector of observed attributes that vary with both community and dwelling (e.g., workplace accessibility) and Y_i is the vector of attributes that vary only with community (e.g., availability of community recreation facilities); α and β are vectors of unknown parameters. We can write

$$P_{ij} = P_{j|i} \cdot P_i$$

The conditional probability $P_{j|i}$ can be seen to be

$$P_{j|i} = e^{V_{ij}} \left/ \sum_{k=1}^{N_i} e^{V_{ik}} = e^{\beta' X_{ij}} \right/ \sum_{k=1}^{N_i} e^{\beta' X_{ik}} \tag{3.10}$$

and

$$P_i = \sum_{j=1}^{N_i} e^{V_{ij}} \left/ \sum_{m=1}^{C} \sum_{n=1}^{N_m} e^{V_{mn}} \right.$$

$$= e^{\alpha' Y_i} \sum_{j=1}^{N_i} e^{\beta' X_{ij}} \left/ \sum_{m=1}^{C} e^{\alpha' Y_m} \sum_{n=1}^{N_m} e^{\beta' X_{mn}} \right. \tag{3.11}$$

We define an inclusive value

$$I_i = \log\left(\sum_{j=1}^{N_i} e^{\beta' X_{ij}} \right) \tag{3.12}$$

Then we can write equations (3.10) and (3.11) compactly as

$$P_{j|i} = e^{\beta'X_{ij}}/e^{I_i} \tag{3.13}$$

$$P_i = e^{\alpha'Y_i + I_i} \bigg/ \sum_{m=1}^{C} e^{\alpha'Y_m + I_m} \tag{3.14}$$

One method of estimating model (3.8) is to estimate the parameters β from the conditional-choice model (3.10), calculate the values I_i, and finally estimate α from equation (3.14), given the values of I_i. This sequential approach can be applied in all problems in which the number of choices is very large but the decision process has a tree structure.

The extension of this model to cases involving several branches of a tree is obvious. For instance, in the example in Figure 3.1, there are three levels of choice. Analogous to (3.8), we have

$$P_{ijk} = e^{V_{ijk}} \bigg/ \sum_{l} \sum_{m} \sum_{n} e^{V_{lmn}} \tag{3.15}$$

We assume that

$$V_{ijk} = \beta'X_{ijk} + \alpha'Y_{ij} + \gamma'Z_i \tag{3.16}$$

where X_{ijk}, Y_{ij}, and Z_i refer to the vectors of explanatory variables specific to categories (i,j,k), (i,j), and (i), respectively. Here the index i refers to the different attributes of the entrée (meat or fish), j refers to the different attributes of the meals (beef, lamb, sole, or trout), and k refers to the attributes of different types of beef (steak or roast beef). In this example, $i=1,2$, $j=1,2,3,4$, and $k=1,2$. We write

$$P_{ijk} = P_{k|i,j} \cdot P_{j|i} \cdot P_i \tag{3.17}$$

The conditional probability $P_{k|i,j}$ will involve only the parameters β:

$$P_{k|i,j} = e^{\beta'X_{ijk}} \bigg/ \sum_{n} e^{\beta'X_{ijn}} \tag{3.18}$$

We define the inclusive values

$$I_{ij} = \log\left(\sum_{n} e^{\beta'X_{ijn}}\right) \tag{3.19}$$

Then

$$P_{j|i} = e^{\alpha'Y_{ij} + I_{ij}} \bigg/ \sum_{m} e^{\alpha'Y_{im} + I_{im}} \tag{3.20}$$

We define another set of inclusive values

$$J_i = \log\left(\sum_{m} \sum_{n} e^{\beta'X_{imn} + \alpha'Y_{im}}\right) = \log\left(\sum_{m} e^{\alpha'Y_{im} + I_{im}}\right) \tag{3.21}$$

Then

$$P_i = e^{\gamma' Z_i + J_i} \bigg/ \sum_l e^{\gamma' Z_l + J_l} \tag{3.22}$$

The sequential estimation procedure is as follows:

1. Get estimates of β from (3.18).
2. Calculate the inclusive values I_{ij} from (3.19).
3. Estimate α from (3.20), given the values I_{ij}.
4. Calculate the inclusive values J_i from (3.21).
5. Estimate γ from (3.22), given the values J_i.

The *nested logit model* is a model that is obtained by allowing the inclusive values to have a coefficient other than 1. For instance, equation (3.14) will be modified as

$$P_i = e^{\alpha' Y_i + (1-\sigma) I_i} \bigg/ \sum_{m=1}^{C} e^{\alpha' Y_m + (1-\sigma) I_m} \tag{3.23}$$

McFadden (1978) showed that this nested logit model can be derived from a theory of stochastic utility maximization, in a manner analogous to that of the multinomial logit model. The multinomial logit model was derived on the assumption that the residuals ϵ in the stochastic utility function have independent extreme-value distributions. The nested multinomial logit model can be derived from the assumption that the residuals $(\epsilon_1, \epsilon_2, \ldots, \epsilon_n)$ have a generalized extreme-value distribution. Thus, it allows for a general pattern of dependence among the choices and avoids the red-bus/blue-bus problem (the IIA property) referred to earlier, which is the main limitation of the Luce model.

3.7   The generalized extreme-value model

The generalized extreme-value distribution is defined as

$$F(\epsilon_1, \epsilon_2, \ldots, \epsilon_n) = \exp[-G(e^{-\epsilon_1}, e^{-\epsilon_2}, \ldots, e^{-\epsilon_n})] \tag{3.24}$$

where $G(Y_1, Y_2, \ldots, Y_n)$ is a nonnegative function (homogeneous of degree 1) of $(Y_1, Y_2, \ldots, Y_n) \geq 0$. Also,

$$\lim_{Y_i \to \infty} G(Y_1, Y_2, \ldots, Y_n) = +\infty \quad \text{for } i = 1, 2, \ldots, n$$

and for any distinct $(i_1, i_2, \ldots, i_k)$, $\partial^k G / \partial Y_{i_1} \ldots \partial Y_{i_k}$ is nonnegative for k odd and nonpositive for k even. The special case

$$G(Y_1, Y_2, \ldots, Y_n) = \sum_{i=1}^{n} Y_i$$

yields the multinomial logit model, because in this case, $(\epsilon_1, \epsilon_2, \ldots, \epsilon_n)$ have independent extreme-value distributions.

A simple bivariate extreme-value distribution is

$$G(Y) = (Y_1^{1/(1-\sigma)} + Y_2^{1/(1-\sigma)})^{1-\sigma} \tag{3.25}$$

For this distribution, σ is approximately equal to the correlation between Y_1 and Y_2.[3]

McFadden (1978) proved that the generalized extreme-value distribution (3.24) implies that the probabilistic-choice model that is consistent with utility maximization gives choice probabilities of the form

$$P_i = e^{V_i} G_i(e^{V_1}, e^{V_2}, \ldots, e^{V_n}) / G(e^{V_1}, e^{V_2}, \ldots, e^{V_n}) \tag{3.26}$$

We shall not go through the details of this proof here.

With the bivariate extreme-value distribution (3.25), the choice probabilities according to (3.26) are

$$P_1 = e^{V_1/(1-\sigma)} / (e^{V_1/(1-\sigma)} + e^{V_2/(1-\sigma)})$$

and

$$P_2 = e^{V_2/(1-\sigma)} / (e^{V_1/(1-\sigma)} + e^{V_2/(1-\sigma)})$$

If $\sigma = 0$, these are the same as the multinomial logit probabilities. As $\sigma \to 1$, P_1 and $P_2 \to 1/2$.

For the case of three alternatives, with alternatives 2 and 3 being very similar (e.g., alternative 1 represents a dwelling in one community, and alternatives 2 and 3 represent dwellings of a similar type in a second community), we can define the G function

$$G(Y_1, Y_2, Y_3) = Y_1 + (Y_2^{1/(1-\sigma)} + Y_3^{1/(1-\sigma)})^{1-\sigma} \tag{3.27}$$

The choice probabilities will then be

$$P_1 = \frac{Y_1}{G(Y_1, Y_2, Y_3)}$$
$$P_2 = Y_2^{1/(1-\sigma)}(Y_2^{1/(1-\sigma)} + Y_3^{1/(1-\sigma)})^{-\sigma} / G(Y_1, Y_2, Y_3) \tag{3.28}$$

with an expression for P_3 similar to that for P_2. For compactness of notation, we have written Y_j for $\exp(V_j)$.

If only alternatives 1 and 2 are available, then P_1 and P_2 have the binomial logit form

---

[3] McFadden informed me that after failing to find a proof that σ in (3.25) is equal to the correlation between Y_1 and Y_2, he computed the correlation ρ numerically and found that they are not equal but $\sigma \leqslant \rho \leqslant \sigma + 0.045$.

$$P_1 = e^{V_1}/(e^{V_1} + e^{V_2}), \quad P_2 = e^{V_2}/(e^{V_1} + e^{V_2}) \tag{3.29}$$

If only alternatives 2 and 3 are available, then P_2 has the binomial logit form

$$P_2 = e^{V_2/(1-\sigma)}/(e^{V_2/(1-\sigma)} + e^{V_3/(1-\sigma)})$$

With the availability of alternative 3, it is easy to see from (3.28) and (3.29) that the odds ratio P_1/P_2 changes, unlike the case of the multinomial logit model with the IIA property. Thus, the generalized extreme-value (GEV) model enables us to get around the red-bus/blue-bus problem.

Suppose the total number of alternatives N can be classified into m groups with N_i alternatives in the ith group, so that $\sum_i N_i = N$. Then a generalized functional form, corresponding to (3.27), would be

$$G(Y) = \sum_{i=1}^{m} a_i \left(\sum_{j=1}^{N_i} Y_{ij}^{1/(1-\sigma_i)} \right)^{1-\sigma_i} \tag{3.30}$$

with $a_i > 0$, $0 \leqslant \sigma_i < 1$. Equation (3.27) is a special case of this, with $m = 2$, $N_1 = 1$, $N_2 = 2$, and $a_1 = a_2 = 1$.

We denote the probability of choosing the jth alternative in the ith group by P_{ij}. Then, writing $P_{ij} = P_{j|i} \cdot P_i$, we have

$$P_{j|i} = e^{V_{ij}/(1-\sigma_i)} \left/ \sum_{k=1}^{N_i} e^{V_{ik}/(1-\sigma_i)} \right. \tag{3.31}$$

and

$$P_i = a_i \left(\sum_{j=1}^{N_i} e^{V_{ij}/(1-\sigma_i)} \right)^{1-\sigma_i} \left/ \sum_{k=1}^{m} a_k \left(\sum_{j=1}^{N_k} e^{V_{kj}/(1-\sigma_k)} \right)^{1-\sigma_k} \right. \tag{3.32}$$

3.8   The relationship between the NMNL model and the GEV model

Suppose we set $a_i = a$ and $\sigma_i = \sigma$ for all i in (3.31) and (3.32). We assume that i indexes the community and that j indexes the jth dwelling in the ith community, and we write, as in (3.9),

$$V_{ij} = \beta' X_{ij} + \alpha' Y_i$$

with X_{ij} and Y_i denoting the attributes specific to the (i,j)th dwelling and the ith community, respectively. Then formulas (3.31) and (3.32) can be written as

$$P_{j|i} = e^{\beta' X_{ij}/(1-\sigma)}/e^{I_i} \tag{3.33}$$

$$P_i = e^{\alpha' Y_i + (1-\sigma)I_i} \left/ \sum_j e^{\alpha' Y_j + (1-\sigma)I_j} \right. \tag{3.34}$$

where
$$I_i = \log\left(\sum_{k=1}^{N_i} e^{\beta' X_{ik}/(1-\sigma)} \right) \tag{3.35}$$

These formulas are seen to be the same as those for the nested logit model defined earlier in (3.23). Note that β in (3.33) is estimable only up to a scale factor $1 - \sigma$. Thus, nested logit models are consistent with stochastic utility maximization, and the coefficient of the inclusive value provides an estimate of the similarity of the observed choices at the lower level of the tree structure. The GEV models can be estimated using the sequential multinomial logit models and inclusive values.

For the case of three levels to be indexed by (i, j, k) considered in equations (3.18) to (3.22), all we have to change for the nested multinomial logit model is equations (3.20) and (3.22), which will, respectively, read as

$$P_{j|i} = e^{\alpha' Y_{ij} + (1-\sigma) I_{ij}} \Big/ \sum_m e^{\alpha' Y_{im} + (1-\sigma) I_{im}}$$

and

$$P_i = e^{\gamma' Z_i + (1-\delta) J_i} \Big/ \sum_l e^{\gamma' Z_l + (1-\delta) J_l}$$

where σ is the measure of similarity at the lowest (k) level, and δ is the measure of similarity at the next higher (j) level. Note that the parameters β are estimable only up to a scale factor $1 - \sigma$, and the parameters σ are estimable up to a scale factor $1 - \delta$, and hence we did not redefine equations (3.18), (3.19), and (3.21).

The theorem proved by McFadden (1978) relating the generalized extreme-value distribution to stochastic utility maximization implies that a sufficient condition for a nested logit model to be consistent with stochastic utility maximization is that the coefficient of each inclusive value lie in the unit interval. Thus, in the estimation of the sequential multinomial logit models, if the estimated coefficient of the inclusive value is outside the unit interval, we can view this as evidence of a specification error and reexamine the model.

3.9   Estimation methods

Estimation of the multinomial logit model (MNL) can be easily carried out using the ML method. In large samples these estimates have been proved to have all the usual desirable statistical properties. See the work of McFadden (1973) for proofs.

Consider the MNL model given by (3.7). Initially, let us assume $\alpha_j = 0$

for all j (i.e., the individual characteristics do not enter the choice model). Suppose that β is a k-dimensional vector. Define the $k \times m$ matrix

$$X_t = (X_{t1}, X_{t2}, \ldots, X_{tm})$$

Also, define

$$Y_t = \begin{bmatrix} Y_{t1} \\ Y_{t2} \\ \vdots \\ Y_{tm} \end{bmatrix} \quad \text{and} \quad P_t = \begin{bmatrix} P_{t1} \\ P_{t2} \\ \vdots \\ P_{tm} \end{bmatrix}$$

where Y_{ti} and P_{ti} are as defined in section 3.1. The log-likelihood function is

$$\log L = \sum_t \sum_j Y_{tj} \log P_{tj}$$

$$= \sum_t \sum_j Y_{tj}(\beta'X_{tj}) - \sum_t \log\left(\sum_k e^{\beta'X_{tk}}\right)$$

(We have used the condition that $\sum_j Y_{tj}=1$, i.e., the assumption that the individual chooses only one alternative.) After differentiation and simplification, we can write the first-order condition as

$$\frac{\partial \log L}{\partial \beta} = \sum_t X_t(Y_t - P_t) = 0 \tag{3.36}$$

Also

$$-E\left(\frac{\partial^2 \log L}{\partial \beta \partial \beta'}\right) = E\left(\frac{\partial \log L}{\partial \beta} \cdot \frac{\partial \log L}{\partial \beta'}\right) = \sum_t X_t A_t X_t' \tag{3.37}$$

where

$$A_t = E(Y_t - P_t)(Y_t - P_t)' = D(P_t) - P_t P_t' \tag{3.38}$$

and $D(P_t)$ is a diagonal matrix with its jth diagonal element $=P_{tj}$. Hence, the covariance matrix of $\hat{\beta}_{ML}$ is $(\sum_t X_t A_t X_t')^{-1}$.

The ML estimates can be obtained by any of the usual methods: Newton–Raphson, method of scoring, or the Berndt et al. (1974) method. In the method of scoring, the iterative procedure will be

$$\beta_{r+1} = \beta_r + [I(\beta_r)]^{-1}S(\beta_r) \tag{3.39}$$

where $I(\beta_r)$ and $S(\beta_r)$ are, respectively, the expressions in (3.37) and (3.36) evaluated at $\beta=\beta_r$ and β_r is the estimate of β at the rth iteration.

Estimation of the parameters α_j [coefficients of the individual-specific characteristics in equation (3.7)] in this model is handled by creating a set of dummy variables. Let

$$\alpha' = (\alpha_1', \alpha_2', \ldots, \alpha_{m-1}')$$

Note that we have to use a normalization rule, and we have used $\alpha_m = 0$. Define Z_{tj}^* as a vector with Z_t as the jth element, all other elements being equal to 0. Then $\alpha' Z_{tj}^* = \alpha_j' Z_t$. Now define

$$\theta = \begin{bmatrix} \beta \\ \alpha \end{bmatrix} \quad \text{and} \quad W_{tj} = \begin{bmatrix} X_{tj} \\ Z_{tj}^* \end{bmatrix}$$

Then the model is in the same form as the one considered earlier (with no individual characteristics), with θ replacing β and W_{tj} replacing X_{tj}. Formulas (3.36) to (3.39) all hold, with θ replacing β and W replacing X.

Estimation of the multinomial probit model was discussed in section 3.3. Also, in section 3.6 we discussed the estimation of sequential logit models with inclusive values estimated from earlier stages of the model. However, when we use the sequential estimation procedure, the estimate of the covariance matrix of the ML estimates obtained is not the correct one, except at the first stage. The subsequent stages are based on the "inclusive values," which are based on estimates from the previous stage. Amemiya (1978*a*) provided the correct asymptotic covariance matrix for the estimates obtained from the second stage of the sequential estimation method. The model he considered is that in equations (3.9) to (3.14), with $C = n$ and $N_i = m$. The first-stage estimation is based on equation (3.10). This is the same as the ML estimation of the McFadden logit model considered earlier, except that the effective number of observations is the number of individuals multiplied by the number of choices at level i. The estimation of (3.14) after calculation of the inclusive values is again done by using the ML estimation for the McFadden logit model. Because the correct asymptotic covariance matrices derived by Amemiya (1978*a*) require many definitions, they will not be presented here.

Another problem that has received considerable attention in the estimation of probabilistic-choice models is the estimation from choice-based samples. It has been found, in models of choices of transportation modes, that instead of conducting household surveys it is much cheaper to obtain data from samples of individuals at bus stops, train stations, car parks, and so forth. Such samples are called choice-based samples because the sampling is from individual data stratified by choice. Because choice of mode of transport is an endogenous variable, this is a case of stratification by an endogenous variable. Manski and Lerman (1977) showed that treating choice-based samples as if they were random and calculating estimators appropriate to random samples will generally yield inconsistent estimates. They introduced a weighted likelihood func-

Table 3.1. *Prediction success table for probabilistic-choice models*

		Predicted choice					Observed count
		1	2	3	$\cdots$	m	
Observed	1	N_{11}	N_{12}	N_{13}	$\cdots$	N_{1m}	$N_{1.}$
choice	2	N_{21}	N_{22}	N_{23}	$\cdots$	N_{2m}	$N_{2.}$
	3	N_{31}	N_{32}	N_{33}	$\cdots$	N_{3m}	$N_{3.}$
	$\vdots$						
	m	N_{m1}	N_{m2}	N_{m3}	$\cdots$	N_{mm}	$N_{m.}$
Predicted count		$N_{.1}$	$N_{.2}$	$N_{.3}$	$\cdots$	$N_{.m}$	$N_{..}$

tion whose maximization has been shown to yield consistent estimates. In this method we modify the familiar exogenous sampling ML estimator by weighting each observation's contribution to the log-likelihood by $Q(j)/H(j)$, where $Q(j)$ is the fraction of the decision-making population selecting the jth alternative and $H(j)$ is the analogous fraction for the choice-based sample.

3.10   Goodness-of-fit measures

In probabilistic-choice models we can use the same goodness-of-fit measures as those discussed in section 2.11. In addition to this, we can look at the proportion of successful predictions of the choices made. One can prepare a success table (Table 3.1) for a case of m alternatives. In this table, N_{ij} refers to the number of individuals who chose alternative i but had been predicted to choose alternative j. N_{ii} refers to the number of correct predictions for alternative i.

McFadden et al. (1977) suggested the use of an overall prediction success index

$$\sigma = \sum_{i=1}^{m} \left[\frac{N_{ii}}{N_{..}} - \left(\frac{N_{.i}}{N_{..}} \right)^2 \right] \tag{3.40}$$

This index is nonnegative, with a maximum value of

$$1 - \sum_{i=1}^{m} \left(\frac{N_{.i}}{N_{..}} \right)^2$$

and can be normalized to have a value of 1 if desired.

The reasoning behind formula (3.40) is as follows: $N_{.i}/N_{..}$ is the proportion of sample observations predicted to choose alternative i. $N_{ii}/N_{.i}$

is the proportion of predictions for alternative i that were correct. For the ith choice, McFadden took the success index as $N_{ii}/N_{.i} - N_{.i}/N_{..}$. The expression in (3.40) is a weighted average of these success indexes with weights $N_{.i}/N_{..}$.

One other alternative is to compute

$$S_1 = \frac{1}{N_{..}} \left(\sum_{i=1}^{m} N_{ii} \right) \tag{3.41}$$

This is the total number of choices made that were predicted correctly. We can prepare a table like Table 3.1 for the second choice instead of the first choice and compute an index like (3.41). Call this S_2. Then $S_1 + S_2$ will give the proportion of times that the actual choice made was predicted as the first or second choice by the model. Nelson and Noll (1980) used this measure as a criterion of adequacy of their model.

It is also customary to compare $N_{.i}$ with $N_{i.}$ (i.e., the number of predicted choices and actual choices for each alternative i). However, this is not a good measure of the performance of the model. For instance, take the case $N_{.1} = N_{1.} = 4$ and $N_{.2} = N_{2.} = 4$. This could be interpreted as perfect prediction. However, this is consistent with $N_{12} = N_{21} = 4$, and thus all individual choices being predicted wrongly. Thus, comparing $N_{.i}$ with $N_{i.}$ is not a good way of judging the adequacy of a model. Carroll and Relles (1976) compared predictions from their models with those obtained from the conditional logit model by using the numbers $N_{.i}$ and $N_{i.}$.

3.11   Some tests for specification error

Earlier, in section 3.8, we argued that tests of significance applied to the coefficients of the inclusive values can be used to test the IIA property or the validity of the model. If this coefficient is significantly different from 1, then this is evidence that the IIA property does not hold. If this coefficient is outside the unit interval, then this is evidence of other specification errors and an argument for reexamining the model.

Hausman and McFadden (1980) suggested an alternative specification-error test for the IIA property. An implication of this property is that the model structure and parameters are unchanged when choice is analyzed conditional on a restricted subset of the full choice set. Let C be the full choice set, and D a proper subset of C. Let $\hat{\beta}_C$ be the parameter estimate obtained by ML on the full choice set, and $\hat{V}_C$ the estimate covariance matrix. Let $\hat{\beta}_D$ and $\hat{V}_D$ be the corresponding estimates for ML applied to the restricted choice set D. Under the null hypothesis that the IIA property holds, $\hat{\beta}_D - \hat{\beta}_C$ is a consistent estimator of zero. Under the alternative specifications where the IIA fails, it is not. Under the null hypothesis, $\hat{\beta}_D - \hat{\beta}_C$ has an estimated covariance matrix $\hat{V}_D - \hat{V}_C$. Hence, the statistic

$$S = (\hat{\beta}_D - \hat{\beta}_C)'(\hat{V}_D - \hat{V}_C)^{-1}(\hat{\beta}_D - \hat{\beta}_C)$$

is asymptotically chi-square with degrees of freedom equal to the rank of $\hat{V}_D - \hat{V}_C$.

Note that $\hat{\beta}_C$ and $\hat{\beta}_D$ are, respectively, the ML estimates for the full and restricted choice sets of the subvector of parameters identified in both cases. Hence, $(\hat{V}_D - \hat{V}_C)^{-1}$ is an ordinary inverse, and the rank of $\hat{V}_D - \hat{V}_C$ is the same as the order of $\hat{\beta}$.

3.12   Concluding remarks

There have been numerous applications of the probabilistic-choice models described in this chapter in transportation studies, residential-choice studies, studies of college-going behavior, studies of choices of appliances, studies of energy use, and so on. The references to these examples can be found in the several studies by McFadden cited earlier. Because these problems have been surveyed exhaustively in the earlier literature, we shall not dwell on them at length. However, there have also been many applications in which the logit model of probabilistic choice has been misapplied. A case in point is the study by Levin (1978), which was criticized by Braeutigam and Noll (1981), who argued that the logit model used was inappropriate for the problem.

There are also some distribution-free estimators that have been suggested for qualitative-choice models. These are the maximum-score estimator suggested by Manski (1975) and the improvement on this estimator made by Cosslett (1980). However, these estimators can be used only in very simple models; further, the standard errors of these estimators are not yet known. Therefore, we shall not go into the details of this work, although these methods are interesting.

CHAPTER 4

Discriminant analysis

4.1   Introduction

In section 2.3 we considered the problem of constructing a linear discriminant function that provides the best discrimination between two groups. In section 2.4 we outlined the analogy with multiple regression and the relationship between the linear probability model and the discriminant function. In this chapter we shall consider how the classification rules change when costs of misclassification are considered, and we shall extend the analysis to several groups. We shall also examine the relationship between the discriminant function and logit analysis.

4.2   The case of two populations

We shall initially consider the case of two populations. Our problem is to classify an individual into one of two populations π_1 and π_2 based on a vector of characteristics $x = (x_1, x_2, \ldots, x_k)$. Let $f_1(x)$ and $f_2(x)$ be the densities (or probability functions) of the distributions of the characteristics x in the two populations. Fisher (1936) suggested using a linear combination of the observations

$$y = \lambda_1 x_1 + \lambda_2 x_2 + \cdots + \lambda_k x_k \tag{4.1}$$

and choosing the coefficients so that the ratio of the squared difference between $\bar{y}_1$ and $\bar{y}_2$ (the means of y in the two groups) to the variance of y is maximized.

Let the means of x in the two groups be μ_1 and μ_2, respectively, and the covariance matrices of x in the two groups be Σ_1 and Σ_2, respectively (note that we are not making the assumption of normality). The means of the linear function y in the two groups are $\lambda'\mu_1$ and $\lambda'\mu_2$, respectively, and if we assume $\Sigma_1 = \Sigma_2 = \Sigma$, then the variance of y is $\lambda'\Sigma\lambda$. Thus we have to maximize

$$\phi = \frac{[\lambda'(\mu_1 - \mu_2)]^2}{\lambda'\Sigma\lambda}$$

Differentiating ϕ with respect to λ and equating the derivative to zero, we get

$$\frac{2[\lambda'(\mu_1 - \mu_2)](\mu_1 - \mu_2)\lambda'\Sigma\lambda - 2\Sigma\lambda[\lambda'(\mu_1 - \mu_2)]^2}{(\lambda'\Sigma\lambda)^2} = 0$$

or

$$(\mu_1 - \mu_2)\lambda'\Sigma\lambda = \Sigma\lambda[\lambda'(\mu_1 - \mu_2)] \tag{4.2}$$

This gives the solution $(\mu_1 - \mu_2) = \Sigma\lambda$, or

$$\lambda = \Sigma^{-1}(\mu_1 - \mu_2) \tag{4.3}$$

If the parameters are not known, it is the usual practice to estimate them by the corresponding sample quantities. The formula in terms of sample quantities is equation (2.4) in Chapter 2.

4.3   Prior probabilities and costs of misclassification

Let p_1 be the proportion of the group π_1 and p_2 the proportion of the group π_2 in the total population. Let us choose regions R_1 and R_2 such that if the sample point falls in R_1 we classify the individual into π_1, and if it falls in R_2 we classify the individual into π_2. Let C_1 be the cost of misclassifying a member of π_1 into π_2 and C_2 the cost of misclassifying a member of π_2 into π_1. The expected total cost of misclassification is

$$C = C_1 p_1 \int_{R_2} f_1(x)\, dx + C_2 p_2 \int_{R_1} f_2(x)\, dx$$

Because

$$\int_{R_2} f_1(x)\, dx + \int_{R_1} f_1(x)\, dx = 1$$

we have

$$C = C_1 p_1 \left[1 - \int_{R_1} f_1(x)\, dx\right] + C_2 p_2 \int_{R_1} f_2(x)\, dx$$

$$= C_1 p_1 + \int_{R_1} \left[C_2 p_2 f_2(x) - C_1 p_1 f_1(x)\right] dx$$

This is minimized if R_1 is chosen so that

$$C_2 p_2 f_2(x) < C_1 p_1 f_1(x)$$

or

$$\frac{f_1(x)}{f_2(x)} > \frac{C_2 p_2}{C_1 p_1} \tag{4.4}$$

If x is normally distributed with means μ_1 and μ_2, respectively, and covariance matrix Σ, because

$$f_i(x) = (2\pi)^{-k/2} |\Sigma|^{-1/2} \exp[-\tfrac{1}{2}(x - \mu_i)'\Sigma^{-1}(x - \mu_i)]$$

we have

$$\frac{f_1(x)}{f_2(x)} = \exp[-\tfrac{1}{2}(x - \mu_1)'\Sigma^{-1}(x - \mu_1) + \tfrac{1}{2}(x - \mu_2)'\Sigma^{-1}(x - \mu_2)]$$

$$= \exp[(\mu_1 - \mu_2)'\Sigma^{-1}x - \tfrac{1}{2}(\mu_1 - \mu_2)'\Sigma^{-1}(\mu_1 + \mu_2)] \tag{4.5}$$

Thus, condition (4.4) gives, after taking logs,

$$(\mu_1 - \mu_2)'\Sigma^{-1}x > \ln \frac{C_2 p_2}{C_1 p_1} + \tfrac{1}{2}(\mu_1 - \mu_2)'\Sigma^{-1}(\mu_1 + \mu_2)$$

Defining λ as in (4.3), we get

$$\lambda'x > \ln \frac{C_2 p_2}{C_1 p_1} + \tfrac{1}{2}\lambda'(\mu_1 + \mu_2)$$

If we substitute $\bar{x}_1$ for μ_1, $\bar{x}_2$ for μ_2, and S for Σ, and if $C_2 p_2 = C_1 p_1$, then this condition is the same as the condition we derived earlier in equation (2.4) of Chapter 2. Welch (1939) studied the discrimination problem from the point of view of minimizing the total probability of misclassification. This amounts to the case $C_1 = C_2$.

In the foregoing discussion, if $\Sigma_1 \neq \Sigma_2$, then the discriminant function will not be linear in x. We then get

$$\ln \frac{f_1(x)}{f_2(x)} = -\tfrac{1}{2}x'(\Sigma_1^{-1} - \Sigma_2^{-1})x + x'(\Sigma^{-1}\mu_1 - \Sigma_2^{-1}\mu_2) + \text{a constant}$$

Thus the discriminant function is quadratic in x.

4.4   Nonnormal data and logistic discrimination

The linear discriminant function and the assignment rule depend on the following assumptions:

1. Both $f_1(x)$ and $f_2(x)$ are multivariate normal.
2. The covariance matrices are equal (i.e. $\Sigma_1 = \Sigma_2$).

3. The prior probabilities p_1 and p_2 are known.
4. The means μ_1 and μ_2 and the covariance matrix Σ are known.

We saw that when assumption 4 is not satisfied (it rarely is), we substitute the corresponding sample values. If assumption 3 is not satisfied, we can again use the sample proportions as estimates if the sample is chosen at random from the whole population (rather than choosing samples separately from the two groups). If assumption 2 is violated, we saw that the discriminant function is quadratic rather than linear. As for assumption 1, there is scattered evidence to show that the linear discriminant function does not perform well with discrete data of various types.

Consider again the case of two populations. The probability of being a member of π_i, given x, is, according to the Bayes theorem,

$$P(\pi_i | x) = \frac{P(x | \pi_i)p_i}{P(x | \pi_1)p_1 + P(x | \pi_2)p_2} \qquad (i = 1, 2)$$

If $P(x | \pi_i)$ is multivariate normal, with mean μ_i and covariance matrix Σ, we can write

$$\frac{P(\pi_1 | x)}{P(\pi_2 | x)} = \frac{P(x | \pi_1)}{P(x | \pi_2)} \cdot \frac{p_1}{p_2} = \exp(\alpha + \beta' x) \qquad (4.6)$$

where α and β are, from equation (4.5) earlier, given by

$$\alpha = \ln \frac{p_1}{p_2} - \tfrac{1}{2}(\mu_1 - \mu_2)' \Sigma^{-1}(\mu_1 + \mu_2)$$

and

$$\beta = \Sigma^{-1}(\mu_1 - \mu_2)$$

From (4.6) we get

$$P(\pi_1 | x) = \frac{\exp(\alpha + \beta' x)}{1 + \exp(\alpha + \beta' x)} \qquad (4.7)$$

$$P(\pi_2 | x) = \frac{1}{1 + \exp(\alpha + \beta' x)}$$

The model given by (4.6) is commonly called the *logistic model*. Although it was derived from the assumption of normality of the two populations, Cox (1966) and Day and Kerridge (1967) noted that this model holds for a variety of situations, including (a) multivariate normal with equal covariance matrices in π_1 and π_2, (b) multivariate independent dichotomous, (c) multivariate dichotomous following the log-linear model with equal second- and higher-order effects, (d) a combination of (a) and (c). Cox suggested estimating the parameters of (4.7) by the ML method. Let

$$y_i = 1 \quad \text{if } x_i \in \pi_1$$
$$y_i = 0 \quad \text{if } x_i \in \pi_2$$

Then the likelihood function is

$$L = \prod_{y_i=1} \frac{\exp(\alpha + \beta' x_i)}{1 + \exp(\alpha + \beta' x_i)} \prod_{y_i=0} \frac{1}{1 + \exp(\alpha + \beta' x_i)} \tag{4.8}$$

The likelihood equations must be solved by iterative methods, and a good starting value is the set of discriminant-function coefficients. It has sometimes been argued that it is not worthwhile to use the more complicated ML method because the ML estimates often are very close to the discriminant-function estimates, which can be obtained using the standard multiple-regression programs and using formula (2.13) in Chapter 2. Unless one has a really large number of observations, the ML estimation of the logistic model is really not that time-consuming. Halperin et al. (1971) compared the discriminant-function approach and the ML approach. They presented convincing evidence to show that if x does not come from a normal population, the ML estimates from (4.8) are preferable to the discriminant-function estimates $\hat{\lambda}$. In particular, they showed that if the components of x are dummy variables, the discriminant-function estimates $\hat{\lambda}$ will not be consistent. To see this, consider the case of only one explanatory variable x, which is dichotomous. Suppose that the probability of an event occurring is $e^{\alpha+\beta x}/(1+e^{\alpha+\beta x})$. Denote by P_0 and P_1 the values of this probability for $x=0$ and $x=1$, respectively, so that

$$P_0 = \frac{e^\alpha}{1 + e^\alpha} \quad \text{and} \quad P_1 = \frac{e^{\alpha+\beta}}{1 + e^{\alpha+\beta}}$$

Hence,

$$\alpha = \log \frac{P_0}{1 - P_0} \quad \text{and} \quad \beta = \log \left(\frac{P_1(1 - P_0)}{P_0(1 - P_1)} \right) \tag{4.9}$$

Define the dummy variable

$$y = 1 \quad \text{if the event occurs}$$
$$y = 0 \quad \text{otherwise}$$

Let the distribution of the observations be

		y		
		1	0	
x	1	n_1	$N_1 - n_1$	N_1
	0	n_0	$N_0 - n_0$	N_0
		n	$N - n$	N

The likelihood function is

$$L = P_0^{n_0}(1 - P_0)^{N_0 - n_0}P_1^{n_1}(1 - P_1)^{N_1 - n_1}$$

and the ML estimates are

$$\hat{\alpha}_{ML} = \log \frac{n_0}{N_0 - n_0} \quad \text{and} \quad \hat{\beta} = \log \frac{n_1(N_0 - n_0)}{n_0(N_1 - n_1)} \quad (4.10)$$

As $N \to \infty$, $N_1 \to \Pi_1 N$ and $N_0 \to \Pi_0 N$, where Π_1 and Π_0 are population proportions for which $x=1$ and $x=0$, respectively. Also, $n_1 \to \Pi_1 P_1 N$ and $n_0 \to \Pi_0 P_0 N$. Thus, $\hat{\alpha} \to \alpha$ and $\hat{\beta} \to \beta$.

As for the discriminant-function coefficients, they are given by formula (2.4) in Chapter 2. To obtain them, we have to find the regression coefficients in the linear probability model and the residual sum of squares. The regression model is

$$y = \alpha + \beta x + u$$

Thus we have

$$1 = \alpha + \beta + u \quad \text{for } n_1 \text{ observations}$$
$$0 = \alpha + \beta + u \quad \text{for } N_1 - n_1 \text{ observations}$$
$$1 = \alpha + u \quad \text{for } n_0 \text{ observations}$$
$$0 = \alpha + u \quad \text{for } N_0 - n_0 \text{ observations}$$

The normal equations are

$$\Sigma(y - \alpha - \beta x) = 0 \Rightarrow (n_1 + n_0) - (N_1 + N_0)\alpha - N_1\beta = 0$$
$$\Sigma x(y - \alpha - \beta x) = 0 \Rightarrow n_1 - N_1\alpha - N_1\beta = 0$$

These equations give the OLS estimates

$$\hat{\alpha}_{OLS} = \frac{n_0}{N_0} \quad \text{and} \quad \hat{\beta}_{OLS} = \frac{n_1}{N_1} - \frac{n_0}{N_0} \quad (4.11)$$

$$\text{Plim } \hat{\alpha}_{OLS} = P_0 \quad \text{and} \quad \text{Plim } \hat{\beta}_{OLS} = P_1 - P_0 \quad (4.12)$$

The residual sum of squares is

$$\text{RSS} = n_1\left(1 - \frac{n_1}{N_1}\right)^2 + (N_1 - n_1)\left(-\frac{n_1}{N_1}\right)^2 + n_0\left(1 - \frac{n_0}{N_0}\right)^2$$

$$+ (N_0 - n_0)\left(-\frac{n_0}{N_0}\right)^2$$

$$= n_1\left(1 - \frac{n_1}{N_1}\right) + n_0\left(1 - \frac{n_0}{N_0}\right)$$

The discriminant-function coefficient β^* is given by

$$\beta^* = \frac{(N-2)\hat{\beta}_{\text{OLS}}}{\text{RSS}}$$

As $N \to \infty$, $\text{RSS}/(N-2) \to \Pi_1 P_1(1-P_1) + \Pi_0 P_0(1-P_0)$. Hence,

$$\text{Plim }\beta^* = \frac{P_1 - P_0}{\Pi_1 P_1(1-P_1) + \Pi_0 P_0(1-P_0)} \tag{4.13}$$

which is quite different from β given in (4.9). One can evaluate the expression (4.13) for different values of Π_1, Π_0, P_0, and P_1. This result can also be extended to the case of several dichotomous variables, but we shall not present it here. See the work of Halperin et al. (1971) for details.

Of greater interest is the relationship between the estimates of the logit model and the linear probability model. Note that the ML estimates (4.10) can be derived directly from the OLS estimates (4.11). However, with more variables, one must be careful in deriving the relationships.[1] Consider the case of two dichotomous variables x_1 and x_2. The linear probability model is

$$y = \alpha_0 + \alpha_1 x_1 + \alpha_2 x_2 + u$$

This model implies that the probability of the event occurring is $\alpha_0 + \alpha_1 x_1 + \alpha_2 x_2$. The logit models says that this probability is $e^{\beta'Z}/(1+e^{\beta'Z})$. The questions are the value of Z and the relationship between the α's and β's. We write $\beta'Z = \beta_0 + \beta_1 x_1 + \beta_2 x_2 + \beta_3 x_1 x_2$. Then,

$$\log\left(\frac{\alpha_0 + \alpha_1 x_1 + \alpha_2 x_2}{1 - (\alpha_0 + \alpha_1 x_1 + \alpha_2 x_2)}\right) = \beta_0 + \beta_1 x_1 + \beta_2 x_2 + \beta_3 x_1 x_2$$

Hence,

$$\beta_0 = \log\left(\frac{\alpha_0}{1-\alpha_0}\right)$$

$$\beta_0 + \beta_1 = \log\left(\frac{\alpha_0 + \alpha_1}{1 - \alpha_0 - \alpha_1}\right)$$

---

[1] There appears to be some misconception among some empirical researchers in this area. For instance, Marantz et al. (1976) wrongly asserted that Halperin et al. (1971) showed that the logit coefficients can be derived directly from the OLS estimates. This reference is often quoted by others working with discrimination in housing markets. Halperin et al. only showed that when the x variables are not normal, the discriminant-analysis estimates are inconsistent. They did not show that the logit coefficients can be derived directly from OLS.

$$\beta_0 + \beta_2 = \log\left(\frac{\alpha_0 + \alpha_2}{1 - \alpha_0 - \alpha_2}\right)$$

$$\beta_0 + \beta_1 + \beta_2 + \beta_3 = \log\left(\frac{\alpha_0 + \alpha_1 + \alpha_2}{1 - \alpha_0 - \alpha_1 - \alpha_2}\right)$$

Note that if $\beta'Z$ is taken to be $\beta_0 + \beta_1 x_1 + \beta_2 x_2$, then the last equation gives

$$\beta_0 + \beta_1 + \beta_2 = \log\left(\frac{\alpha_0 + \alpha_1 + \alpha_2}{1 - \alpha_0 - \alpha_1 - \alpha_2}\right)$$

and thus we have four equations to determine β_0, β_1, and β_2.

This example illustrates that there are some simple relationships between the logit coefficients and the coefficients of the linear probability model in the case in which the explanatory variables are dichotomous.

In our discussion of the logit model, we are considering the binary and multinomial logit models discussed in Chapter 2. Earlier, in Chapter 2, we mentioned that the multinomial logit model discussed there is related to the discriminant function but that the conditional logit model is not. In essence, discriminant analysis and multinomial logit analysis, as discussed in Chapter 2, can be regarded as analysis of reduced forms, whereas the models considered in Chapter 3 are structural models. Given data on individual characteristics and the choices made, discriminant analysis and the multinomial logit analysis discussed in Chapter 2 can be used to predict the choices of a new individual with given characteristics. However, these models do not permit such predictions if a new choice is introduced. The models in Chapter 3 permit such predictions. McFadden (1976b) discussed the relationship between discriminant analysis and the conditional logit model in greater detail, but the essential difference is that between reduced-form models and structural models.

4.5   The case of several groups

Suppose that instead of only two groups we have m groups $\pi_1, \pi_2, \ldots, \pi_m$. Corresponding to equation (4.7), we can specify

$$P(\pi_j | x) = \frac{\exp(\alpha_j + \beta_j' x)}{C} \tag{4.14}$$

where $C = \sum_{j=1}^{m} \exp(\alpha_j + \beta_j' x)$. Because the conditional probabilities (4.14) remain unchanged, if one multiplies the numerator and denominator by $\exp(a + b'x)$, we see that not all α_j and β_j are estimable. In practice, one imposes a condition such as $\alpha_m = \beta_m = 0$. In the ML method we maximize the likelihood function

$$L = \prod_{i=1}^{n} \prod_{j=1}^{m} [P(\pi_j \mid x)]^{y_{ij}}$$

where

$$y_{ij} = 1 \quad \text{if } x_i \in \pi_j$$
$$y_{ij} = 0 \quad \text{otherwise}$$

A computer program to estimate the α_j and β_j has been given by Nerlove and Press (1973).

As in the case of two groups, we can start with prior probabilities p_j that an individual belongs to π_j. Then the conditional probabilities $P(\pi_j \mid x)$ are given by

$$P(\pi_j \mid x) = p_j f_j(x) \bigg/ \left[\sum_{j=1}^{m} p_j f_j(x) \right] \tag{4.15}$$

where $f_j(x)$ is the density of x in π_j. If the densities $f_j(x)$ are multivariate normal, with mean μ_j and a common covariance matrix Σ, then

$$f_j(x) = (2\pi)^{-k/2} \Sigma^{-1/2} \exp(-\tfrac{1}{2} Q_j)$$

where

$$Q_j = (x - \mu_j)' \Sigma^{-1} (x - \mu_j)$$
$$= x'\Sigma^{-1}x - 2\mu_j'\Sigma^{-1}x + \mu_j'\Sigma^{-1}\mu_j$$

Substituting this expression in (4.15), because

$$(2\pi)^{-k/2} \Sigma^{-1/2} \exp(-\tfrac{1}{2} x'\Sigma^{-1}x)$$

cancels throughout, we get expression (4.14), where

$$\alpha_j = \log p_j - \tfrac{1}{2} \mu_j' \Sigma^{-1} \mu_j$$
$$\beta_j = \Sigma^{-1} \mu_j$$

For an individual with characteristics x, the quantities $\alpha_j + \beta_j' x$ are called the *linear discriminant scores* for the individual. The procedure that minimizes the total probability of misclassification assigns the individual to π_j if $P(\pi_j \mid x)$ is greater than the other conditional probabilities. This is the same as classifying the individual into the group for which the discriminant score is the maximum. In actual practice we have to estimate the parameters in α_j and β_j by their corresponding sample quantities. If we draw a sample of size n, and n_j of these observations fall in the jth group, then

$$\hat{p}_j = n_j/n \quad \text{if } p_j \text{ are not known}$$
$$\hat{\mu}_j = \bar{x}_j \quad \text{(the mean of the observations in the } j\text{th group)}$$
$$\hat{\Sigma} = S = \frac{1}{n-m} \sum_{j=1}^{m} \sum_{i=1}^{n_j} (x_{ji} - \bar{x}_j)(x_{ji} - \bar{x}_j)'$$

Given a value x_0 of characteristics for a new individual, we compute the linear discriminant scores

$$\hat{\alpha}_j + \hat{\beta}_j'x_0 \quad (j = 1, 2, \ldots, m)$$

and assign the individual to that group for which the score is highest.

Another approach to the multiple-group problem, based on Fisher's original method (which is a distribution-free method), would be to choose the linear function

$$y = \lambda'x$$

where λ is determined so that the variance of y between groups relative to the variance of y within groups is maximized.

If the means of x in the different groups are μ_j and the variance of x is Σ (the same in all groups), and if we define

$$\bar{\mu} = \frac{1}{m} \sum_j \mu_j$$

$$B = \frac{1}{m} \sum_j (\mu_j - \bar{\mu})(\mu_j - \bar{\mu})'$$

and

$$W = \Sigma$$

then the variance of y between groups is $\lambda'B\lambda$, and the variance of y within groups is $\lambda'W\lambda$. Thus, we have to maximize $\theta = \lambda'B\lambda/\lambda'W\lambda$. The solution to this problem is that λ is the characteristic vector corresponding to the maximum characteristic root of the determinantal equation $|B - \theta W| = 0$.

4.6   Bayesian methods

Throughout our analysis we derived the optimal classification procedures assuming that the parameters μ_1, μ_2, and Σ were known, and after deriving these we substituted the corresponding sample quantities. In practice, this produces an error, and there is a considerable amount of literature on the analysis of these errors.

In the Bayesian approach, because μ_1, μ_2, and Σ are not known, we assume a prior distribution for these parameters. Then we derive the posterior mean of the distribution of the true discriminant function, which is optimal if we assume a squared error loss function. This is what Geisser (1966) did.

Let $D_T(x)$ denote the true discriminant function $\alpha + \beta x$:

$$D_T(x) = \ln \frac{p_1}{p_2} - \tfrac{1}{2}(\mu_1 - \mu_2)'\Sigma^{-1}(\mu_1 + \mu_2) + (\mu_1 - \mu_2)'\Sigma^{-1}x$$

Similarly, the sample discriminant function $D_S(x) = \hat{\alpha} + \hat{\beta}x$ is given by

$$D_S(x) = \ln \frac{p_1}{p_2} - \tfrac{1}{2}(\bar{x}_1 - \bar{x}_2)'S^{-1}(\bar{x}_1 - \bar{x}_2) + (\bar{x}_1 - \bar{x}_2)'S^{-1}x$$

Geisser showed that if we use the noninformative prior

$$g(\mu_1, \mu_2, \Sigma^{-1}) \propto |\Sigma|^{(k+1)/2} \tag{4.16}$$

then the posterior mean of $D_T(x)$ is given by

$$ED_T(x) = D_S(x) + \tfrac{1}{2}k\left(\frac{1}{n_2} - \frac{1}{n_1}\right)$$

This justifies the discriminant function $D_S(x)$ we have been using. Note, however, that there is a correction term for differences in sample sizes.

However, this is not really the full Bayesian approach. The full approach would be to derive the predictive densities

$$f(x \mid \bar{x}_1, \bar{x}_2, S, \pi_1) \quad \text{and} \quad f(x \mid \bar{x}_1, \bar{x}_2, S, \pi_2)$$

and use these in formula (4.5). This is what Geisser (1970) did using the prior (4.16). The predictive densities are given by

$$f(x \mid \bar{x}_1, \bar{x}_2, S, \pi_i)$$
$$= \int f(x \mid \mu_1, \mu_2, \Sigma^{-1}, \pi_i) g(\mu_1, \mu_2, \Sigma^{-1} \mid \bar{x}_1, \bar{x}_2, S) \, d\mu_1 \, d\mu_2 \, d\Sigma^{-1}$$

Geisser showed that

$$\ln \frac{f(x \mid \bar{x}_1, \bar{x}_2, S, \pi_1)}{f(x \mid \bar{x}_1, \bar{x}_2, S, \pi_2)} = \frac{k}{2}\ln\frac{n_1}{n_2} + \frac{v - k + 1}{2}\ln\frac{n_1 + 1}{n_2 + 1}$$
$$+ \frac{v + 1}{2}\ln\frac{(n_2 + 1)v + n_2(x - \bar{x}_2)'S^{-1}(x - \bar{x}_2)}{(n_1 + 1)v + n_1(x - \bar{x}_1)'S^{-1}(x - \bar{x}_1)} \tag{4.17}$$

where $v = n_1 + n_2 - 2$. This is the ratio we use in formula (4.4). If $n_1 = n_2$, the first two terms in (4.17) drop out, and if v is large, using the approximation $\ln(1 + x) \approx x$, the last term in (4.17) simplifies to

$$\tfrac{1}{2}[(x - \bar{x}_2)'S^{-1}(x - \bar{x}_2) - (x - \bar{x}_1)'S^{-1}(x - \bar{x}_1)]$$
$$= (\bar{x}_1 - \bar{x}_2)'S^{-1}x - \tfrac{1}{2}(\bar{x}_1 - \bar{x}_2)'S^{-1}(\bar{x}_1 + \bar{x}_2)$$

which is the expression in (4.5) with $\bar{x}_1$, $\bar{x}_2$, and S substituted for μ_1, μ_2, and Σ, respectively.

4.7   Separate-sample logistic discrimination

Throughout the preceding analysis it has been assumed that a random sample is drawn from the total population and we observe whether the individual observation belongs to one or the other group. There are many situations in which separate samples are drawn from the different groups.[2] An example of this is the problem of discriminating between loan applications accepted and rejected, as considered in section 2.5, where the results of the linear probability model, the logit model, and the probit model were presented in Table 2.1. The data were analyzed there as if the sample was a random sample, but the sample was actually a stratified sample. There were 4,600 observations in the loans-granted category and 250 observations in the rejected category. To have enough observations on females and blacks in the rejected category, it was decided to include all the 250 observations from the rejected category and get a random sample of 500 observations from the accepted category. Thus, the sampling rate was 100% for the rejected group and 10.87% for the accepted group.

To see how the case of nonproportionate sampling is handled, suppose that there are only two groups. Extension of the analysis to the case of several groups is fairly straightforward. Let p_1 and p_2 be the proportions sampled from the two groups. Also, let

$$y_i = 1 \quad \text{if the } i\text{th observation belongs to the first group}$$
$$y_i = 0 \quad \text{otherwise}$$

Because p_1 is the probability that an observation from the first group will be selected and p_2 is the probability that an observation from the second group will be selected, the logit model we specify will be

$$\text{Prob}(y_i = 1) = \frac{p_1 e^{\beta' X_i}}{p_2 + p_1 e^{\beta' X_i}}$$

$$\text{Prob}(y_i = 0) = \frac{p_2}{p_2 + p_1 e^{\beta' X_i}}$$

Define $p = p_2 / p_1$. Then

$$\text{Prob}(y_i = 1) = \frac{e^{\beta' X_i}}{p + e^{\beta' X_i}}$$

Let $\gamma = -\log p$ or $p = e^{-\gamma}$. Then we have

---

[2] The situation is similar to the case of choice-based sampling mentioned in section 3.9 and stratification by endogenous variables discussed in section 6.10.

$$\text{Prob}(y_i = 1) = \frac{e^{\gamma + \beta' X_i}}{1 + e^{\gamma + \beta' X_i}}$$

$$\text{Prob}(y_i = 0) = \frac{1}{1 + e^{\gamma + \beta' X_i}}$$

With random or equiproportionate sampling, we have $p = 1$ and $\gamma = 0$, and we have the usual logit model. Thus, the result of drawing separate samples from the two populations is that the constant term in the logistic discriminant function changes. It increases by $\gamma = \log p_1 - \log p_2$. But the slope coefficients are all unaltered.[3] Thus, in Table 2.1 the logit coefficients are all correct, except for the constant term, which needs to be increased by $\log p_1 - \log p_2 = \log(0.1087) - \log(1.0)$.

The effect of such sampling procedures on the linear probability model (the linear discriminant function) or the probit model is not as simple as in the case of the logit model. That is why in these cases the logistic discriminant model is more appealing.[4] In the case of the probit model, we denote $\Phi(\beta' X_i)$ by Φ_i. Then we have

$$\text{Prob}(y_i = 1) = p_1 \Phi_i / D_i^*$$
$$\text{Prob}(y_i = 0) = p_2 (1 - \Phi_i) / D_i^*$$

where $D_i^* = p_1 \Phi_i + p_2 (1 - \Phi_i)$. Because only $p = p_2 / p_1$ is relevant, we have

$$\text{Prob}(y_i = 1) = \Phi_i / D_i$$
$$\text{Prob}(y_i = 0) = p(1 - \Phi_i) / D_i$$

where $D_i = p + (1 - p)\Phi_i$. The log-likelihood function is

$$\log L = \sum_{y_i = 1} \log \Phi_i + \sum_{y_i = 0} \log(1 - \Phi_i) + N_2 \log p$$
$$- \sum \log[p + (1 - p)\Phi_i] \tag{4.18}$$

where N_2 is the number of observations for which $y_i = 0$. Because p is a given constant, it is the last term in (4.18) that makes the difference. If $p_1 = p_2$, this term is zero.

For any alternative distribution, we just substitute the appropriate distribution function F_i for Φ_i (the distribution function of the standard normal) in formula (4.18).

---

[3] Further discussion of this problem can be found in the work of Anderson (1972).

[4] McFadden informed me that on the basis of some numerical experiments he concluded that whereas the ML estimate of the unweighted probit model using stratified data was technically inconsistent for all parameters, the bias was almost all concentrated in the intercept.

CHAPTER 5

Multivariate qualitative variables

5.1 Introduction

In the preceding chapters we discussed univariate qualitative variables. In this chapter we shall discuss multivariate qualitative variables. One obvious way of generalizing the univariate models formulated in terms of latent variables in the preceding chapters is to consider a general simultaneous-equations model in terms of latent variables. Consider the model

$$By_t^* + \Gamma X_t = u_t \tag{5.1}$$

where u_t are serially independent, with zero mean and covariance matrix Σ, and B is a $G \times G$ nonsingular matrix with unitary diagonal elements. Γ is a $G \times K$ matrix, y_t^* and u_t are $G \times 1$ vectors, and X_t is a $K \times 1$ vector; y_t^* is the vector of "latent" endogenous variables. Also define $E(u_t u_t') = \Sigma$. The identification problems in this model are the same as those in the usual simultaneous-equations model, except for the fact that because some (or all) elements of y_t^* are observed as qualitative variables, the parameters (B, Γ, Σ) are estimable only up to certain scale factors.[1] For simplicity, let us consider the case in which some elements of y_t^* are observed as dichotomous variables.

We partition the endogenous variables y_t^* into two sets of y_{1t}^* and y_{2t}^*. The variables y_{2t}^* are observed, but the variables y_{1t}^* are not. Instead, we observe y_{1t}, each element of which is 1 or 0, depending on whether or not the corresponding element of y_{1t}^* is $\geqslant$ or < 0.

[1] The following discussion is based on prior work by Maddala and Lee (1976).

93

Now consider the reduced form for the system

$$y_t = \Pi X_t + v_t$$

where

$$\Pi = -B^{-1}\Gamma$$

$$v_t = B^{-1}u_t$$

The covariance matrix of v_t is

$$\Omega = B^{-1}\Sigma(B')^{-1}$$

Note that the rows of Π corresponding to y_{1t}^* are estimable only up to a proportionality factor. Define

$$\Lambda = \begin{bmatrix} D & 0 \\ 0 & I \end{bmatrix}$$

where D is a diagonal matrix whose ith element is $1/\lambda_i$, where λ_i^2 is the variance of the reduced-form residual corresponding to the ith element of y_{1t}^*. Thus, $\Lambda\Pi$ and $\Lambda\Omega\Lambda$ are the reduced-form parameters that can be estimated in this model.

To see what structural parameters are estimable, we can write the condition

$$B\Pi + \Gamma = 0 \quad \text{as} \quad (B\Lambda^{-1})(\Lambda\Pi) + \Gamma = 0 \tag{5.2}$$

Because Λ is a diagonal matrix, the usual rank conditions for Π are applicable to $\Lambda\Pi$. However, the normalization rule $\beta_{ii}=1$ does not help in the identification for the first set of equations because the diagonal elements have a multiplicative factor $1/\lambda_i$, where λ_i are unknown. Hence, to have all diagonal elements unity, we have to write equation (5.2) as

$$(\Lambda B\Lambda^{-1})(\Lambda\Pi) + \Lambda\Gamma = 0 \tag{5.3}$$

Under the usual rank conditions, $\Lambda B\Lambda^{-1}$ and $\Lambda\Gamma$ are estimable. Also, the condition

$$\Sigma = B\Omega B'$$

can be written as

$$\Lambda\Sigma\Lambda = (\Lambda B\Lambda^{-1})(\Lambda\Omega\Lambda)(\Lambda B\Lambda^{-1})'$$

Thus, from the estimable reduced-form parameters $\Lambda\Pi$ and $\Lambda\Omega\Lambda$, we see that in this model, under the usual rank conditions, we can get estimates of $\Lambda B\Lambda^{-1}$, $\Lambda\Gamma$, and $\Lambda\Sigma\Lambda$ only.

The situation is different, however, when we have known nonzero threshold values for the unobserved variables. That is, suppose we have

$$y_{it} = 1 \quad \text{if } y^*_{it} \geqslant c_{it}$$
$$y_{it} = 0 \quad \text{otherwise}$$

where c_{it} are known nonzero values. In this case the reduced-form parameters are estimable, and the conditions for identification are the same as in the usual simultaneous-equations models.

To illustrate which parameters are estimable, consider the following two-equations model:

$$y_1^* = \beta_{12} y_2 + \gamma_1 x_1 + u_1$$
$$y_2 = \beta_{21} y_1^* + \gamma_2 x_2 + u_2$$

Here y_1^* is not observed. Instead, we observe y_1, defined by

$$y_1 = 1 \quad \text{iff } y_1^* > 0$$

Let the variance of the reduced-form residual for y_1^* be λ^2, and let the covariance matrix of the residuals (u_1, u_2) be

$$\Sigma = \begin{bmatrix} \sigma_1^2 & \sigma_{12} \\ \sigma_{12} & \sigma_2^2 \end{bmatrix}$$

We have

$$\Lambda = \begin{bmatrix} \frac{1}{\lambda} & 0 \\ 0 & 1 \end{bmatrix}$$

The parameters that are estimable in this model are

$$\frac{\beta_{12}}{\lambda}, \quad \lambda\beta_{21}, \quad \frac{\gamma_1}{\lambda}, \quad \gamma_2, \quad \frac{\sigma_1}{\lambda}, \quad \frac{\sigma_{12}}{\lambda}, \quad \text{and} \quad \sigma_2^2$$

As far as the estimation of these models is concerned, one can use the ML method. But for every partially observed variable, the likelihood function involves the evaluation of an integral. Thus, ML estimation will not be computationally feasible if we have more than one or two partially observed variables.

As an alternative to the ML method, one can use the two-stage estimation method. This consists of estimating the reduced forms by the probit method, substituting the estimated values of the latent variables, and then estimating the structural equations again by the probit method. Because this two-stage method is discussed in detail in Chapter 8, we shall not discuss it here.

Not all formulations of qualitative-variable models need be in terms of underlying latent variables. In many cases this complication is unnecessary. We shall, therefore, discuss some models, such as the log-linear models, that are not in terms of latent variables. We shall return to the latent-variable formulations later. The important distinction between the latent-variable formulation and the log-linear model discussed by Goodman (1970, 1971, 1973), Nerlove and Press (1973, 1976), and others is that with the log-linear models one cannot specify a structural system like (5.1). In fact, we shall show later what sorts of structural systems are implied by these models. Before we discuss these, we shall briefly review the minimum chi-square methods suggested for grouped data.

5.2   Some minimum chi-square methods for grouped data

As with univariate models, we can have grouped data with multivariate models, and we can use minimum chi-square methods analogous to those in section 2.8. Zellner and Lee (1965) suggested a system method for estimation of equations like (2.31) considered in Chapter 2. They considered the linear probability model and thus considered equation (2.27). Let us, instead, consider the logit model given by equation (2.31).

Suppose there are K jointly dependent dichotomous variables, and for the tth observation there are n_t individuals, and for m_{it} of these the event corresponding to the ith variable occurs. In the Zellner and Lee example, m_{1t} is the number of people buying cars, and m_{2t} is the number of people applying for credit, both in the tth income group. In the Ashford and Snowden (1970) example, m_{1t} is the numer of coal miners experiencing breathlessness, and m_{2t} is the number experiencing wheezing, both in the tth age group. We assume that observations for different t values are independent. We define

$$\hat{p}_{it} = \frac{m_{it}}{n_t} \quad (i = 1, 2, \ldots, K, \ t = 1, 2, \ldots, T)$$

As before (see section 2.8), we can define the logits

$$L_{it} = \log \frac{\hat{p}_{it}}{1 - \hat{p}_{it}}$$

Then we write $L_{it} = \beta' x_{it} + u_{it}$, where

$$u_{it} \simeq \frac{1}{p_{it}(1 - p_{it})} (\hat{p}_{it} - p_{it}) \tag{5.4}$$

The $\simeq$ symbol is used to denote an equality that holds only asymptotically. We can write this system as

$$L = X\beta + u$$

or

$$
\begin{bmatrix} L_1 \\ L_2 \\ \cdot \\ L_K \end{bmatrix} = \begin{bmatrix} X_1 & 0 & 0 & \cdots & 0 \\ 0 & X_2 & 0 & \cdots & 0 \\ \cdot & \cdot & \cdot & \cdots & \cdot \\ 0 & 0 & 0 & \cdots & X_K \end{bmatrix} \begin{bmatrix} \beta_1 \\ \beta_2 \\ \cdot \\ \beta_K \end{bmatrix} + \begin{bmatrix} u_1 \\ u_2 \\ \cdot \\ u_K \end{bmatrix} \tag{5.5}
$$

where L_i is the vector of T observations on variable i and X_i and u_i are defined accordingly. For each i, the model is a univariate model. To obtain the covariance matrix of u, we need the covariance matrix of $V = (V_{it}) = (\hat{p}_{it} - p_{it})$. The covariance matrix of V is

$$
\Sigma = E(VV') = \begin{bmatrix} D_{11} & D_{12} & \cdots & D_{1K} \\ D_{21} & D_{22} & \cdots & D_{2K} \\ \cdot & \cdot & \cdots & \cdot \\ D_{K1} & D_{K2} & \cdots & D_{KK} \end{bmatrix} \tag{5.6}
$$

where D_{ii} is a diagonal matrix corresponding to variable i of order $T \times T$, with the tth diagonal element $p_{it}(1 - p_{it})/n_t$, and D_{ij} is also a diagonal matrix of order $T \times T$, with the tth diagonal element $(p_{ijt} - p_{it} p_{kt})/n_t$, where p_{ijt} is the probability of both the ith and jth events occurring for observation. This is because

$$\text{Cov}(\hat{p}_{it}, \hat{p}_{jt}) = E(\hat{p}_{it} \cdot \hat{p}_{jt}) - E(\hat{p}_{it}) \cdot E(\hat{p}_{jt})$$

and the first term is nothing but the probability of both events occurring jointly. Note that D_{ij} are all diagonal matrices because of the assumption that observations for different t are independent. Now we define the diagonal matrix

$$H = \text{Diag}(h_{it}) = \text{Diag}\left(\frac{1}{p_{it}(1 - p_{it})}\right)$$

Then the covariance matrix of $u = \Omega = H\Sigma H'$.

We now use the Aitken generalized least-squares method to estimate the system of equations (5.5). For the normit model, as discussed in section 2.8, we have $h_{it} = 1/[\phi(p_{it})]$. For the linear probability model, $h_{it} = 1$. Zellner and Lee proved that the estimator $\hat{\beta}$ of β obtained by this method is consistent and asymptotically normally distributed, with covariance matrix $(X'\Omega^{-1}X)^{-1}$.

Amemiya (1974a) discussed a bivariate model considered by Ashford and Snowden (1970). He obtained the appropriate minimum chi-square estimator and called it the full-information minimum chi-square (FIMC) estimator; he showed that the Zellner–Lee method discussed earlier is a limited-information minimum chi-square (LIMC) method. To see what is involved, consider the Ashford–Snowden model: Y_1 and Y_2 are two dichotomous variables, each of which assumes the values 1 and 2. Let

$$p_{ij} = \text{Prob}(Y_1 = i, \ Y_2 = j) \quad (i = 1, 2, \ j = 1, 2)$$

The Ashford–Snowden model is

$$
\begin{aligned}
p_{11} &= F(\beta'x, \gamma'x, \rho) \\
p_{11} + p_{12} &= p_1 = \Phi(\beta'x) \\
p_{21} + p_{22} &= p_2 = \Phi(\gamma'x)
\end{aligned}
\tag{5.7}
$$

where $F(\cdot, \cdot, \rho)$ is the distribution function of the bivariate standard normal with correlation coefficient ρ. As before, we assume that there are n_t observations for each t ($t = 1, 2, \ldots, T$) and that observations are temporally independent. From (5.7) we can derive p_{12}, p_{21}, and p_{22}. Let n_{ij} be the number of observations for which $Y_1 = i$ and $Y_2 = j$ ($i, j = 1, 2$). Then the log-likelihood function is

$$\log L = \sum_{t=1}^{T} \sum_{ij} n_{ijt} p_{ijt} \tag{5.8}$$

To obtain the ML estimates, we need derivatives of $\Phi(\cdot)$ and $F(\cdot, \cdot, \rho)$. We know that $\partial \Phi(x)/\partial x = \phi(x)$. We also use the following:

$$\frac{\partial F(x_1, x_2, \rho)}{\partial x_1} = \phi(x_1) \cdot \Phi\left(\frac{x_2 - \rho x_1}{(1 - \rho^2)^{1/2}}\right)$$

$$\frac{\partial F(x_1, x_2, \rho)}{\partial \rho} = f(x_1, x_2, \rho)$$

where $f(x_1, x_2, \rho)$ is the bivariate density function of standard normal variables with correlation coefficient ρ. Using these, one can write down the first and second derivatives of the likelihood function (5.8) and obtain the ML estimates of β, γ, and ρ by an iterative procedure.

For the minimum chi-square method, the second and third equations in (5.7) give

$$\Phi^{-1}(p_1) = \beta'x \quad \text{and} \quad \Phi^{-1}(p_2) = \gamma'x$$

What Amemiya said is that Zellner and Lee used only these equations and did not consider an equation for ρ. The Zellner–Lee method consists of writing

$$\Phi^{-1}(p_1) = \beta'x + u \quad \text{and} \quad \Phi^{-1}(p_2) = \gamma'x + v \tag{5.9}$$

Table 5.1. *Numbers of subjects responding for the two symptoms in terms of age group: The Ashford–Sowden data*

Age group (years)	Breathlessness		No breathlessness		Total
	Wheezing	No wheezing	Wheezing	No wheezing	
20–24	9	7	95	1,841	1,952
25–29	23	9	105	1,654	1,791
30–34	54	19	177	1,863	2,113
35–39	121	48	257	2,357	2,783
40–44	169	54	273	1,778	2,274
45–49	269	88	324	1,712	2,393
50–54	404	117	245	1,324	2,090
55–59	406	152	225	967	1,750
60–64	372	106	132	526	1,136
Total	1,827	600	1,833	14.022	18,282

and estimating these equations by a system method as described earlier. What Amemiya did was add an equation for ρ. He solved the three equations in (5.7) for ρ. Call it

$$\rho = G(p_{11}, p_1, p_2)$$

Then he expanded $G(\hat{p}_{11}, \hat{p}_1, \hat{p}_2)$ around (p_{11}, p_1, p_2) by a Taylor-series expansion and got an equation

$$G(\hat{p}_{11}, \hat{p}_1, \hat{p}_2) = \rho + w \tag{5.10}$$

Now equations (5.9) and (5.10) are estimated by the Aitken generalized least-squares method to get estimates of β, γ, and ρ. This he called the FIMC estimator, whereas the Zellner–Lee method that is based on equations (5.9) only is called the LIMC estimator. We shall not present the detailed expressions for the covariance matrix of (u, v, w) here. They can be found in Amemiya's study.

Note that this procedure is difficult to generalize to the case of more than two dependent variables, whereas the Zellner–Lee procedure can be used for a large number of dependent variables. In the example considered by Ashford and Snowden, the three models ML, FIMC, and LIMC did not produce much different results. The data are presented in Table 5.1. The parameter estimates are presented in Table 5.2, where

$$\beta'x = \beta_0 + \beta_1 x$$
$$\gamma'x = \gamma_0 + \gamma_1 x$$

Table 5.2. *Comparison of estimates obtained by ML, FIMC,
and LIMC methods*

Parameters	ML	FIMC	LIMC
β_0	−3.6113	−3.5738	−3.5867
β_1	0.05484	0.05465	0.05492
γ_0	−2.4542	−2.4315	−2.4350
γ_1	0.03700	0.03691	0.03698
ρ	0.7709	0.7746	—

and x is the midpoint of the age group. Amemiya showed that the diagonal elements of the covariance matrix of the FIMC estimator were smaller than those of the LIMC estimator, as they should be, but the differences were very small.

Morimune (1979) considered the logistic model

$$p_{11} = D^{-1}\exp(a'x + b'x + c'x)$$
$$p_{12} = D^{-1}\exp(a'x)$$
$$p_{21} = D^{-1}\exp(b'x)$$
$$p_{22} = D^{-1} \tag{5.11}$$

where

$$D = 1 + \exp(a'x) + \exp(b'x) + \exp(a'x + b'x + c'x)$$

We can consider this a generalization of the Ashford–Snowden model, where the correlation coefficient ρ is also made a function of x, so that the first equation in (5.7) becomes

$$p_{11} = F(\beta'x, \gamma'x, \delta'x)$$

Actually, a logistic version of the normal model presented in (5.7) would look like

$$p_{11} = \exp(a'x + b'x + c'x)/[1 + \exp(a'x + b'x + c'x)]$$
$$p_1 = \exp(b'x)/[1 + \exp(b'x)]$$
$$p_2 = \exp(a'x)/[1 + \exp(a'x)] \tag{5.12}$$

The multivariate logit analysis discussed by Grizzle (1971) and Zellner and Lee (1965) corresponds to the use of only the marginal probabilities p_1 and p_2 in (5.12). Thus, they are LIMC logit estimates, whereas those based on all the equations in (5.12) will be the FIMC logit estimates.

The estimation methods for formulations (5.11) and (5.12) are similar, but we shall consider the formulation (5.11), which is in the form of the log-linear models to be discussed in later sections. This formulation also corresponds to that used by Mantel and Brown (1973) and Nerlove and Press (1973), both of whom introduced explanatory variables into the log-linear model framework. Using (5.11), we have

$$\log \frac{p_{12}}{p_{22}} = a'x$$

$$\log \frac{p_{21}}{p_{22}} = b'x$$

$$\log \frac{p_{11}p_{22}}{p_{12}p_{21}} = c'x \qquad (5.13)$$

From the observed frequencies, we get $\hat{p}_{11}$, $\hat{p}_{12}$, $\hat{p}_{21}$, and $\hat{p}_{22}$. We then expand these in a Taylor series around the true probabilities. Omitting higher-order terms (also omitting the subscript t throughout) and using (5.13), we have

$$\log \frac{\hat{p}_{12}}{\hat{p}_{22}} = a'x + \frac{1}{p_{12}}(\hat{p}_{12} - p_{12}) - \frac{1}{p_{22}}(\hat{p}_{22} - p_{22})$$

$$\log \frac{\hat{p}_{21}}{\hat{p}_{22}} = b'x + \frac{1}{p_{21}}(\hat{p}_{21} - p_{21}) - \frac{1}{p_{22}}(\hat{p}_{22} - p_{22})$$

$$\log \frac{\hat{p}_{11}\hat{p}_{22}}{\hat{p}_{12}\hat{p}_{21}} = c'x + \frac{1}{p_{11}}(\hat{p}_{11} - p_{11}) + \frac{1}{p_{22}}(\hat{p}_{22} - p_{22})$$

$$- \frac{1}{p_{12}}(\hat{p}_{12} - p_{12}) - \frac{1}{p_{21}}(\hat{p}_{21} - p_{21})$$

These equations can be written compactly as

$$y_{1t} = a'x_t + u_{1t}$$
$$y_{2t} = b'x_t + u_{2t}$$
$$y_{3t} = c'x_t + u_{3t}$$

which we can write as $Y_t = X_t \beta + u_t$, where $Y_t = (y_{1t}, y_{2t}, y_{3t})'$, $\beta' = (a', b', c')$, $u_t = (u_{1t}, u_{2t}, u_{3t})'$, and

$$X_t = \begin{bmatrix} x_t' & & 0 \\ & x_t' & \\ 0 & & x_t' \end{bmatrix}$$

The covariance matrix of u_t is

$$\Sigma_t = \begin{bmatrix} \dfrac{1}{n_t} \left[\dfrac{1}{p_{12}} + \dfrac{1}{p_{22}} \right. & \dfrac{1}{p_{22}} & -\dfrac{1}{p_{12}} - \dfrac{1}{p_{22}} \\ & \dfrac{1}{p_{21}} + \dfrac{1}{p_{22}} & -\dfrac{1}{p_{21}} - \dfrac{1}{p_{22}} \\ & & \left. \dfrac{1}{p_{11}} + \dfrac{1}{p_{12}} + \dfrac{1}{p_{21}} + \dfrac{1}{p_{22}} \right] \end{bmatrix}$$

and

$$\Sigma_t^{-1} = n_t \begin{bmatrix} (p_{21}+p_{22})(p_{12}+p_{11}) & p_{22}p_{11}-p_{12}p_{21} & p_{11}(p_{22}+p_{21}) \\ & (p_{12}+p_{22})(p_{21}+p_{11}) & p_{11}(p_{22}+p_{21}) \\ & & p_{11}(1-p_{11}) \end{bmatrix}$$

The minimum chi-square estimator of β is

$$\hat{\beta} = \left(\sum_t X_t'\Sigma_t^{-1}X_t \right)^{-1} \sum_t X_t'\Sigma_t^{-1}Y_t$$

with covariance matrix $(\sum_t X_t'\Sigma_t^{-1}X_t)^{-1}$. Unlike the FIMC probit estimator considered by Amemiya, the FIMC logit estimator can be easily generalized and applied to the case of many dichotomous variables. Instead of defining the dichotomous variables as taking on the values 1 and 2, we can assume that they take on the values 1 and 0. Then the specification given in (5.11) can be compactly written as

$$P(Y_1, Y_2) = D^{-1}\exp(a'xY_1 + b'xY_2 + c'xY_1Y_2) \tag{5.14}$$

where Y_1 and Y_2 take on the values 1 or 0 and D is as defined in (5.11). A generalization to the case of three variables will be

$$P(Y_1, Y_2, Y_3) = D^{-1}\exp\left(\sum_{i=1} a_i'xY_i + \sum_{i<j} b_i'xY_iY_j + \sum_{i<j<k} c_{ijk}'xY_iY_jY_k \right)$$
$$\tag{5.15}$$

and D is chosen so that $\sum P(Y_1, Y_2, Y_3) = 1$.

Morimune considered the problem of discrimination between the logit and probit models, and because they are not nested, he proposed Cox-type test statistics based on minimum chi-square estimates. Lee (1979d) pointed out that if the explanatory variables are also qualitative, then either the two models are statistically equivalent (and thus one cannot apply any tests) or they are nested (and thus one can apply likelihood-ratio tests). The detailed derivations can be found in Lee's study and will not be presented here.

5.3 Log-linear models[2]

The models presented in (5.14) and (5.15) are called log-linear probability models. To fix ideas initially, we shall omit the explanatory variables x and consider the case of three dichotomous variables Y_1, Y_2, Y_3. Generalization to polychotomous variables and more variables is straightforward and involves more complex notation that will be introduced later. The dichotomous variables can be defined as taking the values 1 and 2, or 1 and 0, or $+1$ and -1, and we shall use the last notation. The log-linear model is

$$\log[P(Y_1, Y_2, Y_3)] = u_0 + u_1 Y_1 + u_2 Y_2 + u_3 Y_3 + u_{12} Y_1 Y_2$$
$$+ u_{13} Y_1 Y_3 + u_{23} Y_2 Y_3 + u_{123} Y_1 Y_2 Y_3 \qquad (5.16)$$

The $2^3 = 8$ cell probabilities are represented by the eight singly, doubly, and triply subscripted u terms. By analogy with analysis-of-variance models for continuous variables at various levels of K factors, the terms u_1, u_2, and u_3 are commonly interpreted as main effects, the terms u_{12}, u_{13}, and u_{23} are denoted second-order interaction terms, and u_{123} is called the third-order interaction term. These terms can also be made functions of explanatory variables. In fact, equation (5.15) makes main effects and all interaction terms functions of x. Because the probabilities must sum to 1, an obvious constraint is imposed on the overall mean, u_0.

$$D = e^{-u_0} = \sum_{Y_1, Y_2, Y_3} \exp(u_1 Y_1 + u_2 Y_2 + u_3 Y_3 + u_{12} Y_1 Y_2$$
$$+ u_{13} Y_1 Y_3 + u_{23} Y_2 Y_3 + u_{123} Y_1 Y_2 Y_3) \qquad (5.17)$$

Equation (5.16) represents the "fully saturated" log-linear model.[3] It contains as many parameters (the u terms) as there are all probabilities in the 2^3 contingency table. One can economize on the number of parameters by making some assumptions of independence. For example, if all

---

[2] The presentation in this and the next two sections is taken from an unpublished paper by Forrest D. Nelson: "Structural Models for Qualitative Variables." California Institute of Technology, November 1979. I thank him for allowing me to incorporate all that material here.

[3] The dichotomous Y_i case allows for this compact notation, but the results are readily generalized. Suppose, for example, that Y_1 takes on three values. Then the u_1 term will be replaced by $u_{1(i)}$, where the subscript 1 refers to variable Y_1 and the i indicates the value of Y_{1i}. We then require that $\sum u_{1(i)} = 0$, just as $u_1 \cdot (+1) + u_1 \cdot (-1) = 0$ for the dichotomous case. Similarly, the higher-order terms will appear as, for example, $u_{12(ij)}$, with the restriction $\sum_i u_{12(ij)} = \sum_j u_{12(ij)} = \sum_i \sum_j u_{12(ij)} = 0$.

three variables are independent, $P(Y_1, Y_2, Y_3) = P(Y_1) \cdot P(Y_2) \cdot P(Y_3)$, then $u_{12} = u_{13} = u_{23} = u_{123} = 0$. If Y_1 is independent of Y_2 and Y_3, $P(Y_1, Y_2, Y_3) = P(Y_2, Y_3) \cdot P(Y_1)$, and $u_{12} = u_{13} = u_{123} = 0$. The log-linear model (LLM) then provides a convenient means for both testing for independence and economizing on parameters. Given a K-dimensional contingency table of observed frequencies on K variables, we fit the fully saturated LLM and then successively drop the higher-order interaction terms, testing whether or not they are significantly different from zero (i.e., testing the implied independence hypotheses). We then report that unsaturated LLM for which all remaining u terms are significantly nonzero.

Two points should be noted. First, the strategy of testing high-level u terms first is known as hierarchical model fitting and is the strategy most often employed for various intuitive and theoretical reasons. According to that strategy, no lower-level u term is omitted if any of its subscripts are attached to higher-level terms that have been determined to be nonzero. For example, if u_{123} is not eliminated, then neither are any of the terms $u_1, u_2, u_3, u_{12}, u_{13}$, or u_{23}.

The second point to note is that elimination from the model of any u term requires computation (estimation) of all other u terms. Those fitted u terms will remain unchanged if and only if the eliminated u term is precisely zero.

Although the details of estimation and hypothesis testing are of little concern for our purposes, some mention of them is warranted. For the fully saturated model, estimates can be obtained by direct solution from (5.16) after replacing $P(Y_1, Y_2, Y_3)$ on the left with the observed cell proportions. These will be maximum-likelihood estimates. For unsaturated models, closed-form solutions do not exist; iterative procedures are required. The log-likelihood for a sample represented by the cell frequencies $N(Y_1, Y_2, \ldots, Y_K)$ is given by

$$\log L(U_i) = C + \sum_{Y_1} \sum_{Y_2} \cdots \sum_{Y_K} N(Y_1, Y_2, \ldots, Y_K) \log[P(Y_1, \ldots, Y_K)]$$

(5.18)

where U_i is the set of u terms not restricted to be zero and $P(Y_1, \ldots, Y_K)$ is replaced by the right side of (5.16) after imposing the indicated restrictions. Estimates $\hat{U}_i = (\hat{u})$ under any hypothesis i are obtained by maximizing (5.18) by some iterative procedure, say Newton–Raphson.[4]

---

[4] Such procedures can be expensive if large numbers of alternative models are to be estimated. A less expensive procedure, called iterative proportional fitting (IPF) has been described by Bishop et al. (1975). Haberman (1974) presented a convenient program for IPF.

Corresponding to each potential model U_i is a hypothesis H_i that the u terms not included in the set U_i are zero. Suppose for some models i and j that U_i is a proper subset of U_j; that is, $U_i \subset U_j$. Then H_i is nested in H_j, and the likelihood-ratio statistic

$$X^2 = 2[\log L(U_j) - \log L(U_i)]$$

serves as a test of the hypothesis that the u terms in $U_j \cap U_i^c$ are all zero. Under that hypothesis, $X^2 \sim \chi^2_{(K)}$, where K is the number of u terms in $U_j \cap U_i^c$.

In what follows we shall employ notation for the models represented by the sets U_i that has become standard in the LLM literature. Assuming the hierarchical strategy, a particular model can be specified by merely indicating the highest-level terms in which each variable appears. In a four-way table for Y_1, Y_2, Y_3, and Y_4, for example, [1234] will indicate the fully saturated model with all fifteen u terms present, [123][124][124][234] will indicate that all terms are present save the four-way interaction u_{1234}, and [123][14][24] will indicate zero restrictions on u_{34}, u_{124}, u_{134}, u_{234}, and u_{1234}, all other interactions and main effects being nonzero.

5.4   Conditional logistic models

The LLM analysis begins with linear specification of the log of joint cell probabilities. From these we can obtain expressions for conditional probabilities, as will be required, for example, for the prediction of one variable given advance knowledge of the outcomes of other variables. Those conditional-probability expressions involve fewer parameters than the LLM for the full contingency table and can be expressed in the form of log odds ratios, a form in which they appear analogous to the structural equations of simultaneous-equations models. This has led several authors to suggest estimation of and inference from the conditional logistic equations. We shall examine this method of analysis, beginning with the case of three dichotomous variables. Again we assume, for convenience, that these variables take on values $+1$ and -1.

From equation (5.16) we have

$$P(Y_1 \mid Y_2, Y_3) = \frac{P(Y_1, Y_2, Y_3)}{P(+1, Y_2, Y_3) + P(-1, Y_2, Y_3)}$$

$$= \frac{\exp(u_1 Y_1 + u_{12} Y_1 Y_2 + u_{13} Y_1 Y_3 + u_{123} Y_1 Y_2 Y_3)}{\begin{aligned}&\exp(u_1 + u_{12} Y_2 + u_{13} Y_3 + u_{123} Y_2 Y_3)\\ &\quad + \exp(-u_1 - u_{12} Y_2 - u_{13} Y_3 - u_{123} Y_2 Y_3)\end{aligned}}$$

The more convenient representation is the log odds ratio

$$L_{1|23} = \log \frac{P(Y_1 = +1 \mid Y_2, Y_3)}{P(Y_1 = -1 \mid Y_2, Y_3)} = 2u_1 + 2u_{12}Y_2 + 2u_{13}Y_3 + 2u_{123}Y_2Y_3$$
$$= w_0^1 + w_2^1 Y_2 + w_3^1 Y_3 + w_{23}^1 Y_2 Y_3 \quad (5.19)$$

Similar expressions exist for conditional probabilities for Y_2 and Y_3:

$$L_{2|13} = w_0^2 + w_1^2 Y_1 + w_3^2 Y_3 + w_{13}^2 Y_1 Y_3 \quad\quad\quad (5.20)$$

$$L_{3|12} = w_0^3 + w_1^3 Y_1 + w_2^3 Y_2 + w_{12}^3 Y_1 Y_2 \quad\quad\quad (5.21)$$

Expressions (5.19) through (5.21) represent the fully saturated conditional logistic model (CLM). Each equation contains four parameters (the w terms), in contrast with the LLM, which contains seven unconstrained u terms. We note, too, a number of implicit cross-equation parameter constraints, namely

$$w_2^1 = w_1^2 = 2u_{12}$$
$$w_3^1 = w_1^3 = 2u_{13}$$
$$w_3^2 = w_2^3 = 2u_{23}$$
$$w_{23}^1 = w_{13}^2 = w_{12}^3 = 2u_{123} \quad\quad\quad (5.22)$$

Thus the total number of free parameters in the three CLM equations is the same as the number in the LLM. Analysis of the CLM proceeds with estimation and inference from each of the three equations separately, ignoring the cross-equation constraints. The cross-equation constraints need not be imposed, because the parameter estimates will satisfy them automatically. The CLM equations (5.19) through (5.21) all correspond to the same fully saturated LLM [123], and ML estimates for a conditional logistic equation are exactly equal to twice the ML estimates of the corresponding LLM.[5]

Of more interest is the unsaturated model obtained by fixing one or more of the w^1 terms in equation (5.19) at zero. We might examine the relationship between the parameter estimates so obtained and the esti-

---

[5] Nelson (see footnote 2) proved the result as follows: Note that LLM estimates for a particular LLM will fit exactly those observed marginal-probability tables represented by the highest-level interactions in that LLM. Similarly, the CLM estimates will fit exactly the tables of observed conditional probabilities represented by the highest level of interaction in that CLM. Uniqueness of the coefficient estimates in each case, and the fact that the observed conditional probabilities can be obtained uniquely from the relevant observed marginal table, establishes the result. This result has also been proved formally by Kawasaki (1979); that is, with categorical explanatory variables, one does not have to impose cross-equation constraints in CLM.

mates of the corresponding LLM, and also estimates of corresponding parameters of the other CLM equations (5.20) and (5.21). Note that for any particular unsaturated model for (5.19) there is an equivalent LLM. Five such equivalent models for (5.19), noting the conditions (5.22), are

CLM for $Y_1 \mid Y_2, Y_3$		LLM
No constraint	⇔	[123]
$w_{23}^1 = 0$	⇔	[23][12][13]
$w_{23}^1 = w_2^1 = 0$	⇔	[23][13]
$w_{23}^1 = w_3^1 = 0$	⇔	[23][12]
$w_{23}^1 = w_2^1 = w_3^1$	⇔	[22][1]

For these models, estimation of the CLM equations for $Y_1 \mid Y_2, Y_3$ will give the same parameter estimates as those obtained from the corresponding LLM. As for the other two CLM equations, it all depends on whether or not those equations also correspond to the same LLM. If they do, then the separate estimates of the common parameter will be not only consistent and efficient but also exactly the same. If the CLM equations imply different LLMs, the individual estimates will be consistent, but neither identical nor fully efficient. For example, if the true three-way LLM is [12][13][23], then estimates obtained separately from the LLM and the three CLM equations will all be efficient and will satisfy the constraints

$$\hat{w}_0^1 = 2\hat{u}_1, \quad \hat{w}_0^2 = 2\hat{u}_2, \quad \hat{w}_0^3 = 2\hat{u}_3,$$
$$\hat{w}_2^1 = \hat{w}_1^2 = 2\hat{u}_{12}, \quad \hat{w}_3^1 = \hat{w}_1^3 = 2\hat{u}_{13}, \quad \text{and} \quad \hat{w}_3^2 = \hat{w}_2^3 = 2\hat{u}_{23}$$

when the constraints

$$\hat{w}_{23}^1 = \hat{w}_{13}^2 = \hat{w}_{12}^3 = \hat{u}_{123} = 0$$

are imposed. On the other hand, consider the LLM [12][13]. The corresponding CLM will fit

$$L_{1 \mid 23} = w_0^1 + w_2^1 Y_2 + w_3^1 Y_3$$

which corresponds to [23][12][13],

$$L_{2 \mid 13} = w_0^2 + w_1^2 Y_1$$

which corresponds to [13][12], and

$$L_{3 \mid 12} = w_0^3 + w_1^3 Y_1$$

which corresponds to [12][13]. The second two CLM equations will produce efficient estimates that match the LLM estimates, but estimates from the first will not be efficient and will match neither the LLM estimates nor the corresponding interaction terms in the other two equations. Thus, whether or not the different CLM equations have to be estimated jointly to get efficient estimates will depend on whether they correspond to different LLM models or to the same LLM model.

Nerlove and Press (1973) and Schmidt and Strauss (1975a) formulated models with two binary variables as follows:

$$\log \frac{P(Y_1 = +1 \mid Y_2, X)}{P(Y_1 = -1 \mid Y_2, X)} = X\alpha + \lambda Y_2$$

$$\log \frac{P(Y_2 = +1 \mid Y_1, X)}{P(Y_2 = -1 \mid Y_1, X)} = X\beta + \lambda Y_1 \qquad (5.23)$$

This is the same as the CLM where the two main effects u_1 and u_2 are functions of exogenous variables. Note that the coefficients of Y_1 and Y_2 are the same in the two equations, and this equivalence is similar to the one derived in equations (5.22). Nerlove and Press referred to this model as a multivariate logit model, and Schmidt and Strauss labeled it a simultaneous logit model.

There is a strong temptation to interpret the conditional logistic equations as structural. The temptation follows from the similarity between these equations and the structural equations of a simultaneous-equations model for continuous variables. However, as opposed to the situation with classic simultaneous-equations models, the derivation of (5.23) is based on conditional distributions. There are no zero restrictions on the elements of α and β that are needed for identification. Further, the effects of Y_1 on Y_2 and Y_2 on Y_1 are equal. This suggests that the model is more a correlation model than a causal model. In fact, our derivation of the CLM from the LLM makes these points abundantly clear. Thus, to formulate some structural models, we shall have to consider some alternative formulations. In the next section we shall consider recursive models. These have been discussed by Maddala and Lee (1976).

5.5   Recursive logistic models

Let us again consider three binary variables, Y_1, Y_2, and Y_3. It might be the case that Y_1 is determined first, that Y_1 then determines Y_2, and that Y_1 and Y_2 directly influence the third, Y_3. The relevant statistical analysis should therefore model the marginal distribution of the outcome Y_1, the conditional distribution of Y_2 given Y_1, and, finally, the conditional distribution of Y_3 given both Y_1 and Y_2. Because all three variables are qualitative, the relevant distributions are probability distributions, and we write

$$P(Y_1) \cdot P(Y_2 \mid Y_1) \cdot P(Y_3 \mid Y_1, Y_2) = P(Y_1, Y_2, Y_3)$$

Each of the three probability components, one marginal and two conditional probabilities, can be conveniently expressed in log odds form:

$$L_1 = \log \frac{P(Y_1 = +1)}{P(Y_1 = -1)} = 2u_1^1 \tag{5.24}$$

$$L_{2\mid 1} = \log \frac{P(Y_2 = +1 \mid Y_1)}{P(Y_2 = -1 \mid Y_1)} = 2u_2^2 + 2u_{12}^2 Y_1 \tag{5.25}$$

$$L_{3\mid 12} = \log \frac{P(Y_3 = +1 \mid Y_1, Y_2)}{P(Y_3 = -1 \mid Y_1, Y_2)}$$
$$= 2u_3^3 + 2u_{13}^3 Y_1 + 2u_{23}^3 Y_2 + 2u_{123}^3 Y_1 Y_2 \tag{5.26}$$

The u terms appearing in each equation are the relevant u terms from the appropriate LLM, and the superscripts indicate the dimension of the contingency table to which that model applies. For example, u_{13}^3 is the Y_1, Y_3 interaction term for the full three-way table, u_{12}^2 is the Y_1, Y_2 interaction in a LLM fitted to the two-way table for Y_1 and Y_2, and u_1^1 is the (trivial) main effect for Y_1 in the one-way marginal table for Y_1.

Analysis proceeds by fitting each equation separately. Equation (5.24) represents a log-linear logistic model for a one-dimensional contingency table for Y_1. Equations (5.25) and (5.26) represent CLMs for a two-way table with Y_1 and Y_2 and a three-way table with all three variables, respectively. Thus, the discussion of section 5.4 applies to these two equations. Note, for example, that if the fit of (5.25) suggests $u_{12}^2 = 0$ (no interaction between Y_1 and Y_2), we can choose to impose this as a constraint in (5.26). But the CLM for (5.26) corresponds to a LLM represented by [123], [12][13][23], [12][13], [12][23], or [12], depending on which of the interaction terms we fix at zero. The Y_1, Y_2 interaction u_{12} does not occur in this CLM equation and is a free parameter in all cases. Thus, if $u_{12} = 0$, we can estimate the CLM for (5.26), obtaining consistent but inefficient estimates, or we can fit the three-way LLM constraining u_{12}^3 to be zero and obtain a different but more efficient estimate. Finally, note that if we fit the full LLM to the three-way table, the estimated Y_1, Y_2 interaction term u_{12}^3 will not be the same as the u_{12}^2 term for that same Y_1, Y_2 interaction as obtained for equation (5.25). The reason is that the LLM parameters for a three-way table are related to,

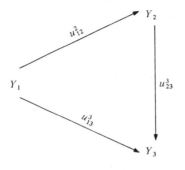

Figure 5.1. Path diagram for three-variable fully recursive model

but distinctly different from, the LLM parameters for a two-way marginal table.

Goodman (1973) gave a causal interpretation to the interaction terms in equations (5.25) and (5.26). Ignoring the third-order interaction, we can present the model in terms of a path diagram, as in Figure 5.1. Each "causal" arrow has an effect, as measured by the appropriate interaction term.

The model we have considered until now is a fully recursive model. One can also consider a partially recursive model, in which Y_1 is determined first, and Y_1 affects both Y_2 and Y_3, which are determined jointly. The relevant statistical model is

$$P(Y_1, Y_2, Y_3) = P(Y_1) \cdot P(Y_2, Y_3 \mid Y_1)$$

$P(Y_2, Y_3 \mid Y_1)$ is itself a LLM given by

$$P(Y_2, Y_3 \mid Y_1) = \frac{1}{D} \exp(u_2 Y_2 + u_3 Y_3 + u_{12} Y_1 Y_2 + u_{13} Y_1 Y_3 \\ + u_{23} Y_2 Y_3 + u_{123} Y_1 Y_2 Y_3)$$

where D is such that

$$\sum_{Y_2, Y_3} P(Y_2, Y_3 \mid Y_1) = 1$$

Note that all terms not involving Y_2 or Y_3 cancel out. One can use this LLM directly or consider the two equivalent CLM equations based on $P(Y_2 \mid Y_1, Y_3)$ and $P(Y_3 \mid Y_1, Y_2)$. Equation (5.26) will stay the same. Equation (5.25) will now change to

$$L_{2|13} = \log \frac{P(Y_2 = +1 \mid Y_1, Y_3)}{P(Y_2 = -1 \mid Y_1, Y_3)} = 2u_2^3 + 2u_{12}^3 Y_1 + 2u_{23}^3 Y_3 + 2u_{123}^3 Y_1 Y_3$$

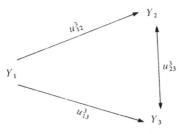

Figure 5.2. Path diagram for three-variable partially recursive model

The path diagram for this model is shown in Figure 5.2. Note the difference in the superscript for the interaction term u_{12}, and also note that there is a two-headed arrow between Y_2 and Y_3 with the same effect.

The partially recursive models are thus again correlation-type models, not structural models. We can argue that it is only fully recursive models that can be given a causal or structural interpretation. However, there are some problems in interpreting the interaction terms as the causal effects, because the models considered here are all models of outcome probabilities rather than models of the process generating the outcomes. We shall therefore revert to the models with latent variables discussed in section 5.1, but before we do that we shall examine whether or not one can empirically distinguish between the fully recursive logistic models (RLM) and the log-linear models (LLM) when the explanatory variables are qualitative and when they are continuous variables.[6]

We have discussed how to estimate the RLM and the LLM (or the equivalent CLM) when the models are specified in that particular form. In practice, however, we shall want to test whether or not the RLM in an adequate representation of the data as compared with the LLM. However, we cannot test such hypotheses using the CLM equations because of the symmetry conditions. For instance, in (5.23) we cannot test whether or not λ in the first equation is zero, because this would imply that λ is zero in the second equation as well. We have to see what the equivalent first equation would be if indeed the model is fully recursive.

---

[6] Note that some of the conclusions we have been stating apply only when the explanatory variables themselves are qualitative, such as the statement that separate estimations of the CLM equations (5.19) to (5.21) yield exactly the same estimates for the parameters that are equal across equations. When there are continuous explanatory variables, there is a gain in estimating the CLM equations jointly, imposing cross-equation constraints.

Consider the fully recursive model, where the main effects are functions of explanatory variables:

$$\log \frac{P(Y_1 = 1)}{P(Y_1 = -1)} = X\alpha \qquad (5.27)$$

$$\log \frac{P(Y_2 = 1 \mid Y_1)}{P(Y_2 = -1 \mid Y_1)} = X\beta + \lambda Y_1 \qquad (5.28)$$

Equation (5.28) is the same as the second equation in (5.23). X denotes a set of explanatory variables. The CLM equation equivalent to (5.27) has been derived by Lee (1981) as

$$\log \frac{P(Y_1 = 1 \mid Y_2)}{P(Y_1 = -1 \mid Y_2)} = X\alpha + \lambda Y_2 + G(X\beta, \lambda) \qquad (5.29)$$

where

$$G(X\beta, \lambda) = \lambda + \log \frac{1 + \exp(X\beta - \lambda)}{1 + \exp(X\beta + \lambda)} \qquad (5.30)$$

To derive this, we write, using Bayes's theorem,

$$\frac{P(Y_1 = 1 \mid Y_2)}{P(Y_1 = -1 \mid Y_2)} = \frac{P(Y_2 \mid Y_1 = 1) \cdot P(Y_1 = +1)}{P(Y_2 \mid Y_1 = -1) \cdot P(Y_1 = -1)}$$

$$= \frac{P(Y_2 \mid Y_1 = +1)}{P(Y_2 \mid Y_1 = -1)} \cdot \exp(X\alpha) \qquad (5.31)$$

Equation (5.28) can be written alternatively as

$$P(Y_2 \mid Y_1) = \frac{\exp[(X\beta + \beta Y_1)I]}{1 + \exp(X\beta + \lambda Y_1)}$$

where

$$I = 1 \quad \text{if} \ \ Y_2 = 1$$
$$I = 0 \quad \text{if} \ \ Y_2 = -1$$

Hence,

$$\frac{P(Y_2 \mid Y_1 = +1)}{P(Y_2 \mid Y_1 = -1)} = \exp(2\lambda I) \cdot \frac{1 + \exp(X\beta - \lambda)}{1 + \exp(X\beta + \lambda)} \qquad (5.32)$$

But $2\lambda I = \lambda + \lambda Y_2$.

Substituting (5.32) into (5.31), we get (5.29). What this suggests is that in the CLM equations (5.23) we modify the first equation by writing it as

$$\log \frac{P(Y_1 = -1 \mid Y_2)}{P(Y_1 = -1 \mid Y_2)} = X\alpha + \lambda Y_2 + \delta G(X\beta, \lambda) \qquad (5.33)$$

Then $\delta = 0$ corresponds to the LLM, and $\delta = 1$ corresponds to the RLM. The identification of δ requires that $G(X\beta, \lambda)$ is not an exact linear function of the variables X. Lee (1981*b*) showed that if all the explanatory variables are qualitative, then $G(X\beta, \lambda)$ may be a linear function of X, and δ will not be identifiable.[7] However, if X contains continuous variables, then δ will be identifiable, and the test can be carried out. Lee (1981) suggested first estimating equation (5.28) by logit ML to obtain estimates $(\hat{\beta}, \hat{\lambda})$ of (β, λ) and then estimating (5.33) again by logit ML after substituting $G(X\hat{\beta}, \hat{\lambda})$ for $G(X\beta, \lambda)$. These two-stage estimates can be shown to be consistent, and the correct asymptotic covariance matrix can be derived, as done by Amemiya (1979). The derivation of covariance matrices of such two-stage estimates is described in Chapter 8 and will not be pursued here. In the empirical illustration, Lee investigated the association between workers' job satisfaction and subsequent job-quitting behavior based on a sample of 2,606 observations from a 1972–3 panel study of income dynamics. The RLM assumes that job satisfaction precedes job-quitting behavior. However, the hypothesis $\delta = 1$ versus $\delta \neq 1$ was rejected, thus rejecting the RLM specification. The hypothesis $\delta = 0$ versus $\delta \neq 0$ (the Nerlove–Press model) was not rejected.

5.6 Some comments on LLM, CLM, RLM, the conditional log-linear models, and simultaneous equations

The discussion in the preceding sections indicates that estimation of the parameters in log-linear models is easiest with the CLM and RLM equations. One can use the standard logit programs, treating the explanatory variables as exogenous. One can use the ML methods or the minimum chi-square methods described in section 5.2. The actual parameter estimates with the two methods will, of course, be different, although they have the same asymptotic distribution.

As explained earlier, in section 5.4, problems do arise if the different CLM equations correspond to different LLMs. In this case, separate estimation of the CLM equations may give consistent estimates for only some parameters. To get the efficient estimates, we will have to estimate the corresponding LLM or carry out the joint estimation of the CLM equations with the cross-equation constraints imposed.

Our preceding discussion also indicates that to infer any causal structures we have to formulate a fully recursive logit model (RLM). For such models, the estimated coefficients can also be given a structural interpretation. We also mentioned briefly some test procedures for testing the RLM versus the LLM. These tests can give us an indication that the particular structure imposed is not the correct one. This leaves the question of finding an alternative RLM or an alternative model that will enable us to measure some structural parameters, as in the case of the usual simultaneous-equations systems in econometrics. One crude way of judging the comparative performances of different causal structures and the noncausal models is to get the predicted cell frequencies for the different formulations and compare the goodness-of-fit measure like the χ^2.

Some alternatives to the RLM that have a structural interpretation have been suggested by Vuong (1980). Our discussion in section 5.1 and the RLM suggest two ways of constructing models with a structural interpretation: One is in terms of some underlying latent variables, and the other is in terms of fully recursive logistic models (RLM). The alternative that Vuong suggested does not depend on any latent variables but depends on equilibrium quantities of qualitative variables. Before we discuss it, we shall state briefly the criticism of the LLM.

Fienberg (1975) pointed out that the LLM does not readily generalize to accommodate continuous endogenous variables, whereas the multivariate normal model can do this.[8] He suggested that such methodology should be developed. We shall discuss in Chapter 9 some models that are mixtures of continuous variables and discrete variables following the multivariate logistic distribution. Heckman's criticism (1978a) was that the LLM is not sufficiently rich in parameters to distinguish structural association among discrete variables from purely statistical association, a distinction that is at the heart of all simultaneous-equations theory. As mentioned earlier, we can use a latent-variable structural model, as in section 5.1. However, what Heckman suggested was models with "structural shift," where both the latent variables and their dichotomous realizations occur in the model simultaneously. We shall discuss these models in the next section, and in section 5.8 we shall point out the deficiencies in Heckman's structural-shift model. We shall also discuss there the example that he considered for comparing the LLM with the model with latent variables.

The alternative models that Vuong (1980)[9] suggested are based on conditional log-linear models (CLLM). Starting from the LLM (5.16), we can derive the CLLM as

---

[8] Fienberg pointed out that Pearson (1900) insisted that it always made sense to assume an underlying continuous variable for a dichotomy or polytomy (even when the dichotomy was death–alive) and that the probability distribution for this continuous variable was normal. Yule (1900), on the other hand, chose to analye the cross-classified data as they are. He can thus be considered the founder of the LLM school.

[9] The notation of Vuong is very complicated, because he considered very general models. Our example with binary variables will simplify it to convey the main ideas.

$$\log P(Y_1 \mid Y_2, Y_3) = \mu_1 + u_1 Y_1 + u_{12} Y_1 Y_2 + u_{13} Y_1 Y_3 + u_{123} Y_1 Y_2 Y_3$$
$$\log P(Y_2 \mid Y_1, Y_3) = \mu_2 + u_2 Y_2 + u_{12} Y_2 Y_1 + u_{23} Y_2 Y_3 + u_{123} Y_1 Y_2 Y_3$$

and

$$\log P(Y_3 \mid Y_1, Y_2) = \mu_3 + u_3 Y_3 + u_{13} Y_3 Y_1 + u_{23} Y_3 Y_2 + u_{123} Y_1 Y_2 Y_3$$

where μ_1, μ_2, and μ_3 are normalizing constants. For instance

$$P(Y_1 = +1 \mid Y_2, Y_3) + P(Y_1 = -1 \mid Y_2, Y_3) = 1$$

gives

$$\mu_1 = -\log[\exp(u_1 + u_{12} Y_2 + u_{13} Y_3 + u_{123} Y_2 Y_3)$$
$$+ \exp(-u_1 - u_{12} Y_2 - u_{13} Y_3 - u_{123} Y_2 Y_3)]$$

We considered the log odds ratios and the conditional logistic models (CLM) because they were easier to estimate. Similarly, we can write

$$\log P(Y_1, Y_2 \mid Y_3) = \eta_1 + u_1 Y_1 + u_2 Y_2 + u_{12} Y_1 Y_2 + u_{13} Y_1 Y_3$$
$$+ u_{23} Y_2 Y_3 + u_{123} Y_1 Y_2 Y_3$$

with similar expressions for $P(Y_1, Y_3 \mid Y_2)$ and $P(Y_2, Y_3 \mid Y_1)$. The normalizing constant η_1 can again be determined so that

$$\sum_{Y_1, Y_2} P(Y_1, Y_2 \mid Y_3) = 1$$

What Vuong did is the following. Take a demand-and-supply model so that Y_1 is quantity and Y_2 is price. Y_{1d} and Y_{2d} refer to quantity and price for the demand function, and Y_{1s} and Y_{2s} refer to quantity and price for the supply function. We shall assume that (Y_{1d}, Y_{2d}) and (Y_{1s}, Y_{2s}) are determined independently. Thus

$$\log P(Y_{1d}, Y_{2d} \mid Y_{1s}, Y_{2s}) = \eta_d + u_{1d} Y_{1d} + u_{2d} Y_{2d} + u_{12d} Y_{1d} Y_{2d}$$

$$\log P(Y_{1s}, Y_{2s} \mid Y_{1d}, Y_{2d}) = \eta_s + u_{1s} Y_{1s} + u_{2s} Y_{2s} + u_{12s} Y_{1s} Y_{2s}$$

The normalizing constants η_d and η_s can be obtained as before. However, the observed quantity Y_1 and price Y_2 are determined by "demand equals supply," that is, $Y_1 = Y_{1d} = Y_{1s}$ and $Y_2 = Y_{2d} = Y_{2s}$. The fact that we observe only equilibrium points and that we cannot observe $Y_{1d} \neq Y_{1s}$ and $Y_{2d} \neq Y_{2s}$ is precisely the crucial hypothesis underlying any simultaneous-equations model. Thus,

$$P(Y_1 = i, \ Y_2 = j)$$
$$= P(Y_{1d} = i, \ Y_{1s} = i, \ Y_{2d} = j, \ Y_{2s} = j \mid Y_{1d} = Y_{1s}, \ Y_{2s} = Y_{2s})$$
$$\text{for } i, j = +1, -1$$

Because (Y_{1d}, Y_{2d}) and (Y_{1s}, Y_{2s}) are assumed to be independent, we have

$$\log P(Y_{1d}, Y_{2d}, Y_{1s}, Y_{2s}) = \log P(Y_{1d}, Y_{2d}) + \log P(Y_{1s}, Y_{2s})$$

Hence, we have

$$\log P(Y_1, Y_2) = \eta + (u_{1d} + u_{1s})Y_1 + (u_{2d} + u_{2s})Y_2 + (u_{12d} + u_{12s})Y_1 Y_2$$

where η is a normalizing factor. Obviously, one cannot identify all the parameters $(U_d, U_s) = (u_{1d}, u_{2d}, u_{1s}, u_{2s})$ separately unless one imposes zero restrictions on some of the coefficients. The situation is not different from the usual simultaneous-equations model in which we are given just quantity and price. But the important thing to note is that the LLM specifying $\log P(Y_1, Y_2)$ and the associated two CLLM equations represent the reduced-form equations, and underlying these are structural equations in the variables Y_{1d}, Y_{1s}, Y_{2d}, and Y_{2s} and the structural parameters (U_d, U_s).

Consider now the case in which there are two dichotomous variables Y_3 and Y_4, where Y_3 influences (Y_{1d}, Y_{2d}) only, and Y_4 influences (Y_{1s}, Y_{2s}) only. We therefore postulate (assuming all third- and higher-order interaction terms are zero)

$$\log P(Y_{1d}, Y_{2d} \mid Y_{1s}, Y_{2s}, Y_3, Y_4)$$
$$= \theta_d + u_{1d}Y_{1d} + u_{2d}Y_{2d} + u_{12d}Y_{1d}Y_{2d} + u_{13d}Y_{1d}Y_3 + u_{23d}Y_{2d}Y_3$$

and

$$\log P(Y_{1s}, Y_{2s} \mid Y_{1d}, Y_{2d}, Y_3, Y_4)$$
$$= \theta_s + u_{1s}Y_{1s} + u_{2s}Y_{2s} + u_{12s}Y_{1s}Y_{2s} + u_{14s}Y_{1s}Y_4 + u_{24s}Y_{2s}Y_4$$

where θ_d and θ_s are normalizing constants. From these two equations we can get $\log P(Y_{1d}, Y_{2d}, Y_{1s}, Y_{2s} \mid Y_3, Y_4)$, and we can also get, as before,

$$\log P(Y_1, Y_2 \mid Y_3, Y_4) = \theta + (u_{1d} + u_{1s})Y_1 + (u_{2d} + u_{2s})Y_2 + (u_{12d} + u_{12s})Y_1 Y_2$$
$$+ u_{13d}Y_1 Y_3 + u_{23d}Y_2 Y_3 + u_{14s}Y_1 Y_4 + u_{24s}Y_2 Y_4$$

where θ is a normalizing constant. Thus, we see that the parameters u_{13d}, u_{23d}, u_{14s}, and u_{24s} are identified, but the parameters pertaining to the main effects and the bivariate interaction between Y_1 and Y_2 still are not identified. We must impose zero restrictions on some of these parameters to achieve identification. Thus, the introduction of exogenous variables Y_3 and Y_4 does not help. The usual exclusion restrictions that are sufficient to identify all the structural parameters of simultaneous-equations models in standard econometrics are, in general, insufficient to identify all the structural parameters of a system of CLLMs.[10]

Vuong next considered some recursive models in which Y_{1d} and Y_{1s} are determined prior to Y_{2d} and Y_{2s}, respectively. This is similar to the case in which price is determined first and then quantity. The formulation that Vuong adopted of interpreting the LLM (or even the RLM) as a reduced form and thinking of underlying structural equations specified in the CLLM or RLM form is interesting, but this needs further work before we can pass judgment on whether or not the LLM can be used for purposes other than describing pure statistical associations.[11]

5.7 Models with mixed structures: some consistent and inconsistent models

In section 5.1 we considered simultaneous-equations models with underlying continuous latent variables Y^*. In sections 5.3 through 5.6 we considered models in terms of only the observed qualitative variables Y. There we saw that the coefficients we estimate measure associations and that we cannot give causal interpretation (as in regression models, or the model considered in section 5.1) unless the models are fully recursive. The models are just descriptions of outcome probabilities and do not (except in the special cases discussed in the last section) enable us to understand the underlying mechanisms generating the observations. We shall now return to the latent-variable formulation and consider cases in which both the latent variables Y^* and their realized qualitative variables Y figure in the model. Consider the following models.

Model 1

$$y_1 = \beta_1 y_2 + \gamma_1' x_1 - u_1 \tag{5.34}$$

$$y_2^* = \beta_2 y_1 + \gamma_2' x_2 - u_2 \tag{5.35}$$

where

---

[10] Throughout our discussion we have considered only the specification of conditional probabilities. The conditions under which these conditional probabilities uniquely determine the joint probabilities can be found in the studies of Vuong and Gourieroux and Monfort (1979a, b).

[11] Koenig et al. (1981) and Nerlove (1981) tested different theories of expectations formation using the log-linear models. Thus, even with correlation-type models, one can draw many conclusions.

$$y_2 = 1 \quad \text{if } y_2^* > 0$$
$$y_2 = 0 \quad \text{otherwise}$$

Here the partially observed variable y_2^* occurs in the observed dichoto-mous form in equation (5.34) and the latent-variable form in equation (5.35). Models of this kind, in which the latent variables as well as their dichotomous or truncated observations occur in different structural equations, need some restrictions on the coefficients to be logically con-sistent. These consistency conditions have ben discussed by Maddala and Lee (1976) and Heckman (1976a, 1978a). An easy way of deriving these conditions is to make use of the following lemma.

Lemma. Let y^* be an unobserved variable, with the corresponding observed variable defined as

$$y = 1 \quad \text{if } y^* > 0$$
$$y = 0 \quad \text{otherwise} \tag{5.36}$$

or

$$y = y^* \quad \text{if } y^* > 0$$
$$y = 0 \quad \text{otherwise} \tag{5.37}$$

Then, an equation of the form $y^* = \gamma x + \beta y - u$, where u is a residual, is logically inconsistent unless $\beta = 0$.

Proof. We shall prove the result for the specification (5.36). The proof is similar when the specification is (5.37). When $y = 1$, we have

$$\gamma x + \beta y > u \quad \text{or} \quad \gamma x + \beta > u$$

When $y = 0$, we have

$$\gamma x + \beta y \leqslant u \quad \text{or} \quad \gamma x \leqslant u$$

Hence,

$$\text{Prob}(y = 0) + \text{Prob}(y = 1) = 1 - F(\gamma x) + F(\gamma x + \beta)$$

which is equal to 1 only if $\beta = 0$.

Consider now the model given by equations (5.34) and (5.35). Elimi-nating y_1, we get

$$y_2^* = \beta_1 \beta_2 y_2 + \beta_2 \gamma_1' x_1 + \gamma_2' x_2 + u_2 + \beta_2 u_1$$

Using this lemma, we note that the model is logically consistent if and only if $\beta_1 \beta_2 = 0$ (i.e., if and only if β_1 or β_2 is equal to zero).

Consider now the following alternative models.

Model 2

$$y_1^* = \beta_1 y_2^* + \gamma_1' x_1 - u_1 \tag{5.38}$$
$$y_2^* = \beta_2 y_1 + \gamma_2' x_2 - u_2 \tag{5.39}$$

where

$$\begin{aligned}
y_1 &= 1 \quad \text{iff } y_1^* > 0 \\
y_1 &= 0 \quad \text{otherwise} \\
y_2 &= 1 \quad \text{iff } y_2^* > 0 \\
y_2 &= 0 \quad \text{otherwise}
\end{aligned} \tag{5.40}$$

Again, the model is not logically consistent unless β_1 or β_2 is equal to zero.

Model 3

$$y_1^* = \beta_1 y_2 + \gamma_1' x_1 - u_1$$
$$y_2^* = \beta_2 y_1 + \gamma_2' x_2 - u_2$$

where y_1 and y_2 are defined by (5.40). For simplicity, and without loss of generality, let us assume that $x_1 = x_2 = 0$ and that u_1 and u_2 are independent. Also, denote by $F_1(\cdot)$ and $F_2(\cdot)$ the distribution functions of u_1 and u_2, respectively. Then we have

$$\begin{aligned}
\text{Prob}(y_1 = 1, \, y_2 = 1) &= F_1(\beta_1)F_2(\beta_2) \\
\text{Prob}(y_1 = 1, \, y_2 = 0) &= F_1(0)[1 - F_2(\beta_2)] \\
\text{Prob}(y_1 = 0, \, y_2 = 1) &= [1 - F_1(\beta_1)]F_2(0) \\
\text{Prob}(y_1 = 0, \, y_2 = 0) &= [1 - F_1(0)][1 - F_2(0)]
\end{aligned}$$

The sum of these probabilities is equal to

$$1 + F_1(0)F_2(0) - F_1(\beta_1)F_2(0) - F_1(0)F_2(\beta_2) + F_1(\beta_1)F_2(\beta_2)$$

This sum is not equal to 1 unless β_1 or β_2 is equal to zero.

The conditions for logical consistency in models with mixtures of latent variables and their partially observed realizations can be checked by considering the corresponding reduced forms, as was done in the case of models 1 and 2, or by considering the sum of the different probabilities, as was done in the case of model 3. The identifiability conditions in such models are also somewhat different from those in the usual simultaneous-equations models.

Consider, for instance, model 1, given by equations (5.34) and (5.35). We saw that it is logically consistent only if β_1 or β_2 is zero. However, the conditions for identification are different for the two resulting models.

Consider first the case $\beta_1 = 0$, model 4.

Model 4

$$y_1 = \gamma_1' x_1 - u_1 \tag{5.41}$$

$$y_2^* = \beta_2 y_1 + \gamma_2' x_2 - u_2 \tag{5.42}$$

In this model the conditions for identification are that u_1 and u_2 be independent, or else there is at least one variable in x_1 not included in x_2. These conditions are the same as those in the usual simultaneous-equations models, where y_2^* is observed.

Consider next the case $\beta_2 = 0$, model 5.

Model 5

$$y_1 = \beta_1 y_2 + \gamma_1' x_1 - u_1 \tag{5.43}$$

$$y_2^* = \gamma_2' x_2 - u_2, \quad \mathrm{Var}(u_2) = 1 \tag{5.44}$$

Now the model is identified even if u_1 and u_2 are not independent and x_1 includes all the variables in x_2. Note that under these conditions we can still distinguish equation (5.43) from linear combinations of equations (5.43) and (5.44), because equation (5.44) involves y_2^* and equation (5.43) involves y_2. This is not the case with equations (5.41) and (5.42).

The two-stage estimation of this model proceeds as follows. We first get an estimate $\hat{\gamma}_2$ of γ_2 by using the probit ML method for equation (5.44). As for equation (5.43), we can write it as

$$y_1 = \beta_1 F_2(\gamma_2' x_2) + \gamma_1' x_1 + w \tag{5.45}$$

where $w = -u_1 + \beta_2[y_2 - F_2(\gamma_2' x_2)]$ and $F_2(\cdot)$ is the distribution function of u_2. Because w has zero mean and is uncorrelated with the regressors, we can estimate equation (5.45) by OLS after substituting $\hat{\gamma}_2$ for γ_2. Because $\hat{\gamma}_2$ is a consistent estimate of γ_2, under some general conditions, it can be shown that the resulting estimates of β_1 and γ_1 are consistent. The two-stage methods are discussed in detail in Chapter 8.

An alternative two-stage estimation procedure is the following. We rewrite model 5 in the form of a switching regression model:

$$y_1 = \beta_1 + \gamma_1' x_1 - u_1 \quad \text{if } y_2^* > 0 \text{ (i.e., } u_2 < \gamma_2' x_2)$$

and

$$y_1 = \gamma_1' x_1 - u_1 \quad \text{if } y_2^* \leq 0 \ (\text{i.e., } u_2 \geq \gamma_2' x_2)$$

Hence,[12]

$$E(y_1 \mid y_2 = 1) = \beta_1 + \gamma_1' x_1 - E(u_1 \mid u_2 < \gamma_2' x_2)$$

$$= \beta_1 + \gamma_1' x_1 + \sigma_{12} \frac{\phi(\gamma_2' x_2)}{\Phi(\gamma_2' x_2)} \tag{5.46}$$

and

$$E(y_1 \mid y_2 = 0) = \gamma_1' x_1 - \sigma_{12} \frac{\phi(\gamma_2' x_2)}{1 - \Phi(\gamma_2' x_2)} \tag{5.47}$$

where $\sigma_{12} = \text{Cov}(u_1, u_2)$ and $\phi(Z)$ and $\Phi(Z)$ are the density function and the distribution function of the standard normal evaluated at Z.

Equation (5.46) suggests the following two-stage estimation procedure. We first get probit ML estimates $\hat{\gamma}_2$ of γ_2. Then, for the subsample corresponding to $y_2 = 1$, we regress y_1 on x_1 and $\phi(\hat{\gamma}_2' x_2)/\Phi(\hat{\gamma}_2' x_2)$, with a constant term, to get estimates of β_1, γ_1, and σ_{12}.

Note that by combining the two equations (5.46) and (5.47), we get

$$E(y_1) = E(y_1 \mid y_2 = 1) \cdot \text{Prob}(y_2 = 1) + E(y_2 \mid y_2 = 0) \cdot \text{Prob}(y_2 = 0)$$

$$= \beta_1 \Phi(\gamma_2' x_2) + \gamma_1' x_1 \tag{5.48}$$

which justifies the two-stage estimation method we mentioned earlier of substituting $\Phi(\hat{\gamma}_2' x_2)$ for y_2. Note that even if x_1 has all the variables in x_2, this does not create a perfect multicollinearity problem in this model, because we substitute for y_2 a nonlinear function $\Phi(\gamma_2' x_2)$, not a linear function $\gamma_2' x_2$ as in the usual simultaneous-equations models.

In the special case in which u_1 and u_2 are independent, we can estimate equation (5.43) by OLS. But if u_1 and u_2 are correlated, then the foregoing two-stage estimation procedures can be used. It can be shown that the resulting estimates are consistent.

For estimation of models 4 and 5 by the ML method, we derive the following joint densities. For model 4, we have

$$g(y_1, y_2 = 1) = \int_{-\infty}^{\beta_2 y_1 + \gamma_2' x_2} f(y_1 - \gamma_1' x_1, u_2) \, du_2$$

$$g(y_1, y_2 = 0) = \int_{\beta_2 y_1 + \gamma_2' x_2}^{\infty} f(y_1 - \gamma_1' x_1, u_2) \, du_2$$

---

[12] See the Appendix at the end of the book for the expressions concerning the means of the truncated distributions.

where $f(u_1, u_2)$ is the joint density function of (u_1, u_2). The likelihood function to be maximized is[13]

$$L(\beta_2, \gamma_1, \gamma_2) = \Pi[g(y_1, y_2 = 1)]^{y_2}[g(y_1, y_2 = 0)]^{1-y_2}$$

If the residuals u_1 and u_2 are independent, then maximizing L amounts to estimation of the two equations separately: equation (5.41) by OLS and equation (5.42) by the probit ML method. For model 5, we have

$$g(y_1, y_2 = 1) = \int_{-\infty}^{\gamma_2' x_2} f(y_1 - \beta_1 y_2 - \gamma_1' x_1, u_2) \, du_2$$

$$g(y_1, y_2 = 0) = \int_{\gamma_2' x_2}^{\infty} f(y_1 - \beta_1 y_2 - \gamma_1' x_1, u_2) \, du_2$$

and the likelihood function to be maximized is

$$L(\beta_1, \gamma_1, \gamma_2) = \Pi[g(y_1, y_2 = 1)]^{y_2}[g(y_1, y_2 = 0)]^{1-y_2}$$

Again, if the residuals u_1 and u_2 are independent, then maximizing L amounts to estimation of the two equations separately: equation (5.43) by OLS and equation (5.44) by the probit ML method.

The case of model 2, given by equations (5.38) and (5.39), is somewhat different. As shown earlier, for logical consistency, we need to impose the condition $\beta_1 = 0$ or $\beta_2 = 0$. The case $\beta_2 = 0$ is similar to that of model 4. Consider the model with $\beta_1 = 0$. We have

Model 6

$$y_1^* = \gamma_1' x_1 - u_1 \tag{5.49}$$

$$y_2^* = \beta_2 y_1 + \gamma_2' x_2 - u_2 \tag{5.50}$$

Of course, because y_1^* and y_2^* are observed as dichotomous variables, we need to impose the conditions $\text{Var}(u_1) = 1$ and $\text{Var}(u_2) = 1$. But if u_1 and u_2 are not independent and x_2 includes all the variables in x_1, the parameters in (5.50) are not identified. This is so even though a linear combination of equations (5.49) and (5.50) does not generate an equation of the form (5.50). To see this, consider the case in which x_1 and x_2 are both constants. We thus have

$$y_1^* = \gamma_1 - u_1$$

$$y_2^* = \beta_2 y_1 + \gamma_2 - u_2$$

---

[13] Maximization of likelihoods of this form and computation of ML estimates will be discussed in the next two chapters.

Define $\mathrm{Cov}(u_1, u_2) = \delta$. The sample information enables us to estimate three probabilities (the fourth is obtained as a residual), and from these three probabilities we cannot estimate four parameters γ_1, γ_2, β_2, and δ. One of the parameters β_2, γ_2, and δ has to be zero. The conditions for identification in this model are the same as those in model 4.

As for the estimation of this model, we can use the ML method. If u_1 and u_2 are independent, then one can estimate both equations separately by the probit ML method. If u_1 and u_2 are not independent, this method does not give consistent estimates of the parameters for the second equation (5.50). We cannot use the two-stage method, in which we first obtain the probit ML estimates $\hat{\gamma}_1$ of γ_1, and we substitute $\Phi(\hat{\gamma}_1', x_1)$ for y_1, as was done in the case of model 5.

Note that in some models it makes more sense to specify equation (5.50) as

$$y_2^* = \beta_2 \bar{y}_1 + \gamma_2' x_2 - u_2 \tag{5.51}$$

where

$$\bar{y}_1 = \mathrm{Probl}(y_1^* > 0)$$

In this case the substitution of $\Phi(\gamma_1' x_1)$ for $\bar{y}_1$ is valid, and the resulting estimates can be shown to be consistent.

For the ML estimation of model 6, we proceed as follows: Denote the joint distribution function of (u_1, u_2) by $F(\cdot, \cdot)$ and assume for simplicity of notation that u_1 and u_2 have symmetric distributions. Then the joint probability distribution of (y_1, y_2) is given by the following expressions:

$$P_{11} = \mathrm{Prob}(y_1 = 1,\ y_2 = 1) = F[(\gamma_1' x_1, \beta_2 + \gamma_2' x_2); \rho)]$$
$$P_{10} = \mathrm{Prob}(y_1 = 1,\ y_2 = 0) = F[(\gamma_1' x_1, -\beta_2 - \gamma_2' x_2); \rho)]$$
$$P_{01} = \mathrm{Prob}(y_1 = 0,\ y_2 = 1) = F[(-\gamma_1' x_1, \gamma_2' x_2); -\rho)]$$
$$P_{00} = \mathrm{Prob}(y_1 = 0,\ y_2 = 0) = F[(-\gamma_1' x_1, -\gamma_2' x_2); -\rho)]$$

and the likelihood function to be maximized is

$$L(\beta_2, \gamma_1, \gamma_2) = \Pi P_{11}^{y_1 y_2} P_{10}^{y_1(1-y_2)} P_{01}^{(1-y_1)y_2} P_{00}^{(1-y_1)(-1-y_2)}$$

The use of the ML method involves evaluation of double integrals.

We shall refer to models 4, 5, and 6 as *recursive models*. Note that in the usual simultaneous-equations literature the term is used for models in which the residuals (u_1, u_2) are independent. We are not making such an assumption in the case of model 5.

In model 6, problems of estimation arise when the occurrence of y_1 is a precondition for y_2. In this case the estimates from the probit estimation of (5.50) will yield an infinite estimate of β_2. If the occurrence of y_1 is a precondition for y_2, we have a contingency table of the following type. The entry for $y_1 = 0$, $y_2 = 1$ will be identically zero.

	$y_1 = 1$	$y_1 = 0$
$y_2 = 1$	X	0
$y_2 = 0$	X	X

Models of this kind are what Amemiya (1975) called sequential models; they were discussed in Chapter 2. Models 4, 5, and 6 are recursive models, not sequential models. If model 6 were a sequential model, the proper estimation procedure would be to estimate equation (5.49) by the probit ML method, using the entire set of data, and estimate equation (5.50) again by the probit ML method, but using the subset of observations for which $y_1 = 1$.

Maddala and Lee (1976) discussed an example of a model like model 6. The model involved the following variables:

$y_1 = 1$ if the individual had heard of the neighborhood youth corps (NYC) program

$y_1 = 0$ otherwise

$y_2 = 1$ if the individual participated in NYC

$y_2 = 0$ otherwise

They did, however, estimate the model by a two-stage method using all the observations. This was a valid procedure, in spite of the fact that the model looked like a sequential model. Logically, in this model y_1 was a precondition for y_2. However, there were many observations in the sample for which y_1 was zero and yet y_2 was nonzero. The reason this was so was that the question regarding having heard of the NYC program was referred to a particular time period. Thus, in this case, the estimate of β_2 in (5.50) need not be infinite.

The preceding discussion shows that models in which latent variables and their dichotomous or truncated realizations occur simultaneously fall in the category of recursive or sequential models. We have discussed some two-stage estimation methods for these models. We shall now discuss briefly the economic rationale behind the formulation of these models.

If we refer to y_1^* as measuring intentions and y_i as the actual actions, then a model of the form

$$y_1^* = \beta_1 y_2^* + \gamma_1' x_1 + u_1$$
$$y_2^* = \beta_2 y_1^* + \gamma_2' x_2 + u_2$$

says that the intentions about y_1 and y_2 are simultaneously determined by the exogenous variables x_1 and x_2. For instance, y_1^* may be the intention to use fertilizer, and y_2^* may be the intention to use hybrid seed. The model

$$y_1 = \beta_1 y_2 + \gamma_1' x_1 + u_1$$
$$y_2 = \beta_2 y_1 + \gamma_2' x_2 + u_2$$

says that the actions about y_1 and y_2 are simultaneously determined.

On the other hand, models 1, 2, and 3 do not have any such interpretation. For instance, model 3 ways that intentions about y_1 depend on actual action on y_2 and that intentions about y_2 depend on actual action on y_1. In the example involving fertilizer and hybrid seed, model 3 says that the intention about using fertilizer depends on whether or not hybrid seed are actually used, and the intention about using hybrid seed depends on whether or not fertilizer is actually used. It is intuitively clear that y_1 or y_2 must precede the other variable. This is what the condition $\beta_1 = 0$ or $\beta_2 = 0$ for logical consistency of the model says. If $y_1 = 1$ is a precondition for $y_2 = 1$, then, of course, we have a sequential model. Otherwise, y_1 merely precedes y_2, and we have a recursive model like model 6.

We have elaborated the different classes of two-equation models so as to fix ideas that are likely to be obscured by elaborate algebra in the case of models with more variables. We have presented what the two-stage and ML estimation methods will be, but we have not gone into the details, because these details will be discussed in the next three chapters. The logical-consistency conditions have also been illustrated with reference to very simple two-equation models; these have been generalized by Schmidt (1982). Such conditions have also been discussed for simultaneous-equations models with truncated dependent variables by Amemiya (1974b); more important, they have been discussed in a very general class of switching simultaneous-equations models by Gourieroux et al. (1980b). These will be discussed in subsequent chapters. In the next section, however, we shall again discuss a two-equation example to illustrate the logical-consistency condition and to show how an examination of the model reveals an alternative formulation for which no logical-consistency condition need be imposed.

5.8 Heckman's model with structural shift and dummy endogenous variables

A good illustration of the ideas in the preceding section can be provided by discussing a model suggested by Heckman (1978a):

$$y_1 = \gamma_1 y_2^* + \delta_1 y_2 + X_1 \beta_1 + u_1 \tag{5.52}$$

$$y_2^* = \gamma_2 y_1 + \delta_2 y_2 + X_2 \beta_2 + u_2 \qquad (5.53)$$

where

$$y_2 = 1 \quad \text{if } y_2^* > 0$$
$$y_2 = 0 \quad \text{otherwise}$$

We shall first discuss the logical consistency of this model and the estimation methods and then discuss under what conditions this model makes sense. We shall also consider alternative formulations of this model for the problem that Heckman suggested.

First, we solve (5.52) and (5.53) for y_2^*. We get

$$y_2^* = \frac{1}{1 - \gamma_1 \gamma_2} [(\gamma_2 \delta_1 + \delta_2) y_2 + X_2 \beta_2 + \gamma_2 X_1 \beta_1 + \gamma_2 u_1 + u_2]$$

$$= \alpha' Z + \frac{\gamma_2 \delta_1 + \delta_2}{1 - \gamma_1 \gamma_2} y_2 + v_2 \quad \text{(say)} \qquad (5.54)$$

By using the lemma in the preceding section, we immediately see that the coefficient of y_2 has to be zero. Hence, if γ_1 and γ_2 are finite, we should have, for logical consistency of the model,

$$\gamma_2 \delta_1 + \delta_2 = 0 \qquad (5.55)$$

Next, to see what the conditions for identification are, we write the model as a switching simultaneous-equations model:

$$\left. \begin{array}{l} y_1 = \gamma_1 y_2^* + X_1 \beta_1 + \delta_1 + u_1 \\ y_2^* = \gamma_2 y_1 + X_2 \beta_2 + \delta_2 + u_2 \end{array} \right\} \quad \text{if } y_2^* > 0 \qquad (5.56)$$

$$\left. \begin{array}{l} y_1 = \gamma_1 y_2^* + X_1 \beta_1 + u_1 \\ y_2^* = \gamma_2 y_1 + X_2 \beta_2 + u_2 \end{array} \right\} \quad \text{if } y_2^* \leqslant 0 \qquad (5.57)$$

It is obvious that in both the regimes the order and rank conditions are the same, and they are the usual rank and order conditions where y_1 and y_2^* are the two endogenous variables and the structure is that given by equation (5.57). The order condition is that there is at least one variable in X_1 not included in X_2, and at least one variable in X_2 not included in X_1.

We next turn to the estimation of the model. Assume that the residuals (u_1, u_2) are jointly normally distributed, with mean vector zero and covariance matrix

$$\begin{bmatrix} \sigma_1^2 & \sigma_{12} \\ & \sigma_2^2 \end{bmatrix}$$

With the condition $\gamma_2 \delta_1 + \delta_2 = 0$ imposed, the reduced-form equation (5.54) for y_2^* is

$$y_2^* = \alpha'Z + v_2 \tag{5.58}$$

Let $\text{Var}(v_2) = \sigma_v^2$. First, we shall see what parameters are estimable. Because y_2 is a dichotomous variable, we can write equation (5.58) as

$$y_2^{**} = \frac{y_2^*}{\sigma_v} = \left(\frac{\alpha}{\sigma_v}\right)' Z + \frac{v_2}{\sigma_v}$$

$$= \alpha^{*'}Z + v_2^* \quad \text{(say)} \tag{5.59}$$

$\text{Var}(v_2^*) = 1$, and the application of probit ML methods to the observations on y_2 gives us an estimate $\hat{\alpha}^*$ of α^*. Equations (5.52) and (5.53) can be written as

$$y_1 = \gamma_1 \sigma_v y_2^{**} + \delta_1 y_2 + X_1 \beta_1 + u_1 \tag{5.60}$$

$$y_2^{**} = \frac{\gamma_2}{\sigma_v} y_1 + \frac{\delta_2}{\sigma_v} y_2 + X_2 \frac{\beta_2}{\sigma_v} + \frac{u_2}{\sigma_v} \tag{5.61}$$

Now it is clear that the estimable parameters in this model are

$$\gamma_1 \sigma_v, \quad \delta_1, \quad \beta_1, \quad \frac{\gamma_2}{\sigma_v}, \quad \frac{\beta_2}{\sigma_v}$$

Note that $\delta_2/\sigma_v = -(\gamma_2/\sigma_v)\delta_1$. As for the error variances and covariances, we can estimate σ_1^2, σ_{12}/σ_v, and σ_2^2/σ_v^2. We can use the two-stage estimation methods outlined in the preceding section to get consistent estimates of these estimable parameters. Although this can be done in several ways, the most straightforward method is the following. We normalize equation (5.61) with respect to y_1. We get

$$y_1 = \frac{\sigma_v}{\gamma_2} y_2^{**} - \frac{\delta_2}{\gamma_2} y_2 - X_2 \frac{\beta_2}{\gamma_2} - \frac{u_2}{\gamma_2} \tag{5.62}$$

First we estimate (5.59) by probit ML methods to get $\hat{\alpha}^*$. Next we substitute $\hat{\alpha}^{*'}Z$ for y_2^{**} and $\Phi(\hat{\alpha}^{*'}Z)$ for y_2 in equations (5.60) and (5.62) and estimate these by OLS. The first equation gives consistent estimates of $\gamma_1 \sigma_v$, δ_1, and β_1, and once these are obtained we can get the estimated residuals $\hat{u}_1$. The second equation gives consistent estimates of

$$\frac{\sigma_v}{\gamma_2}, \quad \frac{\delta_2}{\gamma_2}, \quad \frac{\beta_2}{\gamma_2}$$

and once these are obtained, we can get the estimated residuals $\hat{u}_2/\gamma_2$. From these estimates we get consistent estimates of γ_2/σ_v, δ_2/σ_v, and

β_2/σ_v and estimated residuals $\hat{u}_2/\sigma_v$. From the estimated residuals $\hat{u}_1$ and $\hat{u}_2/\sigma_v$ we can get estimates of σ_1^2, σ_{12}/σ_v, and σ_2^2/σ_v^2.

$$\hat{\sigma}_1^2 = \frac{1}{T}\Sigma\hat{u}_1^2, \qquad \frac{\hat{\sigma}_{12}}{\sigma_v} = \frac{1}{T}\Sigma\hat{u}_1\cdot\frac{\hat{u}_2}{\sigma_v}$$

and so forth. Thus, we get consistent estimates of all the estimable parameters in this model mentioned earlier. The constraint $\delta_2 = -\gamma_2\delta_1$ can be imposed by writing (5.62) as

$$y_1 - \delta_1 y_2 = \frac{\sigma_v}{\gamma_2}y_2^{**} - X_2\frac{\beta_2}{\gamma_2} - \frac{u_2}{\gamma_2} \tag{5.63}$$

Now we use $\hat{\delta}_1$ obtained from the estimation of (5.60) and regress $(y_1 - \hat{\delta}_1 y_2)$ on $\hat{y}_2^{**}$ and X_2 to get estimates of σ_v/γ_2 and β_2/γ_2, and then the residuals $\hat{u}_2/\gamma_2$. The rest of the estimation is as before. This method is preferable to the one described earlier because it explicitly uses the constraint $\gamma_2\delta_1 + \delta_2 = 0$.

Finally, to use the ML method, we derive the likelihood function for this model as follows: After using the condition $\gamma_2\delta_1 + \delta_2 = 0$, we get the reduced forms for y_1 and y_2^* as

$$y_1 = \delta_1 y_2 + \frac{1}{1 - \gamma_1\gamma_2}(X_1\beta_1 + \gamma_1 X_2\beta_2 + \gamma_1 u_2 + u_1)$$

$$y_2^* = \frac{1}{1 - \gamma_1\gamma_2}(X_2\beta_2 + \gamma_2 X_1\beta_1 + \gamma_2 u_1 + u_2)$$

We can rewrite these equations in terms of the estimable parameters mentioned earlier. For this purpose, define

$$\gamma_1^* = \sigma_v\gamma_1, \quad \gamma_2^* = \frac{\gamma_2}{\sigma_v}, \quad \beta_2^* = \frac{\beta_2}{\sigma_v}, \quad u_2^* = \frac{u_2}{\sigma_v}, \quad \text{and} \quad y_2^{**} = \frac{y_2^*}{\sigma_v}$$

where σ_v^2 is as defined earlier, the variance of the residual in y_2^*, that is,

$$\sigma_v^2 = \text{Var}\left(\frac{\gamma_2 u_1 + u_2}{1 - \gamma_1\gamma_2}\right)$$

Now the reduced-form equations written in terms of the estimable parameters are

$$y_1 = \delta_1 y_2 + \frac{1}{1 - \gamma_1^*\gamma_2^*}(X_1\beta_1 + \gamma_1^* X_2\beta_2^* + \gamma_1^* u_2^* + u_1)$$

$$y_2^{**} = \frac{1}{1 - \gamma_1^*\gamma_2^*}(X_2\beta_2^* + \gamma_2^* X_1\beta_1 + \gamma_2^* u_1 + u_2^*)$$

We can write these equations compactly as

$$y_1 = \delta_1 y_2 + \alpha_1' X - v_1$$

$$y_2^{**} = \alpha_2' X - v_2$$

where α_1 and α_2 are functions of $(\gamma_1^*, \gamma_2^*, \beta_1, \beta_2^*)$, X includes all the variables in X_1 and X_2

$$v_1 = -\frac{\gamma_1^* u_2^* + u_1}{1 - \gamma_1^* \gamma_2^*}$$

$$v_2 = -\frac{\gamma_2^* u_1 + u_2^*}{1 - \gamma_1^* \gamma_2^*}$$

and $\mathrm{Var}(v_2) = 1$. Now the model is exactly in the same form as model 5 discussed in the preceding section. The likelihood function is therefore derived similarly. Let $f(v_1, v_2)$ be the joint density function of v_1 and v_2. Then the joint density function of y_1 and y_2 is given by

$$g(y_1, y_2 = 1) = \int_{-\infty}^{\alpha_2' X} f(y_1 - \delta_1 - \alpha_1' X, v_2) \, dv_2$$

and

$$g(y_1, y_2 = 0) = \int_{\alpha_2' X}^{\infty} f(y_1 - \alpha_1' X, v_2) \, dv_2$$

and the likelihood function to be maximized is[14]

$$L(\gamma_1^*, \gamma_2^*, \beta_1, \beta_2^*, \delta_1, \sigma_1, \sigma_{12}^*, \sigma_2^*)$$
$$= \Pi[g(y_1, y_2 = 1)]^{y_2}[g(y_1, y_2 = 0)]^{1-y_2}$$

This completes the discussion of (a) conditions for logical consistency, (b) identification, (c) two-stage estimation, and (d) ML estimation for this model. We now turn to economic interpretation and some alternative formulations.

The motivation behind Heckman's formulation of the model given by (5.52) and (5.53) was a study done by Landes (1968) on the effects of fair-employment legislation on the status of blacks. In Landes's model,

y_1 = wages of blacks relative to those of whites in state i

X_i = vector of exogenous variables

D_i = dummy variable

---

[14] ML estimation from such models will be discussed in the next two chapters.

$$= 1 \text{ if state } i \text{ has a fair-employment law}$$
$$= 1 \text{ otherwise}$$

Landes estimated the equation

$$y_i = X_{1i}\beta_1 + \delta_1 D_i + u_{1i} \tag{5.64}$$

The coefficient δ_1 measures the effect of fair-employment laws. Landes found a marginally positive coefficient for D_i.

Stigler (1973) argued that the passing of a fair-employment law is not an exogenous event. States in which blacks fare well without fair-employment laws may be the states most likely to pass such laws. In such situations the legislation merely ratifies a consensus. This argument suggests that the dummy variable D_i is endogenous. To capture this argument, Heckman defined another equation

$$S_i = X_{2i}\beta_2 + \delta_2 D_i + \gamma_2 y_i + u_{2i} \tag{5.65}$$

where S_i is sentiment favoring fair-employment legislation in state i.

$$D_i = 1 \quad \text{if } S_i > 0$$
$$D_i = 0 \quad \text{otherwise} \tag{5.66}$$

One can also argue for inclusion of the variable S_i in equation (5.64) and rewrite it as

$$y_i = X_{1i}\beta_1 + \delta_1 D_i + \gamma_1 S_i + u_{1i} \tag{5.67}$$

The model in equations (5.65) and (5.67) is now in the form of the model in equations (5.52) and (5.53) that we discussed in detail, with $y_{1i} = y_i$ and $y_{2i}^* = S_i$. Equation (5.67) can be very easily justified, because our objective is to study the effects of passage of fair-employment laws per se after allowing for the sentiment in favor of fair-employment laws. However, it is the "sentiment" equation (5.65) that is difficult to justify the way Heckman has formulated it. Inclusion of the dummy variable D_i in that equation is difficult to justify. How can the passage of the law itself affect sentiment in the same period? One can make an argument that passage of the law affects sentiment, but not in the same period. For instance, the attitude toward sending children to integrated schools changed markedly after passage of the desegregation laws. But such phenomena are described by the following model. There is a threshold level of sentiment that leads to passage of the law. But passage of the law itself leads to a shift in sentiment. This fact is modeled as follows:

$$S_t = X_t\beta + u_t$$

If $S_t > 0$, the law is passed. If $S_t \leqslant 0$, the law is not passed.

$$S_{t+1} = X_{t+1}\beta + u_{t+1} \quad \text{if } S_t \leq 0 \text{ (i.e., no law is passed)}$$
$$S_{t+1} = X_{t+1}\beta + \alpha + u_{t+1} \quad \text{if } S_t > 0 \text{ (i.e., the law is passed)}$$

This models a situation in which the passage of the law itself shifts sentiment in favor of the issue under consideration, but in the next period.

In his model, Heckman talked about "contemporaneous shift."[15] If we write it in the form of switching simultaneous equations, as in equations (5.56) and (5.57), the model says that there is a shift in the structural system if the law is passed. However, this structural shift is peculiar. If we look at the reduced-form equations, there is no shift in the y_2^* equation. In fact, any such shift is logically inconsistent, and the condition for logical consistency, $\delta_2 + \gamma_2\delta_1 = 0$, states this. Thus, the only shift that occurs is in the y_1 equation, this shift being $[(\delta_1 + \gamma_1\delta_2)/(1 - \gamma_1\gamma_2)]y_2$, which, together with the condition $\delta_2 + \gamma_2\delta_1 = 0$, leads to $\delta_1 y_2$. What this captures is the effect of passage of the law on the relative wage level for blacks. We can label this shift as a structural shift with peculiar restrictions, or we can simply view it as a shift in the wage function produced by passage of the law. The latter interpretation is more straightforward.

The logical thing to do in this model is to set $\delta_2 = 0$. If we set $\delta_2 = 0$ in equation (5.65), the logical-consistency condition derived earlier, namely $\delta_2 + \gamma_2\delta_1 = 0$, implies either $\delta_1 = 0$ or $\gamma_2 = 0$. But δ_1 is precisely the coefficient we are interested in. Hence, we have to assume $\gamma_2 = 0$ (i.e., the variable y_i should not be in the sentiment equation). Thus, to capture Stigler's argument, the model should be formulated as:

$$y_i = X_{1i}\beta_1 + \delta_1 D_i + \gamma_1 S_i + u_{1i} \tag{5.67}$$

$$S_i = X_{2i}\beta_2 + u_{2i} \tag{5.68}$$

$$D_i = 1 \quad \text{if } S_i > 0$$
$$D_i = 0 \quad \text{otherwise} \tag{5.66}$$

---

[15] One can justify Heckman's formulation by arguing that the "contemporaneous shift" that he talked about arises from the fact that the observations are on a cross section of "time-averaged" values of S and D. Although there is a dynamic process underlying the generation of the data, this is masked by time-aggregation, and the data can exhibit contemporaneous shift. However, with this interpretation, Heckman's model is no longer a true structural model. If the logical-consistency condition holds, then the time-aggregates tend to behave as if they were being determined by his contemporaneous-shift structural model. On the other hand, if the logical-consistency condition fails, the dynamic model may have cyclic or nonunique solutions, and the time-aggregates do not behave as if they were being determined by Heckman's model.

The reason Heckman included the variable y_i in the sentiment equation was that there is an argument alternative to Stigler's. This, he said, is that "in states with much market discrimination the demand for anti-discrimination on the part of blacks is high, and through logrolling, this leads to a greater incidence of fair employment legislation in these states" (Heckman, 1976a, p. 236). This argument, however, does not lead to the formulation of the sentiment equation as in (5.65). The sentiment that Stigler talked about is the positive sentiment toward blacks. The factors that lead to passage of fair-employment laws are (a) the positive senti-ment in favor of blacks and (b) the pressure from blacks for passage of such laws because of a low value of y_i due to the presence of market dis-crimination. Thus, the sentiment equation still needs to be defined as in (5.68), and it is this S_i that is included in equation (5.67) as an explana-tory variable. On the other hand, it is not S_i that determines the dummy variable D_i (the passage of the law). It is some combination of S_i and y_i^*, where y_i^* is the value of y_i for $D_i=0$ (the wages of blacks relative to whites that would have prevailed in the absence of the law). Instead of (5.66), we now have

$$D_i = 1 \quad \text{if } S_i + \theta y_i^* > 0$$
$$D_i = 0 \quad \text{otherwise} \tag{5.69}$$

where $y_i^* = X_{1i}\beta_1 + \gamma_1 S_i + u_{1i}$ and θ measures the weight attached to the pressure from blacks for legislation of fair-employment laws. Define

$$S_i^* = S_i + \theta y_i^* \tag{5.70}$$

S_i^* is pressure for legislation. We have

$$S_i^* = (1 + \gamma_1\theta)S_i + X_{1i}(\beta_1\theta) + \theta u_{1i} \tag{5.71}$$

Note that in this formulation S_i is not observed even as a dichotomous variable. We have here a model with an unobserved latent variable S_i, which occurs as an explanatory variable in two equations: y_i given by equation (5.67) and S_i^* given by equation (5.71), where S_i^* is observed only as a dichotomous variable. This is similar to the MIMIC model dis-cussed by Jöreskog and Goldberger (1975), except that of the two indi-cators, one is continuous and the other dichotomous.

Equations (5.67), (5.68), and (5.69) can be written, after the necessary substitutions, as follows:

$$y_i = X_{1i}\beta_1 + X_{2i}\beta_2\gamma_1 + \delta_1 D_i + v_{1i} \tag{5.72}$$

$$S_i^* = X_{1i}\beta_1\theta + X_{2i}\beta_2(1 + \gamma_1\theta) + v_{2i} \tag{5.73}$$

$$D_i = 1 \quad \text{if } S_i^* > 0$$
$$D_i = 0 \quad \text{otherwise}$$

where

$$v_{1i} = u_{1i} + \gamma_1 u_{2i}$$
$$v_{2i} = u_{2i} + \theta v_{1i}$$

The model is now in the form of model 5 discussed in the preceding section. One can use the ML method or the two-stage estimation method described for model 5. To see what parameters are estimable, define

$$\text{Cov}(v_1, v_2) = \begin{bmatrix} \lambda_1^2 & \lambda_{12} \\ & \lambda_2^2 \end{bmatrix}$$

The probit estimation of equation (5.73) gives us estimates of

$$\beta_1 \frac{\theta}{\lambda_2} \quad \text{and} \quad \beta_2 \frac{1 + \gamma_1 \theta}{\lambda_2}$$

The two-stage estimation of (5.72) gives us estimates of β_1, $\beta_2 \gamma_1$, δ_1, λ_{12}/λ_2, and λ_1^2. Note that if we allow u_1 and u_2 to be correlated, we shall not be able to exploit the estimates of λ_1^2 and λ_{12}/λ_2 to recover information on any other parameters.

Thus, the estimable parameters in equations (5.72) and (5.73) are

$$\beta_1, \quad \frac{\theta}{\lambda_1}, \quad \frac{\beta_2}{\lambda_2}, \quad \gamma_1 \lambda_2, \quad \text{and} \quad \delta_1$$

The fact that (a) the coefficient γ_1 of S_i in equation (5.67), (b) the coefficient β_2 in the sentiment equation (5.68), and (c) the coefficient θ in equation (5.69) are estimable only up to a scale factor makes intuitive sense and need not bother us. The two important questions are (a) whether or not passage of the law per se has any effect on the relative wages of blacks, that is, whether or not δ_1 in equation (5.67) is significant (this we can easily answer), and (b) whether or not logrolling has an effect on passage of the law, that is, whether or not θ in equation (5.69) is significant. We have to answer this question by testing whether or not θ/λ_2 is significantly different from zero.

In summary, a more fruitful way of looking at Heckman's model with a structural shift is to view it as a switching simultaneous-equations model, as given by equations (5.56) and (5.57). Viewed this way, the generalizations of this model are obvious. One can allow not just for a change in the intercept term but for changes in other coefficients as well. Thus, one can allow not just for *structural shift* but also for *structural change*. The conditions for logical consistency are now derived by noting the fact that we have two reduced-form expressions from the two simultaneous-equations systems, and the condition $y_2^* > 0$ as determined from the first system and $y_2^* < 0$ as determined from the second system should not be inconsistent. As an illustration, consider the model

$$\left.\begin{array}{l} y_1 = \gamma_1 y_2^* + u_1 \\ y_2^* = \gamma_2 y_1 + X_2\beta_2 + u_2 \end{array}\right\} \quad \text{if } y_2^* > 0 \qquad (5.74)$$

$$\left.\begin{array}{l} y_1 = \bar{\gamma}_1 y_2^* + u_1 \\ y_2^* = \gamma_2 y_1 + X_2\beta_2 + u_2 \end{array}\right\} \quad \text{if } y_2^* \leqslant 0 \qquad (5.75)$$

The equation system (5.74) leads to the condition

$$y_2^* > 0 \Rightarrow \frac{1}{1 - \gamma_1\gamma_2}(X_2\beta_2 + \gamma_2 u_1 + u_2) > 0 \qquad (5.76)$$

and equation system (5.75) leads to the condition

$$y_2^* \leqslant 0 \Rightarrow \frac{1}{1 - \bar{\gamma}_1\gamma_2}(X_2\beta_2 + \gamma_2 u_1 + u_2) \leqslant 0 \qquad (5.77)$$

Thus, unless $(1 - \gamma_1\gamma_2)$ and $(1 - \bar{\gamma}_1\gamma_2)$ are of the same sign, conditions (5.76) and (5.77) lead to contradictory results. Estimation of switching simultaneous systems and testing for structural change will be discussed in Chapters 7 and 8.

The point in this lengthy discussion is that mixed models with latent variables and their dichotomous realizations need special care in formulation. One cannot mechanically introduce the dummy variables and then impose a logical-consistency condition. In many cases, careful examination of the model will reveal a better formulation, and then the logical-consistency condition need not be imposed.[16] Sometimes a model does not have to be altered, only interpreted in a different light. As an illustration, let us consider the following problem, also considered by Heckman (1978a). Let there be two dichotomous variables Y_1 and Y_2 defined as follows:

$Y_1 = 1$ if the family has a child
$Y_1 = 0$ otherwise

$Y_2 = 1$ if the family uses contraceptives
$Y_2 = 0$ otherwise

The LLM is

$$P(Y_1, Y_2) = D^{-1}\exp(a_1 Y_1 + a_2 Y_2 + a_3 Y_1 Y_2)$$

where D^{-1} is the normalizing constant. Note that there are only three free parameters. Heckman rightly criticized this model, saying that because it models only purely statistical associations between the vari-

---

[16] Another example of this is given in section 10.10. There, a "coherency" condition appears in one formulation but does not appear in another more meaningful formulation.

ables Y_1 and Y_2, it cannot be used to study the effects of any policies. He suggested the bivariate normal model with structural shift. In this model we assume two underlying sentiments: Y_1^* and Y_2^*. We have $Y_1 = 1$ if and only if $Y_1^* > 0$ and $Y_2 = 1$ if and only if $Y_2^* > 0$. It may happen that because of unmeasured taste and knowledge factors, families more likely to use contraception are more likely not to have children. Hence, Y_1^* and Y_2^* are likely to be negatively correlated. There is, however, a second effect. For obvious reasons, families using birth control will have fewer children. Therefore, the model that Heckman formulated is

$$Y_1^* = X_1\alpha_1 + \beta_1 Y_2 + \gamma_1 Y_2^* + u_1$$
$$Y_2^* = X_2\alpha_2 + \beta_2 Y_2 + \gamma_2 Y_1^* + u_2 \qquad (5.78)$$

and we have to impose the logical-consistency condition $\beta_2 + \beta_1\gamma_2 = 0$. As seen earlier, this condition amounts to saying that there is no structural shift in the reduced-form equation for Y_2^*. We shall write the reduced forms (after normalizing the error variances to be 1) as

$$Y_1^* = X_1\Pi_{11}^* + X_2\Pi_{12}^* + Y_2\Pi_{13}^* + V_1$$
$$= b + Y_2\Pi_{13}^* + V_1 \quad \text{(say)}$$

and

$$Y_2^* = X_1\Pi_{21}^* + X_2\Pi_{22}^* + V_2 = c + V_2 \quad \text{(say)}$$
$$\text{Var}(V_1) = \text{Var}(V_2) = 1 \quad \text{and} \quad \text{Cov}(V_1, V_2) = \rho$$

Note that in the foregoing, b and c include the exogenous variables X_1 and X_2. Also, define $b^* = b + Y_2\Pi_{13}^*$, so that with no structural shift, $b^* = b$.

Denoting the bivariate normal distribution function of (V_1, V_2) by $F(\cdot, \cdot, \rho)$, we get

$$P_{11} = P(Y_1^* > 0, Y_2^* > 0) = F(-b^*, -c, \rho)$$
$$P_{01} = P(Y_1^* \leqslant 0, Y_2^* > 0) = F(b^*, -c, -\rho)$$
$$P_{10} = P(Y_1^* > 0, Y_2^* \leqslant 0) = F(-b^*, c, -\rho)$$
$$P_{00} = P(Y_1^* \leqslant 0, Y_2^* \leqslant 0) = F(b^*, c, \rho) \qquad (5.79)$$

Suppose now that the government forces all families to use contraceptives. The problem is to predict the effect of this policy on the probability of a family having no children. Because $P(Y_1 = 0) = P_{01} + P_{00}$, the normal model with structural shift gives this change in probability as

$$\Delta P(Y_1^* \leqslant 0) = [F(b+\Pi_{13}^*, -c, -\rho) + F(b+\Pi_{13}^*, c, \rho)]$$
$$- [F(b + Y_2\Pi_{13}^*, -c, -\rho) + F(b + Y_2\Pi_{13}^*, c, \rho)] \qquad (5.80)$$

The expression in the first bracket is obtained by setting $Y_2 = 1$ in the expressions for P_{01} and P_{00} in (5.79), because $Y_2=1$ if the government forces families to use contraceptives. If $\Pi^*_{13}=0$, this probability is zero. Thus, it is Π^*_{13} that enables us to measure the effect of this policy. According to the LLM, one can think of measuring the effect of this policy by the difference between the conditional and unconditional probabilities, that is,

$$\Delta P(Y_1=0) = \text{Prob}(Y_1=0\,|\,Y_2=1) - P(Y_1=0)$$

Returning to the model (5.78), it is easy to see that one does not need the involved model with a shift $\beta_2 Y_2$ in the Y^*_2 equation that needs justification regarding not only its inclusion but also its magnitude, namely, that $\beta_2 = -\beta_1\gamma_2$. The structure of the problem leads to the simple formulation

$$Y^*_1 = X_1\alpha_1 + \beta_1 Y_2 + u_1$$
$$Y^*_2 = X_2\alpha_2 + u_2 \tag{5.81}$$

Because u_1 and u_2 incorporate some unobserved taste and knowledge factors, they are correlated. Y_2 is included in the Y^*_1 equation to capture the effect that contraception has on child-bearing. The model (5.81) is now in the form of a simple recursive model (model 6 discussed in the preceding section). The formula (5.80) still holds, with $\Pi^*_{13}=\beta_2$, $b=X_1\alpha_1$, and $c=X_2\alpha_2$. Again, one does not need a model with structural shifts in both equations with a logical-consistency condition superimposed. Heckman was right in arguing that the LLM is not appropriate for this problem. But to capture the arguments in his example, one likewise does not need the model with structural shift with a logical-consistency condition imposed.

The preceding discussion does not mean that the formulation in model (5.78) is not useful. But one needs a substantive example to show its applicability. In the two illustrations we have given here, the structure of the problem leads to alternative models wherein no logical-consistency condition arises.

Returning to the empirical example on measuring the effects of fair-employment laws, although the model suggested by Heckman is designed to estimate the effect of the fair-employment law per se net of sentiment, in the empirical results presented by Heckman (1976a) the latent variable that accounts for passage of the law does not appear in the relative-wage equation. In the notation of (5.52) and (5.53), the model estimated is one with $\gamma_1=\gamma_2=\delta_2=0$ (i.e., model 5 of the preceding section). It is

$$Y_1 = \delta_1 Y_2 + X_1\beta_1 + u_1$$
$$Y^*_2 = X_2\beta_2 + u_2$$

$$Y_2 = 1 \quad \text{if } Y_2^* > 0$$
$$Y_2 = 0 \quad \text{otherwise}$$

where Y_1 are wages of nonwhites relative to wages of whites and X_1 is a set of explanatory variables in the wage equation.

The endogenous-dummy-variable formulation has also been used by Edwards (1978) to estimate the effects of compulsory-school-enrollment laws. She first estimated an equation of the form

$$Y_{1i} = \alpha' X_i + \beta D_i + u_i \tag{5.82}$$

where

$$Y_{1i} = \log[ER_i/(1 - ER_i)]$$
$$ER_i = \text{age- and sex-specific enrollment rate in state } i$$
$$D_1 = 1 \quad \text{if the state has a compulsory schooling law}$$
$$D_i = 0 \quad \text{otherwise}$$
$$X_i = \text{are some explanatory variables}$$

D_i is initially treated as exogenous. Estimation of this exogenous-dummy-variable model helps us predict by how much the enrollment rates will increase if the states that do not have compulsory-schooling laws pass such laws.

After estimating this model, Edwards added an equation to describe the behavior underlying the passage of the law:

$$Y_{2i} = \gamma' Z_i + e_i$$
$$D_i = 1 \quad \text{if } Y_{2i} > 0$$
$$D_i = 0 \quad \text{otherwise} \tag{5.83}$$

Y_{2i} is the net benefit from passage of the law, and Z_i are the explanatory variables measuring benefits and costs. She further assumed u_i and e_i to be independently and normally distributed. (Footnote 38, p. 218, said that attempts to estimate a model where these errors were correlated were unsuccessful.)

Note that if Y_{2i} were indeed observed, and it rather than D_i were included as an explanatory variable in equation (5.82), then the assumption that u_i and e_i are independent implies that the OLS estimation of (5.82) gives efficient estimates. Thus, the endogeneity in this case arises from the fact that Y_{2i} is observed only as a dichotomous variable, not from any correlation between u_i and e_i or the fact that Y_{1i} influences Y_{2i}.

The assumption that u_i and e_i are independent results in a very simple estimation procedure. The coefficients in (5.83) can be estimated by a simple probit model. The coefficients in (5.82) can be estimated by a weighted least-squares method.

The estimation of this simultaneous-equations model did not produce any meaningful results. Many of the explanatory variables in (5.83) had wrong signs. So, in effect, there was not much that could be learned about what leads to passage of the law. On the other hand, because the estimate of the coefficient of D_i (estimated by the two-stage method) was smaller in the simultaneous-equations model, Edwards concluded that the effects of compulsory-schooling laws on enrollment rates were overestimated in an equation that treated the passage of the law as exogenous.

Note that the coefficient of the dummy variable need not always be overestimated in the exogenous-dummy-variable model. The simultaneous-equations bias can go either way.

5.9   Unobserved latent variables and dummy indicators

In the example in the preceding section concerning measuring the effects of fair-employment laws, we noted that the formulation led to a model with two unobserved latent variables and a dummy indicator variable. We shall now discuss models of this nature. The models are extensions of the MIMIC models by Jöreskog and Goldberger (1975) to the case of dummy indicators.

Let y be a vector of p dichotomous variables and y^* the vector of underlying latent variables, so that

$$y_i = 1 \quad \text{if } y_i^* > 0$$
$$y_i = 0 \quad \text{otherwise} \quad (i = 1, 2, \ldots, p)$$

and y^* depends on a vector of m unobservable variables η through the relation

$$y^* = \alpha + \Lambda\eta + \epsilon^* \tag{5.84}$$

where $\alpha(p \times 1)$ and $\Lambda(p \times m)$ are fixed parameters and $p \geqslant m$ and $\epsilon^* \sim N(O, I)$. We also assume that the unobservable variables η are related to a $q \times 1$ vector of observable causal variables x by the relation

$$B\eta + \Gamma x = \xi \tag{5.85}$$

where $B(m \times m)$ and $\Gamma(m \times q)$ are fixed parameters and $\xi \sim N(O, \psi)$ and ψ is an $m \times m$ matrix. This general model has been analyzed in Muthén (1979).

One important assumption that is made is that the latent variables are assumed to account for all the interdependencies among the indicators, so that, conditional on η, the y_i^* are independent.

The reduced form between the observables is

$$y^* = \alpha + \Pi x + \epsilon \qquad (5.86)$$

where

$$\Pi = -\Lambda B^{-1}\Gamma$$
$$\epsilon = \epsilon^* + \Lambda B^{-1}\xi \qquad (5.87)$$

and

$$E(\epsilon\epsilon'\,|\,x) = \Sigma = \Lambda B^{-1}\psi B^{-1}{}'\Lambda' + I \qquad (5.88)$$

Given observations on $Y = (y_1, \ldots, y_p)$ the exogenous variables x, and the structure (5.84) and (5.85), our objective is to estimate the parameters α, Λ, B, Γ, and ψ.

Because y^* are observed only as dummy variables, the parameters α and Π are estimable only up to a scale factor. Define a diagonal matrix D with the ith diagonal term $1/\lambda_i$, where $\lambda_i^2 = \mathrm{Var}(\epsilon_i)$. Then the estimable parameters are

$$\alpha^* = D\alpha, \quad \Pi^* = D\Pi, \quad \text{and} \quad \Sigma^* = D\Sigma D$$

From the estimates of α^*, Π^*, and Σ^* we have to obtain estimates of the structural parameters α, Λ, B, Γ, and ψ using relations (5.87) and (5.88). Note that the assumption of independent indicators can be relaxed and the covariance matrix of ϵ^* substituted in place of I in (5.88), but this can be accomplished only by setting some other parameters to zero.

The general identification rules for this model are difficult to establish. Muthén (1979) gave a set of sufficient conditions and also gave an example in which they are not necessary. Because a detailed discussion of the model would get us into some cumbersome notation, and because no necessary and sufficient conditions can be derived, we shall not pursue it here. The example presented in the preceding section illustrates how one can see which parameters are estimable. We shall present some other examples that illustrate the problems involved. The important thing to note is that, as with all latent-variable models, these models result in cross-equation constraints, and it is this aspect that differentiates them from the models considered in earlier sections.

Even if ϵ^* in (5.84) are assumed to be independent, the residuals ϵ in (5.86) are not. Thus, when we are estimating the reduced-form parameters in (5.86), we end up with a multivariate probit model and p-variate integrals, where p is the number of dichotomous indicators. As is well known, if $p > 2$, this results in severe computational problems. A very and Hotz (1981) suggested an instrumental-variable estimation method that is based on methods developed by Hansen (1982). The method proceeds as follows: Consider the nonlinear regression functions

$$y_i = E(y_i \mid x) + v_i \quad (i = 1, 2, \ldots, p)$$
$$= P(y_i = 1 \mid x) + v_i$$
$$= \Phi(\alpha_i^* + \pi_i^{*\prime}x) + v_i \tag{5.89}$$

where α_i^* is the ith element of α^* and $\pi_i^{*\prime}$ is the ith row of Π^*. We also define $Z_{jk} = y_j y_k$ $(j = 2, 3, \ldots, p, \ k = 1, 2, \ldots, j-1)$:

$$Z_{jk} = E(Z_{jk} \mid x) + w_{jk}$$
$$= P(y_j = 1, \ y_k = 1 \mid x) + w_{jk}$$
$$= F[(\alpha_j^* + \pi_j^{*\prime}x), (\alpha_k^* + \pi_k^{*\prime}x), \rho_{jk}] + w_{jk} \tag{5.90}$$

where $F[a, b, \rho_{jk}]$ is the standardized bivariate normal distribution function with correlation ρ_{jk}, which is the jkth element of Λ^*. Thus, we have p univariate expectation-function equations and $p(p-1)/2$ bivariate equations for a total of $L = p(p+1)/2$. The univariate expectation equations involve the parameters α^* and π^*, and the bivariate expectation equations involve the parameters Σ^* as well. We define

$$u = \begin{bmatrix} v_i \\ w_{jk} \end{bmatrix} \quad \text{and} \quad Z^* = \begin{bmatrix} y_i \\ Z_{jk} \end{bmatrix}$$

as $L \times 1$ vectors. By definition, the residuals u will be orthogonal to each of the independent variables in x. Technically, u is orthogonal to any function of x's. However, Avery and Hotz restricted their attention to x itself. The orthogonality conditions are

$$E(u \otimes x) = 0 \quad \text{and} \quad E(u) = 0 \tag{5.91}$$

where $\otimes$ denotes Kronecker product.

The principle underlying the estimation is to select those estimates of the unknown parameters that set sample analogues to (5.91) to zero (or as close to zero as possible). Hansen (1982) showed that if identification conditions are met, such estimators will be consistent and asymptotically normal, although not efficient. If the number of orthogonality conditions (5.91) is greater than the number of parameters to be estimated, we have to use some weighting schemes. Hansen described the following optimal weighting schemes:

Let θ be the set of parameters to be estimated; θ consists of all the distinct parameters in α^*, Π^*, and Σ^*. Note that u is a function of Z^*, x, and θ. Consider a set of N observations. Define

$$u_n = u(Z_n^*, x_n, \theta) \quad (n = 1, 2, \ldots, N)$$

and $g_n(\theta) = u_n \otimes (x_n, 1)$ as the vector of orthogonality conditions (5.91) corresponding to the nth observation. Next, define

$$g(\theta) = \frac{1}{N} \sum_{n=1}^{N} g_n(\theta)$$

Estimate θ by minimizing $g(\theta)'g(\theta)$. Hansen (1982) showed that the resulting estimator $\hat{\theta}$ will be asymptotically normal, with mean θ_0 (the true parameter value) and covariance matrix

$$V_1 = (G'G)^{-1}G'V_0G(G'G)^{-1}$$

where

$$G = E\left(\frac{\partial g_n(\theta_0)}{\partial \theta}\right) \quad \text{and} \quad V_0 = E[g_n(\theta_0)g_n(\theta_0)']$$

We can consistently estimate these values by their corresponding sample quantities:

$$\hat{G} = \frac{1}{N} \sum_{n=1}^{N} \frac{\partial g_n(\theta)}{\partial \theta}$$

$$\hat{V} = \frac{1}{N} \sum_{n=1}^{N} g_n(\theta)g_n(\theta)'$$

Instead of minimizing $g(\theta)'g(\theta)$, we can minimize a weighted function, $g(\theta)'Wg(\theta)$. The covariance matrix of this weighted estimator $\hat{\theta}_2$ is $V_2 = (G'WG)^{-1}G'WV_0WG(G'WG)^{-1}$. Clearly, the optimal weighting matrix is V_0^{-1}, and the resulting estimator $\hat{\theta}_0$ has a covariance matrix

$$V^* = (G'V_0^{-1}G)^{-1}$$

Because V_0 depends on θ_0, it will not be known, but V_0 can be estimated from some initial parameter estimates, say $\hat{\theta}_1$.

The advantage of the foregoing estimators suggested by Avery and Hotz, called OC (orthogonality condition) estimators, is their computational tractability. In addition to the calculation of univariate and bivariate cumulative normal distribution functions, we need the first derivatives of Φ and F in equations (5.89) and (5.90). Such derivatives are presented in the Appendix at the end of the book.

Note, however, that the foregoing discussion refers to estimation of the reduced-form system (5.86), and there still remains the problem of getting estimates of the structural parameters from the estimates of α^*, Π^*, and Σ^*.

As mentioned earlier, general conditions for identification in this model are difficult to derive. However, one can examine particular cases with ease, as is illustrated by the example in the preceding section. We shall illustrate this with reference to the model on agricultural practices of Filipino farmers considered by Nerlove and Press (1973).

Define X^* as an index of the degree of adoption of modern agricultural methods. We have two indicators for X^*: output, y_1, which is a continuous variable, and use of improved seed, y_2, which is a dichotomous variable. Our objective is to test whether or not certain variables, such as ownership of farm, education of farmer, age of farmer, and so forth, affect X^*. We can formulate the model as

$$X^* = \gamma'Z + u$$
$$y_1 = \alpha_1 + \beta_1 X^* + u_1$$
$$y_2^* = \alpha_2 + \beta_2 X^* + u_2$$
$$y_2 = 1 \quad \text{if } y_2^* > 0$$
$$y_2 = 0 \quad \text{otherwise}$$

We shall assume that all residuals (u, u_1, u_2) are normally distributed. Z includes the explanatory variables that determine good agricultural practice, denoted here by X^*.

Because y_2^* is observed as a dummy variable, we assume $\text{Var}(u_2) = 1$. Also, because X^* is unobserved, we need to normalize by assuming $\gamma'\gamma = 1$ or $\gamma'Z'Z\gamma = 1$ or $\text{Var}(u) = 1$. An alternative (though rather unnatural) normalization is to set $\beta_1 = 1$ (or $\beta_2 = 1$). In what follows, we shall assume $\beta_1 = 1$. The purpose here is to illustrate how one determines what parameters are estimable. The analysis is similar for the other normalizations.

Define $\text{Var}(u) = \sigma^2$ and $\text{Var}(u_1) = \sigma_1^2$. We shall also assume $\text{Cov}(u, u_1) = \text{Cov}(u_1, u_2) = \text{Cov}(u, u_2) = 0$. The reduced-form equations are

$$y_1 = \alpha_1 + \gamma'Z + u + u_1$$
$$y_2^* = \alpha_2 + \beta_2\gamma'Z + u_2 + \beta_2 u \tag{5.92}$$

Because $\text{Var}(u_2 + \beta_2 u) = 1 + \beta_2^2\sigma^2$, we write this as

$$y_2^{**} = \frac{\alpha_2}{(1 + \beta_2^2\sigma^2)^{1/2}} + \frac{\beta_2}{(1 + \beta_2^2\sigma^2)^{1/2}}\gamma'Z + v_2 \tag{5.93}$$

where

$$v_2 = \frac{u_2 + \beta_2 u}{(1 + \beta_2^2\sigma^2)^{1/2}} \quad \text{and} \quad \text{Var}(v_2) = 1$$

Equations (5.92) and (5.93) are now in a form suitable for estimation. One can use the ML method to estimate the parameters. To see what parameters are estimable, consider first the OLS estimation of equation (5.92). This gives us estimates of α_1, γ, and $\sigma^2 + \sigma_1^2$. The probit ML estimation of (5.93) gives us estimates of $\alpha_2 / (1 + \beta_2^2 \sigma^2)^{1/2}$ and $\beta_2 / (1 + \beta_2^2 \sigma^2)^{1/2}$ if we use $\hat{\gamma}'Z$ as the explanatory variable, where $\hat{\gamma}$ is the estimate of γ obtained from the OLS estimation of (5.92). To obtain estimates of α_2, β_2, and σ^2, we need to exploit the covariance between the residuals in (5.92) and (5.93):

$$\text{Cov}(u + u_1, v_2) = \frac{\beta_2 \sigma^2}{(1 + \beta_2^2 \sigma^2)^{1/2}}$$

because $\text{Cov}(u_1, u_2) = 0$. We can obtain an estimate of the covariance between the residuals in (5.92) and (5.93), without going through the ML method, as follows. Note that

$$E(y_1 \mid y_2 = 1) = \alpha_1 + \gamma'Z + E(u + u_1 \mid y_2^{**} > 0)$$

$$= \alpha_1 + \gamma'Z + \sigma_{12}^* \frac{\phi(\Delta)}{1 - \Phi(\Delta)}$$

where

$$\Delta = -\frac{\alpha_2}{(1 + \beta^2 \sigma_2^2)^{1/2}} - \frac{\beta_2}{(1 + \beta_2 \sigma^2)^{1/2}} \gamma'Z$$

and σ_{12}^* is the covariance desired. Thus, we can get consistent estimates of all the parameters $(\alpha_1, \beta_2, \alpha_2, \gamma, \sigma_1^2, \text{ and } \sigma^2)$ by using least squares and probit methods. One can use these initial consistent estimates in the iterative solution of the ML equations. Note that the assumption $\text{Cov}(u_1, u_2) = 0$ is crucial in this model with two indicators. With more indicators, it is possible to introduce correlations among some of the residuals. Suppose that in the previous example we have another indicator y_3, whether or not the farmer used chemicals (fertilizer, pesticides, etc.). We can define

$$y_3^* = \alpha_3 + \beta_3 X^* + u_3$$
$$y_3 = 1 \quad \text{if } y_3^* > 0$$
$$y_3 = 0 \quad \text{otherwise}$$

Again, because y_3^* is observed only as a dichotomous variable, we assume $\text{Var}(u_3) = 1$. The reduced-form equation is

$$y_3^* = \alpha_3 + \beta_3 \gamma'Z + u_3 + \beta_3 u$$

Because $\text{Var}(u_3 + \beta_3 u) = 1 + \beta_3^2 \sigma^2$, we write this as

$$y_3^{**} = \frac{\alpha_3}{(1 + \beta_3^2 \sigma^2)^{1/2}} + \frac{\beta_3}{(1 + \beta_3^2 \sigma^2)^{1/2}} \gamma'Z + v_3 \qquad (5.94)$$

where

$$v_3 = \frac{u_3 + \beta_3 u}{(1 + \beta_3^2 \sigma^2)^{1/2}}$$

has variance 1. Assuming, as before, that u, u_1, and u_2 are mutually uncorrelated, we can get estimates of α_1, α_2, γ, β_2, σ_1^2, and σ^2 with the procedure just described. The probit estimation of equation (5.94) now gives us estimates of α_3 and β_3. Now we have $\text{Cov}(u + u_1, v_3)$ and $\text{Cov}(v_2, v_3)$ to exploit. These will permit us to estimate two of the three covariances $\text{Cov}(u, u_3)$, $\text{Cov}(u_1, u_3)$, and $\text{Cov}(u_2, u_3)$. The number of covariances we have to set equal to zero in the case of this qualitative-indicator model is the same as in the case of the continuous-indicator models. The only difference that is introduced by the fact that y_2^* and y_3^* are observed only as qualitative variables is that we have to set $\text{Var}(u_2) = \text{Var}(u_3) = 1$.

The example concerning agricultural practices of Filipino farmers also illustrates several other problems. Even assuming that there is only one underlying latent variable, X^* (good agricultural practice), the indicators are not independent; for example, y_2^* and y_3^* (whether or not to use improved seed, whether or not to use fertilizer and pesticides) are interrelated. The latent-variable model we have been discussing is one with several latent variables and independent indicators. The example of the Filipino farmers is one with perhaps only one latent variable, but correlated indicators. Further, the dummy variables y_2 and y_3 also should be included in the output equation (5.87).

We shall not go into great detail in estimating this model with correlated indicators. We shall briefly review the findings of Nerlove and Press (1973) and Maddala and Trost (1980). Nerlove and Press estimated a log-linear model with four dichotomous variables defined as follows:

> CHM = 1 if chemicals (fertilizers or insecticides) were
> used (0 otherwise)
>
> LAND = 1 if mechanized methods of land preparation
> were used (0 otherwise)
>
> HYBRID = 1 if a high-yield variety (HYV) was used
> (0 otherwise)
>
> PLNTWD = 1 if modern methods of planting and weeding
> were used (0 otherwise)

There were also exogenous variables in their model:

> AGE = farmer's age, in years
> SCHOOL = highest educational level attained, in years

OWNER = tenure status (1 if owner or part owner, 0 otherwise)

AREA = size of farm, in hectares

IRRIG = 1 if farm is in irrigated area (0 otherwise)

PUMP = 1 if farm is in an area where there is pump irrigation (0 otherwise)

COOP = 1 if farmer is a cooperator (0 otherwise)

Nerlove and Press estimated a LLM with the four main effects being linear functions of the exogenous variables, and the six bivariate interactions being constant (not dependent on the exogenous variables). The three-variable and four-variable interactions were assumed to be zero. Their empirical analysis showed IRRIG, COOP, and AREA as highly significant. PUMP was significant at the 10% level, but not the 5% level, and the remaining variables were not significant even at the 20% level. It was rather disappointing to find that SCHOOL and AGE were not significant.

Maddala and Trost estimated the latent-variable model discussed earlier using three dichotomous indicators, CHM, LAND, and HYBRID. They also used an output equation and introduced the dummy variables and their interactions in the output equation (but these were not significant). Note that for the ML estimation of the model with three dummy indicators, we have to evaluate trivariate integrals. The introduction of the dummy variables and their interactions in the output equation does not cause any extra problems, because the structure of the model is the same as that of model 5 in section 5.7 (i.e., it is a recursive model). To avoid the problems of triple integrals, Maddala and Trost estimated the model excluding the residual u in equation (5.84), and they later verified that the results are not much different if the residual is included and the model is estimated using the output equation with one dummy indicator at a time (this procedure involves only univariate integrals). Dropping the residual u in X^* simplifies the ML estimation considerably, because the residuals in the different equations are now independent, and only cross-equation constraints need be taken into account. With the independence assumption, the estimation is further simplified if we make the logit specification for the dummy-variable equations, and this is what they did. By testing the significance of the coefficients, such as β_1 in (5.85), β_2 in (5.86), and β_3 in (5.90), we can examine which of the variables are good indicators of the variable X^*. The results showed that all the β coefficients were significant, and thus the three dummy variables are good indicators of the unobservable variable X^* (adoption of modern agricultural methods). Among the variables determining X^*, the

variables IRRIG and COOP were significant and had the expected signs
(+ and +). The variable SCHOOL was significant, but its magnitude
was small. AGE (experience) was not significant. Thus the results, except
for the variable SCHOOL, were the same as those obtained by Nerlove
and Press, although the focus of the analysis was different.

Although the results are apparently the same, the focus of analysis in
the log-linear model and that in the latent-variable model are different.
In the log-linear model we are interested in knowing which of the
explanatory variables are significant determinants of the different main
effects and interactions. In the latent-variable model we are interested in
the effects of the different exogenous variables on the unobserved latent
variables, as well as in testing which of the observed dependent variables
are significant indicators of the unobserved latent variables. Very often
the latter question is more interesting. As yet another instance of comparison between the two approaches, we shall briefly review the results
of Maddala and Trost (1981a), who estimated a latent-variable model
for the Vrbsky data analyzed by Nerlove and Press (1976). Vrbsky's data
are from a survey conducted in January 1975 concerning sexual attitudes
of undergraduates at Northwestern University. Data were collected on
four variables: HOMO, ABORT, BCPER, and MAST, which involved
yes or no answers on questions regarding attitudes toward homosex-
uality, abortion, contraceptives, and masturbation, respectively. (A yes
answer denotes sexual permissiveness.) Nerlove and Press (1976) analyzed
these data using multivariate log-linear probability models. They considered the interrelationships between the four attitudinal variables
describing sexual permissiveness (in their analysis, no exogenous variables were used).

Maddala and Trost (1981a) analyzed these data assuming an underlying latent variable X^* that denotes sexual permissiveness and treating
HOMO, ABORT, and MAST as dummy indicators of X^*. (They
dropped BCPER from their analysis.) They found that each of the
dummy variables is a good indicator of X^* (coefficient significant at the
5% or 1% level). As for the determinants of X^*, the religious variables
were significant (more religiousness meant less sexual permissiveness),
but the income variable and the marital status of parents (together,
divorced, separated, etc.) were not significant. The other significant coefficients indicated that juniors and seniors were more permissive than
freshmen and sophomores and that whites were more permissive than
nonwhites.

The foregoing examples illustrate estimations of some simple latent-
variable models that are subject to several limitations. The dummy indicators are all dichotomous. Lee (1982b) considered a model with poly-

chotomous indicators. Another assumption we have often made is that the indicators are independent; however, we have discussed what is involved in relaxing this assumption. Finally, we have not considered a model in which the dummy indicators occur as explanatory variables in the other equations. For instance, in the farming example, the actual observed dummy variables and their interactions are logical candidates for inclusion in the output (continuous indicator) function. Such models can be called interrelated-indicator models with shift variables, and they need further study.

5.10   Summary and conclusions

In this chapter we have reviewed the different methods of analyzing multivariate qualitative data. We have seen that the alternative approaches fall into the categories of those that assume some underlying continuous variables (an approach going back to Pearson, 1900) and those that make no such assumption (an approach going back to Yule, 1900). We have not given much attention to the detailed problems in the latter approach and have given only the main ideas behind the LLM, CLM, RLM, CLLM, RLLM, and other models. There are detailed books on these subjects, such as those of Bishop et al. (1975), Fienberg (1978), and Haberman (1974), as well as the several studies of Goodman (1970, 1971, 1972, 1973) and Nerlove and Press (1973, 1976, 1980). As for the latent-variable approach, we have discussed (a) the usual simultaneous-equations model, (b) the simultaneous-equations model with structural shift, (c) simultaneous-equations models with indicators for linear functions of the latent variables, and (d) models of type (c) with dummy shift variables. We have also outlined some directions in which these models need to be extended.

CHAPTER 6

Censored and truncated regression models

6.1   Introduction

In Chapter 2 we considered regression models in which the dependent variables assumed discrete values. In this chapter we shall consider regression models in which the dependent variable is observed in only some of the ranges. We shall first explain the difference between truncation and censoring and then consider the analysis of this problem in the regression context.

6.2   Censored and truncated variables

Suppose y^* has a normal distribution, with mean μ and variance σ^2. Suppose we consider a sample of size n $(y_1^*, y_2^*, \ldots, y_n^*)$ and record only those values of y^* greater than a constant c. For those values of $y^* \leqslant c$, we record the value c. The observations are

$$y_i = y_i^* \quad \text{if } y_i^* > c$$
$$y_i = c \quad \text{otherwise}$$

The resulting sample $y_1, y_2, \ldots, y_n$ is said to be a *censored sample*. For the observations $y_i = c$, all we know is that $y_i^* \leqslant c$; that is,

$$P(y_i = c) = P(y_i^* \leqslant c)$$

Hence, the likelihood function for estimation of the parameters μ and σ^2 is

$$L(\mu, \sigma^2 \mid y) = \prod_{y_i^* > c} \frac{1}{\sigma} \phi\left(\frac{y_i - \mu}{\sigma}\right) \prod_{y_i^* \leqslant c} \Phi\left(\frac{c - \mu}{\sigma}\right)$$

149

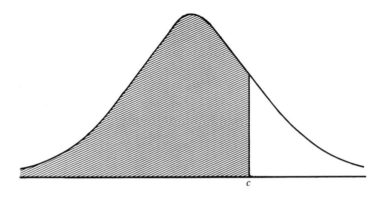

Figure 6.1. Truncated normal distribution

where $\phi(\cdot)$ and $\Phi(\cdot)$ are, respectively, the density function and the distribution function of the standard normal.

Now suppose that before the sample is drawn we truncate the distribution of y^* at the point $y^* = c$, so that no observations are drawn for $y^* > c$. All observations come from the shaded area in Figure 6.1. The density function of the truncated normal distribution from which the samples are drawn is

$$f(y^* \mid y^* < c) = \frac{1}{\sigma} \phi\left(\frac{y^* - \mu}{\sigma}\right) \Big/ \Phi\left(\frac{c - \mu}{\sigma}\right) \quad (-\infty < y^* \leq c)$$

$\Phi[(c - \mu)/\sigma]$ is the normalizing constant, because the integral of the numerator over the range $-\infty < y^* \leq c$ is $\Phi[(c - \mu)/\sigma]$.

A sample from this truncated normal distribution is called a *truncated sample*. An example of this is a sample drawn from families with incomes less than, say, \$10,000.

In practice we can have samples that are doubly truncated, doubly censored, truncated-censored, and so forth. As an example of a truncated-censored sample, consider truncation at the level c_1 and censoring at the level c_2 $(c_2 < c_1)$; that is, only samples of y^* with $y^* \leq c_1$ are drawn, and among these samples only values of $y^* > c_2$ are recorded. For those observations $y^* \leq c_2$, we record c_2; that is,

$$y_i = y_i^* \quad \text{if } y_i^* > c_2$$
$$y_i = c_2 \quad \text{otherwise}$$

The likelihood function for this model is

$$L(\mu, \sigma^2 \mid y_1, y_2, \ldots, y_n) = \left[\Phi\left(\frac{c_1 - \mu}{\sigma}\right)\right]^{-n}$$

$$\times \prod_{y_i^* > c_2} \frac{1}{\sigma} \phi\left(\frac{y_i - \mu}{\sigma}\right) \prod_{y_i^* \leqslant c_2} \Phi\left(\frac{c_2 - \mu}{\sigma}\right)$$

One can consider further combinations of double-truncation and double-censoring, but the details are straightforward. We shall now consider estimation of such models in the regression context, that is, where the mean μ is a linear function $\beta'x$ of explanatory variables x.

6.3   The tobit (censored regression) model

The tobit model is defined as follows:

$$y_i = \beta'x_i + u_i \quad \text{if RHS} > 0$$
$$y_i = 0 \quad \text{otherwise} \tag{6.1}$$

β is a $k \times 1$ vector of unknown parameters; x_i is a $k \times 1$ vector of known constants; u_i are residuals that are independently and normally distributed, with mean zero and a common variance σ^2.

Our problem is to estimate β and σ^2 on the basis of N observations on y_i and x_i. This model was first studied by Tobin (1958). As discussed in Chapter 1, it is a censored normal regression model. As such, its estimation is related to the estimation of the censored and truncated normal distributions.

The literature on estimation of the parameters of the truncated normal distribution is extensive. However, it was Tobin who first discussed this problem in the regression context. Because he related his study to the literature on probit analysis, his model was nicknamed the tobit model (Tobin's probit) by Goldberger (1964).[1]

For the model considered in equation (6.1), let N_0 be the numer of observations for which $y_i = 0$, and N_1 the number of observations for which $y_i > 0$. Also, without any loss of generality, assume that the N_1 nonzero observations for y_i occur first. For convenience, we define the following:[2]

$$F_i = F(\beta'x_i, \sigma^2) = \int_{-\infty}^{\beta'x_i} \frac{1}{\sigma(2\Pi)^{1/2}} e^{-t^2/2\sigma^2} dt \tag{6.2}$$

$$f_i = f(\beta'x_i, \sigma^2) = \frac{1}{\sigma(2\Pi)^{1/2}} e^{-(1/2\sigma^2)(\beta'x_i)^2} \tag{6.3}$$

[1] Presumably there is no connection with the prophet Tobit or the book of Tobit in the Apocrypha.
[2] The notation here follows closely that of Amemiya (1973) and Fair (1977).

$$\Phi_i = F_i = \int_{-\infty}^{\beta'x_i/\sigma} \frac{1}{(2\Pi)^{1/2}} e^{-t^2/2} dt \tag{6.4}$$

$$\phi_i = \sigma f_i = \frac{1}{(2\Pi)^{1/2}} e^{-(\beta'x_i)^2/2\sigma^2} \tag{6.5}$$

ϕ_i and Φ_i are, respectively, the density function and distribution function of the standard normal evaluated at $\beta'x_i/\sigma$.

$$\gamma_i = \frac{\phi_i}{1 - \Phi_i} \tag{6.6}$$

$Y_1' = (y_1, y_2, \ldots, y_{N_1})$ is a $1 \times N_1$ vector of N_1 nonzero observations on y_i

$X_1' = (x_1, x_2, \ldots, x_{N_1})$ is a $k \times N_1$ matrix of values of x_i for nonzero y_i

$X_0' = (x_{N_1+1}, \ldots, x_N)$ is a $k \times N_0$ matrix of values of x_i for $y_i = 0$

$\gamma_0' = (\gamma_{N_1+1}, \ldots, \gamma_N)$ is a $1 \times N_0$ vector of values of γ_i for $y_i = 0$ $\qquad$ (6.7)

For the observations y_i that are zero, all we know is that[3]

$$\text{Prob}(y_i=0) = \text{Prob}(u_i<-\beta'x_i) = (1-F_i)$$

For the observations y_i that are greater than zero, we have

$$\text{Prob}(y_i>0) \cdot f(y_i|y_i>0) = F_i \frac{f(y_i - \beta'x_i, \sigma^2)}{F_i}$$

$$= \frac{1}{(2\Pi\sigma^2)^{1/2}} e^{-(1/2\sigma^2)(y_i - \beta'x_i)^2}$$

Hence, the likelihood function is

$$L = \prod_0 (1 - F_i) \prod_1 \frac{1}{(2\Pi\sigma^2)^{1/2}} e^{-(1/2\sigma^2)(y_i - \beta'x_i)^2}$$

where the first product is over the N_0 observations for which $y_i=0$ and the second product is over the N_1 observations for which $y_i>0$.

$$\log L = \sum_0 \log(1 - F_i) + \sum_1 \log\left(\frac{1}{(2\Pi\sigma^2)^{1/2}}\right) - \sum_1 \frac{1}{2\sigma^2}(y_i - \beta'x_i)^2 \tag{6.8}$$

[3] Because u has a symmetric distribution,

$$\text{Prob}(u_i<-\beta'x_i) = \int_{-\infty}^{-\beta'x_i} f(u) \, du = \int_{\beta'x_i}^{\infty} f(u) \, du = 1 - F(\beta'x_i) = 1 - F_i$$

In what follows, the summation Σ_0 is over the N_0 observations for which $y_i = 0$, and the summation Σ_1 is over the N_1 observations for which $y_i > 0$.

We now write down the first and second derivatives of $\log L$ with respect to β and σ^2. We use the following:

$$\frac{\partial F_i}{\partial \beta} = f_i x_i$$

$$\frac{\partial F_i}{\partial \sigma^2} = -\frac{1}{2\sigma^2} \beta' x_i f_i$$

$$\frac{\partial f_i}{\partial \beta} = -\frac{1}{\sigma^2} \beta' x_i f_i x_i$$

$$\frac{\partial f_i}{\partial \sigma^2} = \frac{(\beta' x_i)^2 - \sigma^2}{2\sigma^4} f_i \tag{6.9}$$

Using these, we get the first-order conditions for a maximum as

$$\frac{\partial \log L}{\partial \beta} = -\sum_0 \frac{f_i x_i}{1 - F_i} + \frac{1}{\sigma^2} \sum_1 (y_i - \beta' x_i) x_i = 0 \tag{6.10}$$

$$\frac{\partial \log L}{\partial \sigma^2} = \frac{1}{2\sigma^2} \sum_0 \frac{\beta' x_i f_i}{1 - F_i} - \frac{N_1}{2\sigma^2} + \frac{1}{2\sigma^4} \sum_1 (y_i - \beta' x_i)^2 = 0 \tag{6.11}$$

Premultiplying (6.10) by $\beta'/2\sigma^2$ and adding the result to (6.11), we get

$$\sigma^2 = \frac{1}{N_1} \sum_1 (y_i - \beta' x_i) y_i = \frac{Y_1'(Y_1 - X_1\beta)}{N_1} \tag{6.12}$$

using the notations in (6.7).

Also, after multiplying throughout by σ, equation (6.10) can be written as

$$-X_0'\gamma_0 + \frac{1}{\sigma} X_1'(Y_1 - X_1\beta) = 0 \tag{6.13}$$

or

$$\beta = (X_1'X_1)^{-1}X_1'Y_1 - \sigma(X_1'X_1)^{-1}X_0'\gamma_0 \tag{6.14}$$

$$= \beta_{LS} - \sigma(X_1'X_1)^{-1}X_0'\gamma_0 \tag{6.15}$$

where β_{LS} is the least-squares estimator for β obtained from the N_1 nonzero observations on y.

Equation (6.15) shows the relationship between the maximum-likelihood estimator for β and the least-squares estimator obtained from the nonzero observations on y.

Fair (1977) suggested an iteration method for obtaining the maximum-likelihood estimates of β and σ^2 using equation (6.15).[4] The method he suggested is the following:

Step 1: Compute β_{LS}, and calculate $(X_1'X_1)^{-1}X_0$.

Step 2: Choose a value of β, say $\beta^{(1)}$, and compute σ^2 from (6.12). If this value of σ^2 is less than or equal to zero, take for the value of σ^2 some small positive number. Let $\sigma^{(1)}$ denote the square root of this chosen value of σ^2.

Step 3: Compute the vector γ_0 using $\beta^{(1)}$ and $\sigma^{(1)}$. Denote this by $\gamma_0^{(1)}$. (A standard FORTRAN function is available to compute the distribution function Φ_i.)

Step 4: Compute β from equation (6.15) using $\sigma^{(1)}$ and $\gamma_0^{(1)}$. Denote this value by $\tilde{\beta}^{(1)}$. Let

$$\beta^{(2)} = \beta^{(1)} + \lambda(\tilde{\beta}^{(1)} - \beta^{(1)}) \quad (0 < \lambda \leqslant 1)$$

λ is just a damping factor used in procedures of this sort.

Step 5: Using $\beta^{(2)}$, go to step 2, and repeat the process until the iterations converge.

Fair tried this iterative procedure in two cases, one with 601 observations (150 nonzero) and another with 6,366 observations (2,053 nonzero),[5] and found that although the number of iterations needed was larger than with the Newton–Raphson method, the computer time was much less (about one-sixth). He suggested using zero as the starting value for $\beta^{(1)}$ if there is a large number of zero observations and using the least-squares estimator β_{LS} as the starting value if there is a large number of nonzero observations. He also suggested using $\lambda = 0.4$ and an iteration limit of twenty as a good initial strategy (these values worked best in the examples he looked at).

The Newton–Raphson method uses the matrix of second derivatives. These are as follows:

$$\frac{\partial^2 \log L}{\partial \beta \partial \beta'} = -\sum_0 \frac{f_i}{(1-F_i)^2} \left[f_i - \frac{1}{\sigma^2}(1-F_i)\beta'x_i \right] x_i x_i' - \frac{1}{\sigma^2} \sum_1 x_i x_i'$$

$$ (6.16) $$

$$\frac{\partial^2 \log L}{\partial \sigma^2 \partial \beta} = -\frac{1}{2\sigma^2} \sum_0 \frac{f_i}{(1-F_i)^2} \left[\frac{1}{\sigma^2}(1-F_i)(\beta'x_i)^2 - (1-F_i) \right]$$

---

[4] This is essentially the EM algorithm discussed by Dempster et al. (1977). Blight (1970) suggested a similar algorithm for all exponential densities (this was pointed out to me by A. S. Deaton). Cohen (1957) also suggested a similar algorithm for normal populations.

[5] Fair suggested choosing $\beta^{(1)}$ as zero or β_{LS}, depending on the numbers of observations that are zero and nonzero.

$$- \beta' x_i f_i \bigg] x_i - \frac{1}{\sigma^4} \sum_1 (y_i - \beta' x_i) x_i \qquad (6.17)$$

$$\frac{\partial^2 \log L}{\partial (\sigma^2)^2} = \frac{1}{4\sigma^4} \sum_0 \frac{f_i}{(1-F_i)^2} \bigg[\frac{1}{\sigma^2} (1-F_i)(\beta' x_i)^3 - 3(1-F_i)\beta' x_i$$

$$- (\beta' x_i)^2 f_i \bigg] + \frac{N_1}{2\sigma^4} - \frac{1}{\sigma^6} \sum_1 (y_i - \beta' x_i)^2 \qquad (6.18)$$

In the method of scoring, one uses the probability limits of these second derivatives used in the Newton–Raphson method of iteration. This simplifies the expressions considerably. Using the first-order conditions for the maximum given by equations (6.10) and (6.11), and substituting

$$\sum (1 - F)Z \quad \text{for} \quad \sum_0 Z$$

and

$$\sum FZ \quad \text{for} \quad \sum_1 Z$$

(where the summations now run over all the observations), the second derivatives can be written compactly (Amemiya, 1973, p. 1007) as

$$\frac{\partial^2 \log L}{\partial \beta \partial \beta'} = -\sum a_i x_i x_i' \qquad (6.19)$$

$$\frac{\partial^2 \log L}{\partial \sigma^2 \partial \beta} = -\sum b_i x_i \qquad (6.20)$$

and

$$\frac{\partial^2 \log L}{\partial (\sigma^2)^2} = -\sum c_i \qquad (6.21)$$

The summations now run over all the N observations, and

$$a_i = -\frac{1}{\sigma^2} \left(Z_i \phi_i - \frac{\phi_i^2}{1 - \Phi_i} - \Phi_i \right) \qquad (6.22)$$

$$b_i = \frac{1}{2\sigma^3} \left(Z_i^2 \phi_i + \phi_i - \frac{Z_i \phi_i^2}{1 - \Phi_i} \right) \qquad (6.23)$$

$$c_i = -\frac{1}{4\sigma^4} \left(Z_i^3 \phi_i + Z_i \phi_i - \frac{Z_i^2 \phi_i^2}{1 - \Phi_i} - 2\Phi_i \right) \qquad (6.24)$$

where

$$Z_i = \frac{\beta' x_i}{\sigma} \qquad (6.25)$$

ϕ_i and Φ_i are, as defined earlier, the density function and distribution function of the standard normal evaluated at Z_i.

The asymptotic covariance matrix of the estimates of (β, σ^2) can be estimated as V^{-1}, where

$$V = \begin{bmatrix} \sum a_i x_i x_i' & \sum b_i x_i \\ \sum b_i x_i' & \sum c_i \end{bmatrix} \tag{6.26}$$

where a_i, b_i, and c_i are as defined earlier.

6.4   A reparametrization of the tobit model

In his study, Tobin (1958) reparametrized the model given by equation (6.1) by dividing throughout by σ. We can write the reparametrized model as

$$hy_i = \beta_0' x_i + v_i \quad \text{if RHS} > 0$$
$$hy_i = 0 \quad \text{otherwise}$$

where $h = 1/\sigma$, $\beta_0 = \beta/\sigma$, and $v_i = u_i/\sigma$ has the standard normal distributions $N(0,1)$. The log-likelihood function can now be written as

$$\log L = \sum_0 \log F(-\beta_0' x_i) + N_1 \log h - \frac{1}{2} \sum_1 (hy_i - \beta_0' x_i)^2 \tag{6.27}$$

Let

$$\theta = \begin{bmatrix} \beta_0 \\ h \end{bmatrix}$$

Olsen (1978b) showed that for the foregoing likelihood function, the matrix $\partial^2 \log L / \partial\theta\partial\theta'$ is negative semidefinite.

For the reparametrized version, the expressions for the second derivatives are less cumbersome than the expressions in equations (6.16) through (6.18). The normal equations for the model are

$$\frac{\partial \log L}{\partial \beta_0} = -\sum_0 \frac{f(-\beta_0' x_i)}{F(-\beta_0' x_i)} x_i + \sum_1 (hy_i - \beta_0' x_i) x_i = 0 \tag{6.28}$$

and

$$\frac{\partial \log L}{\partial h} = \frac{N_1}{h} - \sum_1 (hy_i - \beta_0' x_i) y_i = 0 \tag{6.29}$$

The second derivatives are

$$\frac{\partial^2 \log L}{\partial \beta_0 \partial \beta_0'} = \sum_0 \frac{f(-\beta_0' x_i)}{F(-\beta_0' x_i)} \left(\beta_0' x_i - \frac{f(-\beta_0' x_i)}{F(-\beta_0' x_i)} \right) x_i x_i' - \sum_1 x_i x_i' \tag{6.30}$$

$$\frac{\partial^2 \log L}{\partial \beta_0 \partial h} = \sum_1 y_i x_i \tag{6.31}$$

$$\frac{\partial^2 \log L}{\partial h^2} = -\frac{N_1}{h^2} - \sum_1 y_i^2 \tag{6.32}$$

To show that the matrix of second partials is negative semidefinite, we proceed as follows:

As defined in (6.7), let X_1 be the $N_1 \times k$ matrix of explanatory variables corresponding to the observations for which $y_i > 0$, and X_0 the $N_0 \times k$ matrix of explanatory variables corresponding to the observations for which $y_i = 0$, and similarly Y_1 and Y_0. Let

$$X = \begin{bmatrix} X_0 \\ X_1 \end{bmatrix}, \quad Y = \begin{bmatrix} Y_0 \\ Y_1 \end{bmatrix}, \quad \theta = \begin{bmatrix} \beta_0 \\ h \end{bmatrix}$$

Then the matrix of second derivatives given by equations (6.30) and (6.31) can be written as

$$\frac{\partial^2 \log L}{\partial \theta \partial \theta'} = -\begin{bmatrix} X' \\ Y' \end{bmatrix} \begin{bmatrix} D & 0 \\ 0 & I \end{bmatrix} [XY] - \begin{bmatrix} 0 & 0 \\ 0 & N_1/h^2 \end{bmatrix} \tag{6.33}$$

where D is a diagonal matrix whose ith diagonal element is

$$D_i = -\frac{f(-\beta_0' x_i)}{F(-\beta_0' x_i)} \left(\beta_0' x_i - \frac{f(-\beta_0' x_i)}{F(-\beta_0' x_i)} \right) \tag{6.34}$$

Thus, all that needs to be shown is that D_i is positive.

If w follows a standard normal distribution, and if we consider values of $w > c$, then, obviously,

$$E(w \mid w > c) > c$$

Also,

$$E(w \mid w > c) = \frac{\phi(c)}{1 - \Phi(c)}$$

Hence,

$$c - \frac{\phi(c)}{1 - \Phi(c)} < 0 \tag{6.35}$$

Substituting $\beta_0' x_i$ for c, we see that D_i as given by equation (6.34) is positive. This proves the required result.

The implication of this result is that the likelihood function for the tobit model has a single maximum. Thus, no matter what the starting value, as long as the iterative process is continued to a solution, that solution will be the global maximum of the likelihood function. Also, as proved by Amemiya (1973), this estimator is consistent and asymptotically normal.

6.5   Two-stage estimation of the tobit model

Amemiya (1973) criticized Tobin's initial estimator, saying that it was not consistent, and he suggested an initial consistent estimator.[6] He also showed that the second-round estimator that results from taking one iteration from this initial consistent estimator is asymptotically equivalent to the maximum-likelihood estimator. Many empirical researchers found Tobin's initial estimator satisfactory, and Olsen's proof that the likelihood function for the tobit model has a single maximum explains why they did not have trouble with their initial estimator. However, even though the estimation method suggested by Amemiya is not useful for the tobit model, it will be useful for more complicated models in which the likelihood function is likely to have multiple maxima. Hence, we shall review the method and some of its extensions here.

Considering the model given by equation (6.1) and the nonzero observations y_i we get

$$E(y_i \mid y_i > 0) = \beta' x_i + E(u_i \mid u_i > -\beta' x_i) = \beta' x_i + \sigma \frac{\phi_i}{\Phi_i} \qquad (6.36)$$

where ϕ_i and Φ_i are the density function and distribution function of the standard normal evaluated at $\beta' x_i / \sigma$. Also, using the formulas in the Appendix for the second moments of the truncated normal and simplifying, we get $E(y_i^2 \mid y_i > 0) = \beta' x_i \cdot E(y_i) + \sigma^2$, which we can write as

$$y_i^2 = \beta' x_i y_i + \sigma^2 + \eta_i$$

where $E(\eta_i) = 0$. However, this equation cannot be estimated by OLS, because $\text{Cov}(\eta_i, x_i y_i) \neq 0$. What Amemiya suggested is to regress y_i on x_i and higher powers of x_i, get $\hat{y}_i$ (the estimated value of y_i) from this equation, and use $x_i \hat{y}_i$ as instrumental variables to estimate this equation. Although it is theoretically appealing, the practical usefulness of this instrumental-variable approach is not known.[7]

An alternative procedure first used by Heckman (1976b) is the fol-

---

[6] Tobin suggested taking a linear approximation of the first term in (6.28), solving equations (6.28) to get an estimate of β_0, and then substituting this in (6.29) to get a quadratic equation in h. Because the use of even OLS estimates as starting values assures convergence, we shall not go into the details of Tobin's method here.

[7] However, one study in which the method seems to have given some encouraging results is that of Dubin and McFadden (1980).

lowing: Because the likelihood function for the probit model is well-behaved, we define a dummy variable

$$I_i = 1 \quad \text{if} \quad y_i > 0$$
$$I_i = 0 \quad \text{otherwise}$$

Then, using the probit model, we get consistent estimates of β/σ. Using these, we get estimated values of ϕ_i and Φ_i. Now we get consistent estimates of β and σ by estimating equation (6.36) by OLS, with $\hat\phi_i/\hat\Phi_i$ as the explanatory variable in place of ϕ_i/Φ_i.

Instead of using only the nonzero observations on y_i, if we use all the observations, we get

$$E(y_i) = P(y_i > 0) \cdot E(y_i \mid y_i > 0) + P(y_i = 0) \cdot E(y_i \mid y_i = 0)$$

$$= \Phi_i \left(\beta' x_i + \sigma \frac{\phi_i}{\Phi_i} \right) + (1 - \Phi_i) 0$$

$$= \Phi_i \beta' x_i + \sigma \phi_i \tag{6.37}$$

Thus, after getting estimates of ϕ_i and Φ_i, we estimate equation (6.37) by OLS.

Note that the threshold value in equation (6.1) is zero. This is not a very restrictive assumption, because if the model is

$$y_i = \beta' x_i + u_i \quad \text{if} \quad y_i > c_i$$
$$y_i = c_i \quad \text{otherwise}$$

we can define

$$y_i^* = y_i - c_i, \quad x_i^* = \begin{bmatrix} x_i \\ c_i \end{bmatrix}, \quad \beta^* = \begin{bmatrix} \beta \\ -1 \end{bmatrix}$$

and the model in (6.1) applies with y, x, and β replaced by y^*, x^*, and β^*.

Similarly, for models with an upper constraint, so that

$$y_i = \beta' x_i + u_i \quad \text{if} \quad \text{RHS} < 0$$
$$y_i = 0 \quad \text{otherwise}$$

we multiply y, x, and u by -1, and this reduces to the model in equation (6.1). Thus the tobit model can be specified as in equation (6.1) without any loss of generality. Problems arise where the thresholds c_i are known only as stochastic functions of some other variables. Such models will be considered in the next chapter.

6.6 Prediction in the tobit model

The prediction of y_i, given x_i, can be obtained from the different expectations functions we have given. Note that if we define the model in (6.1) in a latent-variable framework, with

$$y_i^* = \beta' x_i + u_i \quad \text{and} \quad E(u_i) = 0$$

defining the latent variable y_i^* (say desired or potential expenditures), and if we define y_i, the observed variable, as

$$y_i = y_i^* \quad \text{if} \quad y_i^* > 0$$
$$y_i = 0 \quad \text{otherwise}$$

then clearly $E(y_i^*) = \beta' x_i$.

Thus, after estimating β, we can get predictions of the latent variable from this equation. There are, in addition, two other predictions we can make, and these are predictions about the observed y_i, given the information that it is greater than zero and not given any such information. These predictions are given by equations (6.36) and (6.37). What (6.36) gives is $E(y_i^* | y_i^* > 0)$ or $E(y_i | y_i^* > 0)$, that is, the mean of the positive y's. What (6.37) gives is $E(y_i)$, that is, the mean of all observed y's, positive and zero. Note that this is not $E(y_i^*)$ which is the mean of potential y's. Thus, there are three predictions: one for the latent variable and two for the observed variable (with and without the information that the observed variable is greater than zero). Note that $E(y_i) = \Phi_i E(y_i | y_i^* > 0)$. Corresponding to these three expectations functions we have the following derivatives to predict the effects of changes in the exogenous variables.

Denote $z = \beta' x / \sigma$ and β_j the jth component of β. We drop the subscript i, which refers to the ith observation. Then, using the formulas for derivatives in the Appendix at the end of the book, we have, after simplifications,

$$\frac{\partial E(y^*)}{\partial x_j} = \beta_j$$

$$\frac{\partial E(y)}{\partial x_j} = \Phi(z)\beta_j$$

and

$$\frac{\partial E(y | y^* > 0)}{\partial x_j} = \beta_j \left[1 - z \frac{\phi(z)}{\Phi(z)} - \left(\frac{\phi(z)}{\Phi(z)} \right)^2 \right]$$

6.7   The two-limit tobit model

There are many examples in which the dependent variable will be truncated at both high and low values. For instance, in commodity trading there are upper and lower limits on the price movements (these upper and lower limits are usually fixed at levels based on the previous day's closing price). In the problem of insurance coverage, there is a minimum coverage, a maximum coverage, and values in between. The model then becomes

$$y_i^* = \beta'x_i + u_i$$

where y_i^* is the latent variable. If we denote by y_i the observed dependent variable,

$$
\begin{aligned}
y_i &= L_{1i} \quad \text{if } y_i \leqslant L_{1i} \\
&= y_i^* \quad \text{if } L_{1i} < y_i^* < L_{2i} \\
&= L_{2i} \quad \text{if } y_i^* \leqslant L_{2i}
\end{aligned}
\tag{6.38}
$$

Here L_{1i} and L_{2i} are, respectively, the lower and upper limits. The likelihood function for this model is given by

$$L(\beta, \sigma \,|\, y_i, x_i, L_{1i}, L_{2i})$$

$$
= \prod_{y_i=L_{1i}} \Phi\left(\frac{L_{1i}-\beta'x_i}{\sigma}\right) \prod_{y_i=y_i^*} \frac{1}{\sigma}\phi\left(\frac{y_i-\beta'x_i}{\sigma}\right) \prod_{y_i=L_{2i}} \left[1 - \Phi\left(\frac{L_{2i}-\beta'x_i}{\sigma}\right)\right]
\tag{6.39}
$$

The detailed expressions for the first and second derivatives of this likelihood function need not be presented here. The expressions will be similar to those for the simple tobit model. For a computer program, see the work of Nelson (1976). The proof for the concavity of the log-likelihood function also follows the same lines as that for the simple model. Because this involves only some algebraic detail, it is omitted here. See the work of Pratt (1981) for some general theorems.

Denoting $\Phi[(L_{1i}-\beta'x_i)/\sigma]$ and $\Phi[(L_{2i}-\beta'x_i)/\sigma]$ by Φ_{1i} and Φ_{2i}, respectively, with corresponding definitions for ϕ_{1i} and ϕ_{2i}, we get the expressions for $E(y_i)$ as

$$E(y_i \,|\, L_{1i} < y_i^* < L_{2i}) = \beta'x_i + E(u_i \,|\, L_{1i}-\beta'x_i < u_i < L_{2i}-\beta'x_i)$$

$$= \beta'x_i + \sigma\frac{\phi_{1i}-\phi_{2i}}{\Phi_{2i}-\Phi_{1i}}
\tag{6.40}$$

See the formulas in the Appendix. The unconditional expectation of y_i is given by

$$
\begin{aligned}
E(y_i) &= P(y_i=L_{1i}) \cdot L_{1i} + P(L_{1i}<y_i^*<L_{2i}) \cdot E(y_i \,|\, L_{1i}<y_i<L_{2i}) \\
&\quad + P(y_i=L_{2i}) \cdot L_{2i} \\
&= \Phi_{1i}L_{1i} + \beta'x_i(\Phi_{2i}-\Phi_{1i}) + \sigma(\phi_{1i}-\phi_{2i}) + (1-\Phi_{2i})L_{2i}
\end{aligned}
\tag{6.41}
$$

Equations (6.40) and (6.41) can be used for obtaining the appropriate conditional and unconditional predictions of y_i given x_i. They can be also used for a two-stage estimation procedure, but note that in this case the limits L_{1i} and L_{2i} are known. Hence, a two-limit probit model that uses just the number of observations at the limits L_{1i} and L_{2i} and the number of observations between the limits will give consistent estimates of the parameters β and σ. This model has been illustrated by Rosett and Nelson (1975). The likelihood function for this model is

$$L(\beta, \sigma) = \prod_{n_1} \Phi_{1i} \prod_{n_2} (\Phi_{2i} - \Phi_{1i}) \prod_{n_3} (1 - \Phi_{2i}) \qquad (6.42)$$

where n_1 is the number of observations at the lower limit L_{1i}, n_2 is the number of observations between the limits L_{1i} and L_{2i}, and n_3 is the number of observations at the upper limit L_{3i}. In the medical-insurance example, for instance, what this says is that we know if each individual buys minimum coverage, partial coverage, or maximum coverage, and given the incomes for all individuals we can estimate the income elasticity of demand for insurance. The two-limit probit model is a special case of the ordinal probit model discussed in section 2.13.

6.8   Models of friction

There are many instances in which the dependent variable responds to only large values of the exogenous variables. Such models are called models of friction. One familiar example of this is that of dividend payments. Define y_t^* as the desired dividend payments in period t. Here y_t^* will depend on variables like cash flow, earnings, and so forth. It is not feasible for the company to make changes in dividend payments continuously. Hence, the observed dividend rate y_t can be modeled as follows:

$$y_t = 0 \quad \text{if } y_t^* < L_0$$
$$y_t = L_0 \quad \text{if } L_0 \leqslant y_t^* < L_1$$
$$y_t = L_1 \quad \text{if } L_1 \leqslant y_t^* < L_2 \qquad (6.43)$$

Because we have no observations for $y_t \geqslant L_2$, we have to consider our observations as a sample from a truncated distribution. Let

$$y_t^* = \beta' x_t + u_t \quad [u_t \sim IN(0, \sigma^2)]$$

Then the likelihood function for this model can be written as

$$L(\beta, \sigma \,|\, L_0, L_1, L_2, x)$$

$$= \prod_{y_t=0} \frac{\Phi_{0t}}{\Phi_{2t}} \prod_{y_t=L_0} \frac{\Phi_{1t} - \Phi_{0t}}{\Phi_{2t}} \prod_{y_t=L_1} \frac{\Phi_{2t} - \Phi_{1t}}{\Phi_{2t}}$$

where Φ_{0t}, Φ_{1t}, and Φ_{2t} are defined as in the two-limit tobit model. If, in the model given by (6.43), L_2 is not known, we shall in effect assume it to be ∞, and now the likelihood function is

$$L(\beta, \sigma \mid L_0, L_1, x) = \prod_{y_1=0} \Phi_{0t} \prod_{y_t=L_0} (\Phi_{1t} - \Phi_{0t}) \prod_{y_t=L_1} (1 - \Phi_{1t})$$

This is the same as the likelihood function for a two-limit probit model discussed in the preceding section.

Econometric studies of dividend behavior usually have been based on a lagged-adjustment model of the sort

$$y_t - y_{t-1} = \lambda(y_t^* - y_{t-1})$$

This model still assumes that dividends can be changed continuously. It does not capture the fact that dividends are increased in discrete jumps, as given in model (6.43). Thus, the model described in (6.43) is a more appropriate one to model dividend behavior and is more meaningful than the partial-adjustment models. Another example of the friction model is the model considered by Rosett (1959). Consider the problem of investigating the effects of changes in yield on changes in the asset holdings of a particular asset by a certain class of investors. Because of transactions costs, small changes in yield will have no effect on the changes in asset holdings.

Rosett's model can be written as

$$y_i^* = \beta'x_i + u_i$$
$$y_i = y_i^* - \alpha_1 \quad \text{if } y_i^* < \alpha_1$$
$$y_i = 0 \quad \text{if } \alpha_1 \leqslant y_i^* \leqslant \alpha_2$$
$$y_i = y_i^* - \alpha_2 \quad \text{if } \alpha_2 < y_i^* \qquad (6.44)$$

where $\alpha_1 < 0$ and $\alpha_2 > 0$. Here y_i^* is the desired change in asset holdings, y_i is the actual change in asset holdings, and x_i is the change in yield. Actual holdings do not change for small negative or positive changes in desired holdings. α_1 represents a desired decrease, and α_2 represents a desired increase. The likelihood function for this model is

$$L(\alpha_1, \alpha_2, \beta, \sigma \mid y, x) = \prod_1 \frac{1}{\sigma} \phi\left(\frac{y_i + \alpha_1 - \beta'x_i}{\sigma}\right)$$
$$\times \prod_2 \left[\Phi\left(\frac{\alpha_2 - \beta'x_i}{\sigma}\right) - \Phi\left(\frac{\alpha_1 - \beta'x_i}{\sigma}\right)\right]$$

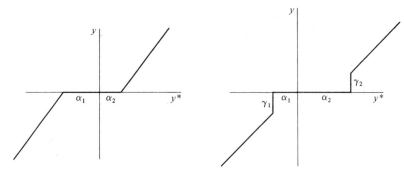

Figure 6.2. Friction models

$$\times \prod_3 \frac{1}{\sigma} \phi\left(\frac{y_i + \alpha_2 - \beta' x_i}{\sigma}\right) \qquad (6.45)$$

The product is over the sets 1, 2, and 3 of observations for which $y_i^* < \alpha_1$, $\alpha_1 \leqslant y_i^* \leqslant \alpha_2$, and $\alpha_2 < y_i^*$, respectively. This model is, again, similar to the two-limit probit model, except that for the first and third groups we have observations on y_i as well.

The model given by equations (6.44) is represented by the first diagram in Figure 6.2. The model allows for a change in the intercept, but no changes in the slope coefficients. But one can easily generalize the model to allow for shifts in the slope coefficients as well. Because this is very straightforward, details will not be presented here.

Another generalization we can consider is to define (6.44) as

$$y_i = y_i^* - \alpha_1 + \gamma_1 \quad \text{if } y_i^* < \alpha_1$$
$$y_i = 0 \quad \text{if } \alpha_1 \leqslant y_i^* \leqslant \alpha_2$$
$$y_i = y_i^* - \alpha_2 + \gamma_2 \quad \text{if } \alpha_2 < y_i^* \qquad (6.46)$$

Here γ_1 and γ_2 are themselves parameters to be estimated. This model is shown in the second diagram in Figure 6.2.[8] The likelihood function for this model is obtained by changing y_i to $y_i - \gamma_1$ and $y_i - \gamma_2$, respectively, in the first and last expressions of (6.45). Dagenais (1975) considered this model, but the likelihood functions he presented are very messy.

One other type of friction model is the model of expectations in the studies of Fishe and Lahiri (1981) and Maddala et al. (1982). The data are from surveys conducted by the Survey Research Center at the University of Michigan. The survey asks two questions: The first is a direc-

---

[8] Note that γ_1 is negative and γ_2 is positive in Figure 6.2.

tional question asking respondents if they expect prices to go up, stay the same, or go down. The second is a quantitative question on the magnitude of the anticipated price rise, asked of those who say that prices will go up. In constructing the model appropriate to these data, we need to know what "stay the same" means. We shall assume that respondents give this answer if their expectation is the range $(-\delta, +\delta)$.

Let P_i^* be the forecast of the ith individual and P_i^0 the reported value. Then we assume

$$P_i^* = \mu + u_i \quad \text{and} \quad \text{Var}(u_i) = \sigma^2$$

and

$$
\begin{aligned}
P_i^0 &= P_i^* && \text{iff } \delta - \mu < u_i && (N_1 \text{ observations}) \\
&= 0 && \text{iff } -\delta - \mu \leqslant u_i \leqslant \delta - \mu && (N_2 \text{ observations}) \\
&= 0 && \text{iff } u_i < -\delta - \mu && (N_3 \text{ observations})
\end{aligned}
$$

Defining $C = (1/\sigma)(-\delta - \mu)$ and $D = (1/\sigma)(\delta - \mu)$, the likelihood function for this model is

$$L = \prod_{\psi_1} \phi\left(\frac{P_i^0 - \mu}{\sigma}\right) \prod_{\psi_2} [\Phi(D) - \Phi(C)] \cdot \prod_{\psi_3} \Phi(C)$$

where ψ_1, ψ_2, and ψ_3 are the sets of observations in the three groups ("go up," "stay the same," and "go down").

Maximizing this likelihood with respect to μ, σ, and δ, we get a set of nonlinear equations that give the following solution:

$$\hat{\mu} = \left(1 - \frac{2}{D+C}\frac{\phi(D)}{1-\Phi(D)}\right)^{-1} \frac{1}{N_1}\sum_{\psi_1} P_i^0$$

$$\hat{\sigma} = \frac{-2}{D+C}\hat{\mu}$$

$$\hat{\delta} = \frac{D-C}{2}\hat{\sigma}$$

The foregoing model is a friction model in the sense that a range of $(-\delta, \delta)$ is imperceptible in the mind of the respondent.

6.9 Truncated regression models

The models considered in the previous sections are censored regression models. There are many situations in which the appropriate model is a truncated regression model. One can also have both elements (truncation and censoring) present in any problem, but we shall discuss these models later. A good example of the truncated regression model is the earnings equation estimated from the data for the negative-income-tax experiment. There families with income levels above a certain limit (1.5 times the 1967 poverty line) were eliminated from the study. The truncation thus takes the form $y_i < L_i$, where L_i depends on family size. Hausman and Wise (1976, 1977) estimated earnings functions based on these data. Without any loss of generality, we can discuss the truncated regression model with reference to this problem. We assume that in the population the relationship between earnings and exogenous variables is of the form

$$y_i = \beta' x_i + u_i \tag{6.47}$$

where y_i are earnings, x_i is a vector of k exogenous variables (including education, intelligence, etc.), i indexes individuals, and u_i are disturbances assumed to be $IN(0, \sigma^2)$.

Families were selected at random, but those with incomes higher than the limit L_i (1.5 times the 1967 poverty line) were eliminated from the study. Thus, L_i is a function of family size. Equation (6.47) refers to individual income, and the truncation refers to family income, but let us ignore this for the present.

The density function of y_i is the truncated normal defined earlier:

$$f(y_i) = \frac{(1/\sigma)\phi[(y_i - \beta' x_i)/\sigma]}{\Phi[(L_i - \beta' x_i)/\sigma]} \quad \text{if } y_i \leqslant L_i$$

$$f(y_i) = 0 \quad \text{otherwise}$$

where $\phi(\cdot)$ and $\Phi(\cdot)$ are, respectively, the density function and the distribution function of the standard normal.

That the estimation of equation (6.47) by OLS from the truncated sample leads to biased estimates is fairly obvious. This can be clearly seen from Figure 6.3, where L_i is assumed to be a constant. The log-likelihood function for the model is given by

$$\log L = -N \log[(2\pi)^{1/2}\sigma] - \frac{1}{2}\sum \left(\frac{y_i - \beta' x_i}{\sigma}\right)^2$$

$$- \sum \log \Phi\left(\frac{L_i - \beta' x_i}{\sigma}\right) \tag{6.48}$$

The likelihood function is quite similar in structure to that of the censored regression model presented in (6.8). The main difference arises from the fact that in the censored regression model the exogenous variables x_i are observed even for the observations for which $y_i > L_i$. In the truncated regression model, such observations are completely eliminated from the sample. Define

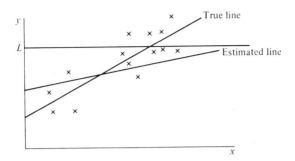

Figure 6.3. Truncated regression model

$$d_i = \frac{L_i - \beta' x_i}{\sigma} \tag{6.49}$$

Then the first-order conditions are

$$\frac{\partial \log L}{\partial \beta} = \frac{1}{\sigma^2} \sum (y_i - \beta' x_i) x_i + \sum \frac{x_i \phi(d_i)}{\sigma \Phi(d_i)} = 0 \tag{6.50}$$

$$\frac{\partial \log L}{\partial \sigma^2} = -\frac{N}{2\sigma^2} + \frac{1}{2\sigma^4} \sum (y_i - \beta' x_i)^2 + \frac{1}{2\sigma^2} \sum \frac{d_i \phi(d_i)}{\Phi(d_i)} = 0 \tag{6.51}$$

The second derivatives of $\log L$ can be derived the same way they were derived for the tobit model in section 6.3. Further, we can use the Newton–Raphson method or the method of scoring for computing the ML estimates. Hausman and Wise used the method of Berndt et al. (1974), based only on the first derivatives (6.50) and (6.51). The initial values used were the OLS estimates. The likelihood function in this model can also be shown to be globally concave, as in the censored regression model. Hence, it does not matter if the iterations are started with the inconsistent OLS estimates.

The two-stage methods available for the censored regression model, as described in section 6.5, are not feasible in the truncated regression model, because no observations are available for $y_i > L_i$. The expected value of y_i and variance of y_i are given by

$$E(y_i | x_i) = \beta' x_i - \sigma \frac{\phi_i}{\Phi_i} \tag{6.52}$$

$$\text{Var}(y_i | x_i) = \sigma^2 - \sigma^2 \left(\frac{d_i \phi_i}{\Phi_i} + \frac{\phi_i^2}{\Phi_i^2} \right) \tag{6.53}$$

where, for compactness, we have written ϕ_i and Φ_i for $\phi(d_i)$ and $\Phi(d_i)$, respectively, and d_i is defined in equation (6.49).

Equation (6.52) can be used to get predicted values of y_i once the parameters β and σ^2 have been estimated. The expected value of y_i in the sample is less than that in the whole population. For compactness, denote by B_i the bias term $-\sigma\phi_i/\Phi_i$ in (6.52). Then

$$\frac{\partial B_i}{\partial L_i} = -\frac{\phi_i d_i}{\Phi_i} - \frac{\phi_i^2}{\Phi_i^2} < 0$$

and

$$\frac{\partial B_i}{\partial \sigma} = \frac{\phi_i d_i^2}{\Phi_i} + \frac{\phi_i^2 d_i}{\Phi_i^2} > 0$$

Thus, the bias decreases with increase in L_i, but it increases with an increase in the variance σ^2.

Regarding the nature of the biases produced in the estimates of the regression parameters β when estimated by OLS, it is not possible to say anything definite, except in the case in which β is a scalar. In that case, if x is positive, note from equation (6.50) that

$$\hat{\beta}_{ML} = \frac{\Sigma y_i x_i}{\Sigma x_i^2} + \text{a positive number}$$

or $\hat{\beta}_{OLS} = \hat{\beta}_{ML} -$ a positive number. However, Goldberger (1981) showed that the situation is different in the special case in which the explanatory variables are multinormally distributed along with the dependent variables. In that case the OLS estimates of all the regression parameters β are biased toward zero.

In this case the conditional distribution of y, given x, is as before:

$$y\,|\,x \sim N(\beta'x, \sigma^2)$$

But we also assume that the regressors have a multivariate normal distribution

$$x \sim N(0, \Sigma)$$

These assumptions imply that the $(k+1)\times 1$ vector $(x', y)'$ has a multivariate normal distribution, with covariance matrix

$$\begin{bmatrix} \Sigma & \Sigma\beta \\ \beta'\Sigma & \eta^2 \end{bmatrix}$$

where $\eta^2 = \text{Var}(y) = \sigma^2 + \beta'\Sigma\beta$. The marginal distribution of y is $N(0, \eta^2)$, and the conditional distribution of x, given y, is normal, with

$$E(x\,|\,y) = \gamma y \quad \text{and} \quad V(x\,|\,y) = \Omega$$

where

$$\gamma = \Sigma\beta/\eta^2 \quad \text{and} \quad \Omega = \Sigma - \eta^2\gamma\gamma' \tag{6.54}$$

Now consider the truncated population $y < L$. Then, for the truncated population,

$$E^*(y|x) = \beta'x - \sigma \frac{\phi(d)}{\Phi(d)}$$

where $d = (L - \beta'x)/\sigma$. Following Goldberger, we have used the asterisk to identify expectations and moments in the truncated population.

The conditional-expectation function is nonlinear in x. The linear regression function can be considered the best linear approximation to this conditional-expectation function. If we estimate the linear regression function

$$\alpha^* + x'\beta^*$$

then

$$\beta^* = [V^*(x)]^{-1}\text{Cov}^*(y,x) \quad \text{and} \quad \alpha^* = E^*(y) - E^*(x)'\beta^* \tag{6.55}$$

What we have to do is obtain $E^*(y)$, $E^*(x)$, $V^*(x)$, and $\text{Cov}^*(y,x)$ for the truncated population.

Because $y \sim N(0, \eta^2)$, we have

$$E^*(y) = -\eta \frac{\phi(L/\eta)}{\Phi(L/\eta)}$$

$$V^*(y) = \theta\eta^2$$

where

$$\theta = 1 - \frac{\phi(L/\eta)}{\Phi(L/\eta)} \left(\frac{L}{\eta} + \frac{\phi(L/\eta)}{\Phi(L/\eta)} \right)$$

Note that $0 \leqslant \theta \leqslant 1$. These formulas for the mean and variance for the truncated normal are from Johnson and Kotz (1970, pp. 81–3). See also the equations in the Appendix.

The conditional distributions of x, given y, are unaffected by the truncation. Hence,

$$E^*(x|y) = \gamma y \quad \text{and} \quad V^*(x|y) = \Omega$$

where γ and Ω are as defined in (6.54). Hence, we have

$$V^*(x) = V^*(\gamma y) + E^*(\Omega)$$
$$= \theta\eta^2\gamma\gamma' + \Omega = (\theta - 1)\eta^2\gamma\gamma' + \Sigma$$

Finally,

$$\text{Cov}^*(x,y) = \text{Cov}^*[E^*(x|y),y] = \theta\eta^2\gamma = \Sigma\theta\beta$$

$$[V^*(x)]^{-1} = \Sigma^{-1} - \frac{(\theta-1)\eta^2}{1+(\theta-1)\eta^2\gamma'\Sigma^{-1}\gamma}\Sigma^{-1}\gamma\gamma'\Sigma^{-1}$$

$$= \Sigma^{-1} + \frac{(1-\theta)}{1-(1-\theta)\delta^2}\frac{\beta\beta'}{\eta^2}$$

using (6.54), where $\delta^2 = \beta'\Sigma\beta/\eta^2$ and $0 \leqslant \delta^2 \leqslant 1$. Hence,

$$\beta^* = [V^*(x)]^{-1}\text{Cov}^*(x,y) = [V^*(x)]^{-1}\Sigma\theta\beta$$

$$= \left(I + \frac{1-\theta}{1-(1-\theta)\delta^2}\frac{\beta\beta'\Sigma}{\eta^2}\right)\theta\beta$$

$$= \left(\theta + \frac{(1-\theta)}{1-(1-\theta)\delta^2}\cdot\theta\delta^2\right)\beta$$

$$= \lambda\beta$$

where $\lambda = \theta/[1-(1-\theta)\delta^2]$ lies in the unit interval.

Thus, in the special case in which x also has a multivariate normal distribution, the OLS estimates of all the regression parameters β are biased toward zero. This assumption may not be satisfied in practice.

Hausman and Wise (1977) estimated an earnings equation using the truncated regression model. The dependent variable was log earnings. The results, shown in Table 6.1, suggest that the OLS method produces biased estimates. In this particular case they are all biased toward zero.

6.10   Endogenous stratification and truncated regression models

In the preceding section we discussed a truncated regression model in which all observations came from the population $y < L$. Suppose we divide the population into two strata, $y < L$ and $y > L$, and then draw separate random samples of predetermined proportions from these two strata. This is called endogenous stratified sampling.

The problem of regression analysis based on stratified samples is a common one. Very often a weighted least-squares method is used when analyzing such data. Suppose that there are m strata with numbers $N_1, N_2, \ldots, N_m$. Suppose the sizes of the samples drawn from these strata are $n_1, n_2, \ldots, n_m$, respectively. Let the regression of y on x be denoted by

$$y_{ij} = \alpha + \beta x_{ij} + u_{ij}, \quad u_{ij} \sim IN(0, \sigma^2) \quad (i=1,2,\ldots,m, \ j=1,2,\ldots,n_m)$$

The weighted least-squares method that is commonly suggested is to estimate α and β by minimizing

$$\sum_{ij}\frac{1}{p_i}(y_{ij} - \alpha - \beta x_{ij})^2$$

Table 6.1. *Earnings equations estimated from the New Jersey negative-income-tax experiment*

Variable	OLS	ML
Constant	8.203 (0.091)	9.102 (0.026)
Education	0.010 (0.006)	0.015 (0.007)
IQ	0.002 (0.002)	0.006 (0.005)
Training	0.002 (0.001)	0.006 (0.003)
Union	0.090 (0.030)	0.246 (0.089)
Illness	−0.076 (0.038)	−0.226 (0.107)
Age (linear)	−0.003 (0.002)	−0.016 (0.005)

Note: Figures in parentheses are standard errors.

where $p_i = n_i / N_i$. We shall discuss later a justification for the weighted least-squares procedure, which is, however, only asymptotic. Note that the weighted least-squares procedure is the appropriate one to use even for small samples if $\text{Var}(u_{ij}) = p_i \sigma^2$. However, there is no reason why this should be a consequence of the fact that samples drawn from the different strata are not equiproportionate.

The correct procedure depends on how the stratification is done. If the stratification is by some exogenous variable (say north–south, east–west, race, sex, etc.), then there is no reason why the weighted least-squares method needs to be used. The likelihood function in this case is exactly the same whatever the values of $n_1, n_2, \ldots, n_m$. Thus, in this case of stratification by exogenous variables, the appropriate procedure is just to use ordinary least squares;[9] that is, estimate α and β by minimizing

$$\sum_{ij} (y_{ij} - \alpha - \beta x_{ij})^2$$

Turning next to endogenous stratification, suppose we have a situation in which high-income families are undersampled and income is the

[9] For a discussion of the applicability of probability weighted least-squares estimation, see Holt et al. (1980).

explained variable. Hausman and Wise (1982) discussed such a situation. The New Jersey negative-income-tax experiment was a case of truncated sampling in which high-income families were not sampled at all. The income maintenance experiments in Gary and Seattle and Denver were less extreme. The high-income families were not discarded. They were just undersampled. The University of Michigan panel study of income dynamics, as well as the 1967 survey of economic opportunity, also undersampled high-income families.

Consider, for simplicity, two strata: $y < L$ and $y > L$. Suppose the proportions sampled are p_1 and p_2, respectively. The truncated regression model discussed in the preceding section corresponds to $p_1 = 1$, $p_2 = 0$. Let $f(y)$ be the density function of y in the population. Then the density function of a sample observation y_i can be written as

$$h(y_i) = \frac{p_1 f(y_i)}{p_1 \Pr(y_i \leqslant L) + p_2 \Pr(y_i > L)} \quad \text{if } y_i \leqslant L$$

$$= \frac{p_2 f(y_i)}{p_1 \Pr(y_i \leqslant L) + p_2 \Pr(y_i > L)} \quad \text{if } y_i > L$$

The denominator is just the normalizing constant. Suppose the regression model we consider is

$$y_i = \beta' x_i + u_i, \quad u_i \sim IN(0, \sigma^2)$$

Then, defining $d_i = (L - \beta' x_i)/\sigma$ and $p = p_2/p_1$, and denoting $\phi(d_i)$ and $\Phi(d_i)$ by ϕ_i and Φ_i, respectively, we can write the density function of y_i as

$$h(y_i) = \frac{1}{p + (1-p)\Phi_i} \frac{1}{\sigma} \phi\left(\frac{y_i - \beta' x_i}{\sigma}\right) \quad \text{if } y_i \leqslant L$$

$$= \frac{p}{p + (1-p)\Phi_i} \frac{1}{\sigma} \phi\left(\frac{y_i - \beta' x_i}{\sigma}\right) \quad \text{if } y_i > L$$

Dividing the sample of N observations into N_1 for $y_i \leqslant L$ and N_2 for $y_i > L$, the log-likelihood function can be written as

$$\log L = N_2 \log p - N \log \sigma - \frac{1}{2\sigma^2} \sum_{i=1}^{N} (y_i - \beta' x_i)^2$$

$$- \sum_{i=1}^{N} \log[p + (1-p)\Phi_i] \tag{6.56}$$

If p is known, this likelihood function is maximized with respect to β and σ. If p is not known, it is maximized with respect to p, β, and σ. We can then test the hypothesis $p = 1$. The case $p = 1$ denotes random sampling. If $p = 1$ we can use ordinary least squares.[10] For prediction purposes, we need $E(y_i | x_i)$. We can obtain conditional as well as unconditional predictions as follows: Define a dummy variable

$$I_i = 1 \quad \text{if } y_i \leqslant L$$
$$I_i = 0 \quad \text{otherwise}$$

Then we have

$$E(y_i | x_i, I_i = 1) = \beta'x_i + E(u_i | I_i = 1) = \beta'x_i - \sigma \frac{\phi_i}{\Phi_i}$$

$$E(y_i | x_i, I_i = 0) = \beta'x_i + E(u_i | I_i = 0) = \beta'x_i + \sigma \frac{\phi_i}{1 - \Phi_i}$$

The unconditional mean is a weighted average of these means, with weights proportional to $p_1 \Phi_i$ and $p_2(1 - \Phi_i)$, respectively. Hence,

$$E(y_i | x_i) = \beta'x_i - \sigma \frac{p_1 \phi_i - p_2 \phi_i}{p_1 \Phi_i + p_2(1 - \Phi_i)} \tag{6.57}$$

If the sample proportions are known, we can use weighted least squares and minimize

$$\sum_{i=1}^{N_1} \frac{1}{p_1} (y_i - \beta'x_i)^2 + \sum_{i=1}^{N_2} \frac{1}{p_2} (y_i - \beta'x_i)^2$$

However, the weighted least-squares (WLS) estimate will be biased in small samples. Consider the case in which β is a scalar. Then, because

$$E(u_i | I_i = 1) = -\sigma \frac{\phi_i}{\Phi_i} \quad \text{and} \quad E(u_i | I_i = 0) = \sigma \frac{\phi_i}{1 - \Phi_i}$$

We have

$$E(\hat{\beta}_{\text{WLS}}) = \beta - \sigma \left(\frac{1}{p_1} \sum_{i=1}^{N_1} x_i^2 + \frac{1}{p_2} \sum_{j=1}^{N_2} x_j^2 \right)^{-1}$$
$$\times \left(\frac{1}{p_1} \sum_{i=1}^{N_1} \frac{x_i \phi_i}{\Phi} - \frac{1}{p_2} \sum_{j=1}^{N_2} \frac{x_j \phi_j}{1 - \Phi_j} \right)$$

In the special case in which x_i are all equal to 1, Hausman and Wise (1982) showed that the bias term simplifies to

$$-\sigma \left(\frac{N_1}{p_1} + \frac{N_2}{p_2} \right)^{-1} \left(\frac{N_1}{p_1} \frac{\phi}{\Phi} - \frac{N_2}{p_2} \frac{\phi}{1 - \Phi} \right)$$

---

[10] We shall not present here the first and second derivatives of $\log L$, because they can be obtained in the same manner as for the truncated and censored regression models.

and as $N \to \infty$, $N_1 \to p_1 \Phi N/D$, and $N_2 \to p_2(1-\Phi)N/D$, where $D = p_1\Phi + p_2(1-\Phi)$, and hence the bias tends to zero. Thus, the weighted least-squares estimator can be given an asymptotic justification in this particular case.

The preceding discussion can all be generalized to the case in which the limits of stratification L_i vary with the observation (as in the case of the income-maintenance experiments in which L_i depends on family size). In this case the preceding expressions all hold, except that the definition of d_i is $(L_i - \beta'x_i)/\sigma$ instead of $(L - \beta'x_i)/\sigma$.

The extension to the case of several strata is also straightforward. Consider m strata, and the proportions sampled are $P_1, P_2, \ldots, P_m$. As before, we normalize these by dividing by P_1 and write P_2 for P_2/P_1, P_3 for P_3/P_1, and so forth. Let the dividing points between the m strata be $L_1, L_2, \ldots, L_{m-1}$. Define

$$d_{ji} = \frac{L_j - \beta'x_i}{\sigma} \quad (j = 1, 2, \ldots, m-1)$$

Denote $\phi(d_{ji})$ and $\Phi(d_{ji})$ by ϕ_{ji} and Φ_{ji}, respectively. Then the log-likelihood function corresponding to (6.56) is

$$\log L = -N \log \sigma - \frac{1}{2\sigma^2} \sum_{i=1}^{n} (y_i - \beta'x_i)^2 + \sum_{j=2}^{m} N_j \log P_j$$
$$- \sum_{i=1}^{N} \log[\Phi_{1i} + P_2(\Phi_{2i} - \Phi_{1i}) + \cdots + P_{m-1}(\Phi_{m-1,i} - \Phi_{m-2,i})$$
$$+ P_m(1 - \Phi_{m-1,i})]$$

where $N_1, N_2, \ldots, N_m$ are the numbers of observations in the m strata and $N = \sum_{j=1}^{m} N_j$.

Formula (6.57) also becomes

$$E(y \mid x)$$
$$= \beta'x - \sigma \frac{(1-P_2)\phi_1 + (P_2-P_3)\phi_2 + \cdots + (P_{m-1}-P_m)\phi_{m-1}}{(1-P_2)\Phi_1 + (P_2-P_3)\Phi_2 + \cdots + (P_{m-1}-P_m)\Phi_{m-1} + P_m}$$

6.11   Truncated and censored regression models with stochastic and unobserved thresholds

The censored regression model discussed in section 6.3 is

$$Y_i = \beta'x_i + u_i \quad \text{if } Y_i > 0$$
$$Y_i = 0 \quad \text{otherwise}$$

Consider now the model

$$Y_{1i} = \beta' x_i + u_i$$
$$Y_{1i} \text{ observed only if } Y_{1i} \geqslant Y_{2i} \tag{6.58}$$

Y_{2i} is unobserved and stochastic, but we observe the variables that determine it, that is,

$$Y_{2i} = \beta_2' X_{2i} + u_{2i} \tag{6.59}$$

In the following discussion we shall drop the subscript i when it is not necessary.

We shall assume that (u_{1i}, u_{2i}) are IN, with means zero and covariance matrix

$$\Sigma = \begin{pmatrix} \sigma_1^2 & \sigma_{12} \\ \sigma_{12} & \sigma_2^2 \end{pmatrix}$$

This is a censored regression model with unobserved stochastic threshold. This model was discussed by Nelson (1977), who estimated it by the ML method. The model was considered earlier by Gronau (1974) and Lewis (1974). In Chapter 8 we shall discuss two-stage estimation of this model (section 8.4) and also derive the conditions for identification of the parameters in this model. There it will be shown that we need one of the following two conditions for identification: (a) $\sigma_{12} = 0$; (b) at least one variable in X_1 is not included in X_2. In his empirical work, Nelson imposed the condition $\sigma_{12} = 0$, because all the variables in X_1 were also included in X_2.

To derive the likelihood function for this model, we partition the sample observations into two groups: Y_1 observed and Y_1 not observed. For the first group, we know that $Y_1 = \beta_1' X_1 + u_1$ and that $Y_2 < Y_1$, or $u_2 < Y_1 - \beta_2' X_2$. Thus, for the first group we have

$$u_1 = Y_1 - \beta_1' X_1 \quad \text{and} \quad u_2 < Y_1 - \beta_2' X_2$$

For the second set we do not observe either Y_1 or Y_2, and all we know is that $Y_1 < Y_2$ or $\beta_1' X_1 + u_1 < \beta_2' X_2 + u_2$. Also note that $(u_1 - u_2) \sim N(0, \sigma^2)$, where $\sigma^2 = \sigma_1^2 + \sigma_2^2 - 2\sigma_{12}$. Hence, in our usual notation, we can write

$$P(Y_1 < Y_2) = \Phi\left(\frac{\beta_2' X_2 - \beta_1' X_1}{\sigma}\right)$$

If $f(u_1, u_2)$ is the joint density of u_1 and u_2, then the likelihood function is

$$L(\beta_1, \beta_2, \Sigma) = \prod_{Y_1 \neq 0} \int_{-\infty}^{Y_1 - \beta_2' X_2} f(Y_1 - \beta_1' X_1, u_2)\, du_2 \prod_{Y_1 = 0} \Phi\left(\frac{\beta_2' X_2 - \beta_1' X_1}{\sigma}\right)$$

$$\tag{6.60}$$

We can simplify this expression by writing $f(u_1, u_2)$ as $f(u_1) \cdot f(u_2 | u_1)$. Note that $u_2 | u_1$ is normal, with mean $(\sigma_{12}/\sigma_1^2)u_1$ and variance $\sigma_{2.1}^2 = \sigma_2^2 - \sigma_{12}^2/\sigma_1^2$. Hence, $P(u_2 < Y_1 - \beta_2' X_2 | u_1 = Y_1 - \beta_1' X_1) = \Phi(W)$, where

$$W = \frac{1}{\sigma_{2.1}} \left[Y_1 - \beta_1' X_2 - \frac{\sigma_{12}}{\sigma_1^2} (Y_1 - \beta_1' X_1) \right]$$

Thus the log-likelihood function can be written as

$$\log L = -N_1 \log \sigma_1 - \frac{1}{2\sigma_1^2} \sum_1 (Y_1 - \beta_1' X_1)^2 + \sum_1 \log \Phi(W)$$

$$+ \sum_0 \log \Phi\left(\frac{\beta_2' X_2 - \beta_1' X_1}{\sigma} \right) \tag{6.61}$$

where $\sum_1$ denotes summation over the N_1 observations for which Y_1 is observed and $\sum_0$ denotes summation over the remaining $(N - N_1)$ observations for which Y_1 is not observed.

We shall not present the first and second derivatives of this likelihood function, because they can be derived in similar manner as in the other models, once we use the standard formulas for the derivatives of $\Phi(W)$ with respect to W. It is the derivatives of W with respect to the several parameters that produce tedious expressions that we need not present here in detail.

There are many examples of the use of this model. The standard example is that of labor supply, where Y_1 is the wage offer (or market wage) and Y_2 is the reservation wage. If $Y_1 > Y_2$, we observe that the individual is in the labor force. If $Y_1 < Y_2$, we observe that the individual is not employed, and we do not observe either Y_1 or Y_2. Note that Y_2 is never observed. Other examples of this model will be discussed in Chapter 9, which deals with models of self-selection. The reason this is called a model of self-selection is that the partitioning of the sample into the employed and unemployed is based on the "self-selection" of individuals into the two groups based on the relationship between wage offers and reservation wages.

The truncated regression model in this case corresponds to the situation in which the sample is drawn entirely from those who are employed (i.e., the unemployed persons are discarded). The likelihood function in this case will consist of only the first part of (6.60), with a divisor equal to Prob$(Y_1 > Y_2)$ or $\Phi[(\beta_1' X_1 - \beta_2' X_2)/\sigma]$, because only observations with $Y_1 > Y_2$ are sampled. The log-likelihood function is therefore given by

$$\log L = -N \log \sigma_1 - \frac{1}{2\sigma_1^2} \sum (Y_1 - \beta_1' X_1)^2 + \sum \log \Phi(W)$$

$$- \sum \log \Phi\left(\frac{\beta_1' X_1 - \beta_2' X_2}{\sigma}\right) \tag{6.62}$$

where the summations now run over all the observations.

The only problem with this truncated regression model as compared with the censored regression model is that in the latter we can obtain initial consistent estimates using two-stage methods (to be described in detail in section 8.4) to start the iterative solution of the likelihood equations. In the case of the truncated regression model, use of the probit method to get estimates of $(\beta_1' X_1 - \beta_2' X_2)/\sigma$ is ruled out because we do not have observations on the unemployed. It is not known whether or not the log-likelihood function (6.62) is well-behaved in the sense of having a unique global maximum. Thus, in empirical applications, it is desirable to start the iterative solution of the ML equations with different starting values.

In the case of the likelihood function (6.61) for the censored regression model, the problems are similar, and it is also desirable to start with different initial values. However, because initial consistent estimates are available using the two-stage methods, we can be sure that the estimates obtained by the first iteration of the likelihood equations using the initial consistent estimates have the usual desirable asymptotic properties (Cox and Hinkley, 1974, p. 308).

Note that one can try to extend Amemiya's procedure (section 6.5) to the truncated regression model with stochastic thresholds discussed here to get initial consistent estimates, but the procedure gets very messy. There is always some loss of information in the truncated regression model, where observations with $Y_1 < Y_2$ are completely discarded, as compared with the censored regression model. Amemiya's procedure is as follows:

We first write the criterion function $Y_1 > Y_2$ as $\gamma'Z > u$, where $\gamma'Z = (\beta_1' X_1 - \beta_2' X_2)/\sigma$ and $u = (u_2 - u_1)/\sigma$. We will also define a dummy indicator variable

$$I = 1 \quad \text{if } Y_1 > Y_2$$
$$I = 0 \quad \text{otherwise}$$

Then, defining $\text{Cov}(u_1, u) = \sigma_{1u}$, we can write, using the standard expressions for the first two moments of a variable with a truncated normal distribution,

$$E(u_1 | I = 1) = -\sigma_{1u} W_1$$
$$E(u_1^2 | I = 1) = \sigma_1^2 - \sigma_{1u}^2 W_1(\gamma'Z)$$

where $W_1 = \phi(\gamma'Z)/\Phi(\gamma'Z)$. Hence, we have

$$E(Y_1 \mid X_1, I=1) = \beta_1'X_1 - \sigma_{1u}W_1$$
$$E(Y_1^2 \mid X_1, I=1) = (\beta_1'X_1)^2 + 2\beta_1'X_1(-\sigma_{1u}W_1) + \sigma_1^2 - \sigma_{1u}^2 W_1(\gamma'Z)$$

Because W_1 is a variable on which we do not have any observations, we eliminate it, and then we get

$$E(Y_1^2) = (\beta_1'X_1)^2 + 2\beta_1'X_1[E(Y_1) - \beta_1'X_1] + \sigma_1^2$$
$$+ \sigma_{1u}\gamma'Z[E(Y_1) - \beta_1'X_1]$$

and hence we can write

$$Y_1^2 = \sigma_1^2 + 2\beta_1'X_1Y_1 + \sigma_{1u}\gamma'ZY_1 - \sigma_{1u}(\gamma'Z)(\beta_1'X_1) - (\beta_1'X_1)^2 + \eta$$

where $E(\eta) = 0$. We can, as Amemiya suggested for the tobit model, regress Y_1 on X_1, Z, and higher powers of these variables and get $\hat{Y}_1$ and then use $X_1\hat{Y}_1$ and $Z\hat{Y}_1$ as instrumental variables. This still does not give us consistent estimates of all the parameters as in the simple tobit model.

In summary, estimation of the truncated regression model with unobserved stochastic thresholds is more complicted than that for the corresponding censored regression model. However, Wales and Woodland (1980) presented results to show that the parameter estimates obtained by using ML methods are almost the same when data are used on employed persons only. But more such evidence is needed to judge the relative performances of the estimates from the two models.

Many data sets commonly encountered conform to the truncated regression model. For instance, suppose there are usury laws limiting the rates of interest, and we have data only on loans granted. Then this is a truncated regression model, not a censored regression model.

6.12   Specification errors: heteroscedasticity

Although substantial developments have been made in recent years in the estimation of different classes of limited-dependent-variable models, there has not been much work on (a) studying the effects of violations of the different assumptions, (b) checking the adequacy of the model assumed, and (c) developing criteria for choosing between different models. In this section we shall discuss one such problem: heteroscedasticity of the residuals. In the general linear model, OLS estimates are consistent but not efficient when the disturbances are heteroscedastic. In the case of the limited-dependent-variable models, Maddala and Nelson (1975) showed that if we ignore heteroscedasticity, the resulting estimates are not even consistent.

Consider the model

$$Y_i = \beta'X_i + u_i \quad \text{if RHS} > 0$$
$$Y_i = 0 \quad \text{otherwise}$$

Then, as derived in equation (6.37), the locus of expected values for Y_i is given by

$$E(Y_i) = \Phi_i\beta'X_i + \sigma\phi_i \tag{6.63}$$

where Φ_i and ϕ_i are, respectively, the distribution function and the density function of the standard normal evaluated at $\beta'X_i/\sigma$. Now suppose that the "true" model is heteroscedastic, with parameters σ_{0i} and β_0, and designate the "true" locus as $E_0(y_i)$. Then

$$E_0(y_i) = \beta_0'X_i \cdot \Phi\left(\frac{\beta_0'X_i}{\sigma_{0i}}\right) + \sigma_{0i}\phi\left(\frac{\beta_0'X_i}{\sigma_{0i}}\right) \tag{6.64}$$

and the "misspecified" locus is given by equation (6.63). It is clear that the presence of the variance term σ_{0i} in the expected-value locus is the source of the difference and, in turn, the estimation bias. One can study the direction of the bias by making some special assumptions about $\text{Var}(u_i)$. But this does not lead us too far. For instance, Maddala and Nelson (1975) assumed that the true variance of the error term was proportional to the square of one of the regressors (without loss of generality, the last regressor X_{ik}); that is,

$$\sigma_{0i}^2 = \lambda^2 X_{ik}^2$$

It was then shown that if we ignore heteroscedasticity and estimate the model by the usual tobit method, and if β_k is the coefficient of X_{ik}, then

$$\text{Plim } \hat{\beta}_k > \beta_k$$

That is, the estimate of the corresponding regression coefficient is upward-biased. But nothing can be said about the other coefficients.

Thus, even in the case of special assumptions made about the residual variances, all we can say is that the usual tobit estimates are inconsistent. We cannot say much about the direction of the bias.

Hurd (1979) argued, in similar manner, that in a truncated regression model heteroscedasticity produces inconsistent estimates when the usual ML method is used. Again, there are no general results about the direction of the bias. He concluded, however, that modest heteroscedasticity caused the parameters to be misestimated by a substantial amount.

The solution to the heteroscedasticity problem is to make some reasonable assumption about the nature of the heteroscedasticity. In the case of the linear regression model, Prais and Houthakker (1955) considered a model in which σ_i^2 is assumed to be proportional to the square of the regression function; that is,

$$\sigma_i^2 = \sigma^2(\alpha + \beta X_i)^2$$

This specification was generalized by Rutemiller and Bowers (1968), who suggested the specification

$$\sigma_i^2 = (\gamma + \delta Z_i)^2 \tag{6.65}$$

A test for heteroscedasticity reduces to a test for $\delta = 0$. One can use the likelihood-ratio test or the Wald test after obtaining the ML estimates of all the parameters. The assumption (6.65) is an appealing one to make in the tobit model as well.[11] Z_i may include some or all of the variables in X_i. The log-likelihood function is given by

$$\log L = \sum_0 \log\left[1 - \Phi\left(\frac{\beta'X_i}{\sigma_i}\right)\right] + \sum_1 \log\left[\frac{1}{\sigma_i}\,\phi\left(\frac{y_i - \beta'X_i}{\sigma_i}\right)\right]$$

where the first summation refers to the set of observations for which $y_i = 0$ and the second summation refers to the set of observations for which $y_i > 0$.

Let us, for compactness, denote

$$\phi_i = \phi\left(\frac{\beta'X_i}{\sigma_i}\right) \quad \text{and} \quad \Phi_i = \Phi\left(\frac{\beta'X_i}{\sigma_i}\right)$$

Then we have

$$\frac{\partial \log L}{\partial \beta} = -\sum_0 \frac{\phi_i X_i}{\sigma_i(1 - \Phi_i)} + \sum_1 \frac{1}{\sigma_i^2}(y_i - \beta'X_i)X_i = 0$$

$$\frac{\partial \log L}{\partial \gamma} = -\sum_0 \frac{(\beta'X_i)\phi_i}{\sigma_i^2(1 - \Phi_i)} + \sum_0 \frac{(y_i - \beta'X_i)^2 - \sigma_i^2}{\sigma_i^3} = 0$$

$$\frac{\partial \log L}{\partial \delta} = \sum_0 \frac{(\beta'X_i)\phi_i Z_i}{\sigma_i^2(1 - \Phi_i)} + \sum_1 \frac{[(y_i - \beta'X_i)^2 - \sigma_i^2]Z_i}{\sigma_i^3} = 0 \tag{6.66}$$

We shall omit the presentation of the second derivatives, for the sake of brevity.

The likelihood equations (6.66) can be solved by an iterative procedure like the Newton–Raphson method. However. Fishe et al. (1979) solved them by the procedure of Berndt et al. (1974). As an illustrative example, they considered the determinants of "eating out" (restaurant expenditures). The data are for the year 1970 from the Michigan panel

---

[11] This was the assumption made by Fishe et al. (1979). The discussion that follows is drawn from that study.

on income dynamics. There were 5,856 observations, and of these, 3,204 were those for which restaurant expenditures were greater than 0. The results for the simple tobit model and the heteroscedastic tobit model showed that restaurant expenditures increase with income and decrease with the age of the head of the household and family size. They were also lower for blacks than for whites. There were no surprises in either set of results, but the heteroscedastic model led them to reject the hypothesis of homoscedasticity.

In the usual linear model it is common practice to make a log transformation of the variables, and this "solves" the heteroscedasticity problem. To examine the usefulness of this procedure, Fishe et al. re-estimated both the simple tobit and heteroscedastic tobit after making a log transformation of the expenditures and income variables. They assumed restaurant expenditures to be one dollar for those with zero expenditures in the sample. Again, the hypothesis of homoscedasticity was rejected. Although there were no sign reversals, the differences in the coefficient estimates between the simple tobit and the heteroscedastic tobit were more pronounced than in the case of the linear specification. The results indicate that ignoring heteroscedasticity results in underestimation of the income elasticity of restaurant expenditures.

The variables used were

$y = $ log(restaurant expenditures)
$X_1 = $ log(income)
$X_2 = $ family size
$X_3 = $ age of head of household
$X_4 = $ dummy variable (1 for blacks, 0 for whites)

The results (asymptotic t ratios in parentheses) were as follows:

Tobit

$$y = -14.31 + 2.25X_1 - 0.35X_2 - 0.05X_3 - 1.46X_4$$
$$\quad (-17.0) \quad (25.1) \quad (-13.9) \quad (-11.2) \quad (-10.5)$$

Heteroscedastic tobit

$$y = -20.81 + 2.97X_1 - 0.31X_2 - 0.06X_3 - 1.35X_4$$
$$\quad (-24.8) \quad (33.4) \quad (-14.1) \quad (-11.4) \quad (-10.1)$$

$$\sigma = 17.68 - 1.69X_1 + 0.04X_2$$
$$\quad (29.0) \quad (-24.3) \quad (8.0)$$

In yet another example, Bomberger and Denslow (1980) analyzed the demand for money and other assets. Define

M = money holdings

Y = income

W = wealth

The data are drawn from interviews with more than 2,000 households. More than 30% of the sample held no demand deposits. The estimates from OLS (using observations with nonzero money holdings) tobit and heteroscedastic tobit (asymptotic t ratios in parentheses) were as follows:

OLS

$$M = -1180.4 + 0.188Y + 0.00536W \quad (R^2 = 0.403)$$
$$\quad\;\; (3.4) \qquad (17.1) \quad\;\; (12.2)$$

Tobit

$$M = -1596.7 + 0.197Y + 0.00539W$$
$$\quad\;\; (2.4) \qquad (49.2) \quad\;\; (60.0)$$

Heteroscedastic tobit

$$M = -115.5 + 0.029Y + 0.0172W$$
$$\quad\; (3.0) \qquad (5.8) \qquad (7.8)$$

$$\sigma = 297.6 + 0.0032Y + 0.0279W$$
$$\quad\; (37.5) \quad (2.5) \qquad (46.5)$$

The main conclusion that follows is that the wealth effect is underestimated and the income effect is overestimated when heteroscedasticity is ignored in the tobit model.

The preceding examples suggest the usefulness of introducing heteroscedasticity explicitly into the tobit model. The estimation procedures are similar for the truncated regression model and will not be pursued here. It is more practicable to make some reasonable assumptions about the nature of heteroscedasticity and estimate the model than just to say that the ML estimates are inconsistent if heteroscedasticity is ignored.

6.13   Problems of aggregation

Very often a model is derived (on the basis of microtheory) that has the structure of the censored or truncated regression model. Then the model is estimated from macrodata, because microdata are not available. This is usually the case even with linear models, and there has been some discussion of aggregation problems in linear models. The problem of aggregation in the tobit (or censored regression) model has been studied by Maddala and Nelson (1975).

Consider the following microlevel model:

$$y_{it} = \beta' X_t + u_{it} \quad \text{if RHS} < L_t$$
$$y_{it} = L_t \quad \text{otherwise}$$
$$u_{it} \sim IN(0, \sigma^2) \tag{6.67}$$

To motivate the model, let y_{it} be the interest rate paid by bank i in time period t on time deposits, let X_t be a vector of observations at time t on a set of exogenous variables that affect savings-account interest rates, and let L_t be the regulation Q ceiling on such rates.

Suppose there are N_t banks (i.e., $i=1, 2, \ldots, N_t$). If microlevel data are available on all N_t banks during each period t ($t=1, 2, \ldots, T$), estimation of β and σ can be handled by the usual tobit analysis. But if only aggregate measures of savings-account interest rates are available, neither tobit nor straightforward OLS analysis is suitable. Suppose observed interest rates amount to the unweighted mean of interest rates paid by all N_t banks during each period t, so that

$$y_t = \frac{1}{N_t} \sum_1 y_{it} \tag{6.68}$$

Let n_t be the number of banks at period t paying an interest rate less than the ceiling rate L_t, and reorder the observations within each period so that those banks are the first n_t. Then (6.68) becomes

$$y_t = \frac{1}{N_t} \left[\sum_{i=1}^{n_t} (\beta' X_t + u_{it}) + (N_t - n_t) L_t \right]$$
$$= \frac{n_t}{N_t} \beta' X_t + \left(1 - \frac{n_t}{N_t}\right) L_t + \frac{1}{N_t} \sum_{i=1}^{n_t} u_{it} \tag{6.69}$$

If n_t were observable, and if the last term on the right-hand side of (6.69) had zero expectation, we could proceed by OLS; but neither of these conditions obtains. Thus, we might proceed by finding $E(y_t)$ and fitting

$$y_t = E(y_t) + w_t$$

by nonlinear least-squares methods. Now

$$E(y_t) = L_t + E\left(\frac{n_t}{N_t}\right)(\beta' X_t - L_t) + E\left(\frac{1}{N_t} \sum_{i=1}^{n_t} u_{it}\right)$$

We define the binomial variable

$$D_{it} = 1 \quad \text{if } i \leqslant n_t$$
$$D_{it} = 0 \quad \text{if } i > n_t$$

Then $\Pr(D_{it}=1) = \Pr(\beta'X_t + u_{it} < L_t) = \Phi[(L_t - \beta'X_t)/\sigma] = E(D_{it})$, where $\Phi(\cdot)$ is the CDF of the standard normal distribution. Now

$$n_t = \sum_{i=1}^{N_t} D_{it}$$

$$E\left(\frac{n_t}{N_t}\right) = \frac{1}{N_t} N_t E(D_{it}) = \Phi\left(\frac{L_t - \beta'X_t}{\sigma}\right) \tag{6.70}$$

Next, note that for each u_{it} such that $i \leqslant n_t$, we have

$$u_{it} < L_t - \beta'X_t$$

Thus, this subset of n_t u_{it}'s pertaining to banks that paid an interest rate less than L_t follows a truncated conditional distribution given by

$$g(u_{it} \mid i \leqslant n_t) = \frac{1}{\sigma} \phi\left(\frac{u_{it}}{\sigma}\right) \Big/ \Phi\left(\frac{L_t - \beta'X_t}{\sigma}\right) \quad \text{for } -\infty < u_{it} < \frac{L_t - \beta'X_t}{\sigma}$$

$$g(u_{it} \mid i \leqslant n_t) = 0 \quad \text{otherwise}$$

where $\phi(\cdot)$ is the PDF of the standard normal. It is easily verified that

$$E(u_{it} \mid i \leqslant n_t) = -\sigma\phi\left(\frac{L_t - \beta'X_t}{\sigma}\right) \Big/ \Phi\left(\frac{L_t - \beta'X_t}{\sigma}\right)$$

Thus,

$$E\left(\frac{1}{N_t} \sum_{i=1}^{n_t} u_{it}\right) = E\left(\frac{n_t}{N_t}\right) \frac{-\sigma\phi(L_t - \beta'X_t)/\sigma}{\Phi(L_t - \beta'X_t)/\sigma}$$

$$= -\sigma\phi\left(\frac{L_t - \beta'X_t}{\sigma}\right) \tag{6.71}$$

An alternative way of getting the same result is the following: Define

$$u_{it}^* = u_{it} \quad \text{if } u_{it} < L_t - \beta'X_t$$
$$u_{it}^* = 0 \quad \text{otherwise}$$

Then $E(u_{it}^*) = -\sigma\phi[(L_t - \beta'X_t)/\sigma]$, and

$$E\left(\frac{1}{N_t} \sum_{i=1}^{n_t} u_{it}\right) = E\left(\frac{1}{N_t} \sum_{i=1}^{N_t} u_{it}^*\right)$$

$$= \frac{N_t}{N_t}\left[-\sigma\phi\left(\frac{L_t - \beta'X_t}{\sigma}\right)\right]$$

Using (6.70) and (6.71), we get

$$y_t = L_t + \Phi\left(\frac{L_t - \beta' X_t}{\sigma}\right)(\beta' X_t - L_t) - \sigma\phi\left(\frac{L_t - \beta' X_t}{\sigma}\right) + w_t \quad (6.72)$$

where w_t now has zero expectation and is uncorrelated with each of the other terms on the right.

A much easier derivation of (6.72) is obtained by noting that

$$E(y_t) = \Phi\left(\frac{L_t - \beta' X_t}{\sigma}\right)\beta' X_t - \sigma\phi\left(\frac{L_t - \beta' X_t}{\sigma}\right)$$

$$+ L_t\left[1 - \Phi\left(\frac{L_t - \beta' X_t}{\sigma}\right)\right] \quad (6.73)$$

which yields (6.72) directly. Estimates of β and σ can be obtained using nonlinear squares on (6.72). There is, however, the further problem of taking the heteroscedasticity of w_t into account.

The important thing to note is that the correct procedure is not the estimation of the tobit model with aggregated data but estimation of an equation of the form (6.72). Note that the additional term in the locus of expected values is the last term in equation (6.73), compared with equation (6.37) for the tobit model.

6.14 Miscellaneous other problems

We can discuss all the problems that we encounter in the linear regression model in the context of the censored and truncated regression models. These are heteroscedasticity, autocorrelated errors, lagged dependent variables, departures from normality, and so forth. In the preceding section we discussed the heteroscedasticity problem. We shall now briefly comment on the other problems.

Autocorrelated errors

Consider the tobit model with the errors following a first-order autoregressive process:

$$u_t = \delta u_{t-1} + e_t$$

where $e_t \sim IN(0, \sigma^2)$. The likelihood function based on T observations involves a T-dimensional integral. Thus, even in this simple case the estimation of the parameters by the ML method is computationally intractable. It is therefore desirable to know if the usual ML estimates obtained on the assumption of independence of the errors have any desirable properties.

In the usual regression model, if the errors are autocorrelated, the OLS estimator is not efficient, but it is still consistent. A similar property holds in the tobit model. Robinson (1982) has proved that the ML estimator obtained on the assumption that the residuals are independent is not efficient but is still consistent. Robinson assumed that the error term follows a stationary autoregressive moving-average process of a finite order; that is,

$$A(L)u_t = B(L)\epsilon_t$$

where L is the lag operator defined as $LX_t = X_{t-1}$ and $\epsilon_t \sim IID(0, 1)$. Robinson also derived an expression for the limiting covariance matrix. The expression is rather cumbersome and will not be reproduced here.

Lagged dependent variables

Consider the distributed-lag model

$$Y_t^* = \beta x_t + \lambda Y_{t-1}^* + u_t \tag{6.74}$$

where Y_t^* is not observed. What we observe is Y_t, defined as

$$Y_t = Y_t^* \quad \text{if } Y_t^* > 0$$
$$Y_t = 0 \quad \text{otherwise}$$

We can write this model as

$$Y_t^* = \frac{\beta}{1 - \lambda L} x_t + \frac{u_t}{1 - \lambda L} \tag{6.75}$$

where L is the lag operator. Ignoring the serial correlation in the residuals, we can estimate equation (6.75) by Klein's method for estimating distributed-lag models. For each λ, we construct $[\beta/1 - \lambda L)]x_t$ and estimate (6.75) by the tobit method. We choose the value of λ that maximizes the likelihood. The only difference is that in the usual distributed-lag model we use the OLS method for each λ, whereas in this case we use the tobit method.

Sometimes it is more reasonable to have a model of the form

$$Y_t^* = \beta x_t + \lambda Y_{t-1} + u_t \tag{6.76}$$

The difference between models (6.74) and (6.76) is that in (6.74) it is the lagged value of the latent variable that appears as an explanatory variable, whereas in (6.76) it is the lagged value of the observed (truncated) variable that appears as an explanatory variable. If the residuals are serially independent, then there is no problem in the estimation of equation (6.76). We can use the usual tobit ML to estimate the parameters.

If the residuals are serially correlated, then the estimation gets very complicated.

Grether and Maddala (1982) used the lagged-latent-variable model (6.74), but with pooled cross-sectional time-series data, where the number of cross-sectional units is large but the number of time periods is small. Further work needs to be done on estimation of models of the form (6.74) and (6.76).

With serially correlated residuals, it is clear that one must be content with some consistent estimates, and hence it will be desirable to develop methods alternative to the tobit ML method.[12]

Nonnormal error distributions

Throughout our discussion of the censored and truncated regression models we have made the assumption that the distribution of the error term is normal. There are two choices open for relaxing this assumption: (a) devise methods of estimation for nonnormal distributions or (b) use transformations to normality. We shall now discuss these in turn.

Regarding nonnormal distributions, Amemiya and Boskin (1974) considered the estimation of a censored regression model when the errors are distributed as log-normal. The model they considered is the following.

The latent variables Y_i^* are assumed to be independent log-normal, with $E(Y_i^*) = \beta' X_i$ and $\mathrm{Var}(Y_i^*) = \eta^2 (\beta' X_i)^2$. We assume that $\beta' X_i > 0$ for all i. These assumptions imply that $\log Y_i$ are independent normal, with $E(\log Y_i^*) = \log(\beta' X_i) - \sigma^2/2$ and $V(\log Y_i^*) = \sigma^2 = \log(1 + \eta^2)$.

The observed variables Y_i are defined as

$$Y_i = Y_i^* \quad \text{if} \quad Y_i^* < \alpha$$
$$Y_i = \alpha \quad \text{if} \quad Y_i^* \geqslant \alpha$$

where α is a known positive constant. It is mathematically convenient in this model to estimate (β', σ^2) rather than (β', η^2).

Let us denote by f and F the density function and distribution function of $N(0, \sigma^2)$ (we have been using the symbols ϕ and Φ for the standard normal). For the observations with $Y_i = \alpha$, we have

$$P(Y_i^* \geqslant \alpha) = P(\log Y_i^* \geqslant \log \alpha)$$
$$= F\left(-\log \alpha + \log \beta' X_i - \frac{\sigma^2}{2}\right)$$

---

[12] A method that gives consistent estimates is the orthogonality-condition (OC) method proposed by Avery et al. (1982).

For the observations $Y_i < \alpha$, the density function is

$$g(Y_i) = \frac{1}{(2\pi)^{1/2}\sigma Y_i} \exp\left[-\frac{1}{2\sigma^2}\left(\log Y_i - \log \beta' X_i + \frac{\sigma^2}{2}\right)^2\right]$$

Hence, the log-likelihood function is (aside from some constants)

$$\log L = \sum_1 \log F_i - \frac{1}{2}\sum_2 \log(\sigma^2 Y_i^2) - \frac{1}{2\sigma^2}\sum_2 V_i^2$$

where

$$\mu_i = -\log \alpha + \log \beta' X_i - \frac{\sigma^2}{2}$$

$$V_i = \log Y_i - \log \beta' X_i + \frac{\sigma^2}{2}$$

$$F_i = F(\mu_i) \tag{6.77}$$

and $\sum_1$ denotes summation over all observations for which $Y_i = \alpha$, and $\sum_2$ denotes summation over all observations for which $Y_i < \alpha$.

$$\frac{\partial \log L}{\partial \beta} = \sum_1 \frac{f_i}{F_i} \frac{1}{\beta' X_i} X_i + \frac{1}{\sigma^2}\sum_2 \frac{V_i}{\beta' X_i} X_i = 0$$

$$\frac{\partial \log L}{\partial \sigma^2} = -\frac{1}{\sigma^2}\sum_1 \frac{\mu_i f_i}{F_i} - \frac{N_2}{2\sigma^2} + \frac{1}{2\sigma^4}\sum_2 V_i^2 - \frac{1}{2}\sum_1 \frac{f_i}{F_i}$$

$$- \frac{1}{2\sigma^2}\sum_2 V_i = 0$$

where N_2 is the number of observations for which $Y_i < \alpha$, $f_i = f(\mu_i)$ and $F_i = F(\mu_i)$, and V_i and μ_i are defined in (6.77).

If one uses the procedure of Berndt et al. (1974), one needs only the first derivatives of $\log L$. If one uses the Newton–Raphson method or the method of scoring, one needs the second derivatives as well. Because the second derivatives can be found in the study by Amemiya and Boskin, they will not be reproduced here.

One of the problems that can arise in this model is that at some stages of iteration $\beta' X_i$ can turn negative, in which case $\log \beta' X_i$ will not be defined. In such cases we can arbitrarily put $\log \beta' X_i = 0$.

Some alternative error distributions can also be suggested for the censored and truncated regression models; for instance, the exponential or the gamma distribution. In each of these cases one will have to specify the parameters carefully so that the variances of the error distribution will also be functions of the exogenous variables.

As an illustration, consider the model in which y_i^* follows an exponential distribution $0 \leqslant y_i^* < \infty$, with mean $\beta' X_i$. We then have

$$E(y_i^*) = \beta' X_i$$
$$V(y_i^*) = (\beta' X_i)^2$$

Note that in this model $\beta' X_i$ has to be positive. The model is useful in those instances in which the dependent variable is always positive and heteroscedasticity is a problem. To see how this model is estimated, suppose y_i^* is observed as a truncated variable. The observations y_i are given by

$$y_i = y_i^* \quad \text{if } y_i^* < c$$
$$y_i = c \quad \text{if } y_i^* > c$$

where c is a known constant. Then, for observations $y_i < c$, we have the density function

$$f(y_i) = \frac{1}{\beta' X_i} \exp\left(-\frac{y_i}{\beta' X_i}\right)$$

and for observations $y_i = c$, we have

$$P(y_i = c) = P(y_i^* > c)$$
$$= \exp\left(-\frac{c}{\beta' X_i}\right)$$

Hence, the log-likelihood function is

$$\log L = -\sum_1 \log(\beta' X_i) - \sum_1 \frac{y_i}{\beta' X_i} - \sum_2 \frac{c}{\beta' X_i}$$

where $\sum_1$ denotes summation over observations $y_i < c$ and $\sum_2$ denotes summation over observations $y_i = c$.

$$\frac{\partial \log L}{\partial \beta} = -\sum_1 \frac{1}{\beta' X_i} X_i + \sum_1 \frac{y_i X_i}{(\beta' X_i)^2} + \sum_2 \frac{c X_i}{(\beta' X_i)^2} = 0 \qquad (6.78)$$

If β is a scalar, then equation (6.78) simplifies to

$$\hat{\beta} = \frac{\sum_1 y_i / X_i + \sum_2 c / X_i}{N_1}$$

where N_1 is the number of observations for which $y_i < c$.

In the general case we have

$$\hat{\beta} = \left(\sum_1 \frac{1}{w_i^2} X_i X_i'\right)^{-1} \left(\sum_1 \frac{1}{w_i^2} y_i X_i + \sum_2 \frac{1}{w_i^2} c X_i\right) \qquad (6.79)$$

where $w_i = \beta'X_i$. Equation (6.79) will have to be solved by an iterative procedure, starting with some estimate of β, computing w_i, and then getting a new estimate of $\hat{\beta}$. The asymptotic covariance matrix can be obtained by evaluating $(-\partial^2 \log L/\partial\beta\partial\beta')^{-1}$. We shall not present the matrix of second derivatives, because it can be derived easily from (6.78).

The foregoing model is only illustrative, and it suggests how we can go about analyzing censored and truncated regression models with alternative error distributions.

Transformations to normality

A common transformation to normality is the one suggested by Box and Cox. The transformation T is define by

$$y^* = T(y, \lambda) = \frac{y^\lambda - 1}{\lambda} \quad \text{if } \lambda \neq 0$$

$$= \log y \quad \text{if } \lambda = 0 \tag{6.80}$$

The family of transformations is well defined for all $y > 0$. It is assumed that $y^* = \beta'X + u$ and that the u's are $IN(0, \sigma^2)$. The method of estimation suggested by Box and Cox is to maximize the likelihood

$$L = J(\lambda, y) \prod_{i=1}^{n} \frac{1}{\sigma} \phi\left(\frac{T(y_i, \lambda) - \beta'X_i}{\sigma}\right) \tag{6.81}$$

where $\phi(\cdot)$ is the density function of the standard normal, and $J(\lambda, y)$ is the Jacobian of the transformation from y^* to y:

$$J(\lambda, y) = \prod_{i=1}^{n} \left|\frac{dy_i^*}{dy}\right| = \prod_{i=1}^{n} y_i^{\lambda-1}$$

The likelihood function (6.81) has frequently been used to determine the value of λ, that is, the correct functional form for the dependent variable. Strictly speaking, the assumption of normality cannot hold for u_i, because the transformation (6.80) imposes restrictions on the range of u_i except in the case $\lambda = 0$. Because $y_i > 0$, we have

$$y_i^* > -\frac{1}{\lambda} \quad \text{if } \lambda > 0$$

$$y_i^* < -\frac{1}{\lambda} \quad \text{if } \lambda < 0$$

There are no restrictions on y_i^* only in the case $\lambda = 0$. These restrictions, in turn, imply

$$u_i > -\frac{1}{\lambda} - \beta'X_i \quad \text{if } \lambda > 0$$

$$u_i < -\frac{1}{\lambda} - \beta'X_i \quad \text{if } \lambda < 0$$

Thus, the proper specification is to assume that the residuals have a truncated normal distribution, with the limits of truncation dependent on both X_i and λ. This suggests that instead of maximizing the likelihood function (6.81) we should be maximizing

$$L^* = J(\lambda, y) \prod_{i=1}^{n} \frac{1}{\sigma} \phi\left(\frac{y_i^* - \beta'X_i}{\sigma}\right)/P_i \tag{6.82}$$

where

$$P_i = 1 - \Phi(-c_i) \quad \text{if } \lambda > 0$$
$$P_i = 1 \quad \text{if } \lambda = 0$$
$$P_i = \Phi(c_i) \quad \text{if } \lambda > 0$$

and

$$c_i = \frac{-(1/\lambda) - \beta'X_i}{\sigma}$$

Thus, in searching over λ, one should use a truncated regression model.[13]

Poirier (1978a) considered the case in which the variable y_i is truncated such that $A_i < y_i < B_i$, with $A_i \geqslant 0$. He then considered the estimation of this truncated regression model using the Box–Cox transformation. The effect of this truncation on the truncation of y_i^* can be derived easily.

Define $A_i^* = T(A_i, \lambda)$ and $B_i^* = T(B_i, \lambda)$, where the transformation T is defined in (6.80). Also define

$$a_i = \frac{A_i^* - \beta'X_i}{\sigma} \quad \text{and} \quad b_i = \frac{B_i^* - \beta'X_i}{\sigma}$$

Then

$$f(y_i^*) = \{\sigma[\Phi(b_i) - \Phi(a_i)]\}^{-1}\Phi\left(\frac{y_i^* - \beta'X_i}{\sigma}\right) \quad \text{if } A_i^* < y_i^* < B_i^*$$

---

[13] Olsen (1980b) estimated λ by maximizing the likelihood function (6.82) and found $\hat{\lambda} = 1.2$, whereas maximizing (6.81) gave $\hat{\lambda} = 0.8$. Amemiya and Powell (1980) showed that the value of λ that maximizes the pseudolikelihood (6.81) is biased toward zero.

$f(y_i^*) = 0$ elsewhere

Because the Jacobian of the transformation from y_i^* to y_i is $y_i^{\lambda-1}$, the density function of y_i is

$$g(y_i) = y_i^{\lambda-1} f(y_i^*) \quad \text{if } A_i < y_i < B_i$$
$$g(y_i) = 0 \quad \text{elsewhere}$$

Poirier suggested estimating $(\beta, \lambda, \sigma^2)$ by maximizing the log-likelihood:

$$L(\beta, \sigma^2, \lambda) = \sum_{i=1}^{n} \log g(y_i)$$

Note that in the special case $A_i = 0$ and $B_i = \infty$ we have

$$A_i^* = -\frac{1}{\lambda}, \quad B_i^* = \infty \quad \text{for } \lambda > 0$$

$$A_i^* = -\infty, \quad B_i^* = -\frac{1}{\lambda} \quad \text{for } \lambda < 0$$

which are the limits derived earlier. Note also that once A_i and B_i are specified and A_i^* and B_i^* are derived, the limits derived earlier, produced by the transformation itself, need not be imposed again, because they are automatically satisfied.

6.15   A general specification test

In preceding sections we discussed methods of handling heteroscedasticity and nonnormality by making some alternative assumptions about departures from the standard model. Recently, Nelson (1981) derived a test of the standard assumptions against a general misspecified alternative in the tobit regression model. Computational ease and freedom from specification of a specific alternative hypothesis are the major merits of this test.

The test Nelson derived is based on the asymptotic specification test derived by Hausman (1978), which is as follows: Let $\hat{\theta}_0$ and $\hat{\theta}_1$ be two estimators of the parameter vector θ such that under the null hypothesis they are both consistent and asymptotically normal, with asymptotic variances V_0 and V_1. Also, let $\hat{\theta}_0$ be asymptotically efficient, so that $V_1 - V_0$ is nonnegative definite. Then $(N)^{1/2}(\hat{\theta}_1 - \hat{\theta}_0)$ is asymptotically normal, with variance $V_1 - V_0$. Letting $\hat{V}_1$ and $\hat{V}_0$ be consistent estimates of V_1 and V_0, respectively, Hausman constructed the test statistic $N(\hat{\theta}_1 - \hat{\theta}_0)'(\hat{V}_1 - \hat{V}_0)^{-1}(\hat{\theta}_1 - \hat{\theta}_0)$, which, he argued, is asymptotically χ^2 with degrees of freedom K (which is the dimensionality of θ). Consider the alternative hypothesis H_1, such that under H_1, Plim $\hat{\theta}_0 \neq \theta$, but Plim $\hat{\theta}_1 = \theta$. Under these conditions, $\hat{\theta}_1 - \hat{\theta}_0$ does not converge to zero, and the test statistic has a noncentral χ^2 distribution.

To implement this test, Nelson constructed two estimators: the ML estimator and the MOM (method of moments) estimator. Both are consistent under the null hypothesis, and the former is also efficient. Under the alternative hypothesis, the MOM estimator is consistent, but the ML estimator is not. The details of the test are as follows. We consider the usual tobit model

$$y_i = \beta'X_i + u_i \quad \text{if RHS} > 0$$
$$y_i = 0 \quad \text{otherwise}$$
$$u_i \sim IN(0, \sigma^2) \quad (i = 1, 2, \ldots, N)$$

For compactness, we define the following: X is the $N \times K$ matrix with X_i' in the ith row. Y is the $N \times 1$ vector with ith element y_i. ϕ is an $N \times 1$ vector with $\phi_i = \phi(\beta'X_i/\sigma)$ as the ith element. Φ is an $N \times N$ diagonal matrix with $\Phi_i = \Phi(\beta'X_i/\sigma)$ as the ith diagonal element. Also, as shown in (6.37),

$$E(y_i) = (\beta'X_i)\Phi_i + \sigma\phi_i$$
$$E(y_i^2) = (\beta'X_i)^2\Phi_i + \sigma^2\Phi_i + (\beta'X_i)\sigma\phi_i \tag{6.83}$$

Hence,

$$E_{xy} = E\left(\frac{1}{N} X'Y\right) = \frac{1}{N} (X'\Phi X\beta + \sigma X'\phi) \tag{6.84}$$

and the variance of $(1/N)X'Y$ is

$$V_1 = \frac{1}{N^2} X'V_y X \tag{6.85}$$

where V_y is an $N \times N$ diagonal matrix with diagonal elements $E(y_i^2) - [E(y_i)]^2$, as defined in (6.83).

The MOM estimator of E_{xy} is $(1/N)X'Y$, which is consistent under both H_0 and H_1, and whose variance under H_0 is given by (6.85). The corresponding efficient estimator under H_0 is the ML estimator obtained by evaluating (6.84) at the ML estimates $\hat{\beta}$ and $\hat{\sigma}$. To obtain its variance, expand (6.84). We have

$$\hat{E}_{xy} - E_{xy} = \frac{1}{N} [X'\Phi X(\hat{\beta} - \beta) + X'\phi(\hat{\sigma} - \sigma) + O(N^{-1/2})]$$

The covariance matrix V_0 is therefore given by

$$V_0 = \frac{1}{N^2} (X'\Phi XX'\phi)V \begin{bmatrix} X'\Phi X \\ X'\phi \end{bmatrix} \qquad (6.86)$$

where V is the covariance matrix of the ML estimates $(\hat{\beta}, \hat{\sigma})$ given in (6.26). The test statistic is now

$$m = N\left(\frac{1}{N} X'Y - \hat{E}_{xy}\right)(\hat{V}_1 - \hat{V}_0)^{-1}\left(\frac{1}{N} X'Y - \hat{E}_{xy}\right)$$

where $\hat{V}_1$ and $\hat{V}_0$ are (6.85) and (6.86) evaluated at the ML estimates $\hat{\beta}$ and $\hat{\sigma}$. This statistic will follow, asymptotically, a χ^2 distribution with degrees of freedom K.[14]

6.16   Mixtures of truncated and untruncated distributions

The discussion in the preceding sections can be extended to regression models in which the error terms are convolutions of truncated and untruncated normal distributions. The major application of this method has been in the area of stochastic frontier estimation and efficiency measurement, although the method can be applied in any situation in which a dummy shift variable is assumed to be random with a skewed distribution. Because the literature on stochastic frontier production functions is vast, we shall not go through it in detail here.[15] We shall discuss only the salient features of these models.

Consider the production function

$$y = f(x, \beta) + \epsilon$$

where y is output, x is a vector of inputs, β is a set of parameters to be estimated, and ϵ is the error term. The usual assumption we make is that $\epsilon \sim N(0, \sigma^2)$. The procedure suggested by Aigner, Lovell, and Schmidt (1977), to be referred to as ALS, is to decompose the error term into two components:

$$\epsilon = -u + v$$

where v follows the usual normal distribution $N(0, \sigma_v^2)$ and u follows the truncated normal

---

[14] Some extensions and amendments of the Nelson test have recently been proposed by Rudd (1982).

[15] See the work of Aigner et al. (1976, 1977) for initial studies, the work of Stevenson (1980) for some generalizations, the work of Førsund et al. (1980) for a survey, and that of Maddala and Fishe (1979) for a skeptical note on some aspects of these models.

$$f(u) = \frac{2}{\sigma_u(2\pi)^{1/2}} \exp\left(-\frac{u^2}{2\sigma_u^2}\right) \quad (u \geq 0) \tag{6.87}$$

The term $-u$ is the one-sided error, which says that each observation should lie on or below the frontier. This residual represents "technical inefficiency." The term v is the usual two-sided error that represents random shifts in the frontier due to favorable and unfavorable external events such as "luck, climate, and machine performance." It also captures measurement error in output y.

Assuming u and v to be independently distributed, and using the result by Weinstein (1964), we get

$$g(\epsilon) = \frac{2}{\sigma}\phi\left(\frac{\epsilon}{\sigma}\right)\left[1 - \Phi\left(\frac{\epsilon\lambda}{\sigma}\right)\right] \tag{6.88}$$

where $\sigma^2 = \sigma_u^2 + \sigma_v^2$, $\lambda = \sigma_u/\sigma_v$, and $\phi(\cdot)$ and $\Phi(\cdot)$ are, respectively, the density function and distribution function of the standard normal. This is obtained by writing the joint density of u and v, substituting $v = \epsilon + u$, and integrating the resulting expression with respect to u.

Once the functional form for the production function $f(x, \beta)$ is specified, then the ALS procedure shows that the ML method can be used to estimate all the parameters. As for the measure of average inefficiency, ALS suggested using $\lambda = \sigma_u/\sigma_v$ and $E(-u) = (2^{1/2}/\pi^{1/2})\sigma_u$. Lee and Tyler (1978) computed the following measure, suggested by Afriat (1972). If the production function being estimated is Cobb–Douglas, with multiplicative error terms, that is,

$$y = AK^\alpha L^\beta e^{-u}e^v$$

then the appropriate technical efficiency is

$$e^{-u} = y/(AK^\alpha L^\beta e^v)$$

Because v is unobservable, computing this measure for each firm is not possible. Afriat therefore suggests using $E(e^{-u})$ as a measure of mean technical efficiency. Because $-u$ is half normal, we get

$$E(e^{-u}) = 2\exp\left(\frac{\sigma_u^2}{2}\right)[1 - \phi(\sigma_u)]$$

ALS also suggested a one-parameter exponential distribution for u, namely,

$$f(u) = \frac{1}{\theta}\exp\left(-\frac{u}{\theta}\right) \quad (u \geq 0)$$

For this distribution, $E(u) = \theta$, and the Afriat measure of inefficiency $E(e^{-u}) = 1/(1+\theta)$.

ALS reported some Monte Carlo studies suggesting that the separation of the residual variance into its component parts cannot be satisfactorily accomplished even for sample sizes as large as 100. Further, the measures of efficiency can be very sensitive to the degree of skewness assumed. One flexible functional form is to assume the distribution of u to be truncated at an unknown point rather than at zero as in (6.87). Stevenson (1980) suggested the function

$$f(u) = \frac{1}{\sigma_u (2\pi)^{1/2}[1 - \Phi(\mu/\sigma_u)]} \exp\left[-\frac{1}{2}\left(\frac{u-\mu}{\sigma_u}\right)^2\right] \quad \text{for } \mu > 0$$

This is the same as (6.87) with the truncation $u > -\mu$. Stevenson also considered a gamma distribution for u instead of the exponential as in the ALS procedure.

CHAPTER 7

Simultaneous-equations models with truncated and censored variables

7.1 Introduction: A general simultaneous-equations model

In Chapter 5 we discussed some simultaneous-equations models with qualitative variables. In Chapter 6 we discussed single-equation models with censored and truncated variables. In this chapter we shall discuss some simultaneous-equations models with discrete censored and truncated variables.

A very general model similar to the one presented in equation (5.1) is

$$BY^* + \Gamma X = U \tag{7.1}$$

where Y^*, X, U, B, and Γ are as defined there. In Chapter 5 we assumed that each element of Y^* is observed either as a continuous variable or as a discrete variable. We shall now relax that assumption and assume that each element is observed as a continuous, discrete, censored or truncated variable. The identification conditions derived there still hold, except that the variables in the set Y_{2t} that were assumed to be observed as continuous variables can be continuous, censored, or truncated. Note that for these variables we need no normalization, because the error variances are estimable. The only difference lies in the estimation methods to be used. In the application of two-stage methods, the reduced forms corresponding to the censored and truncated variables will now be estimated as censored and truncated regression models, as described in Chapter 6. Because these two-stage methods will be described in section 8.8, we shall not elaborate on them here.

An example of this type of model is that presented in Nelson and Olsen (1978). Their model is

$$y_1^* = \gamma_1 y_2^* + \beta_1' X_1 + u_1$$
$$y_2^* = \gamma_2 y_1^* + \beta_2' X_2 + u_2 \tag{7.2}$$

where y_1 is observed, y_2 is truncated so that $y_1 = y_1^*$, and $y_2 = y_2^*$ if $y_2^* > 0$ ($y_2 = 0$ otherwise).

Because in this model only one variable is censored, the ML estimation will not be very difficult. The likelihood function to maximize will be

$$L = \prod_{y_2 > 0} f(y_1, y_2) \cdot \prod_{y_2 = 0} \int_{-\infty}^{0} f(y_1, y_2^*) \, dy_2^* \tag{7.3}$$

where $f(y_1^*, y_2^*)$ is the joint density of y_1^* and y_2^* obtained from (7.2), y_1 is substituted for y_1^*, and y_2 is substituted for y_2^* when $y_2 > 0$. One can decompose the latter part of (7.3) into $f_1(y_1) \cdot f_2(y_2^* | y_1)$, as done in (6.60) and (6.61) in Chapter 6. The detailed derivation of the likelihood equations need not be presented here. With more truncated and censored variables, the ML estimation method becomes cumbersome, because each truncated or censored variable introduces an integral sign in the likelihood function (7.3). In the empirical example considered by Nelson and Olsen there were two latent variables: one observed as a censored variable, the other as a categorical variable. The model referred to simultaneous choices among time spent on vocational school, college, and work (the first variable was censored and the second was categorical).

The model considered by Nelson and Olsen is applicable to several other situations. One example is that of disequilibrium models with fixed supply. Although disequilibrium models will be discussed in detail in Chapter 10, we shall present this particular model here. The model can be written as

$$D_t = \alpha_0 P_t + \alpha_1' X_t + \epsilon_{1t} \qquad \text{(demand function)}$$
$$S_t = \bar{S}_t \qquad \text{(fixed supply)}$$
$$\Delta P_t = \gamma_0 (D_t - S_t) + \gamma_1' X_t + \epsilon_{2t} \quad \text{(price-change equation)}$$
$$Q_t = \text{Min}(D_t, S_t)$$

Q_t is quantity, P_t is price, X_t is a set of exogenous variables, D_t is demand, and S_t is supply. Only $\bar{S}_t$, Q_t, ΔP_t, and X_t are observed. Letting $Y_t^* = D_t - S_t$ (excess demand), the model can be written in the form

$$\Delta P_t = \gamma_0 Y_t^* + \gamma_1' X_t + \epsilon_{2t}$$
$$Y_t^* = -S_t + \alpha_0 P_t + \alpha_1' X_t + \epsilon_{1t}$$

and

$$Y_t = Y_t^* \ (= Q_t - \bar{S}_t) \quad \text{if } Y_t^* < 0$$
$$Y_t = 0 \quad \text{otherwise}$$

Now the model is in the form of the model in equations (7.2) and can be estimated by the same two-stage or ML methods.

The main feature that characterizes the model in (7.1) is that the same latent variables y_i^* occur throughout the model. As with the models considered in section 5.7, we shall consider later (in sections 7.4 and 7.5) models with mixed structures, that is, models of the form

$$B_0 y^* + B_1 y + \Gamma X = U$$

where both the latent variables y^* and their observed counterparts y occur in the model. Before we consider these, we shall discuss some simultaneous-equations models with censoring and truncation.

7.2 Simultaneous-equations models with truncation and/or censoring

We shall discuss the problems that arise in simultaneous-equations models with truncation and censoring with reference to two examples: the analysis of labor-supply functions from the negative-income-tax experiment of Hausman and Wise (1976, 1977) and the analysis of labor-supply models of Heckman (1974), Hanoch (1980a, b), and others. Although the latter studies fall into the class of selectivity models (to be discussed at length in Chapter 9), we shall go through them here.

In the Hausman and Wise study mentioned in section 6.9, we considered estimation of earnings functions where earnings were truncated according to $y_i < L_i$. In the two-equation model, they wrote $y_i = h_i w_i$, where h_i is hours worked and w_i is hourly wage rate.[1] Then $\log y_i = \log h_i + \log w_i$. They assumed that

$$\log w_i = X_{1i}\delta_1 + \epsilon_{1i}$$
$$\log h_i = X_{2i}\delta_2 + \beta_1 \log w_i + \epsilon_{2i}$$

where $(\epsilon_{1i}, \epsilon_{2i})$ have a bivariate normal distribution, with means zero and covariance matrix

---

[1] This model also appears in an unpublished study by Crawford (1975, p. 33). Crawford did this work independently, unaware of the work by Hausman and Wise. However, the data set he used was different. His samples were taken from the five-year panel data set collected by the Survey Research Center at the University of Michigan.

$$\Sigma = \begin{bmatrix} \sigma_{11} & \sigma_{12} \\ \sigma_{12} & \sigma_{22} \end{bmatrix}$$

The reduced form for the model is

$$\log w_i = X_{1i}\delta_1 + \epsilon_{1i}$$
$$\log h_i = X_{1i}\delta_1\beta_1 + X_{2i}\delta_2 + (\epsilon_{1i}\beta_1 + \epsilon_{2i})$$

Let

$$\Omega = \begin{bmatrix} \omega_{11} & \omega_{12} \\ \omega_{12} & \omega_{22} \end{bmatrix}$$

be the covariance matrix of the reduced-form residuals. The truncation condition is $\log y_i < \log L_i$, where $\log y_i = \log w_i + \log h_i$. Because $\log w_i + \log h_i$ is univariate normal, with mean $X_{1i}\delta_1 + X_{1i}\delta_1\beta_1 + X_{2i}\delta_2$ and variance $\omega_{11} + \omega_{22} + 2\omega_{12} = \sigma_1^2(1+\beta_1)^2 + \sigma_2^2 + 2\sigma_{12}(1+\beta_1)$, we have

$$\text{Prob}(\log w_i + \log h_i < \log L_i) = \Phi(Z_i)$$

where

$$Z_i = \frac{\log L_i - X_{1i}\delta_1 - X_{1i}\delta_1\beta_1 - X_{2i}\delta_2}{[\sigma_1^2(1+\beta_1)^2 + \sigma_2^2 + 2\sigma_{12}(1+\beta_1)]^{1/2}}$$

The joint density function of $(\log w_i, \log h_i)$ is just $f(\log w_i, \log h_i)/\Phi(Z_i)$, where $f(\cdot, \cdot)$ is the joint density of $(\log w_i, \log h_i)$ derived in the usual way from the distribution of ϵ_{1i} and ϵ_{2i}. We shall not go through the details of the maximization of the likelihood function here. Because all these problems are similar, we shall present the details for one of the models.

Heckman's model (1974) also considers hours of work and wages, but there is censoring, because some are employed and others are not. The problem considered by Hausman and Wise is merely one of truncated samples. We shall see that both these problems can be analyzed simultaneously.

We start with the model of reservation and market wages presented in section 6.11. We now add hours worked as an extra variable and assume that hours worked adjust to the point where market wage is equal to the reservation (shadow) wage. Let the reservation-wage equation be

$$W_R = \gamma_0 + \gamma_1 H + \gamma_2 X_1 + u_1 \quad (\gamma_1 > 0) \tag{7.4}$$

and the market-wage (wage-offer) equation be

$$W = \beta_0 + \beta_1 X_2 + u_2 \tag{7.5}$$

X_1 and X_2 are exogenous variables.

Heckman assumed that if at $H = 0$, $W_R > W$, then the individual does not work. Otherwise, hours worked adjust to the point where $W_R = W$. In this case we get

$$H = \frac{\beta_0 + \beta_1 X_2 - \gamma_0 - \gamma_1 X_1}{\gamma_1} + \frac{u_2 - u_1}{\gamma_1}$$

$$= \delta' X + V \quad \text{(say)} \tag{7.6}$$

The model, therefore, is

$$\left. \begin{array}{l} W = \beta_0 + \beta_1 X_2 + u_2 \\ H = \delta' X + V \end{array} \right\} \quad \text{if } H > 0$$

$$W = H = 0 \quad \text{otherwise}$$

$$\text{Prob}(H \leqslant 0) = \text{Prob}(V \leqslant -\delta' X) = \Phi\left(\frac{-\delta' X}{\sigma}\right) \tag{7.7}$$

where $\sigma^2 = \text{Var}(V)$. The likelihood function for this model is

$$L = \prod_{H > 0} f(W, H) \cdot \prod_{H \leqslant 0} \Phi\left(\frac{-\delta' X}{\sigma}\right) \tag{7.8}$$

where $f(W, H)$ is the joint density of W and H as obtained from (7.4) and (7.5) after substituting $W_R = W$. The two-stage estimation method for this model and the identification conditions will be discussed in section 8.5. There it will be shown that the model in (7.4) and (7.5) is identified if $\sigma_{12} = 0$ or if there is at least one variable in X_2 not included in X_1.

If we are estimating the Heckman model with the negative-income-tax experiment data used by Hausman and Wise, we need to take account of the truncation by income.[2] To do this, note that the probability of an observation being in the sample is

$$\text{Prob}(\log W + \log H \leqslant \log L)$$

where L is the limit on income (subscript i for observation is omitted for convenience of notation). To use this condition, equations (7.4) and (7.5) have to be specified in the log form (assuming that anyone working for $H \leqslant 1$ hour is unemployed, so that the condition for censoring is $\log H = 0$). Then, once we have the reduced forms for $\log W$ and $\log H$, assuming that in equations (7.5) and (7.6) the dependent variables are $\log W$ and $\log H$, we can get

$$\text{Prob}(\log W + \log H < \log L)$$

---

[2] In an unpublished study by Hotz (1976), the Heckman model was applied ignoring the income constraint.

$$= \text{Prob}\left(u_2 + \frac{u_2 - u_1}{\gamma_1} < \log L - \beta_0 - \beta_1 X_2 - \delta'X \right)$$

$$= \Phi\left(\frac{\log L - \beta_0 - \beta_1 X_2 - \delta'X}{\sigma^*} \right) = \Phi(\Delta) \quad \text{(say)} \qquad (7.9)$$

where

$$\sigma^* = \left[\text{Var}\left(u_2 + \frac{u_2 - u_1}{\gamma_1} \right) \right]^{1/2}$$

The likelihood function for this model with truncated samples is obtained by dividing (7.8) by $\Phi(\Delta)$ in (7.9), and the log-likelihood function is

$$\log \mathcal{L} = -\sum \log \Phi(\Delta) + \sum_{H>0} \log f(W, H) - \sum_{H=0} \Phi\left(\frac{-\delta'X}{\sigma} \right)$$

The first summation is over all observations.

There are other types of truncation and censoring in the context of the labor-supply model. For instance, suppose that data are available only for working individuals. The truncation is that observations with $H \leq 0$ are omitted. Then the likelihood function (7.8) changes to

$$L^* = \prod \frac{f(W, H)}{1 - \Phi(-\delta'X/\sigma)} \qquad (7.10)$$

The denominator is $\text{Prob}(H>0)$, and the product is over all observations. Maximization of (7.10) is carried out by the same iterative procedures used for (7.8). However, the two-stage estimation methods need some modification in this case. The methods to be described in section 8.5 apply to this case as well, except that now equation (7.6) must be estimated as a truncated regression model, as described in section 6.9. The reason for using the two-stage methods is that they give consistent estimates that can be used as initial values in the iterative solution of the likelihood equations.[3] Another extension made of the labor-supply model we are considering is to raise the cutoff point on H to H^* (>0). H^* is the minimum number of hours the individual wants to work. H^* depends on money and time costs of participation.[4] In equation (7.7) the

[3] Wales and Woodland (1980) presented some evidence on ML estimation from data on only employed persons. The results are sampling experiments. However, they did not explain how the ML procedure was carried out.

[4] This was the model used by Cogan (1980). Although Cogan introduced L^* and X^* (time and money costs of participation), these variables were not observed. Thus, the final model involves just H, H^*, and W, as presented here.

condition is now $H > H^*$, instead of $H > 0$. If we write $H^* = \theta'X + V_1$, then

$$\text{Prob}(H < H^*) = \text{Prob}(V - V_1 < \theta'X - \delta'X)$$
$$= \Phi\left(\frac{\theta'X - \delta'X}{\sigma^*}\right)$$

where $\sigma^{*2} = \text{Var}(V - V_1)$. The likelihood function is now of the same form as (7.8). It is

$$L = \prod_{H \geqslant H^*} f(W, H) \prod_{H < H^*} \Phi\left(\frac{\theta'X - \delta'X}{\sigma^*}\right)$$

Hanoch (1980a, b) considered some other kinds of truncation and censoring. This is what he called the survey-week selectivity bias. In data sources such as the Survey of Economic Opportunity (SEO) and the census, information on wages and hours of work is available only for individuals who work (any positive number of hours) during the week prior to their survey interviews. For individuals intending to work K weeks in the current year, therefore, the probability of working in a week is equal, on the average, to $K/52$ (ignoring seasonal effects). Thus, the selection probability is proportional to the endogenous variable K, and the method discussed in section 6.10 is applicable here.

The model that Hanoch (1980b) considered consists of the following equations:

$W = \alpha'x + u_2$ (market-wage equation)

$W_R = \beta'y + u_1$ (reservation-wage equation)

$A = \gamma_1'Z + \delta_1 W + u_3$ if $W \geqslant W_R$ (annual-hours supply equation)
$= 0$ if $W < W_R$

$K = \gamma_2'Z + \delta_2 W + u_4$ if $W \geqslant W_R$ (annual-weeks supply equation)
$= 0$ if $W < W_R$ $(0 < K \leqslant 52)$ (7.11)

The first three equations can be written as

$$\left.\begin{array}{l} W = \alpha'x + u_2 \\ A = \gamma_1'Z + \delta_1 W + u_3 \end{array}\right\} \text{ if } \alpha'x + u_2 \geqslant \beta'y + u_1$$

$$W = A = 0 \quad \text{otherwise}$$

If there is no survey-week selection bias, the model is similar to the labor-supply model considered earlier. The likelihood function is, as in (7.8),

$$L = \prod_{A>0} f(A, W) \prod_{A=0} \text{Prob}(W < W_R) \tag{7.12}$$

The way the survey is conducted, all individuals have different probabilities of being in the sample. These probabilities can be derived from (7.11). Because equation (7.11) can be written as

$$K = \gamma_2' Z + \delta_2(\alpha'x) + (\delta_2 u_2 + u_4) \quad \text{if } W \geqslant W_R$$
$$K = 0 \quad \text{otherwise} \tag{7.13}$$

the probability of being in the sample is proportional to

$$\text{Prob}(W \geqslant W_R) \cdot f(K \mid W \geqslant W_R) \tag{7.14}$$

which can be obtained from (7.13). The appropriate likelihood function is obtained by dividing (7.12) by (7.14) for each observation. The log-likelihood function is

$$\log L = \sum_{A>0} \log f(A, W) + \sum_{A=0} \log \text{Prob}(W < W_R)$$
$$- \sum \log \text{Prob}(W \geqslant W_R) - \sum \log f(K \mid W \geqslant W_R)$$

The last two summations are over all observations.[5] We could consider several other modifications of this model, but we shall not pursue all of them here.

Although the foregoing discussion has been in terms of labor-supply models, there are several problems in which the structures of the problems are very similar. For instance, consider a loan model with interest-rate ceilings (a labor-supply model with minimum-wage laws would be exactly similar). The model, to be considered later in section 10.7, is as follows: Each individual has a demand function giving the combinations of loan amounts and interest rates at which the individual is willing to borrow the stated amounts. Similarly, the bank has a schedule of the maximum amounts it is willing to lend at the different rates. If the equilibrium interest rate R is less than the interest ceiling $\bar{R}$, then a loan transaction takes place. Otherwise, no transaction takes place. The model is given by

$$L_i = a_1 R_i + b_1' X_{1i} + u_{1i} \quad \text{if } R_i \leqslant \bar{R} \quad \text{(loan demand)}$$
$$L_i = a_2 R_i + n_2' X_{2i} + u_{2i} \quad \text{if } R_i \leqslant \bar{R} \quad \text{(loan supply)}$$
$$L_i = 0 \quad \text{otherwise} \tag{7.15}$$

---

[5] Hanoch did not derive the appropriate likelihood function. He actually used a series of corrections using the two-stage methods.

The likelihood function is similar to (7.8). The method for computing the ML estimates is presented in the Appendix at the end of this chapter. The methods are similar for all the other models discussed in this section.

7.3 Simultaneous-equations models with probit- and tobit-type selectivity

In the preceding section we considered several simultaneous-equations models in which the criterion function determining the censoring is of the probit type in some cases and the tobit type in others. The labor-supply model in (7.7) and the loan model in (7.15) are examples in which the criterion function is of the tobit type. The model in (7.11) is an example in which the criterion function is of the probit type, because it has to be estimated by the probit method. The estimation problems are of the same level of complexity whether the criterion function is of the probit or tobit type. In the likelihood functions of the form (7.8), it is only the last term that changes; for example, see (7.12). As for two-stage estimation methods, there are only minor differences. These will be explained in section 8.7, with further examples of the two types of censoring criteria. One point that is worth mentioning is that it may be more realistic to formulate the censoring (or selection) criterion in a very general form, in which case it can be estimated only by the probit method. For instance, in the loan model considered in the preceding section, the criterion by which the loan is granted or denied may not be simply a function of whether or not the rate of interest is less than or equal to $\bar{R}$. If the criterion involves other variables besides R and $\bar{R}$, then it cannot be estimated by the tobit method, and the parameters in the criterion function are estimable only up to a scale factor. But for many practical purposes, estimating the parameters up to a scale factor may be all that is required. Because these problems will be dealt with in the next chapter, they will not be elaborated here.

7.4 Models with mixed latent and observed variables

In section 5.7 we considered models that involve both the latent variables and their observed qualitative counterparts. We shall now consider similar models, with the observed counterparts being the truncated or censored latent variables, and show that again there are some logical-consistency conditions to be imposed.

Amemiya (1974b) was the first to consider such mixed models. For the sake of ease of exposition and notational simplicity, we shall consider a two-equation model. The model is, for $t = 1, 2, \ldots, T$,

$$y_{1t} = \gamma_1 y_{2t} + \beta_1' x_{1t} + u_{1t} \quad \text{if RHS} > 0$$
$$y_{1t} = 0 \quad \text{if RHS} \leqslant 0$$
$$y_{2t} = \gamma_2 y_{1t} + \beta_2' x_{2t} + u_{2t} \quad \text{if RHS} > 0$$
$$y_{2t} = 0 \quad \text{if RHS} \leqslant 0 \tag{7.16}$$

where y_{1t} and y_{2t} are the endogenous variables. We rewrite this model in the following equivalent form:

$$y_{1t}^* = \gamma_1 y_{2t} + \beta_1' x_{1t} + u_{1t}$$
$$y_{2t}^* = \gamma_2 y_{1t} + \beta_2' x_{2t} + u_{2t} \tag{7.17}$$

and

$$y_{1t} = y_{1t}^* \quad \text{if } y_{1t}^* > 0$$
$$y_{1t} = 0 \quad \text{otherwise}$$
$$y_{2t} = y_{2t}^* \quad \text{if } y_{2t}^* > 0$$
$$y_{2t} = 0 \quad \text{otherwise} \tag{7.18}$$

If the variables on the right-hand side of equation (7.17) are y_{2t}^* and y_{1t}^*, then the model is of the form (7.1), or the model considered by Nelson and Olsen (1978). But the fact that both the latent variables and their censored observed counterparts given by (7.18) occur simultaneously is what makes this model different.

Divide the observations into four sets:

$$S_1: \quad y_{1t} > 0, \quad y_{2t} > 0$$
$$S_2: \quad y_{1t} > 0, \quad y_{2t} = 0$$
$$S_3: \quad y_{1t} = 0, \quad y_{2t} > 0$$
$$S_4: \quad y_{1t} = 0, \quad y_{2t} = 0$$

Then, denoting the joint density of (u_1, u_2) by $f(\cdot, \cdot)$, we get the likelihood function as

$$L = \prod_1 (1 - \gamma_1 \gamma_2) f(y_{1t} - \gamma_1 y_{2t} - \beta_1' x_{1t}, \, y_{2t} - \gamma_2 y_{1t} - \beta_2' x_{2t})$$

$$\prod_2 \int_{-\infty}^{-\gamma_2 y_{1t} - \beta_2' x_{2t}} f(y_{1t} - \beta_1' x_{1t}, \, u_2) \, du_2$$

$$\prod_3 \int_{-\infty}^{-\gamma_1 y_{2t} - \beta_1' x_{1t}} f(u_1, \, y_{2t} - \beta_2' x_{2t}) \, du_1$$

$$\prod_4 \int_{-\infty}^{-\beta_2' x_{2t}} \int_{-\infty}^{-\beta_1' x_{1t}} f(u_1, u_2) \, du_1 \, du_2$$

where Π_j denotes product over all observations in S_j ($j=1,2,3,4$). Because of the last term, the ML estimation involves numerical evaluation of double integrals at each stage of iteration.

For the purpose of writing the reduced forms, partition x_1 and x_2 as $x_1' = (x_{11}', x_{12}')$ and $x_2' = (x_{22}', x_{12}')$; x_{12} is the set of exogenous variables common to both equations. Partition β_1 and β_2 accordingly, so that $\beta_1' = (\beta_{11}', \beta_{12}')$ and $\beta_2' = (\beta_{22}', \beta_{12}')$. Define $x' = (x_{11}', x_{22}', x_{12}')$, $v_1 = u_1 + \gamma_1 u_2$, $v_2 = \gamma_2 u_1 + u_2$, and

$$\alpha_1' = \frac{1}{1 - \gamma_1 \gamma_2} (\beta_{11}', \gamma_1 \beta_{22}', \beta_{12}' + \gamma_1 \beta_{21}') = \frac{1}{\Delta} \theta_1' \quad \text{(say)}$$

$$\alpha_2' = \frac{1}{1 - \gamma_1 \gamma_2} (\gamma_2 \beta_{11}', \beta_{22}', \gamma_2 \beta_{12}' + \beta_{21}') = \frac{1}{\Delta} \theta_2' \quad \text{(say)} \quad (7.19)$$

where $\Delta = 1 - \gamma_1 \gamma_2$.

Amemiya considered the reduced form

$$y_{1t}^* = \alpha_1' x_t + v_{1t} \quad \text{and} \quad y_{2t}^* = \alpha_2' x_t + v_{2t}$$

if the right-hand sides of both equations are simultaneously positive,

$$y_{1t}^* = y_{2t}^* = 0$$

otherwise.[6] Thus, he considered only one of the several reduced forms. However, note that there are four reduced forms, which are as follows:

	$y_{1t} > 0$	$y_{1t} = 0$
$y_{2t} > 0$	$y_{1t} = \alpha_1' x_t + (1/\Delta) v_{1t}$ $y_{2t} = \alpha_2' x_t + (1/\Delta) v_{2t}$	$y_{1t} = \theta_1' x_t + v_{1t}$ $y_{2t} = \beta_2' x_{2t} + u_{2t}$
$y_{2t} = 0$	$y_{1t} = \beta_1' x_{1t} + u_{1t}$ $y_{2t} = \theta_2' x_t + v_{2t}$	$y_{1t} = \beta_1' x_{1t} + u_{1t}$ $y_{2t} = \beta_2' x_{2t} + u_{2t}$

Here, α_1, α_2, θ_1, θ_2, and Δ are as defined in (7.19).

Consider now the two reduced forms for y_{1t} corresponding to the case $y_{2t} > 0$. The case $y_{1t} > 0$ implies $y_{1t}^* > 0$. This gives the condition

$$\frac{1}{\Delta} (\theta_1' x_t + v_{1t}) > 0 \tag{7.20}$$

---

[6] See Amemiya (1974b), equation (4.5). Note also that v_{1t} and v_{2t} in Amemiya's study should both be divided by $\Delta = 1 - \gamma_1 \gamma_2$.

The case $y_{1t} = 0$ corresponds to $y_{1t}^* \leqslant 0$. This gives the condition

$$\theta_1' x_t + v_{1t} \leqslant 0 \tag{7.21}$$

The two conditions (7.20) and (7.21) are mutually exclusive only if $\Delta > 0$, that is, $1 - \gamma_1 \gamma_2 > 0$. This is the condition for logical consistency of this model. Amemiya (1974b) derived the condition in the general case that every principal minor of Γ must be positive, where Γ is the matrix of coefficients of the endogenous variables. He derived it by appealing to a theorem of Samelson et al. (1958). General coherency conditions in such models have also been derived by Gourieroux et al. (1980b). Further examples of this will be presented in section 10.5.

In addition to this logical-consistency condition, we have to impose the usual identifiability conditions in this model, namely, that there is at least one variable in each of x_1 and x_2 that is not included in the other. Finally, as an example of the applicability of this model, Amemiya gave the case of joint determination of work hours of a husband and wife, where the hours are naturally constrained to be nonnegative. However, it is difficult to give any economic interpretation to the condition that $\gamma_1 \gamma_2 < 1$, which suggests that this model is not appropriate for this problem. We shall consider in the next section an example in which a proper formulation of a model leads to one like the Amemiya model, but the condition $\gamma_1 \gamma_2 < 1$ is automatically satisfied. Amemiya considered a two-stage estimation procedure for this model, but he used only the observations in S_1. His procedure can be easily extended so as to include all the observations in the sample (for details, see Maddala (1977b)], but because the procedure is computationally not much simpler than the ML method, we shall not go into the details here. It is, however, somewhat instructive to consider a model in which only some variables are truncated.

Lee (1976a, b) and Sickles and Schmidt (1978) considered the model given in (7.17), with only one variable truncated; $y_{2t} = y_{2t}^*$, but

$$y_{1t} = y_{1t}^* \quad \text{if } y_{1t}^* > 0$$
$$y_{1t} = 0 \quad \text{otherwise}$$

For convenience, let us write the model as

$$y_{1t}^* = \gamma_1 y_{2t} + \beta_1' X_t + u_{1t}$$
$$y_{2t}^* = \gamma_2 y_{1t} + \beta_2' X_t + u_{2t} \tag{7.17'}$$

where X is now the set of all exogenous variables. Let S_1 denote the set of observations for which $y_{1t} > 0$ and S_2 the set of observations for which $y_{1t} = 0$. Again this gives us two reduced forms (with the previous definitions):

For $y_{1t} > 0$: $\quad y_{1t} = \dfrac{1}{\Delta}(\beta_1' + \gamma_1\beta_2')X_t + \dfrac{1}{\Delta}v_{1t}$

$$y_{2t} = \frac{1}{\Delta}(\beta_2' + \gamma_2\beta_1')X_t + \frac{1}{\Delta}v_{2t} \tag{7.22}$$

For $y_{1t} = 0$: $\quad y_{1t} = (\beta_1' + \gamma_1\beta_2')X_t + v_{1t}$

$$y_{2t} = \beta_2'X_t + u_{2t} \tag{7.23}$$

By an argument similar to the one given earlier, comparing the two reduced-form equations for y_{1t}, we arrive at the logical-consistency condition $\Delta > 0$ or $1 - \gamma_1\gamma_2 > 0$.

The important differences, however, are in the conditions for identifiability of the parameters and the ease in the estimation. It can be shown that the parameters of the second equation are always identified, whereas one needs the usual exclusion restrictions to identify the parameters in the first equation. To see this, note that from the observations in S_1 the reduced-form parameters

$$\pi_1' = \frac{1}{1-\gamma_1\gamma_2}(\beta_1' + \gamma_1\beta_2') \quad \text{and} \quad \pi_2' = \frac{1}{1-\gamma_1\gamma_2}(\gamma_2\beta_1' + \beta_2') \tag{7.24}$$

are estimable. The question is whether or not equations (7.23) give any more information that will help the identification of the structural parameters. Define $u_t = (1/\sigma^*)(u_{1t} + \gamma_2 u_{2t})$, with $\sigma^{*2} = \mathrm{Var}(u_{1t} + \gamma_2 u_{2t})$. Then $E(u_{2t} \mid y_{1t} < 0) = E(u_{2t} \mid u_t < Z_t) = -\sigma_{2u}\phi(Z_t)/\Phi(Z_t)$, where $Z_t = (1/\sigma^*)(\beta_1' + \gamma_1\beta_2')X_t$ and $\sigma_{2u} = \mathrm{Cov}(u_{2t}, u_t)$. Thus, in the set S_2, we have

$$y_{2t} = \beta_2'X_t - \sigma_{2u}\frac{\phi(Z_t)}{\Phi(Z_t)} + \epsilon_t \tag{7.25}$$

where $E(\epsilon_t) = 0$. If we can get a consistent estimate of Z_t, we can estimate this equation by OLS and get consistent estimates of β_2 and σ_{2u}. Fortunately, in this case, a probit estimation based on the dummy variable

$I_t = 1 \quad \text{if } y_{1t} > 0$

$I_t = 0 \quad \text{otherwise}$

gives us consistent estimates of the parameters in Z_t, and thus we can get a consistent estimate $\hat{Z}_t$ for Z_t. With β_2 identified, we can now go back to equations (7.24) to see what other parameters are identified. Rewriting them as

$$\begin{bmatrix} 1 & -\gamma_1 \\ -\gamma_2 & 1 \end{bmatrix}\begin{bmatrix} \pi_1' \\ \pi_2' \end{bmatrix} = \begin{bmatrix} \beta_1' \\ \beta_2' \end{bmatrix}$$

we note that

$$(-\gamma_2, 1)\begin{bmatrix} \pi_1' \\ \pi_2' \end{bmatrix} = \beta_2'$$

Hence γ_2 is identified. Thus, in this model the parameters of the second equation, namely β_2 and γ_2, are identified without the usual exclusion restrictions. On the other hand, the parameters of the first equation are not identified without the usual restrictions.

To see that the first equation is not identified without further restrictions, add the second equation to the first. We get

$$y_{1t}^* = (\gamma_1 - 1)y_{2t} + \gamma_2 y_{1t} + (\beta_1' + \beta_2')X_t + u_{1t} + u_{2t} \qquad (7.26)$$

Note that this equation does not at first sight appear to be of the same form as the first structural equation.[7] However, we can show that it satisfies the same conditions by considering the cases $y_{1t}^* > 0$ and $y_{2t}^* \leqslant 0$ separately.

For $y_{1t}^* > 0$, because $y_{1t}^* = y_{1t}$, equation (7.26) is indistinguishable in form from the first structural equation. For $y_{1t}^* \leqslant 0$, because $y_{1t} = 0$, note that equation (7.26) implies

$$(\gamma_1 - 1)y_{2t} + (\beta_1' + \beta_2')X_t + u_{1t} + u_{2t} \leqslant 0 \qquad (7.27)$$

But because the second structural equation implies

$$y_{2t} = \beta_2'X_t + u_{2t}$$

by subtraction we get

$$\gamma_1 y_{2t} + \beta_1'X_t + u_{1t} \leqslant 0 \qquad (7.28)$$

Thus, conditions (7.27) and (7.28) are equivalent. In this case equation (7.26) implies the same inequality as the first structural equation and is indistinguishable from it in this sense. [Note that we cannot just argue that equation (7.26) is of the same form as the first structural equation.] This equivalence proves that the first equation is not identified without any further restrictions.

The details of two-stage estimation of this model will not be pursued here, because the model can be written as a switching simultaneous sys-

---

[7] Sickles and Schmidt (1978, p. 15) considered a linear combination of the two equations and solved for y_{2t}. They argued that this resulting equation is distinguishable from the second structural equation because it contains y_1^* as a right-hand-side variable. Obviously, we can use a similar argument for the first structural equation as well, saying it contains y_1 as a right-hand-side variable. Thus, one must be careful about such arguments in this class of models.

tem, and two-stage estimation in such models will be discussed in the next chapter. As for ML estimation, it is easy in this model, because there is only one truncated variable. The likelihood function can be easily written down. Denoting by $f(\cdot, \cdot)$ the joint density of u_1 and u_2, we have

$$L = \prod_1 (1 - \gamma_1\gamma_2)f(y_1 - \gamma_1 y_2 - \beta_1'X, y_2 - \gamma_2 y_1 - \beta_2'X)$$

$$\times \prod_2 \int_{-\infty}^{-\gamma_1 y_2 - \beta_1'X} f(u_1, y_2 - \beta_2'X)\, du_1$$

where we have omitted the subscript t, and $\prod_j$ denotes the product over all observations in S_j ($j = 1, 2$).

The problem with this model is the same as that mentioned earlier. The condition $\gamma_1\gamma_2 < 1$ needs to be imposed, and this condition very often has no economic interpretation. There are very few examples in which the model has had meaningful economic applications. However, one such application will be discussed in section 7.5.

Before we present a meaningful model, there are two illustrations of this model that are worth discussing, even though they are formulated somewhat incorrectly: one by Sickles, Schmidt, and Witte (1979) and the other by Sickles and Yezer (1981). In the former study the data consisted of information on individuals who had been released from prison. The main variables of interest were the criminal behavior of these individuals and their wage rates after release. Sickles et al. denoted these variables as y_1^* and y_2 and defined them as follows: y_1^*, total time sentenced during a follow-up period after release; y_2, wage rate for the first job after release. According to Sickles and Schmidt, y_1^* was zero for several observations, and hence they defined a variable y_1 as

$$y_1 = y_1^* \quad \text{if } y_1^* > 0$$
$$y_1 = 0 \quad \text{otherwise}$$

They then argued that it was y_1, not y_1^*, that should be used as an explanatory variable for y_2, so that the model is given by equations (7.17'). However, note that the way Sickles et al. defined the variables, y_1 and y_1^* are the same variable. Actually, y_1^*, which is an unobserved variable, should be defined as "a propensity to engage in criminal activity," and y_1, the observed counterpart, as "total time sentenced during a follow-up period after release." With these proper definitions of variables, we can discuss how the model needs to be formulated.

If y_1^*, which is a measure of the propensity to engage in criminal activity, and y_2, a measure of alternative opportunities, are mutually dependent, a model of the type considered by Nelson and Olsen is appropriate. Sickles et al. argued that the reason for including y_1 instead of y_1^* is that the individual's actions depend on perceptions of the effects (the releasee's observations concerning sentencing practices), not on the sentiment y_1^* toward these practices. Note, however, that y_1^* was not defined as a "sentiment" initially in their model. Moreover, this argument is fallacious, because y_1 is the sentence received by the individual and thus is observed only after the event. Thus, it cannot be used as an explanatory variable for y_2. One possible alternative candidate for inclusion in the y_2 equation is $\bar{y}_1 = \text{Prob}(y_1^* > 0)$. Such a model was discussed in equation (5.51) in Chapter 5. Implicitly, there are more variables in this model than have been considered (as in the example we discussed in section 5.8). But if y_1^* and y_2 are the only variables considered, a model like that of Nelson and Olsen is the one that is appropriate for this problem. One important variable missing from the analysis is the time taken to find the first job. It is also not clear whether or not everyone found a job after release. (Are there any observations on y_2 that are zero?) Another factor that is relevant is the job stability of the individual. In any case, Sickles and Schmidt found that the coefficient of y_1 in the y_2 equation was not significant and that there was no evidence of simultaneity. As argued here, this could be merely a consequence of the way they formulated the simultaneous-equations model and their not using all the relevant variables.

The second application, by Sickles and Yezer (1981), is also very instructive. Sickles and Yezer considered a model to study the effects of interest-rate ceilings. However, their data are based only on loans granted. The specification they adopted was:

$$R^* = b_0 + b_1 L + b_2 X + u \quad \text{(supply function)}$$
$$L = a_0 + a_1 R + a_2 Z + v \quad \text{(demand function)}$$

where L is the amount loaned, R^* is the "latent" interest rate, and X and Z are exogenous variables. If there is an interest-rate ceiling of $\bar{R}$, the observed interest rate R is given by

$$R = R^* \quad \text{if } R^* < \bar{R}$$
$$R = \bar{R} \quad \text{if } R^* \geqslant \bar{R}$$

This formulation says that if $R^* < \bar{R}$, the interest rate and the amount of loan granted are simultaneously determined by the intersection of demand and supply. If $R^* \geqslant \bar{R}$, then the amount loaned is determined by the demand function; that is, the bank will loan all the amount demanded at that rate of interest. Presumably, because the bank cannot conceivably have such an unlimited supply of funds, the implicit assumption is that the bank will limit the number of borrowers (how and by what criterion must be specified) and give the selected borrowers whatever amounts they want to borrow at the rate of interest $\bar{R}$.

Sickles and Yezer reversed the roles of latent and observed interest rates in the demand and supply functions. If the latent interest rate enters the demand function and the observed interest rate enters the supply function, then when $R^* \geqslant \bar{R}$, $\bar{R}$ determines the amount loaned through the supply function. Although this assumption appears more reasonable than to say that $\bar{R}$ determines the loans granted through the demand function, Sickles and Yezer rejected this model, saying it gave wrong signs for the estimated coefficients.

Again, one reason that a more reasonable model has been rejected by the data could be the problems of the particular estimation method used. It is true that the rate of interest is a truncated variable, but it is not reasonable to include the truncated variable in the demand function and the untruncated variable in the supply function or vice versa. The effect of the truncation on the demand side actually shows up in the form of expectations about loan rejection, and this should be built in explicitly [see, for instance, equation (10.67) in Chapter 10], rather than by including the truncated variable in the model. Another problem is with the data. The data consist only of loans granted. Thus, the sample is a truncated sample. Hence, one should formulate a theory of how loans are rejected. In addition, there should be a discussion of what role the interest-rate ceiling plays in the rejection of loan applications. One model in this direction is presented in equation (7.15), which must be estimated by taking account of the fact that the sample is a truncated sample and thus using likelihood functions of the form (7.10). There are also further modifications to this that can be made (see section 10.7), and we can also change the selection criterion to include other factors besides the interest-rate ceiling.[8]

The main point in both these illustrative examples is that one should be careful in formulating simultaneous-equations models with truncated variables. It is often tempting to introduce the truncated variables mechanically into a simultaneous-equations framework and talk of logical consistency and so forth, but it is desirable to model more carefully the process that produces the truncation. Some further discussion of this point will be presented in Chapter 11. In the next section we shall discuss an example in which a model of the kind suggested by Amemiya is

[8] Alternative demand-and-supply models with interest-rate ceilings for negotiated and nonnegotiated loans, with truncated and untruncated samples, and assuming interest rates to be exogenous and endogenous, have been discussed by Maddala and Trost (1982).

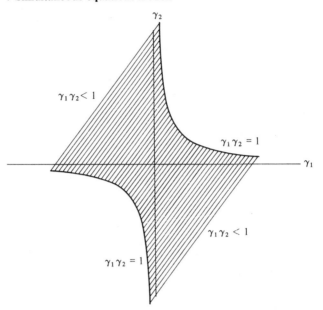

Figure 7.1. Admissible range of the parameter space in a two-equation model with truncated variables

derived from more basic behavioral equations and in which the logical-consistency condition is automatically satisfied.

7.5   The question of logical consistency

The model given by (7.16) is meaningful only if $\gamma_1\gamma_2 < 1$. The range of this parameter space is shown in Figure 7.1. Although it is tempting to formulate model (7.16) directly and impose the logical-consistency condition extraneously, one would be hard pressed to give an economic justification to this condition. Furthermore, the estimation problems that result from imposing the inequality condition are complex. On the other hand, if the model is derived from more basic considerations, it is easy to examine what this condition implies.

As an example of one formulation in terms of basic behavioral relationships, consider the model of Waldman (1981). He constructed a model in which y_1 and y_2 are, respectively, hours of work and hours of schooling. The equation system is

$$w_1 = \beta_1' X + \alpha y_1 + \epsilon_1$$
$$w_2 = \beta_2' X + \gamma y_2 + \epsilon_2$$

$$w_3 = \beta_3' X + \delta(y_1 + y_2) + \epsilon_3 \tag{7.29}$$

where w_1 is market wage, w_2 is marginal productivity of schooling, and w_3 is reservation wage. X is a set of exogenous explanatory variables. We assume that $\alpha = 0$ or is slightly positive; that is, either market wages are independent of hours of work or they rise slightly with hours worked. If income–leisure indifference curves are convex δ will be greater than zero. We shall also assume that $\delta > \alpha$; that is, reservation wages rise faster than market wages with hours of work. Finally, we assume that γ is less than zero; that is, the marginal productivity of schooling declines with years of schooling (perhaps a questionable assumption).

As in the case of Heckman's model, we assume that if at zero hours of work ($y_1 = 0$) we have $w_1 > w_3$, then hours worked adjust to the point $w_1 = w_3$. Hence, either $y_1 = 0$ or, if $y_1 > 0$, we have $w_1 = w_3$, which implies that [from equations (7.29), after solving for y_1]

$$y_1 = -\frac{\delta}{\delta - \alpha} y_2 + \frac{1}{\delta - \alpha}(\beta_1' - \beta_3')X + \frac{1}{\delta - \alpha}(\epsilon_1 - \epsilon_3)$$

Similarly, we assume that if at zero hours of schooling $w_2 > w_3$, hours devoted to schooling will rise to the point where $w_2 = w_3$. Hence, $y_2 = 0$, or, if $y_2 > 0$, we have $w_2 = w_3$. Again, using (7.29) and solving for y_2, we get an equation for y_2 similar to the equation for y_1. Thus we have the model

$$y_1 = -\frac{\delta}{\delta - \alpha} y_2 + \frac{1}{\delta - \alpha}(\beta_1' - \beta_3')X + \frac{1}{\delta - \alpha}(\epsilon_1 - \epsilon_3) \quad \text{if } y_1 > 0$$

$$y_1 = 0 \quad \text{otherwise}$$

$$y_2 = -\frac{\delta}{\delta - \gamma} y_1 + \frac{1}{\delta - \gamma}(\beta_2' - \beta_3')X + \frac{1}{\delta - \gamma}(\epsilon_2 - \epsilon_3) \quad \text{if } y_2 > 0$$

$$y_2 = 0 \quad \text{otherwise} \tag{7.30}$$

This equation system is exactly in the form of equations (7.16). The condition for logical consistency is

$$-\frac{\delta}{\delta - \alpha}\left(-\frac{\delta}{\delta - \gamma}\right) < 1 \tag{7.31}$$

If $\alpha = 0$ (i.e., market wages do not depend on hours of work), then $\gamma < 0$ is a necessary and sufficient condition for the model to be consistent. This implies that marginal productivity of schooling should decline with hours of schooling. In this case the model is easily interpretable. However, if $\alpha \neq 0$, (7.31) gives

$$\gamma < -\frac{\delta\alpha}{\delta-\alpha} \tag{7.32}$$

which implies a stronger condition on γ if $\alpha>0$ and $\delta>\alpha$. Further, it is difficult to interpret what (7.32) means. Equation (7.30) is a sort of semireduced form derived from the structural system (7.29). The observed variables will be w_1, y_1, and y_2, where w_1 is observed only if $y_1>0$, and w_2 and w_3 are never observed. We shall not go into the details of either the identification problem or the estimation problem here. The important point to note is that if $\alpha=0$ in equations (7.29), the logical-consistency condition has an easy interpretation, and one can easily see under what assumptions it is satisfied.

7.6   Summary and conclusions

In this chapter we have considered a series of simultaneous-equations models involving truncated and censored variables and also models with mixed structures, where the latent variables and their truncated observed counterparts occur simultaneously. In the latter models there are some conditions that the parameters must satisfy in order that the model be meaningful, and it is argued that writing down simultaneous-equations models mechanically (which is a very tempting thing to do) results in models whose economic meaning is questionable. There are, as yet, not many examples of these models that have substantive economic interpretations. In addition to the example discussed in the preceding section, we can mention the watermelon-market model analyzed by Goldfeld and Quandt (1975). This model will be discussed in section 10.5. Clearly, more work needs to be done in this area.

Appendix: ML estimation of the supply-and-demand model in section 7.2

The model[9]

Loan demand: $L_i = a_1 R_i + b_i' X_{1i} + u_{1i}$ ⎫
                                                              ⎬ if $R_i < \bar{R}$
Loan supply: $L_i = a_2 R_i + b_2' X_{2i} + u_{2i}$ ⎭

$L_i = 0$ otherwise

---

[9] Heckman's labor-supply model with the likelihood function (7.8) has the same structure.

The likelihood function

$$L = \prod_{L_i>0} f(L_i, R_i) \cdot \prod_{L_i=0} \int_{\bar{R}}^{\infty} g(R_i)\, dR_i \tag{A.1}$$

Assume that u_{1i} and u_{2i} are bivariate normal, and define

$$\Lambda = \text{Cov}(u_{1i}, u_{2i}) = \begin{bmatrix} \sigma_1^2 & \rho\sigma_1\sigma_2 \\ \rho\sigma_1\sigma_2 & \sigma_2^2 \end{bmatrix}, \quad Z_i = \begin{bmatrix} L_i - a_1 R_i - b_1' X_{1i} \\ L_i - a_2 R_i - b_2' X_{2i} \end{bmatrix}$$

$$J = \begin{bmatrix} \dfrac{\partial u_{1i}}{\partial L_i} & \dfrac{\partial u_{1i}}{\partial R_i} \\ \dfrac{\partial u_{2i}}{\partial L_i} & \dfrac{\partial u_{2i}}{\partial R_i} \end{bmatrix} = \begin{bmatrix} 1 & -a_1 \\ 1 & -a_2 \end{bmatrix}$$

Then the bivariate density $f(L_i, R_i)$ is

$$f(L_i, R_i) = \frac{1}{2\Pi} \frac{1}{|\Lambda|^{1/2}} \exp(-\tfrac{1}{2} Z'\Lambda^{-1}Z) \cdot \text{Abs}(|J|) \tag{A.2}$$

where Abs is the absolute value function and $|J|$ is the determinant of the Jacobian of the transformation. Because a_2 is expected to be positive and a_1 is expected to be negative, we get

$$f(L_i, R_i) = \frac{a_2 - a_1}{2\Pi} \frac{1}{|\Lambda|^{1/2}} \exp(-\tfrac{1}{2} Z'\Lambda^{-1}Z) \tag{A.2$'$}$$

To find the marginal density of R_i, $g(R_i)$, we first solve for the reduced form of R_i and get

$$R_i = \frac{1}{a_2 - a_1}(b_1' X_{1i} - b_2' X_{2i}) + \frac{u_{1i} - u_{2i}}{a_2 - a_1} \tag{A.3}$$

So R_i has a normal distribution, with

$$\text{mean} = M = \frac{1}{a_2 - a_1}(b_1' X_{1i} - b_2' X_{2i})$$

$$\text{variance} = \sigma^2 = \frac{\sigma_1^2 + \sigma_2^2 - 2\rho\sigma_1\sigma_2}{(a_2 - a_1)^2}$$

and

$$\int_{\bar{R}}^{\infty} g(R_i)\, dR_i = 1 - \Phi\left(\frac{\bar{R} - M}{\sigma}\right) \tag{A.4}$$

where Φ is the standard normal cumulative function. Finally, dropping the i subscript, we get the log-likelihood function as

$$\log L = -n_1 \log \sigma_1 - n_1 \log \sigma_2 - \frac{n_1}{2} \log(1-\rho^2) + n_1 \log(a_2-a_1)$$

$$- \frac{1}{2(1-\rho^2)} \sum_1 \left(\frac{Z_1^2}{\sigma_1^2} - \frac{2\rho Z_1 Z_2}{\sigma_1\sigma_2} + \frac{Z_2^2}{\sigma_2^2} \right)$$

$$+ \sum_2 \log \left[1 - \Phi\left(\frac{(a_2-a_1)\bar{R} - b_1'X_1 + b_2'X_2}{(\sigma_1^2+\sigma_2^2-2\rho\sigma_1\sigma_2)^{1/2}} \right) \right] \tag{A.5}$$

where n_1 is the number of observations for which $L_i > 0$, n_2 is the number of observations for which $L_i = 0$, $Z_1 = L - a_1 R - b_1'X_1$, $Z_2 = L - a_2 R - b_2'X_2$, $\sum_1$ means summation over the n_1 observation where $L_i > 0$, and $\sum_2$ means summation over the n_2 observation where $L_i = 0$.

The first derivatives of $\log L$

To use the method described in Berndt et al. (1974), we only need the first derivates of $\log L$ with respect to the parameters ($\sigma_1, \sigma_2, \rho, a_1, a_2, b_1$, and b_2). In what follows, define

$$\Delta = \frac{(a_2-a_1)\bar{R} - b_1'X_1 + b_2'X_2}{(\sigma_1^2+\sigma_2^2-2\sigma\rho_1\sigma_2)}$$

and note that

$$\frac{\partial \log[1-\Phi(\Delta)]}{\partial \theta} = - \frac{\phi(\Delta)}{1-\Phi(\Delta)} \cdot \frac{\partial \Delta}{\partial \theta}$$

where ϕ is the standard normal density function. The first derivatives are

$$\frac{\partial \log L}{\partial \sigma_1} = -\frac{n_1}{\sigma_1} - \frac{1}{2(1-\rho^2)} \sum_1 \left(-\frac{2Z_1^2}{\sigma_1^3} + \frac{2\rho Z_1 Z_2}{\sigma_1^2\sigma_2} \right)$$

$$+ \sum_2 \frac{\phi(\Delta)}{1-\Phi(\Delta)} \Delta\left(\frac{\sigma_1-\rho\sigma_2}{\sigma_1^2+\sigma_2^2-2\rho\sigma_1\sigma_2} \right)$$

$$\frac{\partial \log L}{\partial \sigma_2} = -\frac{n_1}{\sigma_2} - \frac{1}{2(1-\rho^2)} \sum_1 \left(-\frac{2Z_2^2}{\sigma_2^3} + \frac{2\rho Z_1 Z_2}{\sigma_2^2\sigma_1} \right)$$

$$+ \sum_2 \frac{\phi(\Delta)}{1-\Phi(\Delta)} \Delta\left(\frac{\sigma_2-\rho\sigma_1}{\sigma_1^2+\sigma_2^2-2\rho\sigma_1\sigma_2} \right)$$

$$\frac{\partial \log L}{\partial \rho} = \frac{n_1\rho}{1-\rho^2} + \frac{\rho}{(1-\rho^2)^2} \sum_1 \left(\frac{Z_1^2}{\sigma_1^2} - \frac{2\rho Z_1 Z_2}{\sigma_1\sigma_2} + \frac{Z_2^2}{\sigma_2^2} \right)$$

$$+ \frac{1}{(1-\rho^2)} \sum_1 \frac{Z_1 Z_2}{\sigma_1 \sigma_2} + \sum_2 \frac{\phi(\Delta)}{1-\Phi(\Delta)} \Delta \left(\frac{\sigma_1 \sigma_2}{\sigma_1^2 + \sigma_2^2 - 2\rho\sigma_1\rho_2} \right)$$

$$\frac{\partial \log L}{\partial a_1} = - \frac{n_1}{a_2 - a_1} + \frac{1}{1-\rho^2} \sum_1 \left(\frac{Z_1 R}{\sigma_1^2} - \frac{\rho R Z_2}{\sigma_1 \sigma_2} \right)$$

$$- \sum_2 \frac{\phi(\Delta)}{1-\Phi(\Delta)} \frac{\bar{R}}{(\sigma_1^2 + \sigma_2^2 - 2\rho\sigma_1\sigma_2)^{1/2}}$$

$$\frac{\partial \log L}{\partial a_2} = - \frac{n_1}{a_2 - a_1} + \frac{1}{1-\rho^2} \sum_1 \left(\frac{Z_2 R}{\sigma_2^2} - \frac{\rho R Z_1}{\sigma_1 \sigma_2} \right)$$

$$- \sum_2 \frac{\phi(\Delta)}{1-\Phi(\Delta)} \frac{\bar{R}}{(\sigma_1^2 + \sigma_2^2 - 2\rho\sigma_1\sigma_2)^{1/2}}$$

$$\frac{\partial \log L}{\partial b_1} = \frac{1}{1-\rho^2} \sum_1 \left(\frac{Z_1}{\sigma_1^2} - \frac{\rho Z_2}{\sigma_1 \sigma_2} \right) X_1$$

$$- \frac{1}{(\sigma_1^2 + \sigma_2^2 - 2\rho\sigma_1\sigma_2)^{1/2}} \sum_2 \frac{\phi(\Delta)}{1-\Phi(\Delta)} X_1$$

$$\frac{\partial \log L}{\partial b_2} = \frac{1}{1-\rho^2} \sum_1 \left(\frac{Z_2}{\sigma_2^2} - \frac{\rho Z_1}{\sigma_1 \sigma_2} \right) X_2$$

$$+ \frac{1}{(\sigma_1^2 + \sigma_2^2 - 2\rho\sigma_1\sigma_2)^{1/2}} \sum_2 \frac{\phi(\Delta)}{1-\Phi(\Delta)} X_2$$

Using the preceding derivatives, one can easily get the ML estimates with the method described in Berndt et al. (1974).

CHAPTER 8

Two-stage estimation methods

8.1 Introduction

Throughout our discussion in many of the preceding chapters we mentioned two-stage estimation methods. In this chapter we shall bring together all these results. The two-stage estimates can be used as final estimates or initial values in the iterative solution of the likelihood equations.

If the models we consider involve a large number of interdependent truncated variables, then estimation by maximum-likelihood methods is very cumbersome and in some cases even infeasible, because it involves the evaluation of multiple integrals. In such cases, some two-stage estimation methods can be used. These methods give us estimates that are consistent. A two-stage method was suggested by Heckman (1976*b*) for his labor-supply model. It was further extended to a wide class of models by Lee (1976*a*). Amemiya (1978*b*, 1979) suggested some further modifications of these procedures. In this chapter we shall review these two-stage procedures.

8.2 Two-stage method for the tobit model

Consider the model

$$y_i = \beta' X_i + u_i \quad \text{if RHS} > 0$$
$$y_i = 0 \quad \text{otherwise} \tag{8.1}$$

The problem with the OLS estimation of equation (8.1) is that $E(u_i) \neq 0$ because of the truncation. The basic idea behind the two-stage method is

221

to evaluate $E(u_i)$, substitute in equation (8.1), and estimate it by ordinary least squares.

Consider the model given by equation (8.1) and the nonzero observations y_i:

$$E(y_i \mid y_i > 0) = \beta'X_i + E(u_i \mid u_i > -\beta'X_i)$$

$$= \beta'X_i + \sigma \frac{\phi_i}{\Phi_i} \tag{8.2}$$

where ϕ_i and Φ_i are the density function and the distribution function of the standard normal evaluated at $\beta'X_i/\sigma$. Thus, equation (8.1) can be written as

$$y_i = \beta'X_i + \sigma \frac{\phi_i}{\Phi_i} + v_i \tag{8.3}$$

where $E(v_i) = 0$. The problem with the OLS estimation of (8.3) is that the variable ϕ_i/Φ_i is not known. Note, however, that its computation involves the parameters β and σ only in the ratio form (i.e., β/σ).

What Heckman (1976b) suggested is the following: Because the likelihood function for the probit model is well-behaved, we define a dummy variable

$$I_i = 1 \quad \text{if } y_i \geqslant 0$$
$$I_i = 0 \quad \text{otherwise}$$

Then, using the probit model, we get the ML estimates of β/σ. Using these, we get estimated values of ϕ_i and Φ_i. Now we get consistent estimates of β and σ by estimating (8.3) by OLS, using $\hat{\phi}_i/\hat{\Phi}_i$ in place of ϕ_i/Φ_i as an explanatory variable. This procedure can be iterated using new estimates of β and σ, and because this is effectively the EM algorithm, the iteration will lead, on covergence, to the ML estimates.

If we use all the observations y_i, and not just the nonzero observations as Heckman suggested, we have

$$E(y_i) = \text{Prob}(y_i > 0) \cdot E(y_i \mid y_i > 0) + \text{Prob}(y_i \leqslant 0) \cdot E(y_i \mid y_i \leqslant 0)$$

$$= \Phi_i \left(\beta'X_i + \sigma \frac{\phi_i}{\Phi_i} \right) + 0$$

$$= \beta'(\Phi_i X_i) + \sigma \phi_i \tag{8.4}$$

Thus, after getting estimates of ϕ_i and Φ_i, we estimate equation (8.4) to get estimates of β and σ. Note that when estimating (8.4), we use all the observations, including the zeros on the left-hand side.

In the case of the tobit model, because the likelihood function is well-behaved and the computation of the ML estimates is easy, there is no need for the two-stage method. In more complicated models in which ML methods are computationally burdensome the two-stage methods are worthwhile.

8.3 Two-stage methods for switching regression models

There is a wide variety of models in which the behavior of the agents is described by two regression equations, and there is a criterion function that determines which of these two equations is applicable. We have the model

$$\text{Regime 1:} \quad y_i = \beta_1' X_{1i} + u_{1i} \quad \text{iff } \gamma' Z_i \geq u_i \tag{8.5}$$

$$\text{Regime 2:} \quad y_i = \beta_2' X_{2i} + u_{2i} \quad \text{iff } \gamma' Z_i < u_i \tag{8.6}$$

We assume that u_i are correlated with u_{1i} and u_{2i}. The model is like a switching regression model considered by Goldfeld and Quandt (1973), but because u_i are correlated with u_{1i} and u_{2i}, we can call it a "switching regression model with endogenous switching," as suggested by Maddala and Nelson (1975). The following are a few examples:

1. The union–nonunion-wage model of Lee (1978). Here the two regimes are the union sector and the nonunion sector. The criterion function determines whether or not an individual joins the union. The two equations describe wage determination in the two sectors.
2. The housing-demand model of Trost (1977). Here the two regimes are owner-occupied housing and rental housing. The two equations describe expenditures on housing services in the two sectors, and the criterion function determines whether the individual owns or rents the house.
3. The disequilibrium market model. Here the two regimes are demand and supply. The criterion function determines whether the observation is one the demand function or the supply function.

There are several other examples in later chapters. The foregoing examples should suffice to provide enough motivation for the model considered.

We define a dummy variable

$$I_i = 1 \quad \text{if } \gamma' Z_i \geq u_i$$
$$I_i = 0 \quad \text{otherwise}$$

In those cases in which the sample separation is observed, we have the observations I_i, and we can use the probit ML to estimate the parameters γ. Because γ is estimable only up to a scale factor, we shall assume that $\text{Var}(u_i) = 1$. We assume that u_{1i}, u_{2i}, and u_i have a trivariate normal distribution, with mean vector zero and covariance matrix

$$\Sigma = \begin{bmatrix} \sigma_1^2 & \sigma_{12} & \sigma_{1u} \\ & \sigma_2^2 & \sigma_{2u} \\ & & 1 \end{bmatrix} \tag{8.7}$$

The likelihood function for this model is

$$L(\beta_1, \beta_2, \sigma_1^2, \sigma_2^2, \sigma_{1u}, \sigma_{2u})$$
$$= \prod \left[\int_{-\infty}^{\gamma'Z_i} g(y_i - \beta'X_{1i}, u_i)\, du_i \right]^{I_i} \left[\int_{\gamma'Z_i}^{\infty} f(y_i - \beta_2'X_{2i}, u_i)\, du_i \right]^{1-I_i} \tag{8.8}$$

where g and f are, respectively, the bivariate normal density functions of (u_{1i}, u_i) and (u_{2i}, u_i). Note that σ_{12} does not occur at all in this expression, and thus σ_{12} is not estimable. Only σ_{1u} and σ_{2u} are estimable. In the case of the disequilibrium market model, if we say that the quantity observed is the minimum of demand and supply, then this criterion function implies that u_i is given by $u_i = (u_{2i} - u_{1i})/\sigma$, where $\sigma^2 = \text{Var}(u_{2i} - u_{1i})$. In this case, from the estimates of σ_1^2, σ_2^2, σ_{1u}, and σ_{2u}, we can obtain an estimate of σ_{12}.

Maximization of the likelihood function (8.8) can be cumbersome, even though not infeasible. Lee (1976a) discussed a simple two-stage method for this, as follows:

Note that what we have to do is obtain the expected values of the residuals u_{1i} and u_{2i} in (8.5) and (8.6). To obtain $E(u_i \leqslant \gamma'Z_i)$, note that the conditional distribution of u_{1i}, given u_i, is normal, with mean $\sigma_{1u}u_i$ and variance $\sigma_1^2 - \sigma_{1u}^2$ (note the variance of $u_i = 1$). Hence,

$$E(u_{1i} \mid u_i \leqslant \gamma'Z_i) = E(\sigma_{1u}u_i \mid u_i \leqslant \gamma'Z_i)$$
$$= -\sigma_{1u}\frac{\phi(\gamma'Z_i)}{\Phi(\gamma'Z_i)} \tag{8.9}$$

Similarly,

$$E(u_{2i} \mid u_i \geqslant \gamma'Z_i) = E(\sigma_{2u}u_i \mid u_i \geqslant \gamma'Z_i) = \sigma_{2u}\frac{\phi(\gamma'Z_i)}{1 - \Phi(\gamma'Z_i)} \tag{8.10}$$

Let us define, for convenience,

$$W_{1i} = \phi(\gamma'Z_i)/\Phi(\gamma'Z_i) \quad \text{and} \quad W_{2i} = \phi(\gamma'Z_i)/[1 - \Phi(\gamma'Z_i)] \tag{8.11}$$

Then we can write equations (8.5) and (8.6) as

$$y_i = \beta_1'X_{1i} - \sigma_{1u}W_{1i} + \epsilon_{1i} \quad \text{for } I_i = 1 \tag{8.12}$$
$$y_i = \beta_2'X_{2i} + \sigma_{2u}W_{2i} + \epsilon_{2i} \quad \text{for } I_i = 0 \tag{8.13}$$

where ϵ_{1i} and ϵ_{2i} are the new residuals, with zero conditional means:

$$\epsilon_{1i} = u_{1i} + \sigma_{1u} W_{1i}$$
$$\epsilon_{2i} = u_{2i} + \sigma_{2u} W_{2i}$$

The two-stage estimation procedure is now clear. We first obtain an estimate of γ using the probit ML method, with observations I_i. Call this $\hat{\gamma}$. We then obtain estimates $\hat{W}_{1i}$ and $\hat{W}_{2i}$ of W_{1i} and W_{2i}, respectively (by substituting $\hat{\gamma}$ for γ). We next estimate equations (8.12) and (8.13) by OLS, substituting $\hat{W}_{1i}$ and $\hat{W}_{2i}$ for W_{1i} and W_{2i}, respectively. This procedure gives us consistent estimates of β_1, β_2, σ_{1u}, and σ_{2u}. To obtain estimates of σ_1^2 and σ_2^2, we need to look at the variances of ϵ_{1i} and ϵ_{2i} in equations (8.12) and (8.13).

Note that the residuals ϵ_{1i} and ϵ_{2i} are heteroscedastic, and thus one should, in principle, estimate equations (8.12) and (8.13) by weighted least squares rather than ordinary least squares. To obtain $\text{Var}(\epsilon_{1i})$ and $\text{Var}(\epsilon_{2i})$, we make use of the following relations for the moments of the truncated bivariate normal derived from Johnson and Kotz (1972, pp. 112–13):

$$E(u_{1i} \mid I_i = 1) = -\sigma_{1u} W_{1i}$$
$$E(u_{1i}^2 \mid I_i = 1) = \sigma_1^2 - \sigma_{1u}^2 (\gamma' Z_i) W_{1i}$$
$$E(u_{2i} \mid I_i = 0) = \sigma_{2u} W_{2i}$$
$$E(u_{2i}^2 \mid I_i = 0) = \sigma_2^2 + \sigma_{2u}^2 (\gamma' Z_i) W_{2i} \tag{8.14}$$

Hence,

$$E(\epsilon_{1i} \mid I_i = 1) = E(\epsilon_{2i} \mid I_i = 0) = 0$$

and

$$\text{Var}(\epsilon_{1i} \mid I_i = 1) = \sigma_1^2 - \sigma_{1u}^2 W_{1i}(\gamma' Z_i + W_{1i}) \tag{8.15}$$
$$\text{Var}(\epsilon_{2i} \mid I_i = 0) = \sigma_2^2 + \sigma_{2u}^2 W_{2i}(\gamma' Z_i + W_{2i}) \tag{8.16}$$

Note that, unlike the case of the tobit model, the second-stage regression of the two-stage method does not give us estimates of all the parameters. We have estimates of only β_1, β_2, σ_{1u}, and σ_{2u}. We still have to get estimates of σ_1^2 and σ_2^2. For this, we proceed as follows: After obtaining $\hat{\beta}_1$ and $\hat{\beta}_2$, compute the residuals:

$$\hat{u}_{1i} = y_i - \hat{\beta}_1' X_{1i} \quad \text{for } I_i = 1$$
$$\hat{u}_{2i} = y_i - \hat{\beta}_2' X_{2i} \quad \text{for } I_i = 0$$

Then equations (8.14) and (8.15) suggest that we estimate σ_1^2 and σ_2^2 by

$$\hat{\sigma}_1^2 = \frac{1}{N_1} \sum_{i=1}^{N_1} [\hat{u}_{1i}^2 + \hat{\sigma}_{1u}^2 (\hat{\gamma}' Z_i) \hat{W}_{1i}] \tag{8.17}$$

$$\hat{\sigma}_2^2 = \frac{1}{N_2} \sum_{i=1}^{N_2} [\hat{u}_{2i}^2 + \hat{\sigma}_{2u}^2 (\hat{\gamma}'Z_i) \hat{W}_{2i}] \tag{8.18}$$

where N_1 is the number of observations for which $I_i = 1$ and N_2 is the number of observations for which $I_i = 0$. There is, however, no guarantee that $\hat{\sigma}_1^2$ and $\hat{\sigma}_2^2$ will be always positive.[1] This completes the estimation of all parameters by the two-stage method for the switching regression model with endogenous switching. To take care of the heteroscedasticity problem, we can use the estimated parameters to compute the error variances in (8.15) and (8.16) and use the weighted least-squares method.

For the two-stage estimation, as mentioned earlier, we get a probit ML estimate of γ, compute the predicted values of $\hat{W}_1$ and $\hat{W}_2$ from equations (8.11), and estimate equations (8.12) and (8.13) by OLS after substituting $\hat{W}_1$ and $\hat{W}_2$ for W_1 and W_2. We can derive the covariance matrix of these two-stage estimates as follows: Let us assume that there are N_1 observations for which $I_i = 1$ and N_2 observations for which $I_i = 0$. The total sample size is $N = N_1 + N_2$. Also define

$$H = \begin{bmatrix} Z_1' \\ Z_2' \\ \vdots \\ Z_N' \end{bmatrix}$$

which can be partitioned into

$$H = \begin{bmatrix} H_1 \\ H_2 \end{bmatrix}$$

corresponding to the N_1 observations for which $I_i = 1$ and the N_2 observations for which $I_i = 0$, respectively. Similarly, define W_1 as the vector of N_1 observations W_{1i} corresponding to $I_i = 1$ and W_2 the vector of N_2 observations W_{2i} corresponding to $I_i = 0$.

Let Λ be an $N \times N$ diagonal matrix whose ith diagonal term is $W_{1i} W_{2i}$ (note that W_{1i} and W_{2i} can be defined for all observations). Let D_i be an $N_1 \times N_1$ diagonal matrix whose ith diagonal term is $W_{1i}(W_{1i} + \gamma'Z_i)$. Let D_2 be an $N_2 \times N_2$ diagonal matrix whose ith diagonal term is $W_{2i}(W_{2i} - \gamma'Z_i)$. Also, let X_1 be the $N_1 \times K_1$ matrix of observations on X_{1i} and X_2 be the $N_2 \times K_2$ matrix of observations on X_{2i}. Let Y_1 be the

---

[1] Lee and Trost (1978) listed two alternative methods of estimating σ_1^2 and σ_2^2. One of these guarantees that the estimates $\hat{\sigma}_1^2$ and $\hat{\sigma}_2^2$ are always positive.

vector of N_1 observations on Y_i corresponding to $I_i = 1$ and Y_2 be the vector of N_2 observations on Y_i corresponding to $I_i = 0$.

Finally, define $G_1 = (X_1, -W_1)$ and $G_2 = (X_2, -W_2)$. Then the two-stage estimates are given by

$$\begin{bmatrix} \hat{\beta}_1 \\ \hat{\sigma}_{1u} \end{bmatrix} = (\hat{G}_1' \hat{G}_1)^{-1} \hat{G}_1' Y_1$$

and the covariance matrix of the two-stage estimates (detailed derivation is in the Appendix at the end of the chapter) is

$$\mathrm{Var}\begin{bmatrix} \hat{\beta}_1 \\ \hat{\sigma}_{1u} \end{bmatrix} = \sigma_1^2 (G_1' G_1)^{-1}$$
$$- \sigma_{1u}^2 (G_1' G_1)^{-1} G_1' [D_1 - D_1 H_1 (H' \Lambda H)^{-1} H_1' D_1] G_1 (G_1' G_1)^{-1}$$

For the other equation we just change the subscript 1 to 2.

It is tempting to use the estimated variances from the OLS estimation of equations (8.12) and (8.13), ignoring the fact that W_{1i} and W_{2i} are estimated. It is shown in the Appendix that this procedure underestimates the true variances.[2]

Finally, it is possible and often desirable to estimate equations (8.5) and (8.6) simultaneously, using all the observations on y_i. The two-stage method for this is as follows: Note that

$$E(y_i) = E(y_i \mid I_i = 1) \cdot P(I_i = 1) + E(y_i \mid I_i = 0) \cdot P(I_i = 0)$$
$$= \beta_1' X_{1i} \Phi_i + \beta_2' X_{2i} (1 - \Phi_i) + \phi_i (\sigma_{2u} - \sigma_{1u}) \tag{8.19}$$

where $\phi_i = \phi(\gamma' Z_i)$ and $\Phi_i = \Phi(\gamma' Z_i)$. Thus, regressing y_i on $X_{1i} \hat{\Phi}_i$, $X_{2i}(1 - \hat{\Phi})$, and $\hat{\phi}_i$, we get estimates of β_1, β_2, and $\sigma_{2u} - \sigma_{1u}$. In the chapter on selectivity problems we shall see how interest centers on $\sigma_{2u} - \sigma_{1u}$, and not on σ_{2u} and σ_{1u} separately, and thus estimation of (8.19) is more convenient than separate estimation of (8.12) and (8.13).

Very often, the variables X_{1i} and X_{2i} are the same, so that we can define $X_i = X_{1i} = X_{2i}$. We can then write equation (8.19) as

$$E(y_i) = \beta_2' X_i + (\beta_1' - \beta_2') X_i \Phi_i + \phi_i (\sigma_{2u} - \sigma_{1u}) \tag{8.20}$$

Estimating this equation enables us to test which coefficients are different in β_1 and β_2. What we do is regress y_i on X_i, $\hat{\phi}_i$, and the interaction variables $X_i \hat{\Phi}_i$. Some of these may be significant and others not. This procedure enables us to delete the nonsignificant variables and thus

---

[2] The estimated variances from the OLS estimation, taking into account heteroscedasticity, will underestimate the true variances. This is not true if heteroscedasticity has not been taken into account in the OLS estimation.

implicitly impose restrictions on equality on some coefficients between the regression coefficients in the two regimes (8.5) and (8.6). This is a convenient procedure to impose cross-equation restrictions in switching regression models with endogenous switching. An illustrative example is given in a report on D methods by Lee et al. (1979).

8.4   Two-stage estimation of censored models

Throughout the discussion in the preceding section we assumed that y_i is observed in at least one of the two regimes. This is not necessarily the case. Very often we have a model of the type

$$y_1 = \beta_1' X_1 + u_1 \tag{8.21}$$
$$y_2 = \beta_2' X_2 + u_2 \tag{8.22}$$

and we observe

$$y = y_1 \quad \text{if } y_1 \geqslant y_2$$
$$y = 0 \quad \text{otherwise} \tag{8.23}$$

This is the case with the labor-supply model analyzed by Gronau (1974). Here, y_1 is the market wage, and y_2 is the reservation wage. Nelson (1977) estimated this model by the ML method and also provided several other examples in which this type of model is applicable. For instance, in the case of the automobile-demand model, we can define y_1 as expenditures the family can afford to make and y_2 as the value of the minimum acceptable car to the family (threshold value). The actual expenditures will be

$$y = y_1 \quad \text{if } y_1 \geqslant y_2$$
$$y = 0 \quad \text{otherwise}$$

Another example is that of bank-borrowing behavior. Here one hears of the needs-versus-reluctance hypothesis, which argues that banks are reluctant to frequent the discount window too often for fear of adverse sanctions from the Federal Reserve (Polakoff and Sibler, 1967). One can define y_2 as the threshold level below which banks will not use the discount window. y_1 is the desired borrowing. The structure of this model is somewhat different from that given in equation (8.23). For this model we have

$$y = y_1 \quad \text{for all observations} \tag{8.24}$$

We know, however, whether $y_1 > y_2$ or $y_2 > y_1$, because all banks do borrow, but not always from the discount window. We shall now discuss two-stage estimation in these models.

Consider first the labor-supply model analyzed by Gronau and Nelson. We can write the criterion function (8.23) in the form we considered in the preceding section, given by equations (8.5) and (8.6). This is

$$\gamma' Z_i = \frac{\beta_1' X_{1i} - \beta_2' X_{2i}}{\sigma} \quad \text{and} \quad u = \frac{u_2 - u_1}{\sigma} \tag{8.25}$$

where

$$\sigma^2 = \text{Var}(u_2 - u_1) = \sigma_1^2 + \sigma_2^2 - 2\sigma_{12} \tag{8.26}$$

From the probit model, based on the dichotomous variable I_i, we get consistent estimates of β_{1j}/σ and β_{2j}/σ for the elements of β_1 and β_2 corresponding to nonoverlapping variables in X_1 and X_2, and $(\beta_{1k} - \beta_{2k})/\sigma$ corresponding to the common variables in X_1 and X_2. Next, from the estimation of equations (8.12), we can get consistent estimates of β_1 and $\sigma_{1u} = (\sigma_{12} - \sigma_1^2)/\sigma$. Because we now have estimates of all the elements of β_1, if there is at least one variable in X_1 not included in X_2, then from the estimate of β_{ij}/σ corresponding to this variable we now get a consistent estimate of σ and hence consistent estimates of all the elements of β_2. Next we use equation (8.17), as before, to get a consistent estimate of σ_1^2, and given estimates of σ, σ_1^2, and σ_{1u}, we can now get an estimate of σ_{12}. Finally, from an estimate of σ^2 we can get an estimate of σ_2^2. Thus we can get consistent estimates of all parameters.

Alternatively, if $\sigma_{12} = 0$, we have $\sigma^2 = \sigma_1^2 + \sigma_2^2$ and $\sigma_{1u} = -\sigma_1^2/\sigma$. From the estimates of $(\beta_1 - \beta_2)/\sigma$ obtained from the probit regression, β_1 and σ_1^2/σ from equation (8.12), and σ_1^2 from equation (8.17), we can get estimates of all the parameters.

In summary, for the censored regression model given by equations (8.21), (8.22), and (8.23), we need one of the following conditions for identification:

1. $\sigma_{12} = 0$.
2. There is at least one variable in X_1 not included in X_2. (In the context of the labor-supply model, there is at least one explanatory variable in the market-wage function not included in the reservation-wage function.)

These conditions for identification in this model were first derived by Nelson (1975), who derived them considering the reduced form and structural form for this model.[3] The foregoing discussion in terms of estimation of the probit equation and estimation of equation (8.12) is much easier to follow (Maddala, 1977a). In his empirical work, Nelson imposed the condition $\sigma_{12} = 0$, because all the variables in X_1 were also

---

[3] See Kiefer and Neumann (1979a, b) and Heckman (1979) for more recent discussions.

included in X_2 in his model. Nelson used the ML method in his work. The likelihood function for this model is

$$L(\beta_1, \beta_2, \sigma_1^2, \sigma_2^2, \sigma_{12}) = \prod_i \left(\int_{-\infty}^{g_{2i}} (g_{1i}, u_{2i}) \, du_{2i} \right)^{I_i} \left(1 - \Phi_i \right)^{1-I_i} \qquad (8.27)$$

where

$$g_{1i} = y_i - \beta_1' X_{1i}$$
$$g_{2i} = y_i - \beta_2' X_{2i}$$
$$\Phi_i = \Phi\left(\frac{\beta_1' X_{1i} - \beta_2' X_{2i}}{\sigma} \right)$$

Consider next the bank-borrowing model. Here the estimation of the probit model and the parameter estimates it yields is the same as before. As for equation (8.21), we can now estimate it by OLS, because we have all observations on y_1. It can be easily verified that the conditions for identification are the same as those in the Gronau–Nelson model. The likelihood function for this model is

$$L(\beta_1, \beta_2, \sigma_1^2, \sigma_2^2, \sigma_{12})$$
$$= \prod_i \left[\frac{1}{\sigma_1} \exp\left(-\frac{1}{2\sigma_1^2} (y_{1i} - \beta_1' X_{1i})^2 \right) \right] \left(\Phi_i \right)^{I_i} \left(1 - \Phi_i \right)^{1-I_i} \qquad (8.28)$$

where Φ_i is defined in (8.27).

Note that the conditions for identification in the switching regression model considered in the preceding section will be the same as those for the censored regression model considered here if there are not enough observations in the second regime to be able to estimate the parameters in (8.13).

Finally, note that the two-stage estimation procedure can be applied using the observations on all the individuals – working and nonworking. The procedure is the same as that suggested for the tobit model in equation (8.4). We note that

$$E(y_{1i} \,|\, I_i = 1) = \beta_1' X_{1i} - \sigma_{1u} \frac{\phi_i}{\Phi_i}$$

Hence, the unconditional expectation of y_{1i} is

$$E(y_{1i}) = E(y_{1i} \,|\, I_i = 1) P(I_i = 1) + E(y_{1i} \,|\, I_i = 0) P(I_i = 0)$$
$$= \beta_1' \Phi_i X_{1i} - \sigma_{1u} \phi_i$$

We estimate this equation by the two-stage method, substituting $\hat{\Phi}_i$ and $\hat{\phi}_i$ for Φ_i and ϕ_i, respectively, instead of equation (8.12). In this procedure we use the observations on all individuals, not just the working ones as in the estimation of (8.12).

8.5   Two-stage estimation of Heckman's model

Heckman (1974) considered a model of labor supply in which wages and hours worked are the two endogenous variables. The model consists of the shadow-wage equation

$$S = \gamma_0 + \gamma_1 H + \gamma_2 Z + u_1 \qquad (8.29)$$

and the market-wage equation

$$W = \beta_0 + \beta_1 X + u_2 \qquad (8.30)$$

where X and Z are exogenous variables. Heckman assumed that hours worked H adjust, so that $S=W$. Hence, from equations (8.29) and (8.30), we get

$$H = \frac{\beta_0 + \beta_1 X - \gamma_0 - \gamma_2 Z}{\gamma_1} + \frac{u_2 - u_1}{\gamma_1} \qquad (8.31)$$

If $H>0$, the person is in the labor force, and we observe H and W. If $H \leqslant 0$, the person is not in the labor force. For the observations for which $H \leqslant 0$, we have

$$\frac{u_2 - u_1}{\gamma_1} < \frac{\gamma_0 - \beta_0 + \gamma_2 Z - \beta_1 X}{\gamma_1}$$

or

$$u_2 - u_1 < \gamma_0 - \beta_0 + \gamma_2 Z - \beta_1 X$$

because γ_1 is expected to be positive. If $\mathrm{Var}(u_2 - u_1) = \sigma^2$, then

$$\mathrm{Prob}(H \leqslant 0) = \Phi\left(\frac{\gamma_0 - \beta_0 + \gamma_2 Z - \beta_1 X}{\sigma}\right) \qquad (8.32)$$

where $\Phi(\cdot)$ is the distribution function of the standard normal. Thus, the likelihood function for this model is

$$L = \prod_{H>0} F(W, H) \cdot \prod_{H \leqslant 0} \Phi(\Delta) \qquad (8.33)$$

where

$$\Delta = \frac{\gamma_0 - \beta_0 + \gamma_2 Z - \beta_1 X}{\sigma} \qquad (8.34)$$

Heckman (1974) estimated this model by ML methods. Later (Heckman, 1976b), he suggested a two-stage estimation method.[4] For the two-stage method we need to evaluate $E(u_2 \,|\, H>0)$ in equation (8.30). This is

---

[4] The discussion of the two-stage method that follows is not exactly the same as that exposited by Heckman. We shall follow the line of reasoning in the preceding sections.

$$E\left(u_2 \left| \frac{u_2 - u_1}{\sigma} > \Delta\right.\right)$$

Denoting $\text{Var}(u_2) = \sigma_2^2$ and $\text{Cov}(u_2, u_1) = \sigma_{12}$, we get this [see equation (8.10)] as

$$\frac{\sigma_2^2 - \sigma_{12}}{\sigma} \frac{\phi(\Delta)}{1 - \Phi(\Delta)}$$

Thus, the wage equation (8.30) can be written as

$$W = \beta_0 + \beta_1 X + \frac{\sigma_2^2 - \sigma_{12}}{\sigma} \frac{\phi(\Delta)}{1 - \Phi(\Delta)} + V_2 \tag{8.35}$$

where V_2 is the new residual with the property that $E(V_2) = 0$.

The two-stage procedure that Heckman suggested is to get estimates of the parameters in Δ from a probit ML estimation and then estimate equation (8.35) by OLS after substituting $\phi(\hat{\Delta})/[1 - \Phi(\hat{\Delta})]$ for $\phi(\Delta)/[1 - \Phi(\Delta)]$. This gives us consistent estimates of β_0, β_1, and $(\sigma_2^2 - \sigma_{12})/\sigma$. To see how we can get estimates of all the parameters, note that the probit ML gives estimates of $(\gamma_0 - \beta_0)/\sigma$:

$$\frac{\gamma_{2j} - \beta_{1j}}{\sigma} \quad \text{for the common variables in } X \text{ and } Z$$

$$\frac{\gamma_{2j}}{\sigma} \quad \text{for the variables in } Z \text{ not in } X$$

$$\frac{\beta_{1j}}{\sigma} \quad \text{for the variables in } X \text{ not in } Z$$

Now, examining equations (8.29) and (8.30), we note that (if we assume $\sigma_{12} \neq 0$) the condition for identification is that there be at least one variable in X not included in Z. For this excluded variable we get an estimate of β_{1j}/σ from the probit equation, and because we have an estimate of β_{1j} from the wage equation, we can get an estimate of σ. Once we have an estimate of σ and estimates of β_0 and β_1, it is easy to see that all elements of γ_0 and γ_2 can now be estimated. Also, because $\sigma^2 = \sigma_1^2 + \sigma_2^2 - 2\sigma_{12}$, we have an estimate of $\sigma_1^2 - \sigma_{12}$ (from the estimates of σ^2 and $\sigma_2^2 - \sigma_{12}$). The problem now is to get separate estimates of σ_1^2, σ_2^2, and σ_{12}. For this purpose we have to use the estimated residuals in the wage equation, as we did in the preceding section for the switching regression model.

Note that we have, in a fashion analogous to equation (8.15),

$$E(u_{2i}^2 | H > 0) = E\left(u_{2i}^2 \left| \frac{u_{2i} - u_{1i}}{\sigma} > \Delta_i\right.\right)$$

$$= \sigma_2^2 + \left(\frac{\sigma_2^2 - \sigma_{12}}{\sigma}\right)^2 \Delta_i \frac{\phi(\Delta_i)}{1 - \Phi(\Delta_i)} \qquad (8.36)$$

Thus, after computing the residuals

$$\hat{u}_{2i} = W_i - \hat{\beta}_0 - \hat{\beta}_1 X_i \qquad (8.37)$$

we estimate σ_2^2 by

$$\hat{\sigma}_2^2 = \frac{1}{N_1} \sum_{i=1}^{N_1} \left[\hat{u}_{2i}^2 - \left(\frac{\sigma_2^2 - \sigma_{12}}{\sigma}\right)^2 \hat{\Delta}_i \frac{\phi(\hat{\Delta}_i)}{1 - \Phi(\hat{\Delta}_i)} \right] \qquad (8.38)$$

where N_1 is the number of observations for which $H > 0$. Once we obtain an estimate of σ_2^2, we have estimates of σ_{12} and σ_1^2, because we have earlier estimated $\sigma_2^2 - \sigma_{12}$ and $\sigma_1^2 - \sigma_{12}$. Finally, to obtain an estimate of γ_1, we have to estimate equation (8.31) by the tobit method.

The essential features of the two-stage methods are clear. First we obtain the expected values of the residuals that are truncated. These expected values involve unknown parameters, but these usually can be estimated by the probit method. We then introduce the estimated values of these variables into the original equation and estimate it by ordinary least squares (or weighted least squares if we take account of the heteroscedasticity problems). Note that to obtain estimates of the residual variances we have to compute the estimated residuals and use formulas like (8.17) and (8.18).

In the foregoing discussion of Heckman's model, we assumed $\sigma_{12} \neq 0$. If $\sigma_{12} = 0$, then we do not need the condition (for identification) that there be at least one variable in X not included in Z. But now the procedure for getting consistent estimates of the parameters is different. From two-stage estimation of the wage equation (8.35) we get estimates of β_0, β_1, and σ_2^2/σ. We next estimate σ_2^2 from the computed residuals for the wage equation according to formula (8.38), using $\sigma_{12} = 0$. We can thus get an estimate of σ, and now the estimates from the probit ML lead us to estimates of γ_0 and γ_2. Because $\sigma^2 = \sigma_1^2 + \sigma_2^2$, we also have an estimate of σ_1^2. As before, γ_1 has to be estimated by using the tobit method for equation (8.31).

Note that the Heckman model can be written as

$$\left.\begin{array}{l} y_1 = \gamma_0 + \gamma_1 y_2 + \gamma_2 Z + u_1 \\ y_2 = \beta_0 + \beta_1 X + u_2 \end{array}\right\} \text{ if } y_2 > 0$$

$$y_1 = y_2 = 0 \quad \text{otherwise} \qquad (8.39)$$

The conditions for identification for the simultaneous-equations model (8.39) are well known; namely, $\text{Cov}(u_1, u_2) = 0$, or there is at least one variable in X not included in Z. These are the conditions for identification in Heckman's model.

Finally, note that the two-stage estimation of the wage equation, as described in equation (8.35), uses only the working individuals. One can easily extend this to cover data on all individuals (working and non-working), along the lines described at the end of the preceding section.

8.6   Two-stage estimation of structural equations

What we discussed in the preceding section was probit and tobit estimation of the hours-worked equation and two-stage estimation of the wage equation (which is anyhow in its reduced form). Thus, both the equations being estimated are reduced-form equations, and we discussed how to recover the structural parameters from the estimates of these reduced-form parameters. One can, however, think of estimating the structural equation (8.29) directly by two-stage methods to obtain estimates of γ_0, γ_1, and γ_2. To do this, note that $S = W$ and

$$E(u_1 \mid H > 0) = E\left(u_1 \left| \frac{u_2 - u_1}{\sigma} > \Delta\right.\right) = \frac{\sigma_{12} - \sigma_1^2}{\sigma} \frac{\phi(\Delta)}{1 - \Phi(\Delta)}$$

where Δ is defined in (8.34). We can now write equation (8.29) as

$$W = \gamma_0 + \gamma_1 H + \gamma_2 Z + \frac{\sigma_{12} - \sigma_1^2}{\sigma} \frac{\phi(\Delta)}{1 - \Phi(\Delta)} + v_1 \qquad (8.40)$$

where v_1 is the residual u_1 corrected for its mean, and hence $E(v_i) = 0$. However, we cannot estimate equation (8.40) by OLS, because H is an endogenous variable. What we have to do is get an estimate of H for the subsample $H > 0$. Note that

$$E\left(\frac{u_2 - u_1}{\gamma_1} \middle| H > 0\right) = \frac{\sigma}{\gamma_1} E\left(\frac{u_2 - u_1}{\sigma} > \Delta\right) = \frac{\sigma}{\gamma_1} \frac{\phi(\Delta)}{1 - \Phi(\Delta)}$$

Hence, equation (8.31) for $H > 0$ can be written as

$$H = \frac{\beta_0 - \gamma_0}{\gamma_1} + \frac{\beta_1 X - \gamma_1 Z}{\gamma_1} + \frac{\sigma}{\gamma_1} \frac{\phi(\Delta)}{1 - \Phi(\Delta)} + v \qquad (8.41)$$

where $E(v) = 0$. We estimate this equation by OLS after substituting $\hat{\Delta}$ for Δ. After estimating the parameters in (8.41) by this two-stage method, we get the estimated values $\hat{H}$. Note that these are obtained from (8.41), not (8.31). We substitute these values of $\hat{H}$ in place of H in equation (8.40) and estimate that equation by OLS. Alternatively, we can use $\hat{H}$ as an instrumental variable in estimating (8.40). This will also produce consistent estimates.

It can be easily shown that the resulting two-stage estimates of the structural parameters are consistent. Their asymptotic covariance matrix can be derived by the methods in the Appendix at the end of this chapter. The method suggested here is the appropriate analogue of the usual two-stage least-squares method for the case of truncated variables. Briefly, what we do is (a) evaluate the expected values of the residuals in both the structural and reduced-form equations, (b) estimate the reduced-form equations by the two-stage estimation method, and (c) substitute the estimated values of the endogenous variables on the right-hand side of each structural equation, as obtained from step (b), and use OLS to estimate the parameters of the structural equations.

The main difference between the ordinary two-stage least-squares (2SLS) procedure and the one suggested here lies in noting the fact that the residuals in the structural equations and the reduced-form equations do not have zero means and that the estimates from the reduced forms (to be substituted in the structural equations) should take this into account.

The advantage of the procedure described here, which was suggested by Lee et al. (1980), is that it can be used in any simultaneous-equations model with truncation. For instance, suppose that hours worked also occurs as an explanatory variable in the market-wage equation (8.20); then this equation also is in a structural form (not a reduced form as in Heckman's model). Again, one can proceed via the reduced-form estimation, as outlined in the preceding section. But this creates problems of multiple solutions for the structural parameters if the equations are overidentified. Hence, it will be desirable to estimate the structural equations by the two-stage methods. Equation (8.35) will now be changed to

$$W = \beta_0 + \beta_1 H + \beta_2 X + \frac{\sigma_2 - \sigma_{12}}{\sigma} \frac{\phi(\Delta)}{1 - \Phi(\Delta)} + v_2 \qquad (8.42)$$

and we estimate this equation by OLS after substituting $\hat{H}$ for H, as obtained from a two-stage estimation of (8.41), and $\hat{\Delta}$ for Δ, as obtained from the probit ML method.

The procedure described is very general and can be used in the estimation of all simultaneous-equations systems with censored dependent variables. The procedure gets complicated, however, if there is more than one condition to determine the censoring. In the Heckman model, for instance, there is only one condition: $H > 0$. Amemiya (1974b) considered a model in which there are two censoring conditions involved:

$$y_1 = \gamma_1 y_2 + \beta_1' X_1 + u_1 \quad \text{if } y_1 > 0$$
$$y_1 = 0 \quad \text{otherwise}$$

$$y_2 = \gamma_2 y_1 + \beta_2' X_2 + u_2 \quad \text{if } y_2 > 0$$
$$y_2 = 0 \quad \text{otherwise}$$

Amemiya showed that this model is logically consistent only if $\gamma_1 \gamma_2 < 1$. We can divide the observations into the following sets:

$$S_1: \quad y_1 > 0, \quad y_2 > 0$$
$$S_2: \quad y_1 > 0, \quad y_2 = 0$$
$$S_3: \quad y_1 = 0, \quad y_2 > 0$$
$$S_4: \quad y_1 = 0, \quad y_2 = 0$$

Consider, as Amemiya did, only observations in S_1. To apply the two-stage methods described earlier, we need to evaluate the expectations of the residuals in the structural equations and the reduced forms under the condition $y_1 > 0$, $y_2 > 0$. These obviously involve double integrals. The first stage of the two-stage method in this case involves estimation of a bivariate probit equation. The rest of the steps, of course, are straightforward. In this model, as with two-stage estimation of the simple tobit model, there is not much to be gained in using the two-stage method as compared with the maximum-likelihood method.

There is another case in which two-stage estimation involves substitution of estimated endogenous variables in an equation prior to estimation. This is the case of the switching regression model considered earlier in equations (8.5) and (8.6), where the criterion function involves the values of y_1 in the two regimes. Specifically, the model in (8.5) and (8.6) is changed as follows:

$$\text{Regime 1:} \quad y_{1i} = \beta_1' X_{1i} + u_{1i} \tag{8.43}$$

$$\text{Regime 2:} \quad y_{2i} = \beta_2' X_{2i} + u_{2i} \tag{8.44}$$

and

$$C_i = \gamma' Z_i + \delta(y_{1i} - y_{2i}) - u_i \tag{8.45}$$

Only one of y_{1i} or y_{2i} is observed for each individual i, depending on whether $C_i \geqslant 0$ or $C_i < 0$. The criterion function (8.45), however, involves $y_{1i} - y_{2i}$, and to estimate δ we need to estimate y_{1i} and y_{2i} for all the observations. Examples of this model are the following:

1. The union model by Lee (1978), where y_{1i} are wages in the union sector, y_{2i} are wages in the nonunion sector, and the criterion function that determines whether or not an individual joins the union depends on, in addition to other factors, the expected benefit as measured by $y_1 - y_2$. Interest centers on whether or not $y_1 - y_2$ is a significant variable in the

decision function, that is, whether or not the coefficient of δ in (8.45) is significant.

2. The college-education model by Willis and Rosen (1979), where y_{1i} are earnings of college graduates, y_{2i} are earnings of those who are not college graduates, and the criterion function that determines whether or not an individual goes to college depends on, in addition to other factors, the expected benefit as measured by $y_1 - y_2$. Interest again centers on whether or not this variable is a significant variable in the decision function, that is, whether or not δ is significant.

Estimation of this model proceeds along the lines described earlier. We first write the criterion function in its reduced form:

$$C_i = \gamma' Z_i + \delta(\beta_1' X_{1i} - \beta_2' X_{2i}) + \delta(u_{1i} - u_{2i}) - u_i \qquad (8.46)$$

We can write this as

$$C_i = \gamma^{*\prime} Z_i^* - u_i^* \qquad (8.47)$$

where γ^* is defined suitably. Now the two-stage estimation of the two wage equations proceeds as before. We define

$$I_i = 1 \quad \text{if } C_i > 0$$
$$I_i = 0 \quad \text{otherwise}$$

Based on the observations on I_i, we use the probit method to get an estimate of γ^*.

Next we estimate equations of the form (8.12) and (8.13) (adding the superscript asterisk where applicable) and get estimates of the parameters β_1 and β_2. Everything is as before except the estimation of the parameters γ and δ in the criterion function (8.45). (Note that these parameters are estimable only up to a proportionality factor.) For this, we obtain predicted values of y_{1i} and y_{2i} for all observations as

$$\hat{y}_{1i} = \hat{\beta}_1' X_{1i} \quad \text{and} \quad \hat{y}_{2i} = \hat{\beta}_2' X_{2i} \qquad (8.48)$$

Note that we do not use equations (8.12) and (8.13) as we did in the two-stage estimation of structural equations described earlier. There the reason these equations were used, and not (8.48), was that only a subset of the observations was used. We next estimate δ by using the probit ML method applied to equation (8.45) based on the dichotomous observations I_i. This method is called the *structural probit method* (it is the use of probit method to estimate a structural equation after substituting the estimates of the endogenous variables in the equation). Lee (1979a) showed that the resulting estimates of γ and δ are consistent and derived the asymptotic covariance matrix.

The question of which estimates of the endogenous variables have to be used in the structural equations depends on whether the structural equation is being estimated on the basis of all observations or only a subsample. For instance, in the structural probit estimation of (8.45), all observations are used, and hence the estimates of the endogenous variables are obtained from (8.48). In the estimation of the Heckman model we discussed earlier, only the observations for which $W > 0$ and $H > 0$ were used, and hence the estimate of $\hat{H}$ to be substituted in the shadow-wage equation is obtained from (8.41), not (8.31).

In all these two-stage methods it is tempting simply to use the standard errors from the second stage (OLS) of the two-stage procedure in judging whether or not the coefficients are significant. This procedure, of course, is incorrect, because it ignores the fact that some of the explanatory variables are estimated. The computation of the correct covariance matrices (shown in the Appendix at the end of this chapter) is not very cumbersome. It might, however, be interesting to know how far off are the estimates obtained from the second stage of the two-stage procedure. Lee (1978) presented some results for the union-and-wages model. The model consists of the union-wage equation, the nonunion-wage equation, and the choice function involving the union–nonunion wage differential. For the two wage equations, the standard errors obtained from the second stage (OLS) of the two-stage method were very close to the correct standard errors (computed from the expressions in the Appendix). It was for the structural probit estimates of the choice function that the standard errors were substantially underestimated. Even here, this was mostly the case with the coefficient of $y_{1i} - y_{21}$, that is, δ in equation (8.45). The estimated coefficient was 2.455, with the (erroneous) standard error of 0.205 from the second stage, but the correct standard error in this case was 0.401. Some other studies in which such comparisons were made also seem to indicate that the standard errors for the second stage of the two-stage procedure were not far off from the correct standard errors for two-stage estimation of reduced-form equations but were far off from the correct standard errors for two-stage estimation of structural equations.

A more general formulation of the model in equations (8.43), (8.44), and (8.45) is the model considered by Westin (1976), for which Lee (1976a) derived both the identifiability conditions and two-stage estimation methods. In the model Westin considered, the choice function (8.45) is changed to

$$C_i = \gamma' Z_i + \delta_1 Y_{1i} + \delta_2 Y_{2i} - u_i \tag{8.49}$$

The reduced form becomes

$$C_i = \gamma^{*\prime} Z_i^* - u_i^*$$

where

$$u_i^* = (u_i - \delta_1 u_{1i} - \delta_2 u_{2i})/\sigma^*$$
$$\sigma^{*2} = \text{Var}(u_i - \delta_1 u_{1i} - \delta_2 u_{2i}) \tag{8.50}$$

and Z_i^* combines the elements in Z_i, X_{1i}, and X_{2i}. Note that

$$I_i = 1 \quad \text{if } C_i > 0$$
$$I_i = 0 \quad \text{otherwise}$$

and we need the normalization $\text{Var}(u_i^*) = 1$.

As long as there are enough observations on y_{1i} and y_{2i}, we can get consistent estimates of β_1, β_2, σ_1^2, and σ_2^2. The problems are with the estimation of the parameters in the choice function (8.49) and the elements of the covariance matrix

$$\Sigma = \text{Cov}(u_1, u_2, u) = \begin{bmatrix} \sigma_1^2 & \sigma_{12} & \sigma_{1u} \\ \sigma_{12} & \sigma_2^2 & \sigma_{2u} \\ \sigma_{1u} & \sigma_{2u} & \sigma_u^2 \end{bmatrix} \tag{8.51}$$

Regarding the estimation of γ, δ_1, and δ_2 in the choice function (8.49), note that the probit equation being estimated is

$$\hat{\gamma}' Z_i + \hat{\delta}_1 (\hat{\beta}_1' X_{1i}) + \delta_2 (\hat{\beta}_2' X_{2i})$$

Thus, if Z_i includes all the variables in X_{1i} and X_{2i}, this introduces perfect multicollinearity, and δ_1 and δ_2 are not estimable. In order that δ_1 be estimable, there should be at least one variable in X_{1i} not included in Z_i. Similarly, in order that δ_2 be estimable, there should be at least one variable in X_{2i} not included in Z_i. Note also that for the model in which the criterion function is given by (8.45), the corresponding condition that δ be estimable is that there be at least one variable in X_{1i} or X_{2i} that is not included in Z_i. These conditions are usually satisfied in practice, and they are being stated here only for completeness of our discussion of these models.

It is the estimation of the residual variances that poses problems. Note from the earlier discussion that we can get estimates of σ_1^2, σ_2^2, σ_{1u^*}, and σ_{2u^*}. From (8.50) we have

$$\sigma_{1u^*} = \frac{\sigma_{1u} - \delta_1 \sigma_1^2 - \delta_2 \sigma_{12}}{\sigma^*} \tag{8.52}$$

and

$$\sigma_{2u^*} = \frac{\sigma_{2u} - \delta_1 \sigma_{12} - \delta_2 \sigma_2^2}{\sigma^*} \tag{8.53}$$

Also, we have the normalization condition

$$\sigma_u^2 + \delta_1^2 \sigma_1^2 + \delta_2^2 \sigma_2^2 - 2\delta_1 \sigma_{1u} - 2\delta_2 \sigma_{2u} + 2\delta_1 \delta_2 \sigma_{12} = \sigma^{*2} \quad (8.54)$$

Thus, from the equations (8.52), (8.53), and (8.54) we have to estimate four parameters: σ_{12}, σ_{1u}, σ_{2u}, and σ_u^2. This shows that we need to impose one more condition to be able to estimate the parameters in the covariance matrix (8.51). Thus, in the model given by equations (8.43) and (8.44), with the choice function specified as (8.45) or (8.49), we need to impose one restriction on the elements of the covariance matrix of the errors given in (8.51). Of course, σ_1^2 and σ_2^2 are always estimable. It is the estimation of the other elements that poses a problem.

A natural assumption to make is $\sigma_{12} = 0$. Note that in the switching regression model given by equations (8.51) and (8.6), the parameter σ_{12} is not estimable.

8.7   Probit two-stage and tobit two-stage methods

At this point it is interesting to distinguish between two types of two-stage estimation methods, termed the probit two-stage (P2SLS) method and the tobit two-stage (T2SLS) method by Lee et al. (1979). Consider, for instance, the labor-supply model of Heckman. The criterion that determines whether or not an individual is in the labor force is whether $H > 0$ or $H < 0$, where H is given by equation (8.31). Heckman suggested estimating the parameters in (8.31) by the probit method, substituting the resulting $\hat{\Delta}$ for Δ in equation (8.35), and estimating (8.35) by OLS. This method we call the *probit two-stage method*. Note that this method uses only the observations on I_i:

$$I_i = 1 \quad \text{if in labor force } (H > 0)$$
$$I_i = 0 \quad \text{otherwise}$$

We can as well use the data on hours worked H and estimate the parameters in (8.31) by the tobit method. We can then substitute the resulting $\hat{\Delta}$ for Δ in equation (8.35) and estimate (8.35) by OLS. This method we call the *tobit two-stage method*. The tobit two-stage method is applicable whenever there are observations on the variable determining the sample separation. This is the case with the labor-supply model considered by Heckman. This is not the case with the switching regression model or the censored regression model considered in earlier sections or the union-and-wages model. In all these models, the function giving the sample separation is of the probit type.

An example considered by Lee et al. (1980) illustrates the difference. The model considers the estimation of the effects of college education on earnings, based on the project TALENT data. Let S be years of college education and E be earnings. X, Z_1, and Z_2 are sets of (possibly overlapping) exogenous variables. These are variables like scores on achievement tests, father's education, mother's education, location of family (urban or rural), number of children in the family in which the respondent grew up, whether or not the parents were split, and so forth.

The model consists of two equations: years of college education and earnings. There is a sample-separation criterion that determines whether or not an individual goes to college. We can consider two types of models:

Model 1: Criterion function of the probit type. Let the choice function be

$$C = X\delta - \epsilon \qquad (8.55)$$

The model is

$$\left.\begin{array}{l} S = Z_1\beta_1 + \epsilon_{11} \\ E = \gamma S + Z_2\beta_2 + \epsilon_{12} \end{array}\right\} \text{ if } C > 0 \qquad (8.56)$$

$$\left.\begin{array}{l} S = 0 \\ E = Z_2\beta_3 + \epsilon_{22} \end{array}\right\} \text{ otherwise} \qquad (8.57)$$

The choice whether or not to go to college depends on expected returns from college education and several family-background variables. The variables in X in (8.55) include family-background variables and some proxies for expected returns to college education. Equation system (8.56) describes the determinants of years of college education and earnings for those who decide to go to college. Equation system (8.57) describes determinants of earnings for those who decide not to go to college. C is not observed. All we observe is

$$I_i = 1 \quad \text{if individual } i \text{ has college education } (C > 0)$$
$$I_i = 0 \quad \text{otherwise}$$

Thus, the criterion function is of the probit type, and we use the probit two-stage method to estimate this model.

Model 2: Criterion function of the tobit type. Define S^* as the "desired" years of college education. S^* obviously depends on both the family-background variables and expected earnings. We can now formulate our model as follows:

$$\left.\begin{array}{l} S = S^* = Z_1\beta_1 + \epsilon_{11} \\ E = \gamma S + Z_2\beta_2 + \epsilon_{12} \end{array}\right\} \text{ if } S^* > 0 \qquad (8.58)$$

$$\left. \begin{array}{l} S = 0 \\ E = Z_2\beta_3 + \epsilon_{22} \end{array} \right\} \quad \text{otherwise} \tag{8.59}$$

In this model the criterion function is

$$S^* = Z_1\beta_1 + \epsilon_{11}$$

We do have observations on S^*, namely, S defined by

$$S = S^* \quad \text{if } S^* > 0$$
$$S = 0 \quad \text{otherwise}$$

Thus, the criterion function is of the tobit type, and we can estimate the criterion function by the tobit method and use the tobit two-stage method. Note that in this model we can use the probit two-stage method as well by ignoring the observations on S and just using the information on I_i defined by

$$I_i = 1 \quad \text{if } S^* > 0$$
$$I_i = 0 \quad \text{otherwise}$$

Lee et al. (1980) derived the asymptotic covariance matrices for the probit two-stage and tobit two-stage methods. One important conclusion that emerges concerns the comparison of the correct standard errors with the (incorrect) standard errors from the second stage (OLS) of the two-stage method. They showed that in the case of the probit two-stage method, the standard errors from the second stage unambiguously underestimate the correct standard errors. In the case of the tobit two-stage method, this is so only for the second regime described by equations (8.59), whereas for the first regime described by equations (8.58) we cannot make any such assertion.

8.8   Two-stage methods for models with mixed qualitative, truncated, and continuous variables

Consider, for ease of exposition, a two-equation model:

$$y_1^* = \gamma_1 y_2^* + \beta_1' X_1 + u_1$$
$$y_2^* = \gamma_2 y_1^* + \beta_2' X_2 + u_2 \tag{8.60}$$

The two-stage procedures considered in this section are different from the two-stage procedures discussed in the previous sections. Often the second stage involves the ML estimation by probit or tobit methods, and the likelihood function to be maximized is of the form $L(\hat{\theta}_1, \theta_2)$, where $\hat{\theta}_1$ is a consistent estimate of θ_2. The derivation of the asymptotic covariance matrix of the two-stage estimates follows the method used by

Amemiya (1979) for the Nelson–Olsen model. This method uses the fact that the asymptotic covariance matrix of the estimator obtained by maximizing the likelihood function $L(\hat{\theta}_1, \theta_2)$, where some of the parameters have been replaced with their consistent estimates, can be obtained from the following relationship:

$$\hat{\theta}_2 - \theta_2 \overset{A}{=} -\left(E\frac{\partial^2 \log L}{\partial\theta_2 \partial\theta_2'}\right)^{-1}\left[\frac{\partial \log L}{\partial\theta_2} + E\frac{\partial^2 \log L}{\partial\theta_2 \partial\theta_1'}(\hat{\theta}_1 - \theta_1)\right]$$

where $\overset{A}{=}$ means that both sides of this equation have the same asymptotic distribution. We shall not present the details of the derivations (which follow the paper by Amemiya), but we shall give the appropriate expressions wherever they are not very cumbersome. Often these expressions can be programmed easily.

We shall denote the observed variables corresponding to y_1^* and y_2^* by y_1 and y_2. We can have the following types of situations and the corresponding two-stage estimation procedures:

Model 1. Both variables observed:

$$y_1 = y_1^*, \quad y_2 = y_2^*$$

This is the case of the usual two-stage least squares.

Model 2. y_1 observed, y_2 censored:

$$y_1 = y_1^*$$
$$y_2 = y_2^* \quad \text{if } y_2^* > 0$$
$$y_2 = 0 \quad \text{otherwise}$$

This is the model considered by Nelson and Olsen (1978). The procedure they suggested is as follows: Write the reduced forms for y_1 and y_2^*:

$$y_1 = \Pi_1 X + v_1$$
$$y_2^* = \Pi_2 X + v_2$$

where X includes all the exogenous variables in X_1 and X_2. Estimate the reduced form for y_1 by OLS and the reduced form for y_2^* by the tobit method. Next, estimate the equation for y_1 by OLS using $\hat{y}_2^*$ for y_2^* and the equation for y_2^* by tobit using $\hat{y}_1$ for y_1.

Amemiya (1979) derived the asymptotic covariance matrix for the Nelson–Olsen estimator and suggested an alternative method of estimation. We shall discuss this alternative method in the next section. The detailed derivation of the asymptotic covariance matrix can be found in

Amemiya's study and will not be reproduced here. The expression for the covariance matrix is as follows: Define

$$\alpha_1' = (\gamma_1, \beta_1')$$
$$\alpha_2' = (\gamma_2, \beta_2')$$
$$\text{Cov}(v_1, v_2) = \begin{bmatrix} \sigma_1^2 & \sigma_{12} \\ \sigma_{12} & \sigma_2^2 \end{bmatrix}$$

Also define $H = (\Pi_2, J_1)$ and $G = (\Pi_1, J_2)$, where J_1 and J_2 are matrices consisting of 1's and 0's so that $XJ_1 = X_1$ and $XJ_2 = X_2$. The asymptotic covariance matrix of the Nelson–Olsen estimator of α_1 is

$$V(\hat{\alpha}_1) = c(H'X'XH)^{-1} + \gamma_1^2(H'X'XH)^{-1}H'X'XV_0X'XH(H'XH)^{-1}$$

where

$$c = \sigma_1^2 - 2\gamma_1\sigma_{12} \quad \text{and} \quad V_0 = \text{Var}(\hat{\Pi}_2)$$

V_0 can be obtained from the tobit estimation of Π_2. Also,

$$V(\hat{\alpha}_2) = (G'V_0G)^{-1} + d(G'V_0G)^{-1}G'V_0^{-1}(X'X)^{-1}V_0^{-1}G(G'V_0G)^{-1}$$

where $d = \gamma_2^2\sigma_1^2 - 2\gamma_2\sigma_{12}$.

Model 3. y_1 observed, y_2 dichotomous: Here the model is

$$y_1 = y_1^*$$
$$y_2 = 1 \quad \text{if } y_2^* > 0$$
$$y_2 = 0 \quad \text{otherwise}$$

The reduced forms are

$$y_1 = \Pi_1 X + v_1$$
$$y_2^* = \Pi_2 X + v_2$$

Because y_2^* is observed only as a dichotomous variable, we can only estimate Π_2/σ_2, where $\sigma_2^2 = \text{Var}(v_2)$. Hence, we write

$$y_2^{**} = \frac{y_2^*}{\sigma_2} = \frac{\Pi_2}{\sigma_2}X + \frac{v_2}{\sigma_2} = \Pi_2^* X + v_2^* \tag{8.61}$$

The structural equations (8.60) are now written as

$$y_1 = \gamma_1\sigma_2 y_2^{**} + \beta_1'X_1 + u_1 \tag{8.62}$$

$$y_2^{**} = \frac{\gamma_2}{\sigma_2}y_1 + \frac{\beta_2'}{\sigma_2}X_2 + \frac{u_2}{\sigma_2} \tag{8.63}$$

The two-stage procedure would be to estimate Π_1 by OLS, estimate Π_2^* by probit ML, estimate equation (8.62) by OLS after substituting $\hat{\Pi}_2^* X$ for y_2^{**}, and estimate equation (8.63) by probit ML after substituting $\hat{\Pi}_1 X$ for y_1. Note that the estimable parameters in this model are $\gamma_1 \sigma_2$, γ_2/σ_2, β_1, β_2/σ_2, σ_1, and σ_{12}/σ_2.

The asymptotic covariance matrix can be derived by using a procedure similar to the one used by Amemiya for the Nelson–Olsen model (model 2). Given the estimable parameters in this model, we define

$$\alpha_1' = (\gamma_1 \sigma_2, \beta_1')$$

$$\alpha_2' = \left(\frac{\gamma_2}{\sigma_2}, \frac{\beta_2'}{\sigma_2} \right)$$

The definitions of H and G are as before. Then the covariance matrix of the two-stage estimates of α_1 is

$$\text{Var}(\hat{\alpha}_1) = c(H'X'XH)^{-1}$$
$$+ (\gamma_1 \sigma_2)^2 (H'X'XH)^{-1} H'X'XV_0 X'XH(H'X'XH)^{-1}$$

where V_0 is now the covariance matrix of the probit ML estimate of Π_2. For the two-stage probit estimate of α_2, the covariance matrix is

$$\text{Var}(\hat{\alpha}_2) = (G'V_0^{-1}G)^{-1}$$
$$+ d(G'V_0^{-1}G)^{-1} G'V_0^{-1}(X'X)^{-1} V_0^{-1} G(G'V_0^{-1}G)^{-1}$$

where V_0 is again the covariance matrix of the probit ML estimate of Π_2 and

$$d = \left(\frac{\gamma_2}{\sigma_2} \right)^2 \sigma_1^2 - 2\left(\frac{\gamma_2}{\sigma_2} \right)\left(\frac{\sigma_{12}}{\sigma_2} \right)$$

Model 4. y_1 and y_2 are both censored: Here we have

$$y_1 = y_1^* \quad \text{if } y_1^* > 0$$
$$y_1 = 0 \quad \text{otherwise}$$

$$y_2 = y_2^* \quad \text{if } y_2^* > 0$$
$$y_2 = 0 \quad \text{otherwise}$$

Note that this model is different from the two-equation model considered by Amemiya (1974b). The estimation procedure for this model is to estimate the reduced-form equations by the tobit method and the structural equations by the second-stage tobit method, as done by Nelson and Olsen. The derivation of the asymptotic covariance matrix of the two-stage estimates is very complicated and will not be attempted here.

Model 5. y_1 censored, y_2 binary: Here the situation is the same as in model 3. The reduced forms for y_1^* and y_2^* are estimated by the tobit and probit methods, respectively; the structural equations are estimated by the second-stage tobit and the two-stage probit methods, respectively. As in model 3, note that it is only $\gamma_1\sigma_2$, γ_2/σ_2, β_1, β_2/σ_2, and σ_1 that are estimable. The derivation of the asymptotic covariance matrix of the two-stage estimates is very complicated and will not be attempted here.

Model 6. y_1 and y_2 both binary: We have

$$y_1 = 1 \quad \text{if } y_1^* > 0$$
$$y_1 = 0 \quad \text{otherwise}$$

$$y_2 = 1 \quad \text{if } y_2^* > 0$$
$$y_2 = 0 \quad \text{otherwise}$$

This is the model considered by Mallar (1977), although his formulation of the model is not as transparent. Now the reduced forms are

$$y_1^* = \Pi_1 X + v_1$$
$$y_2^* = \Pi_2 X + v_2$$

If $\text{Var}(v_1) = \sigma_1^2$ and $\text{Var}(v_2) = \sigma_2^2$, because y_1^* and y_2^* are observed only as dichotomous variables, we can estimate only Π_1/σ_1 and Π_2/σ_2. Thus, writing $y_1^{**} = y_1^*/\sigma_1$ and $y_2^{**} = y_2^*/\sigma_1$, we note that the estimable structural functions are

$$y_1^{**} = \gamma_1 \frac{\sigma_2}{\sigma_1} y_2^{**} + \frac{\beta_1'}{\sigma_1} X_1 + \frac{u_1}{\sigma_1}$$

$$y_2^{**} = \gamma_2 \frac{\sigma_1}{\sigma_2} y_1^{**} + \frac{\beta_2'}{\sigma_2} X_2 + \frac{u_2}{\sigma_2}$$

We first estimate the reduced forms by probit ML. Then we substitute the predicted values of y_2^{**} and y_1^{**} and estimate the structural equations by the probit ML method. Note that the estimable parameters in this model are

$$\gamma_1 \frac{\sigma_2}{\sigma_1}, \quad \gamma_2 \frac{\sigma_1}{\sigma_2}, \quad \frac{\beta_1}{\sigma_1}, \quad \text{and} \quad \frac{\beta_2}{\sigma_2}$$

We again omit the detailed derivation and present the covariance matrices. Define

$$\alpha_1' = \left(\gamma_1 \frac{\sigma_2}{\sigma_1}, \frac{\beta_1'}{\sigma_1} \right)$$

$$\alpha_2' = \left(\gamma_2 \frac{\sigma_2}{\sigma_1}, \frac{\beta_2'}{\sigma_2} \right)$$

Let

$$a_1 = \frac{\phi_1}{\Phi_1(1 - \Phi_1)}, \quad a_2 = \frac{\phi_2}{\Phi_2(1 - \Phi_2)},$$

$$A_1 = \phi_1 a_1, \quad A_2 = \phi_2 a_2, \quad Z = \begin{bmatrix} \Pi_2^* X \\ X \end{bmatrix}$$

$$W_1 = \frac{1}{N} \sum_1^N A_1 Z Z'$$

$$W_2 = \frac{1}{N} \sum_1^N A_2 X X'$$

$$W_3 = \frac{1}{N} \sum_1^N A_1 \left(\gamma_1 \frac{\sigma_2}{\sigma_1} \right) Z X'$$

$$W_4 = \frac{1}{N} \sum^N a_1 a_2 E[(y_1 - \Phi_1)(y_2 - \Phi_2)] X Z'$$

Then the covariance matrix of $N^{1/2}(\hat{\alpha}_1 - \alpha_{01})$ (where α_{01} is the true value of α_1 and $\hat{\alpha}_1$ is the two-stage estimator) is

$$W_1^{-1}[W_1 - W_3 W_2^{-1} W_4 - W_4' W_2^{-1} W_3' + W_3 W_2^{-1} W_3'] W_1^{-1}$$

The covariance matrix of $\hat{\alpha}_2$ will be a similar expression, with the subscripts 1 and 2 interchanged in the definitions of Z, W_1, W_2, W_3, and W_4.

8.9   Some alternatives to the two-stage methods

Amemiya (1979) suggested some estimators alternative to the two-stage estimator used by Nelson and Olsen. The procedure Amemiya suggested is to obtain by regression methods estimates of the structural parameters from the estimates of the reduced-form parameters. To see what is involved, consider the two-equation model

$$y_{1i} = \gamma_1 y_{2i} + \beta' x_{1i} + u_{1i}$$
$$y_{2i} = \gamma_2 y_{1i} + \beta' x_{2i} + u_{2i}$$

In vector and matrix notation, we write these as

$$y_1 = \gamma_1 y_2 + X_1 \beta_1 + u_1 \tag{8.64}$$

$$y_2 = \gamma_2 y_1 + X_2 \beta_2 + u_2 \tag{8.65}$$

Let the reduced forms be

$$y_1 = X\Pi_1 + v_1 \tag{8.66}$$
$$y_2 = X\Pi_2 + v_2 \tag{8.67}$$

Define the matrices J_1 and J_2 (consisting of 1's and 0's at the appropriate places) by

$$XJ_1 = X_1 \quad \text{and} \quad XJ_2 = X_2$$

Substituting (8.67) into (8.64), we get

$$y_1 = \gamma_1 X\Pi_2 + XJ_1\beta_1 + \gamma_1 v_2 + u_1$$

Comparing this with (8.66), we get

$$\Pi_1 = \gamma_1 \Pi_2 + J_1\beta_1 \tag{8.68}$$

Similarly, we get

$$\Pi_2 = \gamma_2 \Pi_1 + J_2\beta_2 \tag{8.69}$$

Amemiya suggested estimating equations (8.68) and (8.69) directly by regression methods, writing $\hat{\Pi}_1$ for Π_1 and $\hat{\Pi}_2$ for Π_2. For instance, equation (8.68) will be written as

$$\hat{\Pi}_1 = \gamma_1 \hat{\Pi}_2 + J_1\beta_1 + \eta_1 \tag{8.70}$$

where

$$\eta_1 = \hat{\Pi}_1 - \Pi_1 - \gamma_1(\hat{\Pi}_2 - \Pi_2)$$

Amemiya observed that the GLS estimation of (8.70) indeed gives the usual 2SLS estimates of γ_1 and β_1 in this case. It is important to see why this is true to understand the procedure that Amemiya suggested for the Nelson–Olsen model.

Consider equation (8.64). It can be written as

$$X'y_1 = \gamma_1 X'y_2 + (X'X)J_1\beta_1 + x'u_1 \tag{8.71}$$

It is well known that GLS estimation of the equation gives the 2SLS estimates of γ_1 and β_1. We can premultiply (8.71) throughout by $(X'X)^{-1}$ to get

$$(X'X)^{-1}X'y_1 = \gamma_1(X'X)^{-1}X'y_2 + J_1\beta_1 + (X'X)^{-1}X'u_1 \tag{8.72}$$

The GLS estimation of (8.72) is the same as the GLS estimation of (8.71). But (8.72) is the same as (8.70). Thus, the 2SLS estimates and the GLS estimates of (8.70) are identical.

Returning to the Nelson–Olsen model, what Amemiya showed is that in models of the type Nelson and Olsen considered, GLS estimation of an equation of the type (8.72) yields more efficient estimates than the two-stage estimation of equation (8.64). The Nelson–Olsen model is

$$y_1 = \gamma_1 y_2^* + X_1\beta_1 + u_1 \tag{8.73}$$

$$y_2^* = \gamma_2 y_1 + X_2\beta_2 + u_2 \tag{8.74}$$

$$y_{2i} = y_{2i}^* \quad \text{if } y_{2i}^* > 0$$

$$y_{2i} = 0 \quad \text{otherwise}$$

The reduced forms are

$$y_1 = X\Pi_1 + v_1$$

$$y_2^* = X\Pi_2 + v_2$$

$$\hat{\Pi}_1 = (X'X)^{-1}X'y_1 \tag{8.75}$$

But $\hat{\Pi}_2$ is not $(X'X)^{-1}X'y_2$. $\hat{\Pi}_2$ is obtained by the tobit estimation of (8.75). Now write equation (8.73) as

$$y_1 = \gamma_1 X\hat{\Pi}_2 + X_1\beta_1 + v_1 = \gamma_1 X(\hat{\Pi}_2 - \Pi_2) = X\hat{H}\alpha_1 + w_1 \tag{8.76}$$

where

$$w_1 = v_1 - \gamma_1 X(\hat{\Pi}_2 - \Pi_2)$$

$$\hat{H} = (\hat{\Pi}_2, J_1) \tag{8.77}$$

and

$$\alpha_1 = \begin{bmatrix} \beta_1 \\ \gamma_1 \end{bmatrix}$$

Denote $\mathrm{Var}(w_1)$ by Σ_1. The Nelson–Olsen estimator is OLS applied to (8.76), which is

$$\hat{\alpha}_1 = (\hat{H}'X'X\hat{H})^{-1}\hat{H}'X'y_1 \tag{8.78}$$

The GLS estimator from (8.76) is

$$\hat{\alpha}_1^G = (\hat{H}'X'\Sigma_1^{-1}X\hat{H})^{-1}\hat{H}'X'\Sigma_1^{-1}y_1 \tag{8.79}$$

The problem with this, as Amemiya noted, is that unlike the case of the usual simultaneous-equations model, the matrix Σ_1 is a complicated matrix when $\hat{\Pi}_2$ is obtained by the tobit method. Thus, a matrix of a high order ($T \times T$, where T is the number of observations) needs to be inverted. To see what Amemiya suggested, premultiply equation (8.76) by X'. We get

$$X'y_1 = (X'X)\hat{H}\alpha_1 + X'w_1$$

or

$$(X'X)^{-1}X'y_1 = \hat{H}\alpha_1 + (X'X)^{-1}X'w_1 \tag{8.80}$$

This is nothing but equation (8.70), which Amemiya suggested estimating by OLS and GLS. Denote by V_1 the covariance matrix of the residuals in (8.80):

$$V_1 = (X'X)^{-1}X'\Sigma_1 X(X'X)^{-1} \tag{8.81}$$

The OLS and GLS estimates of α_1 from (8.80) are

$$\alpha_1^L = (\hat{H}'\hat{H})^{-1}\hat{H}'y_1 \tag{8.82}$$

$$\alpha_1^G = (\hat{H}'V_1^{-1}\hat{H})^{-1}\hat{H}'V_1^{-1}y_1 \tag{8.83}$$

Comparing equation (8.83) with equation (8.78), Amemiya concluded that the Nelson–Olsen estimator is the same as the GLS estimator applied to equation (8.80), using the "wrong" covariance matrix $(X'X)^{-1}$ in place of V_1. α_1^L also uses the "wrong" covariance matrix I in place of V_1. Hence, we can conclude that $V(\hat{\alpha}_1) - V(\alpha_1^G)$ is nonnegative definite and $V(\hat{\alpha}_1) - V(\alpha_1^L)$ is indefinite. The GLS estimator $\hat{\alpha}_1^G$ given by (8.79) is, however, more efficient than the GLS estimator of α_1^G given by (8.83). However, as noted earlier, this is difficult to implement in these models. The GLS estimator (8.83) requires inversion of the matrix $(X'\Sigma_1 X)$, which is of a much lower dimension than Σ_1.

To show that $\hat{\alpha}_1^G$ is more efficient than α_1^G, note that

$$V(\hat{\alpha}_1^G) = (\hat{H}'X'\Sigma_1^{-1}X\hat{H})^{-1}$$
$$V(\alpha_1^G) = (\hat{H}'V_1^{-1}\hat{H})^{-1}$$
$$X'\Sigma_1^{-1}X - V_1^{-1} = X'\Sigma_1^{-1}X - (X'X)(X'\Sigma_1 X)^{-1}(X'X)$$
$$= X'\Sigma_1^{-1/2}[1 - \Sigma_1^{1/2}X(X'\Sigma_1 X)^{-1}X'\Sigma_1^{1/2}]\Sigma_1^{-1/2}X$$

and the expression in square brackets is nonnegative definite.

In summary, Nelson and Olsen suggested estimating equation (8.76) by OLS. Amemiya suggested premultiplying this equation by $(X'X)^{-1}X'$ and estimating the resulting equation (8.80) by GLS. This completes our discussion of the estimation of the first equation of the Nelson–Olsen model.

Regarding the second equation (8.74), Nelson and Olsen substituted $X\hat{\Pi}_1$ for Y_1 and estimated the resulting equation by the tobit method. We write equation (8.74) as

$$y_2^* = \gamma_2 X \hat{\Pi}_1 + X_2 \beta_2 + v_2 - \gamma_2 X(\hat{\Pi}_1 - \Pi_1)$$
$$= X \hat{G} \alpha_2 + w_2 \tag{8.84}$$

where

$$w_2 = v_2 - \gamma_2 X(\hat{\Pi}_1 - \Pi_1)$$
$$\hat{G} = (\hat{\Pi}_1, J_2) \tag{8.85}$$

and

$$\alpha_2 = \begin{bmatrix} \gamma_2 \\ \beta_2 \end{bmatrix}$$

This time the procedure Amemiya suggested is not obtained by premultiplying (8.84) throughout by $(X'X)^{-1}X'$, because $\hat{\Pi}_2$ is not $(X'X)^{-1}X'y_2^*$. The equation Amemiya suggested estimating is

$$\hat{\Pi}_2 = G \alpha_2 + \eta_2 \tag{8.86}$$

Amemiya showed that in this case, as well, the GLS estimation applied to (8.86) gives estimates more efficient than the tobit estimation of (8.84) that Nelson and Olsen suggested (details of the proof are omitted here).

There is, of course, an alternative way of estimating the parameters in equation (8.74). This is two write it in the form

$$y_1 = \frac{1}{\gamma_2} y_2^* - X_2 \frac{\beta_2}{\gamma_2} - \frac{u_2}{\gamma_2}$$

Now the same procedure used for the estimation of (8.73) can be used to estimate the parameters of this equation. From the estimates of $1/\gamma_2$ and $-\beta_2/\gamma_2$, one can obtain estimates of γ_2 and β_2.

The procedures that Amemiya suggested, using the regression methods to get estimates of the structural parameters from the estimates of the reduced-form parameters, can be generalized to the case of other models. These generalizations, as well as a discussion of some generalized instrumental-variable estimators, can be found in the study by Lee (1982b), who showed that although the GLS estimators derived by Amemiya's method are more efficient than the two-stage estimation procedures, there exist some generalized instrumental-variable estimators that are asymptotically more efficient than the GLS estimator derived from Amemiya's principle.[5] Thus, it is possible to improve on the two-

---

[5] Because discussion of these estimators would involve reproducing most of the study of Lee (1982b), it will not be undertaken here.

stage estimation methods in the case in which some of the endogenous variables are observed only as truncated or dichotomous variables.

8.10   Some final comments

We have reviewed the two-stage estimation methods in a wide class of models involving censored and qualitative endogenous variables. Some of the applications of the two-stage methods not discussed here (e.g., those involving disequilibrium models) will be discussed in other chapters. Because of their computational simplicity, as compared with the ML methods, these methods are likely to be popular in much the same way that the two-stage least-squares (2SLS) method became popular in the 1950s and 1960s. Like the 2SLS method, the two-stage methods described here often have been found to create severe multicollinearity problems. For instance, estimation of equations of the type (8.12) and (8.13) has sometimes been found to yield poor estimates of the parameters because of multicollinearity between the W's and the X's. A discussion of some of these problems will be found in Chapter 9. Those interested in using the different two-stage methods described in this chapter should be careful to use the correct asymptotic covariances rather than the covariances from the second stage. As can be seen from the expressions presented for the different models, very often these expressions have to be derived separately for each model.[6] For this reason, unless the model being used falls in the category of the simple models discussed here, it might be appropriate to use the two-stage estimates as starting values for iterative computation of maximum-likelihood estimates. The methods described here would be useful for that purpose.

Appendix: Asymptotic covariance matrices for the different two-stage estimators

In this appendix we shall derive the asymptotic covariance matrix of the two-stage estimates for the switching regression model in section 8.3. We shall next derive the asymptotic covariance matrix for the parameters of structural equations. These results are from the work of Lee et al. (1980), which follows the methods of Amemiya (1978b).

Consider equation (8.5) and the two-stage estimation discussed there. In the first stage we get the probit ML estimate $\hat{\gamma}$ of γ. Let us, for compactness, write ϕ_i for $\phi(\gamma'Z_i)$ and Φ_i for $\Phi(\gamma'Z_i)$. Then, as defined in

---

[6] There is, however, more generality in the derivation of the asymptotic covariance matrices of the generalized IV estimators discussed by Lee (1982b).

(8.11), we have $W_{1i} = \phi_i/\Phi_i$ and $W_{2i} = \phi_i(1 - \Phi_i)$. Also, recall that we defined Λ as the $N \times N$ diagonal matrix whose ith diagonal term is $W_{1i}W_{2i}$, D_1 as the $N_1 \times N_1$ diagonal matrix whose ith diagonal term is $W_{1i}(W_{1i} + \gamma'Z_i)$, and D_2 as the $N_2 \times N_2$ diagonal matrix whose ith diagonal term is $W_{2i}(W_{2i} - \gamma'Z_i)$. Further, we defined $G_1 = (X_1, -W_1)$, $G_2 = (X_2, -W_2)$, and

$$H = \begin{bmatrix} Z_1' \\ Z_2' \\ \vdots \\ Z_N' \end{bmatrix}$$

with the partitioning

$$H = \begin{bmatrix} H_1 \\ H_2 \end{bmatrix}$$

corresponding to the N_1 observations for which $I_i = 1$ and N_2 observations for which $I_i = 0$, respectively.

The equation being estimated at the second stage is

$$Y_i = \beta_1' X_{1i} - \sigma_{1u} \hat{W}_{1i} + \tilde{\epsilon}_{1i}$$

where

$$\tilde{\epsilon}_{1i} = \epsilon_{1i} + \sigma_{1u}(\hat{W}_{1i} - W_{1i}) \quad \text{and} \quad \epsilon_{1i} = u_{1i} + \sigma_{1u} W_{1i}$$

Expanding $\hat{W}_1$ around γ, we get

$$\hat{W}_1 - W_1 \simeq B_\gamma(\hat{\gamma} - \gamma)$$

where

$$B_\gamma = \begin{bmatrix} (W_{11}Z_1'\gamma + W_{11}^2)Z_1 \\ \vdots \\ (W_{1N_1}Z_{N_1}'\gamma + W_{1N_1}^2)Z_{N_1} \end{bmatrix} = D_1 H_1$$

Hence, it follows that[7]

$$\begin{bmatrix} \hat{\beta}_1 \\ \hat{\sigma}_{1u} \end{bmatrix} - \begin{bmatrix} \beta_1 \\ \sigma_{1u} \end{bmatrix} \overset{A}{=} (G_1'G_1)^{-1}G_1'[\epsilon_1 + \sigma_{1u}B_\gamma(\hat{\gamma} - \gamma)]$$

The asymptotic covariance matrix is therefore

---

[7] In the discussion that follows, the notation $\overset{A}{=}$ means that the two expressions have the same asymptotic distribution.

$$\text{Var}\begin{bmatrix} \hat{\beta}_1 \\ \hat{\sigma}_{1u} \end{bmatrix} = (G_1'G_1)^{-1}G_1'[\text{Var}\,\epsilon_1 + \sigma_{1u}^2 B_\gamma \,\text{Var}(\hat{\gamma})B_\gamma'$$

$$+ \sigma_{1u}B_\gamma \,\text{Cov}(\hat{\gamma},\epsilon_1') + \sigma_{1u}\,\text{Cov}(\hat{\gamma}',\epsilon_1)B_\gamma']G_1(G_1'G_1)^{-1} \tag{A.1}$$

We have now to obtain $\text{Var}(\hat{\gamma})$, $\text{Var}(\epsilon_1)$, and $\text{Cov}(\hat{\gamma},\epsilon_1)$.

The probit ML method uses all the N observations. Following Amemiya (1978b), we can write

$$(\hat{\gamma}-\gamma) \stackrel{A}{=} \left[\sum_{i=1}^{N}\frac{\phi_i^2}{\Phi_i(1-\Phi_i)}Z_iZ_i'\right]^{-1}\sum_{i=1}^{N}\frac{\phi_i}{\Phi_i(1-\Phi_i)}Z_i(I_i-\Phi_i)$$

where I_i is the dummy variable defined as

$$I_i = 1 \quad \text{if } \gamma'Z_i > u_i$$
$$I_i = 0 \quad \text{otherwise}$$

If we now define Λ_1 as an $N\times N$ diagonal matrix with the ith diagonal term $\phi_i/[\Phi_i(1-\Phi_i)]$, then we can write

$$(\hat{\gamma}-\gamma) \stackrel{A}{=} (H'\Lambda H)^{-1}H'\Lambda_1 \begin{bmatrix} I_1 - \Phi_1 \\ I_2 - \phi_2 \\ \vdots \\ I_N - \Phi_N \end{bmatrix} \tag{A.2}$$

and $\text{Var}(\hat{\gamma}) = (H'\Lambda H)^{-1}$. It follows that

$$E(\hat{\gamma}-\gamma)\epsilon_1'$$
$$= (H'\Lambda H)^{-1}H'\Lambda_1$$
$$\times E\begin{bmatrix} I_1 - \Phi_1 \\ \vdots \\ I_{N_1} - \Phi_{N_1} \end{bmatrix} (u_{11} + \sigma_{1u}W_{11}, \ldots, u_{1N_1} + \sigma_{1u}W_{1N_1}) \begin{bmatrix} I_1 = 1 \\ I_2 = 1 \\ \vdots \\ I_{N_1} = 1 \end{bmatrix}$$

$$= 0$$

Finally, from equation (8.15), we have $\text{Var}(\epsilon_1) = \sigma_1^2 I - \sigma_{1u}^2 D_1$, where I is an $N_1 \times N_1$ identity matrix and D_1 is as defined earlier. Hence, substituting these expressions in (A.1) and simplifying, we get

$$\text{Var}\begin{bmatrix} \hat{\beta}_1 \\ \hat{\sigma}_{1u} \end{bmatrix} = \sigma_1^2(G_1'G_1)^{-1} - \sigma_{1u}^2(G_1'G_1)^{-1}G_1'$$

$$\times [D_1 - D_1H_1(H'\Lambda H)^{-1}H_1'D_1]G_1(G_1'G_1)^{-1} \tag{A.2}$$

which is the expression reported in section 8.3

For two-stage estimation of (8.6), the difference is in the expansion of $\hat{W}_2 - W_2$ around γ, and we get

$$\hat{W}_2 - W_2 \simeq C_\gamma(\hat{\gamma} - \gamma)$$

where $C_\gamma = D_2 H_2$. Hence, using the same simplifications as before, and noting that $E[\hat{\gamma} - \gamma, \epsilon_2'] = 0$, we get

$$\text{Var}\begin{bmatrix} \hat{\beta}_2 \\ \hat{\sigma}_{2u} \end{bmatrix} = \sigma_2^2(G_2'G_2)^{-1} - \sigma_{2u}^2(G_2'G_2)^{-1}G_2'$$

$$\times [D_2 - D_2 H_2(H'\Lambda H)^{-1}H_2'D_2]G_2(G_2'G_2)^{-1} \qquad (\text{A.3})$$

If in the second stage of the two-stage estimation we ignore the fact that $\hat{\gamma}$ has been estimated, then in expression (A.1) the terms $\text{Var}(\hat{\gamma})$ and $\text{Cov}(\hat{\gamma}, \epsilon_1')$ drop out, and the asymptotic covariance matrix is given by

$$(G_1'G_1)^{-1}G_1'\text{Var}(\epsilon_1)G_1(G_1'G_1)^{-1}$$
$$= \sigma_1^2(G_1'G_1)^{-1} - \sigma_{1u}^2(G_1'G_1)^{-1}G_1'D_1G_1(G_1'G_1)^{-1} \qquad (\text{A.4})$$

Clearly, the difference between (A.2) and (A.4) is

$$\sigma_{1u}^2(G_1'G_1)^{-1}G_1'D_1H_1(H'\Lambda H)^{-1}H_1'D_1G_1(G_1'G_1)^{-1}$$

which is positive semidefinite. Thus, ignoring the fact that $\hat{\gamma}$ has been estimated will result in an underestimation of the true variances.

Two-stage estimation of structural equations

The expressions for the covariance matrices of two-stage estimates of the structural equations are similar to those in (A.2) and (A.3), with proper definitions of the involved matrices.

Without any loss of generality, let us consider the first structural equation in the first regime, corresponding to $I_i = 1$:

$$Y_{1i} = \beta_{12}Y_{2i} + \cdots + \beta_{1m}Y_{mi} + \gamma_{1i}X_{1i} + u_{1i} \qquad (\text{A.5})$$

Because $E(u_{1i} \mid I_i = 1) = -\sigma_{1u}(\phi_i/\Phi_i)$, we can write (A.5) as

$$Y_{1i} = \beta_{12}Y_{2i} + \cdots + \beta_{1m}Y_{mi} + \gamma_{1i}X_{1i} - \sigma_{1u}\frac{\phi_i}{\Phi_i} + \epsilon_{1i} \qquad (\text{A.6})$$

The two-stage method consists of estimating the reduced forms of $Y_{2i}, \ldots, Y_{mi}$ by the methods suggested earlier for single-equation models. After obtaining these estimates, we get the predicted values of Y_{ji}. Note that if the reduced-form equation for Y_j is

$$Y_j = X_j\Pi_j + v_j$$

and

$$\text{Cov}(v_j, u) = \sigma_{v_j u}$$

then the predicted values of Y_{ji} are

$$\hat{Y}_{ji} = X_{ji}\hat{\Pi}_j - \hat{\sigma}_{v_j u}\frac{\hat{\phi}_i}{\hat{\Phi}_i}$$

The two-stage estimates of the parameters in (A.5) are given by

$$\hat{\theta} = (G_1^{*\prime}G_1^*)^{-1}G_1^{*\prime}Y_1$$

where

$$\theta' = [\beta_{12}, \beta_{13}, \ldots, \beta_{1m}, \gamma_{11}, \sigma_{1u}]$$

and

$$G_1^* = [\hat{Y}_2, \hat{Y}_3, \ldots, \hat{Y}_m, X_1, -W_1]$$

The asymptotic covariance matrix of this estimator is the same as expression (A.2), with G_1^* substituted for G_1.

CHAPTER 9

Models with self-selectivity

9.1 Introduction

There are many problems in which the data we have are generated by individuals making choices of belonging to one group or another (i.e., by individual self-selection). An early discussion of this problem of self-selectivity was that of Roy (1951), who discussed the problem of individuals choosing between two professions, hunting and fishing, based on their productivity in each. The observed distribution of incomes of hunters and fishermen was determined by these choices.

Suppose Y_{1i} is the output of the ith individual in hunting and Y_{2i} the output in fishing. Individual i will choose to be a hunter if $Y_{1i} > Y_{2i}$. Output here is defined in dollar terms. Assume that (Y_1, Y_2) have a joint normal distribution, with means (μ_1, μ_2) and covariance matrix

$$\begin{bmatrix} \sigma_1^2 & \sigma_{12} \\ \sigma_{12} & \sigma_2^2 \end{bmatrix}$$

Define

$$u_1 = Y_1 - \mu_1, \quad u_2 = Y_2 - \mu_2, \quad \sigma^2 = \mathrm{Var}(u_1 - u_2),$$

$$Z = \frac{\mu_1 - \mu_2}{\sigma} \quad \text{and} \quad u = \frac{u_2 - u_1}{\sigma}$$

The condition $Y_1 > Y_2$ implies $u < Z$. The mean income of hunters is given by

$$E(Y_1 \mid u < Z) = \mu_1 - \sigma_{1u} \frac{\phi(Z)}{\Phi(Z)} \tag{9.1}$$

257

where $\sigma_{1u} = \text{Cov}(u_1, u)$ and $\phi(\cdot)$ and $\Phi(\cdot)$ are, respectively, the density function and the distribution function of the standard normal. The mean income of fishermen is given by

$$E(Y_2 \mid u > Z) = \mu_2 + \sigma_{2u} \frac{\phi(Z)}{1 - \Phi(Z)} \tag{9.2}$$

where $\sigma_{2u} = \text{Cov}(u_2, u)$. Because

$$\sigma_{1u} = \frac{\sigma_{12} - \sigma_1^2}{\sigma} \quad \text{and} \quad \sigma_{2u} = \frac{\sigma_2^2 - \sigma_{12}}{\sigma}$$

we have $\sigma_{2u} - \sigma_{1u} > 0$. We can now consider different cases.

Case 1. $\sigma_{1u} < 0$, $\sigma_{2u} > 0$. In this case the mean income of hunters is greater than μ_1 and the mean income of fishermen is greater than μ_2; that is, those who chose hunting are better than average hunters, and those who chose fishing are better than average fishermen.

Case 2. $\sigma_{1u} < 0$, $\sigma_{2u} < 0$. In this case the mean income of hunters is greater than μ_1, and the mean income of fishermen is less than μ_2. In this case those who chose hunting are better than average in both hunting and fishing, but they are better in hunting than in fishing. Those who chose fishing are below average in both hunting and fishing, but they are better in fishing than in hunting.

Case 3. $\sigma_{1u} > 0$, $\sigma_{2u} > 0$. This is the reverse of case 2.

Case 4. $\sigma_{1u} > 0$, $\sigma_{2u} < 0$. This is not possible, given the definitions of σ_{1u} and σ_{2u}.

Note that case 2 typically occurs if σ_1 is very large compared with σ_2. Thus, the individuals with better skills go into the profession with higher variance in earnings.

The more detailed analysis of this model can be found in the work of Roy (1951). The important thing to note here is the importance of the covariance terms σ_{1u} and σ_{2u} in the interpretation of the results. We shall see later how they play an important role in discussions of selectivity bias.

The econometric discussion of the consequences of self-selectivity began with the studies by Gronau (1974), Lewis (1974), and Heckman (1974). In this case the problem is about women choosing to be in the labor force or not. The observed distribution of wages is a truncated distribution. It is the distribution of wage offers truncated by reservation wages. The Gronau–Lewis model consisted of two equations:

$$W_o = X\beta_1 + u_1$$
$$W_r = X\beta_2 + u_2 \tag{9.3}$$

We observe $W = W_o$ if and only if $W_o \geqslant W_r$. Otherwise, $W = 0$. We discussed the estimation of this model in Chapter 8, and we shall not repeat it here. The term *selectivity bias* refers to the fact that if we estimate equation (9.3) by OLS, based on the observations for which we have wages W, we get inconsistent estimates of the parameters. Note that

$$E(u_1 \mid W_o \geqslant W_r) = -\sigma_{1u} \frac{\phi(Z)}{\Phi(Z)}$$

where $Z = (X\beta_1 - X\beta_2)/\sigma$ and the other terms are as defined earlier. Hence, we can write (9.3) as

$$W = X\beta_1 - \sigma_{1u} \frac{\phi(Z)}{\Phi(Z)} + V \tag{9.4}$$

where $E(V) = 0$. A test for selectivity bias is a test for $\sigma_{1u} = 0$. Heckman (1976b) suggested a two-stage estimation method for such models. First, get consistent estimates for the parameters in Z by the probit method applied to the dichotomous variable (in the labor force or not). Then estimate equation (9.4) by OLS, using the estimated values $\hat{Z}$ for Z. This two-stage method has been discussed in detail in Chapter 8.

The self-selectivity problem has more recently been analyzed in different contexts by several people. Lee and Trost (1978) applied it to the problem of housing demand, with choices of owning and renting. Willis and Rosen (1979) applied the model to the problem of education and self-selection. These are all switching regression models. Griliches et al. (1978) and Kenny et al. (1979) considered models with both selectivity and simultaneity. These models are switching simultaneous-equations models. As for methods of estimation, both two-stage and maximum-likelihood methods have been used. For two-stage methods, the study by Lee et al. (1980) gave the asymptotic covariance matrices when the selectivity criterion was of the probit and tobit types (see Chapter 8).

In the literature on self-selectivity, a major concern has been with testing for selectivity bias. These are tests for $\sigma_{1u} = 0$ and $\sigma_{2u} = 0$ in equations of the form (9.1) and (9.2). However, a more important issue concerns the signs and magnitudes of these covariances, and often not much attention is devoted to this. In actual practice, we ought to have $\sigma_{2u} - \sigma_{1u} > 0$, but σ_{1u} and σ_{2u} can have any signs.[1] It is also important to

---

[1] Trost (1981) discussed this point in reference to returns from college education.

estimate the mean values of the dependent variables for the alternative choice. for instance, in the case of college education and income, we should estimate the mean income of college graduates had they chosen not to go to college and the mean income of non-college-graduates had they chosen to go to college. In the example of hunting and fishing, we should compute the mean income of hunters had they chosen to be fishermen and the mean income of fishermen had they chosen to be hunters. Such computations throw light on the effects of self-selection and also reveal deficiencies in the model that are not revealed by simple tests for the existence of selectivity bias. In the example concerning hunting and fishing, the mean income of hunters, had they chosen fishing, would be

$$E(Y_2 \mid Y_1 > Y_2) = E(Y_2 \mid u_2 > Z)$$

$$= \mu_2 - \sigma_{2u} \frac{\phi(Z)}{\Phi(Z)}$$

and the mean income of fishermen, had they chosen hunting, would be

$$E(Y_1 \mid Y_1 < Y_2) = \mu_1 + \sigma_{1u} \frac{\phi(Z)}{1 - \Phi(Z)}$$

Also, if we denote by $\overline{Y}_1$ and $\overline{Y}_2$ the actual mean incomes of hunters and fishermen, then from (9.1) and (9.2) we have

$$E(\overline{Y}_1 - \overline{Y}_2) = \mu_1 - \mu_2 - \sigma_{1u} \frac{\phi(Z)}{\Phi(Z)} - \sigma_{2u} \frac{\phi(Z)}{1 - \Phi(Z)}$$

If σ_{1u} and σ_{2u} are both negative, then $\overline{Y}_1 - \overline{Y}_2$ is an upward-biased estimate of $\mu_1 - \mu_2$. If σ_{1u} and σ_{2u} are both positive, then $\overline{Y}_1 - \overline{Y}_2$ is a downward-biased estimate of $\mu_1 - \mu_2$. If $\sigma_{1u} < 0$ and $\sigma_{2u} > 0$, the direction of bias is not unambiguous.[2]

The foregoing discussion generalizes easily to models with explanatory variables. All we do is substitute $\mu_1 = \beta_1' X_1$ and $\mu_2 = \beta_2' X_2$ in all the expressions.

9.2   Self-selection and evaluation of programs

One major use of the self-selection models is in evaluating the benefits of social programs. To evaluate the benefit from a program, a model commonly employed is the following:

$$Y = X\beta + \alpha I + u \tag{9.5}$$

---

[2] Some illustrative examples are given by Maddala (1977a). Because the examples can be worked out easily, they will not be repeated here.

where Y is the outcome (test score, earnings, etc.), X is a vector of exogenous personal characteristics, and I is a dummy variable ($I=1$ if the individual participates in the program; $I=0$ otherwise). For this model, the effect of the program is measured by the estimate of α. However, the dummy variable I cannot be treated as exogenous if the decision of an individual to participate or not participate in the program is based on individual self-selection. If the variable I is endogenous, equation (9.5) must be estimated by instrumental-variable techniques.

The foregoing model is very restrictive, because the program may create interaction effects with observed or unobserved personal characteristics; a more general model is the following:

$$y_{1i} = X_i\beta_1 + u_{1i} \quad \text{(for participants)}$$
$$y_{2i} = X_i\beta_2 + u_{2i} \quad \text{(for nonparticipants)}$$
$$I_i^* = Z_i\gamma = \epsilon_i \quad \text{(participation decision function)}$$

$$I_i = 1 \quad \text{iff } I_i^* > 0$$
$$I_i = 0 \quad \text{iff } I_i^* \leqslant 0$$

The observed y_i is defined as

$$y_i = y_{1i} \quad \text{iff } I_i = 1$$
$$y_i = y_{2i} \quad \text{iff } I_i = 0$$
$$\text{Cov}(u_{1i}, u_{2i}, \epsilon_i) = \begin{bmatrix} \sigma_{11} & \sigma_{12} & \sigma_{1\epsilon} \\ \sigma_{12} & \sigma_{22} & \sigma_{2\epsilon} \\ \sigma_{1\epsilon} & \sigma_{2\epsilon} & 1 \end{bmatrix}$$

To evaluate the benefit of the program that has already been created, we need to consider the total gross benefit for all the participants. For each participant with characteristics X_i and Z_i, we can compare the outcome y_{1i} in the program and the expected potential outcome without the program, that is, $E(y_{2i} | I_i=1)$. Under the normality assumption, the gross benefit for participants i is

$$y_{1i} - E(y_{2i} | I_i = 1) = y_{1i} - X_i\beta_2 + \sigma_{2\epsilon} \frac{\phi(Z_i\gamma)}{\Phi(Z_i\gamma)} \tag{9.6}$$

The total benefit is the summation of (9.6) over all the participants. Thus, to evaluate the success of a program from the cost–benefit point of view, the conditional expectation of u_{2i} for the participants needs to be evaluated. Note that, under self-selection, those individuals who have a comparative advantage with the program will be joining the program and thus will benefit more from it than would a randomly selected individual with the same characteristics. The expected gross benefit for participant i is

$$E(y_{1i} \,|\, I_i = 1) - E(y_{2i} \,|\, I_i = 1) = X_i(\beta_1 - \beta_2) + (\sigma_{2\epsilon} - \sigma_{1\epsilon}) \frac{\phi(Z_i \gamma)}{\Phi(Z_i \gamma)} \qquad (9.7)$$

If self-selection is based on comparative advantage, as in Roy's example on hunting and fishing in the preceding section, $\sigma_{2\epsilon} - \sigma_{1\epsilon}$ is greater than zero.[3] Thus, the program will produce greater benefit under self-selection than under a random assignment. The difference is measured by the summation of the last term in (9.7) over all participants.

The preceding discussion assumes that there are only two groups of individuals, one participating in the program (treatment group) and the other not participating (control group), and the assignment of individuals to the two groups is by self-selection rather than by random assignment. There can be other types of self-selection. Suppose that there is a social experiment (say a time-of-day pricing experiment) for which we draw a random sample. Some of the individuals in the sample may not wish to participate. Among those who participate, the assignment to the control or treatment group could be a random assignment. In this case the self-selection is at the stage of entering an experiment. What one will do is estimate an equation of the form (9.5) using the method of the censored or truncated regression models described in Chapter 6. What we have is a model of the form

$$I^* = Z\gamma - \epsilon \qquad (9.8)$$

The individual is in the experiment, and $I = 1$ if and only if $I^* > 0$. Otherwise, the individual is not in the experiment. Also,

$$Y = X\beta + \alpha D + u \qquad (9.9)$$

where $D = 1$ if the individual is in the treatment group and $D = 0$ if in the control group. Because the assignment to the treatment and control groups is random, D is an exogenous dummy variable. However, there is censoring or truncation produced by (9.8). If data on Z are available on all individuals, we shall estimate (9.9) as a censored regression model. If data on Z are available only for the participants in the experiment, we shall estimate equation (9.9) as a truncated regression model. If the residuals ϵ and u in equations (9.8) and (9.9) are independent, of course we can estimate (9.9) by the OLS method. The important thing, however, is that D is exogenous, because individuals are randomly assigned to the control and treatment groups.

What if there is self-selection at the stage of choosing whether or not to participate in the experiment and also at the stage of choosing

---

[3] See also the work of Lee (1979b) on self-selection and comparative advantage.

between the treatment and control groups. There is the question whether we want to treat this as a trichotomous-choice model or a sequential self-selection model. In the trichotomous-choice model, the individual has to choose among three alternatives: to belong to the treatment group, to belong to the control group, not to participate in the experiment at all. In the sequential self-selection model, the individual first chooses whether or not to participate in the experiment, and those who decide to participate then decide whether to go into the treatment group or the control group. Such selectivity models with polychotomous choices and sequential choices will be discussed later in this chapter (section 9.4).

A third alternative is where the assignment of individuals to the control and treatment groups is made by the program administrator on the basis of a screening variable that is itself correlated with X in equation (9.9). Goldberger (1972) analyzed this problem and pointed out that there are some misconceptions about the biases in the estimates of treatment effects in such cases. For example, suppose the selection procedure is to put lower-ability students into the treatment group and higher-ability students into the control group, as in the Head Start compensatory educational programs. Because ability is not measurable, the program administrator uses the pretest score, say Z (measured as deviations from the mean). So the assignment is

$$D = 1 \quad \text{if } Z < 0$$
$$D = 0 \quad \text{otherwise} \tag{9.10}$$

After completion of the program, one looks at the posttest score Y. If Y is then regressed on Z and D, that is

$$Y = \beta Z + \alpha D + \epsilon \tag{9.11}$$

and the estimate of α is not significantly different from zero, it is often argued that this is not really proof that the program is not working, because the students assigned to the treatment group are students with lower ability. What Goldberger pointed out is that the estimation of equation (9.11) nevertheless produces an unbiased estimate of α, the coefficient of D, or the treatment effect. The reasoning behind this fact is that controlling for Z eliminates any correlation of D with the other variables.

The formal argument runs as follows: Let us denote the unobserved ability variable by X. Because it affects the posttest score Y, we have

$$Y = \gamma_1 X + \alpha D + \epsilon_1 \tag{9.12}$$

The pretest score Z also depends on ability. Hence,

$$Z = \gamma_2 X + \epsilon_2 \tag{9.13}$$

Suppose ability X is indeed measurable. Then, of course, estimation of (9.12) by OLS will give inconsistent estimates of the parameters γ_1 and α so long as ϵ_1 and ϵ_2 are correlated. But we also know the methods of obtaining consistent estimates of the parameters in this case by correcting for the selection bias. Consider now the case in which X is not observed, but we know its determinants W, so that

$$X = \theta W + v$$

Substituting this in equations (9.12) and (9.13), we get equations of the form

$$Y = \theta_1 W + \alpha D + u_1 \tag{9.14}$$
$$Z = \theta_2 W + u_2 \tag{9.15}$$

Again, estimation of (9.14) by OLS gives inconsistent estimates of the parameters if u_1 and u_2 are correlated, but again we know how to get consistent estimates. The model is again a model with sample selectivity that has been considered earlier. This is the case considered by Barnow et al. (1981).

Consider, finally, the case in which all we have are equations (9.12) and (9.13) and X is not observable; that is, we have pretest score, posttest score, and the dummy variable D, which is itself determined by the pretest score. Eliminating X, we get

$$
\begin{aligned}
Y &= \frac{\gamma_1}{\gamma_2}(Z - \epsilon_2) + \alpha D + \epsilon_1 \\
&= \gamma Z + \alpha D + (\epsilon_1 - \gamma\epsilon_2) \tag{9.16}
\end{aligned}
$$

where $\gamma = \gamma_1/\gamma_2$. Now the question is what we can say about the estimate of α when (9.16) is estimated by OLS. The answer, as shown by Goldberger (1972), is that Plim $\hat{\alpha} = \alpha$.

The preceding discussion referred to the program administrator's assignment of individuals to the treatment and control groups. In practice, in many programs with eligibility requirements and so on, we can have the twin problems of individual decision whether or not to participate and the program administrator's decision whether or not to choose. This is a sequential-decision model with partial observability, and we shall discuss it in a later section. There are two decision variables, I_1 and I_2, and we observe the variable Y if and only if $I_1 > 0$ and $I_2 > 0$. In such problems there is the further complication that the pool of applicants may be only a self-selected subsample of all those who wish to participate, because many may not apply if they know that there is a long waiting list. However, there is no easy way to deal with this problem of the discouraged applicants.

Yet another complication is that of attrition of dropout of people from the experiment. Some participants inevitably drop out of the experiment before the treatment response is measured. One way of modeling this phenomenon is as follows: Define

$$I_i^* = Z_i\gamma - \epsilon_1$$
$$A_i^* = Z_i\delta - \epsilon_2$$
$$Y_{1i} = X_{1i}\beta_1 + \epsilon_3$$
$$Y_{2i} = X_{2i}\beta_2 + \alpha T + \epsilon_4 \qquad (9.17)$$

where

$I_i = 1$ and the individual participates in the experiment iff $I_i^* > 0$

$I_i = 0$ otherwise

$A_i = 1$ and the individual continues in the experiment iff $A_i^* > 0$

$A_i = 0$ otherwise (the individual drops out)

If $I_i = 0$, neither Y_{1i} nor Y_{2i} is observed. If $I_i = 1$, $A_i = 0$, we observe only Y_{1i}. If $I_i = 1$, $A_i = 1$, we observe both Y_{1i} and Y_{2i}.

An example of the estimation of this model is that of Venti and Wise (1980). We shall discuss some limitations of such models later in the section on multiple criteria of selectivity.

In summary, in evaluating the effects of several social programs, we must consider the selection and truncation that can occur at different levels. We can depict the situation by a decision tree (Figure 9.1). In practical situations, one must assume randomness at certain levels, or else the model can get too unwieldy to be of any use. As to the level at which selection and truncation bias needs to be introduced, this is a question that depends on the nature of the problem. Further, in Figure 9.1 the individual's decision to participate preceded the administrator's decision to select. This situation can be reversed, or the decisions can be simultaneous. Problems of sequential versus joint selection will be discussed in section 9.6. Another problem is that caused by the existence of multiple categories, such as no participation, partial participation, or full participation, or different types of treatment. These cases fall in the class of models with polychotomous choice and selectivity that will be discussed in section 9.5.

Finally, there is the problem of truncated samples. Very often we do not have data on all the individuals, participants and nonparticipants. If the data involve only participants in a program, but we know nevertheless that there is self-selection and we have data on the variables determining the participation decision function, then we can still correct for selectivity bias, although the two-stage methods described in the previous chapters are not applicable. What we have is the model

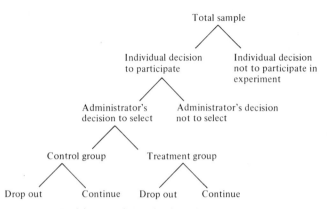

Figure 9.1. Decision tree for evaluation of social experiments

$$y_{1i} = X_i \beta_1 + u_{1i}$$
$$I_i^* = Z_i \gamma - \epsilon_i$$

As before,

$$I_i = 1 \quad \text{iff} \quad I_i^* > 0$$
$$I_i = 0 \quad \text{otherwise}$$

We are given only those observations for which $I_i = 1$, and for these we observe y_{1i}, X_i, and Z_i. The probit estimates of γ cannot be obtained because we do not have the observations corresponding to $I_i = 0$. Thus, we cannot use the two-stage methods. But we can use the ML method to correct for the selectivity bias. The model is different from the truncated regression model considered in section 6.9 in that the truncation is now based on an unobserved indicator I_i^* rather than the variable y_{1i}.

The likelihood function for the model is

$$L = \prod_i \frac{\int_{-\infty}^{Z_i \gamma} f(u_{1i}, \epsilon_i) \, d\epsilon_i}{\text{Prob}(I_i = 1)}$$

where $f(u_1, \epsilon)$ is the joint density function of u_1 and ϵ. If we assume that u_1 and ϵ are jointly normally distributed, with mean vector zero and covariance matrix

$$\Sigma = \begin{bmatrix} \sigma_1^2 & \rho \sigma_1 \\ \rho \sigma_1 & 1 \end{bmatrix}$$

then by writing $f(u_i, \epsilon)$ as $f_1(u_1) \cdot f_2(\epsilon | u_1)$, we can simplify the likelihood function as

$$L = \prod_i [\Phi(Z_i \gamma)]^{-1} \frac{1}{\sigma_1} \exp\left[-\frac{1}{2\sigma_1^2} (y_{1i} - X_i \beta_1)^2 \right]$$

$$\times \ \Phi\left(\frac{[Z_i\gamma - \rho(y_{1i} - X_i\beta_1)]/\sigma_1}{(1-\rho^2)^{1/2}}\right)$$

The first expression is $\mathrm{Prob}(I_i = 1)$. The second is $f_1(u_1)$. The third is $\mathrm{Prob}(\epsilon < Z\gamma)$, derived from the conditional density $f_2(\epsilon \mid u_1)$. Note that $\mathrm{Var}(\epsilon) = 1$, by normalization.

The problem of truncated samples can be handled in a similar manner with the other problems of self-selection and hence will not be elaborated here. The important thing to note is that although, theoretically, truncation does not change the identifiability of the parameters, there is nevertheless a loss of information. It is usually the case that even though we are able to correct for the selectivity bias in the OLS estimates β_1, the estimates of the parameters γ in the selectivity criterion are not reliable. Muthén and Jöreskog (1981) reported the results of some simulated experiments they did with a simple selectivity model with truncated data and censored data. They conducted two studies, one with a sample size of 1,000 and the other with a sample size of 4,000. For each study they considered two cases. In case 1 the proportion of observations with $I_i = 1$ was roughly 50%. In case 2 the proportion of observations with $I_i = 1$ was roughly 75%. The difference between the censored and truncated samples was that in the case of the censored sample, data were assumed to be available on the variable Z for all observations, whereas in the truncated case, data were assumed to be available on only the subsample for which $I_i = 1$. In both cases, data on X_i were assumed to be available for only the subsample for which $I_i = 1$. Their finding was that even with such large samples, in the truncated case it was not possible to get good estimates of the parameters γ in the selectivity criterion, although it was possible to correct for selectivity bias in the β coefficients. Table 9.1 presents the results for the case in which $N = 1,000$ and $I_i = 1$ for about 50% of the observations.

In summary, even if the available data are for subgroups and are thus truncated samples, one can try to correct for the selectivity bias in the OLS estimates by using the ML method described here, provided one has a clear notion of what variables affect the selectivity criterion. However, one cannot expect to have good estimates for the parameters in the selectivity criterion itself.

9.3   Selectivity bias with nonnormal distributions

In the preceding sections, and in the several examples in Chapter 8, we discussed the selectivity-bias problem under the assumption that the disturbances are normally distributed. We shall now consider methods of relaxing this assumption.

Table 9.1. *Estimation of selectivity models from truncated and censored samples* (*simulated data*)

Parameter	Population value	OLS estimates	Probit estimates	ML (truncated sample)	ML (censored sample)
β_0	0.0	−0.373		−0.209	0.074
		(0.054)		(0.119)	(0.179)
β_1	1.0	0.788		0.931	1.033
		(0.052)		(0.095)	(0.114)
σ_1^2	1.0	0.985		0.982	1.126
		(0.065)		(0.076)	(0.131)
γ_0	0.0		0.011	0.991	0.013
			(0.046)	(1.599)	(0.046)
γ_1	−1.0		−1.033	−3.448	−1.040
			(0.067)	(4.542)	(0.068)
ρ	−0.5			−0.248	−0.522
				(0.413)	(0.164)

Note: Standard errors in parentheses. $N = 1{,}000$ and $I_i = 1$ for 503 observations.
Source: Muthén and Jöreskog (1981, Table 3).

Consider the simple two-equation model

$$Y_1 = X\beta + u \qquad (9.18)$$
$$Y^* = Z\gamma - \epsilon \qquad (9.19)$$

where X and Z are exogenous variables. Equation (9.19) is the selectivity criterion. The dependent variable Y^* is never observable, but it has a dichotomous realization I that is related to Y^* as follows:

$$I = 1 \quad \text{iff} \quad Y^* \geqslant 0$$
$$I = 0 \quad \text{otherwise}$$

The dependent variable Y_1 conditional on X and Z has a well-defined marginal distribution, but Y_1 is not observed unless $Y^* > 0$. Thus, the observed distribution of Y_1 is truncated.

Regarding the disturbances, we assume that

$$E(u \mid X, Z) = 0, \quad V(u \mid X, Z) = \sigma_u^2, \quad \text{Cov}(u, \epsilon \mid X, Z) = \rho\sigma_u\sigma_\epsilon$$
$$E(\epsilon \mid X, Z) = \mu_\epsilon, \quad \text{and} \quad V(\epsilon \mid X, Z) = \sigma_\epsilon^2$$

In all the examples in the preceding section, as well as in Chapter 8, we assumed $\mu_\epsilon = 0$ and $\sigma_\epsilon = 1$. But here we shall not make that assumption as yet. Following Olsen (1980a), we also assume that the conditional expectation of u, given ϵ, is linear, so that

$$u = \frac{\rho \sigma_u}{\sigma_\epsilon}(\epsilon - \mu_\epsilon) + v \qquad (9.20)$$

and $E(v|\epsilon) = 0$ and $\text{Var}(v|\epsilon) = \sigma_u^2(1-\rho^2)$.

Consider now the censored sample of Y_1. From (9.20) we get

$$E(Y_1|I=1) = X\beta + E(u|\epsilon < Z\gamma) = X\beta + \frac{\rho \sigma_u}{\sigma_\epsilon}[g(Z\gamma) - \mu_\epsilon] \qquad (9.21)$$

where $g(Z\gamma)$ is the truncated mean $E(\epsilon|\epsilon < Z\gamma)$. Also,

$$V(Y_1|I=1) = \frac{\rho^2 \sigma_u^2}{\sigma_\epsilon^2} V(\epsilon|\epsilon < Z\gamma) + \sigma_u^2(1-\rho^2) \qquad (9.22)$$

In the usual selectivity model we have been discussing, $\mu_\epsilon = 0$ and $\sigma_\epsilon = 1$. Further, ϵ is assumed to be normal, so that

$$g(Z\gamma) = -\frac{\phi(Z\gamma)}{\Phi(Z\gamma)} = \lambda \quad \text{(say)} \qquad (9.23)$$

and $V(\epsilon|\epsilon < Z\gamma) = 1 - \lambda(Z\gamma - \lambda)$. Hence, equations (9.21) and (9.22) become

$$E(Y_1|I=1) = X\beta + \rho\sigma_u\lambda \qquad (9.24)$$
$$V(Y_1|I=1) = \sigma_u^2[1 - \rho^2\lambda(Z\gamma - \lambda)] \qquad (9.25)$$

Note that in the derivation of (9.24) and (9.25) we have not made any assumption about the distribution of u. The only assumptions made are that ϵ is normal and that the conditional expectation of u, given ϵ, is linear, as given in equation (9.20). If u and ϵ are bivariate normal, this condition follows automatically.

One question we might ask is how well the expression λ, defined in (9.23) under the assumption of normality, approximates the true truncated mean $g(Z\gamma)$ if ϵ is not normal. Goldberger (1980a) made some calculations with alternative error distributions and showed that the normal selection-bias adjustment is quite sensitive to departures from normality. This suggests that one should use a more general functional form for the truncated mean function in practice.

Before we move on to the generalized functional forms, we should note two points about the selectivity-bias adjustment:

1. One problem that has often been pointed out is that if Z includes some variables in X (or variables highly correlated with those in X), then given that the function $g(Z\gamma)$ is a nonlinear function of Z, it is likely to pick up any nonlinear terms omitted in equation (9.18), and the variable $g(Z\gamma)$ could be significant, thus indicating the presence of selection bias, even when there is no selection bias. The solution to this problem is to include nonlinear terms in (9.18), if that does indeed make

economic sense, and then examine whether or not the variable $g(Z\gamma)$ is significant.

2. Another problem occurs when $(Z\gamma)$ is constant. In this case the two-stage method described in Chapter 8 breaks down if there is a constant term in (9.18), because $g(Z\gamma)$ is constant for all observations.[4] However, the ML estimator does exist if we make the assumption that u and ϵ are jointly normally distributed, and thus one can test for the presence of selectivity bias.

Returning to the question of nonnormal distributions, Olsen (1982a) suggested that the distribution of ϵ in (9.19) be assumed to be generated from a bivariate normal (ϵ, v), with v truncated so that $v \le K$, a given constant. (Here v is another variate introduced to produce nonnormality.) By varying K, we get a variety of skewed distributions. Specifically, what he suggested is to consider the distribution of (u, ϵ, v) to be tri-variate normal, with correlation matrix

$$\begin{bmatrix} 1 & \rho_1 & \rho_2 \\ \rho_1 & 1 & \rho_1\rho_2 \\ \rho_2 & \rho_1\rho_2 & 1 \end{bmatrix}$$

The extent and direction of selection are governed by ρ_1. The parameters ρ_2 and K allow for nonnormality. The model falls in the category of multiple criteria of selectivity, because what it implies is that Y_1 is observed if and only if $\epsilon \le Z\gamma$ and $v \le K$. We shall be discussing these models in the next section. Because K is a constant, we have to use the ML method of estimation, and thus will involve evaluation of double integrals.

In another study, Olsen (1980a) suggested the use of uniform distribution for ϵ in the range $(0, 1)$. In this case, $E(\epsilon) = 1/2$, and $v(\epsilon) = 1/12$. Hence, using equation (9.20), we get

$$E(u \mid \epsilon < Z\gamma) = E\left[\frac{\rho\sigma_u}{\rho_\epsilon} \left(\epsilon - \frac{1}{2} \right) \middle| \epsilon < Z\gamma \right]$$

$$= \frac{\rho\sigma_u}{\sigma_\epsilon} \left(\frac{Z\gamma}{2} - \frac{1}{2} \right) = \rho\sigma_u (3)^{1/2} (Z\gamma - 1)$$

Thus,

$$E(Y_1 \mid I = 1) = X\beta + \rho\sigma_u (3)^{1/2} (Z\gamma - 1) \tag{9.26}$$

---

[4] There are some cases that the two-stage method would break down when $Z\gamma$ is a combination of dichotomous variables (not just the case in which $Z\gamma$ is a constant).

Also,

$$V(Y_1 \mid I = 1) = \sigma_u^2(1 - \rho^2) + \rho^2\sigma_u^2(Z\gamma)^2 \tag{9.27}$$

Given this specification of ϵ, the preliminary consistent estimates of $Z\gamma$ can be obtained from the linear probability model, and then the model derived from equation (9.26) that is estimated by ordinary least squares after substituting $Z\hat{\gamma}$ for $Z\gamma$ is

$$Y_1 = X\beta + \alpha(Z\hat{\gamma} - 1) + v$$

where

$$\alpha = \rho\sigma_u(3)^{1/2}$$

and

$$v = -\alpha Z(\hat{\gamma} - \gamma) + \eta$$

Olsen derived the asymptotic covariance matrix for these two-stage estimates of β and α.

One important distinction between the corrections for selectivity bias based on the linear probability model and the probit model is that in the probit model the function $g(Z\gamma)$ in (9.23) is a nonlinear function of Z, whereas in the linear probability model it is a linear function of Z. Hence, for the selectivity-bias adjustment when the probit model is used, we can have Z contain the same variables as in X and not cause any problems of identification, but when we use the linear probability model we cannot have the same variables as in X. If we believe that the same variables are important in both equations (9.18) and (9.19), we have to use nonlinear functions of these variables in Z. On the other hand, if X contains nonlinear functions of these variables, we shall have some problems of identification even if the probit method is used. Thus, in a practical sense, problems of identification will arise even if the probit model is used for the selectivity-bias adjustment. In the empirical illustration that Olsen (1980a) used, the two models (probit and linear probability) gave similar results.

Finally, there are the implications about the distributions of u and ϵ in equations (9.18) and (9.19). Assuming ϵ to be uniform, and assuming that the conditional expectation of u, given ϵ, is linear in ϵ, implies some outrageous assumptions about the distribution of u. If u is assumed to be a convolution of a uniform density and a normal density, the distribution of u will be symmetric, but with a broader peak and narrower tails. If $|\rho| < 0.5$, this distribution does not differ much from the normal, and in the extreme case $|\rho| = 1$ the distribution is uniform, which is a very unlikely distribution for a regression model.

9.4   Some general transformations to normality

In the preceding section we considered some particular alternatives to the probit method of correcting for selectivity bias. We shall now discuss some general transformations to normality suggested by Lee (1982c, in press).

Consider the model given in equations (9.18) and (9.19). Let $G(u)$ and $F(\epsilon)$ be the distribution functions of u and ϵ. Let $\Phi(\cdot)$ be the distribution function of the standard normal, and let $B(\cdot, \cdot; \rho)$ be the bivariate normal distribution, with zero means, unit variances, and correlation coefficient ρ. Because the distributions of ϵ and u are specified, each of them can be transformed to a standard normal random variable $N(0,1)$. Let

$$\epsilon^* = J_1(\epsilon) \equiv \Phi^{-1}[F(\epsilon)] \tag{9.28}$$
$$u^* = J_2(u) \equiv \Phi^{-1}[G(u)] \tag{9.29}$$

Then ϵ^* and u^* have $N(0,1)$ distributions. The transformations J_1 and J_2 involve the inverse of the standard normal distribution function. Computationally simple and accurate methods involving the use of approximation functions for this can be found in Appendix IIC of Bock and Jones (1968) and in the work of Hildebrand (1956). Errors of approximation for these methods are less than 3×10^{-4}.

A bivariate distribution having the marginal distributions $F(\epsilon)$ and $G(u)$ can be specified as

$$H(\epsilon, u; \rho) = B[J_1(\epsilon), J_2(u); \rho] \tag{9.30}$$

If $f(\epsilon)$ and $g(u)$ are the marginal density functions of ϵ and u, respectively, then the joint density function of ϵ and u corresponding to the distribution function (9.30) is

$$h(\epsilon, u; \rho) = (1 - \rho^2)^{-1/2} f(\epsilon) g(u)$$
$$\times \exp(-\rho[2(1-\rho^2)]^{-1}\{\rho[J_1^2(\epsilon) + J_2^2(u)] - 2J_1(\epsilon)J_2(u)\})$$
$$\tag{9.31}$$

When the marginal distributions of u and ϵ are normally distributed, the foregoing bivariate distribution will be a bivariate normal distribution.

With this specification, one can easily derive the likelihood function for the censored regression model in (9.18) and (9.19). Let us denote the observations on Y_1 for $I=1$ by Y. Then, for this group, we have $\epsilon < Z\gamma$ and $u = Y - X\beta$. But

$$\int_{-\infty}^{Z\gamma} h(\epsilon, Y - X\beta) = \frac{\partial}{\partial u} H(\epsilon, u; \rho)\Big|_{\substack{u = Y - X\beta \\ \epsilon = Z\gamma}}$$

$$= \frac{\partial B[J_1(\epsilon), J_2(u); \rho]}{\partial J_2(u)} \cdot \frac{g(u)}{\phi[J_2(u)]} \bigg|_{\substack{u=Y-X\beta \\ \epsilon = Z\gamma}} \qquad (9.32)$$

where $\phi(\cdot)$ is the standard normal density function. Because

$$\frac{\partial B(t, s; \rho)}{\partial s} \frac{1}{\phi(s)} = \Phi\left(\frac{t-\rho s}{(1-\rho^2)^{1/2}}\right)$$

the expression in (9.32) simplifies to

$$\Phi\left(\frac{J_1 Z(\gamma) - \rho J_2(Y - X\beta)}{(1-\rho^2)^{1/2}}\right) \cdot g(Y - X\beta) \qquad (9.33)$$

The log-likelihood function can therefore be written as

$$\log L(\beta, \gamma, \theta_1, \theta_2, \rho)$$

$$= \sum_{i=1}^{N} \left\{ I_i \log g(Y_i - X_i\beta) + I_i \log \Phi\left(\frac{J_1(Z_i\gamma) - \rho J_2(Y_{1i} - X_i\beta)}{(1-\rho^2)^{1/2}}\right) \right.$$

$$\left. + (1 - I_i) \log[1 - F(Z_i\gamma)] \right\} \qquad (9.34)$$

where θ_1 and θ_2 are the unknown parameters in $F(\epsilon)$ and $G(u)$, respectively. The maximum-likelihood method can be applied to this likelihood function.

One can also use two-stage estimation methods to obtain initial consistent estimates. Specifically, assume that u are $N(0, \sigma^2)$, whereas the distribution of ϵ is arbitrary. In this case, $J_2(u) = u/\sigma$, and $g(u) = (1/\sigma)\phi(u/\sigma)$. For the ML estimation, we make these substitutions in (9.34). For two-stage estimation, note that

$$I = 1 \Leftrightarrow \epsilon < Z\gamma$$

$$\Leftrightarrow J_1(\epsilon) < J_1(Z\gamma) \qquad (9.35)$$

Also, $\text{Prob}(I=1) = \Phi[J_1(Z\gamma)] = F(Z\gamma)$. The usual methods of two-stage estimation (discussed in Chapter 8) apply by substituting $J_1(Z\gamma)$ for $Z\gamma$. Thus, conditional on $I=1$, we can write

$$Y = X\beta = \sigma\rho\phi[J_1(Z\gamma)]/F(Z\gamma) + \eta \qquad (9.36)$$

where $E(\eta \mid I=1, X, Z) = 0$ and

$$\text{Var}(\eta \mid I=1, X, Z) = \sigma^2 - (\sigma\rho)^2\{J_1(Z\gamma) + \phi[J_1(Z\gamma)]/F(Z\gamma)\}$$
$$\times \phi[J_1(Z\gamma)]/F(Z\gamma)$$

We have substituted $F(Z\gamma)$ for $\Phi[J_1(Z\gamma)]$. In the two-stage method, we first estimate γ by maximizing the likelihood function

$$\log L_1(\gamma) = \sum_{i=1}^{N} \{I_i \log F(Z_i\gamma) + (1 - I_i) \log[1 - F(Z_i\gamma)]\}$$

Let $\hat{\gamma}$ be the ML estimate of γ. We then substitute $\hat{\gamma}$ for γ in (9.36) and estimate the equation by ordinary least squares. The asymptotic covariance matrix of the two-stage estimates are the same as those presented in Chapter 8, with $J_1(Z\gamma)$ replacing $Z\gamma$ throughout. Because this can be derived easily, it will not be presented here.

If ϵ follows the normal distribution, then we have the usual probit method of correction for selectivity bias. If $F(\epsilon)$ is the logistic distribution, then we have the logit method of correction for selectivity bias. In this case the estimation of (9.36) gives us the logit two-stage estimates. The methods that can be used to estimate (9.36) are thus very general. However, as explained in the preceding section, the two-stage estimation method does not depend on the assumption of normality of u. The only assumption needed is linearity of the conditional-expectation function, as in equation (9.20). A general class of dependence models suggested by Lee (1982c) that can be used in connection with equations (9.21) and (9.22) is the following: Let J be a specified strictly increasing transformation, so that

$$\epsilon < Z\gamma \Leftrightarrow J(\epsilon) < J(Z\gamma)$$

Also let

$$\mu_J = D[J(\epsilon)]$$
$$\sigma_J^2 = V[J(\epsilon)]$$

A general specification for the distribution of u is

$$u = \lambda[J(\epsilon) - \mu_J] + v$$

where v and $J(\epsilon)$ are independent. If $\lambda = 0$, then ϵ and u will be uncorrelated. If we write

$$M_1 = E[J(\epsilon) \mid J(\epsilon) < J(Z\gamma)]$$
$$M_2 = E[J^2(\epsilon) \mid J(\epsilon) < J(Z\gamma)]$$

then equations (9.21) and (9.22) can be written as

$$Y = X\beta + \frac{\rho\sigma_u}{\sigma_J}\left(\frac{M_1}{F(Z\gamma)} - \mu_J\right) + \eta \tag{9.37}$$

where

$$E(\eta \mid X, Z, I = 1) = 0$$

$$V(\eta \mid X, Z, I = 1) = \frac{\rho^2\sigma_u^2}{\sigma_J^2}\left[\frac{M_2}{F(Z\gamma)} - \left(\frac{M_1}{F(Z\gamma)}\right)^2\right] + \sigma_u^2(1 - \rho^2)$$

The transformation to normality given by equation (9.28) is one convenient candidate for J. The equation (9.37) is more general and can be used if some other transformations are considered.

The foregoing discussion shows that correction for selectivity bias and estimation of models with selectivity can be done with very general error distributions. The additional computational burden involved is that of computing the transformations in (9.28) and (9.29).

9.5   Polychotomous-choice models and selectivity bias

Throughout the preceding discussion we considered the case of two choices and a potential regression equation in each category. We shall now consider generalizations of this to multiple choices. An illustration of the multiple-choice problem was provided by Hay (1980). The example considered by Hay involved simultaneous estimation of specialty choice and specialty income for physicians. He considered a model with three alternatives: GP (general or family practice), IM (internal medicine), and OT (all other specialties).

There are two approaches to the analysis of polychotomous-choice models with mixed continuous and discrete data.[5] The first approach is to formulate them as models with multiple binary-choice rules and partial observations. The second approach depends on order statistics for polychotomous-choice models. We shall now elaborate both these approaches.

Consider the following polychotomous-choice model, with M categories and one potential regression outcome in each category:

$$y_{si} = x_{si}\beta_s + u_{si} \quad (s = 1, 2, \ldots, M)$$
$$I_{si}^* = z_{si}\gamma + \eta_{si} \quad (i = 1, 2, \ldots, N)$$

The subscript i refers to the ith observation; x_s and z_s are exogenous variables; $E(u_s \mid x_s, z_s) = 0$; y_s is observed only if the sth category is chosen. Let I be a polychotomous variable with values 1 to M and $I = s$ if the sth category is chosen.

$$I = s \quad \text{iff} \quad z_s\gamma - z_j\gamma > \eta_j - \eta_s \quad \text{for all} \quad j = 1, 2, \ldots, M \quad (j \neq s) \qquad (9.38)$$

This formulation relates the polychotomous-choice model as a model with $M-1$ binary-decision rules (9.38) with partial observations. This is the approach followed by Hay (1980) and Dubin and McFadden (1980).

In the second formulation we write

$$I = s \quad \text{iff} \quad I_s^* > \text{Max } I_j^* \quad (j = 1, 2, \ldots, M, \ j \neq s) \qquad (9.39)$$

Let

$$\epsilon_s = \text{Max } I_j^* - \eta_s \quad (j = 1, 2, \ldots, M, \ j \neq s) \qquad (9.40)$$

It follows that

[5] The subsequent discussion here is based on the work of Lee (1982c).

$$I = s \quad \text{iff} \quad \epsilon_s < z_s \gamma \tag{9.41}$$

This second approach leads to tractable results if the distribution function of ϵ_s can be specified. For example, suppose that η_j $(j=1,2,\ldots,M)$ are independently and identically distributed, with the type I extreme-value distribution with cumulative distribution function.

$$F(\eta_i < c) = \exp[-\exp(-c)]$$

Then, as shown in section 3.1, or as shown by Domencich and McFadden (1975),

$$\text{Prob}(\epsilon_s < z_s \gamma) = \text{Prob}(I = s) = \frac{\exp(z_s \gamma)}{\sum_j \exp(z_j \gamma)}$$

Thus, the distribution function of ϵ_s is given by

$$F_s(\epsilon) = \text{Prob}(\epsilon_s < \epsilon) = \frac{\exp(\epsilon)}{\exp(\epsilon) + \sum_{\substack{j=1,2,\ldots,M \\ j \neq s}} \exp(z_j \gamma)} \tag{9.42}$$

Thus, what we have is that for each choice s we now have the model

$$y_s = x_s \beta_s + u_s$$

where y_s is observed if and only if $\epsilon_s < z_s \gamma$. The distribution function of ϵ_s is given by (9.42). The estimation is now exactly the same as in the binary-choice model discussed in the preceding section. We consider a transformation as in (9.28):

$$\epsilon_s^* = J_s(\epsilon_s) = \Phi^{-1}[F_s(\epsilon)]$$

The condition $\epsilon_s < z_s \gamma \Leftrightarrow \epsilon_s^* < J_s(z_s \gamma)$, and we estimate a model like (9.36) by the two-stage method. We estimate the equation

$$y_s = x_s \beta_s - \sigma_s \rho_s \phi[J_s(z_s \gamma)] / F_s(z_s \gamma) + v_s \tag{9.43}$$

by ordinary least squares after substituting $\hat{\gamma}$ for γ; $\sigma_s^2 = \text{Var}(u_s)$, and ρ_s is the correlation coefficient between u_s and ϵ_s^*.

The only difference between this estimation of the polychotomous-choice model and the estimation of the binary-choice model considered in the preceding section is that the preliminary estimate of γ is obtained by the conditional logit model (described in Chapter 3).

Returning to the first approach, as followed by Hay (1980) and given by equation (9.38), let us define

$$\omega_{sj} = \eta_j - \eta_s \quad \text{and} \quad t_{sj} = z_j \gamma - z_s \gamma \tag{9.44}$$

so that the condition (9.38) becomes $\omega_{sj} < t_{sj}$. If we assume, as before, that η_j are independently and identically distributed, with the type I extreme-value distribution, then the $M-1$ random variables ω_{sj} will have the multivariate logistic distribution of Gumbel (1961). The joint distribution is[6]

$$F(\omega_{s1}, \omega_{s2}, \ldots, \omega_{s,s-1}, \omega_{s,s+1}, \ldots, \omega_{sm})$$

$$= \left[1 + \sum_{\substack{j=1,2,\ldots,m \\ j \neq s}} \exp(-\omega_{sj})\right]^{-1} \quad (9.45)$$

If $l' = (1, 1, \ldots, 1)$ is an $M-1$ vector with all 1's, the covariance matrix of the $M-1$ variables ω_{sj} is

$$\Sigma_\omega = \frac{\pi^2}{6}(I + ll')$$

Consider now the two-stage estimation method. For simplicity of notation, let us consider choice 1. We have the equations

$$y_1 = x_1\beta_1 + u_1$$

and y_1 is observed if and only if $\omega_{1j} < t_{1j}$ $(j=2,3,\ldots,M)$, where ω_{1j} follow the distribution (9.45). Denoting the vector $(\omega_{12}, \omega_{13}, \ldots, \omega_{1M})'$ by ω_1 we next write, as in section 9.3,

$$u_1 = \mathrm{Cov}(u_1, \omega_1)[\mathrm{Var}(\omega_1)]^{-1}[\omega_1 - E(\omega_1)] + v_1$$

$$= \sum_{j=2}^{M} \lambda_j \omega_{ij} + v_1 \quad (9.46)$$

where $E(v_1 \mid \omega_1) = 0$ and $E(\omega_1) = 0$. Hence,

$$E(y_1 \mid \omega_{1j} < t_{1j}) = x_1\beta_1 + \sum_{j=2}^{M} \lambda_j E(\omega_{1j} \mid \omega_{1k} < t_{1k})$$

$$(j=2,3,\ldots,M, \ k=2,3,\ldots,M) \quad (9.47)$$

Once we evaluate the conditional expectation in (9.47), we can use the equation for two-stage estimation. For this, we use the following result:[7] If $v_1, v_2, \ldots, v_J$ have a multivariate logistic distribution

$$F(v_1, v_2, \ldots, v_J) = \left(1 + \sum_{j=1}^{J} e^{-v_j}\right)^{-1} \quad (9.48)$$

then

---

[6] Further details of this distribution can be found in Chapter 42 of Johnson and Kotz (1972).

[7] See the study by Lee (1982c), where $E(v_i)$, $E(v_i^2)$, and $E(v_i v_j)$ are presented. The variance and covariance terms are needed for deriving the correct asymptotic covariance matrices of the two-stage estimates.

$$E(v_1 \mid v_1 < x_1, v_2 < x_2, \ldots, v_J < x_J)$$
$$= [1 - e^{-x_1} F(x_1, x_2, \ldots, x_J)]^{-1}$$
$$\times [\log F(x_1, x_2, \ldots, x_J) - x_1 e^{-x_1} F(x_1, x_2, \ldots, x_J)] \tag{9.49}$$

Thus, (9.47) can be written as

$$E(y_1 \mid \omega_{1j} < t_{1j}) = x_1 \beta_1$$
$$+ \sum_{j=2}^{M} \lambda_j [1 - e^{-t_{1j}} F(t_1)]^{-1} [\log F(t_1) - t_{1j} e^{-t_{1j}} F(t_1)]$$
$$(j = 2, 3, \ldots, M) \tag{9.50}$$

where $F(t_1) = F(t_{12}, t_{13}, \ldots, t_{1M})$ and $F(\cdot)$ is the multivariate logistic distribution (9.48). Note that t_{ij} are functions of $z_j \gamma$. Thus, we first estimate γ using the conditional logit model. We substitute the estimate $\hat{\gamma}$ of γ in t_{1j}, calculate the values of the variables with coefficients λ_j in (9.50), and estimate this equation by ordinary least squares to get estimates of β_1 and λ_j $(j = 2, 3, \ldots, N)$. This procedure is repeated for each of the variables y_s $(s = 1, 2, \ldots, M)$.

The expressions for the asymptotic covariance matrices of the two-stage estimates are very complicated and will not be presented here.[8] Clearly, this approach is more cumbersome than the alternative approach based on equations (9.41) through (9.43).

9.6   Multiple criteria for selectivity

There are several practical instances in which selectivity can be due to several sources, rather than just one, as considered in the examples in the preceding section. Griliches et al. (1978) cited several problems with the NLS data on young men that could lead to selectivity bias. Prominent among these are attrition and other missing-data problems. In such cases we need to formulate the model as a switching regression model or a switching simultaneous-equations model, where the switch depends on more than one criterion function. One such example is that by Abowd and Farber (1982), who considered the union-and-wages example of Lee (1978). The model consists of a union-wage equation (Y_1) and a nonunion-wage equation (Y_2). There are two decision functions: the decision of individuals to join a queue for union jobs (I_1^*) and the deci-

[8] Dubin and McFadden (1980) derived the covariance matrix for the case of M alternatives and corrected some slips in Hay's (1980) calculation. Lee (1981b) gave expressions for the second moments of the truncated multivariate logistic distribution.

sion of employers to draw individuals from the queue (I_2^*). The specification of the model is

$$Y_1 = X_1\beta_1 + u_1 \tag{9.51}$$
$$Y_2 = X_2\beta_2 + u_2 \tag{9.52}$$
$$I_1^* = Z_1\gamma_1 - \epsilon_1 \tag{9.53}$$
$$I_2^* = Z_2\gamma_2 - \epsilon_2 \tag{9.54}$$

If $I_1^* > 0$, the individual decides to join the queue for union jobs. If $I_2^* > 0$, the individual is chosen from the queue for a union job. Here we observe Y_1 only if $I_1^* > 0$ and $I_2^* > 0$. In this example, the set $I_1^* < 0$ and $I_2^* > 0$ will be empty.

When we talk of multiple criteria for selectivity, we should distinguish two cases: the joint case and the sequential case. In the joint-decision model, (9.53) and (9.54) are defined over the entire set of observations. In the sequential-decision model, (9.54) is defined over only the subset of observations for which $I_1^* > 0$. In this example, the choice of drawing from the queue arises only for those who are in the queue.

We also have to consider whether the choices are completely observed or partially observed. Define the indicator variables

$$I_1 = 1 \quad \text{iff } I_1^* > 0$$
$$I_1 = 0 \quad \text{otherwise}$$
$$I_2 = 1 \quad \text{iff } I_2^* > 0$$
$$I_2 = 0 \quad \text{otherwise}$$

The question is whether we observe I_1 and I_2 separately or only as a single indicator variable $I = I_1 I_2$. The latter is the case with the example of Abowd and Farber. Poirier (1980) also considered a bivariate probit model with partial observability, but his model was a joint model, not a sequential model as in the example of Abowd and Farber. An example of a joint model is that of estimating the probability that an on-the-job trainee will be retained by the sponsoring agency after training. In this situation the employer must decide whether or not to make a job offer, and the applicant must decide whether or not to seek a job offer. We do not observe these individual decisions. What we observe is whether or not the trainee continues to work after training. If either the employer or the employee makes his decision first, then the model will be a sequential model.

Tunali et al. (1980) also considered a sequential-decision model, given by (9.51), (9.53), and (9.54). Here, y_1 is observed only if $I_1 = 1$ and $I_2 = 1$. However, in their model, both I_1 and I_2 are observed. Their example was one of labor-force participation by women in Managua, Nicaragua. Of the 1,247 women in the sample, only 579 were labor-force participants. Of these, only 525 reported earnings. The first decision is whether or not to participate in the labor force, and the second decision is whether or not to report earnings.

In the joint-decision model with partial observability (i.e., where we observe $I = I_1 \cdot I_2$ only, not I_1 and I_2 individually), the parameters γ_1 and γ_2 in equations (9.53) and (9.54) are estimable only if there is at least one nonoverlapping variable in either one of Z_1 and Z_2. Because $V(\epsilon_1) = V(\epsilon_2) = 1$, by normalization, let us define $\mathrm{Cov}(\epsilon_1, \epsilon_2) = \rho$. Also, write

$$\mathrm{Prob}(I_1^* > 0,\ I_2^* > 0) = \mathrm{Prob}(\epsilon_1 < Z_1\gamma_1, \epsilon_2 < Z_2\gamma_2)$$
$$= F(Z_1\gamma_1, Z_2\gamma_2, \rho)$$

Then the ML estimates of γ_1, γ_2 and ρ are obtained by maximizing the likelihood function

$$L_1 = \prod_{I=1} F(Z_1\gamma_1, Z_2\gamma_2, \rho) \cdot \prod_{I=0} [1 - F(Z_1\gamma_1, Z_2\gamma_2, \rho)] \qquad (9.55)$$

With the assumption of bivariate normality of ϵ_1 and ϵ_2, this involves the use of bivariate probit analysis.

In the sequential-decision model with partial observability, if we assume that the function (9.54) is defined only on the subpopulation $I_1 = 1$, then, because the distribution of ϵ_2 that is assumed is considered on $\epsilon_1 < Z_1\gamma_1$, the likelihood function to be maximized will be

$$L_2 = \prod_{I=1} [\Phi(Z_1\gamma_1)\Phi(Z_2\gamma_2)] \cdot \prod_{I=0} [1 - \Phi(Z_1\gamma_1)\Phi(Z_2\gamma_2)] \qquad (9.56)$$

Again, the parameters γ_1 and γ_2 are estimable only if there is at least one nonoverlapping variable in either one of Z_1 and Z_2 (otherwise, we would not know which estimates refer to γ_1 and which refer to γ_2). In their example on job queues and union status of workers, Abowd and Farber (1982) obtained their parameter estimates using the likelihood function (9.56). One can, perhaps, argue that even in the sequential model the appropriate likelihood function is still (9.55), not (9.56). It is possible that there are persons who do not join the queue ($I_1 = 0$) but to whom employers would want to offer union jobs. The reason we do not observe these individuals in union jobs is because they decided not to join the queue. But we also do not observe in the union jobs all those with $I_2 = 0$. Thus, we can argue that I_2^* exists and is, in principle, defined even for the observations $I_1 = 0$. If the purpose of the analysis is to examine what factors influence an employer's choice of employees for union jobs, then possibly the parameter estimates should be obtained from (9.55). The difference between the two models is in the definition of the distribution of ϵ_2. In the case of (9.55), the distribution of ϵ_2 is defined over the whole population. In the case of (9.56), it is defined over the subpopulation $I_1 = 1$. The latter allows us to make only conditional inferences.[9] The former allows us to make both conditional and marginal inferences. To make marginal inferences, we need estimates of γ_2. To make conditional inferences, we consider the conditional distribution $f(\epsilon_2 \mid \epsilon_1 < Z_1\gamma_1)$, which involves γ_1, γ_2, and ρ. We shall discuss this issue of marginal versus conditional inferences in the next section.

Yet another type of partial observability arises in the case of truncated samples discussed earlier in section 9.2. An example is that of measuring discrimination in loan markets. Let I_1^* refer to the decision of an individual whether or not to apply for a loan, and let I_2^* refer to the decision of the bank whether or not to grant the loan.

$I_1 = 1$ if the individual applies for a loan

$I_1 = 0$ otherwise

$I_2 = 1$ if the applicant is given a loan

$I_2 = 0$ otherwise

Rarely do we have data on the individuals for whom $I_1 = 0$. Thus, what we have is a truncated sample. We can, of course, specify the distribution of I_2^* only for the subset of observations $I_1 = 1$ and estimate the parameters γ_2 by, say, the probit ML method and then examine the significance of the coefficients of race, sex, age, and so forth to see if there is discrimination by any of these variables. This does not, however, allow for self-selection at the application stage, say for some individuals not applying because they feel they will be discriminated against. For this purpose, we define I_2^* over the whole population and analyze the model from the truncated sample. The argument is that, in principle, I_2^* exists even for the nonapplicants. The parameters γ_1, γ_2, and ρ can be estimated by maximizing the likelihood function

$$L_3 = \prod_{I_2=1} \frac{F(Z_1\gamma_1, Z_2\gamma_2, \rho)}{\Phi(Z_1\gamma_1)} \cdot \prod_{I_2=0} \frac{\Phi(Z_1\gamma_1) - F(Z_1\gamma_1, Z_2\gamma_2, \rho)}{\Phi(Z_1\gamma_1)} \tag{9.57}$$

In this model, the parameters γ_1, γ_2, and ρ are, in principle, estimable

---

[9] The conditional model does not permit us to allow for the fact that changes in Z_2 also might affect the probability of being in the queue. Also, the decision whether or not to join the queue can be influenced by the perception of the probability of being drawn from the queue.

even if Z_1 and Z_2 are the same variables. In practice, however, the estimates are not likely to be very good.[10]

Fishe et al. (1981) considered a two-decision model, but it is a model of joint decisions, and with both I_1 and I_2 observed. The model is one that determines wages of young women, some of whom have college education and some of whom do not. The two decision equations (9.53) and (9.54) refer to the decisions whether or not to go to college and whether or not to join the labor force.

The analysis of the model in equations (9.51) and (9.54) will depend crucially on whether the two decisions are independent or correlated, that is, whether or not $\text{Cov}(\epsilon_1, \epsilon_2) = 0$. In the case $\text{Cov}(\epsilon_1, \epsilon_2) = 0$, we can easily extend the Heckman–Lee two-stage estimation methods to this model. We define

$$\lambda_{ij} = \text{Cov}(u_i, \epsilon_j) \quad (i=1,2, \ j=1,2)$$

Then,

$$E(u_1 \mid I_1^* > 0, I_2^* > 0) = -\lambda_{11} \frac{\phi(Z_1 \gamma_1)}{\Phi(Z_1 \gamma_1)} - \lambda_{12} \frac{\phi(Z_2 \gamma_2)}{\Phi(Z_2 \gamma_2)} \tag{9.58}$$

Thus, we get preliminary consistent estimates of γ_1 and γ_2 by estimating equations (9.53) and (9.54) by the probit method. Next, we regress Y_1 on X_1 and the constructed variables

$$\frac{\phi(Z_1 \hat{\gamma}_1)}{\Phi(Z_1 \hat{\gamma}_1)} \quad \text{and} \quad \frac{\phi(Z_2 \hat{\gamma}_2)}{\Phi(Z_2 \hat{\gamma}_2)}$$

In case ϵ_1 and ϵ_2 are correlated, so that $\text{Cov}(\epsilon_1, \epsilon_2) = \sigma_{12}$, the expressions get very messy. In this case we have to use bivariate probit methods to estimate γ_1, γ_2, and σ_{12}. Further,

$$E(u_1 \mid I_1^* > 0, I_2^* > 0) = \lambda_{11} M_{12} + \lambda_{12} M_{21}$$

where

$$M_{ij} = (1 - \sigma_{12}^2)^{-1}(P_i - \sigma_{12} P_j)$$

$$P_j = \frac{\int_{-\infty}^{Z_1 \gamma_1} \int_{-\infty}^{Z_1 \gamma_1} \epsilon_j f(\epsilon_1 \epsilon_2) \, d\epsilon_2 \, d\epsilon_1}{F(Z_1 \gamma_1, Z_2 \gamma_2)} \tag{9.59}$$

---

[10] See the evidence presented in section 9.2 on estimation of the parameters in the selectivity criterion from truncated samples. See also the work of Bloom et al. (1981), who reported that attempts at estimating this model did not produce good parameter estimates.

These expressions can still be evaluated numerically.[11]

Fishe et al. estimated the parameters in equatiions (9.53) and (9.54) by the bivariate probit method and evaluated expressions of the form (9.59) by numerical methods. They then used the extension of the Heckman–Lee two-stage method.

9.7 Endogenous switching models and mixture-distribution models

The models of self-selection discussed in this chapter (as well as the dis-equilibrium models discussed in the next chapter) fall in the general class of switching models with endogenous switching (Maddala and Nelson, 1975). In a recent study, Poirier and Rudd (1981) argued that there has been substantial confusion in the econometric literature over switching regression models with endogenous switching and that this confusion can cause serious interpretation problems when the model is employed in applied work. They argued that the problems of interpretation arise because there is an observational equivalence between two fundamentally different specifications: the mixture model of conditional densities and the switching regression model with endogenous switching. Because their study can convey misleading impressions about the practical usefulness of the models discussed in this chapter, we shall discuss the two models here.

The switching regression model with endogenous switching is defined as follows:

$$y_{1i} = X_{1i}\beta_1 + u_{1i} \tag{9.60}$$
$$y_{2i} = X_{2i}\beta_2 + u_{2i} \tag{9.61}$$
$$I_i^* = Z_i\gamma - \epsilon_i \tag{9.62}$$

$$I_i = 1 \quad \text{iff} \ I_i^* > 0$$
$$I_i = 0 \quad \text{iff} \ I_i^* \leqslant 0 \tag{9.63}$$

The observed y_i is defined as

$$y_i = y_{1i} \quad \text{iff} \ I_i = 1$$
$$y_i = y_{2i} \quad \text{iff} \ I_i = 0 \tag{9.64}$$
$$(u_1, u_2, \epsilon)' \sim N(0, \Sigma)$$

---

[11] See the work of Rosenbaum (1961) for moments of a truncated bivariate normal distribution. These are also reported in the Appendix at the end of the book.

with

$$\Sigma = \begin{bmatrix} \sigma_{11} & \sigma_{12} & \sigma_{1\epsilon} \\ \sigma_{12} & \sigma_{22} & \sigma_{2\epsilon} \\ \sigma_{1\epsilon} & \sigma_{2\epsilon} & 1 \end{bmatrix}$$

If $\sigma_{1\epsilon} = \sigma_{2\epsilon} = 0$, we have the switching regression model with exogenous switching. Otherwise, we have endogenous switching.

Equations (9.60) and (9.61) define the marginal distributions of y_{1i} and y_{2i}.[12] From the specification of the model we can derive the conditional distributions $f(y_{1i} | I_i = 1)$ and $f(y_{2i} | I_i = 0)$. For instance,

$$f(u_1 | I = 1) = \int_{-\infty}^{Z\gamma} f(u_1 \epsilon) \, d\epsilon / \Phi(Z\gamma)$$

and writing $f(u_1 \epsilon) = f(u) \cdot f(\epsilon | u)$, we can write

$$f(y_1 | I = 1) = [\Phi(Z\gamma)]^{-1} \sigma_{11}^{-1/2} \phi[\sigma_{11}^{-1/2}(y_1 - X_1 \beta_1)]$$
$$\times \Phi\left\{\left(1 - \frac{\sigma_{1\epsilon}^2}{\sigma_{11}}\right)^{-1/2} \left[Z\gamma - \frac{\sigma_{1\epsilon}}{\sigma_{11}}(y_1 - X_1 \beta_1)\right]\right\}$$

Similarly,

$$f(y_2 | I = 0) = [1 - \Phi(Z\gamma)]^{-1} \sigma_{22}^{-1/2} \phi[\sigma_{22}^{-1/2}(y_2 - X_2 \beta_2)]$$
$$\times \left(1 - \Phi\left\{\left(1 - \frac{\sigma_{2\epsilon}^2}{\sigma_{22}}\right)^{-1/2} \left[Z\gamma + \frac{\sigma_{2\epsilon}}{\sigma_{22}}(y_2 - X_2 \beta_2)\right]\right\}\right)$$

$$(9.65)$$

We can decompose the error terms u_{1i}, u_{2i}, and ϵ_i into a set of correlated and noncorrelated components. We can write

$$y_{1i} = X_{1i} \beta_1 + \alpha_{1i} + w_{1i}$$
$$y_{2i} = X_{2i} \beta_2 + \alpha_{2i} + w_{2i}$$
$$I_i^* = Z_i \gamma + \alpha_{3i} + w_{3i} \qquad (9.66)$$

where $w_i' = (w_{1i}, w_{2i}, w_{3i}) \sim N(0, \Omega)$ and $\alpha_i' = (\alpha_{1i}, \alpha_{2i}, \alpha_{3i}) \sim N(0, \Lambda)$ and w_i' are independent of α_i'. Ω is a diagonal matrix

---

[12] Poirier and Rudd claimed that some studies have defined (9.60) and (9.61) as conditional on $I_i = 1$ and $I_i = 0$, respectively. However, we need not go into this issue in detail, because those who read the studies carefully can see that equations (9.60) and (9.61) were always meant to be marginal distributions, with the observed y_i being defined by (9.64).

$$\Omega = \begin{bmatrix} \omega_{11} & 0 & 0 \\ 0 & \omega_{22} & 0 \\ 0 & 0 & \omega_{33} \end{bmatrix}$$

and

$$\Lambda = \begin{bmatrix} \lambda_{11} & \lambda_{12} & \lambda_{13} \\ \lambda_{12} & \lambda_{22} & \lambda_{23} \\ \lambda_{13} & \lambda_{23} & \lambda_{33} \end{bmatrix}$$

This method is identical with that for the model in equations (9.60) through (9.62), with

$$\lambda_{11} + \omega_{11} = \sigma_{11}, \quad \lambda_{22} + \omega_{22} = \sigma_{22}, \quad \lambda_{33} + \omega_{33} = 1,$$
$$\lambda_{12} = \sigma_{12}, \quad \lambda_{13} = \sigma_{1\epsilon}, \quad \text{and} \quad \lambda_{23} = \sigma_{2\epsilon} \tag{9.67}$$

Note that the models given by (9.66) and (9.60) through (9.62) are not different models.[13] The α_i now capture the correlations between the residuals, and conditional on α_i, the variables y_{1i}, y_{2i}, and I_i^* are independent.

The mixture-distribution model that Poirier and Rudd considered is

$$(y_{1i} \mid I_i = 1, \alpha_i) \sim N(X_{1i}\beta_1 + \alpha_{1i}, \omega_{11})$$
$$(y_{2i} \mid I_i = 0, \alpha_i) \sim N(X_{2i}\beta + \alpha_{2i}, \omega_{22})$$
$$(I_i^* \mid \alpha_i) \sim N(Z_i\gamma + \alpha_{3i}, \omega_{33}) \tag{9.68}$$

where $\alpha_i \sim N(0, \Lambda)$, as before. They showed that, unconditional on α_i, we have

$$I_i^* \sim N(Z_i\gamma, 1)$$

and that $f(y_{1i} \mid I_i = 1)$ and $f(y_{2i} \mid I_i = 0)$ are the conditional densities given by (9.65), with the parameter equivalence (9.67). From this, they argued that it is possible to construct two different observationally equivalent models, which produces an ambiguity in inferences. They argued that "although the interpretations of the parameters in each formulation are entirely different, the observed data cannot distinguish between these two different interpretations" (Poirier and Rudd, 1981, p. 255).

However, as can be seen from the equivalence of models (9.66) and (9.60) through (9.63), there are not two different models. *They are just two different ways of writing the same model. Thus, there is no ambi-*

---

[13] The likelihood function for this model is presented in equation (8.8) in Chapter 8. As noted there, the parameter σ_{12} is not estimable.

guity of inferences. Note that although it appears from (9.68) as though Poirier and Rudd defined only the conditional distributions, this is not so. Because, as mentioned earlier, conditional on α_i, the variables y_{1i}, y_{2i}, and I_i^* are independent, equations (9.66) and (9.68) are exactly equivalent. That is,

$$f(y_{1i} \mid \alpha_i, I_i = 1) = f(y_{1i} \mid \alpha_i, I_i^* > 0)$$
$$= f(y_{1i} \mid \alpha_i)$$

Thus, it is not true that Poirier and Rudd constructed a different model based on a specification of conditional distributions that gives the same likelihood function.

Another argument Poirier and Rudd made (1981, p. 250) was that "the contrast between a trivariate model and bivariate data suggests a major limitation of the model." Note, however, that the data do refer to three variables, each of which is partially observed. I^* is observed as a dichotomous variable; y_i is observed only when $I^* > 0$, and y_2 is observed only when $I^* < 0$. The only problem that arises is that y_1 and y_2 are not observed simultaneously. As a consequence, σ_{12} is not estimable. But apart from this, there are no identifiability problems.[14] Thus, the problem is not one of a trivariate model and bivariate data, but one of partial observability, and there are many such models that are of practical use.

Poirier and Rudd also seem to have argued that because y_1 is observed only if $I = 1$, and y_2 only if $I = 0$, we should model only these conditional distributions. As shown earlier, the conditional specification they suggested is not indeed a specification of the distributions over the subpopulations. In the next section we shall discuss such a specification. However, just because y_1 is observed only if $I = 1$ does not mean that we should specify the distribution of y_1 only on this subset. To push the analogy further, consider the tobit model: Just because y_i is observed if and only if $y_i > 0$ does not mean that the distribution of the disturbance term need be specified for this subpopulation alone! In the case of sequential-decision models, of course, we might specify distributions of residuals on subpopulations only.

Of more practical importance is the issue raised by Poirier and Rudd concerning the interpretation of coefficient estimates. The selectivity

---

[14] Some other identification problems arise in the model in which only y_1 or y_2 is observed (see section 8.4). The fact that σ_{12} is not estimable means that there can be any number of models with different values of correlations between u_1 and u_2 in equations (9.60) and (9.61) that are observationally equivalent. But the problem is not one of conditional versus marginal distributions, but one of covariance between the errors of marginal distributions.

model permits two types of inferences: conditional and marginal. For instance, with respect to the parameters in equation (9.60), we can consider $\partial E(y_{1i})/\partial X_{1i}$ for inferences from the marginal distribution and $\partial E(y_{1i}|I_i=1)/\partial X_{1i}$ for inferences from the conditional distributions. The former are given by the estimates of the parameter β_1 in (9.57). For the latter, we note that under the assumptions of normality of the residuals,

$$E(y_{1i}|I_i=1) = X_{1i}\beta_1 - \sigma_{1\epsilon}\frac{\phi(Z_i\gamma)}{\Phi(Z_i\gamma)}$$

where $\sigma_{1\epsilon} = \text{Cov}(u_1, \epsilon)$ and $\phi(\cdot)$ and $\Phi(\cdot)$ are, respectively, the density and distribution functions of the standard normal.

If there is a variable that appears in both X_{1i} and Z_i (say in the jth position for each), then

$$\frac{\partial E(y_{1i}|I_i=1)}{\partial X_{1ij}} = \beta_{1j} + \gamma_j\sigma_{1\epsilon}\frac{\phi(Z_i\gamma)}{\Phi(Z_i\gamma)}\left(Z_i\gamma + \frac{\phi(Z_i\gamma)}{\Phi(Z_i\gamma)}\right)$$

Note that the sign changes on $\sigma_{1\epsilon}$ in our equations, as compared with those in the study of Poirier and Rudd, arise from the way equation (9.63) is defined.

Poirier and Rudd pointed out that given that sex is a variable included in both X_{1i} and Z_i, Lee and Trost (1978, p. 374) incorrectly argued from the sign of β_{1j} that "females tend to spend more than males if they own houses." However, a reading of Lee and Trost's study indicates that what they had in mind all along was potential expenditures, and thus they meant to say "if they were to own houses" rather than "if they own houses." There is, thus, no confusion or misinterpretation. The substantive issue here is what type of inference is of practical interest in this problem. Is it inference from the marginal distribution (potential expenditures on housing) or from the conditional distributions (actual expenditures on housing)? The answer to this question is that it depends on the problem at hand. If we are considering the effects of tax incentives, as did Rosen (1979), then we have to consider potential as well as actual expenditures. Poirier and Rudd (1981, p. 283) argued that if only conditional inferences are needed, then one should model directly the conditional densities and not bother about the selectivity model. But certainly the housing-decision model that they cited is not one in which our interest is only in conditional inferences. We can perhaps find examples in which only conditional inferences are of interest. In the next section we shall give examples in which the selectivity model makes sense but the mixture model does not.

9.8   When can the selection model be used, but not the mixture model?

In the preceding section we argued that the main difference between the selection model and the mixture model is in the specification of the distributions of the disturbances over the entire population versus subpopulations. We shall now give examples of cases in which the mixture model is not applicable.

To be specific, the selection model (S) is

$$I^* = Z\gamma - \epsilon$$
$$Y_1 = X_1\beta_1 + u_1$$
$$Y_2 = X_2\beta_2 + u_2$$

where ϵ, u_1, and u_2 have well-defined distributions on the whole population. The mixture-distribution model (M) is

$$I^* = Z\gamma - \epsilon$$
$$Y_1 = X_1\beta_1 + u_1$$
$$Y_2 = X_2\beta_2 + u_2$$

where ϵ has a well-defined distribution on the whole population. The distribution of u_1 is defined only on the subpopulation for which $I=1$, and the distribution of u_2 is defined only on the subpopulation for which $I=0$.

The M model is not appropriate for modeling the problems in which y_1 and y_2 are explicitly factors in the decision process, as in the union-decision model of Lee (1978). Here we have

$$I^* = \alpha(y_1 - y_2) + Z\gamma - \epsilon \tag{9.69}$$

This implies

$$I^* = \alpha(X_1\beta_1 - X_2\beta_2) + Z\gamma - v$$

where $v = \epsilon - \alpha(u_1 - u_2)$. The disturbance term v does not have a well-defined distribution in the M model, because the distributions of u_1 and u_2 are defined only on subpopulations. The main interest in such models centers on the decision process, in particular the significance or nonsignificance of α in (9.69); see, for instance, the work of Willis and Rosen (1979). These situations can be modeled only by the selection models, not the mixture models. For each individual, $y_{1i} - y_{2i}$ represents the net gain (or net loss) from the choice between the two options. If y_{1i} is the return of the outcome from choosing option 1, y_{2i} will be the foregone outcome from option 2 (and vice versa). Any econometric models involving discrete choice and foregone outcomes (or earnings) are meaningless to be modeled as M models. The selection model is the appropriate one to be used.

The selection models are also useful for evaluating many government programs. These cannot be analyzed by the mixture-distribution model. These problems have been discussed in section 9.2.

In many activities (or choices) involving productivity or earnings, such as job choices, we observe that individuals engage in one activity rather than others. A possible reason from the productivity (or earnings) point of view, as suggested by Roy (1951), Sattinger (1975), Rosen (1978), and Willis and Rosen (1979), is that the individual has comparative advantage in an activity that, as compared with the other options, increases the well-being of the individual. To infer the implications of comparative advantage in discrete-choice behavior, one needs to have information on the potential outcomes from the unchosen alternative options. For this purpose, the selectivity model is useful. The mixture-distribution model does not permit any inferences to be made in such cases. An example cited by Roy (1951) was discussed in section 9.1.

9.9 Summary and conclusions

The preceding discussion suggests the usefulness of the selectivity model in a number of situations. The selectivity model has been applied in the following types of studies, among others:

1. Studies of participation in the labor force: Heckman (1974, 1979), Nelson (1977), Cogan (1980), Hanoch (1980*a, b*)
2. Studies of retirement decisions: Gordon and Blinder (1980)
3. Studies of returns to education: Griliches et al. (1978), Kenny et al. (1979), Willis and Rosen (1979)
4. Studies of the effects of unions on wages: Lee (1978), Abowd and Farber (1982)
5. Studies of the effects of employment services: Katz (1977)
6. Studies of migration and income: Nakosteen and Zimmer (1980)
7. Studies of physician behavior: Poirier (1981); studies of lawyer behavior: Weisbrod (1980)
8. Studies of electric utility rates: Roberts et al. (1978)
9. Studies of tenure choice and the demand for housing: Trost (1977), Lee and Trost (1978), Rosen (1979), King (1980)

We shall discuss the union-and-wages problem in Chapter 11. The studies on labor supply are far too numerous to review here. Regarding the area of tenure choice and demand for housing, the traditional literature treats the discrete tenure choice and the continuous housing-demand choice separately. Trost (1977), Lee and Trost (1978), and Rosen (1979) recognized that the two decisions are interdependent, and they specified error terms of the discrete- and continuous-choice models to be correlated. King (1980) extended this analysis further in two important directions. First, he noted that because tenure choice and housing demand are based on maximization of the same utility function, the two models can involve some of the same parameters. In that case, joint estimation will involve imposing cross-equation constraints on the parameters of the tenure-choice and housing-demand equations, as well as recognizing that error terms are correlated. Second, King incorporated into the model estimates of the impact of rationing in the mortgage market and in the local-authority rental market in the United Kingdom. Because going through these aspects would involve reproducing most of King's study, it will not be done here.

CHAPTER 10

Disequilibrium models

10.1 Introduction

There have been many studies analyzing disequilibrium from both the theoretical and empirical points of view. The early studies on disequilibrium dealt with partial-adjustment models of the following sort.

Let y_t^* be the desired or optimum value of y at period t. Because of costs of adjustment, the firm does not adjust y_t to its desired level. We hypothesize that the firm makes only a partial adjustment, given by

$$y_t = y_{t-1} + \lambda(y_t^* - y_{t-1}) \tag{10.1}$$

where λ is some number between 0 and 1.

As Griliches (1967, p. 43) pointed out, the parameter λ in (10.1) can be interpreted in terms of the relative costs of being out of equilibrium and of making the adjustment to the desired value. Assume that the firm incurs two types of costs: a cost of being out of equilibrium (foregone profits) and a cost of change. If both cost functions can be approximated by quadratic terms, we can write the firm's overall loss function as

$$L = \alpha(y_t - y_t^*)^2 + \beta(y_t - y_{t-1})^2$$

The first term measures the cost of being out of equilibrium, and the second term measures the cost of making a change. The problem is to choose y_t, given y_{t-1} and y_t^*, so as to minimize the loss. We get

$$\frac{dL}{dy_t} = 2\alpha(y_t - y_t^*) + 2\beta(y_t - y_{t-1}) = 0$$

Solving for y_t, we get

$$y_t = y_{t-1} + \frac{\alpha}{\alpha + \beta} (y_t^* - y_{t-1}) \qquad (10.2)$$

Comparing (10.2) with (10.1), we note that the adjustment coefficient λ depends on the ratio of the marginal out-of-equilibrium costs to the marginal adjustment costs. Obviously, the higher the adjustment costs, the slower the rate of adjustment.

In these partial-adjustment models, the term *disequilibrium* refers to a state that is not the optimum. But the optimum value is first derived without any consideration of costs or adjustment, and then the adjustment costs are superimposed through the partial-adjustment specification. If the model is properly formulated, taking into account the costs of adjustment in the derivation of the optimum value y_t^*, then the disequilibrium disappears. In this sense, the disequilibrium model is an imperfectly specified model.

Disequilibrium models incorporating partial adjustment have been discussed by such authors as Rosen and Nadiri (1974), Bergstrom and Wymer (1976), and Johnson and Taylor (1977). In this chapter we shall consider a different type of disequilibrium model – one whose statistical analysis makes use of the probit and tobit methods outlined in earlier chapters (although we shall incorporate some elements of the partial-adjustment models as well). The essence of these models is that markets are characterized by excess demands or supplies. The first empirical study in this direction, one that sparked a lot of later work, was that by Fair and Jaffee (1972). However, that study did not use the limited-dependent-variable methods, nor did the further analyses of their data by Quandt (1972) and Goldfeld and Quandt (1972), who suggested switching regression methods. The studies by Amemiya (1974c) and Maddala and Nelson (1974) showed how the correct statistical analysis of these models depends on the use of limited-dependent-variable methods.

10.2   The Fair and Jaffee model

Fair and Jaffee (1972) considered the following model:

$$D_t = \alpha_1 P_t + X'_{1t}\beta_1 + u_{1t} \quad \text{(demand function)} \qquad (10.3)$$
$$S_t = \alpha_2 P_t + X'_{2t}\beta_2 + u_{2t} \quad \text{(supply function)} \qquad (10.4)$$

X_1 and X_2 are sets of exogenous variables determining demand and supply, respectively. We observe X_{1t}, X_{2t}, P_t, and the quantity transacted, Q_t.

In an equilibrium model,

$$Q_t = D_t = S_t \qquad (10.5)$$

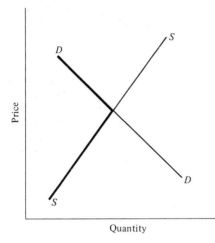

Figure 10.1. A simple disequilibrium model with rationing

and equations (10.3) and (10.4) form a simultaneous-equations system with two endogenous variables, Q_t and P_t. This system of equations can be estimated by the usual simultaneous-equations methods, provided they are identified.

In the Fair–Jaffee model, the equation (10.5) is replaced by the equation

$$Q_t = \text{Min}(D_t, S_t) \tag{10.6}$$

If $D_t > S_t$, then the observed quantity Q_t is on the supply function, and if $D_t < S_t$, then the observed quantity Q_t is on the demand function. This is shown in Figure 10.1, where the heavy line shows the observed values of Q_t.

The problem now is to estimate the parameters of the demand and supply equations, given the data on Q_t and P_t and the exogenous variables X_{1t} and X_{2t}. In the specification given by equations (10.3), (10.4), and (10.6), P_t is also an exogenous variable. It is endogenous only in the equilibrium model, or some modifications of the disequilibrium model to be considered later.

Even if we know which observations on Q_t belong to the demand function (10.3) and the supply function (10.4), we cannot estimate these equations by ordinary least squares. This is because the residuals in these truncated samples do not have zero means and also are correlated with the exogenous variables.

Fair and Jaffee (1972) used six methods of estimation that can be classified into three categories:

Equilibrium method. Here $D_t = S_t$. As mentioned earlier, now Q_t and P_t are both endogenous variables.

Directional method. This says that if $\Delta P_t = P_t - P_{t-1} > 0$, then we have excess demand, and if $\Delta P_t < 0$, then we have excess supply. Thus, we use the sign of ΔP_t to sort out the sample into two groups: one in which there is excess demand and hence $Q_t = S_t$, and another in which there is excess supply, and hence $Q_t = D_t$. Those observations for which $\Delta P_t = 0$ can be put into both groups for estimation purposes. Fair and Jaffee (1972, pp. 503–4) did point out that applying OLS methods to the two groups separately gives inconsistent estimates of the parameters, because the means of the resulting residuals are nonzero, and the residuals are correlated with the explanatory variables in the model.

Quantitative methods. These depend on assuming that the change in price is proportional to excess demand; that is $\Delta P_t = \gamma(D_t - S_t)$.

Fair and Jaffee used the OLS method and two-stage least-squares method of estimation, allowing for serial correlation in the residuals. Because the subsequent studies by Amemiya (1974c) and Maddala and Nelson (1974) discussed the appropriate statistical methods for these models, we shall not dwell at length on the estimation methods used by Fair and Jaffee. There is, of course, the difference that the serial-correlation problem analyzed by Fair and Jaffee becomes difficult to handle in the limited-dependent-variable framework, as will be discussed later.

The empirical example of the housing market considered by Fair and Jaffee merits some discussion. The demand for housing starts during month t, HS_t^D, is assumed to be a function of (a) population growth and income trend, both of which are approximated by a time trend, (b) the stock of houses in existence, and (c) mortgage rate lagged by two months RM_{t-2}. The equation is thus

$$HS_t^D = \alpha_0 + \alpha_1 t + \alpha_2 \sum_{i=1}^{t-1} HS_i + \alpha_3 RM_{t-2} + u_{1t} \tag{10.7}$$

The summation of HS_i in equation (10.7) arbitrarily assumes that the initial stock of houses in month 0 is zero. Fair and Jaffee claimed that this error is absorbed in the constant term, because $\alpha_2 \sum_{i=-\infty}^{0} HS_i$ is a constant. The time trend t in equation (10.7) is picking up the growth in population and income as well as the effect of past removals.

The supply of housing starts in month t, HS_t^S, is specified as

$$HS_t^S = \beta_0 + \beta_1 t + \beta_2 DF6_{t-1} + \beta_3 DHF3_{t-2} + \beta_4 RM_{t-1} + u_{2t} \qquad (10.8)$$

where $DF6_t$ is a six-month moving average of DF_t. $DHF3_t$ is a three-month moving average of DHF_t. DF_t denotes the flow of private deposits into savings and loan associations (SLA) and mutual savings banks during period t, and DHF_t denotes the flow of borrowings by the SLAs from the federal home-loan bank during month t. Finally, the actual number of housing starts, HS_t, is assumed to be determined by

$$HS_t = Min(HS_t^D, HS_t^S) \qquad (10.9)$$

Because RM_t is used as the price variable, in the quantitative method Fair and Jaffee used

$$\Delta RM_t = \gamma(HS_t^D - HS_t^S) \qquad (10.10)$$

The estimation was based on data for June 1959 to November 1969, a total of 126 observations. None of the data, however, were seasonally adjusted. The equilibrium method and the quantitative method used all the data. In the directional method, there were 85 observations used to estimate the demand function and 108 to estimate the supply function. This implies that there were 18 observations that could be classified as belonging to the demand function and 41 belonging to the supply function, and 67 were equilibrium points. The noteworthy conclusions from their empirical results are the following: (a) Use of the disequilibrium methods gave parameter estimates that were not much different from those obtained under the assumption of full equilibrium. (b) On the other hand, the coefficients of ΔRM_t in the quantitative method were significant, thus indicating that the housing market is not always in equilibrium. These apparently conflicting results may be due to deficiencies in the method of estimation. But, more important, it is questionable that the mortgage-rate variable RM_t really can be considered as the sole "price" of housing.

Maddala and Nelson (1974) reestimated the Fair and Jaffee model using seasonal adjustment and the OLS and tobit methods. The sample separation used was that in Directional Method I of Fair and Jaffee. The results showed that the OLS estimates and the tobit estimates were not significantly different from each other in the case of the supply equation, and in the case of the demand equation, none of the coefficients was significant (some of them had the wrong signs). This suggests that the data possibly were not informative at all about the parameters of the demand function. This also explains why more elaborate methods of estimation used on these data did not yield any improved results.

10.3   Maximum-likelihood methods: sample separation unknown

Fair and Kelejian (1974) later suggested maximum-likelihood methods for estimation of the Fair-Jaffee model. However, their likelihood function did not consider the correct conditional distributions, and thus they will not be discussed at length here. Amemiya (1974c) discussed the appropriate maximum-likelihood estimation for the quantitative method of the Fair–Jaffee study, and Maddala and Nelson (1974) gave the appropriate maximum-likelihood methods for the other formulations. We shall follow the discussion in the latter study.

Because initially the price P_t will be considered as exogenous, we shall include it in the list of exogenous variables. The model now consists of the following equations:

$$D_t = X'_{1t}\beta_1 + u_{1t}$$
$$S_t = X'_{2t}\beta_2 + u_{2t}$$
$$Q_t = \text{Min}(D_t, S_t) \tag{10.11}$$

D_t denotes the quantity demanded during period t; S_t denotes the quantity supplied during period t; X_{1t} and X_{2t} denote the variables that influence demand and supply, respectively (as noted earlier, P_t is included in these variables); u_{1t} and u_{2t} are residuals. Q_t is the quantity transacted during period t. We shall now consider the following four models.

Model 1. Equations (10.11). Q_t is observed.

Model 2. Equations (10.11) and

$$\Delta P_t > 0 \quad \text{if } D_t > S_t$$
$$\Delta P_t < 0 \quad \text{if } D_t < S_t$$

Q_t and ΔP_t are observed. P_t is price in period t, and $\Delta P_t = P_t - P_{t-1}$. This is the model Fair and Jaffee called Directional Method I.

Model 3. Equations (10.11) and

$$\Delta P_t = \gamma(D_t - S_t)$$

Q_t and ΔP_t are observed. This is the model Fair and Jaffee called the Quantitative Method.

Model 4. Equations (10.11) and

$$\Delta P_t = \gamma(D_t - S_t) + u_{3t}$$

Q_t and ΔP_t are observed. This is the same as model 3, except that the price equation is made stochastic.

Model 1 will be considered in this section. Models 2 and 3 will be considered in section 10.4. Model 4 will be considered in section 10.5.

Consider the simplest disequilibrium model, with sample separation unknown (model 1):

$$D_t = X_{1t}\beta_1 + u_{1t} \quad \text{(demand function)}$$
$$S_t = X_{2t}\beta_2 + u_{2t} \quad \text{(supply function)}$$
$$Q_t = \text{Min}(D_t, S_t)$$

The probability that observation t belongs to the demand function is

$$\lambda_t = \text{Prob}(D_t < S_t)$$
$$= \text{Prob}(u_{1t} - u_{2t} < X_{2t}\beta_2 - X_{1t}\beta_1) \tag{10.12}$$

Let $f(u_1, u_2)$ be the joint density of u_1 and u_2 and $g(D, S)$ the joint density of D and S derived from it. If observation t is on the demand function, we know that $S_t = Q_t$ and $S_t > Q_t$. Hence,

$$h(Q_t \mid Q_t = D_t) = \int_{Q_t}^{\infty} g(Q_t, S_t)\, dS_t / \lambda_t \tag{10.13}$$

The denominator λ_t in (10.13) is the normalizing constant. It is equal to the numerator integrated over Q_t over its entire range. Similarly, if observation t is on the supply function, we know that $S_t = Q_t$ and $D_t > Q_t$. Hence,

$$h(Q_t \mid Q_t = S_t) = \int_{Q_t}^{\infty} g(D_t, Q_t)\, dD_t / (1 - \lambda_t) \tag{10.14}$$

Hence, the unconditional density of Q_t is

$$h(Q_t) = \lambda_t h(Q_t \mid Q_i = D_t) + (1 - \lambda_t) h(Q_t \mid Q_t = S_t)$$
$$= \int_{Q_t}^{\infty} g(Q_t, S_t)\, dS_t + \int_{Q_t}^{\infty} g(D_t, Q_t)\, dDt \tag{10.15}$$

The likelihood function is

$$L = \prod_t h(Q_t) \tag{10.16}$$

As will be shown later, the likelihood function for this model is unbounded for certain parameter values.

Once the parameters in the model have been estimated, we can estimate the probability that each observation is on the demand function or the supply function. Maddala and Nelson (1974) suggested estimating the expressions λ_t in (10.12). These were the probabilities calculated in Sealey (1979) and Portes and Winter (1980). Kiefer (1980) pointed out that (10.12) does not use all the sample information, namely, the data on Q_t. He therefore suggested calculating

$$P(D_t < S_t | Q_t) \tag{10.17}$$

Kiefer derived this probability in a model in which u_1 and u_2 are uncorrelated. We shall derive it for a general model. Noting that

$$\frac{P(AB)}{P(B)} = \frac{P(B|A) \cdot P(A)}{P(B)}$$

we can write (10.17) as

$$\text{Prob}(D_t < S_t | Q_t) = \frac{\text{Prob}(Q_t | D_t < S_t) \cdot \text{Prob}(D_t < S_t)}{\text{Prob}(Q_t)} \tag{10.18}$$

But the numerator of (10.18), from (10.13), is just

$$\int_{Q_t}^{\infty} g(Q_t, S_t) \, dS_t$$

Hence,

$$\text{Prob}(D_t < S_t | Q_t) = \int_{Q_t}^{\infty} g(Q_t, S_t) \, dS_t / h(Q_t) \tag{10.19}$$

where $h(Q_t)$ is defined in (10.15). If u_1 and u_2 are independent, so that $g(D_t, S_t)$ can be written as $g_1(D_t) \cdot g_2(S_t)$ and G_1 and G_2 are the distribution functions corresponding to the density functions g_1 and g_2, respectively, then (10.19) simplifies to

$$\text{Prob}(D_t < S_t | Q_t) = \frac{g_1(Q_t)[1 - G_2(Q_t)]}{g_1(Q_t)[1 - G_2(Q_t)] + g_2(Q_t)[1 - G_1(Q_t)]} \tag{10.20}$$

The likelihood function (10.16) simplifies in this case to

$$L = \prod_t \{ g_1(Q_t)[1 - G_2(Q_t)] + g_2(Q_t)[1 - G_1(Q_t)] \} \tag{10.21}$$

Noting the relationship between (10.20) and the likelihood function (10.21), or between (10.19) and the corresponding likelihood function (10.16), it is clear that calculation of the conditional probabilities (10.16) is computationally feasible. Even in a complicated model these relationships hold good. Note that in a more complicated model (say with stochastic price-adjustment equations), to calculate λ_t, as in (10.12), we

have to derive the marginal distributions of D_t and S_t. To compute
(10.19), we need to derive the joint distribution of D_t and S_t. This is the
main difference between the expressions (10.12) and (10.19).

There are two major problems with the models with unknown sample
separation, one conceptual and the other statistical. The conceptual
problem is that we are asking too much from the data when we do not
know which observations are on the demand function and which are on
the supply function. Goldfeld and Quandt (1975) analyzed the value of
sample-separation information by Monte Carlo methods, and Kiefer
(1979) analyzed analytically the value of such information by comparing
the variances of the parameter estimates in a switching regression model
from the joint density of (y, D) and the marginal density of y (where y is
a continuous variable and D is a discrete variable). These results show
that there is considerable loss of information if sample separation is not
known. In view of this, some of the empirical results being reported for
estimation of disequilibrium models with unknown sample separation
are surprisingly good. Very often, if we look more closely into the
reasons why disequilibrium exists, then we may be able to say something
about the sample separation itself. This point will be mentioned later in
our discussion of tests for disequilibrium.

The statistical problem is that the likelihood functions for this class of
models usually are unbounded, unless some restrictions (usually unjusti-
fiable) are imposed on the error variances (e.g., Day, 1969; Goldfeld and
Quandt, 1975; Quandt, 1978a). As an illustration, consider the model in
which the observed value y is generated by two different probability
laws:

$$y_1 = X\beta_1 + u_1$$
$$y_2 = X\beta_2 + u_2$$

Define

$$\text{Prob}(y = y_1) = \Pi$$
$$\text{Prob}(y = y_2) = 1 - \Pi$$

The conditional density of y, given $y = y_1$, is

$$f(y \mid y_1) = f_1(y - X\beta_1)/\Pi$$

Similarly, $f(y \mid y_2) = f_2(y - X\beta_2)/(1 - \Pi)$. Hence, the unconditional
density of y is

$$f(y) = [f_1(y - X\beta_1) + f_2(y - X\beta_2)]$$

where f_1 and f_2 are the density functions of u_1 and u_2, respectively.
Thus, the distribution of y is the mixture of two normal distributions.

Given n observations y_i, we can write the likelihood function as

$$L = (A_1 + B_1)(A_2 + B_2) \cdots (A_n + B_n) \tag{10.22}$$

where

$$A_i = \frac{1}{\sigma_1} \exp\left[-\frac{1}{2\sigma_1^2} (Y_i - X_i\beta_1)^2 \right]$$

and

$$B_i = \frac{1}{\sigma_2} \exp\left[-\frac{1}{2\sigma_1^2} (Y_i - X_i\beta_2)^2 \right]$$

Take $\sigma_2 \neq 0$, and consider the behavior of L as $\sigma_1 \to 0$. If $X_1\hat{\beta}_1 = y_1$, then $A_1 \to \infty$, and $A_2, A_3, \ldots, A_n$ all approach zero. But $B_1, B_2, \ldots, B_n$ are finite. Hence, $L \to \infty$. Thus, as $\sigma_1 \to 0$, the likelihood function tends to infinity if $X_i\hat{\beta}_1 = y_i$ for any value of i. Similarly, if $\sigma_1 \neq 0$, then as $\sigma_2 \to 0$ the likelihood function tends to infinity if $X_t\hat{\beta}_2 = y_i$ for any value of i.

The case of the disequilibrium model with unknown sample separation is similar. Consider the simplest formulation, with only one exogenous variable P_t:

$$D_t = \beta_1 P_t + u_{1t}$$
$$S_t = \beta_2 P_t + u_{2t}$$
$$Q_t = \text{Min}(D_t, S_t)$$

with u_{1t} and u_{2t} both contemporaneously and serially uncorrelated. If Q is on the demand function, $D=Q$ and $S>Q$. Similarly, if Q is on the supply function, $S=Q$ and $D>Q$. Hence, the likelihood function for this model is of the form (10.22), with

$$A_i = f_1(Q_i)[1 - F_2(Q_i)]$$
$$B_i = f_2(Q_i)[1 - F_1(Q_i)]$$

where f_1 and f_2 are the density functions of u_1 and u_2, respectively, and F_1 and F_2 are the corresponding distribution functions. Take

$$\hat{\beta}_1 = \text{Max}\left(\frac{Q_t}{P_t} \right)$$

Suppose this maximum is Q_k/P_k. Suppose $\sigma_2 \neq 0$, and consider the behavior of A_i and B_i as $\sigma_1 \to 0$. Because $Q_k - \beta_1 P_k = 0$ and $Q_j - \beta_1 P_j < 0$ for $j \neq k$, we have $f_1(Q_k) \to \infty$ and $f_1(Q_j) \to 0$ for $j \neq k$; $f_2(Q_j)$ and $F_2(Q_j)$ are finite for all j. Thus, all B_i will be finite. $A_k \to \infty$, and all the other A_i will be finite. Hence, $L \to \infty$ as $\sigma_1 \to 0$.

In more complicated models, for instance the watermelon-market model considered by Goldfeld and Quandt (1975), where unbounded-ness of the likelihood function is demonstrated, the proof is more complicated, but the structure of the proof is the same as in this simple model.

This unboundedness does not occur in models with known sample separation, nor does it occur if we assume $\sigma_2^2 = c\sigma_1^2$, where c is known. In this case, if one of the $A_i \to \infty$, we can show that some of the other factors $(A_j + B_j) \to 0$. The consequence of the unboundedness of the likelihood function is that in practical work the maximization of the likelihood function might pose problems in that successive iterations might produce higher and higher values of the likelihood without ever converging. This is the reason that Goldfeld and Quandt imposed the condition $\sigma_2^2 = c\sigma_1^2$, with c known. We can see this problem occurring if the successive higher values of the likelihood correspond to lower and lower values of one of the residual variances. In such cases we might want to fix the values of these residual variances so as to prevent them from declining and then maximize with respect to the other parameters. The maximum we locate this way will, of course, be a local maximum rather than a global maximum. However, Amemiya and Sen (1977) showed that even if the likelihood function diverges, a consistent estimate of the true parameter value in this model corresponds to a local maximum of the likelihood function, rather than a global maximum. Thus, the fact that we have located a local maximum rather than a global maximum need not worry us, but this result does not ensure that the particular local maximum we have located will give us a consistent estimate of the true parameter value.[1]

Another problem in this model, as pointed out by Goldfeld and Quandt (1978), is the possibility of convergence to a point where the correlation between the residuals is either $+1$ or -1. They examined in detail the simple disequilibrium model with unknown sample separation and with $\text{Cov}(u_1, u_2) = \xi\sigma_1\sigma_2$. They derived the likelihood function (10.16) and simplified it by factoring the joint density $g(D_t, S_t)$ into the marginal density of one variable (D_t or S_t, whichever was equal to Q_t) and the conditional density of the other variable.

Define, for compactness of notation,

$$W_{1t} = \frac{Q_t - X_{1t}\beta_1}{\sigma_1}$$

---

[1] Hartley and Mallela (1977) proved the strong consistency of the maximum-likelihood estimator, but on the assumption that σ_1 and σ_2 are bounded away from zero.

$$W_{2t} = \frac{Q_t - X_{2t}\beta_2}{\sigma_2}$$

$$Z_{1t} = \frac{1}{(1 - \zeta^2)^{1/2}} (W_{2t} - \zeta W_{1t})$$

$$Z_{2t} = \frac{1}{(1 - \zeta^2)^{1/2}} (W_{1t} - \zeta W_{2t}) \tag{10.23}$$

Then $h(Q_t)$ in (10.15) can be written as

$$h(Q_t) = \frac{1}{\sigma_1} \phi(W_{1t})[1 - \Phi(Z_{1t})] + \frac{1}{\sigma_2} \phi(W_{2t})[1 - \Phi(Z_{2t})] \tag{10.24}$$

where $\phi(\cdot)$ and $\Phi(\cdot)$ are the density function and distribution function of the standard normal. Goldfeld and Quandt then showed that if values for β_1, β_2, σ_1, and σ_2 are chosen such that

$$W_{1t} + W_{2t} < 0 \quad \text{for all } t \tag{10.25}$$

then the likelihood function (10.24) can only increase as $\zeta \rightarrow -1$. Similarly, if

$$W_{2t} > W_{1t} \quad \text{if } \frac{1}{\sigma_2} \phi(W_{2t}) > \frac{1}{\sigma_1} \phi(W_{1t})$$

$$W_{2t} < W_{1t} \quad \text{otherwise} \tag{10.26}$$

then the likelihood function (10.24) increases as $\zeta \rightarrow +1$. Goldfeld and Quandt claimed that conditions (10.24) and (10.25) are often encountered in empirical estimation of this model and, in fact, that this problem is more frequent than the problem of unboundedness of the likelihood function.

The disequilibrium model with unknown sample separation that we have been discussing is a switching regression model with endogenous switching. The case of a switching regression model with exogenous switching and unknown sample separation has been extensively discussed by Quandt and Ramsey (1978) and the commentators on their study. The model in this case is

Regime 1: $y_i = X_{1i}\beta_1 + \epsilon_{1i}$ with probability λ

Regime 2: $y_i = X_{2i}\beta_2 + \epsilon_{2i}$ with probability $(1 - \lambda)$

$\epsilon_{1i} \sim IN(0, \sigma_1^2)$, $\quad \epsilon_{2i} \sim IN(0, \sigma_2^2)$

As noted earlier, the likelihood function for this model becomes unbounded for certain parameter values. However, the following results are known for this model:

1. Kiefer (1978) showed that a root of the likelihood equations corresponding to a local maximum is consistent, asymptotically normal, and efficient.

2. Hartley (1977) suggested an algorithm for the iterative solution of the likelihood equations that can be shown to be equivalent to the EM algorithm of Dempster et al. (1977) for this problem. He found, in the limited Monte Carlo experiments he conducted, that covergence to a solution of the likelihood equations corresponding to a local maximum of the likelihood function always obtains and that point estimates are very close to the parameter values (for moderate sample sizes of 100 observations). However, the experience of others with the EM algorithm has not been very good, and it is doubtful that one can place much credence in these limited Monte Carlo results of Hartley.[2]

The EM method involves substitution of expected values for the missing variables (E part) and then maximization of the likelihood function (M part). To implement it in this case, Hartley suggested defining an auxiliary variable $Z_i \sim IN(\mu, 1)$. If $Z_i < 0$, then y_i belongs to regime 1. If $Z_i > 0$, y_i belongs to regime 2. Thus, $\lambda = \text{Prob}(Z_i < 0) = \Phi(-\mu)$. The case in which Z_i are observed corresponds to known sample separation. Because Z_i are "missing," Hartley suggested evaluating $E(Z_i \mid y_i)$ and substituting these missing values for Z_i. The details of this method have been described for a more general case (where λ varies with each observation) by Hartley (1977, 1979) and need not be reproduced here.

3. Quandt and Ramsey (1978) suggested a moment-generating function (MGF) estimator for this model. Note that the moment-generating function of y is

$$E(e^{\theta y}) = \lambda \exp\left(x_1'\beta_1\theta + \frac{\theta^2 \sigma_1^2}{2}\right)$$

$$+ (1-\lambda) \exp\left(x_2'\beta_2\theta + \frac{\theta^2 \sigma_2^2}{2}\right) \qquad (10.27)$$

Select a set of θ_j $(j = 1, 2, \ldots, k)$, and in equation (10.27) replace

$$E(e^{\theta_j y}) \quad \text{by} \quad \frac{1}{n}\sum_{i=1}^{n} e^{\theta_j y_i}$$

$$\exp(\theta_j x_1'\beta_1) \quad \text{by} \quad \frac{1}{n}\sum_{i=1}^{n} \exp(\theta_j x_{1i}'\beta_1)$$

---

[2] Kiefer has informed me in correspondence that his experience is that the iterations by the EM algorithm tend to wander away in models with unbounded likelihood functions. In fact, he found this to happen even when the starting values were the true parameter values.

and

$$\exp(\theta_j x_2' \beta_2) \quad \text{by} \quad \frac{1}{n} \sum_{i=1}^{n} \exp(\theta_j x_{2i}' \beta_2)$$

Quandt and Ramsey's MGF method is to estimate the parameters $\gamma = (\lambda, \beta_1, \beta_2, \sigma_1^2, \sigma_2^2)$ by minimizing

$$\sum_{j=1}^{k} \left(\frac{1}{n} \sum_{i=1}^{n} Z_i(\theta_j) - \frac{1}{n} \sum_{i=1}^{n} G(\gamma, x_i, \theta_j) \right)^2 \tag{10.28}$$

where $Z_i(\theta_j) = \exp(\theta_j y_i)$ and $G(\gamma, x_i, \theta_j)$ is the value of the expression on the right-hand side of (10.27) for $\theta = \theta_j$ and the ith observation.

The normal equations obtained by minimizing (10.28) with respect to γ are the same as those obtained by minimizing

$$\sum_{j=1}^{k} \sum_{i=1}^{n} [Z_i(\theta_j) - G(\gamma, x_i, \theta_j)]^2 \tag{10.29}$$

The normal equations in both cases are

$$\sum_i \sum_j [Z_i(\theta_j) - G(\gamma, x_i, \theta_j)] \frac{\partial G}{\partial \gamma} = 0 \tag{10.30}$$

One major problem with the MCF method is the choice of the θ_j values. Quandt and Ramsey said that the θ_j should be chosen so as to ensure nonsingularity of the equation system (10.30). They derived the asymptotic distribution of the MGF estimates and presented some Monte Carlo evidence to show that its performance is satisfactory. The discussants of the Quandt and Ramsey study pointed out that the authors had perhaps exaggerated the problems with the ML method, that they should compare their method with the ML method and perhaps use the MGF estimates as starting values for the iterative solution of the likelihood equations.

In summary, there are many problems with the estimation of switching models with unknown sample separation, and much more work needs to be done before we can judge either the practical usefulness of the model or the empirical results already obtained in this area. The literature on self-selection deals with switching models with known sample separation, but the literature on disequilibrium models contains several examples of switching models with unknown sample separation; see the studies of Sealey (1979), Rosen and Quandt (1978), and Portes and Winter (1980). Apart from the computational problems mentioned earlier, there is also the problem that these studies have all been based on the hypothesis of the minimum condition holding on the aggregate, so that the aggregate quantity transacted switches between being on the demand curve and being on the supply curve. The validity of this assumption could be as much a problem in the interpretation of the empirical results as the estimation problems discussed earlier. Although the "minimum condition" can be justified at the microlevel, it will no longer be valid at the macrolevel. Muellbauer argued that at the macro-level a more reasonable assumption is that

$$Q_t \leqslant \text{Min}(D_t, S_t)$$

The problems of aggregation are as important as the problems of estimation with unknown sample separation that were discussed at length earlier.

10.4   Maximum-likelihood methods: sample separation known

Model 2: The directional model. Unlike the case with model 1, we can now use the information on ΔP_t to classify the observations into those belonging to the demand category and the supply category.[3] Consider the joint density of D_t and S_t, say $g(D_t, S_t)$. Then the conditional densities of Q_t in the two regimes are

$$g_{1t} = \int_{Q_t}^{\infty} g(Q_t, S_t) \, dS_t / \lambda_t$$

and

$$g_{2t} = \int_{Q_t}^{\infty} g(D_t, Q_t) \, dD_t / (1 - \lambda_t)$$

where λ_t is defined in (10.12). The likelihood function to be maximized is

$$L = \prod_{\Delta P < 0} g_{1t} \cdot \prod_{\Delta P > 0} g_{2t} \cdot \prod_{\Delta P < 0} (\lambda_t) \cdot \prod_{\Delta P > 0} (1 - \lambda_t) \qquad (10.31)$$

The last factor is the probability of obtaining this particular sample separation. The only requirements for validity of expression (10.31) are that there be no equilibrium observations and that the residuals be serially independent. The second is a serious assumption, and we see no way of relaxing it. The first assumption will be valid if u_1 and u_2 are continuous. In that case, Prob($\Delta P_t = 0$) is zero. In practice, however, we

---

[3] Strictly speaking, the directional method does not make sense, because P_t cannot be exogenous if it gives information on whether there is excess demand or excess supply, and we do not have an equation for P_t. The directional method makes sense only for estimation of the reduced-form equations for D_t and S_t in a model with a price-adjustment equation. There are cases in which this is needed, and they are discussed at the end of section 10.6.

might observe equilibrium points. In that case, we should include them in one or the other of the expressions corresponding to $\Delta P_t > 0$ and $\Delta P_t < 0$.

It should be noted that the expression that Fair and Kelejian (1974) advocated maximizing is the first part of L given in (10.31):

$$L^* = \prod_{\Delta P < 0} g_{1t} \cdot \prod_{\Delta P > 0} g_{2t} \tag{10.32}$$

The essential difference between these two likelihood functions can be seen as follows: Define the dummy variable Z_t as

$$Z_t = 1 \quad \text{if } \Delta P_t < 0$$
$$Z_t = 0 \quad \text{otherwise}$$

Then, L^* defined in (10.32) is based on the joint distribution of $Q_1, Q_2, \ldots, Q_T$ conditional on $Z_1, Z_2, \ldots, Z_T$. L defined in (10.31) is based on the joint distribution of $Q_1, Q_2, \ldots, Q_T$ and $Z_1, Z_2, \ldots, Z_T$. Because Z_t is an endogenous variable by virtue of relations (10.11), Fair and Kelejian were looking at the density of one endogenous variable (Q_t) conditioned on another endogenous variable (Z_t). The model does give information on the probability of observing the sequence $Z_1, Z_2, \ldots, Z_T$. This information is ignored in (10.32) but is used in (10.31). The variable Z_t does give information on the sample partitioning into demand and supply regimes, but this does not imply that our inferences about the parameters in the model are conditional on the observed Z_t series. What we need to do is to obtain the joint density of the observed endogenous variables Q_t and Z_t,

$$f(Q_1, Q_2, \ldots, Q_T, Z_1, \ldots, Z_T, \ldots, Z_T)$$

$$= \prod_{t \in \psi_1} f(Q_t \mid Z_t = 1) \cdot \text{Prob}(Z_t = 1) \prod_{t \in \psi_0} f(Q_t \mid Z_t = 0) \cdot \text{Prob}(Z_t = 0)$$

where ψ_1 is the set of points for which $Z_t = 1$ and ψ_0 is the set of points for which $Z_t = 0$. This is the density function used in the likelihood function (10.31).

Model 3: The quantitative model. In model 1 we can include the price variable P_t in both D_t and S_t in (10.11), so long as we treat it as exogenous. In model 2 it is not possible to include the price variable contemporaneously in D_t or S_t, because, given the specification of the model, P_t is endogenous, and we do not have enough equations to determine the joint density of Q_t and P_t. In models 3 and 4, however, we can include the price variable P_t in these equations. Hence, let us change model 3 to the following:

$$D_t = X'_{1t}\beta_1 + \alpha_1 P_t + u_{1t}$$
$$S_t = X'_{2t}\beta_2 + \alpha_2 P_t + u_{2t}$$
$$Q_t = \text{Min}(D_t, S_t)$$
$$\Delta P_t = \gamma(D_t - S_t) \tag{10.33}$$

The appropriate ML method for this model has been presented by Amemiya (1974c). Let $f_1(Q_t, P_t)$ be the joint density of Q_t and P_t when $Q_t = D_t$, and let $f_2(Q_t, P_t)$ be the corresponding density when $Q_t = S_t$. To obtain $f_1(Q_t, P_t)$, note that

$$D_t = Q_t = \beta'_1 X_{1t} + \alpha_1 P_t + u_{1t}$$
$$\Delta P_t = \gamma(D_t - S_t) = \gamma(Q_t - \beta'_2 X_{2t} - \alpha_2 P_t - u_{2t})$$

From these equations we obtain the joint density of Q_t and P_t, given the joint density of u_{1t} and u_{2t}. Similarly, to obtain $f_2(Q_t, P_t)$, note that

$$S_t = Q_t = \beta'_2 X_{2t} + \alpha_2 P_t + u_{2t}$$

and

$$\Delta P_t = \gamma(D_t - S_t) = \gamma(\beta'_1 X_{1t} + \alpha_1 P_t + u_{1t} - Q_t)$$

The conditional joint density of Q_t and P_t when $\Delta P_t < 0$ is $f_1(Q_t, P_t)/\lambda_t$, where λ_t denotes, as before, $\text{Prob}(D_t < S_t)$.

Similarly, the conditional joint density of Q_t and P_t when $\Delta P_t > 0$ is $f_2(Q_t, P_t)/(1 - \lambda_t)$. The likelihood function that Amemiya suggested maximizing is

$$L = \prod_{\Delta P < 0} f_1(Q_t, P_t) \cdot \prod_{\Delta P > 0} f_2(Q_t, P_t) \tag{10.34}$$

whereas the likelihood function that Fair and Kelejian suggested maximizing is

$$L^* = \prod_{\Delta P < 0} \frac{f_1(Q_t, P_t)}{\lambda_t} \cdot \prod_{\Delta P > 0} \frac{f_2(Q_t, P_t)}{1 - \lambda_t} \tag{10.35}$$

Equation (10.34) is obtained by multiplying (10.35) by the probability of obtaining the particular sample separation observed. Thus, the estimates of the parameters obtained by maximizing (10.34) are based on more sample information than those obtained from (10.35).

Because in many problems the maximum-likelihood method will be cumbersome, it should be interesting to discuss some variants of least-squares methods that will give consistent estimates. These estimates can be used either as final estimates or as starting values in iterative solutions of the likelihood equations. These methods will be labeled two-stage methods.

We shall first discuss two-stage estimation methods for the model in which sample separation is available. We shall consider the problems when sample separation is not available in the next section.

Consider first the case of model 2, the directional model. What we have here is a switching regression model with endogenous switching and sample separation known. We can write the model as

Regime 1: $Q_t = \beta_1' X_{1t} + u_{1t}$ iff $\beta_1' X_{1t} + u_{1t} < \beta_2' X_{2t} + u_{2t}$
Regime 2: $Q_t = \beta_2' X_{2t} + u_{2t}$ iff $\beta_1' X_{1t} + u_{1t} \geqslant \beta_2' X_{2t} + u_{2t}$

We can write the criterion function as

$$\gamma' Z_t > u_t$$

where

$$\frac{\beta_1' X_{1t} - \beta_2' X_{2t}}{\sigma} = \gamma' Z_t, \qquad \frac{u_{2t} - u_{1t}}{\sigma} = u_t$$

and $\sigma^2 = \mathrm{Var}(u_{1t} - u_{2t})$. Then, as discussed in Chapter 8, we have

$$Q_t = \beta_1' X_{1t} - \sigma_{1u} \frac{\phi(\gamma' Z_t)}{\Phi(\gamma' Z_t)} + \epsilon_{1t}$$

for observations in regime 1, and

$$Q_t = \beta_2' X_{2t} + \sigma_{2u} \frac{\phi(\gamma' Z_t)}{1 - \Phi(\gamma' Z_t)} + \epsilon_{2t} \tag{10.36}$$

for observations in regime 2. After getting estimates of γ by the probit method, we can estimate equation (10.36) by ordinary least squares. These give consistent estimates of β_1, β_2, σ_{1u}, and σ_{2u}. Because the details of the estimation of residual variances are explained in Chapter 8, they will not be pursued here.

Consider next model 3, the quantitative model discussed earlier. Fair and Jaffee (1972) noted that we can derive the following equations. For $\Delta P_t > 0$, we know from (10.33) that $D_t > S_t$. Hence, $S_t = Q_t$, and we have

$$Q_t = \beta_2' X_{2t} + \alpha_2 P_t + u_{2t} \tag{10.37}$$

Also, equation (10.33) can be written as $Q_t = D_t - (1/\gamma)\Delta P_t$. Hence, we have

$$Q_t = \beta_1' X_{1t} + \alpha_1 P_t + u_{1t} - \frac{1}{\gamma} \Delta P_t \qquad (10.38)$$

Similarly, for $\Delta P_t < 0$, we have $D_t < S_t$, and hence $D_t = Q_t$. Thus,

$$Q_t = \beta_1' X_{1t} + \alpha_1 P_t + u_{1t} \qquad (10.39)$$

Also, writing equation (10.33) as $Q_t = S_t + (1/\gamma)\Delta P_t$, we get

$$Q_t = \beta_2' X_{2t} + \alpha_2 P_t + u_{2t} + \frac{1}{\gamma} \Delta P_t \qquad (10.40)$$

Combining equations (10.38) and (10.39), we get

$$Q_t = \beta_1' X_{1t} + \alpha_1 P_t + \frac{1}{\gamma} Z_{1t} + u_{1t} \qquad (10.41)$$

where

$$Z_{1t} = -\Delta P_t \quad \text{if } \Delta P_t > 0$$
$$Z_{1t} = 0 \quad \text{if } \Delta P_t < 0$$

Similarly, combining (10.37) and (10.40), we get

$$Q_t = \beta_2' X_{2t} + \alpha_2 P_t + \frac{1}{\gamma} Z_{2t} + u_{2t} \qquad (10.42)$$

where

$$Z_{2t} = 0 \quad \text{if } \Delta P_t > 0$$
$$Z_{2t} = \Delta P_t < 0$$

Amemiya (1974a) suggested the following two-stage estimation method: Regress P_t, Z_{1t}, and Z_{2t} on all the exogenous variables (using all the observations). Substitute the estimated P_t, Z_{1t}, and Z_{2t} in equations (10.41) and (10.42), and estimate these by OLS. The resulting two-stage estimates can be shown to be consistent.

Hartley (1976) considered a special case of the models described in the Maddala–Nelson (1974) study. He considered the case of fixed supply (S_t is a constant $\bar{S}$), pointing out that the fixed-supply case is useful for analyzing short-run demand for sporting events, plays, concerts, airline flights, and so forth. Because the models considered in his study are special cases of the models discussed earlier, we need not discuss them here. Likewise, the nonlinear least-squares methods suggested in Hartley's study are not very useful, particularly when it is easy to apply the maximum-likelihood methods in this case of known sample separation. Also, the two-stage methods described earlier are available.

10.5   Some generalized disequilibrium models

Again adding the price variable P_t to the first two equations of the model considered earlier, we have our model 4, called the generalized model by Fair and Kelejian (1974):

$$D_t = X'_{1t}\beta_1 + P_t\beta_2 + u_{1t}$$
$$S_t = X'_{2t}\beta_3 + P_t\beta_4 + u_{2t}$$
$$\Delta P_t = \beta_5(D_t - S_t) + X_{3t}\beta_6 + u_{3t} \tag{10.43}$$

and

$$Q_t = \text{Min}(D_t, S_t) \tag{10.44}$$

The methods outlined earlier can be easily extended to this model. From equations (10.43) we can determine the joint density of the three endogenous variables D_t, S_t, and P_t, given the set of exogenous variables, to be denoted henceforth by X_t. Call this $g(D_t, S_t, P_t | X_t)$. This is nothing but the joint density of (u_{1t}, u_{2t}, u_{3t}) multiplied by the Jacobian of the transformation from (u_{1t}, u_{2t}, u_{3t}) to (D_t, S_t, P_t), as in any simultaneous-equations model. Now, utilizing the condition (10.44), we note that the conditional joint density $g_1(Q_t, P_t | X_t)$ of Q_t and P_t, given that Q_t is on the demand function, is given by

$$g_1(Q_t, P_t | X_t) = \frac{\int_{Q_t}^{\infty} g(Q_t, S_t, P_t)\, dS_t}{N_t} \tag{10.45}$$

where N_t is the normalization factor given by the integral of the numerator of (10.45) with respect to Q_t. It should also be noted that N_t is nothing but the probability that $D_t < S_t$, given the model (10.43). Similarly, the conditional joint density $g_2(Q_t, P_t | X_t)$ of Q_t and P_t, given that Q_t is on the supply function, is given by

$$g_2(Q_t, P_t | X_t) = \frac{\int_{Q_t}^{\infty} g(D_t, Q_t, P_t)\, dD_t}{1 - N_t}$$

Because Q_t is on the demand function, with probability N_t, and on the supply function, with probability $1 - N_t$, the unconditional joint density of the observed endogenous variables Q_t and P_t is given by

$$f(Q_t, P_t | X_t) = N_t g_1(Q_t, P_t | X_t) + (1 - N_t)g_2(Q_t, P_t | X_t)$$
$$= \int_{Q_t}^{\infty} g(Q_t, S_t, P_t | X_t)\, dS_t + \int_{Q_t}^{\infty} g(D_t, Q_t, P_t | X_t)\, dD_t \tag{10.46}$$

The ML estimates of the parameters $\bar{\beta}$ and Σ, where $\bar{\beta}$ is the vector of β's and Σ is the covariance matrix of (u_1, u_2, u_3), are obtained by maximizing the log likelihood

$$L = \sum_{i=1}^{n} \log f(Q_t, P_t \mid X_t)$$

The expressions for the first and second derivatives of L will indeed be very complicated, but again we can use the iterative procedures by evaluating these derivatives numerically. The calculation of the probabilities N_t will also be complicated, because they are no longer given by such simple expressions as (10.12).

The procedure outlined here is the appropriate full-information ML procedure to use in this class of problems and is also derived in a more straightforward manner than the one outlined by Fair and Kelejian. They worked in terms of several conditional expectations and finally derived a simultaneous-equations system of two equations in P_t and Q_t. Because these are complicated to handle, they suggested some approximations based on polynomial expansions. We shall discuss some limited-information methods in a later section.

The expression given in (10.46) is also valid if there are other endogenous variables Z_t in the system besides P_t. In that case, the joint density of the observed endogenous variables Q_t, P_t, and Z_t is given by

$$f(Q_t, P_t, Z_t \mid X_t) = \int_{Q_t}^{\infty} g(D_t, Q_t, P_t, Z_t \mid X_t)\, dD_t$$

$$+ \int_{Q_t}^{\infty} g(Q_t, S_t, P_t, Z_t \mid X_t)\, dS_t$$

In general, consider a model consisting of n endogenous variables $y_1, y_2, \ldots, y_n$ and m exogenous variables $Z_1, Z_2, \ldots, Z_m$. Let $g(y_1, y_2, \ldots, y_n \mid Z_1, \ldots, Z_m)$ be the joint density. Classify the endogenous variables into two sets $Y_1 = (y_1, y_2, \ldots, y_{n_1})$ and $Y_2 = (y_{n_1} + 1, \ldots, y_n)$. Suppose we observe only one endogenous variable y in the set Y_1, where $y = \text{Min}(y_1, y_2, \ldots, y_{n_1})$. (The argument is similar for Max instead of Min.) Define $\bar{Y}_1$ as the set Y_1 excluding y_1, $\bar{Y}_2$ as the set Y_1 excluding y_2, and so forth. Also, let g_1 be the density g if y_1 is replaced by y, let g_2 be the density of g if y_2 is replaced by y, and so forth. Then the joint density of the observed endogenous variables (y_1, Y_2) is given by

$$L(y_1, Y_2) = \int_{y}^{\infty} g_1(y, \bar{Y}_1, Y_2)\, d\bar{Y}_1 + \int_{y}^{\infty} g_2(y, \bar{Y}_2, Y_2)\, d\bar{Y}_2$$

$$+ \cdots + \int_y^\infty g_{n_1}(y, \bar{Y}_{n_1}, Y_2) \, d\bar{Y}_{n_1}$$

where the integrals are $(n_1 - 1)$-tuple integrals, the limits for each variable being y and ∞. Obviously, if n_1 is greater than 2, this is a very complicated problem to tackle; this is, in fact, the problem we face with serially correlated residuals in the disequilibrium model. If n_2 is greater than 2, again the computational burden will increase greatly. Hence, it might be of some interest to consider some limited-information methods for these models.

The watermelon-market model

Goldfeld and Quandt (1975) extended the methods developed by Maddala and Nelson (1974) to analyze the watermelon-market model studied by Suits (1955). The model is complicated by the existence of a truncated variable in the Min condition. Otherwise, the methods of writing the likelihood functions are the same as in model 4 considered here. Because the derivation of the likelihood function in the Goldfeld–Quandt study is somewhat complicated, we shall present it here in a straightforward manner in line with the discussion here. Let

$q =$ crop of watermelons
$p =$ price of watermelons
$x =$ desired harvest $(x \leqslant q)$
$y =$ actual harvest

The distinction between crop and harvest in this model arises from the fact that some of the crop can be left unharvested. The model consists of the following equations:

$$q = b_1 Z_1 + b_2 + u_1 \tag{10.47}$$

$$x = b_3 p + b_4 q + b_5 Z_2 + b_6 + u_2 \quad \text{if } x < q$$

$$x = q \quad \text{otherwise} \tag{10.48}$$

$$p = b_7 Z_3 + b_8 y + b_9 + u_3 \tag{10.49}$$

$$y = \text{Min}(x, q) \tag{10.50}$$

We have rewritten equations (10.48) in a more illuminating way than did Goldfeld and Quandt. The other equations are the same as in their study. Equation (10.47) explains the determination of the crop. The "exogenous" variables Z_1 include lagged prices of watermelons and other competing crops. Equation (10.49) is a standard demand function. The exogenous variables Z_3 include variables like income and freight rates. Price depends also on the quantity y of watermelons in the market. Equation (10.48) is the harvest equation, which depends on price p, crop q, and the exogenous variables Z_2, which include farm wage rates.

Note that depending on whether $x < q$ or $x = q$, we have two structural systems. We shall consider three cases:

Case 1: q is not observed, and sample separation is not known
Case 2: q is not observed, but, somehow, sample separation is known
Case 3: q is observed, and thus sample separation is also known

We shall now discuss these in detail.

Case 1: q is not observed. Here the observed variables are y, p, Z_1, Z_2, and Z_3. Suppose $x < q$. Then $y = x$, and the model is

$$q = b_1 Z_1 + b_2 + u_1$$
$$y = b_3 p + b_4 q + b_5 Z_2 + b_6 + u_2$$
$$p = b_7 Z_3 + b_8 y + b_9 + u_3 \tag{10.51}$$

When $x < q$, we have $q > x = y$. Hence, the conditional density of (y, p), given $x < q$, is given by

$$h_1(y, p \mid x < q) = \int_y^\infty g_1(q, y, p)\, dq / N \tag{10.52}$$

where g_1 is the joint density of (q, y, p) derived from (10.51) and N is the integral of this over the range $q > x = y$, which is nothing but $\text{Prob}(x < q)$. We shall simplify this integral later.

When $x = y$, we have $y = q$, and the structural system consists of

$$y = b_1 Z_1 + b_2 + u_1$$
$$x = b_3 p + b_4 y + b_5 Z_2 + b_6 + u_2$$
$$p = b_7 Z_3 + b_8 y + b_9 + u_3 \tag{10.53}$$

and

$$h_2(y, p \mid x > q) = \int_y^\infty g_2(y, x, p)\, dx / (1 - N) \tag{10.54}$$

where $N = \text{Prob}(X < q)$ and g_2 is the joint density of (q, x, p) derived from (10.53). The density of (y, p) is now given from (10.52) and (10.54):

$$h(y, p) = \int_y^\infty g_1(q, y, p)\, dq + \int_y^\infty g_2(y, x, p)\, dx \tag{10.55}$$

This is precisely the expression that Goldfeld and Quandt had in their study. This expression is similar to equation (10.46).

The value of the Jacobian is

$$\left| \frac{\partial(u_1, u_2, u_3)}{\partial(q, y, p)} \right| = 1 - b_3 b_8$$

in the first regime and

$$\left| \frac{\partial(u_1, u_2, u_3)}{\partial(y, x, p)} \right| = 1$$

in the second regime. Hence, we can write (10.55) as

$$h(y, p) = (1 - b_3 b_8) \int_y^\infty f_1(u_1, u_2, u_3) \, dq + \int_y^\infty f_2(u_1, u_2, u_3) \, dx$$

Assuming that (u_1, u_2, u_3) are independently normally distributed, with means zero and variances σ_1^2, σ_2^2, and σ_3^2, respectively, we can write down $f_1(u_1, u_2, u_3)$ from equations (10.51) and $f_2(u_1, u_2, u_3)$ from (10.53). Because the integration is straightforward algebra and has been reported in the Goldfeld–Quandt study, we shall not present it here.

Case 2: q unobserved, but, somehow, sample separation is known. This case is similar to model 2, considered in the Maddala–Nelson study and in the preceding section. The appropriate likelihood function to maximize is

$$L_2 = \prod_1 h_1(y, p \mid x < q) \cdot \prod_2 h_2(y, p \mid x = q)$$

$$\times \left[\prod_1 \text{Prob}(x < q) \cdot \prod_2 \text{Prob}(x = q) \right] \tag{10.56}$$

where subscript 1 denotes the set of observations for which $x < q$ and 2 denotes the set of observations for which $x = q$. The bracketed term in (10.56) is the probability of observing this particular sample separation. On using equations (10.52) and (10.54), equation (10.56) simplifies to

$$L_2 = \prod_1 \int_y^\infty g_1(q, y, p) \, dq \prod_2 \int_y^\infty g_2(y, x, p) \, dx \tag{10.57}$$

Case 3: q observed. For the regime $x < q$, we have the joint density $g_1(q, y, p)$ given by (10.51). For the regime $x = q$, the joint density is $g_2(y, x, p)$ given by (10.53). Hence, the likelihood function for this case is

$$L_3 = \prod_1 g_1(q, y, p) \cdot \prod_2 g_2(y, x, p) \tag{10.58}$$

The model considered by Goldfeld and Quandt is essentially a switching simultaneous-equations system that can be written as follows:

Regime 1: $x < q$, $y = x$, and p observed	Regime 2: $x > q$, $y = q$, and p observed
$q = b_1 Z_1 + b_2 + u_1$	$q = b_1 Z_1 + b_2 + u_1$
$x = b_3 p + b_4 q + b_5 Z_2 + b_6 + u_2$	$x = b_3 p + b_4 q + b_5 Z_2 + b_6 + u_2$
$p = b_7 Z_3 + b_8 x + b_9 + u_3$	$p = b_7 Z_3 + b_8 q + b_9 + u_3$

In such switching simultaneous-equations systems, one needs to impose some conditions for logical consistency. In the present model, this condition turns out to be $1 - b_3 b_8 > 0$, and luckily this condition is satisfied, because b_3 is expected to be positive and b_8 is expected to be negative. To see this, consider the reduced forms for q and x in the two regimes. In regime 1,

$$q = b_1 Z_1 + b_2 + u_1$$

$$x = \frac{1}{1 - b_3 b_8}(b_4 b_1 Z_1 + b_5 Z_2 + b_3 b_7 Z_3 + b_6 + b_3 b_9 + b_4 b_2 \\ + b_4 u_1 + u_2 + b_3 u_3)$$

so that the condition $x < q$ gives

$$\frac{1}{1 - b_3 b_8}(b_4 u_1 + u_2 + b_3 u_3) - u_1$$

$$< b_1 Z_1 + b_2 - \frac{1}{1 - b_3 b_8}(b_4 b_1 Z_1 + b_5 Z_2 + b_3 b_7 Z_3 + b_6 + b_3 b_9 + b_4 b_2)$$

If we assume $1 - b_3 b_8 > 0$, we can multiply throughout by this factor and get

$$(b_4 + b_3 b_8 - 1)u_1 + u_2 + b_3 u_3 \\ < (1 - b_3 b_8 - b_4)(b_1 Z_1 + b_2) - (b_5 Z_2 + b_6) - b_3(b_7 Z_3 + b_9) \quad (10.59)$$

Similarly, in regime 2, we have

$$q = b_1 Z_1 + b_2 + u_1$$

$$x = (b_3 b_8 + b_4)(b_1 Z_1 + b_2) + (b_5 Z_2 + b_6) + b_3(b_7 Z_3 + b_9) \\ + (b_3 b_8 + b_4)u_1 + u_2 + b_3 u_3$$

so that the condition $x > q$ gives

$$(b_4 + b_3 b_8 - 1)u_1 + u_2 + b_3 u_3 \\ > (1 - b_3 b_8 - b_4)(b_1 Z_1 + b_2) - (b_5 Z_2 + b_6) - b_3(b_7 Z_3 + b_9) \quad (10.60)$$

Conditions (10.59) and (10.60) are thus mutually exclusive. On the other hand, if $1 - b_3 b_8 < 0$, we have both the conditions $x < q$ in regime 1 and $x > q$ in regime 2 producing the condition (10.60), thus leading to contradictions.

Such conditions for logical consistency have been pointed out by Amemiya (1974*b*), Maddala and Lee (1976), and Heckman (1978*a*). They need to be imposed in switching simultaneous systems in which the switch depends on some of the endogenous variables. Gourieroux et al. (1980*b*) derived some general conditions that they called coherency conditions, and they illustrated them with a number of examples. These conditions are derived from a theorem by Samelson et al. (1958) that gives a necessary and sufficient condition for a linear space to be partitioned in cones. We shall not go into these conditions in detail here. In the case of the switching simultaneous system considered here, the condition they derived is that the determinants of the matrices giving the mapping from (q, x, p) to (u_1, u_2, u_3) be of the same sign. In regime 1 $(x < q)$, we have

$$
A_1 \begin{bmatrix} q \\ x \\ p \end{bmatrix} = \begin{bmatrix} 1 & 0 & 0 \\ -b_4 & 1 & -b_3 \\ 1 & -b_8 & 1 \end{bmatrix} \begin{bmatrix} q \\ x \\ p \end{bmatrix} = \begin{bmatrix} u_1 \\ u_2 \\ u_3 \end{bmatrix}
$$

In regime 2 $(x > q)$, we have

$$
A_2 \begin{bmatrix} q \\ x \\ p \end{bmatrix} = \begin{bmatrix} 1 & 0 & 0 \\ -b_4 & 1 & -b_3 \\ 1 & -b_8 & 1 \end{bmatrix} \begin{bmatrix} q \\ x \\ p \end{bmatrix} = \begin{bmatrix} u_1 \\ u_2 \\ u_3 \end{bmatrix}
$$

Hence, $|A_1| = 1 - b_3 b_8$ and $|A_2| = 1$. The condition that both have the same sign gives the condition that $1 - b_3 b_8 > 0$ derived earlier. We shall use the conditions derived by Gourieroux et al. (1980*b*) again in our discussion of multimarket-disequilibrium models (section 10.8).

As yet another example, consider the model

$$
Y_1 = \gamma_1 Y_2 + \beta_1' x_1 + u_1
$$
$$
Y_2 = \gamma_2 Y_1 + \beta_2' x_2 + u_2 \quad \text{if } Y_1 < c
$$
$$
Y_2 = \gamma_2' Y_1 + \beta_2' x_2 + u_2 \quad \text{if } Y_1 \geqslant c
$$

The two determinants under consideration are $(1 - \gamma_1 \gamma_2)$ and $(1 - \gamma_1 \gamma_2')$. The condition for logical consistency of the model is that they be of the same sign, or $(1 - \gamma_1 \gamma_2)(1 - \gamma_1 \gamma_2') > 0$. A question arises about what to do with this condition. One can impose it and then estimate the model. Alternatively, because the condition is algebraic, if it cannot be given an economic interpretation it is important to check the basic structure of the model.[4]

An interesting feature of the switching simultaneous systems is that it is possible to have underidentified systems in one of the regimes. As an illustration, consider the following "disequilibrium" model estimated by Avery (1982):

$$
\left.
\begin{aligned}
D &= \beta_1' X_1 + \alpha_1 Y + u_1 \quad \text{(demand for durables)} \\
Y_1 &= \beta_2' X_1 + \alpha_2 D + u_2 \quad \text{(demand for debt)} \\
Y_2 &= \beta_3' X_3 + \alpha_3 D + u_3 \quad \text{(supply of debt)}
\end{aligned}
\right\} \tag{10.61}
$$

$$
Y = \mathrm{Min}(y_1, y_2) \quad \text{(actual quantity of debt)} \tag{10.62}
$$

D, Y_1, and Y_2 are the endogenous variables, and X_1 and X_3 are sets of exogenous variables. Note that the exogenous variables in the demand-for-durables equation and the demand-for-debt equation are the same. The model is a switching simultaneous-equations model with endogenous switching. We can write the model as follows:

Regime 1: $Y_1 < Y_2$	Regime 2: $Y_2 < Y_1$
$D = \beta_1' X_1 + \alpha_1 Y + u_1$	$D = \beta_1' X_1 + \alpha_1 Y + u_1$
$Y = \beta_2' X_1 + \alpha_2 D + u_2$	$Y = \beta_3' X_3 + \alpha_3 D + u_3$

If we get the reduced forms for Y_1 and Y_2 in the two regimes and simplify the expression $Y_1 - Y_2$, we find that

$$
(Y_1 - Y_2) \text{ in Regime 2} = \frac{1 - \alpha_1 \alpha_3}{1 - \alpha_1 \alpha_2} [(Y_1 - Y_2) \text{ in Regime 1}]
$$

Thus, the condition for logical consistency of this model is that $(1 - \alpha_1 \alpha_3)$ and $(1 - \alpha_1 \alpha_3)$ be of the same sign – a condition that can also be derived by using the theorems of Gourieroux et al. (1980b).

The interesting thing to note is that the simultaneous-equations system in regime 1 is underidentified. However, if the system of equations in regime 2 is identified, the fact that we can get consistent estimates of the parameters in the demand equation for durables from regime 2 enables us to get consistent estimates of the parameters in the Y_1 equation. Thus, the parameters in the simultaneous-equations system in regime 1 are identified. We could construct a formal and rigorous proof, but that will

---

[4] This is illustrated in our discussion of Heckman's example of measuring the effect of fair-employment laws in Chapter 5, and also in section 10.10.

not be attempted here. Avery (1982) found that he could not estimate the parameters of the structural equation for Y_1, but that may have been because of the estimation methods he used.

The likelihood function for this model is

$$L = \Pi\left[\int_Y^\infty f(D, Y, Y_2)\, dY_2 + \int_Y^\infty f(D, Y_1, Y)\, dY_1\right]$$

where $f(D, Y_1, Y_2)$ is the joint density of (D, Y_1, Y_2) derived from equations (10.61).

Although computationally it is no simpler than the ML estimation, it might be of some interest to note here what a two-stage estimation method for models like this involves. Two-stage estimation involves the following steps:

1.   Write equations for Y_1 and Y_2 in their reduced form and estimate these with equation (10.61) using the ML method. However, note that the residuals in these reduced forms are correlated even if the residuals in the structural equations are not.

2.   Next, obtain predicted values $\bar{Y}_1$ and $\bar{Y}_2$ of Y_1 and Y_2 from the estimates of these reduced-form equations. Also, let $\hat{\sigma}_1^2$, $\hat{\sigma}_2^2$, and $\hat{\sigma}_{12}$ be the estimates of the variances and covariance between the residuals in these reduced forms. Then a predicted value of Y is

$$\bar{Y} = \lambda\bar{Y}_1 + (1 - \lambda)\bar{Y}_2 - \hat{\sigma}\phi\left(\frac{\bar{Y}_1 - \bar{Y}_2}{\hat{\sigma}}\right)$$

where

$$\lambda = \Phi\left(\frac{\bar{Y}_1 - \bar{Y}_2}{\hat{\sigma}}\right)$$

$\Phi(\cdot)$ and $\phi(\cdot)$ are, respectively, the distribution function and the density function of the standard normal, and

$$\hat{\sigma}^2 = \hat{\sigma}_1^2 + \hat{\sigma}_2^2 - 2\hat{\sigma}_{12}$$

3.   Substitute $\bar{Y}$ in the equation for D in (10.61), and estimate it by OLS. This gives the two-stage estimates of the parameters in this equation.

4.   Next, obtain the predicted value $\bar{D}$ of D, and reestimate the equations for Y_1 and Y_2 by ML, using the same procedure as in step 1.

This procedure gives consistent estimates of all the structural parameters. The major problem with this procedure is that the standard errors obtained in the second stage are not the correct standard errors. Further, the derivation of the correct asymptotic covariance matrix of the two-stage estimates is much more involved than the derivation of Lee et al. (1980), which was for the switching simultaneous system with known sample separation. In view of all this, and the fact that the two-step procedure itself involves the use of the ML procedure twice, it is preferable to estimate this model by the ML method. Of course, all the problems mentioned in the preceding section apply to these models too. In fact, until the problems of estimation with simple switching regression models with sample separation unknown are resolved, it is not worth undertaking estimation of switching simultaneous-equations models with sample separation unknown. The purpose in bringing up this model here is to point out some interesting identification problems in such models.

In summary, switching simultaneous-equations models often involve the imposition of constraints on parameters so as to avoid some internal inconsistencies in the model. But it is also very often the case that such logical inconsistencies arise when the formulation of the model is mechanical. In many cases it has been found that a reexamination and a more careful formulation will lead to an alternative model in which such constraints need not be imposed.

There are also some switching simultaneous-equations models in which a variable is endogenous in one regime and exogenous in another, and, unlike the cases considered by Richard (1978) and Davidson (1978), the switching is endogenous. An example is a disequilibrium model in a study by Maddala (1979) that will be discussed in section 10.7.

10.6   Price adjustment and disequilibrium

In our discussion of the Fair–Jaffee model, we considered two methods: the directional method and the quantitative method given by equation (10.33). There are two meanings one can give to these price-adjustment equations. Suppose we argue, as Fair and Jaffee did, that if there is excess demand, prices rise, and if there is excess supply, prices fall. The question, however, is when. In this case it may be more meaningful to substitute $\Delta P_{t+1} = P_{t+1} - P_t$ for ΔP_t in equation (10.33), so that we have

$$\Delta P_{t+1} > 0 \quad \text{if} \ D_t > S_t$$
$$\Delta P_{t+1} < 0 \quad \text{if} \ D_t < S_t$$

This is what Laffont and Garcia (1977) did. What this does to estimation is that in models 2 and 3 considered in section 10.4, P_t is exogenous, not endogenous, at time t. Laffont and Garcia also allowed for different speeds of price adjustment for periods of excess demand and excess supply in their quantitative methods. In their reformulation, equation (10.33) is written as

$$\Delta P_t = \gamma_1 (D_t - S_t) \quad \text{if} \ D_t > S_t$$
$$\Delta P_t = \gamma_2 (D_t - S_t) \quad \text{if} \ D_t < S_t$$

If we argue that it is $\Delta P_{t+1} = P_{t+1} - P_t$, and not $\Delta P_t = P_t - P_{t-1}$, that is affected by excess demand or excess supply in period t, these equations will be written as

$$\Delta P_{t+1} = \gamma_1(D_t - S_t) \quad D_t > S_t$$
$$\Delta P_{t+1} = \gamma_2(D_t - S_t) \quad D_t < S_t \tag{10.33'}$$

The method of estimation does not change much with these reformulations. The only difference is that there is one extra parameter.

In the case of the specification (10.33′) used by Laffont and Garcia, where we use ΔP_{t+1} instead of ΔP_t in the price-adjustment equation, we note that P_t is exogenous, and it is now P_{t+1} that is endogenous. But the procedure of deriving the likelihood function is the same as in the previous case. The Jacobians will now be different. To see this, let $f_1(Q_t, P_{t+1})$ be the joint density of Q_t and P_{t+1} when $Q_t = D_t$. We then have the equations

$$u_{1t} = Q_t - \beta_1' X_{1t} - \alpha_1 P_t$$
$$u_{2t} = Q_t - \beta_2' X_{2t} - \left(\alpha_2 - \frac{1}{\gamma_2}\right)P_t - \frac{P_{t+1}}{\gamma_2} \tag{10.63}$$

The Jacobian of the transformation from (u_{1t}, u_{2t}) to (Q_t, P_{t+1}) is now

$$\begin{vmatrix} 1 & 0 \\ 1 & -1/\gamma_2 \end{vmatrix} = \frac{1}{\gamma_2}$$

Hence, $f_1(Q_t, P_{t+1}) = (1/\gamma_2)g_1(u_1, u_2)$. In the density $g_1(u_1, u_2)$ of (u_1, u_2), we substitute the expressions in (10.63) in the observed variables.

The derivation of f_2 is similar. We have

$$Q_t = S_t = \beta_2' X_{2t} + \alpha_2 P_t + u_{2t}$$

and

$$P_{t+1} - P_t = \gamma_1(D_t - S_t) = \gamma_1(\beta_1' X_{1t} + \alpha_1 P_t + u_{1t} - Q_t)$$

These equations can be written as

$$u_{1t} = Q_t - \beta_1' X_{1t} - \left(\alpha_1 - \frac{1}{\gamma_1}\right)P_t - \frac{1}{\gamma_1}P_{t+1}$$
$$u_{2t} = Q_t - \beta_2' X_{2t} - \alpha_2 P_t \tag{10.64}$$

The Jacobian of the transformation from (u_{1t}, u_{2t}) to (Q_t, P_{t+1}) is $1/\gamma_1$. Hence,

$$f_2(Q_t, P_{t+1}) = \frac{1}{\gamma_1}g_2(u_1, u_2)$$

where $g_2(u_1, u_2)$ is the density of (u_1, u_2), with the expressions in (10.64) substituted for u_1 and u_2. Finally, the likelihood function to be maximized is

$$L = \prod_{\Delta P_{t+1} < 0} f_1(Q_t, P_{t+1}) \prod_{\Delta P_{t+1} > 0} f_2(Q_t, P_{t+1})$$

Thus, the likelihood function and estimation problems are not much altered by making the alternative assumptions in equations (10.33′) instead of (10.33).[5]

Although the modifications of the price-adjustment equations suggested by Laffont and Garcia, given by equations (10.33′), make sense, there is an alternative interpretation of the price-adjustment equation under which equation (10.33) is more meaningful. This interpretation actually goes to the root of the question why disequilibrium exists at all.

Let P_t^* be the price that equilibrates demand and supply. If there are no costs of price adjustment, then $P_t = P_t^*$, and we have an equilibrium model. On the other hand, if firms cannot adjust prices immediately (even though they know the market-clearing price), we have a partial-adjustment model:

$$P_t - P_{t-1} = \lambda(P_t^* - P_{t-1}) \quad (0 < \lambda < 1)$$
$$= \lambda(P_t^* - P_t + P_t - P_{t-1})$$

Hence,

$$P_t - P_{t-1} = \frac{\lambda}{1-\lambda}(P_t^* - P_t) \tag{10.65}$$

If $P_t < P_t^*$, there will be excess demand, and if $P_t > P_t^*$, there will be excess supply. Hence, if $\Delta P_t < 0$, we have a situation of excess supply.

Note that in this case it is ΔP_t (not ΔP_{t+1} as in the Laffont–Garcia case) that gives the sample separation. *The interpretation is not that prices rise in response to excess demand* (as implicitly argued by Fair and Jaffee) *but that there is excess demand* (or excess supply) *because prices do not fully adjust to the equilibrating values.*[6]

Equation (10.65) can also be written as

[5] The two-stage least-squares methods described in section 10.4 can be easily applied for these models as well. We replace ΔP_t by ΔP_{t+1} in the definitions of Z_{1t} and Z_{2t}, γ by γ_1 in equation (10.41), and γ by γ_2 in equation (10.42). Also, P_t is no longer endogenous. Only Z_{1t} and Z_{2t} are endogenous.

[6] The formulation in terms of partial adjustment toward P^* was suggested by Bowden (1978a), although he did not use the interpretation of the Fair-Jaffee equation given here. Bowden (1978b) discussed this approach in greater detail under the title "The PAMEQ Specification."

$$P_t - P_{t-1} = \gamma(D_t - S_t)$$

if we assume that the excess demand $D_t - S_t$ is proportional to the difference $P_t^* - P_t$, that is, the difference between the equilibrating price and the actual price. The interpretation of the coefficient γ is, of course, different from what Fair and Jaffee gave to the same equation.

Thus, there are two interpretations of the price-adjustment equations:

1. Prices rise or fall in response to excess demand or excess supply. Here the formulation of Laffont and Garcia using ΔP_{t+1} makes more sense than the formulation of Fair and Jaffee using ΔP_t.
2. Excess demand or excess supply exists because prices do not adjust fully (because of costs of adjustment) to the equilibrium level. Here the formulation of Fair and Jaffee makes more sense than that of Laffont and Garcia.

Different speeds of upward and downward adjustments, as in equation (10.33) can also be derived in the partial-adjustment framework. Consider the following formulation:

$$P_t - P_{t-1} = \lambda_1 (P_t^* - P_{t-1}) \quad \text{if } P_t^* > P_{t-1}$$
$$P_t - P_{t-1} = \lambda_2 (P_t^* - P_{t-1}) \quad \text{if } P_t^* < P_{t-1}$$

These equations imply

$$P_t - P_{t-1} = \frac{\lambda_1}{1-\lambda_1}(P_t^* - P_t) \quad \text{if } P_t^* > P_t$$

$$P_t - P_{t-1} = \frac{\lambda_2}{1-\lambda_2}(P_t^* - P_t) \quad \text{if } P_t^* < P_t$$

Note first that the conditions $P_t^* > P_{t-1}$, $P_t > P_{t-1}$, $P_t^* > P_t$, and $D_t > S_t$ are all equivalent. Also, assuming that excess demand is proportional to $P_t^* - P_t$, we can write these equations as

$$\Delta P_t = \gamma_1 (D_t - S_t) \quad \text{if } D_t > S_t$$
$$\Delta P_t = \gamma_2 (D_t - S_t) \quad \text{if } D_t < S_t$$

Again, note that we get ΔP_t, and not ΔP_{t+1} in these equations.

Ito and Ueda (1981) used Bowden's formulation with different speeds of adjustment, as given by (10.66), to estimate the rates of adjustment in interest rates for business loans in the United States and Japan. They preferred this formulation to that of Fair and Jaffee or that of Laffont and Garcia because in equation (10.66), λ_1 and λ_2 are pure numbers that can be compared across countries. The same cannot be said about the parameters γ_1 and γ_2 in equation (10.33′).

There is still one disturbing feature about the partial-adjustment equation (10.65) that Bowden adopted and under which we have given a justification for the Fair and Jaffee directional and quantitative methods. This is that ΔP_t unambiguously gives us an idea about whether there is excess demand or excess supply. As mentioned earlier, this does not make intuitive sense. On closer examination, we see that the problem is with equation (10.65), in particular the assumption that λ lies between 0 and 1. This is indeed a very strong assumption, and it implies that prices are sluggish but never change to overshoot P_t^*, the equilibrium prices. There is, however, no a priori reason why this should happen.[7] Once we drop the assumption that λ should lie between 0 and 1, it is no longer true that we can use ΔP_t to classify observations as belonging to excess demand or excess supply. As noted earlier, the assumption $0<\lambda<1$ implies that the conditions $P_t^*>P_{t-1}$, $P_t>P_{t-1}$, $P_t^*>P_t$, and $D_t>S_t$ are all equivalent. With $\lambda>1$, this no longer holds good.

To see the full implications of the partial-adjustment equation (10.65), define Q_t^* as the quantity that would be transacted if the market were to be in equilibrium. Consider the situation in Figure 10.2, where the supply function SS is stable but the demand function shifts to the left. Then $P_t^*<P_{t-1}^*$, and $Q_t^*<Q_{t-1}^*$. As for P_{t-1}, we do not really know whether or not at time $t-1$ the market was in equilibrium. But for any value of P_{t-1} between X and P_t^*, the value of Q_{t-1} will be greater than Q_t^* but less than Q_{t-1}^*. As for Q_t, a partial-adjustment model for P_t given by (10.65) will trace out points along YZ, and so Q_t will be less than Q_t^*. Thus, the partial-adjustment equation for prices given by (10.65) implies a quantity-adjustment equation:

$$Q_t - Q_{t-1} = \mu(Q_t^* - Q_{t-1}) \tag{10.66}$$

where $\mu>1$. Of course, in this particular case, if P_{t-1} is less than P_t^*, then the value of μ in the quantity-adjustment equation (10.66) will also satisfy $0<\mu<1$. But we can show that anything is possible for the parameter μ in the quantity-adjustment equation (10.66).

If Q_t and P_t are simultaneously determined, as the model says they are, then it is inconsistent to have a price-adjustment equation of the form (10.65) in isolation that leads to a quantity-adjustment equation of the form (10.66). The way out of this dilemma is either drop the minimum condition (10.6) or drop the assumption that P_t is endogenous. If we have a market-clearing model, of course, we should not consider equation (10.6) in the first place. But if we are dealing with a rationing

---

[7] Because no economic model has been specified, there is no reason to make any alternative assumption either.

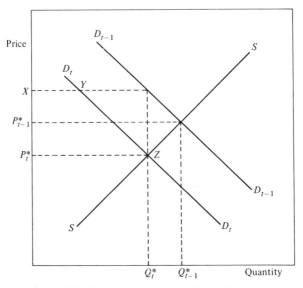

Figure 10.2. Price adjustment and disequilibrium

model, then we have to live with condition (10.6). The logical thing then is to drop equation (10.65). Obviously, equation (10.65) itself implies that prices are being adjusted or set by someone. If this is the case, P_t has to be exogenous, and a price-adjustment equation like (10.33'), suggested by Laffont and Garcia, is more reasonable. But the proper way to look at this equation is as a forecast equation for future prices, in which case equation (10.33') needs some further thinking. The source of disequilibrium now is not imperfect adjustment of prices but imperfect forecasts of market-equilibrating prices.

The preceding discussion refers to alternative formulations of the price-adjustment equation. We can also question the specification of the other equations as well. We shall now discuss alternative specifications of the demand and supply functions. Alternative specifications of the "minimum condition" will be discussed in the next section.

The probability that there will be rationing should affect the demand and supply functions. One such formulation that incorporates this idea in a disequilibrium model with no price adjustment was considered by Eaton and Quandt (1979). The model they considered is as follows:

$$D_t = \beta_1' X_{1t} + \gamma_1 \Pi_t + u_{1t} \quad (\gamma_1 < 0)$$
$$S_t = \beta_2' X_{2t} + u_{2t}$$

$$Q_t = \text{Min}(D_t, S_t)$$
$$\Pi_t = \text{Prob}(D_t > S_t) = \text{Prob}(Q_t = S_t) \tag{10.67}$$

The analysis of this model is similar to that for the usual disequilibrium model,[8] provided we can show that this system of equations determines a unique Π_t for given values of the exogenous variables and the parameters in the system. Eaton and Quandt showed that the solution for Π_t is unique, because $\gamma_1 < 0$. The proof runs as follows:

$$\begin{aligned}
\Pi_t &= \text{Prob}(D_t \leqslant S_t) \\
&= \text{Prob}(u_{2t} - u_{1t} \leqslant \beta_1' X_{1t} - \beta_2' X_{2t} + \gamma_1 \Pi_t) \\
&= \Phi\left(\frac{\beta_1' X_{1t} - \beta_2' X_{2t} + \gamma_1 \Pi_t}{\sigma}\right)
\end{aligned} \tag{10.68}$$

where $\Phi(\cdot)$ is the cumulative distribution function of the standard normal and $\sigma^2 = \text{Var}(u_{1t} - u_{2t})$. Because the right-hand side of (10.68) lies between 0 and 1 and is a monotonically decreasing function of Π_t, and the left-hand side starts at 0 and has a constant slope of 1, we have a unique solution for Π_t in the open interval $(0, 1)$.

If the probability of rationing affects the supply function as well, so that we can write

$$S_t = \beta_2' X_{2t} + \gamma_2(1 - \Pi_t) + u_{2t} \quad (\gamma_2 < 0) \tag{10.69}$$

then it is easy to see that equation (10.68) is changed to

$$\Pi_t = \Phi\left(\frac{\beta_1' X_{1t} - \beta_2' X_{2t} - \gamma_2 + (\gamma_1 + \gamma_2)\Pi_t}{\sigma}\right)$$

and we have a unique solution to Π_t in the open interval $(0, 1)$.

The preceding analysis is for a disequilibrium model with sample separation unknown; as we discussed in a previous section, this poses several problems. However, the same modifications of the demand and supply functions to allow for rationing effects can be done for models with price-adjustment equations where sample separation is known, as discussed earlier in this section. In these models, after some simplifications, we can show that the reduced forms for D_t and S_t are of the same form as equations (10.67) and (10.69), and thus Π_t is uniquely determined. As for estimation, the methods outlined earlier are all valid, except that we substitute $D_t - \gamma_1 \Pi_t$ for D_t and $S_t - \gamma_2(1 - \Pi_t)$ for S_t. We can get estimated values of Π_t once we estimate the reduced-form equa-

----

[8] Although the analysis is similar, the computations are more complex because of the presence of Π_t in the demand function.

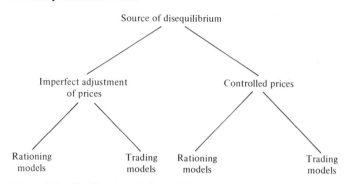

Figure 10.3. Classification of disequilibrium models

tions for D_t and S_t. Note that in this model, because sample separation is known, the reduced-form equations have to be estimated by maximizing the likelihood function for what Fair and Jaffee called the directional method. The likelihood function for this, derived by Maddala and Nelson (1974) and presented in section 10.4, needs to be appropriately modified to include Π_t in both the demand and supply functions, and this does create additional computational problems.

To summarize this section, we have discussed the implications and problems of interpretation with the price-adjustment equations suggested in the recent literature on disequilibrium models, the two-stage and ML estimations of these models, and the modifications of the demand and supply equations to allow for the effects of possible rationing. In the next section we shall discuss some models in which the "minimum condition," valid in only rationing models, needs to be modified as well.

10.7   Models with controlled prices

For convenience of exposition, we can classify the several disequilibrium models in Figure 10.3. By the term *trading models,* we mean models in which

$$Q_t = 0 \quad \text{if } D_t \neq S_t$$

We can also have a combination of rationing elements and trading elements in a particular problem, in which case we have

$$Q_t < \text{Min}(D_t, S_t)$$

Commodity-trading models do not necessarily fall into the category of trading models defined here. On the other hand, models that involve rationing at the aggregate level might fall into the class of trading models defined here at the microlevel. Consider, for instance, the loan-demand problem with interest-rate ceilings. At the aggregate level, there will be an excess demand at the ceiling rate, and there will be rationing. The question is how rationing is carried out. One can argue that for each individual there is a demand schedule giving the loan amounts L the individual will want to borrow at different rates of interest R. Similarly, the bank will also have a supply schedule giving the amounts L it will be willing to lend at different rates of interest R. If the rate of interest at which these two schedules intersect is less than or equal to $\bar{R}$, the ceiling rate, then a transaction takes place. Otherwise, no transaction takes place. This assumption is perhaps more appropriate for mortgage loans than for consumer loans. In this situation, Q is not $\text{Min}(D, S)$. In fact, $Q = 0$ if $D \neq S$. The model can be formulated as follows:

$$\left. \begin{array}{ll} \text{Loan demand:} & L_i = \alpha_1 R_i + \beta_1' X_{1i} + u_{1i} \\ \text{Loan supply:} & L_i = \alpha_2 R_i + \beta_2' X_{2i} + u_{2i} \end{array} \right\} \quad \text{if } R_i^e \leqslant \bar{R}$$

$$L_i = 0 \quad \text{otherwise}$$

R_i^e is the rate of interest that equilibrates demand and supply. If the assumption is that the individual borrows what is offered at the ceiling rate $\bar{R}$, an assumption more appropriate for consumer loans, we have

$$L_i = \alpha_2 \bar{R} - \beta_2' X_{2i} + u_{2i} \quad \text{if } R_i^e > \bar{R}$$

In this case, of course, $Q = \text{Min}(D, S)$, but there is never a case of excess supply.

The most important criticism one can level against the econometric literature on disequilibrium is that usually there is no discussion of why disequilibrium exists in the first place. There are two major sources of disequilibrium: (a) imperfect adjustment of prices and (b) controlled prices. In the preceding section we discussed the case of imperfect adjustment to the market-equilibrating price. In this section we shall discuss the case of controlled prices.

The case of controlled prices is different from the case of fixed prices. The disequilibrium model considered earlier (model 1, section 10.3) is one with fixed prices. With fixed prices, the market is almost always in disequilibrium. With controlled prices, the market is sometimes in equilibrium and sometimes in disequilibrium.[9]

[9] MacKinnon (1978) discussed this problem, but the likelihood functions he presented are incorrect. The correct analysis of this model was presented by Maddala (1979). Further, MacKinnon treated only the "rationing" models.

Consider the following model:

$$D_t = X_{1t}\beta_1 + \alpha_1 P_t + u_{1t}$$
$$S_t = X_{2t}\beta_2 + \alpha_2 P_t + u_{2t} \qquad (10.70)$$

where D_t is quantity demanded, S_t is quantity supplied, P_t is price, X_{1t} and X_{2t} are explanatory variables, and u_{1t} and u_{2t} are residuals that are only contemporaneously correlated. Let P_t be controlled to lie between $\bar{P}_{1t}$ and $\bar{P}_{2t}$ (i.e., $\bar{P}_{1t} < P_t < \bar{P}_{2t}$). The limits are assumed to be exogenous. We shall discuss the case of endogenous limits later. There are several examples of this. In the case of natural gas, $\bar{P}_{2t}$ is the price ceiling. There is no price floor, and hence $\bar{P}_{1t} = -\infty$. In the case of price supports for agricultural commodities, $\bar{P}_{1t}$ is the price floor. There is no price ceiling. Hence, $\bar{P}_{2t} = \infty$. In the case of commodity futures markets, there are both lower and upper limits for the price variation.

In all these models, if the equilibrating price is within the specified limits, we have equilibrium, and the quantity transacted, Q_t, is given by $D_t = S_t = Q_t$. In this case, both P_t and Q_t are endogenous variables. If the price falls outside the specified limits, P_t is exogenous, and we have disequilibrium. We thus have a switching simultaneous system in which P_t is sometimes endogenous and sometimes exogenous. Earlier, Barten and Bronsard (1970) derived some two-stage least-squares estimators for the case in which a regressor may be exogenous or endogenous at different times. Richard (1978) studied some wider aspects of this problem, and Davidson (1978) derived the exact maximum-likelihood estimators for a fairly general class of models involving shifts between the endogenous and exogenous variables. But the switching between regimes considered in these studies was exogenous, rather than endogenous as in the model we are considering; it was a consequence of some abrupt institutional changes or policy changes, such as a shift from fixed to floating exchange rates, a shift in Federal Reserve policy from manipulation of interest rates to control of money supply, and so forth. By contrast, the switch in our model is produced by controls in the market-equilibrating price.

We can classify the observations into three regimes. Figure 10.4 illustrates the three cases.

Regime 1. $\bar{P}_{1t} < P_t < \bar{P}_{2t}$. Denote this set of points by ψ_1. These are the equilibrium points, and Q_t and P_t are both endogenous.

Regime 2. $P_t \geqslant \bar{P}_{2t}$. Denote this set of points by ψ_2. What happens to Q_t depends on whether we are considering a rationing model or a trading model. In the case of natural gas, $Q_t = S_t$ and $D_t \geqslant Q_t$. Also, $\bar{P}_{2t}$ is an

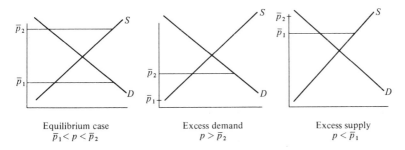

Figure 10.4. Different cases with price controls

exogenous variable. In trading models, because no trading takes place, $Q_t = 0$.

Regime 3. $P_t \leqslant \bar{P}_{1t}$. Denote this set by ψ_3. This set corresponds to excess supply. What happens to Q_t depends on the type of model we are considering. In rationing models, we have $Q_t = D_t$, $S_t \geqslant Q_t$, and $\bar{P}_{1t}$ is exogenous. In the case of agricultural price supports, we observe both D_t and S_t in this regime, because we know the market demand and the surplus purchased by the government. In the case of trading models, because no trading takes place, we have $Q_t = 0$.

The appropriate likelihood functions for the different classes of models are as follows. For a model with price ceiling and rationing, the likelihood function is

$$L = \prod_{\psi_1} f(Q_t, P_t) \cdot \prod_{\psi_2} \int_{Q_t}^{\infty} g(D_t, Q_t) \, dD_t \qquad (10.71)$$

where $f(Q_t, P_t)$ is the joint density of Q_t and P_t derived from the joint density of (u_1, u_2), as in any simultaneous-equations model, and $g(D_t, S_t)$ is the joint density of D_t and S_t derived from the joint density of (u_1, u_2), treating $P_t = \bar{P}$ as exogenous. Note that the Jacobian of transformation for $f(Q_t, P_t)$ is $|\alpha_1 - \alpha_2|$, which is expected to be nonzero, because α_1 and α_2 have opposite signs and are nonzero. The Jacobian of transformation for $g(D_t, S_t)$ is, of course, unity.

For a model with price supports, as in agricultural commodity programs (no rationing), the likelihood function is

$$L = \prod_{\psi_1} f(Q_t, P_t) \prod_{\psi_3} g(D_t, S_t)$$

where $f(Q_t, P_t)$ is as defined in (10.71), and $g(D_t, S_t)$ is the joint density of D_t and S_t derived from the joint density of (u_1, u_2), treating $P_t = P_{1t}$ as exogenous.

For a model with both price ceilings and price floors and rationing, the likelihood function is

$$L = \prod_{\psi_1} f(Q_t, P_t) \cdot \prod_{\psi_2} \int_Q^\infty g_2(D_t, Q_t)\, dD_t \cdot \prod_{\psi_3} \int_Q^\infty g_1(Q_t, S_t)\, dS_t \qquad (10.72)$$

where g_1 and g_2 are the joint densities of D_t and S_t derived from (10.70) after substituting $P_t = \bar{P}_{2t}$.

For a trading model in which no transactions take place,[10] if there is excess demand or excess supply, the likelihood function is

$$L = \prod_{\psi_1} f(Q_t, P_t) \prod_{\psi_2} \int_{\bar{P}_{2t}}^\infty g(P_t)\, dP_t \prod_{\psi_3} \int_{-\infty}^{\bar{P}_{1t}} g(P_t)\, dP_t \qquad (10.73)$$

where $g(P_t)$ is the distribution of the equilibrium price P_t, that is, the distribution of P_t derived from the reduced-form equation for P_t implied by the structural equations (10.70).

In practice, with commodity trading, there will be a series of trades that take place at different prices within the admissible range $\bar{P}_{1t} \leqslant P_t \leqslant \bar{P}_{2t}$. In this case, all we observe is Q_t (the total volume of trading), and all we know is that price P_t is within the admissible range. In this case, the first term in the likelihood function (10.73) should be changed to

$$\prod_{\psi} \int_{\bar{P}_{1t}}^{\bar{P}_{2t}} f(Q_t, P_t)\, dP_t$$

Note that here we have a simultaneous-equations model with two endogenous variables P_t and Q_t. Q_t is observed only if P_t is within a specified range, and P_t is observed only in a qualitative way: to which of the three different sets does it belong? The parameters of the demand and supply functions (10.70) can be estimated with these data.[11]

[10] As we explained earlier, a trading model does not necessarily mean a commodity-trading model in which there is a sequence of trades in a day. It merely means models in which $Q_t = 0$ if $D_t \neq S_t$.

[11] Actually, in studies on commodity trading, the total number of contracts is treated as Q_t and the closing price for the day as P_t. The closing price is perhaps closer to an equilibrium price than the opening, low, and high prices. But it cannot be treated as an equilibrium price. There is the question of what we mean by equilibrium price in a situation in which a number of trades take place in a day. One can interpret it as the price that would prevail if there were to be a Walrasian auctioneer and a single trade took place for a day. If that is the case, then the closing price will be an equilibrium price only if a day is a long enough period for prices at the different trades to converge to some equilibrium. These problems need further work.

We shall now review two-stage methods and estimation of the market-equilibrating price if controls are removed, as discussed by Maddala (1979). Consider the rationing model with price ceilings and price floors, for which the likelihood function is given by (10.72). The reduced form for P_t, which we estimate by the two-limit tobit method, is

$$P_t = \bar{P}_{1t} \quad \text{if } P_t \leqslant \bar{P}_{1t}$$
$$P_t = \Pi X_t + v_t \quad \text{if } \bar{P}_{1t} < P_t < \bar{P}_{2t}$$
$$P_t = \bar{P}_{2t} \quad \text{if } P_t \geqslant \bar{P}_{2t} \tag{10.74}$$

After we get the tobit estimates of Π and σ_v, we next get predicted values of P_t for the observations in regime 1. Define

$$Z_{1t} = \frac{\bar{P}_{1t} - \Pi X_t}{\sigma_v} \quad \text{and} \quad Z_{2t} = \frac{\bar{P}_{2t} - \Pi X_t}{\sigma_v}$$

Then $E(P_t)$ in regime 1 is given by

$$E(P_t \mid \bar{P}_{1t} < P_t < \bar{P}_{2t}) = \Pi X_t - \sigma_v \frac{\phi(Z_{2t}) - \phi(Z_{1t})}{\Phi(Z_{2t}) - \Phi(Z_{1t})} \tag{10.75}$$

Our next step will be to adjust for the means of the residuals u_{1t} and u_{2t} in the different regimes.

Note that the parameters of the demand function are estimated from observations in regimes 1 and 3, and the parameters of the supply function are estimated from observations in regimes 1 and 2. We have the following expressions for the expectations of u_{1t} and u_{2t} in the different regimes. Denote $\sigma_{1v} = \text{Cov}(u_{1t}, v_t)$ and $\sigma_{2v} = \text{Cov}(u_{2t}, v_t)$. Let us, for compactness, define

$$W_{1t} = \frac{-\phi(Z_{2t}) + \phi(Z_{1t})}{\Phi(Z_{2t}) - \Phi(Z_{1t})}$$

$$W_{2t} = \frac{\phi(Z_{2t})}{1 - \Phi(Z_{2t})}$$

and

$$W_{3t} = -\frac{\phi(Z_{1t})}{\Phi(Z_{1t})}$$

Then,

$$E(u_{jt} \mid t \in \psi_1) = \frac{\sigma_{jv}}{\sigma_v} W_{1t} \quad (j = 1, 2)$$

$$E(u_{2t} \mid t \in \psi_2) = \frac{\sigma_{2v}}{\sigma_v} W_{2t}$$

$$E(u_{1t} \mid t \in \psi_3) = \frac{\sigma_{1v}}{\sigma_v} W_{3t}$$

Substituting these expressions in the demand and supply functions, we can write them as follows.

Demand functions:

$$Q_t = X'_{1t}\beta_1 + \alpha_1 P_t + \frac{\sigma_{1v}}{\sigma_v} W_{1t} + \epsilon_{1t} \quad \text{for } t \text{ in } \psi_1$$

$$Q_t = X'_{1t}\beta_1 + \alpha_1 \bar{P}_{1t} + \frac{\sigma_{1v}}{\sigma_v} W_{3t} + \epsilon_{1t} \quad \text{for } t \text{ in } \psi_3$$

(10.76)

Supply functions:

$$Q_t = X'_{2t}\beta_2 + \alpha_2 P_t + \frac{\sigma_{2v}}{\sigma_v} W_{1t} + \epsilon_{2t} \quad \text{for } t \text{ in } \psi_1$$

$$Q_t = X'_{2t}\beta_2 + \alpha_2 \bar{P}_{2t} + \frac{\sigma_{2v}}{\sigma_v} W_{2t} + \epsilon_{2t} \quad \text{for } t \text{ in } \psi_2$$

The new residuals ϵ_{1t} and ϵ_{2t} have zero means. The tobit two-stage method is as follows: We first estimate Π and σ_v from (10.74). Next, we get estimates of Z_{1t} and Z_{2t} and an estimate of P_t in regime 1 from (10.75). We then substitute $\hat{P}_t$ for P_t, $\hat{W}_{1t}$ for W_{1t}, $\hat{W}_{2t}$ for W_{2t}, and $\hat{W}_{3t}$ for W_{3t} in equations (10.76). We then estimate the demand functions together, using observations in ψ_1 and ψ_3, and the supply functions together, using observations in ψ_1 and ψ_2. We now have consistent estimates of $\beta_1, \beta_2, \alpha_1, \alpha_2, \sigma_{1v}, \sigma_{2v}$, and σ_v. The tobit two-stage least-squares estimates are consistent. Their asymptotic covariance matrix, however, is complicated. It can be obtained following the methods of Amemiya (1978b) and Lee et al. (1980). The two-stage estimates can be used as initial values in the iterative solution of the likelihood equations. We have not described the method of obtaining estimates of σ_1^2, σ_2^2, and σ_{12} in the two-stage method, but it can be done following the procedures in Chapter 8.

In this model, so long as there are enough observations in ψ_2 and ψ_3, we do not need the usual exclusion restrictions for identification of either the demand function or the supply function. This is easy to see from equation (10.76). For estimation of the demand function from observations in ψ_2, price is exogenous. The two-stage estimation method can be simplified in cases in which ψ_2 or ψ_3 is empty. For instance, in the case of only price ceilings, ψ_3 is empty. In this case the variables for the supply equation are observed for all the observations. Hence, we can use the usual two-stage least-squares method to estimate the parameters of the supply function (Gourieroux and Monfort, 1980). Similarly, when we have only price floors, we have all observations on the demand function, and we can estimate it by the usual two-stage procedure. (In both cases, the reduced form for P_t is, of course, estimated by the tobit method.)

The two-stage method can be extended to the case of trading models. Consider the model with price ceilings and price floors for which the likelihood function is given in (10.73). In this case, Q_t is not observed in ψ_2 or ψ_3. Thus, in equation (10.76) we use only observations in ψ_1. The estimation of the reduced form for P_t is as before. The conditions for identification of the demand and supply functions in this model are the same as those in the usual simultaneous-equations model.

Finally, one can estimate what the equilibrium price will be if there are no price ceilings or price floors in the regimes for which the controls are operative. These are given by

$$E(P_t \mid P_t \leqslant P_{1t}) = \Pi X_t + \sigma_v W_{3t}$$

and

$$E(P_t \mid P_t \geqslant P_{2t}) = \Pi X_t + \sigma_v W_{2t}$$

where W_{2t} and W_{3t} are as defined earlier. For the values of Π, we can use the reduced-form estimates. The same formulas can be used for the trading models.

The foregoing analysis can easily be extended to the case in which we have no observations on P_t for the equilibrium points. We do have information on $\bar{P}_{1t}$ and $\bar{P}_{2t}$, and we also know which observations belong to regimes 1, 2, and 3. In this case the likelihood function to be maximized is

$$L = \prod_{\psi_1} h(Q_t) \prod_{\psi_2} \int_{Q_t}^{\infty} g_2(D_t, Q_t)\, dD_t \prod_{\psi_3} \int_{Q_t}^{\infty} g_1(Q_t, S_t)\, dS_t \qquad (10.77)$$

where $h(Q_t)$ is the reduced-form equation for Q_t derived from equations (10.70). The only difference between the likelihood functions (10.72) and (10.77) is in the first expression. Although $h(Q_t)$ involves only the reduced-form parameters, the other two expressions in the likelihood function (10.77) enable us to estimate all the structural parameters. Once the structural parameters have been estimated, the prediction of P_t proceeds as before.

There is a difference, however, in the way the initial estimates of Π and σ_v are computed. In this case we do not observe P_t at all. All we know are the numbers of observations that are less than or equal to $\bar{P}_{1t}$, between $\bar{P}_{1t}$ and $\bar{P}_{2t}$, and equal to or greater than $\bar{P}_{2t}$. We can now use the two-limit probit method described by Rosett and Nelson (1975) to get estimates of Π and σ_v. Once this is done, the rest of the two-stage estimation proceeds as in the preceding section.

The preceding discussion refers to models in which the controlled prices $\bar{P}_{1t}$ and $\bar{P}_{2t}$ are exogenous. There are many situations in practice in which the limits are not exactly fixed. What we have are some rules. The exact level at which price controls are imposed depends on some firm-specific historical data. Some price controls depend on transportation costs, and so forth. In view of this, it is more meaningful to assume the price limits as stochastic.[12]

For simplicity, consider the model with price ceiling P_t^c only. Then, in addition to equations (10.70), we assume

$$P_t^c = \beta_3' X_{3t} + u_{3t} \tag{10.78}$$

If u_{3t} is correlated with u_{1t} and u_{2t}, then we term the ceiling price P_t^c endogenous. The analysis of this model is straightforward. Denote by P_t^* the price that equilibrates D_t to S_t, as given by equations (10.70). If Q_t, P_t, and P_t^* are all observed, then we have a switching simultaneous-equations model with (a) Q_t, P_t, and P_t^c as the three endogenous variables if $P_t^* < P_t^c$ or (b) D_t, S_t, and P_t^c as the three endogenous variables if $P_t^* > P_t^c$. In this case, we substitute P_t^c for P_t in equations (10.70) and note that $S_t = Q_t$ and $D_t > Q_t$. The likelihood function is similar to (10.71), except that there is another variable P_t^c in each of the expressions.

In the case in which P_t^c is not observed, but we know when controls are operative and when not, the appropriate likelihood function is that given by (10.71), except that in equations for D and S in (10.70) we substitute $\beta_3' X_{3t} + u_{3t}$ for P_t. The case in which we do not know when controls are operative or not operative falls in the category of the disequilibrium models with sample separation unknown. The likelihood function in this case can be easily derived. In summary, given only the determinants X_{3t} of the price ceilings P_t^c, and observations on P_t and Q_t, we can estimate these models with controlled prices, even when no data are available on the exact level of the controlled prices.

Perhaps the most interesting applications of disequilibrium models are in the area of regulated industries. After all, it is regulations that produce disequilibrium in these markets. The models described in this section are

---

[12] Models with endogenous price limits have been analyzed by Gourieroux and Monfort (1980). Models in which lagged values of D_t and S_t occur can be analyzed in a manner similar to that described by Laffont and Monfort (1979).

appropriate for analysis of these markets. However, as yet there have been no empirical studies applying the models described.

10.8   Tests for disequilibrium

There have been many tests suggested for the "disequilibrium hypothesis," that is, to test whether the data have been generated by an equilibrium model or a disequilibrium model. Quandt (1978b) discussed several tests and said that there does not exist a uniformly best procedure for testing the hypothesis that a market is in equilibrium against the alternative that it is not.

A good starting point for all tests for disequilibrium is to ask the basic question: What causes the disequilibrium? In the case of the partial-adjustment model given by equation (10.65), the disequilibrium is clearly due to imperfect adjustment of prices. In this case the proper test for the equilibrium versus disequilibrium hypothesis is to test whether or not $\lambda = 1$. As discussed in section 10.6, this leads to a test that $1/\gamma = 0$ in the Fair and Jaffee quantitative model, because γ is proportional to $\lambda/(1-\lambda)$. This is the procedure Fair and Jaffee suggested. However, if the meaning of the price-adjustment equation is that prices adjust in response to either excess demand or excess supply, then, as argued in section 10.6, the price-adjustment equation should have ΔP_{t+1}, not ΔP_t, and also it is not clear how one can test for the equilibrium hypothesis in this case. The intuitive reason is that now the price-adjustment equation does not give any information about the source of the disequilibrium.

Quandt (1978b) argued that there are two classes of disequilibrium models: (a) models in which it is known for which observations $D_t < S_t$ and for which $D_t > S_t$ (i.e., the sample separation is known), and (b) models in which such information is not available. He said that in case (a) the question of testing for disequilibrium does not arise at all; it is only in case (b) that it makes sense.

The example of the partial-adjustment model (10.65) is a case in which we have sample separation given by ΔP_t. However, it still makes sense to test for the disequilibrium hypothesis, which in this case merely translates to a hypothesis about the speed of adjustment of prices to levels that equilibrate demand and supply. Adding a stochastic term u_{3t} to the price-adjustment equation does not change the test. When $\lambda = 1$, this says that $P_t = P_t^* + u_{3t}$.

There was considerable discussion in Quandt's study on the question of the nested versus nonnested hypothesis. Quandt argued that very often the hypothesis of equilibrium versus disequilibrium is nonnested;

that is, the parameter set under the null hypothesis that the model is an equilibrium model is not a subset of the parameter set for the disequilibrium model. The problem in these cases may be that there is no adequate explanation of why disequilibrium exists in the first place.

Consider, for instance, the disequilibrium model with the demand and supply functions specified by equations (10.70). Quandt argued that if one takes the limit of the likelihood function for this model, with the price-adjustment equation being

$$\Delta P_t = \gamma(D_t - S_t) + u_{3t} \qquad (10.79)$$

and $\sigma_{23} = \text{Cov}(u_2, u_3) = 0$, $\sigma_{13} = \text{Cov}(u_1, u_3) = 0$, $\sigma_3^2 \neq 0$, and $\gamma \to \infty$, then we get the likelihood function for the equilibrium model ($Q_t = D_t = S_t$), and thus the hypothesis is nested, but that if $\sigma_3^2 = 0$, the likelihood function for the disequilibrium model does not tend to the likelihood function for the equilibrium model even if $\gamma \to \infty$, and thus the hypothesis is not nested. The latter conclusion, however, is counterintuitive, and if we consider the correct likelihood function for this model, as derived by Amemiya (1974) and presented in equation (10.34), and if we take the limits as $\gamma \to \infty$, we get the likelihood function for the equilibrium model.

Quandt also showed that if the price-adjustment equation is changed to

$$\Delta P_{t+1} = \gamma(D_t - S_t) + u_{3t} \qquad (10.80)$$

then the limit of the likelihood function of the disequilibrium model as $\gamma \to \infty$ is not the likelihood function for the equilibrium model. This makes intuitive sense, and it is also clear when we look at the likelihood functions derived in section 10.6. In this case the hypothesis is nonnested, but the problem is that, as discussed earlier, this price-adjustment equation does not tell us anything about what causes the disequilibrium. As shown in section 10.6, the price-adjustment equation (10.79) follows from the partial-adjustment equation (10.65), and thus it throws light on what causes the disequilibrium; but the price-adjustment equation (10.80) says nothing about the source of the disequilibrium. If we view the equation as a forecast equation, then the disequilibrium is due to imperfect forecasts of the market-equilibrating price. In this case it is clear that as $\gamma \to \infty$, we do not get perfect forecasts. What we need in order to have a nested model is a forecasting equation that for some limiting values of some parameters yields perfect forecasts at the market-equilibrating prices.

Consider now the case in which we do not have a price-adjustment equation and the model consists merely of a demand equation and a supply equation. Now, clearly the source of the disequilibrium is that P_t

is exogenous. Hence, the test boils down to testing whether P_t is exogenous or endogenous. The methods developed by Wu (1973) and Hausman (1978) will be of use here.

In summary, tests for disequilibrium should be based on a discussion of the source of disequilibrium. The test will then be a test of a nested hypothesis, and what the appropriate test is will be obvious from a statement of the problem. For some alternative methods of testing for disequilibrium, see the studies of Hwang (1980) and Ducos et al. (1981).

10.9 Multimarket-disequilibrium models

The analysis in the preceding sections on single market-disequilibrium models has been extended to multimarket-disequilibrium models by Gourieroux et al. (1980a) and Ito (1980). Quandt (1978a) first considered a market-disequilibrium model with two markets of the following form (the exogenous variables are omitted):

$$D_{1t} = \alpha_1 Q_{2t} + U_{1t}$$
$$S_{1t} = \beta_1 Q_{2t} + U_{2t}$$
$$D_{2t} = \alpha_2 Q_{1t} + V_{1t}$$
$$S_{2t} = \beta_2 Q_{1t} + V_{2t} \qquad (10.81)$$

$$Q_{1t} = \text{Min}(D_{1t}, S_{1t})$$
$$Q_{2t} = \text{Min}(D_{2t}, S_{2t}) \qquad (10.82)$$

Quandt did not consider the logical consistency of the model. This was considered by Amemiya (1977b) and Gourieroux et al. (1980a). Consider the regimes

$$R_1: \quad D_1 \geqslant S_1, \quad D_2 \geqslant S_2$$
$$R_2: \quad D_1 \geqslant S_1, \quad D_2 < S_2$$
$$R_3: \quad D_1 < S_1, \quad D_2 < S_2$$
$$R_4: \quad D_1 < S_1, \quad D_2 \geqslant S_2 \qquad (10.83)$$

In regime 1, we have $Q_1 = S_1$ and $Q_2 = S_2$, and substituting these in (10.81), we have

$$A_1 \begin{bmatrix} D_1 \\ S_1 \\ D_2 \\ S_2 \end{bmatrix} = \begin{bmatrix} 1 & 0 & 0 & -\alpha_1 \\ 0 & 1 & 0 & -\beta_1 \\ 0 & -\alpha_2 & 1 & 0 \\ 0 & -\beta_2 & 0 & 1 \end{bmatrix} \begin{bmatrix} D_1 \\ S_1 \\ D_2 \\ S_2 \end{bmatrix} = \begin{bmatrix} u_1 \\ u_2 \\ u_3 \\ u_4 \end{bmatrix}$$

Similarly, we can define the corresponding matrices A_2, A_3, and A_4 in regimes R_2, R_3, and R_4, respectively, that give the mapping from (D_1, S_1, D_2, S_2) to (u_1, u_2, u_3, u_4):

$$A_2 = \begin{bmatrix} 1 & 0 & -\alpha_1 & 0 \\ 0 & 1 & -\beta_1 & 0 \\ 0 & -\alpha_2 & 1 & 0 \\ 0 & -\beta_2 & 0 & 1 \end{bmatrix}, \quad A_3 = \begin{bmatrix} 1 & 0 & -\alpha_1 & 0 \\ 0 & 1 & -\beta_1 & 0 \\ -\alpha_2 & 0 & 1 & 0 \\ -\beta_2 & 0 & 0 & 1 \end{bmatrix}$$

$$A_4 = \begin{bmatrix} 1 & 0 & 0 & -\alpha_1 \\ 0 & 1 & 0 & -\beta_1 \\ -\alpha_2 & 0 & 1 & 0 \\ -\beta_2 & 0 & 0 & 1 \end{bmatrix}$$

The logical-consistency or coherency conditions derived by Gourieroux et al. are that the determinants of these four matrices, $(1-\beta_1\beta_2)$, $(1-\alpha_2\beta_1)$, $(1-\alpha_1\alpha_2)$, $(1-\alpha_1\beta_2)$, must have the same sign.

The major problem that the multimarket-disequilibrium models are supposed to throw light on [which the model in equations (10.81) and (10.82) does not] involves the spillover effects – the effects of unsatisfied demand or supply in one market on the demand and supply in other markets. Much of the discussion of spillover effects has been in the context of macromodels; the two markets considered are the commodity market and the labor market. The commodity market is supplied by producers and consumed by households. Labor is supplied by households and used by producers. The quantities actually transacted are given by

$$C = \text{Min}(C^d, C^s)$$
$$L = \text{Min}(L^d, L^s) \tag{10.84}$$

The demands and supplies actually presented in each market are called "effective" demands and supplies, and these are determined by the exogenous variables and the endogenous quantity constraints (10.84). By contrast, the "notional" demands and supplies refer to the unconstrained values. Denote these by $\bar{C}^d$, $\bar{C}^s$, $\bar{L}^d$, $\bar{L}^s$. The different models of multimarket disequilibrium differ in the way the effective demands and spillover effects are defined.

Model I. Gourieroux et al. (1980a) defined the effective demands and spillover effects as follows:

$$C^d = \bar{C}^d \quad \text{if } L = L^s \leq L^d$$
$$C^d = \bar{C}^d + \alpha_1(L - \bar{L}^s) \quad \text{if } L = L^d < L^s \tag{10.85}$$
$$C^s = \bar{C}^s \quad \text{if } L = L^d \leq L^s$$

$$C^s = \bar{C}^s + \alpha_2(L - \bar{L}^d) \quad \text{if } L = L^s < L^d \tag{10.86}$$

$$L^d = \bar{L}^d \quad \text{if } C = C^s \leqslant C^d$$
$$L^d = \bar{L}^d + \beta_1(C - \bar{C}^s) \quad \text{if } C = C^d < C^s \tag{10.87}$$

$$L^s = \bar{L}^s \quad \text{if } C = C^d \leqslant C^s$$
$$L^s = \bar{L}^s + \beta_2(C - C^d) \quad \text{if } C = C^s < C^d \tag{10.88}$$

This specification is based on the work of Clower (1965) and Malinvaud (1977) and assumes that agents on the short side of the market present their notional demand as their effective demand in the other market. For instance, equation (10.85) says that if households are able to sell all the labor they want to, then their effective demand for goods is the same as their notional demand. On the other hand, if they cannot sell all the labor they want to, there is a spillover effect, but note that this is proportional to $L - \bar{L}^s$, not $L - L^s$ (i.e., it is proportional to the difference between actual labor sold and the notional supply of labor).

Model II. The model considered by Ito (1980) is as follows:

$$C^d = \bar{C}^d + \alpha_1(L - \bar{L}^s) \tag{10.85'}$$
$$C^s = \bar{C}^s + \alpha_2(L - \bar{L}^d) \tag{10.86'}$$
$$L^d = \bar{L}^d + \beta_1(C - \bar{C}^s) \tag{10.87'}$$
$$L^s = \bar{L}^s + \beta_2(C - \bar{C}^d) \tag{10.88'}$$

Model III. An alternative model suggested by Portes (1977), based on work by Benassy, is the following:

$$C^d = \bar{C}^d + \alpha_1(L - L^s) \tag{10.85''}$$
$$C^s = \bar{C}^s + \alpha_2(L - L^d) \tag{10.86''}$$
$$L^d = \bar{L}^d + \beta_1(C - C^s) \tag{10.87''}$$
$$L^s = \bar{L}^s + \beta_2(C - C^d) \tag{10.88''}$$

Portes compared the reduced forms for these three models and argued that econometrically there is little to choose between the alternative definitions of effective demand.

The conditions for logical consistency (or coherency) are the same in all the models: $0 < \alpha_i\beta_j < 1$ for $i, j = 1, 2$. Both Gourieroux et al. (1980a) and Ito (1980) derived these conditions, suggested price- and wage-adjustment equations similar to those considered in section 10.6, and discussed the maximum-likelihood estimation of their models. Ito also discussed two-stage estimation, similar to that proposed by Amemiya for the Fair and Jaffee model, and derived sufficient conditions for the uniqueness of a quantity-constrained equilibrium in his model. We cannot go into the details of all these derivations here. The details involve more of algebra than any new conceptual problems in estimation. In particular, the problems mentioned in section 10.6 concerning the different price-adjustment equations apply here as well. There is as yet no empirical example illustrating the estimation of these multimarket-disequilibrium models. There is, on the other hand, an enormous amount of theoretical literature in this area. One major problem, from the empirical point of view, is that discussion of the multimarket-disequilibrium models has been entirely in the context of a macromodel. Thus, when people think of an empirical application, they think of a macromodel. Here the problems of aggregation are very important, and it is not true that the whole economy switches from a regime of excess demand to one of excess supply or vice versa. Only some segments might behave that way. The implications of aggregation for econometric estimation have been studied in some simple models by Malinvaud (1981).

The problems of spillover also tend to arise more at the microlevel than at the macrolevel. For instance, consider two commodities that are substitutes in consumption (say natural gas and coal), one of which has price controls. We can define the demand and supply functions in the two markets (omitting the exogenous variables) as follows:

$$D_1 = \alpha_1 P_1 + \beta_1 P_2 + u_1$$
$$S_1 = \alpha_2 P_1 + u_2 \quad (P_1 \leqslant \bar{P})$$
$$Q_1 = \text{Min}(D_1, S_1)$$
$$D_2 = \gamma_1 P_2 + \delta_1 P_1 + \lambda(D_1 - S_1) V_1$$
$$S_2 = \gamma_2 P_2 + V_2$$
$$Q_2 = D_2 = S_2$$

(i.e., the second market is always in equilibrium). If $P_1 \leqslant \bar{P}$, we have the usual simultaneous-equations model with the two quantities and two prices as the endogenous variables. If $P_1 > \bar{P}$, then there is excess demand in the first market and a spillover of this into the second market. This model is still in a partial-equilibrium framework, but it will have interesting empirical applications. It is at least one step forward from the market-disequilibrium model with a single market, which does not say what happens to the unsatisfied demand or supply.

In actual practice, the unsatisfied demand spills over to other markets. But it will also spill over into future trading sessions of the same market. This implies that the demand function is of the form

$$D_t = \beta_1' X_t + \alpha(D_{t-1} - S_{t-1}) + u_t$$

However, models that consider such "intertemporal" spillovers are more difficult to estimate than those that consider contemporaneous spillovers into other markets.

10.10   Models for regulated markets and models for centrally planned economies

In the preceding sections we have reviewed the recent literature on disequilibrium, the cornerstone of which is the "minimum condition." One of the most disturbing points in the empirical applications is that the models have been mechanically applied, with no discussion of what causes disequilibrium and what the consequences are. In spite of all the limitations mentioned in section 10.3, the model discussed there as model 1 (with slight variation) has been the model with the most empirical applications. For instance, Sealey (1979) used the model to study credit rationing in the commercial-loan market. Portes and Winter (1978) used it to estimate demand for money and savings functions in centrally planned economies (Czechoslovakia, East Germany, Hungary, and Poland). Portes and Winter (1980) used it to study the demand for consumption goods in centrally planned economies. Chambers et al. (1978) used it to study the effects of import quotas on the U.S. beef market. Chambers et al. (1979) used it to study the impact of market regulation in the class 1 dairy-product market in California.

The reason for the popularity of this model is that it requires us to specify very little. The authors of the studies cited specified the demand and supply functions as usual, and then said that there was rationing and disequilibrium because of regulations. But even if the regulations control prices, this does not imply that prices are fixed at certain levels continuously, which is what the model given in equations (10.11) says. Further, there has been no discussion of how the rationing is carried out, and in almost all cases the data used have been macrodata; also, the implications of aggregation have been ignored.

The main application of the method developed here is to regulated markets and centrally planned economies, where there are price and quantity regulations. In section 10.7 we discussed the case of controlled prices and showed how the analysis can be applied to credit markets with interest-rate ceilings (or, equivalently, labor markets with minimum-wage laws).[13] We shall not repeat the arguments presented here.

The case of centrally planned economies has been analyzed by Charemza and Quandt (1982). What they assumed is that the central planners adjust the planned level of output Q_t^* depending on whether

[13]   An application of these models to the analysis of discrimination in loan markets can be found in the work of Maddala and Trost (1982). There, data on home-mortgage loans in Columbia, South Carolina, were analyzed by conventional methods and by the disequilibrium models presented here, and the latter produced more meaningful results. The results regarding the discrimination variables were also quite different. The detailed results need not be reproduced here.

there is excess demand or excess supply and that the planned level of output Q_t^* affects both the actual demand and supply. (What happens to the excess supply? Does it go into next period's supply?)

At first, Charemza and Quandt included Q_t^* in D_t and S_t (i.e., the planned levels have a contemporaneous effect) and argued that the model needed a coherency condition. The problem here is more basic. How can D_t and S_t depend on Q_t^* and the planners make a plan based on D_t and S_t, which cannot be observed until Q_t^* is fixed? Later, they changed the model to the case in which Q_{t-1}^* determines D_t and S_t, which in turn determine Q_t^*. In this latter (more reasonable) model, the coherency condition is automatically satisfied.[14]

The model formulated by Charemza and Quandt is

$$D_t = \beta_1' X_{1t} + \alpha_1 Q_{t-1}^* + u_{1t}$$
$$S_t = \beta_2' X_{2t} + \alpha_2 Q_{t-1}^* + u_{2t}$$
$$Q_t = \text{Min}(D_t, S_t)$$
$$Q_t^* = Q_{t-1}^* + \gamma(D_t - S_t) + u_{3t} \qquad (10.89)$$
$$Q_t^* = Q_t + \gamma(D_t - S_t) + u_{3t} \qquad (10.89')$$

Equations (10.89) and (10.89') are two formulations of the process by which "planned output" is determined.

The derivation of the likelihood function proceeds along the lines presented in previous sections and will not be elaborated here. Charemza and Quandt also included the price variable in D_t and S_t and added a price-adjustment equation of the form

$$p_t - p_{t-1} = \lambda(D_t - S_t) + u_{4t}$$

They also considered some alternative price-adjustment equations. In each case the likelihood function has to be maximized by numerical maximization methods.

Although these formulations provide an improvement over the studies of Portes and Winter, there are still some questions about the practical usefulness of this model. There are two main questions: What happens to unsatisfied demand or unsold goods? The answer depends on whether we are talking of durable or nondurable goods. Thus, the modeling should first consider what sorts of markets one is considering. The second point (a more basic one) concerns the purpose of the model itself: Is it to estimate how planners actually set their targets, or is it something else? Is the

[14] This illustrates the point repeatedly made earlier that it is better to examine the formulation of the model rather than impose the coherency or logical-consistency conditions extraneously.

purpose only a descriptive one, or is the model to be used for policy conclusions as well? If so, how? Equations (10.89) and (10.89′) say that planners use information on $(D_t - S_t)$ to set Q_t^* but we do not have this information (this assumption seems somewhat far-fetched). Our purpose in this case will be to test whether or not planners do use this information. Presumably there is more information on how planners set their targets and also on the amount of unsold goods (in the case of excess supply) than is postulated in the model.

In any case, before a model is presented and estimated, it will be useful to elaborate the following factors: (a) the purpose of the model, (b) the setting of the market under consideration, and (c) the data that we, the analysts, have access to and the data that the decision makers have access to.

10.11 Summary and conclusions

The econometric methods that have been reviewed in this chapter have been criticized recently in two studies by Richard (1980) and Hendry and Spanos (1980). Hendry and Spanos pointed out that the "minimum condition" was actually discussed by Frisch (1949), but that he suggested formulation of "market pressures" that are generated by the inequality between the unobserved latent variables D_t and S_t. These pressures were formulated in the price-adjustment equations discussed in section 10.6, but we also saw the serious limitations of this equation in the presence of the minimum condition.[15] Hendry and Spanos suggested dropping the minimum condition (which is the main source of all the headaches in estimation), concentrating on the "pressures" and dynamic adjustment processes, and modeling the observables directly. Although there is some merit in their argument, the main application of the method described in this chapter is to the analysis of regulated markets and planned economies, and the methods suggested by Hendry and Spanos are not applicable to such problems. Their model, specifically, is as follows: For observed prices, we postulate the equations (all observed variables have tildes above them)

$$p_t = a_0 + a_1 \tilde{p}_{t-1} + a_2 [\tilde{q}_t - d_t(\tilde{p}_t)] + a_3 [s_t(\tilde{p}_t) - \tilde{q}_{t-1}] + a_4 (\eta_t^o - \eta_{t-1})$$
$$(10.90)$$

where

$$d_t(p) = a_0 p_t + a_1' \tilde{z}_t^d + u_{1t}$$
$$s_t(p) = b_0 p_t + b_1' \tilde{z}_t^s + u_{2t}$$

[15] There are some pressure variables in the equations for D_t and S_t as they are formulated in (10.67) and (10.69).

$$\eta_t^o = \sum_{\tau=t-s}^{t} \frac{\tilde{\eta}_\tau}{s} \quad (s>0, \ \tilde{\eta}_t = \text{observed inventories})$$

$$\tilde{p}_{t'} = p_{t'} + \epsilon_{1t} \quad (t' \geqslant t)$$

Equation (10.90) suggests that prices at time t are determined by the observed price at $t-1$, the two pressures of excess demand and supply, and the difference between observed inventories at $t-1$ and some optimum level of inventories η_t^o. As can be seen from (10.90), the excess supply pressure is created by comparing this period's plans and observed quantities transacted at $t-1$. This can be easily justified on various grounds, the simplest of which is that suppliers take longer to respond to quantity changes by changing the price. Also, the reason for the presence of the inventories term in (10.90) is that prices in real life do not jump up and down every time there is an excess demand or supply, but price changes occur so long as accumulated inventories do not reach an optimum level η_t^o (in the foregoing specification, chosen to be some sort of average over the last s periods).

Similarly, we can postulate the following specification for observed quantities:

$$q_t = \beta_0 + \beta_1 \tilde{q}_{t-1} + \beta_2 [\tilde{p}_t - p_t^d(\tilde{q}_t)] + \beta_3 [p_t^s(\tilde{q}_t) - \tilde{p}_{t-1}] + \beta_4 (\tilde{\eta}_{t-1} - \tilde{q}_{t-1}) \tag{10.91}$$

where

$$p_t^d(q) = \frac{1}{\alpha_0} q - \frac{\alpha_1'}{\alpha_0} \tilde{z}_t^d - \frac{1}{\alpha_0} u_{1t}$$

$$p_t^s(q) = \frac{1}{b_0} q - \frac{b_1'}{b_0} \tilde{z}_t^s - \frac{1}{b_0} u_{2t}$$

$$\tilde{q}_{t'} = q_{t'} + \epsilon_{2t'} \quad (t' \geqslant t)$$

with the pressures created by the differences in observed prices at t and $t-1$ and the bid and offer prices correspondingly. Imposing the (testable) restrictions $a_2 = a_3$, $\beta_2 = \beta_3$, $a_1 = 1$, $\beta_1 = 1$, we get

$$\Delta \tilde{p}_t = a_0 + a_2 \Delta \tilde{q}_t + a_2 (b_0 - a_0)(\tilde{p}_t - p_t^*) + a_4 (\eta_t^o - \tilde{\eta}_{t-1}) + \epsilon_{1t}$$

$$\Delta \tilde{q}_t = \beta_0 + \beta_2 \Delta \tilde{p}_t + \beta_2 \frac{b_0 - a_0}{a_0 b_0} (q_t^* - \tilde{q}_t) + \beta_4 (\tilde{\eta}_{t-1} - \tilde{q}_{t-1}) + \epsilon_{2t} \tag{10.92}$$

with the latent variables of equilibrium price and quantity at t as specified by

$$p_t^* = \frac{1}{b_0 - a_0} (a_1' \tilde{z}_t^d + u_{1t} - b_1' \tilde{z}_t^s - u_{2t}) = \frac{1}{b_0 - a_0} (\psi_t^d - \psi_t^s)$$

$$q_t^* = \frac{b_0}{b_0 - a_0} \psi_t^d - \frac{a_0}{b_0 - a_0} \psi_t^s$$

Equations (10.92) are quantity- and price-adjustment equations. The model is thus an extension of our earlier models. However, one can criticize this formulation as well on several grounds: the definitions of supply pressures in equations (10.90) and (10.91), as well as the inclusion of $(\bar{\eta}_{t-1} - \bar{q}_{t-1})$ in equation (10.91). But most important, although there are quantity and price adjustments incorporated into the model, there is no guarantee that $(\bar{p}_t, \bar{q}_t)$ will fall in the region to the left of the heavy lines in Figure 10.1. Any points elsewhere do not make economic sense. Thus, there is no easy way out of some minimum condition in formulating disequilibrium models.

In summary, there are as yet no satisfactory solutions to the several problems mentioned here. However, it is instructive to review the three main limitations of the models considered:

1.   Nothing in the model says what happens to unsatisfied demand or unsold goods. The latter can be taken care of by adding inventories to the model. The former must be handled by allowing some spillover of unsatisfied demand into future periods. The model in equations (10.90) and (10.91) incorporates inventories, but not spillovers of unsatisfied demand.

2.   The minimum condition constrains the observations to lie on the demand curve or the supply curve (i.e., to the points on the heavy lines of Figure 10.1). In practice, the actual trades can take place at any points to the left of these lines. The models considered thus far do not allow for this. As for the model in (10.92), it assures that the observations do not lie on the heavy lines of Figure 10.1, but it does not assure that they lie in the region to the left of these heavy lines.

3.   The models considered do not have a satisfactory formulation of how prices and quantities adjust in response to demand and supply pressures. As reviewed in section 10.6, the price-adjustment equation customarily tagged on to the usual disequilibrium model results in a very peculiar quantity-adjustment equation. Further, there is no reason why ΔP_t should unambiguously determine whether or not there is excess demand or excess supply. We thus need price- and quantity-adjustment equations. Equations (10.29) do this, but not necessarily in a "coherent" way, for the reasons mentioned earlier.

In summary, much more work needs to be done, even in the case of the market-disequilibrium model with a single market, let alone multi-market-disequilibrium models.

CHAPTER 11

Some applications: unions and wages

11.1   Introduction

In the preceding chapters we discussed several methods for analyzing models with qualitative variables and limited dependent variables. We shall illustrate these methods by considering some examples in greater detail. This will also be an aid in understanding how to avoid mechanical use of such models. In this chapter we shall discuss the studies that have assessed the effects of unions on wages.

There have been numerous studies on the effects of unions on wages. These studies have analyzed relative wages of union and nonunion workers and the effects of union membership separately. Examples include the studies of Lewis (1963), Rosen (1969, 1970), and Boskin (1972). Lewis (1963) estimated that unions had raised the average wage rate for union workers 10% to 15% above that for nonunion workers in the period 1957–8. His estimating equation was

$$\ln W_i = \alpha_0 + \alpha_1 U_i + \alpha_2 Z_i + \epsilon_i \tag{11.1}$$

where W_i is average wage rate in industry i, U_i is the extent of unionization in industry i, and Z_i denotes the set of other exogenous variables. The estimated proportional wage advantage of union workers is $\exp(\hat{\alpha}_1) - 1$.

Rosen (1969) estimated union–nonunion wage differentials to be mostly between 16% and 25%, but in another study (Rosen, 1970) the estimates sometimes ranged as high as 35%.[1]

---

[1] Others, like Weiss, Stafford, and Fuchs, also obtained estimates of 25% to 35%. Their studies are referenced in the works cited here.

In none of these studies was the simultaneity between wages and unionization taken into account. Ashenfelter and Johnson (1972) were the first to do this, although the fact that relative wages may affect the probability of unionization and the extent of unionization was noted earlier by Reder (1965).

11.2   The Ashenfelter–Johnson study

The Ashenfelter–Johnson model (1972) is a three-equation model in which wages, degree of unionization, and labor quality are treated as simultaneously determined. The three equations are

$$\ln W_i = \alpha_0 + \alpha_1 E_i + \alpha_2 U_i + \alpha_3 F_i + \epsilon_{1i} \tag{11.2}$$

$$U_i = \beta_0 + \beta_1 \ln W_i + \beta_2 \mathrm{CON}_i + \epsilon_{2i} \tag{11.3}$$

$$E_i = \delta_0 + \delta_1 \mathrm{SK}_i + \delta_2 \mathrm{URB}_i + \epsilon_{3i} \tag{11.4}$$

where

W_i = average wage rate in industry i

E_i = average educational attainment of the work force in industry i

U_i = proportion of production workers in industry i who are employed in establishments covered by collective bargaining

F_i = proportion of female workers in industry i (this is used as an index of discrimination in the industry

CON_i = concentration ratio in industry i

SK_i = index of skill requirement in industry i

URB_i = fraction of workers in industry i who are located in urban areas.

Ashenfelter and Johnson estimated this model by OLS, 2SLS, and 3SLS, based on data for two-digit manufacturing industries in 1960. In the OLS estimation of equation (11.2), U_i had a coefficient of 0.382, with a standard error 0.093, but the 2SLS estimate was 0.176, with a standard error of 0.267. Changing the specification of equation (11.2) with other exogenous variables did not change the pattern of results. In general, the coefficient of U_i in the OLS equation was around 0.4 and was significant, whereas when simultaneity was taken into account, it dropped in magnitude and was not significant. This suggests that one reason for the high estimates of the effects of unions on wages was the fact that the simultaneity between the two variables had not been taken into account.

Ashenfelter and Johnson, however, cautioned that the qualitative and quantitative nature of their data prevented them from giving any firm conclusions. We shall now examine other studies that have taken simultaneity into account.

11.3 The Schmidt and Strauss study

Schmidt and Strauss (1976) used a logit model of union membership mixed with a normal regression model of earnings to study the simultaneous determination of wages and unionization. Let

$X_i = 1$ if individual i is a union member

$X_i = 0$ otherwise

Y_i = wages of individual i

Then the Schmidt–Strauss model, which they called a mixed logit model, is

$$\log_e\left(\frac{P(X_i=1\mid Y_i)}{P(X_i=0\mid Y_i)}\right) = Q_i\gamma + \alpha Y_i \tag{11.5}$$

and

$$Y_i\mid X_i \sim N(Z_i\beta + \delta X_i, \sigma^2) \tag{11.6}$$

where Q_i and Z_i are vectors of exogenous variables. Equation (11.5) is a logit specification for the probability of unionization. Equation (11.6) says that the distribution of Y_i, given X_i, is a normal distribution. From (11.6) we can write

$$f(Y_i\mid X_i=0) = \frac{1}{\sigma(2\pi)^{1/2}}\exp\left[-\frac{1}{2\sigma^2}(Y_i-Z_i\beta)^2\right]$$

$$f(Y_i\mid X_i=1) = \frac{1}{\sigma(2\pi)^{1/2}}\exp\left[-\frac{1}{2\sigma^2}(Y_i-Z_i\beta-\delta)^2\right] \tag{11.6'}$$

The model of Schmidt and Strauss is not different in spirit from that of Ashenfelter and Johnson. The difference is that Schmidt and Strauss used microdata, and thus unionization is not a proportion but a binary variable assuming a value 0 or 1. Hence, they used a logit model for it. But, given that one variable was binary (with a logit specification) and the other continuous, they preferred to specify the two relations among the variables in terms of *conditional distributions*. From the conditional distributions given by (11.5) and (11.6), they derived the joint distribution. Note that the specification in the usual simultaneous-equations models is in terms of the joint distribution, not the conditional distributions. Also, it is customary to look at the marginal distributions of the endogenous variables (these are given by the reduced-form equations), and although one can derive the conditional distributions, one rarely does this, because they are complicated and not very useful.

Schmidt and Strauss derived the joint distribution of Y and X from (11.5) and (11.6') as follows: Note that from (11.5) we get

$$\frac{f(X_i=1, Y_i)}{f(X_i=0, Y_i)} = \frac{P(X_i=1 \mid Y_i)}{P(X_i=0 \mid Y_i)} = \exp(Q_i\gamma + \alpha Y_i) \qquad (11.7)$$

Also,

$$P(X_i=j) = \frac{f(X_i=j, Y_i)}{f(Y_i \mid X_i=j)} \qquad (j=0,1)$$

Because $P(X_i=0) + P(X_i=1) = 1$, we get

$$\frac{f(X_i=0, Y_i)}{f(Y_i \mid X_i=0)} + \frac{f(X_i=1, Y_i)}{f(Y_i \mid X_i=1)} = 1$$

Using (11.7), we get

$$f(X_i=0, Y_i)\left(\frac{1}{f(Y_i \mid X_i=0)} + \frac{\exp(Q_i\gamma + \alpha Y_i)}{f(Y_i \mid X_i=1)}\right) = 1$$

Hence, we get

$$f(X_i=0, Y_i) = \frac{f(Y_i \mid X_i=0) \cdot f(Y_i \mid X_i=1)}{f(Y_i \mid X_i=1) + f(Y_i \mid X_i=0) \cdot \exp(Q_i\gamma + \alpha Y_i)} \qquad (11.8)$$

and, using (11.7),

$$f(X_i=1, Y_i) = \exp(Q_i\gamma + \alpha Y_i) \cdot f(X_i=0, Y_i)$$

where $f(Y_i \mid X_i=1)$ and $f(Y_i \mid X_i=0)$ are given by the expressions (11.6'). Schmidt and Strauss maximized the likelihood function

$$L = \prod_{X_i=0} f(X_i=0, Y_i) \prod_{X_i=1} f(X_i=1, Y_i)$$

numerically with respect to γ, β, α, δ, and σ^2. They used the data from the 1967 Survey of Economic Opportunity. The data consisted of a random sample of 912 observations from the representative portion of the survey, after it had been modified to include only those who were full-time workers over 14 years of age, but less than 66, and who had nonzero annual earnings.

The sets of exogenous variables Q_i and Z_i were identical. Note that this does not pose any problems with identification, because each equation is specified as a conditional distribution. The exogenous variables were education, experience, race, and sex; the locational dummies were N.E., N.C., and West.

The ML estimates of the mixed logit model were

$$\log_e \frac{P(\text{union} \,|\, \text{earnings})}{P(\text{nonunion} \,|\, \text{earnings})} = Q\gamma + 0.000064(\text{earnings})$$
$$(2.30)$$

and

$$\text{earnings} = Q\beta + 470.9(\text{union})$$
$$(1.44)$$

(The coefficients γ and β are not reproduced here, for brevity.) The figures in parentheses are asymptotic t-ratios and are the corrected figures reported by Schmidt (1978). Thus, the coefficient of the union variable in the earnings equation was not significant, but the coefficient of the earnings variable in the union equation was significant. By contrast, if simultaneity is not taken into account, the ordinary logit estimation of the union equation yields a coefficient 0.000059 for the earnings variable, with a t ratio of 2.79, and the OLS estimation of the earnings equation gives a coefficient of 648.3, with a t ratio of 2.12. Thus, the effect of unions on earnings is significant if simultaneity is not taken into account. Schmidt and Strauss concluded that these results support the findings of Ashenfelter and Johnson.

Besides the minor point that the model could have been better specified in terms of ln(earnings), instead of earnings, there are two major problems with the Schmidt–Strauss approach. The first problem is with the specification in terms of conditional distributions. Although this avoids any problems with identification, and also makes the least-squares estimates consistent, it raises the problem of how to interpret the coefficients. Indeed, the coefficients in the Schmidt–Strauss study do not have the same structural-coefficient interpretation as those in the Ashenfelter–Johnson study. The system of equations is not a structural system, and hence it is difficult to interpret the coefficients – indeed, it is not clear what they mean. Further, the specification in terms of conditional distributions imposes some restrictions on the parameters. This was noted by Olsen (1978a). Such restrictions always arise when one specifies the relationships among the endogenous variables in terms of the conditional distributions. From the joint distribution (11.8) we can derive the marginal distribution $P(X_i = 0)$:

$$P(X_i = 0) = \frac{f(X_i = 0, Y_i)}{f(Y_i \,|\, X_i = 0)}$$

$$= \frac{1}{1+\exp(Q_i\gamma+\alpha Y_i)\cdot f(Y_i\,|\,X_i=0)/f(Y_i\,|\,X_i=1)}$$

From (11.6') we have

$$\frac{f(Y_i\,|\,X_i=0)}{f(Y_i\,|\,X_i=1)} = \exp\left(-\frac{1}{2\sigma^2}(2Y_i\delta-2Z_i\beta\delta-\delta^2)\right)$$

Substituting this in the expression for $P(X_i=0)$, and noting that $P(X_i=0)$, being a marginal probability, cannot be a function of Y_i, we get the result that

$$\alpha Y_i - \frac{1}{2\sigma^2}(2Y_i\delta) = 0 \quad \text{or} \quad \alpha\sigma^2 = \delta$$

Olsen argued that this is a very unnatural restriction to impose. Why should σ^2 equal δ/α? The answer to this question, as pointed out by Lee (1979c), lies in the fact that α and δ in equations (11.5) and (11.6) are both measures of correlation between X and Y expressed in different units; they are not distinct simultaneous effects. Specifically, $\delta=\sigma_{XY}/\sigma_X^2$ and $\alpha=\sigma_{XY}/\sigma^2\sigma_X^2$, where σ_X^2 is the variance of X and σ_{XY} is the covariance between X and Y. To see this, consider the following two models.

Model 1: The mixed logit model.[2]

$$\ln\left(\frac{P(X=1\,|\,Y)}{P(X=0\,|\,Y)}\right) = Z\gamma + \alpha Y$$
$$Y\,|\,X \sim N(Z\beta+\delta X, \sigma^2)$$

with parameter set $A=(\gamma, \alpha, \beta, \delta, \sigma^2\,|\,\alpha\sigma^2=\delta,\ \sigma^2>0)$.

Model 2: The recursive model.[3]

$$\ln\left(\frac{P(X=1)}{P(X=0)}\right) = Z\theta$$
$$Y\,|\,X \sim N(Z\beta+\delta, \sigma^2)$$

with parameter set $B=(\theta, \beta, \delta, \sigma^2\,|\,\sigma^2>0)$.

We can show that the two models are algebraically equivalent with the relationship

$$\theta = \gamma + \alpha\beta + \frac{\delta\alpha}{2}e_1$$

---

[2] We have combined the variables Q and Z in equations (11.5) and (11.6) into a single set Z.

[3] These models have been considered by Maddala and Lee (1976).

where $e_1' = (1, 0, \ldots, 0)$. To see this, note that

$$\frac{P(X=1|Y)}{P(X=0|Y)} = \frac{P(Y|X=1)P(X=1)}{P(Y|X=0)P(X=0)}$$

Because

$$P(Y|X) = \frac{1}{\sigma(2\pi)^{1/2}} \exp\left[-\frac{1}{2\sigma^2}(Y - Z\beta - \delta X)^2 \right]$$

We have

$$\frac{P(Y|X=1)}{P(Y|X=0)} = \exp\left[\frac{\delta}{\sigma^2}(Y - Z\beta) - \frac{\delta^2}{2\sigma^2} \right]$$

Hence, from the recursive model, we get

$$\frac{P(X=1|Y)}{P(X=0|Y)} = \exp\left[\frac{\delta}{\sigma^2}(Y - Z\beta) - \frac{\delta^2}{2\sigma^2} + Z\theta \right]$$

Comparing this with the first equation in the mixed logit model, and noting that $\alpha = \delta/\sigma^2$, we get the relationship

$$\theta = \gamma + \alpha\beta + \frac{\delta\alpha}{2} e_1$$

What this equivalence shows is that the concept of simultaneity does not apply to the mixed logit model. There are actually no unnatural prior constraints involved. The constraint $\alpha\sigma^2 = \delta$ simply arises from an attempt to give a simultaneity interpretation to a model that is indeed recursive, not simultaneous.

The second major problem with the Schmidt–Strauss model is that although their model says that the probability of joining the union depends on earnings, it is the actual earnings that is used as an explanatory variable, when in fact it is the expected differential between the union and nonunion earnings that should determine the decision whether or not to join the union. This deficiency was corrected in a subsequent study by Schmidt (1978), but the approach still is not very satisfactory, because it is based on some restrictive assumptions that will be elaborated later. A more satisfactory approach to the problem is that of Lee (1978), which will be discussed in the next section. In any case, we shall discuss the approach taken by Schmidt and later elaborate its relationship to the Lee approach.

The correction that Schmidt used was to make the probability of joining the union a function of the income difference. Thus, equation (11.5) is rewritten as

$$\log \frac{P(X_i=1)}{P(X_i=0)} = Q_i\gamma + \alpha[E(Y_i\,|\,X_i=1) - E(Y_i\,|\,X_i=0)] \tag{11.9}$$

Note that the probability of joining the union is no longer written as a conditional distribution as (11.5) was written.

If we retain equation (11.6), the expression in the square brackets in (11.9) is a constant, and if the union–nonunion wage differential is constant for all individuals, this cannot be used to explain why some individuals are more likely to join the union than others. To avoid this problem, Schmidt rewrote the earnings equation (11.6) as

$$Y_i = Z_i\beta + (X_iZ_i)\delta + \epsilon_i \tag{11.10}$$

where $\epsilon_i \sim IN(0, \sigma^2)$. In this case,

$$(Y_i\,|\,X_i=1) - (Y_i\,|\,X_i=0) = Z_i\delta \tag{11.11}$$

Note that the distribution of X_i in (11.9) no longer depends on Y_i. Schmidt assumed that ϵ_i and X_i are independent. Hence, the joint density of Y_i and X_i is

$$\begin{aligned}
f(Y_i, X_i) &= \frac{1}{\sigma(2\pi)^{1/2}} \exp\left(-\frac{1}{2\sigma^2}(Y_i - Z_i\beta - X_iZ_i\delta)^2\right) \\
&\quad \times \frac{\exp[X_i(Q_i\gamma + \alpha Z_i\delta)]}{1 + \exp(Q_i\gamma + \alpha Z_i\delta)}
\end{aligned} \tag{11.12}$$

Hence, the log likelihood is given by

$$\begin{aligned}
\log L &= \sum_{i=1}^{n} \log f(Y_i, X_i) \\
&= \text{constant} - \frac{N}{2}\log\sigma^2 - \frac{1}{2\sigma^2}\Sigma(Y_i - Z_i\beta - X_iZ_i\delta)^2 \\
&\quad + \Sigma X_i(Q_i\gamma + \alpha Z_i\delta) - \Sigma\log[1 + \exp(Q_i\gamma + Z_i\delta)]
\end{aligned}$$

Maximizing with respect to σ^2 gives

$$\hat{\sigma}^2 = \frac{1}{N}\Sigma(Y_i - Z_i\beta - X_iZ_i\delta)^2$$

Hence, the concentrated log likelihood function is

$$\begin{aligned}
\log L^* &= \text{constant} - \frac{N}{2}\log[\Sigma(Y_i - Z_i\beta - X_iZ_i\delta)^2] \\
&\quad + \Sigma X_i(Q_i\gamma + \alpha Z_i\delta) - \Sigma\log[1 + \exp(Q_i\gamma + Z_i\delta)]
\end{aligned}$$

For conciseness, let us define

$$e_i = Y_i - Z_i\beta - X_iZ_i\delta$$

and

$$P_i = \frac{\exp(Q_i\gamma + \alpha Z_i\delta)}{1 + \exp(Q_i\gamma + \alpha Z_i\delta)}$$

Then,

$$\frac{\partial \log L^*}{\partial \beta} = 0 \quad \text{gives} \quad \Sigma e_i Z_i = 0 \tag{11.13}$$

$$\frac{\partial \log L^*}{\partial \gamma} = 0 \quad \text{gives} \quad \Sigma(X_i - P_i)Q_i = 0 \tag{11.14}$$

$$\frac{\partial \log L^*}{\partial \alpha} = 0 \quad \text{gives} \quad \Sigma(X_i - P_i)Z_i\delta = 0 \tag{11.15}$$

$$\frac{\partial \log L^*}{\partial \delta} = 0 \quad \text{gives} \quad \frac{1}{\hat{\sigma}^2}\Sigma e_i X_i Z_i + \alpha\Sigma(X_i - P_i)Z_i = 0 \tag{11.16}$$

Note that because of the assumption that X_i and ϵ_i are independent, the OLS estimation of equation (11.10) gives consistent estimates $\hat{\beta}$ and $\hat{\delta}$ of β and δ. Also, substituting $\hat{\delta}$ in (11.11), we can get consistent estimates of γ and α by estimating (11.9) as a simple logit model. However, these estimates are not efficient because of the occurrence of δ in both the equations. A comparison of the likelihood equations (11.13) to (11.16) with the equations for this consistent procedure shows that equations (11.14) and (11.15) are the same as those for the logit estimation of γ and α from (11.9). However, the normal equations for OLS estimation of β and δ are (11.13) and

$$\Sigma e_i X_i Z_i = 0 \tag{11.17}$$

and (11.17) is the same as (11.16) only if $\alpha = 0$. The consistent estimates mentioned earlier are, of course, useful as starting values in the iterative solution of the likelihood equations (11.13) to (11.16).

Schmidt reestimated this model (using the same data as in the earlier study) by the ML method and arrived at the conclusion that the union–nonunion wage differential does not significantly affect the probability of unionization. He found that unionism does affect earnings, the effect depending on the individual's level of education and experience. But for individuals of average education and experience, the effect is rather small. However, the findings of Lee (1978), to be discussed in the next section, were quite the opposite. He found that the wage differential has a significant effect on unionization and that the effects of unions on earnings are also significant. We shall discuss the limitations of Schmidt's model after discussing Lee's study.

11.4   Lee's binary-choice model

In most of the studies on unionism, personal-characteristics variables and the unionism dummy variables are used additively in a wage equation implying that the effects of personal characteristics on wage rates are independent of union status. Rosen (1970) allowed for some interactions, and so did Schmidt (1978) in the study discussed with equation (11.10) in the preceding section. Lee assumed complete interactions in the wage equations: one wage equation for union workers and another for nonunion workers. His model is

$$\ln W_{ui} = \theta_{uo} + X_{ui}\theta_{u1} + Z_{ui}\theta_{u2} + \epsilon_{ui} \tag{11.18}$$

$$\ln W_{ni} = \theta_{no} + X_{ni}\theta_{n1} + Z_{ni}\theta_{n2} + \epsilon_{ni} \tag{11.19}$$

$$I_i^* = \delta_0 + \delta_1(\ln W_{ui} - \ln W_{ni}) + \delta_2 X_i + \delta_3 Z_i - v_i \tag{11.20}$$

where

$$\epsilon_u \sim IN(0, \sigma_1^2)$$
$$\epsilon_n \sim IN(0, \sigma_2^2)$$
$$v \sim IN(0, \sigma_v^2)$$

Equation (11.18) is the wage equation for union workers, equation (11.19) is the wage equation for nonunion workers, and equation (11.20) is an equation that determines whether or not the individual belongs to a union.

If $I^* > 0$, then the individual belongs to the union group, and his wage is determined by equation (11.18). Otherwise, he belongs to the nonunion group, and his wage is determined by equation (11.19). The variables X are individual characteristics, and the variables Z are industry characteristics. The X variables include race, sex, education, market experience, health limitation, regional location, city size, and weeks worked per year. All these variables are included as explanatory variables in all the three equations, except the variable weeks worked, which appears only in the union-status equation (11.20). The industries in the sample included mining, construction, manufacturing (durable and nondurable), transportation, communication, utilities, and sanitary services. Industry dummy variables are the Z variables included in both equation (11.18) and equation (11.19). Additional Z variables include percentage of union coverage in the industry, which is used only in the union-wage equation (11.18), and industrial-concentration ratio, which is used only in the choice equation (11.20).

The data used were from the Survey of Economic Opportunity. Lee estimated the model using only those workers whose occupations classify them as operatives, that is, semiskilled workers, because it is for this group that the choice equation is most appropriate. For skilled workers, union restrictions on entry are much stronger, whereas for nonskilled laborers, minimum-wage regulations require an alternative specification of the wage equation. The total sample used by Lee consisted of 3,720 operatives, of whom 1,925 were in the union and 1,795 were not.

Note that the observed wage rate depends on the union status; that is, we observe

$$W_{ui} \quad \text{if } I_i^* > 0$$
$$W_{ni} \quad \text{otherwise}$$

but never both.

Lee estimated his model by two-stage estimation methods, as discussed earlier in Chapter 8. Note that OLS estimation of equations (11.18) and (11.19) gives inconsistent estimates, because

$$E(\epsilon_u \mid I_i^* > 0) \neq 0 \quad \text{and} \quad E(\epsilon_n \mid I_i^* \leqslant 0) \neq 0$$

Substituting the wage equations (11.18) and (11.19) into (11.20), we get a typical probit model:

$$I_i^* = \gamma_0 + \gamma_1 W_i - \epsilon_i^* \tag{11.21}$$

where W_i contains all the exogenous variables in X and Z, and ϵ_i^* has been normalized to have unit variance. We get estimates $\hat{\gamma}_0$ and $\hat{\gamma}_1$ using the probit ML method. Then, conditional on union status, the union wage equation is

$$\ln W_{ui} = \theta_{u0} + X_{ui}\theta_{u1} + Z_{ui}\theta_{u2} - \sigma_{1\epsilon^*} \frac{\phi(\psi_i)}{\Phi(\psi_i)} + \eta_u \tag{11.22}$$

where ϕ is the density function and Φ the distribution function of the standard normal, $\psi_i = \gamma_0 + \gamma_1 W_i$, and $\sigma_{1\epsilon^*} = \text{Cov}(\epsilon_u, \epsilon^*)$. Similarly, conditional on nonunion status, the nonunion wage equation is

$$\ln W_{ni} = \theta_{n0} + X_{ni}\theta_{n1} + Z_{ni}\theta_{n2} - \sigma_{2\epsilon^*} \frac{\phi(\psi_i)}{1 - \Phi(\psi_i)} + \eta_n \tag{11.23}$$

where $\sigma_{2\epsilon^*} = \text{Cov}(\epsilon_n, \epsilon^*)$. After getting $\hat{\psi}$ from the probit estimates of γ_0 and γ_1 and substituting it for ψ_i in equations (11.22) and (11.23), these equations are estimated by OLS. Further details of this two-stage procedure can be found in Chapter 8.

Lee found that almost all the coefficients were significant and had the expected signs. The estimates of $\sigma_{1\epsilon^*}$ and $\sigma_{2\epsilon^*}$ were also significant and were, respectively, -0.168 and 0.136. As discussed in Chapter 9, this suggests that both groups have comparative advantage at the jobs chosen.

After getting consistent estimates of the θ's, these are plugged into equations (11.18) and (11.19). One can then get estimates of $\hat{W}_{ui}$ and $\hat{W}_{ni}$ and calculate $[(\hat{W}_{ui} - \hat{W}_{ni})/\hat{W}_{ui}](100)$ as the percentage increase in the wage rate. Lee found that this was 15.68 for the whole sample. The corresponding figures can be calculated for different groups, industries, educational levels, and so forth. For instance, Lee found the following numbers for different race-sex groups:

	White	Nonwhite
Male	16.2	28.5
Female	2.8	12.7

In the calculation of $\hat{W}$, note that, strictly speaking, we cannot take $\exp(\ln \hat{W})$. What we have to calculate is

$$E\exp(\ln \hat{W}) = \exp(\theta_0 + X\theta_1 + Z\theta_2 + \tfrac{1}{2}\sigma^2)$$

But because $\hat{\sigma}_1^2 = 0.093$ and $\hat{\sigma}_2^2 = 0.120$, Lee said that $\exp(\tfrac{1}{2}\sigma_1^2 - \tfrac{1}{2}\sigma_2^2) \simeq 1 + \tfrac{1}{2}(\sigma_1^2 - \sigma_2^2) = 0.986$, and hence taking the exponent of the estimated $\ln \hat{W}$ is alright in calculating the percentage changes in wages.

Finally, after getting $\ln \hat{W}_u$ and $\ln \hat{W}_n$, Lee substituted them in equation (11.20) and estimated the choice equation by the probit ML method. The resultant structural probit estimates, as Lee (1979a) showed, are consistent. Again, he found most of the coefficients significant and of the right sign. In particular, the coefficient δ_1 was 2.455, with a standard error of 0.205. Thus, the wage difference has a significant impact on the determination of union status.

The results of Lee are at variance with those obtained by Schmidt. Part of the difference in results can be ascribed to a better model that takes all interactions into account. But part of the difference results from taking greater care with the data (separating operatives and taking industry characteristics into account) and greater care in the specification of the relevant variable – in short, greater care in the empirical work. Needless to say, careful handling of the data is as important as careful specification of the model. We turn now to the differences in the model specifications.

11.5 Alternative specifications of the unionism-wages model

In the previous sections we discussed some specifications of the models for studying the relationship between unionization and wages. As discussed earlier, the Schmidt–Strauss model has severe deficiencies arising from the specification in terms of conditional distributions and also the assumption that the union-status equation depends on actual earnings. Let us, therefore, consider the alternative model by Schmidt (1978).

We can write equation (11.10) in the notation of Lee's model (using log wages instead of wages) as follows:

$$\ln W_{ui} = Z_i(\beta + \delta) + \epsilon_i \tag{11.24}$$

$$\ln W_{ni} = Z_i\beta + \epsilon_i \tag{11.25}$$

Also, changing equation (11.9) to the probit specification, we can write

$$I_i^* = Q_i\gamma + \delta_1(\ln W_{ui} - \ln W_{ni}) - v_i \tag{11.26}$$

and

$$X_i = 1 \quad \text{iff } I_i^* > 0$$
$$X_i = 0 \quad \text{otherwise}$$

As explained in Chapter 2, the difference between the probit and logit specifications is merely in the assumption about the distribution of v_i. For the logit model, v_i is assumed to have a sech^2 distribution, and for the probit model it is assumed to have a normal distribution. What, then, is the difference between the models of Schmidt and Lee? Clearly, the differences (apart from the specification of the wage equations in the log form and the explanatory variables included) are that Schmidt assumed the residuals in the two wage equations (11.18) and (11.19) to be identical and ϵ_i in equations (11.24) and (11.25) and u_i in equation (11.26) to be independent. Clearly, these are very restrictive assumptions to make, and these could account in part for the differences in the results. Note that Lee obtained estimates of 0.093 for σ_1^2 and 0.120 for σ_2^2, which confirms the expectation that unionization reduces the payoffs to unobservable components of productivity.

After fixing the union-status equation by including the differences in the wage rates, and after allowing for different slope coefficients in the wage equations, Schmidt assumed that the residuals in the wage equations remain the same for both union and nonunion workers. If the residuals are allowed to differ, as in Lee's model, even assuming that the residuals in the three equations (11.18), (11.19), and (11.20) are independent, we still have a selectivity bias with OLS estimation of the wage equations (11.18) and (11.19), because the reduced-form residual ϵ_i^* in equation (11.21) will necessarily be correlated with the residuals in (11.18) and (11.19). In fact, in this case, as Lee (1978, p. 426) pointed out,

$$\sigma_{1\epsilon^*} = -\delta_1 \sigma_1^2 / \sigma^*$$
$$\sigma_{2\epsilon^*} = \delta_1 \sigma_2^2 / \sigma^*$$

and as δ_1 is expected to be positive, $E(\epsilon_u | I^* > 0)$ and $E(\epsilon_n | I^* \leqslant 0)$ are both positive. In fact, there is no selectivity bias only if $\delta_1 = 0$. Note that in Lee's analysis $\sigma_{1\epsilon^*}$ and $\sigma_{2\epsilon^*}$ were both highly significant. Thus, the assumption that $\epsilon_{ui} = \epsilon_{ni}$, which Schmidt made, although it results in a considerable simplification in the estimation procedure, is an untenable assumption. With the logit specification in the union-choice equation (11.26), relaxing this assumption will result in a hopelessly complicated estimation problem. The reduced-form expression for equation (11.26) will have an error that is the sum of a sech^2 variable and a normal variable.

What if we retain the assumption that $\epsilon_{ui} = \epsilon_{ni}$ but try to relax the assumption that the residuals in the wage equation and the union-choice equation are correlated? Again, this is not possible with the logit specification of the union-choice equation, because now we have to deal with two correlated variables, one with a sech^2 distribution and the other with a normal distribution. On the other hand, if we assume that the residual v_i in equation (11.26) is normally distributed, we can proceed as follows. Equation (11.26) can be written as

$$I^* = Q_i \gamma + \alpha Z_i \delta - v_i$$

As usual, we normalize the coefficients so that v_i are in $IN(0, 1)$. Let $\text{Var}(\epsilon_i) = \sigma_\epsilon^2$ and $\text{Cov}(\epsilon_i, v_i) = \sigma_{\epsilon v}$. The joint distribution of (ϵ_i, v_i) will be normal, and the likelihood function is

$$L = \prod_{X_i = 1} \left(\int_{-\infty}^{Q_i \gamma + Z_i \delta} f(\epsilon_i, v_i) \, dv_i \right) \prod_{X_i = 0} \left(\int_{Q_i \gamma + Z_i \delta}^{\infty} f(\epsilon_i, v_i) \, dv_i \right) \tag{11.27}$$

We can simplify this by writing the joint distribution $f(\epsilon_i, v_i)$ as $f(\epsilon_i) \cdot f(v_i | \epsilon_i)$.

Coming back to the Schmidt–Strauss model, we mentioned earlier that there are two problems with it. One is the fact that the union-choice equation is specified as dependent on current wages. But more important, the equations are specified in terms of conditional distributions, thus making it impossible to give a structural interpretation to the coefficients. Let us, therefore, see what can be done to make them structurally interpretable. Because we shall retain the assumption that the union decision depends on current earnings, the model will not be very meaningful, but the exercise will be illuminating, and the model could be of use in other contexts, though not in this one.

We can leave the earnings equation as it is, except that it is supposed to be interpreted as a structural equation. It is

$$Y_i = Z_i\beta + \delta X_i + \epsilon_i$$
$$\epsilon_i \sim IN(0, \sigma^2) \tag{11.28}$$

For the union-choice equation, we write it in the unobserved-indicator form:

$$X_i^* = Q_i\gamma + \alpha Y_i - v_i \tag{11.29}$$

Note that X_i^* is not observed. What we observe is X_i, defined as

$$X_i = 1 \quad \text{if } X_i^* > 0$$
$$X_i = 0 \quad \text{otherwise} \tag{11.30}$$

If v_i are assumed to have the sech^2 distribution, then this reduces to the logit specification (11.5), except that we view (11.29) as a structural equation, not a specification of a conditional distribution.

The problem with the specification given by (11.28) and (11.29) is that it leads to logical inconsistencies, because, in addition to the relationship between the unobservable variable X_i^* and the observed variable X_i given by (11.30), there is another relationship obtained by substituting (11.28) into (11.29):

$$X_i^* = Q_i\gamma + \alpha Z_i\beta + \alpha\delta X_i + (\alpha\epsilon_i - v_i) \tag{11.31}$$

Unless $\alpha = 0$, these two conditions are inconsistent. Such inconsistencies, where unobserved-indicator variables and their dichotomous realizations occur in different equations, have been discussed by Maddala and Lee (1976, p. 535) and by Heckman (1976a).

One possible way out of this problem is to assume that X_i^*, not X_i, affects earnings. In this case there will be a single reduced form for X_i^*, which is

$$X_i^* = \frac{1}{1-\alpha\delta}(Q_i\gamma + \alpha Z_i\beta) + \frac{\alpha\epsilon_i - v_i}{1-\alpha\delta}$$

However, we should have $1 - \alpha\delta \neq 0$, and although apparently we have the two conditions

$$X_i^* > 0 \Leftrightarrow v_i - \alpha\epsilon_i < Q_i\gamma + \alpha Z_i\beta \quad \text{if } 1 - \alpha\delta > 0$$
$$X_i^* > 0 \Leftrightarrow v_i - \alpha\epsilon_i > Q_i\gamma + \alpha Z_i\beta \quad \text{if } 1 - \alpha\delta < 0$$

these two conditions will not give problems, because $1/(1-\alpha\delta)$ will be absorbed in the reduced form. All this discussion shows that the reformulation of the Schmidt–Strauss model so as to give it a structural interpretation leads to logical difficulties. On the other hand, making the more realistic assumption that the union decision depends on the union–non-union wage differential makes the formulation of the structural system much easier. However, even here one cannot go too far with the logit specification. The model is tractable only under the very restrictive assumptions made by Schmidt (1978), but then there is no simultaneity in the model. The most general model that we have discussed for application with data on individuals is that of Lee (1978), and the other models can be treated as special cases of this model.

11.6   The Abowd and Farber study

The basic assumption in all the studies discussed in the previous sections was that all workers who wish to work on union jobs are able to find such jobs. The study by Abowd and Farber relaxed this assumption. They argued that not everyone who desires a union job gets it. There is usually a queue for union jobs. They formulated two decision equations:

$$I_1^* = X_1\beta_1 - \epsilon_1 \quad \text{(decision to join the queue for union jobs)}$$
$$I_2^* = X_2\beta_2 - \epsilon_2 \quad \text{(decison of employer to choose a worker from the queue)}$$

Let

$$\begin{aligned}
&IQ = 1 \quad \text{if a person is in the queue}\\
&IQ = 0 \quad \text{otherwise}\\
&CFQ = 1 \quad \text{if a person is chosen from the queue}\\
&CFQ = 0 \quad \text{otherwise}\\
&U = 1 \quad \text{if a person is in a union job}\\
&U = 0 \quad \text{otherwise}
\end{aligned}$$

$$\text{Prob}(IQ=1) = \text{Prob}(I_1^* > 0)$$
$$\text{Prob}(CFQ=1 \mid IQ=1) = \text{Prob}(I_2^* > 0)$$
$$\text{Prob}(U=1) = \text{Prob}(IQ=1) \cdot \text{Prob}(CFQ=1 \mid IQ=1)$$
$$= \text{Prob}(\epsilon_1 < X_1\beta_1) \cdot \text{Prob}(\epsilon_2 < X_2\beta_2)$$

Although Abowd and Farber said that their model was the same as the bivariate probit model with partial observability discussed by Poirier (1980), there is a difference between the two models. In the Abowd–Farber study, I_2^* is defined only for the subset of observations for which $I_1^* > 0$. It is actually a sequential-decision model rather than a joint-decision model, as considered by Poirier.

The only observable variable is U = 1 or 0. The parameters β_1 and β_2 are not identified if the same variables occur in X_1 and X_2. This is not the case in their study, because they have seniority variables included in X_1 but not X_2. The seniority in union or nonunion jobs affects the decision of joining the queue or not, because changing jobs will result in the loss of some benefits occurring from seniority. But, more important, Abowd and Farber tried to achieve identification of β_1 and β_2 by the use of another variable, JR (job rights). They assumed that an individual who held a union job in the previous year and has not been involuntarily terminated can retain the union job. For such individuals, JR = 1. For others, JR = 0. For these individuals, Prob(CFQ = 1 | IQ = 1) = 1, and hence Prob(U = 1) = Prob(IQ = 1), and the parameters β_1 can be estimated by the use of a simple probit model for this group.

The data used by Abowd and Farber involved 1,341 males in 1976 from the probability sample of the University of Michigan Panel Study of Income Dynamics who were employed in 1976, were not employed in the construction industry, and were heads of the same households in 1975 and 1976. The JR variable was defined as 1 if the individual held a union job in 1975, was not fired from that job, and did not quit that job to take another union job. The distribution of the sample was as follows:

	Union job	Nonunion job	Total
Job rights	364	25	389
No job rights	75	877	952
Total	439	902	1,341

The likelihood function to maximize is

$$L = \prod_1 \Phi_1^U (1-\Phi_1)^{1-U} \prod_0 (\Phi_1\Phi_2)^U (1-\Phi_1\Phi_2)^{1-U}$$

where the first product is over all observations with JR = 1, the second product is over all observations with JR = 0, U = 1 for union job workers and U = 0 for others, and $\Phi_1 = \Phi(X_1\beta_1)$ and $\Phi_2 = \Phi(X_2\beta_2)$.

In the model in which we assume that everyone who demands a union job gets it, we have

$$\text{Prob}(U=1) = \Phi(X_1\beta_1)$$

Abowd and Farber contrasted the estimates of β_1 from the two models. They found that experience is negatively related to the probability of desiring a union job and positively related to the probability of being chosen from the queue. Such conflicting results will be masked in the estimation of a probit equation for the entire sample (the no-queue model). Another major finding is that most new entrants prefer union jobs but cannot get them. As time goes by, and they accrue nonunion seniority, they become less likely to want union jobs. Thus, the union status of most workers is determined by their success in being selected from the queue early in their working lives.

Abowd and Farber used only the decision functions, not the wage equations, in their analysis. This latter model would be an interesting one to estimate. In Chapter 9 we discussed some of these models.

11.7   Summary and conclusions

The purpose of this chapter has been to review several methods discussed in the previous chapters in relation to a single problem and point out how some mechanical formulations endogenizing dummy variables result in models that are not entirely satisfactory. The proper way to model is to incorporate the choice processes explicitly.

Appendix: Some results on truncated distributions

The truncated normal distribution

We shall use the symbol ϕ to denote the density function and Φ to denote the cumulative distribution function of the standard normal distribution. We shall also use the notation f and F to denote the density function and distribution function for distributions other than the standard normal.

$$\Phi(y) = \int_{-\infty}^{y} \frac{1}{(2\pi)^{1/2}} \exp(-\tfrac{1}{2}u^2) \, du$$

and

$$\phi(y) = \frac{d\Phi(y)}{dy} = \frac{1}{(2\pi)^{1/2}} \exp(-\tfrac{1}{2}y^2)$$

For a normal distribution with mean μ and variance σ^2, the function $\Phi(y)$ becomes $\Phi[(y-\mu)/\sigma]$, and the function $\phi(y)$ becomes $(1/\sigma)\phi[(y-\mu)/\sigma]$.

Mean and variance of the truncated normal

Suppose the random variable X is $N(0,1)$, and we consider the truncated distribution $X \geqslant c_1$. The mean and variance of this truncated distribution are given by

$$E(X) = \frac{\phi(c_1)}{1-\Phi(c_1)} = \frac{\text{ordinate at } X=c_1}{\text{right-hand tail area}} = M_1 \quad \text{(say)}$$

$$V(X) = 1 - M_1(M_1 - c_1)$$

If the truncation is from above, so that we consider the distribution $X \leqslant c_2$, then

$$E(X) = \frac{-\phi(c_2)}{\Phi(c_2)} = M_2 \quad \text{(say)}$$

$$V(X) = 1 - M_2(M_2 - c_2)$$

365

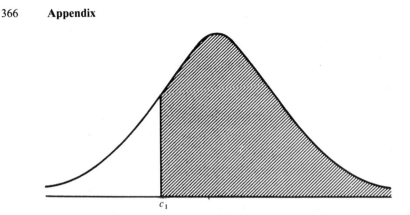

Figure A.1. Normal distribution truncated from below

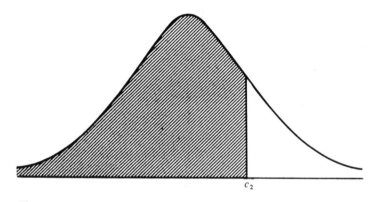

Figure A.2. Normal distribution truncated from above

If the distribution is doubly truncated, so that we consider $c_1 \leqslant X \leqslant c_2$, then

$$E(X) = \frac{\phi(c_1) - \phi(c_2)}{\Phi(c_2) - \Phi(c_1)} = M \quad \text{(say)}$$

$$V(X) = 1 - M^2 + \frac{c_1 \phi(c_1) - c_2 \phi(c_2)}{\Phi(c_2) - \Phi(c_1)}$$

If X has the normal distribution, with mean μ and variance σ^2 (instead of mean 0 and variance 1), then in the preceding formulas we have to substitute $(X-\mu)/\sigma$, $(c_1-\mu)/\sigma$, and $(c_2-\mu)/\sigma$ for X, c_1, and c_2 respectively (Johnson and Kotz, 1970, pp. 81–3).

In equations (5.46) and (5.47) in Chapter 5, we needed expressions of

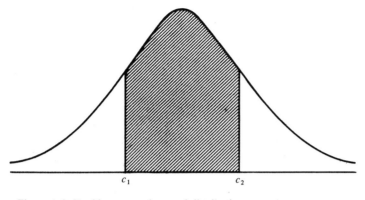

Figure A.3. Doubly truncated normal distribution

the form $E(u_1 \mid u_2 < c)$ and $E(u_1 \mid u_2 > c)$, where (u_1, u_2) are jointly normal, with zero means, unit variances, and covariance σ_{12}. Note that $E(u_1 \mid u_2) = \sigma_{12} u_2$. Thus,

$$E(u_1 \mid u_2 < c) = \sigma_{12} E(u_2 \mid u_2 < c)$$

$$= -\sigma_{12} \frac{\phi(c)}{\Phi(c)}$$

Similarly,

$$E(u_1 \mid u_2 > c) = \sigma_{12} E(u_2 \mid u_2 > c)$$

$$= \sigma_{12} \frac{\phi(c)}{1 - \Phi(c)}$$

These are the expressions used in (5.46) and (5.47).

Derivatives

Very often we need the derivatives of functions of the form $\Phi(\alpha/\lambda)$ and $\phi(\alpha/\lambda)$ with respect to the parameters α and λ. Noting the expressions for Φ and ϕ, it can be verified (using the standard formulas for finding a derivative of an expression with an integral sign) that

$$\frac{\partial \Phi}{\partial \alpha} = \frac{1}{\lambda} \phi\left(\frac{\alpha}{\lambda}\right)$$

$$\frac{\partial \Phi}{\partial \lambda} = -\frac{\alpha}{\lambda^2} \phi\left(\frac{\alpha}{\lambda}\right)$$

$$\frac{\partial \phi}{\partial \alpha} = -\frac{\alpha}{\lambda^2} \phi\left(\frac{\alpha}{\lambda}\right)$$

$$\frac{\partial \phi}{\partial \lambda} = \frac{\alpha^2}{\lambda^3} \phi\left(\frac{\alpha}{\lambda}\right)$$

Moments of the truncated bivariate normal distribution

See the work of Rosenbaum (1961). Let

$$f(x, y, \rho) = \frac{1}{2\pi(1-\rho^2)^{1/2}} \exp\left[-\frac{1}{2(1-\rho^2)}(x^2 - 2\rho xy + y^2)\right]$$

be the standard bivariate normal distribution, with zero means, unit variances, and correlation coefficient ρ.

Consider the truncated distribution $x \geq h$, $y \geq k$. Let

$$F(h, k, \rho) = \text{Prob}(x \geq h, y \geq k)$$

$$m_{ij} = E(x^i y^j \mid x \geq h, y \geq k)$$

$$h^* = \frac{h - \rho k}{(1-\rho^2)^{1/2}}$$

$$k^* = \frac{k - \rho h}{(1-\rho^2)^{1/2}}$$

$$Z = (h^2 - 2\rho hk + k^2)^{1/2}/(1-\rho^2)^{1/2}$$

Then, writing F for $F(h, k, \rho)$, we have

$$Fm_{10} = \phi(h)[1 - \Phi(k^*)] + \rho\phi(k)[1 - \Phi(h^*)]$$
$$Fm_{20} = F + h\phi(h)[1 - \Phi(k^*)] + \rho^2 k\phi(k)[1 - \Phi(h^*)]$$
$$+ \frac{\rho(1-\rho^2)^{1/2}}{(2\pi)^{1/2}}\phi(Z)$$

m_{01} and m_{02} can be obtained by interchanging h and k in these expressions.

$$Fm_{11} = F\rho + \rho h\phi(h)[1 - \Phi(k^*)]$$
$$+ \rho k\phi(k)[1 - \Phi(h^*)] + \frac{(1-\rho^2)^{1/2}}{(2\pi)^{1/2}}\phi(Z)$$

Note that in this example we considered F as $\text{Prob}(x \geq h, y \geq k)$.

Some nonnormal distributions

See the study of Lee (1982c, "Some Approaches to the Correction of Selectivity Bias," Appendix). Let $f(u)$ denote the density function and $F(u)$ the distribution function, so that $F(c) = \text{Prob}(u \leq c)$. Let

$$M_1(c) = E(u \mid u \leq c) \quad \text{and} \quad M_2(c) = E(u^2 \mid u \leq c)$$

Then we have the following results.

(1) *Normal distribution.*

$$\phi(u) = f(u) = (2\pi)^{-1/2} \exp(-\tfrac{1}{2}u^2) \quad (-\infty < u < \infty)$$

As defined earlier, we have

$$M_1(c) = -\phi(c)/\Phi(c), \quad M_2(c) = 1 - c\phi(c)/\Phi(c)$$

(2) *Log-normal distribution.* This would be useful to model variables with a skew distribution; $u = e^v$, where v is a standard normal variate.

$$M_1(c) = e^{1/2}\Phi(\ln c - 1)/F(c)$$
$$M_2(c) = e^2\Phi(\ln c - 2)/F(c)$$

(3) *Logistic distribution.*

$$f(u) = e^{-u}/(1 + e^{-u})^2 \quad (-\infty < u < \infty)$$

$$M_1(c) = c + \ln[1 - F(c)]/F(c)$$

$$M_2(c) = \left[\frac{\pi^2}{3} + \text{sign}(c) \sum_{j=1}^{\infty} (-1)^{j-1}j^{-2}\Gamma_{j|c|}(3)\right] \Bigg/ F(c)$$

where $\Gamma_x(a) = \int_0^x u^{a-1}e^{-u}\,du$ is the incomplete gamma function with parameter a.

(4) *Uniform distribution.*

$$f(u) = 1 \quad (0 \leq u \leq 1)$$
$$M_1(c) = \tfrac{1}{2}c \quad M_2(c) = c^2/3 \quad (0 \leq c \leq 1)$$

(5) *Laplace distribution.*

$$f(u) = \tfrac{1}{2}e^{-|u|} \quad -\infty < u < \infty$$
$$M_1(c) = c - 1 \quad \text{for } c \leq 0$$
$$M_1(c) = -(c + 1)f(c)/F(c) \quad \text{for } c \geq 0$$
$$M_2(c) = c^2 - 2c + 2 \quad \text{for } c \leq 0$$
$$M_2(c) = [\tfrac{3}{2} - (c^2 + c + 1)f(c)]/F(c) \quad \text{for } c \geq 0$$

(6) *Exponential distribution.*

$$f(u) = (1/\sigma)e^{-u/\sigma} \quad (\sigma > 0, \ u > 0)$$

$$M_1(c) = \sigma \Gamma_{c/\sigma}(2)/F(c)$$
$$M_2(c) = 2\sigma^2 \Gamma_{c/\sigma}(3)/F(c)$$

(7) *Gamma distribution.*

$$f(u/\alpha) = u^{\alpha-1}e^{-u}/\Gamma(\alpha) \quad (\alpha > 0, \; u \geqslant 0)$$
$$M_1(c) = \alpha F_\gamma(c|\alpha+1)/F_\gamma(c|\alpha)$$
$$M_2(c) = \alpha(\alpha+1)F_\gamma(c|\alpha+1)/F_\gamma(c|\alpha)$$

where $F_\gamma(Z/a)$ is the distribution function of the gamma variate with parameter a.

Goldberger (1980a) derived $M_1(c)$ for logistic and Laplace distributions. Lee's study should be consulted for other functional forms, as well as sources.

Clark's formulas

Clark's formulas pertain to section 3.3. Assume that y_1, y_2, and y_3 have a trivariate normal distribution, with mean vector $m = (m_1, m_2, m_3)$ and covariance matrix

$$\Sigma = \begin{bmatrix} \sigma_{11} & \sigma_{12} & \sigma_{13} \\ \sigma_{12} & \sigma_{22} & \sigma_{23} \\ \sigma_{13} & \sigma_{23} & \sigma_{33} \end{bmatrix}$$

Let $\tilde{y}_2 = \text{Max}(y_1, y_2)$. In connection with a stochastic network-scheduling problem, Clark (1961) calculated the first four moments of $\tilde{y}_2$ and the covariance of $\tilde{y}_2$ with y_3. The formulas for the first two moments of $\tilde{y}_2$ and the covariance of $\tilde{y}_2$ with y_3 are as follows:

$$E(\tilde{y}_2) = \tilde{m}_2 = m_2 + (m_1 - m_2)\Phi(\alpha) + a\phi(\alpha)$$

$$E(\tilde{y}_2^2) = \tilde{\tilde{m}}_2 = m_2^2 + \sigma_{22} + (m_1^2 + \sigma_{11} - m_2^2 - \sigma_{22})\Phi(\alpha) + (m_1 + m_2)a\phi(\alpha)$$

$$\text{Var}(\tilde{y}_2) = \tilde{\sigma}_{22} = \tilde{\tilde{m}}_2 - \tilde{m}_2^2$$

$$\text{Cov}(\tilde{y}_2, y_3) = \tilde{\sigma}_{23} = \sigma_{23} + (\sigma_{13} - \sigma_{23})\Phi(\alpha)$$

where $a = (\sigma_{11} + \sigma_{22} - 2\sigma_{12})^{1/2}$ and $\alpha = (m_1 - m_2)/a$.

Clark suggested approximating the distribution of $(\tilde{y}_2, y_3)$ by a normal distribution with these first and second moments. The multinomial probit model makes repeated use of this approximation.

A note on computer programs

Amemiya (1981) listed two computer programs available for qualitative variables. Forrest Nelson has a program at Caltech for models with qualitative and limited dependent variables. The program is for the probit model, the multinomial logit model, the two-limit probit model, the ordinal polychotomous probit model, and the tobit model. These are the models discussed in Chapters 2, 3, and 6. For the models discussed in other chapters, programs should be available from the authors of the studies cited. None of these programs is complicated, and thus they can be readily written to suit the particular problem at hand. In fact, as pointed out repeatedly throughout this book, one should avoid mechanical formulations of the models, and the tendency to use a ready-made program often can result in mechanical formulation. For more or less uniform use, the program package written by Nelson, or some similar package, will be adequate.

Bibliography

Abowd, J. M., and H. S. Farber (1982). "Job Queues and the Union Status of Workers." *Industrial and Labor Relations Review* 35(3):354-67.

Afriat, S. N. (1972). "Efficiency Estimation of Production Functions." *International Economic Review* 13(3):568-98.

Aigner, D. J., T. Amemiya, and D. J. Poirier (1976). "On the Estimation of Production Frontiers: Maximum Likelihood Estimation of the Parameters of a Discontinuous Density Function." *International Economic Review* 17(2):377-96.

Aigner, D. J., A. S. Goldberger, and G. Kalton (1975). "On the Explanatory Power of Dummy Variable Regressions." *International Economic Review* 16:503-10.

Aigner, D. J., C. A. Lovell, and P. Schmidt (1977). "Formulation and Estimation of Stochastic Frontier Production Function Models." *Journal of Econometrics* 6:21-37.

Aitchison, J., and J. Bennett (1970). "Polychotomous Quantal Response by Maximum Indicant." *Biometrika* 57:253-62.

Aitchison, J., and J. A. C. Brown (1957). *The Lognormal Distribution.* Cambridge University Press.

Aitchison, J., and S. Silvey (1957). "The Generalization of Probit Analysis to the Case of Multiple Responses." *Biometrika* 44:131-40.

Akerlof, G. A., and B. G. M. Main (1980). "Maximum Likelihood Estimation with Pooled Observations: An Example from Labor Economics." *International Economic Review* 21(3):507-15.

Akin, J., D. K. Guilky, and R. Sickles (1979). "A Random Coefficient Probit Model with an Application to a Study of Migration." *Journal of Econometrics* 11:233-46.

Amemiya, T. (1973). "Regression Analysis When the Dependent Variable Is Truncated Normal." *Econometrica* 41:997-1016.

(1974a). "Bivariate Probit Analysis: Minimum Chi-Square Methods." *Journal of the American Statistical Association* 69:940-4.

(1974b). "Multivariate Regression and Simultaneous Equation Models When the Dependent Variables Are Truncated Normal." *Econometrica* 42:999-1012.

(1974c). "A Note on the Fair and Jaffee Model." *Econometrica* 42:759-62.

(1975). "Qualitative Models." *Annals of Economic and Social Measurement* 4:363-72.

(1976a). "The Maximum Likelihood, the Minimum Chi-Square, and the Non-Linear Weighted Least Squares Estimator in the General Qualitative Response Model." *Journal of the American Statistical Association* 71: 347-51.

373

(1976*b*). "Specification and Estimation of a Multinomial Logit Model." Technical report 211. Institute for Mathematical Studies in the Social Sciences, Stanford University.

(1977*a*). "The Modified Second-Round Estimator in the General Qualitative Response Model." *Journal of Econometrics* 5:295–9.

(1977*b*). "The Solvability of a Two-Market Disequilibrium Model." Working paper 82. Institute for Mathematical Studies in the Social Sciences, Stanford University.

(1978*a*). "On a Two-Step Estimation of a Multivariate Logit Model." *Journal of Econometrics* 8(1):13–21.

(1978*b*). "The Estimation of a Simultaneous Equation Generalized Probit Model." *Econometrica* 46:1193–205.

(1978*c*). "A Note on the Estimation of a Time Dependent Markov Chain Model." Working paper 92. Institute for Mathematical Studies in the Social Sciences, Stanford University.

(1979). "The Estimation of a Simultaneous Equation Tobit Model." *International Economic Review* 20(1):169–81.

(1980). "The η^{-2}-Order Mean Squared Errors of the Maximum Likelihood and the Minimum Logit Chi-Square Estimates." *Annals of Statistics,* 8(3): 488–505.

(1981). "Qualitative Response Models: A Survey." *Journal of Economic Literature* 19(4):483–536.

Amemiya, T., and M. Boskin (1974). "Regression Analysis When the Dependent Variable Is Truncated Normal with an Application to the Determinants of the Duration of Welfare Dependency." *International Economic Review* 15(2):485–96.

Amemiya, T., and F. Nold (1975). "A Modified Logit Model." *Review of Economics and Statistics* 57:255–7.

Amemiya, T., and J. L. Powell (1980). "A Comparison of the Box–Cox ML Estimator and the Nonlinear 2SLS Estimator." Technical Report 322. Institute for Mathematical Studies in the Social Sciences, Stanford University.

Amemiya, T., and G. Sen (1977). "The Consistency of the Maximum Likelihood Estimator in a Disequilibrium Model." Technical report 238. Institute for Mathematical Studies in the Social Sciences, Stanford University.

Andersen, E. B. (1970). "Asymptotic Properties of Conditional Maximum-Likelihood Estimators." *Journal of the Royal Statistical Society* (ser. B) 32(2):283–301.

Anderson, J. A. (1972). "Separate Sample Logistic Discrimination." *Biometrika* 59(1):19–35.

Ashenfelter, O. (1978). "Estimating the Effect of Training Programs on Earnings." *Review of Economics and Statistics* 60(1):47–57.

(1980*a*). "Unemployment as Disequilibrium in a Model of Aggregate Labor Supply." *Econometrica* 48(3):547–64.

(1980*b*). "Discrete Choice in Labor Supply: The Determinants of Participation in the Seattle and Denver Income Maintenance Experiments." Working paper 136. Industrial Relations Center, Princeton University.

Ashenfelter, O., and G. E. Johnson (1972). "Unionism, Relative Wages and Labor Quality in U.S. Manufacturing Industries." *International Economic Review* 13(3):488–508.

Ashford, J. R. (1959). "An Approach to the Analysis of Data for Semi-Quantal Responses in Biological Response." *Biometrics* 15:573–81.

Ashford, J. R., and R. R. Sowden (1970). "Multivariate Probit Analysis." *Biometrics* 26:535–46.

Ashton, W. (1972). *The Logit Transformation.* New York: Hafner.

Avery, R. B. (1982). "Estimation of Credit Constraints by Switching Regressions." In D. McFadden and C. Manski (eds.), *Structural Analysis of Discrete Data: With Econometric Applications.* Cambridge, Mass.: M.I.T. Press.

Avery, R. B., L. P. Hansen, and V. J. Hotz (1982). "Multiperiod Probit Models and Orthogonality Condition Estimation." Working paper 62-80-81. Carnegie Mellon University.

Avery, R. B., and V. J. Hotz (1981). "Estimation of Multiple Indicator Multiple Cause (MIMIC) Models with Dichotomous Indicators." Working paper 60-80-81. Carnegie Mellon University.

Barnow, B. S., G. G. Cain, and A. S. Goldberger (1981). "Issues in the Analysis of Selectivity Bias." In W. E. Stromsdorfer and G. Farkas (eds.), *Evaluation Studies Review Annual, Vol. 5,* pp. 43–59. Beverley Hills: Sage.

Barten, A. P., and L. S. Bronsard (1970). "Two-State Least Squares with Shifts in the Structural Form." *Econometrica* 33(6):938–41.

Batchelor, R. A. (1977). "A Variable-Parameter Model of Exporting Behaviour." *Review of Economic Studies* 44(1):43–58.

Bergstrom, A. R., and C. R. Wymer (1976). "A Model of Disequilibrium Neo-Classical Growth and Its Application to the United Kingdom." In A. R. Bergstrom (ed.), *Statistical Inference in Continuous Time Economic Models.* Amsterdam: North-Holland.

Berkson, J. (1949). "Application of the Logistic Function to Bioassay." *Journal of the American Statistical Association* 39:327–39, 357–65.

(1953). "A Statistically Precise and Relatively Simple Method of Estimating the Bio-Assay with Quantal Response, Based on the Logistic Function." *Journal of the American Statistical Association* 48:565–99.

(1955a). "Estimate of the Integrated Normal Curve by Minimum Normit Chi-Square with Particular Reference to Bio-assay." *Journal of the American Statistical Association* 50:529–49.

(1955b). "Maximum Likelihood and Minimum Chi-Square Estimations of the Logistic Function." *Journal of American Statistical Association* 50:130–61.

(1980). "Minimum Chi-Square, Not Maximum Likelihood." *Annals of Statistics* 8:457–87.

Berndt, E. R., B. H. Hall, R. E. Hall, and J. A. Hausman (1974). "Estimation and Inference in Non-linear Structural Models." *Annals of Economic and Social Measurement* 3(4):653–65.

Bishop, T., S. Fieberg, and P. Holland (1975). *Discrete Multivariate Analysis.* Cambridge, Mass.: M.I.T. Press.

Blight, J. N. (1970). "Estimation from a Censored Sample for the Exponential Family." *Biometrika* 57(2):389–95.

Block, H., and J. Marschak (1960). "Random Orderings and Stochastic Theories of Response." In I. Olkin (ed.), *Contributions to Probability and Statistics.* Stanford: Stanford University Press.

Bloom, D. E., B. J. Preiss, and J. Trussell (1981). "Mortgage Lending Discrimination and the Decision to Apply: A Methodological Note." Manuscript. Carnegie Mellon University.

Bock, R. D. (1968). "Estimating Multinomial Response Relations." In R. C. Bose et al. (eds.), *Essays in Statistics and Probability* (*Essays in Memory of S. N. Roy*). Chapel Hill: University of North Carolina Press.

Bock, R. D., and L. V. Jones (1968). *The Measurement and Prediction of Judgement and Choice.* San Francisco: Holden-Day.

Bomberger, W., and D. Denslow (1980). Some Cross-Sectional Evidence on Demand for Money and other Liquid Assets." Manuscript. University of Florida.

Borjas, G. J., and S. Rosen (1979). "Income Prospects and Job Mobility of Younger Men." Report 7920. Center for Mathematical Studies in Business and Economics, University of Chicago.

Boskin, M. J. (1972). "Unions and Relative Wages." *American Economic Review* 62(1):466–72.

(1974). "A Conditional Logit Model of Occupational Choice." *Journal of Political Economy* 82:389–98.

(1975). "A Markov Model of Turnover in Aid to Families with Dependent Children." *Journal of Human Resources* 10:467–81.

(1977). "Social Security and Retirement Decisions." *Economic Inquiry* 15: 1–25.

Boskin, M. J., and M. D. Hurd (1978). "The Effect of Social Security on Early Retirement." *Journal of Public Economics* 10:361–77.

Bowden, R. J. (1978*a*). "Specification, Estimation and Inference for Models of Markets in Disequilibrium." *International Economic Review* 19(3):711–26.

(1978*b*). *The Econometrics of Disequilibrium.* Amsterdam: North-Holland.

Braeutigam, R. R., and R. G. Noll (1981). "The Regulation of Surface Freight Transportation: The Welfare Effects Revisited." Social Science Working Paper 375, California Institute of Technology.

Burr, I. W. (1942). "Cumulative Frequency Functions." *Annals of Mathematical Statistics* 13:215–32.

Burtless, G., and J. A. Hausman (1978). "The Effect of Taxation on Labor Supply: Evaluating the Gary Negative Income-Tax Experiment." *Journal of Political Economy* 86(6):1103–30.

Buse, A. (1973). "Goodness of Fit in Generalized Least Squares Estimation." *American Statistician* 27:106–8.

Butler, J. S., and R. Moffitt (1982). "A Computationally Efficient Quadrature Procedure for the One-Factor Multinomial Probit Model." *Econometrica* 50(3):761–4.

Carroll, S. J., and D. A. Relles (1976). "A Bayesian Model of Choice among Higher Education Institutions." Report R-2005-NIE/LE, Rand Corporation, Santa Monica, California.

Chamberlain, G. (1980). "Analysis of Covariance with Qualitative Data." *Review of Economic Studies* 47:225–38.

Chambers, R. G., R. E. Just, L. J. Moffitt, and G. A. Rowe (1979). "Disequilibrium Analysis of Fluid Milk." California Agricultural Experiment Station.

Chambers, R. G., R. E. Just, L. J. Moffitt, and A. Schmitz (1978). "International Markets in Disequilibrium: A Case Study of Beef." California Agricultural Experiment Station.

Charemza, W., and R. E. Quandt (1982). "Models and Estimation of Disequilibrium for Centrally Planned Economies." *Review of Economic Studies* 49: 109–16.

Christofferson, A. (1975). "Factor Analysis of Dichotomized Variables." *Psychometrika* 40(1):5-32.

Clark, C. (1961). "The Greatest of a Finite Set of Random Variables." *Operations Research* 9:145-62.

Clower, R. W. (1965). "The Keynesian Counter-Revolution: A Theoretical Appraisal." In F. H. Hahn and F. P. R. Brechling (eds.), *The Theory of Interest Rates*. London: Macmillan.

Cogan, J. (1980). "Labor Supply With Costs of Labor Market Entry." In J. P. Smith (ed.), *Female Labor Supply: Theory and Estimation*. Princeton: Princeton University Press.

Cohen, A. C. (1957). "On the Solution of Estimating Equations for Truncated and Censored Samples from Normal Populations." *Biometrika* 44:225-36.

Cosslett, S. R. (1980). "Distribution-Free Maximum Likelihood Estimator of the Binary Choice Model." Manuscript. Northwestern University.

(1981*a*). "Efficient Estimators of Discrete Choice Models." In C. Manski and D. McFadden (eds.), *Structural Analysis of Discrete Data*. Cambridge, Mass.: M.I.T. Press.

(1981*b*). "Maximum Likelihood Estimator for Choice-Based Samples." *Econometrica* 49(5):1289-316.

Cox, D. R. (1958). "The Regression Analysis of Binary Sequences." *Journal of the Royal Statistical Society* (ser. B) 20:215-42.

(1966). "Some Procedures Connected with the Logistic Response Curve." In F. David (ed.), *Research Papers in Statistics*. New York: Wiley.

(1970). *Analysis of Binary Data*. London: Methuen.

Cox, D. R. (1972*a*). "The Analysis of Multivariate Binary Data." *Applied Statistics* 21:113-20.

(1972*b*). "Regression Models and Life Tables." *Journal of the Royal Statistical Society* (ser. B) 34:187-220.

Cox, D. R., and D. V. Hinkley (1974). *Theoretical Statistics*. London: Chapman and Hall.

Cox, D. R., and E. Snell (1968). "A General Definition of Residuals." *Journal of the Royal Statistical Society* (ser. B) 30:248-65.

(1971). "On Test Statistics Calculated from Residuals." *Biometrika* 58:589-94.

Cragg, J. G. (1971). "Some Statistical Models for Limited Dependent Variables with Application to the Demand for Durable Goods." *Econometrica* 39:829-44.

Cragg, J. G., and R. Uhler (1970). "The Demand for Automobiles." *Canadian Journal of Economics* 3:386-406.

Crawford, D. L. (1975). "Estimating Earnings Functions from Truncated Samples." Discussion paper 287-75. Institute for Research on Poverty, University of Wisconsin.

Daganzo, C. (1980). *Multinomial Probit*. New York: Academic.

Dagenais, M. G. (1975). "Application of a Threshold Regression Model to Household Purchases of Automobiles." *Review of Economics and Statistics* 57:275-85.

Daly, A., and S. Zachary (1979). "Improved Multiple Choice Models." In D. Hensher and O. Dalvi (eds.), *Identifying and Measuring the Determinants of Mode Choice*. London: Teakfield.

Davidson, J. (1978). "FIML Estimation of Models with Several Regimes." Manuscript. London School of Economics.

Day, N. E. (1969). "Estimating the Components of a Mixture of Normal Distributions." *Biometrika* 56:463–74.

Day, N. E., and D. F. Kerridge (1967). "A General Maximum Likelihood Discriminant." *Biometrika* 23:313–23.

Debreu, G. (1960). "Review of R. D. Luce Individual Choice Behavior." *American Economic Review* 50:186–8.

Dempster, A. P. (1973). "Aspects of the Multinomial Logit Model." In P. R. Krishniah (ed.), *Multivariate Analysis III*, pp. 129–42. New York: Academic.

Dempster, A. P., N. M. Laird, and D. B. Rubin (1977). "Maximum Likelihood from Incomplete Data via the E. M. Algorithm." *Journal of the Royal Statistical Society* (ser. B) 39:1–38.

Domencich, T., and D. McFadden (1975). *Urban Travel Demand: A Behavioral Analysis.* Amsterdam: North-Holland.

Dubin, J., and D. McFadden (1980). "An Econometric Analysis of Residential Electrical Appliances Holdings and Usage." Working paper. Department of Economics, Massachusetts Institute of Technology.

Ducos, G., J. Green, and J. J. Laffont (1981). "A Test of the Equilibrium Hypothesis Based on Inventories." Conference paper series 140. National Bureau of Economic Research, Cambridge, Mass.

Duncan, G. (1980). "Formulation and Statistical Analysis of the Mixed Continuous/Discrete Variable Model in Classical Production Theory." *Econometrica* 48(4):839–52.

Eaton, J., and R. E. Quandt (1979). "A Quasi-Walrasian Model of Rationing and Labor Supply: Theory and Estimation." Research memorandum 251. Econometric Research Program, Princeton University.

Edwards, L. N. (1978) "An Empirical Analysis of Compulsory Schooling Legislation 1940–1960." *Journal of Law and Economics* 21(1):203–22.

El Sayyad, G. M. (1973). "Bayesian and Classical Analysis of Poisson Regression." *Journal of the Royal Statistical Society* (ser. B) 35:445–51.

Fair, R. C. (1977). "A Note on the Computation of the Tobit Estimator." *Econometrica* 45(7):1723–7.

Fair, R. C., and D. M. Jaffee (1972). "Methods of Estimation for Markets in Disequilibrium." *Econometrica* 40:497–514.

Fair, R. C., and H. H. Kelejian (1974). "Methods of Estimation for Markets in Disequilibrium: A Further Study." *Econometrica* 42(1):177–90.

Feige, E., and H. W. Watts (1972). "An Investigation of the Consequences of Partial Aggregation of Micro-economic Data." *Econometrica* 40(2): 343–60.

Fienberg, S. E. (1975). "Comment." *Journal of the American Statistical Association* 70:521–4.

(1978). *The Analysis of Cross-Classified Data.* Mass.: M.I.T. Press.

Finney, D. (1971). *Probit Analysis.* Cambridge University Press.

Fishe, R. P. H., and K. Lahiri (1981). "On the Estimation of Inflationary Expectations from Qualitative Responses." *Journal of Econometrics* 16:89–102.

Fishe, R. P. H., G. S. Maddala, and R. P. Trost (1979). "Estimation of a Heteroscedastic Tobit Model." Manuscript. University of Florida.

Fishe, R. P. H., R. P. Trost, and P. Lurie (1981). "Selectivity Bias and Comparative Advantage: A Generalized Approach." *Economics of Education Review* 1:169–91.

Fisher, J. A. (1962). "An Analysis of Consumer Durable Goods Expenditures in 1957." *Review of Economics and Statistics* 27:431–47.

Fisher, R. A. (1936). "The Use of Multiple Measurement in Taxonomic Problems." *Annals of Eugenics* 7:179–88.

Førsund, F. R., C. A. Knox Lovell, and P. Schmidt (1980). "A Survey of Frontier Production Functions and of Their Relationship to Efficiency Measurement." *Journal of Econometrics* 13:5–25.

Frank, R. H. (1978). "How Long Is a Spell of Unemployment?" *Econometrica* 46(2):285–302.

Frisch, R. (1949). "Prolegomena to a Pressure Analysis of Economic Phenomena." *Metroeconomica* 1:135–60.

Gallant, A. R., and D. W. Jorgenson (1979). "Statistical Inference for a System of Simultaneous, Non-linear Implicit Equations in the Context of Instrumental Variable Estimation." *Journal of Econometrics* 11:275–302.

Geisser, S. (1966). "Predictive Discrimination." In P. R. Krishniah (ed.), *Multivariate Analysis,* pp. 149–63. New York: Academic.

(1970). "Discriminatory Practices." In R. Collier and F. Meyer (eds.), *Bayesian Statistics,* pp. 57–70. Itasca, Ill.: Peacock.

Goldberger, A. S. (1964). *Econometric Theory.* New York: Wiley.

(1971). "Econometrics and Psychometrics: A Survey of Communalities." *Psychometrika* 36:83–107.

(1972). "Selection Bias in Evaluating Treatment Effects: Some Formal Illustrations." Discussion paper 123-72. Institute for Research on Poverty, University of Wisconsin.

(1973). "Correlations Between Binary Choices and Probabilistic Predictions." *Journal of the American Statistical Association* 68:84.

(1980a). "Abnormal Selection Bias." Workshop series 8006. Social Systems Research Institute, University of Wisconsin.

(1980b). "An Omitted Variable Problem in Selectivity Bias Adjustment." Manuscript. University of Wisconsin.

(1981). "Linear Regression After Selection." *Journal of Econometrics* 15: 357–66.

Goldfeld, S. M., and R. E. Quandt (1972). *Nonlinear Methods in Econometrics.* Amsterdam: North-Holland.

(1973). "The Estimation of Structural Shifts by Switching Regressions." *Annals of Economic and Social Measurement* 2:475–85.

(1975). "Estimation in a Disequilibrium Model and the Value of Information." *Journal of Econometrics* 3(3):325–48.

(1978). "Some Properties of the Simple Disequilibrium Model with Covariance." *Economics Letters* 1(4):343–6.

(1979). "Estimation in Multi-Market Disequilibrium Models." *Economics Letters* 4(4):341–7.

Goodman, L. A. (1970). "The Multivariate Analysis of Qualitative Data: Interactions Among Multiple Classifications." *Journal of the American Statistical Association* 65:226–56.

(1971). "The Analysis of Multidimensional Contingency Tables: Stepwise Procedures and Direct Estimation Methods for Building Models for Multiple Classifications." *Technometrics* 13:33–61.

(1972a). "A Modified Multiple Regression Approach to the Analysis of Dichotomous Variables." *American Sociological Review* 37:28–46.

(1972*b*). "A General Model for the Analysis of Surveys." *American Journal of Sociology* 77:1035–86.

(1973). "Causal Analysis of Panel Study Data and Other Kinds of Survey Data." *American Journal of Sociology* 78:1135–91.

Gordon, R. H., and A. S. Blinder (1980). "Market Wages, Reservation Wages and Retirement Decisions." *Journal of Public Economics* 14:277–308.

Gourieroux, C., J. J. Laffont, and A. Monfort (1980*a*). "Disequilibrium Econometrics in Simultaneous Equations Systems." *Econometrica* 48(1):75–96.

(1980*b*). "Coherency Conditions in Simultaneous Linear Equations Models with Endogenous Switching Regimes." *Econometrica* 48(3):675–95.

Gourieroux, C., and A. Monfort (1979*a*). "On the Characterization of a Joint Probability Distribution by Conditional Distributions." *Journal of Econometrics* 9:115–18.

(1979*b*). "Compatibility of Conditional Qualitative Response Models." Discussion paper 7912. ENSAE, Paris.

(1980). "Estimation Methods for Markets with Controlled Prices." Working paper 8012. INSEE, Paris.

Greene, W. H. (1981). "On the Asymptotic Bias of the Ordinary Least Squares Estimator of the Tobit Model." *Econometrica* 49(2):505–13.

Grether, D. M., and G. S. Maddala (1982). "A Time Series Model with Qualitative Variables." In M. Diestler, E. Fürst, and G. Schwödiauer (eds.), *Games, Economic Dynamics and Time Series Analysis,* pp. 291–305. Vienna-Wurzburg: Physica Verlag.

Griliches, Z. (1967). "Distributed Lags: A Survey." *Econometrica* 35(1)16–49.

Griliches, Z., B. H. Hall, and J. A. Hausman (1978). "Missing Data and Self-Selection in Large Panels." *Annals de l'INSEE* 30–31:137–76.

Grizzle, J. (1962). "Asymptotic Power of Tests of Linear Hypotheses Using the Probit and Logit Transformations." *Journal of the American Statistical Association* 57:877–94.

(1971). "Multivariate Logit Analysis." *Biometrics* 27:1057–62.

Gronau, R. (1973). "The Effect of Children on the Housewife's Value of Time." *Journal of Political Economy* 81:s168–99.

(1974). "Wage Comparisons—A Selectivity Bias." *Journal of Political Economy* 82:1119–43.

Gumbel, E. J. (1961). "Bivariate Logistic Distributions." *Journal of the American Statistical Association* 56:335–49.

Gunderson, M. (1974). "Retention of Trainees: A Study with Dichotomous Dependent Variables." *Journal of Econometrics* 2:79–93.

Gurland, J., T. Lee, and P. Dahm (1960). "Polychotomous Quantal Reponse in Biological Assay." *Biometrics* 16:382–98.

Haberman, S. (1974). *The Analysis of Frequency Data.* Chicago: University of Chicago Press.

Halperin, M., W. C. Blackwelder, and J. I. Verter (1971). "Estimation of the Multivariate Logistic Risk Function: A Comparison of the Discriminant Function and Maximum Likelihood Approaches." *Journal of Chronic Diseases* 24:125–58.

Hanoch, G. (1980*a*). "Hours and Weeks in the Theory of Labor Supply." In J. P. Smith (ed.), *Female Labor Supply: Theory and Estimation.* Princeton: Princeton University Press.

(1980*b*). "A Multivariate Model of Labor Supply: Methodology for Estimation." In J. P. Smith (ed.), *Female Labor Supply: Theory and Estimation.* Princeton: Princeton University Press.

Hansen, L. P. (1982). "Large Sample Properties of Generalized Methods of Moments Estimator." *Econometrica* 50(4):1029–54.

Hansen, W. L., B. A. Weisbrod, and W. J. Scanlon (1970). "Schooling and Earnings of Low Achievers." *American Economic Review* 60(3):409–18.

Harter, J., and A. Moore (1967). "Maximum Likelihood Estimation, from Censored Samples, of the Parameters of a Logistic Distribution." *Journal of the American Statistical Association* 62:675–83.

Hartley, M. J. (1976). "The Estimation of Markets in Disequilibrium: The Fixed Supply Case." *International Economic Review* 17(3):687–99.

(1977). "On the Estimation of a General Switching Regression Model via Maximum Likelihood Methods." Discussion paper 415. Department of Economics, State University of New York at Buffalo.

(1979). "Comment." *Journal of the American Statistical Association* 73(364): 738–41.

Hartley, M. J., and P. Mallela (1977). "The Asymptotic Properties of a Maximum Likelihood Estimator for a Model of Markets in Disequilibrium" *Econometrica* 45(5):1205–20.

Hausman, J. (1978). "Specification Tests in Econometrics." *Econometrica* 46:1251–71.

(1979*a*). "Individual Discount Rates and the Purchase and Utilization of Energy Using Durables." *Bell Journal of Economics* 10:33–54.

(1979*b*). "The Effect of Wages, Taxes, and Fixed Costs on Women's Labor Force Participation." Discussion paper 238. Department of Economics, Massachusetts Institute of Technology.

(1979*c*). "The Effects of Taxes on Labor Supply." Paper presented at the Brookings Conference on Taxation, October 18–19, 1979.

Hausman, J., B. Hall, and Z. Griliches (1981). "Econometric Models for Count Data With an Application to the Patents—R & D Relationship." Discussion paper. National Bureau of Economic Research.

Hausman, J., and D. McFadden (1980). "A Specification Test for the Multinomial Logit Model." Working paper. Massachusetts Institute of Technology.

Hausman, J. A., and D. A. Wise (1976). "The Evaluation of Results from Truncated Samples: The New Jersey Negative Income Tax Experiment." *Annals of Economic and Social Measurement* 5:421–45.

(1977). "Social Experimentation, Truncated Distributions and Efficient Estimation." *Econometrica* 45:319–30.

(1978). "A Conditional Probit Model for Qualitative Choice: Discrete Decisions Recognizing Interdependence and Heterogeneous Preferences." *Econometrica* 46:403–26.

(1979). "Attrition Bias in Experimental and Panel Data: The Gary Negative Income Maintenance Experiment." *Econometrica* 47(2):445–73.

(1980). "Discontinuous Budget Constraints and Estimation: The Demand for Housing." *Review of Economic Studies* 47:75–96.

(1982). "Stratification on Endogenous Variables and Estimation: The Gary Experiment." In C. Manski and D. McFadden (eds.), *Structural Analysis of Discrete Data: With Econometric Applications.* Cambridge, Mass.: M.I.T. Press.

Hay, J. (1979). *An Analysis of Occupational Choice and Income*. Ph.D. dissertation. Yale University.

(1980). "Selectivity Bias in a Simultaneous Logit-OLS Model: Physician Specialty Choice and Specialty Income." Manuscript. University of Connecticut Health Center.

Heckman, J. (1974). "Shadow Prices, Market Wages, and Labor Supply." *Econometrica* 42:679–94.

(1976a). "Simultaneous Equations Model with Continuous and Discrete Endogenous Variables and Structural Shifts." In S. M. Goldfeld and R. E. Quandt (eds.), *Studies in Non-Linear Estimation*. Cambridge: Ballinger.

(1976b). "The Common Structure of Statistical Models of Truncation, Sample Selection and Limited Dependent Variables and a Simple Estimator for Such Models." *Annals of Economic and Social Measurement* 5:475–92.

(1978a). "Dummy Exogenous Variables in a Simultaneous Equation System." *Econometrica* 46:931–59.

(1978b). "Simple Statistical Models for Discrete Panel Data Developed and Applied to Test the Hypothesis of True State Dependence Against the Hypothesis of Spurious State Dependence." *Annals de l'INSEE* 30–31: 227–70.

(1979). "Sample Selection Bias as a Specification Error." *Econometrica* 47:153–61.

(1982). "Heterogeneity and State Dependence in Dynamic Models of Labor Supply." In S. Rosen (ed.), *Conference on Low Income Labor Markets*. Chicago: University of Chicago Press.

(1982a). "Statistical Models for the Analysis of Discrete Panel Data." In C. Manski and D. McFadden (eds.), *Structural Analysis of Discrete Data: With Econometric Applications*. Cambridge, Mass.: M.I.T. Press.

(1982b). "The Incidental Parameters Problem and the Problem of Initial Conditions in Estimating a Discrete Stochastic Process and Some Monte Carlo Evidence on Their Practical Importance." In C. Manski and D. McFadden (eds.), *Structural Analysis of Discrete Data: With Econometric Applications*. Cambridge, Mass.: M.I.T. Press.

Heckman, J. J., and G. Borjas (1980). "Does Unemployment Cause Future Unemployment? Definitions, Questions and Answers from a Continuous Time Model of Heterogeneity and State Dependence." *Economica* 47: 247–83.

Heckman, J., and T. Macurdy (1979). "A Dynamic Model of Female Labor Supply." *Review of Economic Studies* 47:41–74.

Heckman, J., and B. Singer (eds.) (1982). *Longitudinal Labor Market Studies: Theory, Methods and Empirical Results*. Social Science Research Council monograph. New York: Academic.

Heckman, J., and R. Willis (1976). "Estimation of a Stochastic Model of Reproduction: An Econometric Approach." In N. Terleckyj (ed.), *Household Production and Consumption*. New York: National Bureau of Economic Research.

(1977). "A Beta Logistic Model for the Analysis of Sequential Labor Force Participation of Married Women." *Journal of Political Economy* 85:27–58.

Hendry, D. F., and A. Spanos (1980). "Disequilibrium and Latent Variables." Manuscript. London School of Economics.

Hildebrand, F. B. (1956). *Introduction to Numerical Analysis*. New York: McGraw-Hill.

Holland, P. W. (1973). "Poisson Regression." Manuscript. Educational Testing Service, Princeton University.

Holt, D., T. M. F. Smith, and P. D. Winter (1980). "Regression Analysis of Data from Complex Surveys." *Journal of the Royal Statistical Society* (ser. A) 143:474–87.

Horowitz, J. (1979*a*). "Identification and Diagnosis of Specification Errors in the Multinomial Logit Model." Mimeograph. Environmental Protection Agency.

(1979*b*). "A Note on the Accuracy of the Clark Approximation for the Multinomial Probit Model." Mimeograph. Massachusetts Institute of Technology.

(1980*a*). "The Accuracy of the Multinomial Logit Model as an Aproximation to the Multinomial Probit Model of Travel Demand." *Transportation Research* (part B) 14B:331–41.

(1982). "Sampling, Specification and Data Errors in Probabilistic Discrete Choice Models." In D. Hensher and L. Johnson (eds.), *Applied Discrete Choice Modelling*. London.

Hotz, V. J. (1976). "The Labor Supply of Married Women in the New Jersey Negative Income-Tax Experiments." Technical analysis series 2. Mathematica Policy Research.

Hurd, M. (1979). "Estimation in Truncated Samples when There Is Heteroscedasticity." *Journal of Econometrics* 11:247–58.

Hwang, H. S. (1980). "A Test of a Disequilibrium Model." *Journal of Econometrics* 12:319–33.

Ito, T. (1980). "Methods of Estimation for Multi-Market Disequilibrium Models." *Econometrica* 48(1):97–125.

Ito, T., and K. Ueda (1981). "Tests of the Equilibrium Hypothesis in Disequilibrium Econometrics: An International Comparison of Credit Rationing." *International Economic Review* 22(3):691–708.

Johnson, N. L., and S. Kotz (1969). *Discrete Distributions*. Boston: Houghton Mifflin.

(1970). *Distributions in Statistics: Continuous Univariate Distributions, Vols. 1 and 2*. Boston: Houghton Mifflin.

(1972). *Distributions in Statistics: Continuous Multivariate Distributions*. New York: Wiley.

Johnson, P. D., and J. C. Taylor (1977). "Modelling Monetary Disequilibrium." In M. G. Porter (ed.), *The Australian Monetary System in the 1970's*. Monash University, Australia.

Jöreskog, N., and A. Goldberger (1975). "Estimation of a Model with Multiple Indicators and Multiple Causes of a Single Latent Variable Model." *Journal of the American Statistical Association* 70:631–9.

Jorgenson, D. W. (1961). "Multiple Regression Analysis of a Poisson Process." *Journal of the American Statistical Association* 56:235–45.

Kaplan, R. S., and G. Urwitz (1979). "Statistical Models of Bond Ratings: A Methodological Enquiry." *Journal of Business* 52(2):231–61.

Katz, A. (1977). "Evaluating Contributions of the Employment Service to Applicant Earnings." *Labor Law Journal* 28:472–8.

Kawasaki, S. (1979). "Application of Log-linear Probability Models in Econometrics." Unpublished Ph.D. dissertation. Northwestern University.

Keener, R. W., and D. M. Waldman (1980). "Maximum Likelihood Regression of Rank-Censored Data." Working paper 80-3. University of North Carolina.

Kendall, M. G., and A. Stuart (1967). *Advanced Theory of Statistics, Vols. 1–3.* London: Griffin.

Kenny, L. W., L. F. Lee, G. S. Maddala, and R. P. Trost (1979). "Returns to College Education: An Investigation of Self-Selection Bias Based on the Project Talent Data." *International Economic Review* 20(3):775–89.

Kiefer, N. (1978). "Discrete Parameter Variation: Efficient Estimation of a Switching Regression Model." *Econometrica* 46:427–34.

(1979). "On the Value of Sample Separation Information." *Econometrica* 47:997–1003.

(1980). "A Note on Regime Classification in Disequilibrium Models." *Review of Economic Studies* 47(1):637–9.

Kiefer, N. M., and G. R. Neumann (1979a). "Estimation of Wage Offer Distributions and Reservation Wages." In S. A. Lippman and J. J. McCall (eds.), *Studies in the Economics of Search.* Amsterdam: North-Holland.

(1979b). "An Empirical Job Search Model with a Test of the Constant Reservation Wage Hypothesis." *Journal of Political Economy* 87:89–107.

King, M. (1980). "An Econometric Model of Tenure Choice and Demand for Housing as a Joint Decision." *Journal of Public Economics* 14(2):137–59.

Koenig, H., M. Nerlove, and G. Oudiz (1981). "On the Formation of Price Expectations: An Analysis of Business Test Data by Log-Linear Probability Models." *European Economic Review* 16:103–38.

Kohn, M., C. Manski, and D. Mundel (1976). "An Empirical Investigation of Factors Influencing College Going Behavior." *Annals of Economic and Social Measurement* 5:391–419.

Ladd, G. (1966). "Linear Probability Functions and Discriminant Functions." *Econometrica* 34:873–85.

Laffont, J. J., and Garcia, R. (1977). "Disequilibrium Econometrics for Business Loans." *Econometrica* 45(5):1187–204.

Laffont, J. J., and Monfort, A. (1979). "Disequilibrium Econometrics in Dynamic Models." *Journal of Econometrics* 11(2/3):353–61.

Lancaster, T. (1974). "Some Econometrics of Counts of Events." Manuscript. University of Hull.

(1979). "Econometric Models for the Duration of Unemployment." *Econometrica* 47(4):939–56.

Lancaster, T., and S. Nickell (1980). "The Analysis of Re-employment Probabilities for the Unemployed." *Journal of the Royal Statistical Society* (ser. A) 143:141–65.

Landes, W. (1968). "The Economics of Fair Employment Laws." *Journal of Political Economy* 76:507–52.

Lee, L. F. (1976a). "Estimation of Limited Dependent Variable Models by Two-Stage Methods." Ph.D. dissertation. University of Rochester.

(1976b). "Multivariate Regression and Simultaneous Equations Models with

Some Dependent Variables Truncated." Discussion paper 76-79. University of Minnesota.

(1978). "Unionism and Wage Rates: A Simultaneous Equation Model with Qualitative and Limited Dependent Variables." *International Economic Review* 19:415-33.

(1979a). "Identification and Estimation in Binary Choice Models with Limited (Censored) Dependent Variables." *Econometrica* 47:977-96.

(1979b). "Comparative Advantage in Individuals and Self-Selection." Manuscript. University of Minnesota.

(1979c). "Mixed Logit and Fully Recursive Logit Models." *Economics Letters* 3:363-8.

(1979d). "On Comparisons of Normal and Logistic Models in the Bivariate Dichotomous Analysis." *Economics Letters* 4:151-5.

(1979e). "On the Generalized Berkson's Estimator in the General Qualitative Response Model." *Economics Letters* 4:243-9.

(1980a). "Specification Error in Multinomial Logit Models: Analysis of the Omitted Variable Bias." Working paper. University of Minnesota.

(1980b). "Analysis of Econometric Models for Discrete Panel Data with the Multivariate Log-Linear Probability Models." Discussion paper 23. Center for Econometrics and Decision Sciences, University of Florida.

(1981). "Fully Recursive Probability Models and Multivariate Log-Linear Probability Models for the Analysis of Qualitative Data." *Journal of Econometrics* 16:51-69.

(1982a). "Health and Wage: A Simultaneous Equation Model with Multiple Discrete Indicators." *International Economic Review* 33(1):199-221.

(1982b). "Simultaneous Equations Models with Discrete and Censored Variables." In C. Manski and D. McFadden (eds.), *Structural Analysis of Discrete Data: With Econometric Applications*. Cambridge, Mass.: M.I.T. Press.

(1982c). "Some Approaches to the Correction of Selectivity Bias." *Review of Economic Studies* 49:355-72.

(in press). "Generalized Econometric Models with Selectivity." *Econometrica* 51.

Lee, L. F., G. S. Maddala, and R. P. Trost (1979). "Testing for Structural Change by D-Methods in Switching Simultaneous Equation Models." *Proceedings of the American Statistical Association* (Business and Economics Section), pp. 461-6.

(1980). "Asymptotic Covariance Matrices of Two-Stage Probit and Two-Stage Tobit Methods for Simultaneous Equations Models with Selectivity." *Econometrica* 48:491-503.

Lee, L. F., and R. P. Trost (1978). "Estimation of Some Limited Dependent Variable Models with Applications to Housing Demand." *Journal of Econometrics* 8:357-82.

Lee, L. F., and W. G. Tyler (1978). "The Stochastic Frontier Production Function and Average Efficiency: An Empirical Analysis." *Journal of Econometrics* 7(3):385-90.

Lerman, S. R. (1977). "Location, Housing, Automobile Ownership and Mode to Work: A Joint Choice Model." *Transportation Research Board Record* No. 610.

Lerman, S., and C. Manski (1982). "On the Use of Simulated Frequencies to Approximate Choice Probabilities." In C. Manski and D. McFadden (eds.), *Structural Analysis of Discrete Data: With Econometric Applications*. Cambridge, Mass.: M.I.T. Press.

Levin, R. C. (1978). "Allocation in Surface Freight Transportation: Does Rate Regulation Matter?" *Bell Journal of Economics* 9(1):18–45.

Lewis, H. G. (1963). *Unionism and Relative Wages in the U.S.* Chicago: University of Chicago Press.

(1974). "Comments on Selectivity Biases in Wage Comparisons." *Journal of Political Economy* 82(6):1145–55.

Li, M. (1977). "A Logit Model of Home Ownership." *Econometrica* 45:1081–97.

Luce, R. D. (1959). *Individual Choice Behavior: A Theoretical Analysis*. New York: Wiley.

(1977). "The Choice Axiom After Twenty Years." *Journal of Mathematical Psychology* 15:215–33.

Luce, R. D., and P. Suppes (1965). "Preference, Utility and Subjective Probability." In R. Luce, R. Bush, and E. Galanter (eds.), *Handbook of Mathematical Psychology III*. New York: Wiley.

McFadden, D. (1973). "Conditional Logit Analysis of Qualitative Choice Behavior." In P. Zarembka (ed.), *Frontiers in Econometrics*. New York: Academic.

(1974). "The Measurement of Urban Travel Demand." *Journal of Public Economics* 3:303–28.

(1976a). "A Comment on Discriminant Analysis 'Versus' Logit Analysis." *Annals of Economics and Social Measurement* 5:511–23.

(1976b). "Quantal Choice Analysis: A Survey." *Annals of Economic and Social Measurement* 5:363–90.

(1976c). "The Revealed Preferences of a Public Bureaucracy." *Bell Journal of Economics* 7:55–72.

(1978). "Modelling the Choice of Residential Location." In A. Karlquist et al. (eds.), *Spatial Interaction Theory and Residential Location*, pp. 75–96. Amsterdam: North-Holland.

(1979). "Econometric Analysis of Discrete Data." Fisher-Schultz Lecture, Econometric Society, Athens.

(1980). "Econometric Models for Probabilistic Choice Among Products." *Journal of Business* 53(3):513–29.

(1982). "Econometric Models of Probabilistic Choice." In C. Manski and D. McFadden (eds.), *Structural Analysis of Discrete Data: With Econometric Applications*. Cambridge, Mass.: M.I.T. Press.

(in press). "Qualitative Response Models." In Z. Griliches and M. D. Intrilligator (eds.), *Handbook of Econometrics*. Amsterdam: North-Holland.

McFadden, D., C. Puig, and D. Kirschner (1977). "Determinants of the Long-Run Demand for Electricity." *Proceedings of the American Statistical Association* (Business and Economics Section), pp. 109–17.

McFadden, D., and F. Reid (1975). "Aggregate Travel Demand Forecasting from Disaggregated Behavioral Models." *Transportation Research Board Record* No. 534.

McFadden, D., W. Tye, and K. Train (1976). "An Application of Diagnostic Tests for the Independence from Irrelevant Alternatives Property of the Multinomial Logit Model." *Transportation Research Board Record* No. 637, pp. 39-45.

McGillivray, R. G. (1970). "Estimating the Linear Probability Function." *Econometrica* 38(5):775-6.

(1972). "Binary Choice of Urban Transport Mode in the San Francisco Bay Region." *Econometrica* 40(5):827-48.

McKelvey, R., and W. Zavoina (1975). "A Statistical Model for the Analysis of Ordinal Level Dependent Variables." *Journal of Mathematical Sociology* 4:103-20.

MacKinnon, J. G. (1978). "Modelling a Market which Is Sometimes in Disequilibrium." Discussion paper 287. Department of Economics, Queen's University, Kingston, Ontario, Canada.

MacKinnon, J. G., and N. D. Olewiler (1980). "Disequilibrium Estimation of the Demand for Copper." *Bell Journal of Economics* 11:197-211.

Mandansky, A. (1980). "On Conjoint Analysis and Quantal Choice Models." *Journal of Business* 53:S37-44.

Maddala, G. S. (1977a). "Self-Selectivity Problems in Econometric Models." In P. Krishniah (ed.), *Applications of Statistics,* pp. 351-66. Amsterdam: North-Holland.

(1977b). "Identification and Estimation Problems in Limited Dependent Variable Models." In A. S. Blinder and P. Friedman (eds.), *Natural Resources, Uncertainty and General Equilibrium Systems: Essays in Memory of Rafael Lusky,* pp. 219-39. New York: Academic.

(1978). "Selectivity Problems in Longitudinal Data." *Annals de l'INSEE* 30-31:423-50.

(1979). "Methods of Estimation for Models of Markets with Bounded Price Variation." Social science working paper 296. California Institute of Technology.

(1980). "Simultaneous Probit and Tobit Models with Latent Structures." Discussion paper 15. Center for Econometrics and Decision Sciences, University of Florida.

(in press). "Disequilibrium, Self-Selection and Switching Models." In Z. Griliches and M. D. Intrilligator (eds.), *Handbook of Econometrics.* Amsterdam: North-Holland.

Maddala, G. S., and R. P. H. Fishe (1979). "Technical Change, Frontier Production Functions and Efficiency Measurement." *Proceedings of the American Statistical Association* (Business and Economic Statistics Section), pp. 470-5.

Maddala, G. S., R. P. H. Fishe, and K. Lahiri (1982). "A Time Series Analysis of Popular Expectations Data." In Arnold Zellner (ed.), *Economic Applications of Time Series Analysis.* Washington, D.C.: American Statistical Association.

Maddala, G. S., and L. F. Lee (1976). "Recursive Models with Qualitative Endogenous Variables." *Annals of Economic and Social Measurement* 5(4): 525-45.

Maddala, G. S., and F. Nelson (1974). "Maximum Likelihood Medthods for Markets in Disequilibrium." *Econometrica* 42:1013-30.

(1975). "Switching Regression Models with Exogenous and Endogenous Switching." *Proceedings of the American Statistical Association* (Business and Economics Section), pp. 423-6.

Maddala, G. S., and R. P. Trost (1978). "Estimation of the Logit Model with Randomized Data." Manuscript. University of Florida.

(1980). "Some Extensions of the Nerlove–Press Model." *Proceedings of the American Statistical Association* (Business and Economic Statistics Section), pp. 481–5.

(1981). "Alternative Formulations of the Nerlove–Press Models." *Journal of Econometrics* 16:35–49.

(1982). "On Measuring Discrimination in Loan Markets." *Housing Finance Review* 1(1):245–68.

Malinvaud, E. (1977). *The Theory of Unemployment Reconsidered.* Oxford: Blackwell.

(1981). "Econometric Implications of Macro-disequilibrium Theory." Discussion paper 814, INSEE, Paris.

Mallar, C. D. (1977). "The Estimation of Simultaneous Probability Models." *Econometrica* 45(7):1717–22.

Manski, C. (1975). "Maximum Score Estimation of the Stochastic Utility Model of Choice." *Journal of Econometrics* 3:205–28.

(1977). "The Structure of Random Utility Models." *Theory and Decision* 8:229–54.

(1981). "Structural Models for Discrete Data." *Sociological Methdology,* pp. 58–109.

Manski, C., and S. Lerman. (1977). "The Estimation of Choice Probabilities from Choice-Based Samples." *Econometrica* 45:1977–88.

Manski, C., and D. McFadden (1982). "Alternative Estimates and Sample Designs for Discrete Choice Analysis." In C. Manski and D. McFadden (eds.), *Structural Analysis of Discrete Data: With Econometric Applications.* Cambridge, Mass.: M.I.T. Press.

Mantel, N., and C. Brown (1973). "A Logistic Re-analysis of Ashford and Sowden's Data on Respiratory Symptoms in Coal Miners." *Biometrics* 29:649–55.

Marantz, J. K., K. E. Case III, and H. B. Leonard (1976). *Discrimination in Rural Housing.* Cambridge, Mass.: Ballinger.

Miller, L., and R. Radner (1970). "Demand and Supply in U.S. Higher Education." *American Economic Review* 60:326–34.

Moore, D. H. (1973). "Evaluation of Five Discrimination Procedures for Binary Variables." *Journal of the American Statistical Association* 68:399–404.

Morimune, K. (1979). "Comparisons of the Normal and Logistic Models in the Bivariate Dichotomous Analysis." *Econometrica* 47(4):957–75.

Morrison, D. G. (1972). "Upper Bounds for Correlations Between Binary Outcomes and Probabilistic Predictions." *Journal of the American Statistical Association* 7:68–70.

Muellbauer, J. (1980). "Macro-Models with Regime Changes: Discrete vs. Continuous Formulations of Non-Clearing Markets Approach." Discussion paper. Birbeck College, London.

Muellbauer, J., and D. Winter (1980). "Unemployment, Employment and Exports in British Manufacturing: A Non-Clearing Markets Approach." *European Economic Review* 13:383–409.

Muthén, B. (1978). "Contributions to Factor Analysis of Dichotomous Variables." *Psychometrika* 43:551–60.

(1979). "A Structural Probit Model with Latent Variables." *Journal of the American Statistical Association* 74:807–11.

Muthén, B., and K. G. Jöreskog (1981). "Selectivity Problems in Quasi-experimental Studies." Paper presented at a conference on experimental research in social sciences, University of Florida.

Nakosteen, R. A., and M. Zimmer (1980). "Migration and Income: The Question of Self-Selection." *Southern Economic Journal* 46:840–51.

Nelder, J. A., and R. W. M. Wedderburn (1972). "Generalized Linear Models." *Journal of the Royal Statistical Society* (Ser. A) (Part 3):370–83.

Nelson, F. D. (1975). "Estimation of Economic Relationships with Censored, Truncated and Limited Dependent Variables." Ph.D. dissertation. University of Rochester.

(1976). "On a General Computer Algorithm for the Analysis of Models with Limited Dependent Variables." *Annals of Economic and Social Measurement* 5(4):493–509.

(1977). "Censored Regression Models with Unobserved Stochastic Censoring Thresholds." *Journal of Econometrics* 6:309–27.

(1980). "A Note on Experimental Auction Markets and the Walrasian Hypothesis." Social science working paper 307. California Institute of Technology.

(1981). "A Test for Misspecification in the Censored-Normal Model." *Econometrica* 49(5):1317–29.

Nelson, F. D., and R. Noll (1980). "In Search of Scientific Regulation: The UHF Allocation Experiment." Social Science Working Paper 317, California Institute of Technology.

Nelson, F. D., and L. Olsen (1978). "Specification and Estimation of a Simultaneous Equation Model with Limited Dependent Variables." *International Economic Review* 19:695–710.

Nerlove, M. (1981). "Expectations, Plans and Realization: In Theory and Practice." Presidential address. Econometric Society, Amsterdam meetings.

Nerlove, M., and J. Press (1973). "Univariate and Multivariate Log-Linear and Logistic Models," RAND report R–1306–EDA/NIH.

(1976). "Multivariate and Log Linear Probability Models for the Analysis of Qualitative Data." Discussion paper. Northwestern University.

(1980). "Multivariate Log-Linear Probability Models in Econometrics." Discussion paper. Northwestern University.

Nickell, S. (1979). "Estimating the Probability of Leaving Unemployment." *Econometrica* 47(5):1249–66.

Oliveira, J. T. de (1958). "Extremal Distributions." *Revista de Faculdata de Ciencia, Lisboa* (Ser. A) 7:215–27.

Olsen, R. J. (1978*a*). "Comment on 'The Effect of Unions on Earnings and Earnings on Unions: A Mixed Logit Approach.'" *International Economic Review* 19:259–61.

(1978*b*). "Note on the Uniqueness of the Maximum Likelihood Estimator for the Tobit Model." *Econometrica* 46(5):1211–15.

(1980*a*). "A Least Squares Correction for Selectivity Bias." *Econometrica* 48(7):1815–20.

(1980*b*). "The Method of Box and Cox: A Pitfall." Unpublished manuscript. Yale University.

(1982). "Distributional Tests for Selectivity Bias and a More Robust Likelihood Estimator." *International Economic Review* 23(1):223–40.

Page, E. (1977). "Approximations to the Cumulative Normal Function and Its Inverse for Use on a Pocket Calculator." *Applied Statistics* 26:75–6.

Parks, R. W. (1980). "On the Estimation of Multinomial Logit Models from Relative Frequency Data." *Journal of Econometrics* 13:293–303.

Pearson, K. (1900). "Mathematical Contributions to the Theory of Evolution in the Inheritance of Characteristics Not Capable of Exact Quantitative Measurement, VIII." *Philosophical Transactions of the Royal Society* (Ser. A) 195(1):79–150.

Pearson, K., and A. Lee (1908). "Generalized Probable Error in Multiple Normal Correlations." *Biometrika* 6:59–68.

Pitt, M. M., and L. F. Lee (1981). "The Measurement and Sources of Technical Inefficiency in the Indonesian Weaving Industry." *Journal of Development Economics* 9:43–64.

Plackett, R. L. (1974). *The Analysis of Categorical Data*. London: Charles Griffin.

Poirier, D. J. (1978a). "The Use of Box–Cox Transformation in Limited Dependent Variable Models." *Journal of the American Statistical Association* 73:284–7.

(1978b). A Curious Relationship Between Probit and Logit Models." *Southern Economic Journal* 44:640–1.

(1980). "Partial Observability in Bivariate Probit Models." *Journal of Econometrics* 12:209–17.

(1982). "A Switching Simultaneous Equation Model of Physician Behavior in Ontario." In D. McFadden and C. Manski (eds.), *Structural Analysis of Discrete Data: With Econometric Applications*. Cambridge, Mass.: M.I.T. Press.

Poirier, D. J., and P. A. Rudd (1981). "On the Appropriateness of Endogenous Switching." *Journal of Econometrics* 16(2):249–56.

Polakoff, M. E., and W. L. Sibler (1967). "Reluctance and Member Bank Borrowing: Additional Evidence." *Journal of Finance* 22(1):88–92.

Pollakowski, H. (1980). *Residential Location and Urban Housing Markets*. Lexington, Mass.: D. C. Heath.

Portes, R. D. (1977). "Effective Demand and Spillovers in Empirical Two-Market Disequilibrium Models." Discussion paper 595. Harvard Institute of Economic Research.

Portes, R., and D. Winter (1978). "The Demand for Money and for Consumption Goods in Centrally Planned Economies." *Review of Economics and Statistics* 60(1):8–18.

(1980). "Disequilibrium Estimates for Consumption Goods Markets in Centrally Planned Economies." *Review of Economic Studies* 47(1):137–59.

Prais, S. J., and H. S. Houthakker (1955). *The Analysis of Family Budgets*. Cambridge University Press.

Pratt, J. W. (1981). "Concavity of the Log-Likelihood." *Journal of the American Statistical Association* 76:137–59.

Pregibon, D. (1981). "Logistic Regression Diagnostics." *Annals of Statistics* 9(4):705–24.

Press, S. J., and S. Wilson (1978). "Choosing Between Logistic Regression and

Discriminant Analysis." *Journal of the American Statistical Association* 73:699–705.

Quandt, R. E. (1972). "A New Approach to Estimating Switching Regressions." *Journal of the American Statistical Association* 67:306–10.

(1978*a*). "Maximum Likelihood Estimation of Disequilibrium Models." In T. Bagiotti and G. Franco (eds.), *Pioneering Economics*, pp, 865–96. Padova: Edizioni Cedam.

(1978*b*). "Tests of the Equilibrium vs. Disequilibrium Hypothesis." *International Economic Review* 19(2):435–52.

Quandt, R. E., and J. B. Ramsey (1978). "Estimating Mixtures of Normal Distributions and Switching Regressions." *Journal of the American Statistical Association* 73:730–52.

Quigley, J. M. (1976). "Housing Demand in the Short-Run: An Analysis of Polychotomous Choice." *Explorations in Economic Research* 3:76–102.

Radner, R., and L. Miller (1975). *Demand and Supply in U.S. Higher Education.* New York: McGraw-Hill.

Ramsey, F. L. (1972). "A Bayesian Approach to Bio-Assay." *Biometrics* 28:841–58.

Rao, C. R. (1970). "Inference on Discriminant Function Coefficients." In R. C. Bose et al. (eds.), *Essays in Probability and Statistics,* pp. 587–602. Chapel Hill: University of North Carolina.

(1972). "Recent Trends of Research Work in Multivariate Analysis." *Biometrics* 28:3–22.

Reder, M. W. (1965). "Unionism and Wages: The Problems of Measurement." *Journal of Political Economy* 73:188–96.

Richard, J. F. (1978). "Statistical Analysis of Models with Several Regimes." CORE discussion paper 7822.

(1980). "C-Type Distributions and Disequilibrium Models." Paper presented at the Toulouse conference on economics and econometrics of disequilibrium.

Roberts, R. B., G. S. Maddala, and G. Enholm (1978). "Determinants of the Requested Rate of Return and the Rate of Return Granted in a Formal Regulatory Process." *Bell Journal of Economics* 9(2):611–21.

Robinson, P. M. (1980*a*). "Estimation and Forecasting for Time Series Containing Censored or Missing Observations." In O. D. Anderson (ed.), *Proceedings of the International Time Series Meeting.* Amsterdam: North-Holland.

(1982*a*). "On the Asymptotic Properties of Estimators of Models Containing Limited Dependent Variables." *Econometrica* 50(1):27–41.

(1982*b*). "Analysis of Time-Series from Mixed Distributions." *Annals of Statistics* 10(3):915–25.

Rosen, H. S. (1979). "Housing Decisions and the U.S. Income Tax: An Econometric Analysis." *Journal of Public Economics* 11:1–23.

Rosen, H., and R. E. Quandt (1978). "Estimation of a Disequilibrium Aggregate Labor Market." *Review of Economics and Statistics* 60:371–9.

Rosen, S. (1969). "Trade Union Power, Threat Effects and Extent of Organization." *Review of Economic Studies* 36:185–91.

(1970). "Unionism and the Occupational Structure of the United States." *International Economic Review* 11(2):269–85.

(1978). "Substituting and the Division of Labor." *Economica* 45:235–50.

Rosen, S., and M. I. Nadiri (1974). "A Disequilibrium Model of Demand for Factors of Production." *American Economic Review* 62(2):264–70.

Rosenbaum, S. (1961). "Moments of a Truncated Bivariate Normal Distribution." *Journal of the Royal Statistical Society* (Ser. B) 23(2):405–8.

Rosett, R. N. (1959). "A Statistical Model of Friction in Economics." *Econometrica* 27:263–7.

Rosett, R. N., and F. D. Nelson (1975). "Estimation of a Two-Limit Probit Regression Model." *Econometrica* 43:141–6.

Roy, A. D. (1951). "Some Thoughts on the Distribution of Earnings." *Oxford Economic Papers* 3:135–46.

Rudd, P. A. (1982). "A Score Test for Consistency." Manuscript. Department of Economics, University of California, Berkeley.

Rutemiller, H. C., and D. A. Bowers (1968). "Estimation in a Heteroscedastic Regression Model." *Journal of the American Statistical Association* 63: 552–7.

Samelson, H., R. M. Thrall, and O. Wesler (1958). "A Partition Theorem for Euclidean *n* space." *Proceedings of the American Mathematical Society* 9: 805–7.

Sattinger, M. (1975). "Comparative Advantage and the Distribution of Earnings and Abilities." *Econometrica* 43(3):455–68.

Schmeiser, B. W. (1979). "Approximation to the Inverse Cumulative Normal Function for Use on Hand Calculators." *Applied Statistics* 28:175–6.

Schmidt, P. (1978). "Estimation of a Simultaneous Equations Model with Jointly Dependent Continuous and Qualitative Variables: The Union-Earnings Question Revisited." *International Economic Review* 19(2):453–65.

(1982). "Constraints on the Parameters in Simultaneous Tobit and Probit Models." In C. F. Manski and D. McFadden (eds.), *Structural Analysis of Discrete Data: With Econometric Applications*. Cambridge, Mass.: M.I.T. Press.

Schmidt, P., and R. P. Strauss (1975*a*). "Estimation of Models with Jointly Dependent Qualitative Variables: A Simultaneous Logit Approach." *Econometrica* 43(4): 745–55.

(1975*b*). "The Predictions of Occupation Using Multiple Logit Models." *International Economic Review* 16(2):471–86.

(1976). "The Effect of Unions on Earnings and Earnings on Unions: A Mixed Logit Approach." *International Economic Review* 17(1):204–12.

Schultz, T. P. (1975). "The Determinants of Internal Migration in Venezuela: An Application of the Polytomous Logistic Model." Paper presented at the Third World Congress of the Econometric Society, Toronto, Canada.

(1978). "The Influence of Fertility on Labor Supply of Married Women." In R. G. Ehrenberg (ed.), *Research in Labor Economics II*. Greenwich, Conn.: Jai Press.

Sealey, C. W., Jr. (1979). "Credit Rationing in the Commercial Loan Market: Estimates of a Structural Model Under Conditions of Disequilibrium." *Journal of Finance* 34(2):689–702.

Sickles, R. C., and P. Schmidt (1978). "Simultaneous Equation Models with Truncated Dependent Variables: A Simultaneous Tobit Model." *Journal of Economics and Business* 31:11–21.

Sickles, R. C., P. Schmidt, and Ann D. Witte (1979). "An Application of the

Simultaneous Tobit Model: A Study of the Determinants of Criminal Recidivism." *Journal of Economics and Business* 31(3):166–71.

Sickles, R. C., and A..M. J. Yezer (1981). "An Analysis of Regulated Markets: The Estimation of Markets With Unobservable Equilibria." Discussion paper. George Washington University.

Sjüberg, L. (1977). "Choice Frequency and Similarity." *Scandinavian Journal of Psychology* 18:103–15.

Spilerman, S. (1972). "Extensions of the Mover-Stayer Model." *American Journal of Sociology* 78:599–626.

Stapleton, D. C., and D. J. Young (1981). "Censored Normal Regression with Measurement Error on the Dependent Variable." Discussion paper 81–30. University of British Columbia.

Stevenson, R. E. (1980). "Likelihood Functions for Generalized Stochastic Frontier Estimation." *Journal of Econometrics* 15:57–66.

Stigler, G. J. (1973). "The Sources of Economic Legislation." Manuscript. University of Chicago.

Suits, D. (1955). "An Econometric Model of the Watermelon Market." *Journal of Farm Economics* 37:237–51.

Theil, H. (1969). "A Multinomial Extension of the Linear Logit Model." *International Economic Review* 10:251–9.

   (1970). "On the Estimation of Relationships Involving Qualitative Variables." *American Journal of Sociology* 76:103–54.

Thurstone, L. (1927). "A Law of Comparative Judgement." *Psychological Review* 34:273–86.

Tobin, J. (1958). "Estimation of Relationships for Limited Dependent Variables." *Econometrica* 26:24–36.

Trost, R. P. (1977). "Demand for Housing: A Model Based on Inter-related Choices Between Owning and Renting." Unpublished Ph.D. dissertation. University of Florida.

   (1981). "Interpretation of Error Covariances with Non-Random Data: An Empirical Illustration of Returns to College Education." *Atlantic Economic Journal* 9(3):85–90.

Tsiatis, A. A. (1980). "A Note on a Goodness-of-Fit Test for the Logistic Regression Model." *Biometrika* 67(1):250–1.

Tuma, N. B., and M. T. Hannan (1979). "Approaches to the Censoring Problem in Analysis of Event Histories." In K. Schuessler (ed.), *Sociological Methodology 1979*. San Francisco: Jossey-Boss.

Tuma, N. B., M. T. Hannan, and L. P. Groeneveld (1979). "Dynamic Analysis of Event Histories." *American Journal of Sociology* 84:820–54.

Tuma, N. B., and P. K. Robins (1980). "A Dynamic Model of Employment Behavior: An Application to the Seattle and Denver Income Maintenance Experiment." *Econometrica* 48(4):1031–52.

Tunali, F. I., J. R. Behrman, and B. L. Wolfe (1980). "Identification, Estimation and Prediction Under Double Selection." Paper presented at the ASA meetings, Houston, Texas.

Tversky, A. (1972a). "Choice by Elimination." *Journal of Mathematical Psychology* 9:341–67.

   (1972b). "Elimination by Aspects: A Theory of Choice." *Psychological Review* 79:281–99.

Tversky, A., and S. Sattath (1979). "Preference Trees." *Psychology Review* 86: 542–73.

Uhler, R. S., and J. G. Cragg (1971). "The Structure of Asset Portfolios of Households." *Review of Economic Studies* 38:341–57.

Venti, S., and D. Wise (1980). "Test Scores and Self-Selection of Higher Education." Paper presented to REME conference on discrete econometrics.

Vuong, Q. H. (1980). "Simultaneous Equations and Conditional Log-Linear Probability Models." Manuscript. Northwestern University.

(1982). "Conditional Log-Linear Probability Models: A Theoretical Development with an Empirical Application." Ph.D. dissertation. Department of Economics, Northwestern University.

Waldman, D. M. (1981). "An Economic Interpretation of Parameter Constraints in a Simultaneous Equations Model with Limited Dependent Variables." *International Economic Review* 22(3):731–9.

Wales, T. J., and A. D. Woodland (1980). "Sample Selectivity and the Estimation of Labor Supply Functions." *International Economic Review* 21(2): 437–68.

Walker, S., and D. Duncan (1967). "Estimation of the Probability of an Event as a Function of Several Independent Variables." *Biometrika* 54:167–79.

Warner, J. T. (1978). "The Prediction of Attrition from Military Service." Report CRC 345. Center for Naval Analyses, Alexandria, Virginia.

(1979). "Models of Retention Behavior." Working paper. Center for Naval Analyses, Alexandria, Virginia.

Warner, S. L. (1962). *Stochastic Choice of Mode in Urban Travel*. Evanston: Northwestern University Press.

(1963). "Multivariate Regression of Dummy Variables Under Normality Assumptions." *Journal of the American Statistical Association* 58:1054–63.

(1965). "Randomized Response: A Survey Technique for Eliminating Evasive Answer Bias." *Journal of the American Statistical Association* 60(309): 63–9.

Weinstein, M. A. (1964). "The Sum of Values From a Normal and Truncated Normal Distribution." *Technometrics* 6:104–5.

Weisbrod, B. A. (1980). "Wage Differentials Between the Private For-Profit and Non-Profit Sectors: The Case of Lawyers." Discussion paper 561–79. Institute for Research on Poverty, University of Wisconsin.

Welch, B. L. (1939). "Note on Discriminant Functions." *Biometrika* 31:218–20.

Westin, R. (1974). "Predictions from Binary Choice Models." *Journal of Econometrics* 2:1–16.

(1975). "An Econometric Model of Inter-related Discrete and Continuous Choices." Paper presented at the Third World Congress of the Econometric Society, Toronto.

Westin, R. B., and D. W. Gillen (1978). "Parking Location and Transit Demand: A Case Study of Endogenous Attributes in Disaggregate Mode Choice Functions." *Journal of Econometrics* 8:75–101.

Westin, R. B., and P. L. Watson (1975). "Reported and Revealed Preferences as Determinants of Mode Choice Behavior." *Journal of Marketing Research* 12:282–9.

Willis, R., and S. Rosen (1979). "Education and Self-Selection." *Journal of Political Economy* 87(5, Part 2):507–36.

Winston, C. (1981). "A Disaggregate Model of the Demand for Intercity Freight Transport." *Econometrica* 49(4):981–1006.

Wu, De-Min (1973). "Alternative Tests of Independence Between Stochastic Regressors and Disturbances." *Econometrica* 41(3):733–50.

Yellot, J. (1977). "The Relationship Between Luce's Choice Axiom, Thurstone's Theory of Comparative Judgement, and the Double Exponential Distribution." *Journal of Mathematical Psychology* 15:109–44.

Yule, G. U. (1900). "On the Association of Attributes in Statistics." *Philosophical Transactions of the Royal Society* (Ser. A) 194:257–319.

Zellner, A., and T. Lee (1965). "Joint Estimation of Relationships Involving Discrete Random Variables." *Econometrica* 33:383–94.

Index